DATE DUE

MAY 1 9 '78			
GAYLORD			PRINTED IN U.S.A.

AMERICA'S FAILURE IN CHINA, 1941–50

AMERICA'S FAILURE IN CHINA, 1941–50

AMERICA'S FAILURE IN CHINA
1941-50

TANG TSOU

THE UNIVERSITY OF CHICAGO PRESS
CHICAGO AND LONDON

Library of Congress Catalog Card Number: 63-13072
The University of Chicago Press, Chicago & London
The University of Toronto Press, Toronto 5, Canada
© 1963 by The University of Chicago
All rights reserved
Published 1963. Third Impression 1967
Printed in the United States of America

To my wife, whose unshakable
faith in me has sustained
me in my quest for identity

All nations live by myths. That is, they paint a picture of the past that satisfies their present needs but does violence to the historic record. Some myths are beneficial. They are those that strengthen a nation's confidence in having been, and being, able to do what the tasks of the moment demand of it. The distorting remembrance of great feats, tribulations, and successes is of this kind.

Other myths are pernicious. They draw from a distorted reality lessons for the understanding of the past and the charting of future action which please collective emotions but lead judgment and action astray. They are a spell which the past casts upon the future, a curse with which the dead threaten the living.

The myth of Algeria being an integral part of France was of this pernicious kind. It impressed upon the French mind a wrong conception of reality and corrupted judgment and action. It not only made France pursue disastrous policies in Algeria, but it also afflicted the body politic of France with a seemingly incurable disease. It required the authority, courage, ability, and insight of a great man to restore reality to its rightful place. That man has performed similar operations on French parliamentarism and the Atlantic Alliance. Thus he has been hailed in France as the great "demythologizer," who has made the French to see reality again.

What most of us think about our relations with China partakes of the quality of myth, and it is indeed a pernicious myth. It meets our emotional needs but not the requirements of right judgment and correct action. The communization of China has indeed been the greatest single defeat the foreign policy of the United States has suffered. Yet the very expression, "we have lost China," points to the mythological element in our explanation of the event; for one can lose only what one possesses as one's own, and if one loses what is one's cherished possession the loss must be due to negligence or foul play.

The "loss of China" has been for our collective ego a truly traumatic experience, bringing forth neurotic and psychotic symptoms and calling to mind the story about the distinction between the neurotic and the psychotic: The psychotic believes that two and two make five, the neurotic knows that two and two make four but is unhappy about it. As far as China is concerned, the American people have split into a neurotic and a psychotic party. Only a small and almost inaudible minority has dared to look at the historic record with dispassionate objectivity; for to do so meant looking at ourselves, baring our own errors of judgment and mistaken actions, and thus discovering the cause for the "loss of China" not in the negligence or treachery of an identifiable group of scapegoats but in ourselves, in policies which expressed not only the preferences of the government but the consensus of the people.

It is the great and unique merit of this book to have laid bare the strands of American policy which led to the communization of China and its emergence as a great power. What is revealed is something which is not peculiar to our China policy but has been characteristic of many of our other foreign policies as well: The simultaneous pursuit of contradictory policies and the commitment to ends which could not be achieved with the means employed. The defects of our China policy reveal a style of foreign policy whose roots are embedded in the character of the nation.

This book, prepared under the auspices of the Center for the Study of American Foreign and Military Policy at the University of Chicago, makes a great intellectual contribution in that it combines deep theoretical understanding of foreign policy with meticulous attention to, and judicious interpretation of, the historic evidence. It is both history in the grand style and political science at its best. The book also renders a great public service; for instead of arguing against the myth of our China policy on rational grounds and with impressionistic factual evidence, as others have done, it reconstructs history as it actually has been and thereby exposes the fictitious nature of popular beliefs. It does in the realm of scholarship what great statesmen have done in the sphere of action: It restores truth to its rightful place.

HANS J. MORGENTHAU

This study is an examination of the reasons for the failure of American policy toward China between the time of Pearl Harbor and the collapse of General Douglas MacArthur's "home-by-Christmas" offensive in the Korean War. The measure of this failure is not the loss of China. No one can lose something which he has never possessed. More than any other single person, Generalissimo Chiang Kai-shek was responsible for what happened in China; for responsibility goes with power, and Chiang was the most powerful figure in China. Yet when gauged by her objectives, intentions, and interests, America's policy did fail. In the war against Japan, a Nationalist China was an ally of the United States; in the battle of North Korea, a Communist China emerged as a strong power by defeating American armies.

One way to begin our analysis is to view foreign policy as an integrated structure of assumptions, objectives, and means. This structure can then be examined from two points of view: the interrelations among its various elements and the degree of correspondence between its assumptions and reality. A foreign policy may fail to work out as expected because it contains inconsistent elements. A consistent foreign policy may still fail to promote a nation's interests, if the rational order between political ends and military means is reversed or if its basic assumptions are not in accord with reality or emerging trends. The China policy of the United States provides us with many instructive examples of the reasons why a policy fails.

Obviously, the various elements within a pattern of foreign policy are not of equal importance. Underlying our analysis is a belief that one element stands out as the decisive factor in determining the success and failure of the China policy of the United States from the time of the dispatch of the Open Door notes to the eve of the North Korean aggression. This is the imbalance between end and means. From one point of view, this imbalance takes the form of an unwillingness and, at times, an inability to use military power purposefully to achieve political objectives. From another point of view, it appears as an unwillingness and inability to abandon unattainable goals in order to avoid entanglement in a hopeless cause. The first aspect of the imbalance emerges most clearly in American policy up to 1947, while the second aspect looms large from 1947 to June, 1950. Yet both unwillingness to use military power and espousal of idealistic objectives were integral parts of America's China policy. Together, they turned China into America's dilemma and compelled the United States alternately to advance and retreat in the Far East. Together, they denied the United States any chance for lasting success, while magnifying the consequences of America's ultimate failure. Together, they formed the source of such American illusions as the belief that China under the Nationalists would become a great power, that the Nationalists and Communists could establish a coalition government, and that a Communist China would not pose a serious threat to the United States. Formulated in this simple way, our interpretation sounds rather obvious. But analytical rigor requires a measure of simplicity which helps clarify the meaning of complex events.

Throughout the discussion, an attempt is made to seek an explanation for this unwillingness and inability either to use armed forces purposefully or to relinquish unrealizable goals. Such an examination shows that America's policy was the natural outgrowth of her general approach to Far Eastern affairs — her intellectual assumptions and political and moral considerations. Here and there, hypothetical alternatives to the course of action are explicitly discussed or implicitly posed. These are suggested by hindsight. They were not practical alternatives at the time insofar as they ran counter to the settled assumptions and attitudes which produced the actual policies. Furthermore, no one can prove that an alternative course of action would have succeeded in promoting American ideals and interests or would not have caused even greater damage to the United States. A discussion or suggestion of these hypothetical alternatives serves mainly to emphasize the point that a different course of action could have been followed only if there had been a different set of assumptions.

Implicit in our analysis is the belief that human actions can be viewed from three different perspectives. On the first level they can be seen through the eyes of the actors. From this viewpoint, human actions are not merely occurrences: they are events flowing from human thought, *i.e.*, from the assumptions and considerations of the actors. Thus, a study focusing its attention on the assumptions shaping policies can be a useful supplement to those works which take primarily the form of a narrative of events.

On the second level human actions and their consequences can be understood as the product of a complex of "conditions." The assumptions of the actors constitute one type of "condition." Another type consists of "objective conditions" of which the actors may or may not be fully aware. Some of these "conditions" are totally beyond the control of the actors. On this level of analysis the social scientists look back on past events from the vantage point of the present, trying to discern a pattern and an explanation of human actions. It is from this point of view that the unwillingness and inability either to use military power or to abandon ambitious goals emerge as the most crucial part of the pattern of American policy, whether or not the actors themselves were fully conscious of the importance of this element in determining success or failure. This juxtaposition of a reluctance to use force with a readiness to espouse idealistic principles in international affairs was deeply rooted in American attitudes. Considered by many as the very essence of the American spirit, it constituted an ineluctable and ubiquitous constraint on America's freedom of action and choice. From this second perspective, human actions frequently seem to follow a course of development largely determined by the complex of "conditions" under which they take place.

On still a third level one may ask such questions as the following: Were the assumptions and considerations shaping policies so determined by "objective" factors that the policies were, for all practical purposes, beyond the control of the actors? Can one reasonably argue that the actors — individuals, governments, or nations — could have adopted a different set of assumptions and directed their attention to another group of considerations? If a different set of assumptions and considerations had prevailed, would the course of past events have been different? Where does one draw the line between situations in which the actors can be reasonably regarded as having freedom of choice and those in which they cannot? What were the possible courses of action open to the actors and what other courses of action were ruled out by objective circumstances? Where is the boundary between what could have happened and what could not, or between what was beyond human control and what was due to free human choice? No systematic attempt has been made to answer these questions as they bear on the actions and policies covered by this study. But the raising of these issues, even if only by implication, underscores on the one hand the controlling effect of the prevailing assumptions and considerations and the constraint imposed upon action by man's understanding of himself and his environment. On the other hand, it directs attention to the possibility and limits of a conscious change of human thought through self-knowledge, to the possibility and limits of extending the scope of human control over objective conditions through knowledge of the outer world, and to the possibility and limits of human beings consciously guiding the course of their own history and destiny.

Our study is undertaken primarily from the second perspective, while it starts necessarily from the first and suggests by implication the third. The type of interpretation of a nation's policy over a long period of time such as is attempted here is a hazardous task. At its best, it can be perceptive. Usually it is merely plausible. For it is from a complex total situation that one selects a single element as the focal point of analysis. The selection inevitably reflects the intellectual assumptions, political predisposition, and emotional involvement of the writer, which in turn have been produced by his total milieu. There is a serious danger, too, that analytical rigor may be incompatible with historical complexity. A quest for the meaning of events and an attempt to look at foreign policy as a structure of interrelated elements may impart greater coherence and logic to historical happenings than they actually possess. It is also likely that our present attitudes and mental habits may prevent a full appreciation of the climate of opinion at another time. It is probable that our preoccupation with learning from experience may preclude a complete realization of the objectives restraints and difficulties under which American officials labored. All these inherent limitations to human intelligence are especially serious in such an undertaking as the present venture. It is hoped that by being fully aware of these limits some of the pitfalls can be avoided. Whenever necessary, analytical rigor yields to historical complexity; analysis is intertwined throughout with historical narrative. This work thus falls neither wholly in the field of political science nor wholly in the field of history. It is not a historical narrative, following a strictly chronological order. Nor is it a purely analytical work governed solely by a logical scheme. The chronological order is followed when an account of events is necessary to substantiate an analysis. A logical sequence is adopted when it is necessary to develop an interpretation. This study lies, therefore, in the twilight zone where political science and diplomatic history overlap and where analysis and descriptions are intermingled. Our hope is that, if it does not add much to our knowledge of facts, it does direct our attention to the abstract realm of policy assumptions, sharpen our insight into the wisdom or folly of our action, and systematize the lessons to be learned. Our perspective and indeed our very bias may also direct our attention to a significant aspect of the total situation which has not been sufficiently stressed. Whether such an effort is worthwhile is for others to judge.

This endeavor to interpret American policy has been greatly facilitated by the following outstanding studies of various phases of Sino-American relations during the period from Pearl Harbor to the collapse of General MacArthur's drive for the Yalu. Herbert Feis's *The China Tangle* furnishes us with an authoritative account of American policy toward China between Pearl Harbor and the dispatch of the Marshall mission. The three volumes of the military history of the United States army in China, Burma, and India by Charles F. Romanus and Riley Sunderland give us detailed information about American strategy in the Far East, American military activities in China, and revealing incidents relating to Chinese internal politics as they bore on the war against Japan. H. Bradford Westerfield's *Party Politics and Foreign Policy* ably analyzes the debate over China policy between the "China bloc" in Congress and the Truman administration, which constituted one of the most significant phases of American policy from 1946 to 1950. After the research for the study had been finished, John W. Spanier's *The Truman-MacArthur Controversy and the Korean War* appeared. After the first draft of the chapter on the first six months of the Korean War had been completed, Allen Whiting's *China Crosses the Yalu* was published. Spanier's book contains a perceptive analysis of American policy. Whiting's book is the best work in print on the foreign policy of Communist China. Our findings and conclusions agree often but not always with theirs.

An attempt was made to search through all published documents and other primary sources relating to China policy of this period. The sum total of these materials, when added to numerous articles and secondary works, is staggering. This effort has proved to be rewarding, for it has enabled us to discuss and document fully the assumptions and considerations which lay behind policies and actions. Some use was made of Chinese sources when they threw light on the political realities in China and American policies. Lack of access to materials seriously restricted this effort. But even this limited attempt has produced some interesting results.

The Introduction, which serves as a general interpretation of America's traditional policy before Pearl Harbor, is based primarily on the numerous secondary works covering specific phases of this period. The indebtedness of the author to these writings is acknowledged in footnotes. But four works have been especially helpful. Herbert Feis's *Road to Pearl Harbor* provides a careful account of American policy toward the Far East from 1937 to Pearl Harbor. Paul W. Schroeder's *The Axis Alliance and Japanese-American Relations, 1941*, contains an interesting interpretation of the traditional policy of the United States toward China. William L. Neumann's essay, "Ambiguity and Ambivalence in Ideas of National Interest in Asia," in *Isolation and Security*, edited by Alexander DeConde, gives an analytical treatment of the basic assumptions of American policy. A. Whitney Griswold's *The Far Eastern Policy of the United States* seems to be an ageless book, still unsurpassed in scholarship, style, and breadth of conception by any later works. For this long period only a few selected primary sources are consulted. It is hoped that the Introduction, with its slightly different interpretation and appraisal of the traditional policy of the United States toward China, imparts deeper meaning and a sense of historical continuity to our analysis in the rest of the study.

One great joy in completing a piece of work comes from acknowledging the help graciously given during the uncertain period of essaying the task. This book had its origins in Professor Hans J. Morgenthau's desire to have someone examine the various controversial issues arising out of the wartime and postwar policy of the United States toward China. His concern with concepts and assumptions underlying political action and his profound insight into the intricate interplay of ideas and interests have given this study its general character. Without his guidance, tolerance, and patience, this book would never have been completed. From Robert E. Osgood, I first learned the spirit and the fundamentals of American foreign policy by probing his mind in informal chats within the confining walls of a shared office. His judicious views, conveyed in his extensive and detailed comments on the manuscript, helped me toward a balanced perspective. Dr. Allen S. Whiting read the whole manuscript and his suggestions have led to many improvements. To him, I owe the title of the book. In letters and extensive comments on the manuscript, Mr. Riley Sunderland was kind enough to put at my disposal his detailed knowledge of American military history and allowed me to draw on his penetrating insight into the complex events during the Pacific war. He has become the silent partner in many phases of this intellectual enterprise. The comments of Professor Paul Clyde of Duke University on the first part of an earlier draft alerted me to the importance of a proper blending of analysis and narrative. Professor Knight Biggerstaff of Cornell read the chapters on Hurley and Marshall and gave me the benefit of his vast scholarship and his personal knowledge of the period. Professor John K. Fairbank read the book in galleys and has given me much encouragement and help through the years. I am indebted to Professor Walter Johnson, Professor Herman Finer, Dr. Charles M. Hardin, Mr. Robert Goldwin, and Mrs. David Easton for their perceptive comments on parts of the manuscript. Professor Louis Hartz of Harvard University and Professors Daniel J. Boorstin, Leo Strauss, and Joseph Cropsey of the University of Chicago brought their knowledge of political thought to bear in their comments on an article on the American political tradition and the American image of Chinese communism, published in the December, 1962, issue of the *Political Science Quarterly*, parts of which are incorporated in this book. Mr. John Carter Vincent's two letters commenting on my article on Marshall's China policy, published in the Spring,

1962, issue of *Orbis*, enabled me to understand more accurately and to appreciate more intimately the thinking of American officials at the time. Many suggestions of the anonymous readers and editors of the University of Chicago Press and the various professional journals have been gratefully accepted. On such a controversial issue as the China policy of the United States, it is particularly gratifying to have the benefit of the judgments of these outstanding men to serve as a guide in producing the final version of the book. But the responsibility for the views expressed in the volume is mine alone.

Throughout this hazardous venture in controversial issues, I have been constantly sustained by the unbounded faith, the tremendous courage, and the infinite patience of my wife, Yi, who as a scholar in her own right has a perfect understanding of my problems. She has willingly shared with me all the material hardship and spiritual suffering of a rootless student but has been rewarded with nothing except long hours of silence and protracted periods of anxiety. To her this book is affectionately dedicated.

My search for Chinese materials in other libraries, was greatly facilitated by the efficient services rendered by Miss Helen M. Smith of the University of Chicago Library. In preparing the final draft, I was ably assisted by Mr. Carl Dibble, now a Fulbright fellow in Turkey, who also served as my first critic. Mr. Richard K. Helmbrecht, helped me in proofreading the galleys, checking the footnotes, and compiling the index with utmost thoroughness, indefatigable energy, and a pleasant disposition which was not affected even by these tedious tasks. For typing the manuscript, I wish to thank Miss Linnea Brandwein, Mrs. Marie Fitzmaurice, and Mrs. Margaret Case.

The following publications have kindly given me permission to use materials which I had previously published: *Political Science Quarterly*, edited for the Academy of Political Science by the faculty of political science of Columbia University; *Orbis*, a quarterly journal of world affairs, published by the Foreign Policy Research Institute of the University of Pennsylvania; *Pacific Historical Review*, official journal of the Pacific Coast Branch, American Historical Association.

I would like to thank William Sloane Associates, Inc., for permission to use material from *The Stilwell Papers*, by Joseph W. Stilwell (copyright, 1948, by Winifred A. Stilwell), and William Morrow & Company and S. L. A. Marshall for use of two maps from *The River and The Gauntlet* (copyright 1953 by S. L. A. Marshall).

Acknowledgement is also made to the Committee on Far Eastern Civilizations and to the Social Science Divisional Research Committee of the University of Chicago for research grants to provide for assistants and other expenses.

CONTENTS

INTRODUCTION

ROOTS
IN THE
PAST

CHAPTER I

THE PRINCIPLES

OF THE

OPEN DOOR POLICY

AND

THE PATTERN OF

AMERICA'S

CHINA POLICY

A. The Convergence of Ideals and Interests

In September, 1899, Secretary of State John Hay dispatched the Open Door notes[1] to Germany, Russia, England, Japan, Italy, and France, requesting formal assurances that they would refrain from interfering with any treaty port or any vested interest or the Chinese treaty tariff within their spheres of interest and that they would grant traders of all countries equality of treatment with respect to harbor dues and railroad charges.[2] In July, 1900, during the Boxer Rebellion, he sent a circular to the powers, informing them that "the policy of the Government of the United States is to seek a solution which may bring about permanent safety and peace to China, preserve China's territorial and administrative entity, protect all rights guaranteed to friendly powers by treaty and international law, and safeguard for the world the principle of equal and

[1] The phrase "the principles of the Open Door policy" is borrowed from Henry L. Stimson to denote the principle of equality of economic opportunity for all nations trading in China and the principle of territorial and administrative integrity of China. See Henry L. Stimson, *The Far Eastern Crisis* (New York: Harper & Bros., 1936), p. 13. For the sake of brevity and convenience, the phrases "the principles of the Open Door" and "the Open Door principles" are also used. The phrase "the principle of the Open Door" or "Open Door" is employed to refer to the principle of equality of economic opportunity alone.

[2] Department of State, *Foreign Relations of the United States, 1899* (Washington D.C.: Government Printing Office, 1901), pp. 132–33.

3

impartial trade with all parts of the Chinese Empire."[3] The first pronouncement reasserted in a form applicable to the situation at that time the principle of equality of commercial opportunity for all nations, which lay behind the most-favored-nation clause in the Treaty of Wanghsia, concluded with China in 1844.[4] The second declaration transformed into a guiding principle the hitherto amorphous wish of the United States to preserve the territorial and administrative integrity of China. Together, they publicly and officially defined two objectives which the United States was to pursue, intermittently and not too effectively, in the next fifty years.

As time went on, the United States became increasingly involved in Chinese affairs and gave these two principles progressively broader concrete meaning. The reasons for American involvement and the expansion of the connotation of the Open Door principles are not far to seek. American ideals, sentiments, and interests appeared to converge perfectly on these two principles. The demand for equal opportunity to trade and the opposition to monopoly were traditions antedating the American Revolution. The principle of respect for the integrity of China expressed America's opposition to imperialism and colonialism and the American sympathy for the underdog. As Tyler Dennett observed, "The spirit of the policy [of the Open Door] is as old as the Declaration of Independence."[5] Or, as Walter Lippmann put it, "The Open Door is at bottom a short name for the American way of life, projected abroad."[6]

Another element of the American way of life projected abroad was evangelical Christianity, intertwined with a humanitarian idealism. It found concrete expression in energetic missionary activities and philanthropic and educational works in China. This populous nation seemed to be the most promising country since pagan Rome in which "to plant the shining cross on every hill and in every valley," as the missionaries were invited to do by Anson Burlingame, one-time American minister to Peking who served the Manchu dynasty as a special minister "for the management of China's diplomatic relations."[7] The success of what Secretary of State Henry L. Stimson called "the greatest private missionary effort"[8] was not notable in terms of number of converts, which

[3] Department of State, *Foreign Relations of the United States, 1900* (Washington, D.C.: Government Printing Office, 1902), p. 299.
[4] Earl H. Pritchard, "The Origins of the Most-Favored-Nation and the Open Door Policies in China," *Far Eastern Quarterly*, February, 1942, pp. 161–72.
[5] Tyler Dennett, *Americans in Eastern Asia* (New York: Macmillan, 1922), p. v.
[6] Walter Lippmann, *United States War Aims* (Boston: Little, Brown & Co., 1944), p. 38.
[7] Dennett, *op. cit.*, p. 385; see also Foster Rhea Dulles, *China and America: The Story of Their Relations since 1784* (Princeton, N.J.: Princeton University Press, 1946), pp. 67, 70.
[8] Stimson, *op. cit.*, p. 14.

amounted to only half-a-million baptized Protestants by 1927. But the influence of these Christian Chinese seemed to be great and the social and political changes wrought by the total impact of the missionaries appeared to be profound.[9] As early as 1913 Secretary of State William Jennings Bryan, a fervently religious man, expressed the thought that "the new Chinese civilization was founded upon the Christian movement there."[10] President Woodrow Wilson, a Presbyterian elder, once said that "our Chinese interests were largely in the form of missionary activities and our minister to China should be an evangelical Christian."[11]

A natural desire to see republican, democratic institutions established and prospering was still another facet of the American way of life projected abroad. In hailing the Chinese Revolution of 1911–12, President Wilson declared: "The awakening of the people of China to a consciousness of their possibilities under free government is the most significant, if not the most momentous, event of our generation. With this aspiration the American people are in profound sympathy."[12] America was deeply inspired by the vision of a huge country with an ancient civilization transforming herself into a modern, democratic, Christian nation and following the lead of the United States. Pride in American moral influence in China and hope for Chinese progress fostered benevolent sentiments and a sympathetic attitude toward her and a deep solicitude for her welfare and friendship. Shortly after extending American recognition to the Chinese republic, President Wilson wrote to an American consul in China that "it makes me very proud indeed that they [the Chinese] should look to the United States as their friend and exemplar in the great tasks which lie ahead of them." He expressed the hope that the United States might have the opportunity many times in the future "to show its cordial friendship for China."[13] Giving the reasons for his advocacy of a strong policy against Japan after the Manchurian Incident, Secretary Stimson wrote: "The United States has made a good start in the development of Chinese friendship. It would have been the most short-sighted folly to turn our backs upon her at the time of her most dire need."[14] These American ideals and sentiments, as well as China's welfare and interests, seemed to be best served and satisfied by the principles of the Open

[9] Kenneth S. Latourette, *A History of Christian Missions in China* (New York: Macmillan Co., 1929), pp. 831–43.

[10] Roy Watson Curry, *Woodrow Wilson and Far Eastern Policy, 1913–1921* (New York: Bookman Associates, 1957), p. 36.

[11] *Ibid.*, p. 38. For an excellent study of the American missionary movement in China, see Paul A. Varg, *Missionaries, Chinese, and Diplomats* (Princeton, N.J.: Princeton University Press, 1958).

[12] Quoted by Dulles, *op. cit.*, p. 135.

[13] Quoted by Curry, *op. cit.*, p. 31.

[14] Stimson, *op. cit.*, p. 91.

Door. These noble visions and emotions became the basic driving force behind America's policy toward China.

The twin principles also seemed to foster American interests, both real and imaginary. From 1784 to the middle of the nineteenth century, American trade with China prospered and was a factor in drawing the United States westward in her territorial expansion and population movement.[15] After a period of eclipse, American commerce with China flourished toward the end of the century. The Open Door to equal commercial opportunity was conducive to the trade interests of an economically strong nation, and American business groups played an important part in the episode which resulted in the dispatch of the Open Door notes.[16] Although American trade with China was at no time large, amounting to less than 4 per cent of total American trade even in the 1930's, American businessmen and the public alike were fascinated by the image of a potential market of 400 million people. The principle of respecting the territorial and administrative integrity of China was at first a corollary of the Open Door and a political means to an economic end. For equality of commercial opportunity could best be maintained if the integrity of China was preserved.

With the progressive involvement of the United States in Far Eastern politics, a process which began with the acquisition of the Philippines, American officials became aware of the political importance of the principle of respect for the integrity of China. Meanwhile, the principle of equality of commercial opportunity showed itself to be useful as the basis of a policy with obvious political implications.[17] For, singly or in combination, these two principles served as the foundations of a policy opposing either the dismemberment of China or her domination to the exclusion of the United States. At the turn of the century, the first outcome looked imminent and to avert it Hay's circular of 1900 was issued. Toward the end of the first decade of the twentieth century, the domination of China by other powers to the exclusion of the United States was thought likely, and President Taft's dollar diplomacy was designed to prevent this. In two different periods after 1915 the danger of the subjugation of China to the exclusive control of Japan was real, and the Bryan-Lansing caveat, the Stimson Doctrine, and Secretary Hull's repeated invocation of the time-honored principles were part and parcel of the effort to exorcise it.

Although up to the late thirties the immediate concerns of most American officials were such concrete American interests as trade and missionary activities, some of them were conscious of America's political interest in

[15] Dulles, *op. cit.*, pp. 32–37, and Kenneth S. Latourette, *The United States Moves across the Pacific* (New York: Harper & Bros., 1946), pp. 5–9.

[16] Charles S. Campbell, Jr., "American Business Interests and the Open Door in China," *Far Eastern Quarterly*, November, 1941, pp. 43–58.

[17] Taft's dollar diplomacy was an obvious case in point.

maintaining the balance of power in the Far East and were alive to the adverse political effects of the domination of China by other powers. The State Department, in a memorandum written in September, 1909, to justify dollar diplomacy, noted: "The balancing of power in China is essential to peace in the Orient just as it has been necessary in Turkey to keep Europe quiet. Our interests in Asiatic waters require the prevention of the establishment of predominant interests and influences at Peking on the part of other powers and that American prestige in China be undiminished."[18] But the remoteness of China, the apparent meagerness of American commercial and political interests in the Far East, and the absence of an imperialist tradition rendered it unprofitable if not impossible for the United States to adopt a policy of territorial compensation or to join in the scramble for special privileges with a view to preserving her share of political and commercial interests in China. Furthermore, the dismemberment of China or the struggle for domination of China would entail the possibility of war among the powers and turmoil within China which would inevitably injure American trade and her missionary and philanthropic activities and would probably involve the United States in an unwanted armed conflict. American interest in the Far East, therefore, lay in general stability, not in the acquisition of special privileges in terms of power and territorial gains. It was believed that this over-all objective could be most effectively achieved by securing respect for Chinese territorial and administrative integrity. By denoting American opposition to the designs of the powers and by indicating American desire to provide China with an opportunity to develop her inherent strength, the principles of the Open Door policy seemed to express aptly America's self-interest in the Far East. Guided by them, American policy in the Far East was active, "interventionist." It stood in contrast to the passive, "isolationist" policy toward Europe.[19]

B. Foreign Policy without Force

But despite the convergence of ideals and self-interest on these principles, the United States made no attempt to enforce them by the application of national power. She sought their acceptance primarily by sending diplomatic notes, by making official pronouncements, or by inducing the powers to indorse them in paper agreements. The espousal of these high-sounding principles really meant that the United States was pursuing the very limited immediate objective of preserving and, at times, bolstering slightly what remained of China's territorial and administrative integrity. Even this

[18] Quoted by A. Whitney Griswold, in *The Far Eastern Policy of the United States* (New York: Harcourt, Brace & Co., 1938), p. 145.

[19] Edward Mead Earle, "A Half-Century of American Foreign Policy," *Political Science Quarterly*, June, 1949, p. 172.

limited, immediate objective was not a goal to be achieved by force. On every important occasion up to 1941, the United States invoked the principles but stopped short of using the necessary means to implement them. This feature characterized all major American moves in the Far East, from the Open Door notes and the circular of Secretary Hay through President Theodore Roosevelt's efforts to preserve the neutrality of Manchuria, Secretary Philander C. Knox's attempt to neutralize the Manchurian railways, President Wilson's fight on behalf of China at the Paris Peace Conference, Stimson's non-recognition doctrine, and finally Secretary Cordell Hull's numerous pronouncements, notes, and memoranda up to the time of the imposition of a total embargo on export of oil to Japan. The Nine-Power Treaty appears to be an exception; for, to use A. Whitney Griswold's words, it "constituted the most dynamic and the most comprehensive attempt on the part of the United States to uphold the territorial integrity of China and all that it believed to depend on it; to make the open door in China an enduring principle of international law. . . ."[20] But for all that, it remained, to quote Griswold again, "a self-denying ordinance rather than a collective security pact. The only sanction behind it was the good faith of its signatories."[21]

One need not go very far to seek the reasons for this pattern of persistent verbal effort to implement the limited objectives and the professed principles. In the forty years after the dispatch of the Hay notes, America's progressive loss of her relative geographical isolation was not accompanied by an outright abandonment of her traditional isolationism. Threats to national security appeared to be minor, sporadic, and indirect.[22] America's participation in the first World War proved to be an interlude. It came about as a result of the German decision to resume unrestricted submarine warfare rather than from a conscious American desire to maintain the balance of power in Europe. The return to isolationism and "normalcy," the desire to cut naval expenditures, the peace movement in the twenties, the Great Depression, and the single-minded effort to revitalize the economy — all affected America's policy toward China. In the late thirties, the mounting threat of Nazi Germany drew attention toward Europe. But isolationism was not effectively challenged until the victory of Nazi Germany over Holland and France in May and June of 1940 and the conclusion of the Tripartite Pact between Germany, Italy, and Japan in the following September. Throughout this time, a high degree of economic self-sufficiency lessened the need for foreign markets or for special economic privileges abroad.

[20] Griswold, *op. cit.*, p. 311.
[21] *Ibid.*, p. 326.
[22] Samuel Flagg Bemis, "The Shifting Strategy of American Defense and Diplomacy," *Virginia Quarterly Review*, Summer, 1948, pp. 321–35.

Under these circumstances, American interests in China as reflected in the Open Door principles were not considered essential to the nation, however eagerly businessmen and missionaries in China sought to promote them. The maintenance of a balance of power in the Far East was not a primary consideration in policy-making. If the United States was not prepared to intervene in the affairs of Europe where her stake was infinitely greater, she could not be expected to involve herself in a war in the Far East. Thus, despite the fact that America's ideals imparted to her policy in the Far East an active, "interventionist" character, few American officials saw any reason for going to war to defend or promote American interests in China. To use the succinct statement of Paul W. Schroeder, "It was also a long-standing American policy, equally as traditional as the Open Door and far more consistently observed in practice, that the United States would not go to war for the sake of China."[23] In other words, the idealistic purpose as embodied in the Open Door doctrine lacked the necessary support in perceived self-interest and could not become the basis of a forceful policy.

Only when Japan, by then an ally of Germany, occupied southern Indochina in July, 1941, in preparation for an attack on Singapore and the Netherlands East Indies did the United States risk war by imposing a total embargo on oil. Japan's projected move would have severed the British trade routes in the southern Pacific and might seriously have affected the chance of a successful defense of the British Isles. It would have denied the Western powers important raw materials in Southeast Asia. Under these circumstances the United States took forceful action, but primarily to deter Japan from further advance in Southeast Asia. The embargo was essentially a measure to defend, directly, American interests in Southeast Asia and, indirectly, those in Europe. American interests in China were not the most important consideration in the decision to risk war.[24] Indeed, the United States had abstained from such an embargo from 1937 onward in spite of Japan's action in China.

Yet, despite the unwillingness and inability to implement the principles by force, American interests in China were sufficiently tantalizing and the American ideals as projected to the other shore of the Pacific were appealing enough to prevent the United States from abandoning them. When the principles and the immediate objectives justified by them were put in jeopardy by the powers, the United States would beat a retreat but would never fail to invoke them in order to put her position on record. When the international situation became favorable, she would take a new step for-

[23] Paul W. Schroeder, *The Axis Alliance and Japanese-American Relations, 1941* (Ithaca, N.Y.: Cornell University Press, 1958), p. 181.

[24] Paul Varg, "Alternatives in the Far East," *World Affairs Quarterly*, October, 1955, pp. 247–54. See also pp. 21–23, below.

ward in China and make a new effort to promote the acceptance of the
principles. The principles were, in effect, long-term goals to be sought by
diplomatic, peaceful methods. In this manner, the United States became
increasingly involved in Chinese affairs and the principles fixed the general
course of her policy. Over a period of decades, the pursuit of the long-term
goals could not but impart to American policy a rigidity in its aims. For
the persistent invocation of the Open Door principles inevitably created
strong emotional attachment to them, sentimental concern for China, and
deep hatred for Japan. This development was facilitated by the cluster
of myths surrounding American policy which official pronouncements
helped to create.[25] On occasion, there was in these pronouncements a tendency to represent a setback as a success. At other times, there were discrep-
ancies, between the avowed principles and the actual course of action as,
for example, Secretary Hay's attempt in 1900 to obtain for the United
States a naval base in the province of Fukien.[26] Some of these, such as the
Root-Takahira and Lansing-Ishii agreements, were officially interpreted as
reaffirmations of the Open Door principles, despite the fact that the Root-
Takahira Agreement contained a declaration for the status quo in the
Pacific region and the Lansing-Ishii Agreement recognized Japan's "special
interest in China." These gaps between myths and actuality were the product of the conflict between the unwillingness to abandon the principles and
the inability to enforce them or to achieve the limited objectives pursued

[25] In an early biography of John Hay, William R. Thayer commented on the dispatch
of the Open Door notes as follows: "By what was one of the most adroit strokes of
modern diplomacy, Hay thus accustomed the world to accept the Open Door as the
only decent policy for it to adopt toward China. Not one of the governments concerned wished to agree to it; each saw more profit to itself in exploiting what it had
already secured and in joining in the scramble for more but not one of them, after
Hay had declared for the Open Door, dared openly to oppose the doctrine. It was
as if, in a meeting, he had asked all those who believe in telling the truth to stand
up: the liars would not have kept their seats" (*Life and Letters of John Hay* [Bos-
ton: Houghton Mifflin Co., 1908], II, 243).

This evaluation with its obvious contrast between the moral excellence of the
United States and the viciousness of the powers was repeated with further embellish-
ments by one of the leading publicists eighteen years later; see Mark Sullivan, *Our
Times: The Turn of the Century* (New York: Charles Scribner's Sons, 1926), p. 509.

Analyzing the traditional Far Eastern policy of the United States, a leading his-
torian of American diplomacy observed perceptively that "a nestful of tenacious myths
has grown up about the Open Door." Among them were the misconceptions that all
powers responded affirmatively to John Hay's original request and faithfully respected
the American principles and that the United States saved China. See T. A. Bailey,
Man in the Street (New York: Macmillan Co., pp. 285–90; see also Paul H. Clyde,
"Historical Reflections on Continuity in U.S. Far Eastern Policy," in *Southeast Asia
in the Changing World*, ed. Philip W. Thayer (Baltimore: Johns Hopkins Press,
1953), pp. 17–32, and George F. Kennan, *American Diplomacy 1900–1950* (Chicago:
University of Chicago Press, 1951), chaps. ii and iii. Secretary Stimson himself subscribed to this interpretation of the effectiveness of the Hay notes (Stimson, *op. cit.*,
p. 13).

[26] Griswold, *op. cit.*, p. 83.

in their name. The consequence was an estrangement between political thinking on the popular level and official actions behind the pronouncements. The general public thought about American Far Eastern policy in terms of the high-sounding formulas and mistook the future goals as immediately enforceable principles.

Thus, it came about that the American principles affected the concrete actions of the United States at a crucial moment. After the United States imposed a total embargo on oil, Japan turned to the defensive. She indicated, though ambiguously, her willingness to loosen her ties with the Axis powers and to halt her southward advance. But in the negotiations the United States insisted on enforcing the principle of the integrity of China and demanded the withdrawal of Japanese troops from China. Public opinion was now intensely hostile to Japan, passionately partial to the idealistic formulas, and violently opposed to appeasement. The American people, who had been unwilling to go to war for China, became quite ready to risk an armed clash with Japan. This climate of opinion prevented either a relaxation of the embargo or a retreat from the principles. As Schroeder puts it, "Public opinion was a strong factor in accounting for America's persisting in following a hard, offensive policy toward Japan."[27] At this point, the long-term goals became the immediate aim, unattainable without war.

The Pacific war, occurring at this time, was the natural outcome of the traditional pattern of America's policy toward China. It represented, in effect, the resolution, under the force of circumstances and public opinion, of the basic contradiction in America's China policy between the espousal of the Open Door principles and the refusal to go to war in defense of American interests and principles in China. The clash with Japan was not the final move, used as the last resort, in a planned program to employ military power to enforce America's long-range policy. To make these points clear, it is necessary to see how the United States weighed her interests and principles in China against the risks of war, how she prevented for forty years the potential contradiction in her policy from becoming an actuality, how her traditional policies and her military capabilities were related to each other, how the events gradually brought the contradiction to the fore, and in what military, political, and diplomatic context the force of public opinion resolved the contradiction in favor of the principles.

C. The Changing Environment and the Unchanged Pattern of Policy

When Secretary Hay sent his Open Door notes and his circular, the major powers had already carved out their spheres of influence in China.

[27] Schroeder, *op. cit.*, p. 193.

Taken literally, the Open Door for equal commercial opportunity was clearly incompatible with the existence of the spheres of influence. For within their spheres the powers were granted by China certain special, preferential, and, in some cases, exclusive privileges such as railroad and mining concessions and the first claim to provide "assistance" in personnel, capital, and matériel for a variety of purposes. Hay himself recognized this limitation. For his Open Door notes specifically recognized the existence of the spheres and asked only for equality of trade in consumption merchandise.[28] But even this strictly limited demand was met by evasive and conditional replies from the powers. Much the same can be said about the principle of the integrity of China. Literally speaking, respect for the territorial and administrative integrity of China would have required the outright abolition of the unequal treaties, to which in most aspects the United States herself was a party, and the surrender of all the concessions and special privileges secured by the powers. This was obviously impossible and was not intended by Hay. Instead, the Secretary hoped by his circular to avert the danger of the "breakup" of China, to check further encroachment by the powers, and to preserve what was left of her territorial and administrative integrity. The danger of a partition of China soon faded away, not because of Hay's moral exhortation but as a result of the mutual jealousies of the powers and the resultant stalemate. As a matter of fact, Hay's and his successors' verbal efforts to check the further Russian encroachment before 1904 and the Japanese advance after 1905 were largely futile.

The reason for their failure is not far to seek. The principles of the Open Door and the integrity of China and even the limited objectives pursued in the name of the principles conflicted sharply with the conceived interests of the powers. Their successful implementation would have required the use or the threat of force by the United States. The use of force could have been justified only if the United States had considered her interests in China vital or at least essential. But at no time during this period had the United States either the intention or the power to back up her principles by forcible measures. When, in 1901, the Japanese government inquired whether the United States was willing to put pressure on the Russians to evacuate Manchuria, Secretary Hay replied that the United States was "not at present prepared to attempt singly, or in concert with other powers, to enforce these views in the East as to China's integrity by any demonstrations which could present a character of hostility to any other power."[29] When the Russians promised and then broke their pledge to evacuate Manchuria, Hay told President Theodore Roosevelt that there was noth-

[28] See Paul H. Clyde, "The Open-Door Policy of John Hay," *Historical Outlook*, May, 1931, pp. 212–13, and Earl H. Pritchard, *op. cit.*, pp. 162–72.
[29] Griswold, *op. cit.*, p. 87.

ing the United States could do. "I am sure you will think it is out of the question," he wrote Roosevelt, "that we should adopt any scheme of concerted actions with England and Japan. Public opinion in this country would not support such a course, nor do I think it would be to our permanent advantage."[30] Secretary Hay's views were shared by the President who wrote a British diplomat in February, 1904: "Probably our interests in China are not at the moment so great as to make it possible for us to be drawn into war with them [the Russians]."[31] These judgments by Secretary Hay and President Roosevelt of American interests and intentions set the tone of subsequent evaluations for a long time to come.

Beginning with, if not before, the Taft-Katsura "agreed memorandum" and the Portsmouth Conference which ended the Russo-Japanese War, President Roosevelt followed a policy of maintaining a balance between Russia and Japan and of liquidating the conflict of American and Japanese interests in the Far East.[32] He abandoned, for all practical purposes, any attempts to uphold the Open Door principles, though still giving lip service to them. The rationale behind this shift in policy was revealed in a letter which Roosevelt wrote President Taft in 1910 in response to the latter's request for his advice. Referring to the issue of Japanese immigration to the United States, Roosevelt wrote: "Our vital interest is to keep the Japanese out of our country and at the same time to preserve the good will of Japan."[33] Obviously, he did not consider it a vital or essential interest of the United States to support China and to uphold the Open Door principles.[34] Therefore he advised his successor that since "the vital interest of Japan is in Manchuria and Korea, it is peculiarly our interest not to take any steps as regards Manchuria which will give the Japanese cause to feel, with or without reason, that we are hostile to them, or a menace — in however slight a degree — to their interests."[35]

Then he continued with an appraisal of the feasibility of implementing the Open Door policy in the light of America's military capability:

[A]s I utterly disbelieve in the policy of bluff, in national and international no less than in private affairs, or in any violation of the

[30] Tyler Dennett, *John Hay* (New York: Dodd, Mead & Co., 1934), p. 404.

[31] Howard K. Beale, *Theodore Roosevelt and the Rise of America to World Power* (Baltimore, Md.: Johns Hopkins Press, 1956), pp. 263–64.

[32] *Ibid.*, pp. 269–334; Griswold, *op. cit.*, pp. 122–31; Harley F. McNair and Donald F. Lach, *Modern Far Eastern International Relations* (New York: Van Nostrand Co., 1955), pp. 102–4; and Tyler Dennett, *Roosevelt and the Russo-Japanese War* (New York: Doubleday & Co., 1925), pp. 112–15, 118, 330–33.

[33] Griswold, *op. cit.*, p. 131.

[34] He wrote: "Alliance with China, in view of China's absolute military helplessness, means of course not an additional strength to us, but an additional obligation we must assume" (*ibid.*, pp. 131–32).

[35] Quoted by Griswold, in *ibid.*, p. 131.

old frontier maxim, "Never draw unless you mean to shoot!" I do not believe in our taking any position anywhere unless we can make good; and as regards Manchuria, if the Japanese choose to follow a course of conduct to which we are adverse, we cannot stop it unless we are prepared to go to war, and a successful war about Manchuria would require a fleet as good as that of England, plus an army as good as that of Germany. The Open Door policy in China was an excellent thing, and I hope it will be a good thing in the future, so far as it can be maintained by general diplomatic arrangement; but as has been proved by the whole history of Manchuria, alike under Russia and under Japan, the "Open Door" policy, as a matter of fact, completely disappears as soon as a powerful nation determines to disregard it, and is willing to run the risk of war rather than to forego its intention.[36]

Roosevelt's advice was ignored by President Taft and Secretary of State Philander Knox whose "dollar diplomacy" represented another step to advance the principles of the Open Door. But, failing to judge correctly the international alignment in the Far East and to realize the limits of economic power, Knox's attempt to use economic pressure to eject Japan and Russia from their dominant positions in Manchuria served only to drive them together to conclude two new conventions which gave additional protection to their respective spheres of influence.[37] Despite the ineffective diplomacy of the United States, however, China was not dismembered. Nor was there a complete overturn in the balance of power. The reason for this relative stability is that the conflicts of the powers reached something of an equilibrium in the fourteen years after the dispatch of the Hay notes, although Russia threatened to push ahead before 1904 and Japan poised to gain a greater advantage after 1905. This stalemate among the powers explains the paradox that, while the Open Door policy suffered one setback after another, American interests were not seriously jeopardized by the failures.

During the First World War, the old political balance began to crumble and a new power configuration was taking shape. Preoccupied with the fighting at home, the European powers withdrew to a large extent from the Far East. The European allies of Japan at first depended on her to eliminate German military power in the Far East and later needed the assistance of her navy in the Mediterranean. Japan was quick to take ad-

[36] *Ibid.*, p. 132.
[37] Charles Vevier, *The United States and China, 1906–1913* (New Brunswick, N.J.: Rutgers University Press, 1955), chap. vii, pp. 214–19; Griswold, *op. cit.*, chap. iv, and McNair and Lach, *op. cit.*, pp. 116–17.

vantage of the situation to seize the German leasehold in Kiaochow, to present to China the notorious Twenty-one Demands, and to secure secret promises from Great Britain, France, and Russia to support her claims to the transfer of German rights in Shantung. During this period, the United States also turned her attention to Europe. It was natural that her policy continued to reflect the view that China was not important enough for the United States to risk embroilment with Japan.

At the outbreak of the war, Japan attacked the German leasehold of Kiaochow. Fearful that Japan would extend the war beyond the limits of the leased territory, the Chinese government expressed in an oblique way its hope for the United States to intervene on China's behalf. In instructing the American minister to disabuse China's wishful thinking, Acting Secretary of State Robert Lansing expounded American policy in the following terms:

> The United States desires China to feel that American friendship is sincere and to be assured that this government will be glad to exert any influence which it possesses, to further, *by peaceful methods*, the welfare of the Chinese people, but the Department realizes that *it would be quixotic in the extreme to allow the question of China's territorial integrity to entangle the United States in international difficulties*.[38]

When the Japanese government presented the Twenty-one Demands to China which, if accepted and implemented, would have made China a protectorate of Japan, all that Secretary of State Bryan could do was to send a note to both Tokyo and Peking, informing them that the United States "cannot recognize any agreement or undertaking which has been entered into or which may be entered into between the governments of Japan and China, impairing the treaty rights of the United States and its citizens in China, the political or territorial integrity of the Republic of China, or the international policy relative to China commonly known as the Open Door policy."[39] This Bryan-Lansing caveat later became the model for Secretary of State Stimson's non-recognition doctrine. In 1917, Secretary of State Lansing was forced by circumstances to recognize in the Lansing-Ishii Agreement Japan's "special interests in China" in ex-

[38] Lansing to Paul S. Reinch, November 4, 1914, Department of State, *Foreign Relations of the United States, 1914, Supplement* (Washington, D.C.: Government Printing Office, 1928), p. 190. Emphasis added. For the events leading up to this instruction, see Tien-yi Li, *Woodrow Wilson's China Policy, 1913–1917* (New York: University of Kansas City Press, 1952), pp. 91–99; Curry, *op. cit.*, pp. 104–10; and Russell A. Fifield, *Woodrow Wilson and the Far East* (New York: Thomas Y. Crowell Co., 1952), pp. 14–17.

[39] Department of State, *Foreign Relations of the United States, 1915* (Washington, D.C.: Government Printing Office, 1924, p. 146.

change for a Japanese declaration of respect for the Open Door and the independence and territorial integrity of China.[40]

After the First World War, the fundamental change in the Far Eastern configuration of power which had been in the making during the war crystallized into a clear pattern. The basic feature of the new power structure was the substitution of an American-Japanese opposition for the former shifting equilibrium of conflicting national interests among the powers as the main source of political stability in the Far East. The defeat of Germany, the temporary eclipse of Russia, and the enfeeblement of Great Britain left a strengthened United States to confront an invigorated Japan across the Pacific. In contrast to the balanced antagonism of the powers, the new political constellation at once offered immense possibilities and presented new dangers to the United States. The United States was no longer confronted in the Far East with a group of world powers, antagonistic to each other to be sure, yet ready to protect their special interests and privileges in China, and, if necessary, prepared to join with one another to oppose the Far Eastern policy of the United States. With her enhanced power and prestige, the United States was in a better position than before to initiate effective measures to implement her avowed Far Eastern policy against the sole opposition of Japan, even though Japan's military position in the western Pacific was also strengthened by the acquisition of the former German island possessions north of the equator.

At the same time, the new political balance contained elements of new danger. While the old configuration of power in the Far East excluded the possibility of the United States achieving her proclaimed objectives, the mutual antagonism of the powers also prevented a drastic upset of the political equilibrium, regardless of the commissions and omissions of the United States. Now that this delicate political equipoise had collapsed and the opposition between the United States and Japan had become the main stabilizing factor, the unwillingness or inability of the United States to prevent Japan's further expansion beyond a certain point at the expense of China would lead eventually to the collapse of the political balance in Asia.

But following the tradition of America's Far Eastern policy, most American officials continued to subscribe to the Open Door principles, on the one hand, and to hold the view that America's interests in China were not worth a war with Japan, on the other. Secretary of State Charles Evans Hughes told American delegates to the Washington Conference that the United States "would never go to war over any aggression on the part of

[40] Department of State, *Foreign Relations of the United States, 1917* (Washington, D.C.: Government Printing Office, 1926), pp. 264–65.

Japan in China."[41] Looking back to this earlier period, Elihu Root, who served as secretary of state under Roosevelt and was later a leading member of the American delegation to the Washington Conference, wrote in the thirties that it had "never entered the head" of any American President or secretary of state to send forces to China in defense of the Open Door.[42] One of the main objectives of the United States in the Washington Conference was naval disarmament, compared to which, to cite Griswold, "the Far Eastern dispensations . . . were of secondary importance."[43]

Consequently, the gap between the principles of the Open Door and the available power to defend them was not closed by the Washington Conference. The agreement not to build new naval bases and fortifications in the Pacific and the 5:5:3 ratio in capital ship and aircraft carrier tonnage perpetuated Japan's supremacy in the western Pacific, notwithstanding the dissolution of her alliance with Great Britain.[44] At the time of the Washington Conference Japan's total tonnage was only 50 per cent of American strength.[45] The Washington ratio of 5:5:3 would have represented a gain of 10 per cent for the Japanese navy even if the United States had built her navy up to the treaty limit. Moreover, although there existed in the twenties a broad outline of operations and objectives in the event of war with Japan, this plan was really "more a statement of hopes than a realistic appraisal of what could be done."[46] During the Hoover administration, the President's principal test of the adequate size of the armed forces was whether the defenses were strong enough to prevent a successful landing of foreign soldiers in the continental United States and in the Western Hemisphere.[47]

Japan's conquest of Manchuria in 1931 and her subsequent attempts to detach North China from Nanking caused some soul-searching among American officials. Secretary of State Stimson attributed great importance to China. He saw that the United States was a neighbor of China, since the Pacific Ocean was rapidly losing its character as a natural barrier and

[41] Quoted by William N. Neumann, "Ambiguity and Ambivalence in Ideas of National Interest in Asia," in *Isolation and Security*, ed. Alexander DeConde (Durham, N.C.: Duke University Press, 1957), p. 147.

[42] *Ibid.*

[43] Griswold, *op. cit.*, p. 316.

[44] Harold and Margaret Sprout, *Toward a New Order of Sea Power* (Princeton, N.J.: Princeton University Press, 1940), chap. xv; Merlo J. Pusey, *Charles Evans Hughes* (New York: Macmillan Co., 1951), II, 474–500; Richard M. Van Alstyne, *American Crisis Diplomacy* (Stanford, Calif.: Stanford University Press, 1952), pp. 10–11; Raymond L. Buell, *The Washington Conference* (New York: Appleton Co., 1922), chap. vi.

[45] Commander Dudley W. Knox, Introduction to Samuel Eliot Morison's *The Battle in the Atlantic* (Boston: Little, Brown & Co., 1947), p. lix.

[46] Louis Morton, "War Plan ORANGE: Evolution of a Strategy," *World Politics*, January, 1959, p. 231.

[47] Herbert Hoover, *Memoirs: The Cabinet and the Presidency, 1920–1933* (New York: Macmillan Co., 1952), p. 338.

becoming a means of communication. He concluded that changes in that region would necessarily have direct repercussions on the United States.[48] Accordingly, he recognized a distinct possibility that " a struggle between China and Japan might threaten our own people and their territorial possessions."[49] More important, he was deeply convinced that in the future China would again hold the key to the Far East and that the future of the United States in that region depended on the development of a powerful, yet peace-loving and friendly China acting as "the main stabilizing factor in Asia."[50] True to the tradition of the Far Eastern policy of the United States, President Hoover maintained, however, that "neither our obligation to China, nor our own interest, nor our dignity requires us to go to war over these questions [which arose out of Japan's aggression in Manchuria]."[51] Hoover's refusal to contemplate the use of force to uphold the Kellogg-Briand Pact and the Nine-Power Treaty was also a reflection of the view that world peace should be preserved by the moral force of world public opinion and not by military measures. Moreover, the Great Depression restrained all thoughts of drastic action.[52] Not even Stimson advocated the use of force, although he was willing to go as far as reinforcing America's naval forces in Shanghai and leaving the American fleet at Hawaii in an attempt to bluff Japan.[53]

Furthermore, the United States was powerless to do anything effective. Secretary of State Stimson acknowledged that the Washington treaties "had been intended to make and had made it physically impossible for any single Western nation successfully to intervene by military force in such a matter as the Manchurian dispute even if it should desire so to do."[54] He was, as he himself said, "much alarmed about the present situation of the navy," which appeared to be "more unequal" than he had thought "to [the task of] meeting Japan."[55] President Hoover's military advisers told

[48] Stimson, op. cit., pp. 234–35.

[49] Ibid., p. 89.

[50] Ibid., pp. 89, 236.

[51] Hoover, op. cit., p. 369. See also Ray L. Wilbur and Arthur M. Hyde, The Hoover Policies (New York: Charles Scribner's Sons, 1937), pp. 599–601; William S. Myers, The Foreign Policy of Herbert Hoover (New York: Charles Scribner's Sons, 1946), pp. 195–97. Henry L. Stimson and McGeorge Bundy wrote that Hoover's refusal to use sanction and force to back up the Open Door policy "was squarely in line with the whole tradition of American foreign policy in the Far East. Even Theodore Roosevelt had always insisted that American interests in the Orient were not worth a war" (Henry L. Stimson and McGeorge Bundy, On Active Service in Peace and War [New York: Harper & Bros., 1947], p. 244).

[52] Robert Ferrell, American Diplomacy in the Great Depression, 1929–1933 (New Haven: Yale University Press, 1957).

[53] Stimson and Bundy, op. cit., pp. 245–46; Ferrell, op. cit., p. 280.

[54] Stimson, op. cit., p. 56.

[55] Quoted in Richard N. Current, Secretary Stimson (New Brunswick, N.J.: Rutgers University Press, 1954), p. 103.

him that, on the assumption of full British co-operation and the placing of the entire British fleet under joint command, it would take the United States two years to win a war against Japan. For the United States to fight Japan alone, victory could only be won in four to six years after an initial loss of the Philippines. According to the calculations of Hoover's advisers, the necessary ingredients of military success were, first, a great expansion of the navy to overcome the handicaps placed by the 5 to 3 ratio on the effectiveness of the American fleet in the western Pacific and, second, the building of a large army to land in China or Japan.[56]

The thinking of American officials remained unchanged in the years between 1931 and 1937, during which Japan conquered Jehol, made several attempts to detach North China from Nanking, and put pressure on China to force acceptance of her terms of settlement. As late as January, 1936, Nelson T. Johnson, ambassador to China, whose sympathies for China were well known, wrote Secretary of State Hull: "I do not want to be considered one who believes that the American Government should bestir itself to use force to save China from probable Japanese conquest."[57] By 1936, when the Washington Naval Treaty expired, Japan's total tonnage had risen to 73 per cent of the corresponding strength of the United States.[58]

The outbreak of the Sino-Japanese War in July, 1937, did not bring about an immediate change in America's evaluation of her interests in China and her willingness to take active measures to oppose Japan. On October 5, 1937, President Roosevelt, in the Quarantine Speech, called for a concerted effort on the part of peaceful nations to quarantine the aggressor nations in order to prevent the spread of the epidemic of international lawlessness. The President seemed to have Japan uppermost in his mind.[59] But the congressional and public reaction was so intensely hostile to any hint of forcible action in another part of the world that the President was obliged to beat a hasty retreat. The next day at his press conference he endeavored to explain his speech away by characterizing it as an "expansion" of the Neutrality Act. In a lengthy letter to the *New York Times* on

[56] Hoover, *op. cit.*, pp. 367–68.
[57] Department of State, *Foreign Relations of the United States, 1936, Vol. IV: The Far East* (Washington, D.C.: Government Printing Office, 1954), p. 11.
[58] Morison, *op. cit.*, p. lix.
[59] Sumner Welles wrote: "The President was fully alive to the future menace to the United States in any direct or indirect domination of Europe by Nazi Germany. But I wish to make it unmistakably plain that in 1937 he was far more preoccupied with the threat represented by Japan. It was in the early part of that same summer that he first talked to me of the possibility of creating a naval barrier, later to be spoken of as a 'quarantine' if Japan should persist in her policy of conquering the rest of Asia" (*Seven Decisions That Shaped History* [New York: Harper & Bros., 1950], p. 8).
The German ambassador in Washington told Berlin that the "Quarantine threat was directed principally against Japan" (F. C. Jones, *Japan's New Order in East Asia* [London: Oxford University Press, 1954], p. 51).

October 7, Henry Stimson called for an embargo on the export of oil and metal scrap to Japan. But even he stated explicitly that there should not be "any thought of sending armies to a strife that is going on in Asia."[60]

Thus when the Brussels Conference met to consider the Far Eastern crisis, President Roosevelt found it necessary to instruct Norman Davis, the American delegate, that the American aim was to mobilize the moral force of the nations who wished peace and that he should observe closely the trend of public opinion in the United States to take full account of it. Secretary of State Hull made it clear that the conference should not discuss sanctions against Japan and should endeavor to find a solution by agreement, not force.[61] When Japan bombed the American gunboat "Panay," anchored some twenty-seven miles above Nanking, William Leahy, chief of naval operations, advocated the institution of a blockade against Japan.[62] But nothing came of this proposal because the United States was neither willing to go to war nor militarily prepared for it.

After 1937, the American people became fascinated by the stubborn and heroic resistance of the Chinese against the better-equipped and better-trained Japanese troops.[63] Some officials were more hostile to Japan than to Nazi Germany.[64] But it was not until mid-1940 that a profoundly significant change took place in American-Japanese relations. The German victory over Holland and France and the near defeat of Great Britain produced an acute sense of crisis in the United States, shocked America out of her traditional isolationism, and turned her toward intervention in the European war. Precisely at this juncture, Japan directed her attention from China to Southeast Asia. To pave the way for southward expansion, she concluded in September, 1940, the Tripartite Pact with Germany and Italy, the apparent victors over the powers with colonial possessions in that part of Asia. She also hoped to use the pact to keep the United States from interfering in Asia, to discourage the Western powers from aiding China, and to help her settle the Sino-Japanese War.[65] Coincident with the negotiations leading to the conclusion of the Tripartite Pact, Japan forced on the Vichy government, under the threat of

[60] Stimson's letter to the *New York Times*, October 6, 1937, as reprinted by League of Nations Association, p. 9.

[61] Herbert Feis, *The Road to Pearl Harbor* (Princeton, N.J.: Princeton University Press, 1950), pp. 13–14; Cordell Hull, *The Memoirs of Cordell Hull* (New York: Macmillan Co., 1948), I, 536–53; and William L. Langer and S. Everett Gleason, *The Challenge to Isolation* (New York: Harper & Bros., 1952), pp. 17–24.

[62] William Leahy, *I Was There* (New York: Whittlesey House, 1950), pp. 64, 128–29.

[63] Harold Isaacs, *Scratches on Our Minds* (New York: John Day Co., 1958), pp. 164–76.

[64] Notably Stanley Hornbeck and Norman Davis and Secretary Hull. See Neumann, *loc. cit.*, pp. 153–54.

[65] Schroeder, *op. cit.*, pp. 20–21; Jones, *op. cit.*, pp. 191–220. See also David J. Lu *From the Marco Polo Bridge to Pearl Harbor* (Washington, D.C.: Public Affairs Press, 1961).

a series of ultimatums, an agreement permitting her to station troops in northern Indochina.[66] She redoubled her efforts to draw the Netherlands East Indies into her orbit, but in vain. After the German invasion of the Soviet Union, Japan again advanced southward. In July, 1941, Japanese troops moved into southern Indochina to secure concentration points for an attack on Singapore and the Netherlands East Indies.[67]

Japan's actions in September, 1940, linked the wars in Europe and Asia and brought about a rapid change in America's estimate of the Japanese threat. A memorandum recording a talk between Secretary Hull and his staff on September 30, 1940, reads in part: "It was plain, however, in his [Hull's] own mind that if Japan did move in that quarter [Southeast Asia] the United States could not afford to see the Singapore base fall into the hands of Japan, exposing Australia and New Zealand."[68] Even Joseph Grew, American ambassador to Japan, who had counseled moderation on the American government, urged a show of force against Japan to deter her southward advance. In his famous "green light" message of September 12, 1940, he said:

> Japan today is one of the predatory powers. . . . Her policy of southward expansion is a definite threat to American interests in the Pacific and is a thrust at the British Empire in the East. American security has admittedly depended in a measure upon the existence of the British fleet which in turn has been, and could only have been, supported by the British Empire. If we conceive it to be in our interest to support the British Empire in this hour of her travail, and I most emphatically do so conceive it, we must strive by every means to preserve the status quo in the Pacific at least until the European War has been won or lost. In my opinion this cannot be done nor can our interests be further adequately and properly protected by merely registering disapproval and keeping a careful record thereof. . . . Until such time as there is a complete regeneration of thought in this country, a show of force, together with a determination to employ it if need be, can alone contribute effectively to the achievement of such an outcome and to our future security.[69]

But the United States was confronted with a dilemma. She was obviously far from prepared to fight a two-front war in both the Atlantic and

[66] *Ibid.*, p. 230.
[67] *Ibid.*, p. 363.
[68] Quoted in Feis, *op. cit.*, pp. 111–12.
[69] Joseph Grew, *Turbulent Era*, II (New York: Houghton Mifflin Co., 1952), 1228–29. For a discussion of this message, see Feis, *op. cit.*, pp. 101–2, and William L. Langer and S. Everett Gleason, *The Undeclared War* (New York: Harper & Bros., 1953), pp. 19–21.

the Pacific. In July, 1940, following the collapse of France, a two-ocean navy was authorized by Congress, but it would have taken six years to complete by peacetime methods of construction and two years at least by all-out effort.[70] In a letter written to Harold Ickes at this time, President Roosevelt said: ". . . as you know, it is terribly important for the control of the Atlantic for us to keep the peace in the Pacific. I simply have not got enough navy to go around."[71] A memorandum drafted in September, 1940, by the War Plans Division warned that the United States is "not now prepared and will not be prepared for several years to come" to make a major military effort in the Far East.[72] Up to the months immediately before the attack on Pearl Harbor, the armed services were pleading for time to build up their strength and fortify the line of defense. In particular, the War Department became a strong proponent of the policy of stalling for time in order to establish an effective force of Flying Fortresses in the Philippines and to complete a program of reinforcement there. On October 6, Stimson told Hull that the United States needed three months to secure her position.[73] Even as late as November 27, the Joint Board, the predecessor of the present Joint Chiefs of Staff, sent a memorandum to the White House warning against the dangers of hasty actions by the United States in the event of a Japanese move and stressing the need of the services for time.[74] On the eve of Pearl Harbor, Japan's total tonnage of modern and completed ships had risen to 81 percent of the naval strength of the United States, which had commitments in the Atlantic as well as the Pacific.[75]

Thus, immediate strategic interests required the United States to take the defensive in the Pacific, despite the new evaluation of Japan's threat to American security. American policy in this period was to avoid war with Japan so long as Japanese action in the Far East did not have any important effect on the war in Europe. As Admiral Harold Stark, chief of naval operations, remarked in October, 1940, during a discussion leading to the decision not to send American naval units to Singapore as a deterrent against Japan, "Every day we are able to maintain peace and still support Great Britain is valuable time gained."[76] The concept of the priority of Europe over the Far East was formally incorporated in the "ABC-1 Staff

[70] Morison, *op. cit.*, pp. 227–28; Samuel Eliot Morison, *The Rising Sun in the Pacific Ocean* (Boston: Little, Brown & Co., 1956), pp. 19–30, 31; and T. A. Bisson, *America's Far Eastern Policy* (New York: Macmillan Co., 1945), pp. 44–46.

[71] Quoted in Feis, *op. cit.*, pp. 206–7.

[72] Mark Skinner Watson, *Chief of Staff: Pre-War Plans and Preparations* (Washington, D.C.: Department of the Army, 1956), p. 116.

[73] Stimson and Bundy, *op. cit.*, p. 389.

[74] Langer and Gleason, *Undeclared War*, pp. 899–90.

[75] Knox, in Morison's *The Battle in the Atlantic*, p. lix.

[76] Watson, *op. cit.*, p. 117.

Agreement," which set down the conclusions of the joint American-British staff conferences held between January and March, 1941, and had the tacit approval of the President.[77] The pertinent sections read:

> Since Germany is the predominant member of the Axis Powers, the Atlantic and European Area is considered to be the decisive theatre. The principal United States military effort will be exerted in that theatre. . . . The military strategy in the Far East will be defensive.[78]

Equally revealing is a memorandum submitted on November 5, 1941, to President Roosevelt by General George C. Marshall, chief of staff of the army, and Admiral Stark. General Marshall and Admiral Stark told the President that a Japanese advance on Kunming, which in the opinion of Generalissimo Chiang Kai-shek would bring about the collapse of China, did not warrant America's entry into the war. But they drew a line in Southeast Asia and the western Pacific beyond which Japan should not be allowed to advance without fighting the United States. Stating the matter negatively, Marshall and Stark recommended that military action against Japan should be undertaken only when Japanese forces attacked the territory or mandated territory of the United States, the British Commonwealth, or the Netherlands East Indies, or moved into Thailand to the Isthmus of Kra or into Portuguese Timor, New Caledonia, or the Loyalty Islands.[79] If Japan had not attacked Pearl Harbor, the line drawn by General Marshall and Admiral Stark might have been the boundary between war and peace. An American decision to defend this line would have had essentially the purpose of protecting the strategic resources in Southeast Asia and the essential trade routes on which the survival of Great Britain against German blockade and attack in part depended.

In April, 1941, Secretary Hull began negotiations with the Japanese ambassador to Washington, which lasted until the attack on Pearl Harbor. One of Hull's immediate objectives was to gain time. But, beneath the seemingly unchanged surface, a significant development in America's Far Eastern policy occurred. Secretary Hull broadened the traditional formulas concerning China into universalistic principles, thus making them

[77] Feis, op. cit., p. 168.
[78] Joint Committee on the Investigation of the Pearl Harbor Attack, Hearings on the Pearl Harbor Attack, 79th Cong., 1st and 2d sess. (1945–46), Part 15, p. 1491 (hereafter cited as Pearl Harbor Attack). For an account of the events surrounding the staff agreement, see Feis, op. cit., p. 168, and Langer and Gleason, The Undeclared War, pp. 285–89.
[79] Pearl Harbor Attack, Part 14, p. 1062. For a discussion of this memorandum, see Feis, op. cit., pp. 302–5. Langer and Gleason, Undeclared War, pp. 844–48; and Paul Varg, op. cit.

applicable to Japan's action in Southeast Asia. At the beginning of his conversations with the Japanese ambassador, he laid down four points on which he sought the approval of the Japanese government. They were: "respect for the territorial integrity and the sovereignty of each and all nations; support of the principle of non-interference in the internal affairs of other countries; support of the principle of equality, including equality of commercial opportunity; and non-disturbance of the *status quo* in the Pacific except as the *status quo* may be altered by peaceful means."[80] With some slight changes, they were reiterated in the comprehensive program for a settlement which Hull handed the Japanese ambassador on November 26, 1941, in reply to Japan's minimum terms for a modus vivendi.[81]

Far more important was the fact that they were now, to use Schroeder's words, "no longer to be simply principles which the United States would uphold, but a program which it would finally have to enforce."[82] They formed the basis of a program with three objectives: to stop Japan from any further advance southward, to persuade Japan to withdraw from the Tripartite Pact, and to obtain the evacuation of Japanese troops from China. Up until July, 1941, the first two aims were accorded priority over the third.[83] To enforce this program, the United States froze Japanese assets in July, 1941, and thus imposed a total embargo on oil when Japan moved into southern Indochina.

This drastic action produced the intended effect. Japan went on the defensive and indicated her willingness to halt her southward march. She gave a hint of an inclination to take a course independent of Germany, though she was never ready to make a clear and reliable promise not to join Germany in war. It is a moot point whether war could have been avoided by accepting these Japanese concessions in exchange for an American acquiescence in the continued Japanese occupation of parts of China. In any case, the traditional principles and the force of public opinion after 1941 propelled to the top of America's scheme of priorities the objective of defending the integrity of China and the concomitant demand for the withdrawal of Japanese troops from China. Since Japan would rather accept war with the United States than withdraw her troops from China, the attack on Pearl Harbor ensued. The United States was forced to abandon the policy of refraining from going to war to defend her interests and principles in China.

[80] Memorandum by the Secretary of State, April 16, 1941, Department of State, *Foreign Relations of the United States: Japan: 1931–1941*, II (Washington, D.C.: Government Printing Office, 1943), 407.

[81] Document handed by the Secretary of State to the Japanese ambassador (Nomura) on November 26, 1941, *ibid.*, p. 768.

[82] Schroeder, *op. cit.*, p. 24.

[83] *Ibid.*, p. 174.

D. An Appraisal

The traditional policy of the United States in the Far East up to 1941 consisted of two potentially contradictory aspects: espousal of the Open Door principles and refusal to go to war in the defense of American principles and interests in China. The basic driving force behind it was American idealism. But it was also the product of the view that American interests in China were not essential, though potentially important. While reluctant to pay a heavy price to promote her ideals and to protect her interests, the United States was unwilling to relinquish her principles and her hope of future gains. Thus, she included in her policy two contradictory elements and, up to 1941, prevented the potential contradiction from becoming an actuality by pursuing strictly limited, immediate objectives. Sometimes, these amounted to nothing more than the preservation of what was left of China's territorial and administrative integrity and the Open Door. At other times, they consisted of the restoration of some aspects of China's integrity and some improvements in the conditions protecting equal economic opportunity. At all times, the objectives included the securing of verbal indorsement of the principles by other powers. These immediate, limited objectives were sought by diplomatic, peaceful methods. The principles themselves, were, in effect, long-term goals, again to be achieved by the same methods.

The growth of American influence and potential power enabled the United States, until September, 1931, to pursue progressively greater immediate objectives and to secure a larger measure of observance and a firmer indorsement of her principles. From the demand by Hay for equality of trade in consumption merchandise, the United States went forward, under Secretary Knox and then under President Wilson after November, 1917, to secure equal opportunity for financial investment. She took a further step when Secretary Hughes obtained in the Nine-Power Treaty the pledges of the powers not to seek spheres of influence or mutually exclusive opportunities in designated parts of Chinese territory. The evasive responses of the powers to Hay's circular stood in contrast to the sweeping declarations for the integrity of China and the Open Door in Article I of the Nine-Power Treaty. After the establishment of the Nationalist government in 1927, the slow, tortuous, but discernible progress in China toward political unity enabled the Chinese to take advantage of the American policy in their partly successful attempts to restore Chinese integrity, as for example in the recovery of tariff autonomy in the years between 1929 and 1933.

But there were obvious limits to the possible success of American policy. Although America's pursuit of her immediate, limited objectives by peaceful means did not pose any critical problems for the powers, the vital interests of Japan were threatened by the progressive realization of the Open Door principles. For the principles could not be fully realized unless there was to be a fundamental change in the Far Eastern structure of power in which the special privileges and position of Japan in China would be eliminated and China herself would become a leading power. As an answer to the challenge of rising Chinese nationalism, Japan occupied Manchuria in 1931 and by this action undermined the structure of treaties concluded at the Washington Conference. Since American-Japanese opposition was the sole source of political equilibrium in the Far East after the Washington Conference, conditions favorable to the progressive realization of the Open Door principles could have been maintained only if the United States had been willing and able to use force to oppose Japan. Events from 1931 to Pearl Harbor increasingly sharpened the contradiction between the end and the means of American policy. The coming of the Pacific war meant, finally, that the United States had failed to prevent, by her traditional method, the potential contradiction from becoming an actuality. It signified that this contradiction was resolved in favor of the principles, but more by the compulsion of circumstances and public opinion than by a cool calculation of strategic interests. The American response to Japan's action in 1941 involved no change in the central feature of the basic pattern: the unwillingness and inability to make *purposeful* use of military power to maintain or restore the Far Eastern balance of power. Moreover, when the clash came, the gradual weakening of the Nationalist government in the course of the Sino-Japanese conflict had already challenged the tacit assumption of the Open Door policy that a strong and friendly China would emerge as a stabilizing force in a new structure of power. At the same time, the pressing requirements of a two-ocean war were thought to prevent the adoption of a strategy which might have reversed in time the political trend in China.

Could the potential contradiction in the traditional China policy have been resolved by a deliberate choice between one of its two conflicting aspects at an earlier time, so that war with Japan might have been avoided or, if unavoidable, might have taken place at a more opportune time? [84] Given the American conception of her interests in China, the relinquish-

[84] This speculative question was raised and discussed in the works of a group of able writers and serious thinkers who, during the national mood of self-criticism that developed after the Communist conquest of the mainland and Peking's intervention in the Korean War, expressed profound doubts about the wisdom of the traditional Far Eastern policy of the United States. See works by Kennan and Current, cited above. Also, William L. Neumann, "How American Policy toward Japan Contributed to War in the Pacific," in *Perpetual War for Perpetual Peace*, ed. Harry H. Barnes (Caldwell, Idaho: Canton Printers, 1953); and Louis Halle, *Dream and Reality: Aspects of American Foreign Policy* (New York: Harper & Bros., 1959).

ment, in practice, if not in official pronouncements, of the Open Door principles had much to recommend itself in the period before the First World War. Prior to the war, America's political and economic interests were amply protected by the moving equilibrium among the powers. Theodore Roosevelt's policy of balancing Russia and Japan against each other met two elementary criteria of sound policy. It gave adequate protection to American interests. It did not outrun America's capability.

After the First World War, however, the alternative open to Theodore Roosevelt was, for all practical purposes, excluded by the new structure of power. There was no realistic foundation for the idea that the United States could have maintained the political balance of power in the Far East by balancing Japan and Russia or, as Louis Halle suggests, by refraining from "actively discouraging" Japan from turning her attention toward "the limitless mainland of northeast Asia" where "Japan came into conflict with the Soviet Union. . . ."[85] Nor is there validity in George Kennan's thought that if the United States had not based her policy on the Open Door principles and "had been over a long period of time more circumspect in our attitude toward the Japanese, more considerate of the requirements of their position, more ready to discuss their problems with them on their own terms," something hopeful could have been accomplished in the early phase of Japanese-American relations to arrest the drift toward war, but that in the later phase, after an unspecified point in time, "sheer tragedy overtook human frailty as the determinant of our misfortune."[86]

There is little evidence in this period to show that, if the United States had gracefully acquiesced in the conquest of Manchuria, Japan would have refrained from pushing ever deeper into China and finally into Southeast Asia. On the contrary, as Henry L. Stimson and McGeorge Bundy noted in 1947, "If the Japanese had been content with their Manchurian conquest, they might have remained at peace with the world as they had done after similar conquest of Korea and the non-recognition doctrine must in time have become merely a dead letter."[87] As Schroeder points out, the American policy up to July, 1941, was defensive, no matter how unnecessarily provocative her pronouncements were.

In the early thirties, the Japanese militarists themselves were divided over the fateful question whether Japan should consolidate her position in Manchuria or whether she should continue to push in the direction of China, if for no other reason than to protect her Manchurian conquest.[88]

[85] Halle, *op. cit.*, pp. 246–47.
[86] Kennan, *op. cit.*, p. 51.
[87] Stimson and Bundy, *op. cit.*, p. 261.
[88] Jones, *op. cit.*, p. 18; Delmer M. Brown, *Nationalism in Japan* (Berkeley: University of California Press, 1955), pp. 175–96, 198, 202, 235.

The Kōdōha, or the Imperial Way Group, favored the first course of action while the Tōseiha, or the Control Group, was inclined toward the second. But it was the Control Group which gradually won out in the struggle for power in the army. After the incident of February 26, 1936, the Kōdōha as an organized group was virtually destroyed. Meanwhile, Japan pushed farther and farther into China. Events in the thirties showed that it was military success in China rather than American provocation which was the primary factor in contributing to the rising power of the Japanese army and the eclipse of the influence of the civilian moderates.

It was inevitable, in a very real sense, that Japan would continue to expand in the direction of China and Southeast Asia, even if the conquest of China was thought to be a step in preparation of an eventual war with Russia. In the first place, most empire builders are affected by a general tendency to go a step farther in order to protect what has already been won. The Control Group was no exception to this rule.[89] Second, China and Southeast Asia constituted an attractive prize for a nation with a rapidly growing population but poor natural resources. They were immediately more inviting than Siberia. Third, there was no effective barrier against expansion toward the south. China was still weak and her armies were badly equipped and inadequately trained. The influence and the power of the European nations in the Far East were in rapid decline. America's unwillingness and inability to back up her principles with military power seemed to remove her as a possible source of effective resistance. In order to have turned the expansionist tendency of Japan toward Northeast Asia or simply to have preserved the balance of power in the Far East, it would not have been enough merely to refrain from condemning Japan's conquest of Manchuria and from discouraging Japan's ambitions in Northeast Asia. It would have been necessary to build up and use American power to deter Japan's expansion beyond Manchuria or some other line in China. This would have required the United States to pursue a positive policy of containing Japan, which would have involved a serious risk of war whether in the name of the Open Door principles or on the ground of strategic self-interest.

In the event, Japan's expansion in the direction of North China brought about the Sino-Japanese War in 1937. After the rout of the Central Army of China in the Shanghai-Nanking area, South China was wide open to conquest. Once intrenched in South China and Hainan Island, Japan was in a strategic position to exploit the opportunities to march into Southeast Asia offered by the German victories. The acute threat posed by Japan in the summer of 1941 to British and American positions in the South Seas

[89] Jones, *op. cit.*, p. 18.

was a natural end-product of the overturn of the balance of power in the Far East which began with Japan's attack on China in 1937, if not with the occupation of Manchuria in 1931.

It is interesting to note that the drastic action of the United States in imposing a total embargo on oil was the only American move between 1931 and 1941 which helped to bring about a serious desire on the part of Japan to halt her expansion. It helped the moderates momentarily to take the initiative in the conduct of foreign policy. Only at this point did the traditional principles significantly affect the course of American action by preventing a compromise with Japan and by overriding the policy of refraining from going to war for the sake of China.

Thus the policy of refraining from using force to defend American interests in China merely postponed but did not avoid war. One need not speculate on the question whether the abandonment of this policy at an earlier date would have been in the interests of the United States. What one can reasonably argue is that the United States would have been in a better position to fight a war with Japan in 1937 and the first half of 1938 than in 1941. But, given the American conception of her interests in China, it was out of the question for the United States to go to war with Japan until traditional isolationism had been successfully challenged and Japan had menaced the British trade routes in Southeast Asia and threatened to grasp the essential raw materials there. For the United States conceived of her stake in China primarily in terms of her material and cultural interests rather than as the political interest of maintaining a Far Eastern balance of power. This conception was an expression of isolationism, which denied the primacy of foreign policy and which saw American interests abroad mainly as an extension of American domestic affairs. There was no diplomatic tradition which considered the maintenance of the balance of power in Europe and Asia as primary political objectives of the United States and which sought to evaluate constantly the relations between the two structures of power and to determine the effects on Europe of the collapse of the balance in the Far East. As Neumann puts it: "At no time in the interwar period did any responsible government official make a public and explicit statement of the priorities of American interest in Asia. The relationship of these interests to American interests in other areas remained ambiguous, and which interests in Asia, if any, were vital enough to justify war in their behalf was never clarified."[90] Thus, there could not have been any notion of seeking to preserve the political equilibrium in the Far East by accepting war. Under these circumstances, diplomacy and military power were divorced. The non-military approach to diplomacy

[90] Neumann, "Ambiguity and Ambivalence in Ideas of National Interest in Asia," in DeConde, *op. cit.*, p. 140.

found expression in the gap between America's military capability and her immediate objectives and long-term principles.[91]

Under the influence of the exigencies of war after Pearl Harbor, the United States adopted the policy of making China a great power. But in retrospect it is clear that by this time the prospect for the emergence of China as a strong and friendly nation was already dim. This unpromising situation had come about mainly through Japan's attack on China, which the United States alone could have stopped. Furthermore, the political policy of making China a great power was primarily a means to keep China in the war. It was not effectively implemented by military measures, as we shall see. The non-military approach to diplomacy found a new expression in the failure to make a constant adjustment between political policy and changes in military thinking. The principle of non-intervention, which the United States had invoked against the powers when her political interest in China appeared to be meager, inhibited her from actively intervening in Chinese politics to pursue her positive goals at a time when she became even more deeply involved in China than the powers had ever been. After the war, American policy was consistently governed by her unwillingness to use her armed forces on the mainland of China. Thus, the roots of America's diplomatic disaster in 1949–50 lay deep in the traditions of American policy established since the dispatch of the Open Door notes by Secretary Hay.

[91] For a discussion of the non-military approach to diplomacy, see J. Chalmers Vinson, "Military Force and American Foreign Policy, 1919–1939," in *ibid.*, pp. 56–81.

PART ONE

TO

MAKE

CHINA

A GREAT

POWER

CHAPTER II

AMERICAN

CONCEPTIONS

AND

CHINESE

REALITIES

A. The Web of American Objectives, Policies, and Assumptions

The main American objective in the Far East during the Pacific war was the unconditional surrender of Japan within an over-all strategy of defeating Germany first.[1] As a means to this end, the United States pursued a policy of keeping China in the war in order to make maximum use of her military potential and strategic geographical position in the common war effort. Linked with this policy was another which proved to have far-reaching consequences: the policy of making China a great power and treating her as one of the Big Four for the purpose of building a postwar political order in the Far East. "Toward China we had two objectives," wrote Secretary of State Cordell Hull in his *Memoirs*: "The first was an effective joint prosecution of the war. The second was the recognition and building up of China as a major power entitled to equal rank with the three big Western Allies, Russia, Britain, and the United States, during and after the war, both for the preparation of a postwar organization and for the establishment of stability and prosperity in the Orient."[2] Thus, unlike American wartime activities in Europe, the United States did have a polit-

[1] Cf. Hanson W. Baldwin, *Great Mistakes of the War* (New York: Harper & Bros., 1950).

[2] Cordell Hull, *The Memoirs of Cordell Hull* (New York: Macmillan Co., 1948), II, 1583. The Department of State defined the policy toward China in the following terms: "The principal and immediate objectives of the United States government are to keep China in the war against Japan and to mobilize China's full military and economic strength in the vigorous prosecution of the war.

"The American Government's long range policy with respect to China is based on the belief that the need for China to be a principal stabilizing factor in the Far East is a fundamental requirement for peace and security in that region" (Senate Committee on the Judiciary, *Hearings on the Institute of Pacific Relations*, 82d Cong., 1st and 2d sess. [1951–52], p. 2839 [hereafter cited as *Institute of Pacific Relations*]).

33

ical policy in the Far East other than the military objective of unconditional surrender and the over-all political objective of setting up a general
international organization to preserve peace.[3]

To avert a military collapse of China while making maximum use of her
military potential, the United States endeavored to discourage the Nationalist government from launching a large-scale attack on the Chinese Communists, to use Communist forces and base areas in the common war
effort, and finally to bring the Nationalists and the Communists together in
a coalition government. This policy of bringing about a united and democratic China by peaceful means also derived impetus from the policy of
making China a great power. For China could not fulfil the role assigned
to her by the United States if she was left, in the words of Sumner Welles,
"to welter indefinitely in civil war and anarchy."[4]

The American attempt to make China a great power and to bring about
a political settlement between the Kuomintang and the Chinese Communists was grounded also on her estimate of Russia's intentions toward China
and her hope for continued co-operation with the Soviet Union after the
war, not only in the Far East, but throughout the world. Washington
thought that by giving China the status of a great power; by obtaining a
Soviet pledge to observe certain principles of international conduct; by
bringing China and Russia together in a formal accord; and by uniting the
Chinese Nationalists and Communists in a coalition government — it could
ward off Soviet interference in Chinese affairs, gain Russia's good will toward China, and assure continued American-Soviet co-operation in the
Far East after the war.[5]

Both the grand design for postwar American-Soviet co-operation and
the policy of bringing about a united and democratic China by peaceful
means were consistent with the objective of obtaining the unconditional
surrender of Japan. For, assuming the possibility of continued American-
Soviet concord in the Far East and Nationalist-Communist co-operation
inside China, the most important task was simply to defeat the enemy.
Thus, American military objectives, political policies, and assumptions

[3] The military objective of unconditional surrender of all enemies was consistent
with the assumption that in the postwar world all nations would behave in accordance
with the basic principles of peaceful international conduct; see William H. McNeill,
*Survey of International Affairs, 1939–1946: America, Britain, and Russia: Their Co-
operation and Conflict* (London: Oxford University Press, 1953), pp. 169–70, 269–70,
360–67, 403–5, 532–33, 760–63. It is also consistent with the assumption that China
would emerge as a great power. But this consistency need not mean that American
officials consciously adopted the principle of unconditional surrender to implement
their idealistic program for the postwar world.
[4] Sumner Welles, *Seven Decisions That Shaped History* (New York: Harper &
Bros., 1950), pp. 161–62; and Herbert Feis, *The China Tangle* (Princeton, N.J.: Princeton University Press, 1953), p. 164. See also chap. v, below.
[5] Feis, *op. cit.*, pp. 95–100, 137. See also chaps. iii, vii, below.

about the postwar world formed a coherent whole, linked together by the supreme operational goal of a quick victory over Japan and by the principle of unconditional surrender.

But, unfortunately, this whole structure was founded on a misjudgment of the intentions of the Soviet Union, the world Communist movement, and the Chinese Communist party. It crumbled when neither the Soviet Union nor the Chinese Communists behaved according to the expectations of American officials. Furthermore, the structure took its consistency and its rationale from a military rather than a political objective. In the flux of unfolding events, the political policy became simply a means to achieve the military goal. This reversal of the rational order of political end and military means was the wartime expression of the traditional American divorce of diplomacy from military power. Since the military objective was the paramount goal, the political implications of American military measures were not taken fully into consideration and military strategy was not planned in the light of its political effects on the internal stability of China. The desire to use Chinese Communist forces and base areas became one source of the misjudgment of the nature and intentions of the Chinese Communist party. As a result, the political policy of making China a great power was implemented merely by diplomatic actions. The real nature of the situation was subtly and penetratingly described by Marshall's remark that "President Roosevelt's policy was to *treat* China *as* a great power."[6] The pursuit of the political policy by diplomatic actions alone, with the resulting discrepancy between the declared political objective and the concrete military programs, served only to magnify the consequences of the collapse of the total structure of policy.

B. The Policy of Making China a Great Power: Assumptions and Sentiments

The policy of making China a great power was predicated on the implicit assumption that China would emerge from the Pacific war a powerful nation, friendly to the United States. It embodied a benevolent, noble, and inspiring vision which arose out of a century of seemingly uninterrupted friendship and affection for an oppressed country struggling to free herself from foreign domination and exploitation and to lift herself from backwardness and poverty. It was a policy befitting the generous impulses of the American people who had succeeded in gaining their own independence and establishing a prosperous community of free men in the New World.

The assumption underlying this policy was not entirely unrealistic. Viewed in the long perspective of history, the decrepit state in which

---

[6] Charles F. Romanus and Riley Sunderland, *Stilwell's Mission to China* (Washington, D.C.: Government Printing Office, 1953), p. 62, n. 40. Emphasis added.

China found herself could not but be temporary. A nation which had a record of unbroken cultural continuity over a period of more than three thousand years would certainly find a way to rejuvenate herself sooner or later. In the light of the dynastic cycles characteristic of the long history of China, the present confusion could be easily seen as an interregnum after which a period of restored greatness and glory was sure to come. From the perspective of the movement of world history, it could be interpreted as the twilight before the dawn of a new era in which the traditional grandeur of the Middle Kingdom was to project itself through the power of modernized, industrialized, and democratized China.[7]

This long view on the prospect of China seemed to have been borne out by the recent history of China, which showed substantial progress toward modernization, however slow and halting. The long war of resistance against Japanese aggression, which surprised the Western powers, was considered an indication of the revived political strength of China. It seemed likely, therefore, that the emergence of China as a great power under the aegis of the United States would restore her to her former greatness, herald the end of European imperialism everywhere in the Orient, and usher in a period in which the East and the West would live together on the basis of equality and friendship. This was indeed a noble and inspiring vision.

Of course, there were also seemingly good reasons in the realm of high policy for making China a great power and treating her as one of the Big Four. Indeed, this policy had always been implicit in the twin principles of the Open Door, and its unfolding at this time signalized the apparently impending fulfilment of the traditional policy of the United States toward China. Taking the China policy of the United States as a special case of the Open Door policy toward Asia in general, Tyler Dennett observed early in the twenties that the "corollary of the open door was the policy of promoting an Asia strong enough to be its own door keeper."[8] This view was spelled out in the forties by T. A. Bisson in his *America's Far Eastern Policy,* a work which reflected the prevailing thinking on Far Eastern problems during World War II. He argued that the principles of the American policy toward China as finally embodied in the Nine-Power Treaty were "essentially a stop gap" until China became strong enough to assume full responsibility for her national security. "A strong and united China"

[7] Secretary of State Hull told T. V. Soong, the foreign minister of China, of his belief that Madame Chiang and the Generalissimo "would live to see a great renaissance take place in China in all important lines of human endeavor, such as swept over Europe like a sunburst during the fourteenth and fifteenth centuries" (Department of State, *Foreign Relations of the United States, 1943: China* [Washington, D.C.: Government Printing Office, 1962], p. 66).

[8] Tyler Dennett, *Americans in Eastern Asia* (New York: Macmillan Co., 1922), p. 677.

capable of protecting her independence by her own efforts was "the main requisite for a more stable basis of peace in the Far East." When this condition was realized, "the open door doctrine, in its specifically Chinese application, would become an anachronism and cease to exist."[9]

Even if the United States had not deliberately followed up the implications of the Open Door principles, the logic of events flowing from an American policy based on these principles and from the characteristically American approach to the problem of war and peace would have left the United States with no alternative but to make China a great power. For, in the face of Japan's refusal to abandon her military conquests and her special political and economic positions in China, the American rejection of any solution which might compromise these traditional principles made an armed clash with Japan inevitable, as the negotiations in the second half of 1941 show.[10] Given the wartime aim of unconditional surrender of the enemy and the congruent postwar aims of punishing the aggressor, preventing a revival of the Japanese military threat by the liquidation of the Japanese Empire, and establishing a system of collective security for the preservation of a just and peaceful order, the need for a strong China to fill the resulting power vacuum is clear. As Hull wrote in his *Memoirs*:

> I never faltered in my belief that we should do everything in our power to assist China to become strong and stable. It was obvious to me that Japan would disappear as a great Oriental power for a long time to come. Therefore, the only major strictly Oriental power would be China. The United States, Britain and Russia were also Pacific powers, but the great interests of each were elsewhere. Consequently, if there was ever to be stability in the Far

[9] T. A. Bisson, *America's Far Eastern Policy* (New York: Macmillan Co., 1945), pp. 6–7, 13.

[10] Herbert Feis, *The Road to Pearl Harbor* (Princeton, N. J.: Princeton University Press, 1950), chaps. xxxii–xl; F. C. Jones, *Japan's New Order in East Asia* (London: Oxford University Press, 1954), pp. 457–58; and Paul W. Schroeder, *The Axis Alliance and Japanese-American Relations, 1941* (Ithaca, N.Y.: Cornell University Press, 1958), pp. 168–216. For a different interpretation, see Toshikazu Kase, *Journey to the Missouri* (New Haven: Yale University Press, 1950), p. 56: "The negotiations were indeed hopelessly muddled. It was singular, to say the least, that during the critical period from July to October, 1941, neither the Foreign Office nor the embassy in Washington understood the real issue clearly. They believed that the withdrawal of our armed forces from China constituted the main — and almost the sole — point of disagreement. That is why Tojo could wreck the Konoye cabinet by refusing to consider such withdrawal. Actually the crucial issues, as I have indicated elsewhere, were our alliance with Germany and the pursuit of our expansionist policy, one and the same thing in the mind of the American government. As our government missed this point, the conduct of negotiations was bound to be futile and in several months' time much irreparable harm had been done."

East, it had to be assured with China at the center of any arrangement that was made.[11]

The policy of making China a great power stemmed also from certain assumptions about the postwar world and America's role in it. President Roosevelt was captivated by a vision of an era of international peace, freedom, and justice based upon the moral principles of the Atlantic Charter and the Declaration of the United Nations, ushered in by the establishment of an international organization and policed by the peace-loving powers. To him there did not exist any basic, irreconcilable conflicts of interest between the United States and the Soviet Union or any other countries. Thus, he envisaged his future role as that of arbiter, conciliator, and teacher, adjusting the differences between Great Britain, the Soviet Union, and China and educating them in the new ways of international behavior. Together, these four great powers would be members of a new "Holy Alliance" to defend and enforce a democratic, liberal world order.[12] Such a scheme required a strong China to be a competent partner. China as a member of the highest council in the world organization would give it a world-wide rather than an exclusively European character and would serve to rally Asian loyalty to the new organization. This would also be an advantage for the purposes of American domestic politics,[13] for it would neutralize those who were more concerned with the Far East than with Europe.

President Roosevelt was not totally oblivious to the possibility of differences between the United States and the Soviet Union or the United States and Great Britain. But he seemed to be convinced that the cleavages dividing the other countries from each other ran deeper than those separating the United States from them. In his opinion this would be particularly true with reference to China. Historically, China had always been suspicious of Russia's intentions toward her border areas from Manchuria in the east to Sinkiang in the west. Confronted with a powerful Communist opposition, the Nationalist government was also wary of the possibility of Soviet intervention on the side of its political opponents. As the President told Eden, in insisting on China's membership in the council of great powers, "China, in any serious conflict of policy with Russia, would undoubtedly line up on our side."[14] But the President's postwar policies were also premised upon continued American-Soviet co-operation, which could be disrupted by distrust and conflicts between China and the Soviet Union. By strengthening China's international position, officials in the State De-

---

[11] Hull, *op. cit.*, p. 1587.

[12] McNeill, *op. cit.*, pp. 366–67.

[13] Robert Sherwood, *Roosevelt and Hopkins* (New York: Harper & Bros., 1948), p. 786.

[14] *Ibid.*, p. 718.

partment hoped the Nationalist government would feel more secure in its relations with the Soviet Union and the Chinese Communists and would follow American advice in its policies toward both.[15] As Hull stated, "It would be easier to influence China's development internationally and internally if she were on the inside of any special relationship among the big powers, than if she were on the outside."[16] Furthermore, by obtaining the pledge of the Soviet Union in a joint declaration of basic principles of international conduct, which China also signed in her new status as a great power, America hoped to limit Soviet ambitions toward China and pave the way toward a direct Sino-Soviet accord.[17] Thus, in the Four-Nation Declaration of Moscow, signed on October 30, 1943, the governments of the United States, Great Britain, the Soviet Union, and China jointly declared that "after the termination of hostilities they will not employ their military forces within the territories of other states except for the purposes envisaged in this declaration and after joint consultation."[18] The Moscow Declaration vividly revealed America's faith in the capability of general principles couched in ambiguous language to exorcise the conflicts among nations and to restrain the ambitions of an aggressive revolutionary power.

The President was also certain that China would wholeheartedly support the United States in any conflict with Great Britain. He was thoroughly familiar with the Chinese attitude toward British imperialism — an attitude which he and many Americans heartily approved.[19] Early in the war the conflict between China and Great Britain over the defense of Burma was brought forcefully to his attention.[20] Madame Chiang in her visit to Washington in 1942 acquainted Hopkins with her critical attitude toward the British.[21] The Chinese suspicion of British motives was reciprocated by the British with a curious mixture of condescension, if not contempt, toward the Chinese and a fear of a reinvigorated China. As reported by Hopkins, Eden told Hull in 1943 that he "did not much like the idea of the Chinese running up and down the Pacific."[22] In his visit to Washington right after Pearl Harbor, Churchill had made known to the President that he admired and liked the Chinese as a race and "pitied [them] for their endless misgovernment."[23] Furthermore, the President knew that he would have the

[15] Feis, *The China Tangle*, pp. 95, 98.

[16] Hull, *op. cit.*, p. 1257. See also memorandum from Stanley K. Hornbeck to Hull, in *Foreign Relations of the United States, 1943: China*, p. 822.

[17] Feis, *The China Tangle*, pp. 97, 100.

[18] *Foreign Relations of the United States, 1943: China*, p. 831.

[19] Elliott Roosevelt, *As He Saw It* (New York: Duell, Sloan & Pearce, Inc., 1946), and Sherwood, *op. cit.*, p. 661.

[20] Winston Churchill, *The Second World War*, Vol. IV: *The Hinge of Fate* (London: Cassel, 1951), pp. 119–20.

[21] Sherwood, *op. cit.*, p. 661.

[22] *Ibid.*, p. 716.

[23] Churchill, *op. cit.*, p. 119.

co-operation of China in his policy of liquidating the colonial system in Asia [24] and in his favorite project of setting up a trusteeship system. In a conversation with Molotov in June, 1942, he attributed to Generalissimo Chiang Kai-shek the idea of instituting some sort of interim international trusteeship to administer the colonial possessions of European powers and to prepare them for independence. He asked Mr. Molotov to discuss this system with Stalin.[25]

Many Americans also felt that in China the United States found the most reliable adherent to her idea of establishing a just and peaceful world order through the machinery of an international organization and the spread of international good will. Cosmopolitanism and the idea of a universal order have always been prominent features in Chinese political thought. In "The Program of Resistance and Reconstruction," a quasi-constitutional proclamation of war policy adopted by the Kuomintang party congress in 1938, China solemnly declared herself "prepared to safeguard and strengthen the machinery of peace. . . ."[26] In addressing the People's Political Council, the Generalissimo declared:

> Toward Asia as toward the whole world we wish only to do our duty to the exclusion of any lust for power or other desires incompatible with the moral dictates of love and benevolence that are characteristic of the Chinese national spirit. The aim of the Revolution is, so far as the interests of China herself are concerned, the restoration of her original frontiers and, in regard to the rest of the world, a gradual advance of all nations from the stage of equality to that of an ideal unity.[27]

In answering the question whether a China based on the Three Principles of the People would have any positive proposals to make concerning the subject of world federation or confederation, the Generalissimo said: "In as much as cosmopolitanism and world peace are two of the main aims of San Min Chu I ["The Three Principles of the People"] China will naturally be disposed to participate in any world federation or confederation based on the principle of equality of nations and for the good of mankind."[28] These statements concerning war aims and international order

---

[24] On the President's policy toward colonies, see Sherwood, *op. cit.*, pp. 572–73, 718–19; Hull, *op. cit.*, pp. 1477–78, 1159–1601; Roosevelt, *op. cit.*, pp. 37, 223–24, 74; and Welles, *op. cit.*, pp. 150–51.

[25] Sherwood, *op. cit.*, p. 573.

[26] Paul M. A. Linebarger, *The China of Chiang Kai-shek* (New World: World Peace Foundation, 1941), p. 310. For a slightly different translation, see *China Handbook: 1937–1945* (rev. ed.; New York: Macmillan Co., 1947), p. 79.

[27] Chiang Kai-shek, "The End of Unequal Treaties in China," in *The Collected Wartime Messages of Chiang Kai-shek, 1937–1945* (New York: John Day Co., 1946), II, 719.

[28] Linebarger, *op. cit.*, p. 371.

could not but strike a responsive chord in the hearts of a generation of officials and intellectuals raised in the era of Wilsonian idealism.

Thus President Roosevelt, the formulator and executor of the policy of making China a great power, thought he had good reason to believe that the United States would have the political support of China in the peace settlement and in the postwar world. Chinese leaders lost no opportunity to promote this belief. During her visit to the United States in the winter of 1942–43, Madame Chiang assured Hopkins that "China would line up with us [the United States] at the peace table."[29] She considered this assurance "a commitment in advance which she was willing to make because of China's confidence in the President."[30] Thus the United States assumed that China would be a grateful, friendly, and co-operative partner in the task of building and maintaining a just, peaceful, and stable order in the Far East.

But sentimental impulses, traditional principles, and postwar plans provided only a general framework within which military considerations exerted their decisive influence in pushing the United States to adopt the policy of making China a great power. America's pursuit of unconditional surrender of Japan intensified her interest in China's military potential. These military considerations took the form of an incorrect estimate of the probable contribution of China to the common war effort and an exaggerated fear of a separate peace between China and Japan. Both the hope and the fear were actively fostered and exploited by the Nationalist government as a lever to gain concessions from the United States.

During the early phase of the war it was generally believed by high officials in Washington that China could make significant contributions to the speedy defeat of Japan in several ways. In American strategic planning after Pearl Harbor, the first contribution of China was to provide air bases from which Japanese shipping might be interrupted and destroyed and Japan herself bombed.[31] The existing air bases in China had thus to be guarded against possible Japanese assault, and additional air bases and staging areas had to be established in North China, which was then occupied by Japan. To perform these two tasks, the United States hoped to utilize the immense reservoir of Chinese manpower. This was the second contribution which, in the opinion of many American officials, China could make. Many of those who were far away from the Chinese scene believed that modern weapons and equipment could transform the Chinese armies into a formidable fighting force. As Admiral Ernest J. King told the Combined Chiefs of Staff in January, 1943:

[29] Sherwood, *op. cit.*, p. 706.
[30] *Ibid.*
[31] Romanus and Sunderland, *op. cit.*, p. 357. See chap. iii., below.

In the European theatre, Russia was most advantageously placed for dealing with Germany in view of her geographical position and manpower; in the Pacific, China bore a similar relation to the Japanese. It should be our basic policy to provide the manpower resources of Russia and China with the necessary equipment to enable them to fight.[32]

This hopeful view on the probable contribution of China was in harmony with President Roosevelt's proverbial optimism and pro-Chinese sentiments and was heartily shared by him. As Churchill observed:

At Washington I had found the extraordinary significance of China in American minds, even at the top, strangely out of proportion. I was conscious of a standard of values which accorded China almost an equal fighting power with the British Empire, and rated the Chinese armies as a factor to be mentioned in the same breath as the armies of Russia. I told the President how much I felt American opinion overestimated the contribution which China could make to the general war. He differed strongly. There were five hundred million people in China. What would happen if this enormous population developed in the same way as Japan had done in the last century and got hold of modern weapons? I replied that I was speaking of the present war, which was quite enough to go on with for the time being. I said I would of course always be helpful and polite to the Chinese . . . but that he must not expect me to adopt what I felt was a wholly unreal standard of values.[33]

This prospect of a reformed and reorganized Chinese army under an American commander fighting by the side of the United States also inspired Stimson's many efforts to build up China. To Stimson, the great tradition of American friendship with China constituted the foundation on which a joint military effort could be built, and a great military triumph over a common enemy would in turn further strengthen the traditional friendship, leading to closer co-operation after victory.[34]

The Nationalist government lost no opportunity to promote these hopes. In a conversation with the British ambassador which was relayed to Ambassador Nelson T. Johnson and reported to Washington, Generalissimo Chiang Kai-shek insisted as early as 1940 that the Chinese army, if sup-

[32] Quoted, in Romanus and Sunderland, *op. cit.*, p. 270. Clarence E. Gauss, ambassador to China, expressed an entirely different view; see *Foreign Relations of the United States, 1943: China*, p. 172.

[33] Churchill, *op. cit.*, p. 119.

[34] Henry L. Stimson and McGeorge Bundy, *On Active Service in Peace and War* (New York: Harper & Bros., 1947), pp. 531–32.

plied with equipment, would be able to take the initiative in a decisive way and that Great Britain and the United States would need Chinese manpower sooner or later.[35] During the war Dr. Wellington Koo, the Chinese ambassador to Washington, stated flatly to Admiral William Leahy that, if the United States could provide munitions and supplies for the manpower available in China, the Japanese armies could be destroyed.[36] This line of reasoning was shared by many people in Washington.[37] Even those like General Stilwell and General Marshall who realized the difficulties involved in reorganizing and training the Chinese forces thought it necessary to do everything possible to create a strong and effective Chinese army which would make a major contribution toward the defeat of Japan. For there were no other forces available. Thus in the first two-and-a-half years of the war, General Stilwell was assigned the primary mission of increasing the combat efficiency of the Chinese army.

In the calculations of United States military planners, the third contribution that China could make to the common war effort was a negative one. By simply staying in the fight, China would tie up a large number of Japanese troops which might otherwise be used elsewhere with devastating effect on the Allies. This view of China's importance was shared even by those who were skeptical of the fighting ability of the Chinese army and of the necessity of invading Japan. Commenting on British reluctance to undertake an amphibious operation against the Andaman Islands as a part of the co-ordinated campaign to lift the siege of China, Admiral Leahy observed that

> the defeat of Japan would cost many more ships, lives, not to mention dollars, if Chiang's ill-equipped, ill-fed armies were not kept in the field. The Chinese were not winning many battles. Except for a few American-trained divisions perhaps they didn't fight well, but the fact could not be discounted that Chiang had several million men under arms and was forcing Japan to keep a large standing army in China and to keep it supplied. The American Chiefs of Staff were convinced that support of China was essential to our own safety and to the success of the Allied cause.[38]

American planners were also haunted by the possibility that China might be knocked out of the war and that Japan might use China as a base of operation to hold out against the Allied powers. As General Marshall stated:

[35] Department of State, *Foreign Relations of the United States, 1940*, Vol. IV; *The Far East* (Washington, D.C.: Government Printing Office, 1955), p. 429.
[36] William Leahy, *I Was There* (New York: McGraw-Hill Book Co., 1950), p. 292.
[37] Sherwood, *op. cit.*, p. 504, and Romanus and Sunderland, *op. cit.*, p. 23.
[38] Leahy, *op. cit.*, p. 202. See also Roosevelt, *op. cit.*, pp. 129, 143.

If the armies and government of Generalissimo Chiang Kai-shek had been finally defeated, Japan would have been left free to exploit the tremendous resources of China without harassment. It might have made it possible, when the United States and Britain had finished the job in Europe and assaulted the Japanese homeland, for the government to flee to China and continue the war on a great and rich land mass.[39]

Finally, having China on the side of the Western powers had the negative psychological value of counteracting Japanese propaganda of "Asia for the Asiatics" and the positive value of rallying Asiatic sentiment to the Allied cause. Churchill wrote in January, 1942, to General Wavell on his impression of the importance of China in Washington: "And never forget that behind all looms the shadow of Asiatic solidarity. . . . If I can epitomize in one word the lesson I learned in the United States, it was 'China.'"[40]

These optimistic hopes for China's contributions toward the defeat of Japan brought about exaggerated fears of the loss of China as an ally. These fears were actively cultivated by the Nationalist government, which at crucial moments never failed to remind the United States of the possibility of a loss of morale, a military collapse, a negotiated peace with Japan, or a rupture with the United States. Since the militarily and politically sound policy of defeating Germany first severely limited the amount of military aid to China, the status of a great power and the prospect of future grandeur were held out to China to compensate for the lack of immediate, effective aid and to keep her in the war.[41]

Thus, military exigencies furnished the immediate impetus for the United States to stake her postwar hopes in the Far East on the success of this policy, though it had long been implicit in the principles of the Open Door and was in perfect accord with her sentimental concern for China and her idealistic plans for the postwar world.

This discussion of considerations entering into the policy of making China a great power raises the fundamental question whether a new conception was developing of the importance of China to the United States and of the nature of American interests in China and the Far East. There is little doubt that during the period between Pearl Harbor and the Cairo Conference the United States espoused a new conception of China's importance *as a wartime ally*. It is also clear that the United States saw the necessity of maintaining some sort of balance of power in the Far East and visualized

[39] General George C. Marshall, *The War Records of General George C. Marshall* (New York: J. B. Lippincott Co., 1947), p. 209.

[40] Churchill, *op. cit.*, p. 120.

[41] Feis, *The China Tangle*, pp. 60–61, and chaps. x, xi.

the importance of China in maintaining the power structure. But the conception of China's importance presupposed that China would emerge as a great power after the war. In other words, only to the extent that China could become a great power in the immediate postwar years would she be important to the United States. The implications for American policy are, in retrospect, obvious. If China could emerge a great power, there would be no need for the United States to project her military power in China to maintain the Far Eastern balance of power. If China failed to fulfil the cherished American hope, American political interests in China would be, as they were before the war, relatively unimportant and there would again be no need to become militarily involved. This circular notion made it unnecessary to contemplate the use of American armed forces in China, for, to use Secretary Hull's words, the "great interests" of the United States "were elsewhere."[42]

In any interpretation of American policy toward China it is necessary to remember that during the Pacific war, at least up to the Yalta Conference, the United States did not intend, or feel it necessary, to maintain her forces even in Europe for any length of time after the war. President Roosevelt told Marshal Stalin and Prime Minister Churchill on February 5, 1945, at the Yalta Conference that

> he did not believe that American troops would stay in Europe much more than two years . . . he felt that he could obtain support in Congress and throughout the country for any reasonable measures designed to safeguard the future peace, but he did not believe that this would extend to the maintenance of an appreciable American force in Europe.[43]

Considering the priority given to Europe in Allied strategy and the obviously much higher stake of the United States in Europe, it is reasonable to believe that American policies toward China were influenced by the tacit premise that American armed forces would not be used in China to uphold American interests after the war. Thus, despite President Roosevelt's elevation of China to the status of a great power, the political conception of the United States regarding her interests in the postwar Far East and China was not fundamentally different from that governing the traditional policy and did not imply that the United States would now use her armed forces to uphold her position there. That this was so is clearly demonstrated, as we shall see, by the Marshall mission, Marshall's

[42] Hull, *op. cit.*, p. 1587.
[43] U. S. Department of State, *Foreign Relations of the United States: The Conferences at Malta and Yalta, 1945* (Washington, D.C.: Government Printing Office, 1955), p. 617.

rejection of General Albert C. Wedemeyer's recommendations, and the final withdrawal from China.

In the event, the policy of making China a great power proved no substitute for the direct use of American power to uphold the Far Eastern balance of power. The policy, itself, never had a chance to succeed, for three principal reasons. First of all, the policy of making China a great power and of depending on her to protect American interests in the Far East rested on the implicit assumption that a strong and friendly government would emerge. Four years of war with Japan since 1937 had already, at the time of Pearl Harbor, seriously weakened the Nationalist government and produced internal developments in China which militated against this optimistic assumption.

Second, America's ambitious wartime policy for the postwar Far East stood in sharp contrast to the meager resources which the United States could allocate to the China-Burma-India theater. The original plan of re-opening the Burma Road, the strategic idea of making a landing on the Chinese coast, and the program of reforming and retraining the Chinese army, if effectively implemented, would have increased the possibility of China's being both strong and friendly at the end of the war, but the global shortage of men and resources prevented the early execution of this strategy. At the same time, failure to judge correctly the intentions of the Soviet Union and the Chinese Communist party also prevented American officials from weighing carefully the implications of American military strategies and activities for the internal development and the international position of China. Either the traditional divorce between diplomacy and military power or the misjudgment of Moscow's and Yenan's intentions would have been a sufficient cause for the failure to implement political policy with military means. Together, they made the failure inevitable.

By the time of the Cairo Conference, the success of the island-hopping campaign and the impossibility of implementing the original plans in the CBI theater convinced the United States that Japan could be defeated by American attacks from the Pacific islands without a major land campaign in China. After the Japanese armies had captured the American air bases in "east China,"[44] the United States abandoned all thought of landing American forces in China. The divorce between military strategy and political policy thereby became complete both in conception and in effect.

Third, many American officials were not sufficiently aware of the magnitude of the task of making China a strong and friendly power and of the inevitable obstacles to American endeavors to influence the internal developments of that country. Thus, there were no systematic, deliberate, and

---

[44] The term "east China" is used in American military documents and histories to denote what is known in China as Southwest China. This usage is followed but the term is put in quotation marks to avoid confusion.

concerted efforts to use American power vigorously to produce such effects as the foreign policy and activities of one country might have in another. Instead, purely military projects which promised to produce obvious military results were given priority over military programs which might have had at least an indirect bearing on the political objective. In her pursuit of a quick victory over Japan, the United States forgot in practice her political policy in China, except when it happened also to help promote the military objective.

Furthermore, American commitment to a policy of unconditional surrender weakened her bargaining position vis-à-vis the Nationalist government, whose officials made several hints and threats of a separation. This rendered it difficult to carry through to its logical conclusion a *quid pro quo* policy and a tactic of pressure toward the Nationalist government to bring about sweeping reforms, which constituted an indispensable part of any program to save it from destruction. Thus, the policy of unconditional surrender not only made it necessary for the United States to adopt the policy of making China a great power to fill the political vacuum in the Far East, but it also gave priority to a series of military activities unrelated to the political objective. It doomed the United States to a position of political weakness and guaranteed the failure of a policy which had by this time become very difficult to implement in any case.

Some American officials in China and in Washington realized the difficulties of dealing with the Nationalist government and the necessity of bringing about reforms. But not a few of them misunderstood the nature and intentions of the Chinese Communist party, promoted the schemes of setting up a coalition government including the Communists, and looked hopefully for friendship and co-operation from the Chinese Communist party. Their endeavors dissipated American influence and worked to the disadvantage of the United States.[45]

It can easily be seen that these three inherent weaknesses in the structure of American policies, strategies, and actions were the continuation, under different circumstances, of the pattern of American policies since the dispatch of the Hay notes. The principle of unconditional surrender, the contradiction between the ambitious objective and the meager means allocated to China throughout the war, the widening gap between political policy and military strategy after the Cairo Conference, and the failure effectively to co-ordinate military activities in China with political policy were the new forms which the traditional non-military approach to diplomacy took. Similarly, the tradition of non-intervention in Chinese affairs left the United States without the experience necessary to evaluate correctly the implications of Chinese internal development for American inter-

[45] See Part II, below.

ests and inhibited forceful action at a time when the dependence of the Nationalist government on American support for victory and survival seems to have conferred on the United States the power needed to bring about basic changes in China.

C. The Realities of China in Revolution

What were the political and military realities in China upon which the policy of making China a great power foundered? When the United States declared war on Japan on December 8, 1941, China had been fighting Japan for more than four years. To the surprise of the world, Japan failed to achieve a military decision. The admiration evoked by China's resistance and guilt about the export of vital raw materials to Japan in order to gain time led American officials and the American public to overlook the basic weaknesses of the Nationalist government, which was accentuated under the stress of the war.

From the date of its establishment in Nanking in April, 1927, the Nationalist government suffered from a series of basic contradictions between its program and its practice. Dr. Sun Yat-sen advocated a policy of "land to the tiller," and in 1926 the Nationalist party adopted a program of restricting rent to 37.5 per cent of the annual total produce of the land.[46] But the Nationalist government consistently failed to put its program into effect. The failure to reform land tenure, to reduce interest rates, and to curb usury aliented the peasant. In the theory and program of the Nationalist party, political tutelage by one party was a temporary device to educate and prepare the people for the task of building a constitutional democracy. But the actual trend of the Nationalist government was toward intrenchment of the dictatorship of the party and the concentration of power in the hands of one man. The determination of the Nationalist party to give overwhelming power to the executive and little to the popular assembly in successive revised drafts of the constitution, the rise of such semisecret organizations as the "Blue Shirts," and the imitation of the trappings of Fascist countries disillusioned the Western-educated and Western-oriented liberals. One of the driving forces behind the movement toward a personal dictatorship was the desire for a strong and effective government. Yet Chiang Kai-shek never succeeded in building a united party and an efficient government.

The Nationalist party rose to power on a wave of anti-imperialism among the Chinese people. Its popular support was generated in the first place by its nationalistic program. But, in the years after the Japanese invasion of Manchuria, it consistently refused to face the grave challenge posed by

[46] Ts'ui Shu-ch'ing, *Sun Chung-shan yü kung-chan-chu-i* ["Sun Yat-sen and Communism"] (Hong Kong: Asiatic Press, 1954), pp. 168–73, 177.

Japan to China's territorial integrity and national existence. The government's timidity and vacillation in the face of Japanese aggression stood in sharp contrast to the savage civil war against the Communists, whatever may be said for its policy of "internal pacification before resistance to external attack." As Japan quickly consolidated her control over Manchuria and Jehol and progressively infiltrated Inner Mongolia and North China, the support of the educated class for the Nationalist party began to be dissipated.

Prior to 1937 there were some positive accomplishments. Thirty relatively modern army divisions and a modern air force were created. There were improvements and reforms in the technical fields of administration, finance, and communication. The greatest achievement, however, was the steady extension of the authority of the central government over semi-independent military and political leaders in the various outlying provinces. A semblance of unity had been achieved by the astute use of force and stratagem where feasible and by political compromise when necessary. If Japan had not attacked in 1937, the Nationalist government might have continued to consolidate its power and authority by the sheer weight of its military strength and financial resources.[47] Such a government, though far from popular, might have survived for a substantial period because of the weakness of the opposing forces.

The Sino-Japanese War dealt the Nationalist government crushing blows, which eventually proved fatal. In the first place, it decimated the Nationalist army and drove the Nationalist government from its home base, causing a new surge of the centrifugal tendency in Chinese politics. Secondly, it gave the Communists opportunity to expand their control over the most important regions of China. Third, it greatly weakened the upper classes, which had been the strong and capable supporters of the Nationalist government, and created conditions which alienated the middle classes from the government. Finally, the stresses of war caused a demoralization of the bureaucracy and the army.

During the first year of the war the better-equipped Japanese army succeeded in dealing severe blows to the modern Chinese army which Generalissimo Chiang Kai-shek had painstakingly organized and trained. By the end of 1938, Japan had occupied all the important cities and lines of communication in the coastal area, the North China plain, the middle and lower Yangtze Valley, and the Pearl River Valley. These regions contained the most populous and economically developed provinces of China. Here

[47] Mao recognized that the Japanese occupation of a large part of China created the necessary condition for the ultimate triumph of his party. See Mao's interview in January, 1961, with a leader of the Japanese Socialist party, as reported in *Lien-ho p'ing-lun* (Hong Kong), June 23, 1961, p. 2.

were located all of China's heavy industry, an overwhelming proportion of light industry, and most of the railways and navigable rivers. All this was lost to the Nationalist government when its main forces were pushed into Southwest China.

The loss of the territories directly under the control of the central government gravely weakened its authority over many of the provinces, for the defeat suffered by the Central Army altered the balance of forces between the central and local authorities. The dependence upon the provincial governments for manpower, resources, and supplies greatly increased. The interruption of the normal communication network added to the difficulty of control from the center. The presence of Japanese troops and the enticement of Japanese authorities made defection a real possibility. Over many of the local military commanders, the authority and control of the central government was more precarious than ever. It was maintained chiefly by moving very cautiously to preserve the equilibrium of forces among the various commanders, by yielding a large measure of autonomy to them, and by taking precautionary measures against any open disobedience or revolt. The result was a coalition army of three hundred divisions. The Generalissimo had thirty to forty divisions directly under him. The rest owed their allegiance to their own commanders in the various war areas rather than to the central government. The question of what troops would obey whom under what circumstances could not be answered with certainty.

Chiang Kai-shek's method of dealing with this situation tended to harden rather than to break the existing pattern of disunity. For he looked upon loyalty to himself rather than effectiveness in fighting the war as the most important criterion in allocation of equipment and supply and in promotion and advancement. No matter how successful a commander was in the war against Japan, he was not rewarded with due recognition of his merit if he was not also unquestionably loyal to Chiang Kai-shek as an individual. Conversely, no matter how unsuccessful a commander was, he was not punished or demoted if his personal loyalty was not in doubt. Given the nature of his regime, Chiang's policy was a matter of political necessity. In the institutional void left by the breakdown of the traditional order, Chiang's authority over his political rivals rested, in the last analysis, on his superior military strength which, in turn, depended upon the personal loyalty of his commanders toward him. Seeing no hope of getting a fair share of equipment and supplies on an equal footing with the personal troops of the Generalissimo, the local commanders in the war areas resorted to political pressure and bargaining to get what they wanted and demanded personal loyalty from their own subordinates. They were also compelled by political necessity to practice *Realpolitik* of the crudest sort. Under these conditions unity of military command was impossible. The American military mission to China under Brigadier General John Magruder made many reports on this subject in the fall of 1941.[48]

The resurgence of the centrifugal tendency in Chinese politics confronted the United States with both a grave problem and a new opportunity. On the one hand, if the United States was committed unalterably to the view that no other Nationalist leader could replace Chiang, her policy was seriously jeopardized by the loss of authority on the part of the central government, as turned out to be the case. On the other hand, if the United States was not committed unalterably to Chiang, and if she was searching for other Nationalist leaders to take his place, the rising power of the regional and provincial leaders would have provided her with an opportunity to fashion a new political force. In either case, the task confronting the United States was formidable. But the new situation need not have been considered an unmitigated disaster.

A more serious threat to the authority of the Nationalist government was the phenomenal wartime expansion of the Chinese Communists. In 1937 the Chinese Communists were confined to a small area in an arid and poor region in northern Shensi. They controlled approximately 35,000 square miles of territory with a population of about 1,500,000.[49] By the end of 1943, the Communist-controlled base areas covered 155,000 square miles and contained 54,000,000 people. The Communist party also became the dominant political force in 67,000 square miles of guerrilla territory with 40,000,000 in population.[50] By 1945, the control of the Communists extended over approximately 225,000 square miles of territory with a population of about 65,000,000 people.[51] The strength of Communist regular forces expanded from 100,000 in 1937 to 475,000 in October, 1944. In early 1945 the Communists claimed to have an army of 910,000 troops in addition to local militia forces which numbered about 2,000,000 men.

The remarkable success of the Chinese Communist party was achieved at first by skilfully exploiting the political and military vacuum created by the defeat of the Nationalist forces by the Japanese army, which, pushing ever forward, left large areas behind it without adequate garrison. The political organizers and military units of the Communist party moved into these territories, establishing local governing authorities and organizing the people into militia forces and mass organizations. These activities preserved order in the areas and provided a measure of safety against the marauding Japanese troops. The Communists also took the opportunity to inaugurate a program of rent and interest-rate reduction and to distribute,

[48] Romanus and Sunderland, op. cit., pp. 71, 83.
[49] War Department, Military Intelligence Division, "The Chinese Communist Movement," Institute of Pacific Relations, p. 2355.
[50] Ibid., p. 2369.
[51] Ibid., p. 2355.

for "temporary" use by the peasants, the holdings of landlords who either had fled the area to seek safety from the Japanese and the Communists themselves or had collaborated with the Japanese to preserve their property and status.

In this manner the Chinese Communists succeeded in transforming into active support the passive acquiescence which for generations Chinese peasants had accorded all governments. This enlistment of the active support of the peasant was frequently accomplished at the expense of the gentry, who were under heavy pressure to collaborate with the Japanese and who became easy and legitimate targets for the Communists in a war of national salvation.[52] Frequently the only alternative to collaboration with the Japanese was co-operation with the Communists, by whom the gentry were sometimes given honorable places but little real power. In general, the activities of the Chinese Communists were welcomed by the people in the occupied areas. As the report of the Military Intelligence Division of the War Department stated:

> The Eighth Route Army [the Communist Army] in North China came soon to be considered the benefactor and savior of the people not only against the Japanese, but also against the rule of landlords and the former warlords who had held supreme sway over North China. As one official American observer in Communist-controlled North China recently said, the peasant appears not only willing but even enthusiastic about pay-taxes [sic] "because he is doing it for the Army, which is protecting him and his possessions, and for the first time in centuries he feels that he is getting something in return for his money and goods." It is not the ideology of Communism as such that impresses the people. It is the practical results of Communist leadership.[53]

As the Communists expanded the areas under their control, perfected their techniques of guerrilla warfare and political organization, and received wider and wider popular support, they began to turn their forces against Nationalist troops and bases. Thus, side by side with the Sino-Japanese War, a contest of power between the Communists and the Nationalists took place in the occupied areas. Active popular support is the

[52] For the Communist view of this situation see "The Organization of a Typical Guerrilla Area in South Shantung" by Wang Yu-chuan. Appended in *The Chinese Army* by Evans F. Carlson (New York: Institute of Pacific Relations, 1940), pp. 84–130. For a scholarly study, see Chalmers A. Johnson, *Peasant Nationalism and Communist Power* (Stanford, Calif.: California University Press, 1962). This excellent and provocative work came out too late for the author to take full advantage of it. Johnson's book and the present work emphasize different aspects of the same political process. On many points, they either balance or supplement each other.

[53] "Chinese Communist Movement," p. 2336.

most important condition for success in guerrilla warfare, and in this war-within-a-war, the Communists easily had the upper hand. As had happened many times in the past, war proved again to be the mother of a successful revolution.

The Sino-Japanese War not only weakened the power of the gentry in the occupied area. It sapped the strength of the businessmen, the industrialists, and the financiers, and alienated the middle class from the Nationalist government. The Japanese occupation of the big cities deprived the modern-minded and Western-oriented elements of their bases of operations and often of their wealth. The weakening of this group was reflected in the relative decline of the "Political Science group" and the ascendance of the extreme right wing, the "C.C. clique," in the councils of the Nationalist party and government.

The stresses of the war and the Japanese blockade gave rise to runaway inflation and other problems which the government failed to solve. The inflation hit the salaried classes hardest, wiping out their savings and reducing them to poverty. The rising discontent and disaffection of the middle class found expression through the small parties and political groups and was voiced by many non-party intellectuals. The renewed activities and criticisms of these groups and individuals came at a time when the expansion of the Communists had already alarmed the Nationalist government. Together, these developments generated an intense sense of insecurity in the leaders of the Nationalist government. They feared that their authority in free China would be undermined by adverse criticism while their areas of control in occupied China were threatened by the Communists. They resorted to repressive measures as a means of self-defense. As repression generated more criticism, a vicious circle was created. This trend became obvious in the winter of 1939–40 when the Association of the Comrades of United National Reconstruction was formed by the small parties and groups.[54] The Communists shrewdly abstained from joining this political organization but lent it a helping hand. Thus, the intolerant and repressive policies of the Kuomintang toward these non-Communist groups and individuals played into the hands of the Communists, who pursued a policy of uniting the greatest number of people to isolate and overthrow the smallest number of opponents.

The growing power of the Communist party and the fears and anxieties of the Nationalist government were duly reported to the American government by its diplomatic representatives in China. As early as 1940, Chiang Kai-shek expressed to Ambassador Nelson Johnson his fear of a possible political collapse of the Nationalist government as a result of "the whisper-

[54] Tuan-sheng Ch'ien, *The Government and Politics of China* (Cambridge, Mass.: Harvard University Press, 1950), p. 373.

ing campaign of the Communists."[55] The Chinese leader was reported as taking a more serious view of the threat posed by the Chinese Communists than of the designs of the Japanese. Although Johnson believed that the Nationalists at that time could still win in an open armed clash with the Communists,[56] he warned Washington prophetically that "failure of the United States and Great Britain to afford timely aid to China might in the end result in Communist ascendency in China."[57] Throughout the war the reports of the foreign service officers stationed in China repeatedly pointed out the strength of the Communists and the weakness of the Nationalist government.[58]

These unfavorable political developments, together with wartime hardships, brought about a demoralization of the bureaucracy and the army. At a time when the high officials in the government were increasingly insecure about their hold on the country and inflation had drastically lowered the standard of living for most people, wartime conditions provided numerous opportunities for speculation and graft. The chief of these was the American loan to China. Secretary of the Treasury Henry Morgenthau, Jr., told President Roosevelt in December, 1943, that the Nationalist government's schemes in using the American loan "have had little effect except to give additional profits to insiders, speculators and hoarders. . . ."[59]

For a vast number of civil servants and military officers in the middle and lower echelons, the only way to make ends meet was through irregular channels. This deplorable state of civilian and military administration seriously affected even the most vital activities in connection with the war. For example, in August, 1941, David G. Arnstein, who had been dispatched to inspect the Burma Road, made a depressing report to the President and Mr. Hopkins on the inefficiency and corruption of the agencies operating on the only link between China and the West.[60]

The Chinese army also degenerated greatly over the years because of the malpractices of civilan and military officers. It never developed an effective system of replacement. Purchased exemptions, impressment at gun point, and cruel and inhumane treatment of the recruits characterized the conscription system. The troops were not served by an adequate system of logistics. Ill-clothed, ill-fed, and uncared for when sick, more Chinese soldiers died of disease and malnutrition than on the battlefield after

[55] Department of State, *Foreign Relations of the United States, 1940*, Vol. IV: *The Far East*, p. 674.

[56] *Ibid.*, p. 453.

[57] *Ibid.*, pp. 429–30.

[58] See Part II, chap. vi, below.

[59] Memorandum to President Roosevelt from Secretary of Treasury Morgenthau, Department of State, *United States Relations with China* (Washington, D.C.: Government Printing Office, 1949), p. 489.

[60] Sherwood, *op. cit.*, pp. 404–5, and Romanus and Sunderland, *op. cit.*, pp. 45, 46.

the front had been stabilized in 1938–39. The morale of the Chinese soldier was low and he lost his will to fight.

These conditions pointed to the probability of an imminent revolutionary overturn in China, a problem which the United States had to solve if the policy of making China a great power was to serve her interests. A look at Chinese history suggests that radical changes in China were inevitable. The history of modern China since the Opium War has been punctuated by rebellions and revolutions. These arose out of the profound unrest and turmoil engendered by the impact of the West on China, which had accelerated the growth of elements of instability in Chinese society, destroyed the balance among traditional institutions, and laid bare the inadequacy of the basic concepts of an ancient civilization to solve modern problems. The Nationalist party was itself a revolutionary party. It was instrumental in overthrowing the Manchu Dynasty in 1911. It was borne to power by the revolution of 1925–27. But its failure to find a fundamental solution to the social, economic, and political problems of China prevented it from consummating the revolutionary task. Under the Nationalist regime, dissatisfaction remained widespread. The peasants became restive when the rapid increase of absentee landlords and the destruction of rural handicraft industries, both results of the impact of the West, intensified the evils of the traditional system of land tenure and rural credits, and aggravated the basic poverty due to overpopulation and a shortage of arable land. National humiliation and the failure to resist Japanese aggression alienated a large segment of the middle class from the Nationalist government. Western-oriented individuals were appalled by an obvious trend toward the perpetuation and intensification of the system of "political tutelage" and the building of a personal dictatorship after the Fascist model.

It remained for the Sino-Japanese War to ignite the long fuse that led to the eventual explosion. For resentment against the wartime misdeeds and repressive measures of the Nationalist government solidified public opinion against it. The war also provided an opportunity for the Chinese Communists to demonstrate the feasibility and popularity of a program of reform in areas under their control. Their success inspired trust in Communist political leadership. To the popular demand for change was now added a certain hopefulness of success and the availability of an alternative to the Nationalist regime. The progressive weakening of the Nationalist government and the degeneration of its army and bureaucracy provided the necessary condition for a successful revolution. The conservative forces which constituted the main support of the status quo were so enfeebled and distraught that they were about to lose the ability to preserve the regime. Worst of all, the revolutionary movement challenging the authority of the Nationalist government was led by a party which had been in its first years of existence under complete domination of the Communist party of the Soviet Union and still owed ideological allegiance to it.

If under these circumstances the policy of making China a great power was to serve America's self-interest, the Nationalist government had to be so transformed that it could compete successfully with the Chinese Communist party both on the battlefield and in the realms of political, economic, and social reform. Obviously, the adoption of such a policy required as a fundamental precondition a correct understanding of the nature and intentions of the Chinese Communist party, which was a major force in the world Communist movement, having indigenous roots to be sure, but following consistently the twists and turns of the foreign policy of the Soviet Union. (In Part II, chapter vi, we shall examine in detail the political and intellectual origins of America's misjudgment of the Chinese Communists.) It is obvious that the task confronting the United States was at best an extremely difficult one.[61] It is even likely that no matter what the United States might have done, she could only have postponed but could not have averted the final outcome. But if the United States had had ample resources and manpower to bring overwhelming power to bear on the Chinese situation, if she had subordinated her military activities to political policy, and if she had dealt skilfully with the Nationalist government, the chances of making China a great and friendly power would have been enhanced. Unfortunately, none of these three conditions was fulfilled, as we shall see in the following chapters.

[61] One view on the basic but still open question of the extent to which a foreign power can influence the political developments in another country is developed eloquently by Charles B. Marshall, in *The Limits of Foreign Policy* (New York: Holt, Rinehart & Winston, Inc., 1954).

CHAPTER III

DIPLOMATIC

ACTIONS

AND

MILITARY

STRATEGY

A. The Attempt to Make China a Great Power by Diplomatic Actions

As soon as the United States entered the Pacific war, American officials began to impress upon her allies the importance of treating China as a great power and to assure China the return of lost territory. Churchill's impression of the climate of opinion in Washington on the subject during the winter of 1941–42 has already been referred to. The lifting of the name of China, together with that of the U.S.S.R., out of their alphabetical listing in the original draft of what has become known as the Declaration of the United Nations and placing them with the United States and the United Kingdom in the final listing was trivial in itself but indicative of the mood in Washington.[1] When, on February 9, 1942, General Stilwell called at the White House before leaving for China and asked the President if he had a message for Generalissimo Chiang Kai-shek, Roosevelt told Stilwell to inform the Nationalist leader that "we are in this thing for keeps, and we intend to keep at it until China gets back all her lost territory."[2] The President's informal, oral pledge, though made casually on the spur of the moment, was entirely in harmony with his deep convictions, as his formula of unconditional surrender and the Cairo Declaration readily show. In January, 1943, the United States signed a treaty with China relinquishing her extraterritorial rights and other special privileges. She also persuaded Great Britain to take a similar step.[3] The conclusion

[1] Robert Sherwood, *Roosevelt and Hopkins* (New York: Harper & Bros., 1948), pp. 446–53.

[2] Joseph Stilwell, *The Stilwell Papers* (New York: William Sloane Associates, 1948), p. 152.

[3] Department of State, *United States Relations with China* (Washington, D.C.: Gov-

of these treaties marked the apparent fulfilment of the Open Door principles and the triumph of America's traditional policy. To Eden, during
his visit to Washington in March, 1943, Hull criticized Churchill's failure
in a speech to mention China among the great powers as a serious mistake.[4] In their discussions with Eden at this time about the organization
of the United Nations after the war, the President and Undersecretary of
State Sumner Welles were already proposing that "the real decisions [in
the world organization] should be made by the United States, Great Britain, Russia and China," who together would be the powers to police the
world.[5]

The President and the secretary of state carried their purpose of making China a great power to a series of important international conferences.
At Moscow in October, 1943, Hull overcame Soviet objections to the inclusion of China in the Four-Nation Declaration by hinting at the necessity
of "all sorts of readjustment" by the American government to stabilize the deteriorating political and military situation in the Pacific, in the
event that China's exclusion from the Declaration should result in the
lowering of Chinese morale.[6] As one of the original signatories of the
Moscow Declaration formally and specifically committing the four powers
to the establishment of "a general international organization," China
moved another step toward a position as one of the Big Four in world
affairs. The Cairo Declaration of December 1, 1943, reaffirmed the Casablanca formula of "unconditional surrender." China was solemnly promised the return of all the territories lost to Japan since 1895.[7]

During the Teheran Conference, November 28–December 1, 1943,
President Roosevelt told Marshal Stalin, in a private meeting on November 29, about his plans to preserve the future peace of the world. The
President outlined an organization consisting of three bodies: first, an
assembly composed of all members of the United Nations; second, an

ernment Printing Office, 1949), pp. 34–36, 513–17 (hereafter cited as *United States
Relations with China*).

[4] Sherwood, *op. cit.*, p. 716.

[5] *Ibid.*, p. 717.

[6] Cordell Hull, *The Memoirs of Cordell Hull* (New York: Macmillan Co., 1948), II,
1282; Department of State, *Foreign Relations of the United States, 1943: China* (Washington, D.C.: Government Printing Office, 1957), p. 826.

[7] *United States Relations with China*, pp. 37, 519. At the Cairo Conference, Roosevelt
asked Chiang whether China would want the Ryukyu Islands. Chiang replied that
China would be agreeable to joint occupation by China and the United States and, eventually, joint administration by the two countries under the trusteeship of an international
organization. In January, 1944, Roosevelt informed the Pacific War Council that Stalin
was in complete agreement that the Ryukyu Islands belonged to China and should be
returned to her (Department of State, *Foreign Relations of the United States: Conferences at Cairo and Teheran, 1943* [Washington, D.C.: Government Printing Office,
1961], pp. 324, 869 [hereafter cited as *Cairo Papers*]).

executive committee to deal with all new military questions and to be composed of the U.S.S.R., the United States, the United Kingdom, and China, plus representative nations drawn from the various regions of the world; third, a body which the President termed "The Four Policemen" — the U.S.S.R., the United States, the United Kingdom, and China — whose duty would be to police the world and prevent or check aggression. Stalin expressed his skepticism of China's becoming a powerful nation at the end of the war and playing its assigned role. He also thought the small powers of Europe would resent having China as an enforcement authority for themselves.[8] But Stalin made no issue of the matter and the President left with the impression that his proposal was agreeable to the Soviet Union.

China took part in the Dumbarton Oaks Conference held between August 21 and October 7, 1944, and the "Dumbarton Oaks Proposal for the Establishment of a General International Organization" assigned to China a permanent seat on the Security Council.[9] The efforts on China's behalf culminated in the San Francisco Conference on International Organization, which adopted the Charter of the United Nations. China was named in the Charter as one of the five permanent members of the Security Council. In this process of making China a great power, the United States overcame the skepticism of Great Britain and the reluctance of the Soviet Union.

But diplomatic actions were the only major measures taken by the United States to implement her policy of making China a great power. This policy was not deliberately supported either by the strategy of the Allies in the Far East or by American military activities in China. Thus, China gained only a formal status devoid of the substance of power, while the United States maximized the consequences of her own defeat when the Chinese Communists triumphed in China.

B. The Evolving Strategy in the Far East and the Policy of Making China a Great Power

1. *The Idea of China as an Essential Base of Operations And Its Political Implications*

American strategy in the Far East during the Pacific war consisted of a series of brilliant improvisations in which tactical and strategic opportunities were effectively exploited to achieve a quick victory over Japan within the global strategy of defeating Hitler first. There was no hard-and-

[8] Sherwood, *op. cit.*, pp. 785–86.
[9] Harley A. Notter, *Postwar Foreign Policy Preparation, 1939–1945* (Department of State Publication 3580 [Washington, D.C.: Government Printing Office, 1949]), p. 614.

fast, long-range plan for the defeat of Japan.[10] Each commander of
American forces had his own guiding ideas. The translation of these
ideas into specific plans depended on the exigencies and opportunities of
the moment. In the first half of 1942, the Japanese completed the blockade of China and developed a powerful thrust toward Australia and New
Zealand. To stop Japan's farther advance southward, the United States
deployed a limited number of troops to the Pacific area. Then, having
repulsed the Japanese navy in the battle of the Coral Sea in May and won
a major battle at Midway in June, the United States undertook a tactical offensive within a defensive strategy with her attack on Guadalcanal.[11]
By the end of 1942, the total number of army forces deployed in the Pacific theater was approximately 350,000, a number which slightly exceeded the 347,000 army forces deployed in the United Kingdom and
North Africa. In contrast, 17,000 United States troops were present in or
en route to the China-Burma-India area, which remained essentially an
air and supply theater.[12]

These contrasting developments in the Pacific and the China-Burma-
India theater did not in themselves imply a depreciation of the importance of China as an essential base of future operations against Japan. As
a matter of fact, China's importance was reaffirmed in the Casablanca
Conference of January, 1943. As Maurice Matloff puts it, "On the military
side, the United States Chiefs hoped — as they had from early in the war
— that the manpower and strategic location of China might somehow be
utilized in the struggle with Japan. In that case China might eventually
serve the Allied cause in a position somewhat analogous to that of
U.S.S.R. in the war against Germany."[13] In preparing programs for the
Casablanca Conference, the Joint Chiefs of Staff envisaged a campaign in
Burma in 1943 which would reopen the line of communications to China
and make it possible later to obtain "bases essential to eventual offensive
operations against Japan proper."[14] Staging areas and airfields in North
China were the strategic goal. At this time and for several months there-
after, China appeared to offer the United States greater strategic advantages than the Pacific islands for attacking Japan. To use the words of
Romanus and Sunderland, the differences among American officials "were

[10] Maurice Matloff, *Strategic Planning for Coalition Warfare, 1943–1944* (Washington, D.C.: Government Printing Office, 1959), pp. 336–38, 374.
[11] Samuel Eliot Morison, *Coral Sea, Midway, and Submarine Actions* (Boston: Little,
Brown & Co., 1949), pp. 3–4, 245–48, 261; *The Struggle for Guadalcanal* (Boston:
Little, Brown & Co., 1949); and Matloff, *op. cit.*, p. 15.
[12] *Ibid.*
[13] *Ibid.*, p. 34.
[14] Charles F. Romanus and Riley Sunderland, *Stilwell's Mission to China* (Washington, D.C.: Government Printing Office, 1953), p. 269.

over the timing and sequence of several courses of action rather than over the desirability of attacking Japan from China."[15]

At the Washington Conference in May, 1943, the idea of China as an essential base of operation received further indorsement in the "Strategic Plan for the Defeat of Japan," prepared by the Joint Chiefs, accepted by the Combined Chiefs of Staff, and approved by Roosevelt and Churchill.[16] The Joint Chiefs felt that a sustained, large-scale air offensive against Japan could be mounted only from bases in China.[17] In their proposals air bases in North China played a vital part.[18] To acquire these airfields, a series of steps was envisaged. The British, assisted by Chinese and United States forces, would attempt to recapture Burma. The United States would retake the Philippines and Great Britain would seize the Malacca Strait and Singapore. The Allies would converge on Hong Kong from three routes. The Chinese armies would drive eastward from inland. The United States amphibious forces would come westward through the Celebes and the South China Sea. The British would press eastward through the Malacca Straits.[19] After the seizure of Hong Kong, the Allies would force a way into North China.[20] As late as the Quebec Conferece of August, 1943, the planners still believed that

> China offered the best potentialities for bombing Japan, for attacking Japanese communications to the South Seas, and for mounting an invasion of Japan. . . . The emphasis in the plans for the defeat of Japan . . . still lay in establishing Allied power in North China. Approval of the JCS [Joint Chiefs of Staff] proposal for a drive across the Central Pacific did not minimize the importance of Chinese bases, for the part that Pacific islands could play in strategic aerial bombardment of Japan was not yet realized.[21]

It was this idea of China as an essential base of air operations, and the hope of pinning down Japanese forces in China, which served as the foundation for the policy of making China a great power. But the idea of China as an essential base, if implemented by successful military

[15] Ibid., pp. 269–70.
[16] Matloff, op. cit., p. 135; Philip A. Crowl and Edmund G. Love, Seizure of the Gilberts and Marshalls (Washington, D.C.: Government Printing Office, 1955), p. 12; and Samuel Eliot Morison, Breaking the Bismarcks Barrier (Boston: Little, Brown & Co., 1950), p. 7.
[17] Matloff, op. cit., p. 136.
[18] Romanus and Sunderland, op. cit., p. 328.
[19] Matloff, op. cit., p. 137; Crowl and Love, op. cit., pp. 12–13; Morison, Breaking the Bismarcks Barrier, pp. 7–8; and Samuel Eliot Morison, New Guinea and the Marianas (Boston: Little, Brown & Co., 1953), p. 4.
[20] Romanus and Sunderland, op. cit., p. 328.
[21] Ibid., pp. 357, 359.

action, would have had obvious political implications. The implementation of this idea would have required an early breaking of the Japanese blockade in Burma so that sufficient matériel and equipment could be sent into China. It would have required the creation of a new powerful Chinese army and thus have strengthened the Nationalist government against the Communists. It would have brought the Nationalist armies back to the strategic regions on the China coast and in North China as the war with Japan progressed. It would have firmly re-established the authority of the government in the liberated areas and given the government renewed prestige and influence throughout the country. It would have entailed the landing of American ground forces in substantial numbers on the Chinese coast and their presence over a period of time at key points in China. Thus, it would have brought American military power directly to bear on the Chinese situation. To what extent American officials saw these political implications is not clear.[22] The principal reasons for their endeavors to open a land route to China and to reorganize the Chinese army were military in nature. But, whatever the underlying motivation may have been, the strategic idea of China as an essential base, if carried through, would have maximized the chances for success of the policy of making China a great power.

However, several inherent weaknesses in this strategic idea caused its early demise. The offensive power of the Chinese armies fell far short of American hopes. The political obstacles and practical difficulties encountered in efforts to improve the combat efficiency of the Chinese armies were much greater than most officials had anticipated. The British showed little interest in the Burma campaign and entertained serious doubts about China's military value. To the political complications of coalition warfare were added the formidable military difficulties of opening a land route to China and supplying the Chinese armies. The incontrovertible strategy of defeating Hitler first imposed stringent limits on the amount of men and matériel available for Asia and the Pacific. Even in the Orient itself, the powerful Japanese thrust toward Australia in the early days of the war, the tactical and strategic opportunities for offensive American actions thereafter, and the relatively short line of communications — all combined to make the Pacific the principal area of American operations, with the China-Burma-India theater a purely subsidiary one. The limited amount of manpower and resources allocated to the China-Burma-India theater threw into sharp relief the glaring discrepancy between the ambitious policy of making China a great power and the meager means available for its implementation. This wide gap

[22] Stilwell realized the possibility that the army reform program would strengthen the central government against the local military authorities; see pp. 75–76, below.

and the other weaknesses inherent in this policy and the idea of China as an essential base are most plainly revealed in the repeated postponement or reduction in scale of Stilwell's plan to retake Burma to open a land route to China.

2. The Repeated Postponement and Modification of Stilwell's Original Plan To Reopen the Burma Road

After the Japanese had driven the Allied forces from Burma, Stilwell worked out in July, 1942, a plan for a joint Sino-Anglo-American offensive to break the Japanese blockade. His proposed operation looked toward the re-entry into the port of Rangoon and the reopening of the line of communications from Rangoon to Kunming, which could carry about 30,000 tons of supplies a month into China.[23] To achieve this military objective, Stilwell hoped that United States combat units would be available. The British would be asked to put enough naval strength in the Bay of Bengal to control it and to make a landing at Rangoon. The British army in India and the Chinese forces in Ramgarh, India, would attack Burma from the west, while a Chinese army of twenty picked divisions based in the province of Yunnan would attack from the east.[24] These two forces would converge above Mandalay and push toward South Burma while the landing at Rangoon would cut off Japanese reinforcement via the Bay of Bengal. Marching northward, the newly landed forces would attack the Japanese army from the rear. Such a plan promised a quick and decisive campaign in Burma and the reopening of a ready-made and comparatively short road into China as early as 1943. The reopening of the Rangoon-Kunming line of communication would make possible a continuous flow of supplies to re-equip the Chinese army for an offensive aimed at opening a seaport in South China or Indochina; then there would be a further increase of supplies.

If this objective had been realized, the siege of China could have been broken in 1943. A strong Nationalist army might have come into existence and taken part in the offensive to drive the Japanese army from China. The economic and political deterioration in Nationalist China might have been arrested, and the Nationalist regime might have been in a better position to deal with the Communists. If there was ever a chance to make China a great power, such a chance depended on effective implementation of this plan in Burma.

Stilwell's plan to retake the whole of Burma ran, however, into the stark reality of a shortage of resources, shipping, aircraft, and trained personnel in the face of the requirements of a global war. Neither the

[23] Romanus and Sunderland, *op. cit.*, p. 179.
[24] *Ibid.*, pp. 177–79, 182.

United States nor Great Britain found it possible to allocate to the China-Burma-India theater the necessary armed forces and equipment to carry out the project. In the planning of the War Department, the use of American combat troops on a large scale was not envisioned.[25] Since any effort to retake Burma had to be made principally by the British, with as much help from China as possible, an early lifting of the siege of China depended primarily upon British assent and co-operation and British ability to undertake such an enterprise. But Great Britain's immediate concern was quite naturally the war in Europe and the Middle East. Her second concern was the defense of India. The liberation of Burma, though desirable, was not an objective with high priority.[26] She found it impossible to undertake an amphibious assault on Rangoon without diversion of military forces and equipment from the European theater. Without an amphibious operation to take Rangoon, the British foresaw a prolonged and difficult campaign in the disease-infested jungles and mountains of North Burma.[27] Up to the summer of 1944, British military strategists thought that Burma could be bypassed by a giant enveloping movement aimed at Singapore and Sumatra.

The British lack of enthusiasm for the Burma campaign was only one obstacle which American leaders sought unsuccessfully to overcome. China's inability to exert greater effort to help herself was another handicap which hindered the American attempt to break the Japanese blockade. Intensely conscious of China's weakness, and preoccupied with preserving his forces to maintain himself in power, the Generalissimo wanted

[25] Stilwell, op. cit., p. 152.

[26] For Sherwood's comment on Churchill's views, see Sherwood, op. cit., pp. 772–73.

[27] Prime Minister Churchill intensely disliked and strenuously opposed Stilwell's plan for a Burma campaign on both military and political grounds. These were superbly summarized by Churchill later:

"Certainly we favored keeping China in the war and operating air forces from her territory, but a sense of proportion and the study of alternatives were needed. I disliked intensely the prospect of a large-scale campaign in North Burma. One could not choose a worse place for fighting the Japanese. Making a road from Ledo to China was also an immense, laborious task, unlikely to be finished until the need for it had passed. Even if it were done in time to replenish the Chinese armies while they were still engaged it would make little difference to their fighting capacity. The need to strengthen the American air bases in China would also, in our view, diminish as Allied advances in the Pacific and from Australia gained us airfields closer to Japan. On both counts therefore we argued that the enormous expenditures of man-power and material would not be worth while . . .

"We of course wanted to recapture Burma, but we did not want to have to do it by land advances from slender communications and across the most forbidding fighting country imaginable. The south of Burma, with its port of Rangoon, was far more valuable than the north. But all of it was remote from Japan, and for our forces to become side-tracked and entangled there would deny us our rightful share in a Far Eastern victory" (Winston Churchill, The Second World War, Vol. V: Closing the Ring [London: Cassel, 1952], pp. 494–95).

a full Burma campaign or no campaign at all. For in such a campaign, China's impotence would be concealed in the great strength of the Allied effort. To this end the Generalissimo shrewdly attached several conditions to China's all-out participation in a Burma offensive. The most important of these was British action on a large scale in Burma, particularly an amphibious operation in the Bay of Bengal. Since the United States failed to persuade the British to take the necessary action, the Chinese felt justified in refusing to go forward with the project. Thus, time and again, the Burma offensive was postponed or its scope reduced.

The story of the planning and execution of the Burma campaign has been told in detail in three authoritative volumes of military history of the China-Burma-India theater by Romanus and Sunderland and need not be recapitulated here. Suffice it to say that Stilwell's plan to retake Rangoon and to reopen the Burma Road, originally formulated in July, 1942, was modified at the Washington Conference in May, 1943, into a small operation aiming at the reoccupation of North Burma and the opening of the Ledo Road. The Ledo Road strategy which was substituted for the full Burma offensive promised a long and difficult campaign in the forbidding terrain of North Burma. Ironically, this reduction of the scope of the projected Burma campaign was made at the same time the grandiose "Strategic Plan for the Defeat of Japan" was adopted.[28] The "Strategic Plan," which embodied the idea of China as an essential base, was actually a misnomer. "It was not a plan according to strict military definition, for it gave no estimates of enemy strengths and dispositions, did not mention the types and number of Allied forces that would be required to accomplish the missions it described, said nothing about command or commanders, and did not establish time schedules."[29]

In contrast, the operations in the Pacific moved rapidly forward. One portent of things to come was a decision by the Joint Chiefs that the main effort in the westward advance would be made in the central Pacific, with a subsidiary effort through the south and southwest Pacific.[30] Behind this decision was the thought that, if Allied fleets destroyed or contained the Japanese fleet, they could then strike directly from the Pacific against the Japanese home islands.[31] They could be sent "'north about' on a second and parallel route to Tokyo."[32] At the Quebec Conference in August, 1943, the target date for launching the North Burma offensive was postponed from November, 1943, to mid-February, 1944.[33]

[28] Matloff, op. cit., pp. 135–42.
[29] Crowl and Love, op. cit., p. 2.
[30] Ibid., p. 13.
[31] Ibid., p. 14.
[32] Morison, New Guinea and the Marianas, p. 5.
[33] Romanus and Sunderland, op. cit., pp. 328–32.

3. The Alternatives

This brief review of the planning of the Burma campaign highlights the imbalance between political objectives and military means. From this point of view, the dilemma confronting the United States was obvious. On the one hand, the American policy of making China a great power and relying on a strong China as a stabilizing force and a competent partner in the postwar Far East depended for its success, among other things, on early lifting the siege of China. On the other hand, the meager resources allocated to the China-Burma-India theater rendered it impossible to break the Japanese blockade at an early date.

Looking back, it seems that the United States had three rational alternatives. The first was to allocate sufficient resources and manpower to the China-Burma-India theater to break the Japanese blockade at an early date. Whether the Allies could have made a greater effort in this theater without seriously hampering military operations in Europe and the Atlantic is a difficult question to answer, even today. Admiral Ernest J. King stated at the Casablanca Conference that, according to his estimate, the Allies were engaging only 15 per cent of their total resources against the Japanese in the Pacific (including the Indian Ocean and Burma).[34] At the Quebec Conference in August, 1943, he pointed out that the allocation of another 5 per cent of the Allied resources to the Pacific would add one-third to Allied strength in that region, while decreasing the forces employed against the Axis in Europe by only 6 per cent.[35] Other Allied leaders considered the distribution of resources between Europe and the China theater to be correct, not only in the first two years of the Pacific war, when the prospects of the cross-Channel operations constituted a constant source of deep concern, but also in 1944, after Europe was successfully invaded. Commenting on the recall of Stilwell in October, 1944, Stimson wrote:

> Marshall today said if we had to remove Stilwell he would not allow another American general to be placed in the position of Chief of Staff and Commander of the Chinese armies, for it was so evident that no American would be loyally supported. I am inclined to go further. The amount of effort which we have put into the "Over the Hump" airline has been bleeding us white in transport airplanes — it has consumed so many. Today we are hamstrung in Holland and the mouth of the Scheldt River for lack of transport planes necessary to make new airborne flights in that neighborhood. The same lack is crippling us in northern Italy. This effort over the mountains of Burma bids fair to cost us an

[34] Ernest J. King and Walter Muir Whitehall, *Fleet Admiral King* (New York: W. W. Norton & Co., 1952), p. 417.
[35] *Ibid.*, p. 484.

extra winter in the main theater of the war. And, in spite of it all, we have been unable to save China from the present Japanese attack owing to the failure to support Stilwell in training adequate Chinese ground forces to protect Kunming.[36]

Perhaps the solution to the problem of allocating greater resources to the China-Burma-India theater might have been sought in the diversion of matériel and manpower, not from Europe, but from the American thrust in the Pacific toward Japan. This possibility occurred to Admiral King when he agreed at the Casablanca Conference to divert a number of landing craft to the China-Burma-India theater and when he emphasized to Admiral Chester W. Nimitz, in February, 1943, the importance of doing everything possible in the Pacific prior to October, at which time the United States naval and amphibious forces designated for the Burma campaign would have to be allocated to that operation.[37] But the Burma campaign was reduced in scope in March, 1943, and the limited campaign in North Burma was postponed in August, 1943, and again after the Cairo Conference. The projected diversion never took place.

In view of the military difficulties of opening a land route to China, British reluctance to take aggressive action in Burma, and the inability of the Nationalists to help themselves, it may very well be that even if the United States had allotted a larger amount of men and matériel to the China-Burma-India theater, the outcome could not have been very different. In other words, the idea of China as an essential base, and the accompanying policy of making China a great power, may have been inherently unsound.

Yet while the idea of China as an essential base was soon to be discarded, no thought was given to finding a substitute for the policy of making China a great power and depending on her to protect postwar American interests in the Far East. One of the two alternatives to the policy of making China a great power was to preserve Japan as a significant factor in the Far Eastern balance of power through a compromise peace. This alternative was effectively ruled out by the policy of unconditional surrender and by the oral and written commitments to China on the restoration of the territories lost to Japan.

The other alternative was the direct use of American power, both to stabilize the internal situation in China and to preserve the Far Eastern balance of power. If this political policy had been adopted, the strategy of attacking Japan from the Pacific through the island-hopping campaign would have been the quickest way to end the Pacific war, to acquire an

[36] Henry L. Stimson and McGeorge Bundy, *On Active Service in Peace and War* (New York: Harper & Bros., 1947), p. 538.
[37] King and Whitehall, *op. cit.*, p. 430.

island perimeter surrounding the Asian continent, and from there to establish American power in China at the earliest possible date. There would then have been complete harmony between political and military strategy. But the two prerequisites for the adoption of this alternative were non-existent: a willingness to make heavy military and political commitments to uphold the Far Eastern balance of power, and a firm recognition of the long-term geopolitical importance of China. Furthermore, misjudgment of the intentions of the Soviet Union and the Chinese Communist party prevented a realization of the seriousness of the Communist threat. Without a sense of crisis, no nation will take measures which run counter to her traditions and predispositions.

For these reasons, the United States did not choose between the two alternatives to bring political policy and military strategy into accord. When it became clear that Japan could be defeated through the island-hopping campaign, the United States at first simply relegated the idea of using China as an essential base to a subordinate position and then abandoned it altogether. This gradual adjustment in the planning for the defeat of Japan was not accompanied by the adoption of a new political policy. It thus led to a progressive widening of the discrepancy between political policy and military strategy. In America's management of her political-military affairs, strategic opportunism and the doctrine of flexibility in military strategy,[38] which led to victory in war, were not matched by political realism and wisdom — essential if she was to win the peace.

4. The Widening Gap between Political Policy and Military Strategy after the Cairo Conference

Although at the Quebec Conference of August, 1943, plans for the defeat of Japan still stressed the importance of establishing Allied power in China, a definite trend toward bypassing China was not long in coming. For, according to the calculations of the planners of the Joint Chiefs of Staff, operations against Japan proper could not be undertaken until 1947 if the plan to seize Hong Kong and to march on to North China was followed. The planners feared that delay in a decisive victory over Japan might result in a negotiated peace and urged the preparation of a plan for defeating Japan twelve months after the fall of Germany.[39] At the conference, the Marianas were approved as an objective for the Pacific fleet,[40] though as a part of a subordinate operation.

Seeking a plan to achieve a quick victory, the Operations Division be-

[38] For a discussion of opportunism and flexibility in military strategy, see Matloff, *op. cit.*, pp. 373–74.
[39] Romanus and Sunderland, *op. cit.*, p. 358, and Matloff, *op. cit.*, pp. 240–41, 308–9.
[40] Morison, *New Guinea and the Marianas*, p. 5.

gan, in October, 1943, to think in terms of a "short-term plan for operations against Japan . . . with principal emphasis on approach from the Pacific rather than from the Asiatic mainland."[41] The planners of the Combined Chiefs of Staff prepared at the same time a "short plan for the defeat of Japan," proposing four alternative courses of action, all of them bypassing the mainland of China. The Strategy Section of the Operations Division criticized the current strategy on the mainland of China as too costly and as not sufficiently co-ordinated with the main effort through the central Pacific. A little later, the Joint Strategic Survey Committee advised the Joint Chiefs that "without depreciating the importance of the effort against Japan by way of China, the key to the early defeat of Japan lies in all-out operations through the Central Pacific. . . ."[42] Thus, all the important agencies in the United States were questioning the future importance of China as a base by the time of the Cairo Conference. Meanwhile, the forthcoming B-29 bombers with a radius of 1,500 nautical miles gave the Marianas a new significance. The seizure of the Marianas and the establishment of heavy bomber bases there at the earliest possible date were now stressed.[43] A B-29 base was also to be established at Chengtu, China, but the difficulties involved in using air bases in China were recognized.[44]

The Cairo Conference took place one month after the Moscow Declaration of October, 1943, had formally made China one of the four great powers. At the Cairo Conference itself, China was promised the return of all territories lost to Japan. But it was also at Cairo that President Roosevelt yielded to Churchill's insistence and canceled the amphibious operations in the Bay of Bengal which Chiang had insisted upon as an indispensable component in the projected campaign in Burma, and which Roosevelt had promised to undertake. More important, the concept underlying the military decisions of the Cairo Conference was no longer the future importance of China as an essential base of operation. Rather, it was that the main effort against Japan should be made in the Pacific.[45] Operations in the China-Burma-India theater would be in support of that main effort. This development represented a confirmation in strategic thinking of what had been the actual situation and scheme of priorities from the very beginning of the war. But this crystallization of strategic thinking did have a discernible effect on the future role of China. It decreased the probability that a major campaign against Japan would be

[41] Charles F. Romanus and Riley Sunderland, *Stilwell's Command Problems* (Washington, D.C., Government Printing Office, 1956), p. 53.
[42] *Ibid.*, p. 55.
[43] Morison, *New Guinea and the Marianas*, pp. 6–7.
[44] *Ibid.*, and Romanus and Sunderland, *Stilwell's Command Problems*, p. 54.
[45] *Ibid.*, p. 75, and Matloff, *op. cit.*, p. 374.

undertaken on the Chinese mainland [46] and, as we shall see, it ruled out any increase in allocation of matériel and equipment to Stilwell's army reform program beyond those already planned.

However, the Joint Chiefs of Staff, in March, 1944, still regarded Formosa, Luzon, and some places on the Chinese coast as *alternative* bases from which the final assault on Japan should be made.[47] But in April the Japanese armies launched the "east China" offensive,[48] and by August had forced the American Air Force to retire from forward air-fields in China. The principal air base in Kweilin was threatened. In the next five months, the value of China as a base of operations diminished to the vanishing point. In the Quebec Conference in September, 1944, the over-all strategy of making the main effort in the Pacific was reaffirmed. In their final report the Combined Chiefs of Staff agreed to stress naval and air action and to avoid, where possible, any commitment to a costly land campaign. On October 3, the Joint Chiefs issued a directive to attack Leyte and liberate Luzon and then to take one or more positions in the Bonins and invade the Ryukyus.[49] By early October, the Joint Chiefs were reaching the conclusion that a landing on the East China coast would not be necessary.[50] General Stilwell was informed by General Frank D. Merrill that Admiral Nimitz' repeated statements that the United States required bases on the China coast were purely a cover for projected operations elsewhere in the Pacific and that the United States had no desire to engage in any operations which would involve the use of large American forces on the mainland of China.[51] As Stilwell wrote in his diary on October 4: "War Department is with me apparently, but this theater is written off and nothing expected from us. No [American] troops will be sent."[52] Speaking of the demise of the "Strategic Plan for the Defeat of Japan," approved in May, 1943, Morison says:

> British absorption in the Mediterranean, the weakness and un-reliability of Chiang Kai-shek's government, the difficulty of op-erating a navy in the South China Sea while Japan held the Philippines, and positive factors such as the brilliant success of American amphibious techniques and of fast carrier forces, wrought a complete change of plans in 1944, after the Bismarcks Barrier had been broken and the Marshalls secured. The even-

[46] See Marshall's message of May 27, 1944, to Stilwell, quoted in Romanus and Sunderland, *Stilwell's Command Problems*, pp. 363.

[47] Samuel Eliot Morison, *Leyte* (Boston: Little, Brown & Co., 1958), p. 4.

[48] Romanus and Sunderland, *Stilwell's Command Problems*, p. 322.

[49] Morison, *Leyte*, p. 18.

[50] Herbert Feis, *The China Tangle* (Princeton, N. J.: Princeton University Press, 1953), p. 195.

[51] Romanus and Sunderland, *Stilwell's Command Problems*, p. 457.

[52] Stilwell, *op. cit.*, p. 341.

tual roads to Tokyo were two in number: Marshall-Marianas-Iwo Jima and New Guinea-Leyte-Luzon-Okinawa; neither touched China.[53]

At a meeting of the Combined Chiefs of Staff at Malta on February 1, 1945, General Marshall and Admiral King explained that future operations in the Pacific were designed to avoid full-scale land battles against Japanese forces, which would involve heavy casualties and slow up the conduct of the campaign, and that plans had been prepared aiming for an attack on Kyushu in September of 1945 and the invasion of the Tokyo Plain in December of 1945.[54] In a meeting of the Combined Chiefs of Staff with Roosevelt and Churchill on February 2, 1945, at Malta, the Prime Minister asked whether the President had not been somewhat disappointed at the results achieved by the Chinese in view of the tremendous American efforts which had been made to give them support. Roosevelt answered that "three generations of education and training would be required before China could become a serious factor."[55] A State Department paper on United States policy toward China dated February 27, 1945, asserted that measures "now" to arm China so as to make her a strong power did not appear practicable.[56] Thus, by the time of the Yalta Conference, leading American officials clearly recognized that China would not emerge a great power at the end of the war. But there was no sense of crisis to spur American officials to search for a new policy. It was assumed that the United States could persuade the Nationalists and the Communists to re-establish their co-operation during and after the war and that the Chinese Communists were not implacably hostile to America. It was also assumed that the Soviet Union could be dissuaded from helping the Chinese Communists by bringing her into a formal accord with Nationalist China. These assumptions were part and parcel of President Roosevelt's grand design for postwar American-Soviet co-operation and his plan to attain peace through establishing an international organization to enforce idealistic principles of international conduct. Thus, to support America's projected invasion of Japan and to prevent the Japanese government and armies from making a prolonged last-ditch stand on the Chinese mainland, the United States called in the military might of the Soviet Union to compensate for the inability of China to

[53] Morison, *Breaking the Bismarcks Barrier*, p. 8.

[54] Department of State, *Foreign Relations of the United States: The Conferences at Malta and Yalta, 1945* (Washington, D.C.: Government Printing Office, 1955), pp. 518–19.

[55] *Ibid.*, p. 544.

[56] Charles F. Romanus and Riley Sunderland, *Time Runs Out in CBI* (Washington, D.C.: Government Printing Office, 1959), p. 337.

play her part in the American strategy to win the war. At Yalta in February, 1945, the United States obtained a Soviet promise to enter the Pacific war three months after the defeat of Germany.

In mid-February, 1945, General Wedemeyer worked out a plan to capture the two large seaports in South China, Canton and Hong Kong, in early 1946.[57] This offensive was to be undertaken by Chinese armies alone; no participation by American ground forces was envisaged.[58] The withdrawal in May of Japanese forces from Southwest China to Central and North China in anticipation of Soviet and American thrusts [59] enabled Wedemeyer to advance the schedule for his offensive. In June his plan was revised to provide for the seizure of the small port of Fort Bayard in the former French-leased territory of Kwangchowwan on the Leichou (Luichow) Peninsula, as a preliminary step toward the capture of Canton and Hong Kong. On August 3, the Chinese forces were about twenty miles west of Fort Bayard.[60] But the atomic bomb ended the Pacific war on August 14.[61]

In their authoritative studies of the decision to use the atomic bomb, Louis Morton and Herbert Feis conclude that the compelling consideration behind it was to secure Japan's surrender at the earliest possible moment in order to save American lives. The desire to forestall Soviet intervention in the Pacific war was not a significant reason, although Secretary Stimson did suggest, in July, 1945, that a warning to Japan to surrender, backed by the dropping of the atomic bomb, should come before the Russian attack had progressed too far, if the Soviet Union had already entered the war.[62] It does not appear that any consideration was

[57] *Ibid.*, pp. 330-36.
[58] *Ibid.*, p. 342.
[59] *Ibid.*, p. 352.
[60] *Ibid.*, p. 393, and Feis, *op. cit.*, p. 298.
[61] According to General Chennault, General Stilwell proposed in July, 1945, that part or all of the Tenth Army under his command on Okinawa make a landing on the coast north of Shanghai, and that he arm two hundred or three hundred thousand Communists and turn south to take Shanghai (Senate Committee on the Judiciary, *Hearings on the Institute of Pacific Relations*, 82d Cong., 1st and 2d sess. [1951–52], p. 4769 [hereafter cited as *Institute of Pacific Relations*]). For a more detailed description of this alleged episode, see G. F. Hudson, "The Haichow Plan: A Fragment of Recent History," *Twentieth Century*, May, 1962, pp. 448–49. But neither Romanus and Sunderland nor Feis mentions this episode in their careful studies, which are based on government files and personal papers of participants. It can be safely assumed that nothing in the documents substantiates Chennault's charge. What actually happened seems to have been this: At the end of July, Wedemeyer discussed with Chiang the way in which the United States could assist Chiang in reoccupying Japanese-held China. Chiang made it clear that if American troops from the Pacific landed in China they must not be commanded by Stilwell (Romanus and Sunderland, *Time Runs Out in CBI*, p. 391). This is very different from Chennault's story.
[62] Louis Morton "The Decision To Use the Atomic Bomb," in *Command Decisions*,

given to the implications for the Chinese situation of the projected use of the atomic bomb. Nor was political and military planning in China co-ordinated with its impending employment. To the very end, the quest for a quick victory rather than the achievement of a political objective constituted the paramount guide for most of the important military decisions of the United States throughout the Pacific war.

Thus, after the Cairo Conference, the United States gradually abandoned the idea of China as an essential base of operation, which had given the policy of making China a great power whatever validity it had. In its place the strategy of defeating Japan through the island-hopping campaign in the Pacific was confirmed. The actual strategy pursued did not urgently require the creation of a reorganized and re-equipped Chinese army. It did not enable the Nationalist armies to liberate the occupied areas from Japan, nor did it put them in firm control of Central and North China in the course of the war. It did not envision the use of American ground forces in substantial numbers on the Chinese mainland. The gap between political policy and military policy was rapidly widening, until finally there was a complete divorce. Although at the time of the Yalta Conference American officials began to doubt the validity of the concept of China as a great power, there was no search for an alternative political policy. The end of the Pacific war found the program to train thirty-nine Nationalist divisions still far from completion. The Nationalist armies were confined to a corner in Southwest China. No American ground forces were in China. The air and sea lift of the Nationalist armies to the principal cities and lines of communication in North China and the Yangtze Valley and the hasty landing of American marines in strategic locations in North China temporarily saved the day for the Nationalist government. But these actions did not in any way make up for the basic military weakness of the Nationalist government and the absence of American military power in China over a substantial period of time. Furthermore, the landing of the marines did not imply any departure from the military principle, established in 1944, of avoiding a land campaign on the Chinese mainland;[63] it did not lead to the firm establishment of an American military presence there.

ed. Chief of Military History, Department of the Army (New York: Harcourt, Brace & Co., 1959), pp. 407–8; Herbert Feis, *Japan Subdued* (Princeton, N. J.: Princeton University Press, 1961), pp. 76–79, 89, 121, 181–82; and Stimson and Bundy, *op. cit.*, p. 624.

[63] The Joint Chiefs told Wedemeyer on August 15 that the immediate purpose of occupation operations on the China coast was, by gaining control of key ports and communication points, to extend such assistance to the forces in the China theater as was practicable *without involvement in a major land campaign* (Feis, *Japan Subdued*, p. 143). Emphasis added.

C. Political Policies and Military Activities in China

1. The Political Implications of Stilwell's Army Reform Program

In retrospect, the discrepancy between the ambitious political policy and the insufficient resources allotted to China throughout the war, coupled with the widening gap between political policy and military strategy after the Cairo Conference, constituted only one set of stresses in the structure of American policies. Another set of weaknesses, almost as important as the first, concerned the purposes for which the limited resources available were actually used. Despite the Japanese blockade and the logistical difficulties, America did undertake an impressive series of military activities in the China-Burma-India theater. The airlift over the Hump, Stilwell's army reform program, the expansion of Chennault's air force, the North Burma campaign, the "Matterhorn" project of bombing Japan and Japanese shipping by a group of B-29's stationed in Chengtu, and Wedemeyer's continuation of Stilwell's program — all added up to a notable record of attempts to help China within the framework of America's global strategy. Running through many of these military endeavors was the political objective of supporting Generalissimo Chiang which, in turn, was thought to be an indispensable condition for keeping China in the war. In the next chapter an effort will be made to analyze the impact of both of these aims on the lopsided relationship between the American government and Generalissimo Chiang which paralyzed American efforts to strengthen China. Here our concern is to examine the political implications of Stilwell's army reform program for China's internal stability and for the policy of making China a great power. It is to show how American desire for a quick victory and the concomitant preference for spectacular military actions diverted American attention and resources from Stilwell's project. The lesson seems to be that, if the United States had concentrated the limited resources available on promoting the army reform program, she might have had greater success in strengthening the Nationalist government and in making China a great power.

When Stilwell was dispatched to China as the chief of staff to Generalissimo Chiang Kai-shek, his instructions were to "increase the effectiveness of the United States assistance to the Chinese government for the prosecution of the war and to assist in improving the combat efficiency of the Chinese army."[64] Stilwell construed these and other directives to mean that his *primary* mission was to improve the combat efficiency of the Chinese army. Toward this goal his first proposal, advanced during

[64] Romanus and Sunderland, *Stilwell's Mission to China*, p. 74.

April, 1942, in the perilous moment of the first Burma campaign, was to train in India an elite Chinese army of two corps of three divisions each.[65]

On May 26, 1942, after the Allied rout in Burma, Stilwell presented the Generalissimo with a plan to reorganize the Chinese army by a sharp reduction in the number of divisions and a sweeping purge of inefficient high commanders. His principal aim was to retrain and re-equip thirty picked Chinese divisions as the nucleus of a new Chinese army.[66] Later, in October, 1942, he contemplated a total of sixty re-equipped Chinese divisions.[67] Besides the Chinese divisions at Ramgarh, his scheme was to train thirty divisions in the Chinese province of Yunnan, with Kunming as the center, which would be used for a converging attack to reconquer Burma. The second thirty divisions were to be assembled and begin training in "east China," with Kweilin as the center, as soon as the first thirty-division program was on its way. The War Department told Stilwell that requisitions for his sixty-division program would generally be met within the next six months.[68]

Stilwell's ardor in pushing the Chinese army reform program stemmed quite naturally from military considerations, which in turn arose from the idea of China as an essential base of operations against Japan. But he was not oblivious of the external and internal political effect of his program. In a memorandum dated December 27, 1942, containing the gist of an oral communication to T. V. Soong, Stilwell wrote that the "long range objective" of his program was:

> A powerful independent China, with a modern well-organized Army, in a position to back up all legitimate demands, and with close ties of interest and friendship with the United States. (Under these conditions, peace in the Orient could be assured and China could take the lead in the organization of an Asiatic League of China, Indo-China, Siam, Burma, and India. The Pacific Ocean would be controlled jointly by the United States and China, with no conflicts of interest in the Dutch East Indies, Australia or the Philippine Islands.)

The "immediate objective" was the "reorganization, equipment, and training of the Chinese Army."[69]

Stilwell also saw the army reform program as a means of reversing the centrifugal tendency in Chinese politics and of strengthening the political authority of the central government. As he wrote in a memoran-

[65] *Ibid.*, p. 135.
[66] *Ibid.*, p. 75.
[67] *Ibid.*, p. 225.
[68] *Ibid.*, pp. 225, 264.
[69] Quoted by Romanus and Sunderland, in *ibid.*, p. 256.

dum entitled "Program for China" submitted to Generalissimo Chiang Kai-shek on September 29, 1943:

> The problem of provincial loyalty will disappear as soon as the first and second thirty [divisions] are constituted. These two groups will assure the Central Government of obedience to its orders. . . . With it [a thorough reorganization of the Chinese army] China will emerge at the end of the war with the means of assuring her stability.[70]

In a picturesque entry in his diary on October 5, 1942, Stilwell fumed:

> Troubles of a Peanut dictator [i.e., Generalissimo Chiang Kai-shek]. At first the Peanut thought that military and political function could not be separated, so he combined the authority under the military commanders. *Now* he finds that it makes the boys too powerful, and he's been trying for over a year to shake them loose, without success. . . . The plain fact is that he doesn't dare to take vigorous action — they are sure to be sulky and they may gang up. His best cards are the air force, the artillery, and the ten armies whose training is under the Central Government. Why doesn't the little dummy realize that his only hope is the 30-division plan, and the creation of a separate, efficient, well-equipped and well-trained force?[71]

Notwithstanding Stilwell's observations, there can be no doubt of Chiang's belief in the importance of creating a well-equipped and powerful force. This strong conviction was expressed throughout his career, particularly in his devotion to the task of organizing the Whampoa Military Academy in Canton in the twenties and his endeavors, after the establishment of the Nanking government, to modernize the Nationalist armies with the help of German advisers. In fact, Mr. T. V. Soong, Chiang's personal representative, submitted to the American government in March, 1941, requests for arms which clearly implied a plan to rearm thirty divisions.[72] Why, then, did the Generalissimo fail to co-operate with Stilwell in the latter's effort to train and reform the Chinese armies, and instead frustrate it by delay and evasion? No one can have certain knowledge of Generalissimo Chiang's motives but there is a possible explanation of his behavior. The Chinese armies were in themselves political forces. The implementation of an army training and reform program would necessarily have altered the balance of power among the various political elements in China. The training of the "new army" toward the end of the nineteenth century

---

[70] *Ibid.*, p. 373.
[71] Stilwell, *op. cit.*, p. 157. Stilwell's italics.
[72] Romanus and Sunderland, *Stilwell's Mission to China*, pp. 14, 25.

gave rise to the Peiyang military clique which dominated the political scene in North China for fifteen years after the downfall of the Ch'ing dynasty. Chiang himself owed his political power to the armies commanded by the cadets and officers of the Whampoa Military Academy, of which he was the superintendent.[73] Thus, he had to make certain that the army training program would enhance his own power rather than become the source of a new political force.[74] As for Stilwell's army reform program, he had to be sure that Stilwell's proposal to eliminate inefficient commanders would not militate against his political influence by removing those loyal to him. As Madame Chiang commented on Stilwell's suggestion in the spring of 1942, it was necessary to be "realistic" and "heads cannot be lopped off otherwise nothing would be left."[75] Furthermore, Chiang's power position in China had been deteriorating. The more difficulties he encountered, the more heavily he relied on his control of the army. But, even if selfish political calculation had not been the principal reason for Chiang's delay, the political difficulties of implementing Stilwell's reform program would have remained great. For Stilwell's plan called for drastic reduction of the number of Chinese divisions, and its implementation would have encountered all sorts of resistance from commanders whose troops would be taken away from them.

Since from Chiang's viewpoint the political difficulties and problems created by implementation of Stilwell's proposals of a drastic reduction in the size of the armed forces and a rigid purge of inefficient commanders would be tremendous, he apparently wanted to go slow, and he placed his hope of strengthening his armies primarily on obtaining American arms and equipment. Thus, he gave priority to the increase of the Hump tonnage over the army reform program. In June, 1942, he told Stilwell, as paraphrased by Romanus and Sunderland, that "once a plan had been made to bring in 5,000 tons of supplies a month and to maintain 500 aircraft in China, then attention could be directed to training troops."[76] By countering Stilwell's pressure for reforming and retraining the army with a demand for increased aid to China, Chiang also strengthened his own bargaining position. For this and perhaps other political reasons, Chiang himself placed many obstacles in the way of Stilwell's program.

[73] F. F. Liu, A *Military History of Modern China* (Princeton, N. J.: Princeton University Press, 1956).

[74] Chinese generals and politicians realized that Chiang's fear of a new rival was a major obstacle to Stilwell's army training program. For example, see the memorandum written by John Davies, Jr., recording a conversation with the Chinese air attaché in Washington (Department of State, *Foreign Relations of the United States, 1943, China* [Washington, D.C.: Government Printing Office, 1957], p. 62).

[75] Romanus and Sunderland, *Stilwell's Mission to China*, p. 154.

[76] *Ibid.*, p. 156. See also Romanus and Sunderland, *Stilwell's Command Problems*, p. 26.

2. The Pursuit of a Quick Victory as an Obstacle to Stilwell's Efforts

Stilwell himself realized, as he told Marshall in July, 1943, that "the Generalissimo did not want the regime to have a large, efficient ground force for fear that its commander would inevitably challenge his position as China's leader."[77] Why Stilwell could not overcome Chiang's resistance to his program will be analyzed in the next chapter. It is our concern here to show that Stilwell's program for army reorganization ran not only into Chinese delays but also into the American preference for spectacular military action expected to bring about quick and decisive results. American attitude found an able and forceful spokesman in General Claire L. Chennault. Soon after his arrival in China in the summer of 1937, Captain Chennault, who had retired from the United States Army Air Corps for physical disability and accepted a position as civilian advisor to the Chinese National Aeronautic Commission, perfected a fighter tactic against the vastly superior Japanese air force which exploited the strength of the aircraft flown by the Chinese, the weaknesses of Japanese planes, and errors in Japanese tactics.[78] As early as December, 1940, he had evolved a strategy of using China as a platform for air attack on Japan.[79] His brilliant tactical success in the air over China and Burma as the commander of the Flying Tigers stood in sharp contrast to the humiliating defeats suffered by the Allies in the early months of the Pacific war and won him world-wide fame.

In October, 1942, Chennault, now restored to active service and promoted to brigadier general, claimed that he could "accomplish the downfall of Japan" with "105 fighter aircraft of modern design, 30 medium bombers, and in the last phase, some months from now, 12 heavy bombers."[80] His plan was to attack military objectives in Japanese-held China, to destroy the Japanese air force when it tried to defend them, and then to bomb the Japanese home islands after the Japanese air force had been destroyed. He expounded these views in full in a letter to Wendell Willkie, to be presented directly to the President.[81]

The Chennault plan was a godsend to Generalissimo Chiang. Politically, it provided him with a pretext for resisting Stilwell's insistent demands for an early campaign in Burma and the reorganization and reform of the Chinese army. It enabled the Generalissimo to use Chennault against Stilwell, to counter Stilwell's pressure by weakening his influence

[77] Romanus and Sunderland, *Stilwell's Mission to China*, p. 353.
[78] Claire Lee Chennault, *Way of a Fighter* (New York: G. P. Putnam's Sons, 1949), pp. 49–50, 80, 91.
[79] *Ibid.*, pp. 95–96.
[80] *Ibid.*, p. 214.
[81] *Ibid.*

and authority, and to divide American ranks so that the Chinese leader's will could prevail—a political tactic Chiang had employed time and again in internal political and military maneuvers in China with huge dividends in destruction of his rivals. Militarily, it enabled the Generalissimo to claim a significant contribution to the war without much sacrifice and effort on his part. It also conferred upon him the incidental benefit of providing an effective air defense of Chungking and other principal cities against Japanese raiders. The Generalissimo therefore put the strongest possible support behind the Chennault plan.

Soon after her arrival in the United States in November, 1942, Madame Chiang Kai-shek made it clear that she did not like Stilwell but that she had "the greatest admiration for Chennault."[82] In February, 1943, when the Arnold-Somervell-Dill Mission was in Chungking to persuade the Generalissimo to carry out his part of the Casablanca plan for the reoccupation of Burma, Chiang Kai-shek demanded for China the establishment of an independent air force under Chennault.[83] This wish was granted by President Roosevelt, overriding General Marshall's argument that the success of the Burma offensive and the building of a strong Chinese army were the absolute prerequisites for the expansion of air operations in China. Prophetically, Marshall pointed out that "as soon as our air effort hurts the Japs, they will move in on us, not only in the air but also on the ground. The air situation Chennault can take care of with his fighters, but the ground effort against our bases must be met with men on the ground."[84]

In a letter to Marshall explaining his decision, the President clearly displayed a lack of interest in Stilwell's program to reform the Chinese army and referred to Stilwell's projects as nothing more than local preparations for a Burma campaign.[85] Roosevelt's decision setting up the Fourteenth Air Force under Chennault did not immediately affect Stilwell's scheme to retrain the Chinese forces, for it did not change the priorities in the distribution of the matériel flown over the Hump between Stilwell's and Chennault's projects. But it was a clear indication of the President's preference for the spectacular approach of Chennault over the slow, tedious, and painstaking program of Stilwell. In ruling against Stilwell, Roosevelt did not take into account the immense political implications of the army reform program.

The issue between the two projects was clearly joined when Chennault and Stilwell were recalled by the President to Washington on the eve of the Trident Conference in May, 1943, to present their views—Chennault

[82] Sherwood, *op. cit.*, p. 661.
[83] Romanus and Sunderland, *Stilwell's Mission to China*, p. 275.
[84] *Ibid.*, pp. 280–81.
[85] *Ibid.*, p. 297.

at the request of Chiang Kai-shek, and Stilwell at the suggestion of Marshall. The Generalissimo now made a formal bid for a change in the priorities in the allocation of the Hump tonnage in favor of Chennault's air force.

In presenting their views before the President, Chennault's exaggerated claim for immediate military results greatly impressed the President, while Stilwell's accurate forecast of a Japanese offensive to capture the Chinese air bases was lightly dismissed. Concerning the major point, Chennault recalled: "I replied [to the President] that if we received 10,000 tons of supplies monthly my planes would sink and severely damage more than a million tons of shipping. He banged his fist on the desk and chortled, 'If you can sink a million tons, we'll break their backs.'"[86] To Stilwell's warning that the Chinese air bases could not be defended against a Japanese attack without a reorganized and re-equipped Chinese army, the President retorted, as later recalled by Stilwell, "In a *political fight* it's not good tactics to refrain from doing something because of something your opponent may do in turn."[87] At that time Generalissimo Chiang Kai-shek assured the President that, in the event the enemy attempted to interrupt the air offensive by a ground advance on the air bases, the advance could be halted by the existing Chinese forces.[88]

The upshot was that the President ordered a drastic change in the Hump priorities. Starting July 1, 1943, the first 4,700 tons of supplies per month flown into China were to be allotted to Chennault's air force. After this priority was fully satisfied, the next 2,000 tons per month were to be used for all other purposes including ground forces.[89] By specific agreement between T. V. Soong and General Joseph T. McNarney, deputy chief of staff, 500 tons a month were allotted to the ground forces between July and October, 1943. The War Department's July 8, 1943, program for Chinese lend-lease assigned equipment to the first thirty divisions of Stilwell's army reform program but only 10 per cent of the equipment needed by the second thirty, which were considered token shipments for instructional purposes.[90] Stilwell's second thirty-division project suffered a setback.

The effect of Roosevelt's decision in favor of Chennault was to hamper Stilwell's efforts in reforming and re-equipping the Chinese army either

[86] Chennault, *op. cit.*, pp. 225–26.
[87] Quoted by Romanus and Sunderland in *Stilwell's Mission to China*, p. 324. Stilwell's italics.
[88] *Ibid.*, p. 320.
[89] *Ibid.*, p. 327. Prior to the Trident Conference, Stilwell's announced policy was to allot to Chennault 1,000 tons out of the projected 4,000 tons flown over the Hump. As the actual Hump tonnage at this time fell short of the projected figure, Chennault in fact received only between 600 and 800 tons a month.
[90] Romanus and Sunderland, *Stilwell's Command Problems*, p. 27.

for an offensive in Burma or to defend the "east China" air fields. Commenting on the President's decision, Stilwell wrote in an undated entry: "Nobody was interested in the humdrum work of building a ground force but me. Chennault promised to drive the Japs right out of China in six months, so why not give him the stuff to do it? It was the short cut to victory."[91]

It should be noted that the arguments which both Chennault and Stilwell advanced to support their programs rested purely on military grounds. But in deciding in favor of Chennault's program, President Roosevelt was influenced both by military considerations and by one political judgment. Militarily, he was strongly in favor of air power which promised a short and decisive victory. Politically, he felt obligated to support the Generalissimo unconditionally and to bolster Chinese morale by approving the Chiang Kai-shek–Chennault air program. This method of dealing with Chiang arose basically from Roosevelt's anxiety to keep China in the war, as we shall try to show in the next chapter. At the moment, suffice it to point out that few American officials stressed the immense political implications of the army reform program for the internal stability of China during and after the war, and that the preoccupation with immediate military success and the quest for a quick victory hindered Stilwell's project.

President Roosevelt's decision favoring Chennault's plan on the eve of the Trident Conference at Washington was not the only instance in which the United States preferred a program which promised to bring quick results on the battlefield to another project which might have contributed directly or indirectly to the promotion of the internal stability of China. The Matterhorn project to bomb Japan from Chengtu in China by a task force of B-29's must be included in this category of American military activities.

The project was conceived by American air force planners in August, 1943. After discussions with Major General George E. Stratemeyer of the China-Burma-India theater, it was modified to a plan to base the B-29's in the Calcutta area and to stage them through a Chinese base to bomb the coking facilities in Japan, which were incorrectly believed to be the bottleneck of the Japanese steel industry. The President accepted it with enthusiasm.[92] The B-29's were to be self-supporting, carrying their own supplies to China, and therefore were not to be a burden on the Hump airlift. But, actually, the Air Transport Command had to fly 17,931 tons over the Hump to Chengtu from February to October, 1944, to support this project. The relative importance of the Matterhorn project and the

[91] Stilwell, op. cit., p. 204.
[92] Romanus and Sunderland, Stilwell's Command Problems, pp. 15–17.

army reform program was indicated by the fact that this tonnage was equal to the tonnage flown into China for the Chinese army from May, 1942, to October, 1944.[93] Even Chennault's Fourteenth Air Force was, in practice, assigned second priority in air operations after November, 1943.[94]

In first favoring Chennault's program for defeating Japan by air power in China over Stilwell's program of army reform, and then the B-29 Matterhorn project to bomb Japan over Chennault's plan, the President made two military decisions which subsequent events proved wrong on purely military grounds. The decision on the eve of the Trident Conference giving Chennault first priorities on the Hump tonnage hindered the build-up of a new Chinese army, while it permitted Chennault to inflict such damage on the Japanese that Stilwell's prediction of a Japanese reaction to capture the air bases in "east China" was fulfilled in the large-scale Japanese offensive against the "east China" air bases which was started in April, 1944, and ended in December of that year.

The primary objective of this offensive was to capture and destroy Chennault's bases of operation from the ground. The lack of progress in the army reform program and the diversion of matériel from the ground troops left the Chinese armies ill-prepared to defend the air bases. The Japanese armies not only captured all the air bases in "east China" but at one time appeared to threaten the very existence of the Nationalist government. This was the gravest crisis in the seven years of the Sino-Japanese War. Undoubtedly, the adoption of the Chiang Kai-shek-Chennault air program was primarily responsible for the "east China" disaster. Another factor contributing to the debacle was Generalissimo Chiang's refusal to send supplies to those troops defending "east China" whose commanders were suspected of being disloyal to him and contemplating revolt.[95]

While the operations of Chennault's Fourteenth Air Force brought on the Japanese offensive in "east China" and diverted matériel from the Chinese ground forces, his airmen did make a valiant, though unsuccessful, attempt to stem the Japanese tide by attacks on the Japanese lines of communication and by providing an air cover for the Chinese troops. In contrast, the B-29's of the Matterhorn project, which was a heavy drain on the Hump tonnage, contributed nothing whatever to the defense of "east China" and very little to the final defeat of Japan. Just at the time when the Japanese started the first phase of the "east China" offensive, Stillwell directed that Chennault's primary mission be the defense of the

[93] *Ibid.*, p. 115.
[94] *Ibid.*, p. 25.
[95] *Ibid.*, pp. 401–5, 408–13. See also, Tang Tsou, *"The Historians and the Generals,"* *Pacific Historical Review*, February, 1962, pp. 41–48.

B-29 fields at Chengtu "even at the expense of shipping strikes and support of the Chinese ground forces, dependent upon Japanese reactions to operations from the Chengtu area."[96]

Throughout May and June, Generalissimo Chiang Kai-shek repeatedly requested the diversion of the B-29 stores to the Fourteenth Air Force to support the Chinese ground troops defending Honan and Hunan.[97] In early June, Stilwell yielded to Chiang Kai-shek's entreaties to the extent of asking the War Department's permission to use the B-29 stocks if the situation grew worse.[98] To Stilwell's request the War Department answered:

> It is our view that the early bombing of Japan will have a far more beneficial effect on the situation in China than the long delay in such an operation which would be caused by the transfer of those stocks to Chennault. . . . Furthermore, the Twentieth Bomber Group [the B-29's] represents a powerful agency which must not be localized under any circumstances any more than we would so localize the Pacific Fleet. Please keep this in mind.[99]

On this message, Romanus and Sunderland commented: "Surely here was faith in strategic bombardment at its highest pitch."[100] They might have added that surely here was the clearest indication of the American impulse to achieve a quick victory to the total neglect of political considerations.

At about the same time, Chennault proposed the use of the B-29's in one massive strike against Hankow, the principal supply base for the Japanese offensive in "east China." He was confident that with the help of the B-29's he could stop the Japanese drive. Stilwell gave formal indorsement to this project. But the Joint Chiefs of Staff and General Arnold refused to grant the request.[101] Instead, at a time when the "east China" situation was growing critical, the first mission of the B-29's was flown against the railway workshops in Bangkok, Thailand. Three days before the fall of Changsha, the Chinese bastion in the province of Hunan, the B-29's attacked the steel industry on Kyushu Island. Throughout the period of the Japanese "east China" offensive, the China-based long-range bombers flew many missions against targets on the Japanese home islands, Manchuria, Sumatra, and Formosa.

The operations by the B-29's not only drained off resources which

[96] Chennault, op. cit., p. 285.
[97] Romanus and Sunderland, Stilwell's Command Problems, pp. 325, 366, 368.
[98] Ibid., p. 368.
[99] Quoted by Romanus and Sunderland, ibid., p. 369.
[100] Ibid.
[101] Chennault, op. cit., p. 295.

would otherwise have been available to the Chinese army and Chennault's air force to defend "east China," but their impact on Japanese steel production was negligible. They fell far short of achieving the objective of cutting Japanese steel production in half. On the effectiveness of these operations, the Strategic Bombing Survey concluded: "The reduction in ingot steel supply, excluding electric steel, was not over two percent and in finished steel less than one percent."[102]

Toward the end of the year, General Albert Wedemeyer, who had succeeded Stilwell, finally secured authority from the Joint Chiefs of Staff to use one hundred B-29's against a target in China. The massive air attack on Hankow on December 18, 1944, was a great success.[103] But by now the principal "east China" air bases had been lost for more than a month, the authority and influence of the Nationalist regime had been gravely shaken, and the Japanese were soon to retreat voluntarily from their advanced positions. Thus, success came too late to have much value.

The top priority given the B-29 project was a direct manifestation of the strategy of making the main effort in the Pacific, which received top-level confirmation at the Cairo Conference. It was consonant with the military notion that from now on China's role in the war was to support the island-hopping campaign. The failure to divert resources allocated to the B-29 project or to use the B-29's themselves to slow the Japanese advance was another reflection of the widening gap between military strategy and political policy after the Cairo Conference. Still another expression of this development was the final rejection of Stilwell's second thirty-division program and the diminishing significance which the War Department attached to Stilwell's army reform project. In November, 1943, when Stilwell had had some success in pushing the second thirty-division program in China and the Kweilin center for training the second thirty divisions was about to be established, he asked for a review of the War Department's lend-lease program and wanted a firm commitment to arm the second thirty divisions in full. This request was rejected by the War Department.[104] The rejection of Stilwell's request was again in harmony with the trend of strategic thinking emerging over a period of time in important agencies in the United States. As noted previously, various military planning agencies were thinking in October, 1943, of a major effort through the Pacific, bypassing China. The strategy sections of the Operations Division had recommended that no further commitments be made to the China-Burma-India theater and that no more than thirty Chinese

[102] United States Strategic Bombing Survey, *The Effects of Strategic Bombing on Japan's War Economy*, p. 45, as quoted in Romanus and Sunderland's *Stilwell's Command Problems*, p. 370.

[103] Chennault, *op. cit.*, pp. 328–29.

[104] Romanus and Sunderland, *Stilwell's Command Problems*, p. 27.

divisions be trained and equipped, plus three more divisional sets of equipment to be used in beginning the training of the second thirty divisions in "east China."[105] In making this recommendation, the Operations Division obviously did not see the political implications of Stilwell's sixty-division program. It was oblivious of the United States policy of making China a great power.

At the Cairo Conference the Generalissimo and Stilwell obtained an oral commitment from President Roosevelt to equip ninety divisions eventually. But the less than lukewarm attitude of the army toward the ninety-division program was revealed by its interpretation of the President's promise. The Operations Division told General Marshall: "The commitment regarding the Lend-lease equipping of Chinese divisions the President actually made at SEXTANT is not known. We are proceeding on the assumption the President made no commitment on the timing and flow of equipment."[106] This interpretation was perhaps technically correct but it imposed another obstacle to Stilwell's hope of rebuilding the Chinese army.

After the Cairo Conference, Stilwell's army reform program became even less important in America's scheme of priorities. On May 3, 1944, a directive to Stilwell from the Joint Chiefs of Staff assigned to the China-Burma-India theater a new mission: air support for forthcoming operations in the western Pacific. The Joint Chiefs explicitly conceded that accumulating logistical support for the projected air effort would require major curtailment of Hump support for the ground forces in China.[107] To Stilwell's query on May 24 whether he was to continue on his original mission of increasing the combat effectiveness of the Chinese army, Marshall replied, on May 27, that the United States wished to avoid a major effort on the mainland of Asia and that Stilwell's "paramount" mission for the immediate future was "to conduct such military operations as will most effectively support the main effort directed against the enemy by forces in the Pacific" even if they interfered with his "primary mission" of increasing the combat effectiveness of the Chinese army.[108] These directives were issued at a time when the Japanese armies had already started their offensive to capture the air bases in "east China."

Despite these repeated frustrations, Stilwell's persistent, arduous, and painstaking efforts to rebuild the new Chinese army did result in three elite divisions, trained in Ramgarh, India, two additional divisions which were flown to Burma in April, 1944, and fought under his command, and the fifteen divisions of the Yunnan forces, partly retrained and re-equipped,

[105] *Ibid.*, pp. 54–55.
[106] *Ibid.*, p. 73.
[107] *Ibid.*, pp. 201–2.
[108] *Ibid.*, pp. 363–64.

under General Wei Li-huang, which fought in the Salween campaign. Wedemeyer, who succeeded Stilwell, pursued the same goal. Building on the foundation laid by Stilwell, Wedemeyer's effort to regroup and re-equip the Chinese armies met with some success. Gradually, American officers were placed in all branches of service within the Chinese army as advisers on the high levels and observers on the low. Like Stilwell, Wedemeyer advised Chiang Kai-shek to reduce his 327 divisions to 84, of which the United States would, he proposed, train and equip 39.[109] But as noted above, by February, 1945, both President Roosevelt and the State Department entertained grave doubts about the prospect of China as a great power. On political grounds also, the army reform program had lost its urgency.

Furthermore, time was running out. According to a memo from the acting deputy chief of staff, only about one-third of the necessary equipment for the army reform program of thirty-nine divisions had been given to the Chinese government up to the end of the Pacific war; about one-third was in the China-Burma-India area, but had not yet been turned over to the Chinese government; about one-fifth was on its way to China; the rest was in the United States.[110] On its part, the Nationalist government failed to act with dispatch to train its troops. It was slow in developing an effective system of logistical support and replacement for its armies. Thus, Nationalist China at the end of the war did not have a well-equipped and well-trained force, nor could it sustain one in battle.

Although Stilwell clearly recognized the relationship between his army reform program and the policy of making China a great power, it is doubtful whether he or any other American official saw the potential value of a well-equipped and thoroughly trained ground force as an instrument for dealing with the Communist problem. The American policy was to prevent an outbreak of civil war in China and to bring the Nationalists and Communists together in a coalition government for the purpose both of effectively prosecuting the war and of preserving postwar peace. But, regardless of Stilwell's intentions, the early realization of Stilwell's program might have given the Nationalist government a fighting chance to survive in a part of China if other necessary reforms had been undertaken to provide the minimum political conditions for a major military effort. It might have given the United States a more reliable military instrument in China to counter the threat posed by the Communist bloc, once she had fully

[109] Feis, The China Tangle, pp. 275–76, 296, and Romanus and Sunderland, Time Runs Out in CBI, pp. 231–41, 262, 338, 368.

[110] Feis, The China Tangle, p. 369. At the Potsdam Conference, Marshall stated on July 24 that the American plan was to equip and train fifteen Chinese divisions by August 15 (Department of State, Foreign Relations of the U.S.: The Berlin Conference [The Potsdam Conference], 1945, II [Washington, D.C.: Government Printing Office, 1960], 350).

realized the aggressive intentions of the Soviet Union and had correctly understood the nature of the Chinese Communist party. It is quite true that in 1945 the Nationalist armies outnumbered the Communist armies five to one and were better equipped than their opponents.[111] It is also true that Stilwell's program to reform the Chinese army would not in itself have saved the Nationalist government from destruction. It is also likely that, as one American observer in Communist areas reported, the effectiveness of the American-trained divisions against the Communist type of guerrilla warfare was limited.[112] But well-equipped elite forces would have been one indispensable element in a structure of military and political means to contain Communist expansion in China, had the United States adopted a different policy in China after the war.

To be sure, Chinese apathy and resistance were the primary cause of Stilwell's frustration. But Stilwell's setback also stemmed from the prevailing attitude that the goal of war was exclusively military defeat of the enemy, the inability to grasp firmly the political objective of war in terms of a postwar balance of power, and the failure to co-ordinate military activities with political policy. For our purpose the real significance of the history of Stilwell's army reform program is to provide one of the clearest demonstrations of the American preoccupation with the immediate military aspect of the war to the neglect of making China a great power. Unaccustomed to thinking in terms of the primacy of politics, the United States let the desire to win a quick victory dominate all activities during the war. The result was that it won the war and lost the peace. For one cannot harvest an unsown field.

[111] *United States Relations with China*, p. 311.
[112] Feis, *The China Tangle*, p. 400, n. 6.

CHAPTER IV

THE TACTICS

OF PRESSURE

VERSUS

THE POLICY

OF LIMITED

BUT UNCONDITIONAL

SUPPORT FOR

CHIANG KAI-SHEK

A. The Limits of Foreign Policy and the Method of Dealing with Chiang

In retrospect, it is obvious that no matter how effectively the United States had co-ordinated her military activities and political policy, the use of American ground forces and large-scale aid alone would not have solved the problems of China. Only the Chinese themselves could decide the fate of their country. But American military and economic aid to China could not but strengthen one party against another, and one faction against another. Within certain limits, set primarily by America's method of dealing with Chinese political forces, American policy inevitably influenced the internal development of China.

There were two aspects of America's method of dealing with the internal situation in China. The first was the handling of the military-political conflict between the Nationalists and the Communists. To this question we shall turn in Part II. The second was the method of granting aid to the Kuomintang government and handling the struggle for power within Nationalist China. The essence of this problem was how to deal with Generalissimo Chiang himself. In any analysis of America's approach to the internal politics of China, it is of utmost importance to distinguish between these two problems, for much confusion has been created by the insistence of Generalissimo Chiang and his American friends that to give him unconditional, large-scale economic and military assistance was the only way to fight Chinese communism. This confusion has been compounded by his tendency to see Communist conspiracy or a desire to appease the Communists behind all political opposition to him. In his effort to popularize his case, he was aided by the fact that many American officials and some Chinese politicians misjudged the nature and intentions of the Chinese Communist party.

Actually, his refusal to undertake long-overdue reforms created the very conditions which were exploited by the Communists in their rise to power. His oppression of anti-Communist Chinese politicians as well as of those who entertained illusions of varying degrees about the Communists led them to consider the Communist party the lesser of two evils and drove them into the arms of the Communists. His successful resistance to American advice and pressure for reform produced deep frustrations and despair among American officials, which played an important part in the decision to withdraw from China. As long as the United States failed either to persuade or force him to take the necessary steps to make his regime viable or, alternatively, to bring about his downfall while helping to fashion a new political force to replace him, the necessary condition for the effective use of American aid did not exsist. Nor did saving him from the Communists seem to be a worthy moral cause, — a standard which up to the mid-forties was the popular requisite for making heavy political and military commitments anywhere. The image of a corrupt, oppressive, and moribund regime, headed by a chauvinistic ruler resistant to American advice, was an important factor in the unwillingness to use American forces in postwar China. To this factor, the idealistic tradition of the American policy toward China and the concern for the welfare of the Chinese people gave additional weight.

American experience in dealing with Chiang exemplifies two polar conditions in the range of situations confronting the United States in her relations with governments which she seeks to support and, at the same time, to reform. On the one hand, Chiang's regime and the Generalissimo himself were utterly dependent on American support for victory in the war against Japan and for survival after the war in their struggle with the Communists. This dependence provided the United States with an excellent opportunity to maximize her political influence on the internal development of China. On the other hand, the United States had to cope with Generalissimo Chiang, a master of political maneuvers, who turned his very weakness into a position of diplomatic strength and whose diplomatic adroitness imposed an obstacle to all American endeavors in China.

He employed a threat of rupturing the alliance as a trump card to back his demands and to counter American pressures.

Given the simultaneous existence of these polar conditions, it was American political skill which set the limits of American policy in China. A key factor in Sino-American relations was the inability of the United States either to persuade Chiang to undertake the reform necessary for the survival of his regime or to help fashion a new political force to replace him. This pattern was established during the Pacific war, and the recall of Stilwell was its focal expression.

B. President Roosevelt's Initial Rejection of the "Quid Pro Quo Policy"

During the Pacific war many American officials were pushed by seemingly contradictory impulses toward an identical conclusion as to the proper way of working with their Chinese allies. Imbued with a profound sense of a natural harmony of interests between nations making up the grand coalition, particularly between the United States and China, and exaggerating the dependence of other nations on the United States for postwar economic aid, they overlooked the reality of constant conflict of interests between nations and complacently allowed the policies of the Chinese government to prevail without using every means to effectuate American purposes. When clashes of policies could not be ignored, the United States was impelled to shrink from a contest of wills and to abdicate from a positive assertion of leadership by an exaggerated fear of losing an ally. Under these circumstances, the power and influence of the United States were not fully exerted to implement American policies in China.

On the surface it would seem that convergence of American and Chinese interests could not have been more complete. Did not the United States profess to follow a policy of making China a great power and the stabilizing force in the Far East after the war? Did not the United States insist on treating China as one of the Big Four and on according her a high place in international councils in spite of the skepticism of both Great Britain and the Soviet Union? Did not the United States adopt a policy of unconditional surrender toward Japan and of restoring to China all her lost territories? Did not the United States voluntarily relinquish extraterritorial rights in China and make Great Britain follow its example? Did not the United States revise its immigration law to permit a nominal quota of Chinese immigrants to enter the country and thus remove a source of ill-feeling?

But the United States confronted in China a political leader who turned justified grievances against foreign oppression and legitimate nationalism into xenophobia and chauvinism and who tended to push his interests as far as circumstances permitted. His claims and expectations usually greatly exceeded what others were ready to grant. Further, the two nations were far apart in traditions, historic experience, national character, outlook, and institutional and social structure. Even if there had been complete identity of aims, real differences in methods, procedure, and tempo of doing things would have been inevitable.

During the Second World War, there were several sources of dissension between the United States and China. First of all, there was the conflict between Chinese demands for the allocation of a larger share of equipment and forces to the China-Burma-India theater and the American inability to meet these expectations within the general confines of a global strategy of defeating Hitler first. Second, there was the clash between the American demand for increased effort from China and the Chinese inability to make a greater contribution under the rapidly deteriorating political conditions in China. Third, there was the collision between the natural desire of the ruling group in China to cling to its special privileges and the well-intentioned but, in one major aspect, misguided American attempt to reform its ways by persuasion. Finally, there was the collision between American impatience and Chinese inertia, between American simplicity and Chinese complexity.

Thus, in spite of America's policy of making China a great power, American relations with China during the war were more strained than those with any other ally. The controversies over lend-lease, the Generalissimo's Three Demands, the feud between Stilwell and the Generalissimo, and the row over exchange rate, the army reform program, the Burma campaign—these were the specific issues in which the basic conflicts found expression. While the United States endeavored to submerge or minimize clashes of policies in the community of interests, the Nationalist government pushed its claims as far as possible with an unusual degree of self-righteousness and self-assurance, never shrinking from the possibility of a rupture of the alliance. Since conflicts of interest and policies cannot be wished away or exorcized, the United States was constantly at a disadvantage, and the policies of the Nationalist government frequently prevailed even when the United States occupied an obviously strong bargaining position.

Significantly, most American officials in China, and many in Washington who were familiar with Chinese affairs, did not subscribe to this way of dealing with Generalissimo Chiang. Instead, they urged strongly upon the highest authorities in the United States the adoption of what two authors have called the "quid pro quo" approach, or the tactics of pres-

sure.[1] They were too close to the Chinese scene and too conscious of
their responsibilities in planning and executing American policies in
China to ignore the conflict of purposes and interests. They were familiar
with the high-pressure tactics practiced by the Nationalist government
and the intricate, subtle method of evasion and delay indulged in by
Chinese officials. Thus, they did not believe in the efficacy of advice, persuasion, exhortation, and freely conferred favors to obtain concessions to
American wishes. On the contrary, they were convinced from the very
beginning that the only way to implement American policy and effectuate
American purposes in China was to use lend-lease and American military
activities in the China-Burma-India theater as a lever to move the Nationalist government in the desired direction, exchanging American aid for
Chinese action and conditioning American activities upon Chinese performance.

In July, 1941, well before Pearl Harbor, General Marshall suggested
that the United States obtain guaranties from the Chinese regarding the
command and staff functions of the Americans with Chennault's American Volunteer Group and control over it by General Magruder, the chief
of the American military mission to China, in exchange for a lend-lease
training program for Chinese airmen.[2] In May, 1942, when a controversy
developed between the United States and China over the Chinese share
of lend-lease, General Magruder recommended a tighter control over the
use of lend-lease and its use as a lever to get the Generalissimo's agreement to a specific and limited reorganization of ground and air forces.[3]

The chief and most persistent advocate of the *quid pro quo* policy was,
of course, General Stilwell. When in July, 1942, Stilwell prepared a plan
of operations to retake Burma and proposed to reform a number of Chinese divisions, he explained his approach to the War Department in the
following terms:

> In order to carry out my mission of increasing the combat
> efficiency of the Chinese Army, trading must be the basis of ac-
> tion. Logic and reason, or personal influence, will not produce
> satisfactory results. Pressure and bargaining are the means that
> must be relied on. . . . If it is considered important to keep
> pressure on the Japanese, in spite of tremendous demands on our
> resources in other theaters, the War Department should know
> what the Chinese are prepared to contribute to the effort. The

[1] Charles F. Romanus and Riley Sunderland, *Stilwell's Mission to China* (Washington, D.C.: Government Printing Office, 1953), pp. 278–79, and *Stilwell's Command
Problems* (Washington, D.C.: Government Printing Office, 1956), p. 362.
[2] Romanus and Sunderland, *Stilwell's Mission to China*, p. 41.
[3] *Ibid.*, pp. 159–60.

only way to be sure is to propose a plan under which they would
have to commit themselves.[4]

Later he wrote Marshall, "For everything we do *for* him [Chiang Kai-
shek] we should exact a commitment *from* him."[5]

Colonel Frank Dorn, Stilwell's aide, was even more specific on this
point. In sending one of Stilwell's military plans to the War Department
in August, 1942, he told Major General Thomas T. Handy:

> We all believe that the Generalissimo must be handled on an
> "ultimatum basis," be told in plain language what he must
> do and be given a very short time in which to decide and reply.
> If he threatens to make peace with Japan, tell him to go ahead.
> In all probability the Japanese would laugh at him now. Be-
> sides there exists what amounts to an undeclared peace anyway,
> with mail and a considerable trade going back and forth between
> occupied and unoccupied China. That is why tungsten shipments
> have not been as large as had been expected. The Japs pay a little
> better price.[6]

Besides its strong terms, this passage is also of interest in shedding light
on the attitude of many American officials in China toward the probability and consequences of a negotiated peace between the Nationalist
government and Japan.

Stilwell himself shared the view that Chiang Kai-shek would not conclude a separate peace with Japan but was trying to use the peace maneuvers of Japan "to pull our legs again."[7] Stilwell was an intense
nationalist in his own way. He prided himself on his realistic attitude toward America's allies and his toughness in the game of international politics. In an unfinished paper under the heading "Deck-hand Diplomacy,"
apparently written after the Cairo Conference, Stilwell wrote,

> Our fundamental conception of this game [of international
> politics] is wrong. We are idealists; we have the sporting instinct;
> we want to meet people half-way and shake hands. We forget that
> as the richest nation in the world we are a standing temptation
> for chiselers. We readily forget the experience of the past and
> naively hope that the next time it will come out better. Under
> the actual setup, it can't be anything but a tough game for us.

[4] Memorandum, Stilwell for Marshall, July 30, 1942, as quoted by Romanus and
Sunderland, *ibid.*, p. 179.

[5] *Ibid.*, p. 278.

[6] Dorn to Handy, August 4, 1942, *ibid.*, pp. 182–83.

[7] Joseph Stilwell, *The Stilwell Papers* (New York: William Sloane Associates, 1948),
p. 126.

. . . A little realism is the medicine we need, and we have a
good example in the case of Russia. Have you noticed how they
do it? There you have the direct approach. When they want to
get an idea across instead of saying, "Accept, dear Mr. Ambassador, my sincere hopes that the present harmonious relations between our two great nations will long endure" etc., etc., they
simply say, "If you don't throw these troops out of Shinegazabo
right now, we will have to throw them out." Regrettably crude,
perhaps; remarkably effective, however. Remember that gem of
diplomacy that settled a knotty little problem of Japanese encroachment in Siberia? The message reads: "If you Japs don't
keep your pigs' snouts out of our garden, it will be too bad."
The Japs needed no interpretation by the protocol boys to tell
them just where they stood.

I am not proposing that we assume a truculent or belligerent
attitude; I am merely proposing a readjustment of mental attitude on a basis of realism, because, after all, life is real, life
is earnest. . . . [8]

Stilwell's realism was crude and uncouth; his toughness, undiscriminating;
his understanding of diplomacy, incorrect; his predilection for insisting
on his views and pushing what he conceived to be American interests, too
strong; his language, loose and imprecise; his illustration, inept; and his
diplomatic history, inaccurate. But underlying the passage quoted there
is a grain of truth, to wit: when there is a conflict of interests, an essential
objective in foreign policy must at some point be pursued by the use of
power.

Stilwell's *quid pro quo* policy inevitably entailed a contest of will between the Nationalist government and the United States. It is not difficult
to imagine that the chief source of perpetual crisis in Stilwell's relations
with the Nationalist government was not so much the fluctuating fortunes
of the Burma campaign, the military disaster in "east China," the head-on
collision over the command issue, or even the Communist question, as it
was Stilwell's *quid pro quo* policy and the tactics of pressure.

Stilwell's policy and tactics might have had a better chance to succeed
if they had been accompanied by tact, courtesy, and politeness and if
they had had the sanction and determined support of the highest authorities in the United States. These personal qualities would have strengthened Stilwell's case against the Generalissimo. Had he avoided the
injection of emotional, personal overtones into the situation, this would
have enabled the contestants to maintain a relatively detached and rational view of the issues and to arrive at a settlement on the basis of a cool

[8] *Ibid.*, pp. 257–58.

appraisal of interests and relative strength. As it was, the acid, abusive comments of Vinegar Joe on the Generalissimo and the Chinese government were soon known all over Chungking and aroused intense emotional reactions. They also hurt his policies in Washington. The President had time and again warned him not to be disrespectful toward the Chinese leader.[9] More important, Stilwell's lack of tact tended to confuse the issue of the proper method of dealing with the Nationalist government. Many who rightly condemned Stilwell's personal shortcoming consequently tended to disapprove the correct policy which Stilwell advocated. In any case, Stilwell's policy was at first completely rejected by the President, his confidants, and his envoys to China, although it had the unswerving support of Marshall and Stimson. After the Cairo Conference, the President began to share Stilwell's view and to adopt Stilwell's method, but he failed to follow through in the final crisis leading to Stilwell's recall. As a result the United States failed to accomplish what she intended in China. It was Chiang, despite the asymmetry of power between Nationalist China and the United States, who used Roosevelt for his purposes instead of the other way around.

At first glance, this result seems rather surprising. For Roosevelt had demonstrated that he was the "fox" in American politics, an able tactician and an adroit manipulator.[10] Highly skilful in using other men to achieve his purposes,[11] he was an "artful dodger" who consistently maneuvered to escape commitment to doubtful political positions.[12] But, as James Mac-Gregor Burns notes, "Roosevelt, for all his deviousness, believed in doing good, in showing other people how to do good, and he assumed that ultimately people would do good."[13] In the realm of international affairs, he set out to assert his moral leadership, just as he had in domestic affairs. His greatness, to use the words of Jonathan Daniels, stemmed from his espousal of the "American innocence that the United States had a moral purpose for mankind."[14] But in international affairs, his moral leadership operated within political and institutional contexts totally different from those in domestic politics. Furthermore, his China policy took its place

[9] Robert Sherwood, Roosevelt and Hopkins (New York: Harper & Bros., 1948), p. 739; Romanus and Sunderland, Stilwell's Command Problems, p. 383. Admiral Leahy felt that Stilwell's characterization of the Generalissimo as "Peanut" was not becoming a subordinate officer (Admiral William Leahy, I Was There [New York: Whittlesey House, 1950], pp. 256, 292).

[10] James MacGregor Burns, Roosevelt: The Lion and the Fox (New York: Harcourt, Brace & Co., 1956).

[11] William S. White, Majesty and Mischief (New York: McGraw-Hill Book Co., 1961), p. 24.

[12] Walter Johnson, 1600 Pennsylvania Avenue (Boston: Little, Brown & Co., 1960), p. 194.

[13] Burns, op. cit., p. 475.

[14] Jonathan Daniels, The End of Innocence (New York: J. B. Lippincott Co., 1954), p. 331.

within a framework of traditional principles and practical considerations which set strict limits on his freedom to maneuver.

Upon taking office in 1933, President Roosevelt, with the aid of Cordell Hull and Sumner Welles, crystallized the emergent policy of the United States toward Latin America into the Good Neighbor Policy. The Good Neighbor Policy was a resounding success. It removed the excesses and abuses of "Yankee imperialism," while the predominance of the United States in the Western Hemisphere rendered unnecessary the open use of her power to protect her essential interests. Gradually, this doctrine was thought of as applicable everywhere outside of the Western Hemisphere.[15] The President came to think of himself as the good neighbor of the world, and there is little doubt that the President and his aides believed in the applicability of the Good Neighbor Policy to the quite different setting of China. On several occasions, they based their policy decisions and pronouncements on that foundation. Secretary Hull considered the American moves in 1937 toward the renunciation of extraterritorial rights in China as "merely an extension of the Good Neighbor Policy as applied in the Western Hemisphere."[16] His famous statement of the American position in the Sino-Japanese War issued on July 15, 1937, was based chiefly on his "Eight Pillars of Peace" program which was presented at Buenos Aires in 1936 and was substantially a restatement of the principles of the Good Neighbor Policy. When, on October 1, 1943, President Roosevelt sent a message to Congress urging the repeal of the Chinese exclusion laws, he characterized the requested action as "an earnest of our purpose to apply the policy of the Good Neighbor to our relations with other people."[17]

The desire to be a good neighbor to China was strongly reinforced by the traditional Open Door policy of the United States. This policy embodied the principles of territorial integrity and non-intervention which, according to Hull, were the essence of the Good Neighbor Policy. Before the Pacific war, the principle of non-intervention was one of the many moral thunderbolts which the United States repeatedly hurled at Japan. National self-determination was the cornerstone of the Atlantic Charter. Paragraph 6 of the Moscow Four-Nation Declaration was intended to guard against military intervention in Chinese affairs and rested on the principle of non-interference.

The reiteration of these principles created a powerful deterrent to any actions which smacked of interference in Chinese domestic affairs. The line between intervention and the adoption of Stilwell's tactics of

[15] Cordell Hull, The Memoirs of Cordell Hull (New York: Macmillan Co., 1948), I, 167.

[16] Ibid., p. 566. See also Department of State, Foreign Relations of the United States, 1943: China (Washington, D.C.: Government Printing Office, 1957), p. 12.

[17] Samuel L. Rosenman, The Public Papers and Addresses of Franklin D. Roosevelt: 1943, The Tide Turns (New York: Harper & Bros., 1950), p. 428.

pressure to further such American purposes as the reform of the Chinese army and the appointment of an American to command all Chinese troops seemed tenuous and slender. As a result the rallying cry of the Nationalist government against the infringement of Chinese sovereignty and integrity always secured a respectful hearing in American circles.

In their dealings with the Nationalist government, American officials were influenced by an urge to preserve what was considered a perfect record and by a desire to retain the traditional friendship of China. Harry Hopkins, a close friend of T. V. Soong, an admirer of Chennault, and a critic of Stilwell, wrote: "The United States, through the espousal of the 'Open Door Policy,' has an absolutely clean record in China over the years. We must keep it so."[18] Also well known were the importance which the President placed on the long friendship with China and his gratification over the feeling that the Chinese "really like us."[19] These feelings, which were partly the outgrowth of traditional policy and partly a matter of personal equation, could not but influence his outlook on China policy. Thus, there was a basic contradiction between the traditional principle of non-intervention and the accompanying feeling of friendship for China on the one hand, and, on the other, the necessity to exert pressure on the Chinese government to undertake urgently needed actions.

These considerations, deriving from traditions and principles, were reinforced by two diametrically opposite practical reasons for rejecting Stilwell's tactics of pressure. With the United States emerging during the Second World War as the most powerful nation on earth, American officials were intensely conscious of her tremendous power and the dependence of other nations on her military and economic resources. It was thought that China was so dependent on the United States that it was unnecessary to use pressure. This was the reason for rejecting the Stilwell-Marshall approach given by Lauchlin Currie who, as administrative assistant to the President and assistant to Harry Hopkins in administering lend-lease aid to China, exercised considerable influence over American policy toward China in 1941 and 1942.[20] As Currie wrote in the fall of 1941 in rejecting Marshall's first attempt to use lend-lease as a bargaining device, "In view of the dependence by China upon us for continued aid, it is not anticipated that any difficulty of non-co-operation will be experienced."[21] Hopkins himself was so sure of wholehearted Chinese co-operation that he remarked to Stilwell just before the General left for China on his ill-starred mission: "You are going to command troops, I believe. In fact, I should

[18] Sherwood, *op. cit.*, p. 925.

[19] Stilwell, *op. cit.*, pp. 251–52; Sumner Welles, *Seven Decisions That Shaped History* (New York: Harper & Bros., 1950), pp. 68–69.

[20] Sherwood, *op. cit.*, pp. 208, 284, 286, 404.

[21] Romanus and Sunderland, *Stilwell's Mission to China*, p. 41.

not be surprised if Chiang Kai-shek offered you the command of the Chinese Army." [22] As will be recounted shortly, Stilwell never received the command of the Chinese army then or thereafter, and it was exactly over the issue of the command of the Chinese army that, two-and-one-half years later, the Generalissimo demanded and obtained Stilwell's recall.

In September, 1942, the War Department drafted a message for the President to Generalissimo Chiang Kai-shek asking for the implementation of the thirty-division program and the reorganization of the Chinese army with Stilwell as adviser in exchange for lend-lease aid. Currie again objected to the draft and his objection was sustained by the President.[23] Currie's objection to the War Department's draft was in line with his earlier recommendations to the President: "I do not think we need to lay down any conditions or tie any strings to our support." [24]

Differing basically with Stilwell in his approach to Chinese affairs, Currie was naturally critical of Stilwell and, in late 1942, suggested his recall from the Chinese theater. Although Currie's recommendation for Stilwell's recall was not adopted, his general approach was followed by the President and contributed greatly to the weakening of Stilwell's position in his dealing with the Nationalist government. Currie's view on the proper method of dealing with Chiang Kai-shek was in harmony with the President's temperament. As Stimson and Bundy observed in connection with dealing with the Russians, "Small-minded haggling was no part of Mr. Roosevelt's nature, and in the larger sense this was most fortunate, but it left lesser officials at a considerable disadvantage in trying to make cooperation mutual." [25]

President Roosevelt also rejected the *quid pro quo* policy for another reason, diametrically opposed to the one just mentioned. It was his feeling that a strong policy would be ineffectual and therefore the wrong way to deal with Generalissimo Chiang Kai-shek. This view the President forcefully expressed to General Marshall on March 8, 1943, when the President overruled Marshall and Stilwell and granted Chiang's request to give Chennault command of his own air force and to place air power above the army reform program. This revealing letter from the President to Marshall deserves lengthy quotation:

> . . . Stilwell has exactly the wrong approach in dealing with Generalissimo Chiang who, after all, cannot be expected, as a Chinese, to use the same methods that we do. When Stilwell speaks about the fact that the Generalissimo is very irritable and

[22] Stilwell, *op. cit.*, p. 36.
[23] Romanus and Sunderland, *Stilwell's Mission to China*, p. 185, n. 11, pp. 185–88.
[24] *Ibid.*, p. 186.
[25] Henry L. Stimson and McGeorge Bundy, *On Active Service in Peace and War* (New York: Harper & Bros., 1947), p. 68.

hard to handle, upping his demands, etc., he is, of course, correct; but when he speaks of talking to him in sterner tones, he goes about it just the wrong way.

All of us must remember that the Generalissimo came up the hard way to become the undisputed leader of four hundred million people — an enormously difficult job to attain any kind of unity from a diverse group of all kinds of leaders — military men, educators, scientists, public health people, engineers, all of them struggling for power and mastery, local or national, and to create in a very short time throughout China what it took us a couple of centuries to attain.

Besides that the Generalissimo finds it necessary to maintain his position of supremacy. You and I would do the same thing under the circumstances. He is the Chief Executive as well as the Commander-in-Chief, and one cannot speak sternly to a man like that or exact commitments from him the way we might do from the Sultan of Morocco.[26]

In this letter, President Roosevelt revealed his solicitude for the Generalissimo's political supremacy in China. But he did not give equal weight to the possibility that this supremacy could not be maintained in the face of the Communist challenge by Chiang Kai-shek's methods of government. Nor did he see the consequences for American interests when these methods were allowed to continue and the army reform program was permitted to be sidetracked. The President also showed his appreciation of the political talent and past achievements of the Generalissimo. But he did not fully realize that these achievements could not be long preserved unless sweeping changes were made. Nor did he preceive that the Generalissimo's diplomatic and political skill had to be circumvented if American purposes were to be implemented.

Underlying the President's hesitation to put pressure on the Generalissimo was a fear that, when hard pressed, Chiang Kai-shek would conclude a separate peace with Japan. This exaggerated fear of a separate peace was the principal reason for both the initial rejection of the tactics of pressure and the subsequent failure to carry it through after having adopted it. This was made clear by Robert Sherwood. Commenting on the President's decision to back Chennault rather than Stilwell in the spring of 1943, Sherwood wrote in his *Roosevelt and Hopkins*:

> . . . his [the President's] one overriding concern was to keep China in the war and to hold the friendship of the Chinese people for the United States and he had those objectives in mind in every

[26] Romanus and Sunderland, *Stilwell's Mission to China*, p. 279.

decision that he made. He believed that there was no chance that
the Chinese Communists would surrender to the Japanese as long
as Russia was in the war against the Axis, whereas there was always the possibility that the Kuomintang might make a separate peace. In any case, Chiang Kai-shek was the head of the
government with which the U.S. Government must deal and
the maintenance of good relations was difficult enough under
the circumstances without the frequent disturbances created by
Stilwell. Thus, whether or not Stilwell had the right on his side
— and he certainly had a great deal of it — he was unquestionably
a serious nuisance and there were many times when Roosevelt was
on the verge of ordering his recall.[27]

This fear was shrewdly exploited by the Nationalist government at decisive
moments. It dominated the actions of the United States in and toward
China, since American policy was based upon an overreliance upon the
Chinese in the common war against Japan and for protection of American
interests in the Far East after the war.

The President dealt with the Nationalist government in much the
same way he endeavored to work with the Russians, and in both cases his
efforts ended ultimately in disaster. Instead of bargaining, he was prepared to be generous to the Nationalist government. From the very beginning, he gave his promises freely, without asking anything in return.
Reference has already been made to the President's oral assurances to
the Generalissimo about a fight to the finish to regain for China all lost
territories. Early in February, 1942, a loan of five hundred million dollars
was granted to the Generalissimo with no strings attached and without
asking for a *quid pro quo*. It was hoped that the loan would strengthen
Sino-American relations and ease Stilwell's task.[28] Certainly, the success
or failure of Stilwell's effort in China hinged at least partly on whether
he would be given command of Chinese troops and whether he would
have the means to obtain co-operation from the Nationalist government.[29]
But nothing definite about Stilwell's authority was secured from the
Chinese government to supplement the vaguely worded Soong-Stimson
exchange of letters on January 29 and 30, 1942. These letters merely committed the Nationalist government to appoint the American army representative as the Generalissimo's chief of staff who would command, under
the Generalissimo, "such Chinese forces as may be assigned to him."[30]

[27] Sherwood, *op. cit.*, p. 740.
[28] Stimson and Bundy, *op. cit.*, pp. 530–32; Herbert Feis, *The China Tangle* (Princeton, N.J.: Princeton University Press, 1953), p. 19.
[29] Stimson and Bundy, *op. cit.*, p. 530.
[30] Department of State, *United States Relations with China* (Washington, D.C.:
Government Printing Office, 1949), pp. 15–16 (hereafter cited as *United States Re-*

At about the same time, the air transport service over the Hump was established. In October, the President promised 500 aircraft for the China theater, plus 100 aircraft on the Hump in early 1943. In March, 1943, the Fourteenth Air Force under Chennault was established and China was promised 10,000 tons of supplies a month to be flown over the Hump. At the Trident Conference at Washington in May, 1943, the President decided to comply with the Generalissimo's wishes in giving priority to Chennault's air program over Stilwell's army reform project. After the conference, the United States pledged that "no limits except those imposed by time and circumstances, will be placed on the above operations [i.e., the operations to retake North Burma and the increase of Hump tonnage to 10,000 a month] which have for their object the relief of the siege of China."[31] In November, 1943, the B-29 project was started in China. At the Cairo Conference, China was formally promised the return of all territories lost to Japan. The President also gave an oral promise to equip and train ninety Chinese divisions. All these undertakings on the part of the United States were made without obtaining specific commitments from the Nationalist government to undertake actions and adopt policies desired by the United States.

Stilwell complained bitterly about this method of dealing with Chiang Kai-shek. The freely given promises rendered it impossible for him to exert pressure. When the President told Chiang about the B-29 project, Stilwell wrote: "FDR has undercut me again. Told Peanut [the Generalissimo] all about Twilight [the B-29 project] so I can't bargain on that."[32] Later on, when he was incorrectly told by Madame Chiang that the President had promised to pay all costs for the construction of airfields for the B-29's, he wrote in disgust:

> One more example of the stupid spirit of concession that proves to them that we are suckers. "We'll put in VLR bombers" (no bargaining). Then "we'll pay for the fields" (no bargaining). Same on air freight — promises without bargain. Same on equipment for army — promises without bargain. Same on Chinese Air Force. Same on 14th Air Force. Same on everything.[33]

Worst of all, the promises were so freely given that the United States found it impossible to fulfil them on time. The Hump tonnage and the

lations with China); Romanus and Sunderland, Stilwell's Mission to China, p. 73. For an interesting comment on the difference between the Chinese and American concept of a chief of staff, see William H. McNeill, Survey of International Affairs, 1939–1946: America, Britain, and Russia: Their Co-operation and Conflict, 1941–1946 (London: Oxford University Press, 1953), pp. 159–60, n. 1.
[31] Romanus and Sunderland, Stilwell's Mission to China, p. 332.
[32] Romanus and Sunderland, Stilwell's Command Problems, p. 7.
[33] Ibid., pp. 77–78.

number of aircraft to be maintained in China always fell short of what was pledged. The lend-lease program had to be adjusted and part of the lend-lease supplies already allocated to China were repossessed by the United States, partly due to the demands of other theaters and partly due to the inability to deliver them to China after the fall of Burma. This failure to fulfil his promises caused the President grave concern. To give only one instance, when the Generalissimo sent a strong protest to Washington complaining that the Trident decision to build up the Fourteenth Air Force was not being honored, Roosevelt passed on Chiang's radiogram to Marshall with the note: "I am still thoroughly disgusted with the India-China matter. . . . Everything seems to go wrong. But the worst thing is that we are falling down on our promises every single time. We have not fulfilled one of them."[34] At times even Stilwell himself complained about the breaking of promises. When a group of heavy bombers were diverted from the China-Burma-India theater to Egypt, he wrote on June 5, 1942: "Now what can I say to the Generalissimo? We fail in all our commitments, and blithely tell him to just carry on, old top."[35]

As a result the United States was so busy explaining and apologizing for breaches of promises that bargaining with the Generalissimo was out of the question. Stilwell was put in the impossible position of having to urge the Generalissimo to take action without being able to deliver the goods. Chiang could and did point to the unfulfilled promises in rejecting American suggestions or demands. After the insistence of Prime Minister Churchill forced the cancellation of amphibious operations in the Bay of Bengal, which had been promised the Generalissimo by the President at the Cairo Conference, Stilwell wrote in his diary: "It was fatal to promise anything."[36]

Under these circumstances, it is not surprising that Stilwell's program to reorganize the Chinese army did not yield results proportionate to his efforts. Stilwell himself realized that his inability to apply pressure was one of the major reasons for the lack of progress on his project. He made this point clear to General Marshall in May, 1944:

> My mission vis-à-vis the Chinese is to increase the combat efficiency of the Chinese Army. The basic plan is to equip and train a first group of thirty divisions, followed by a second group of thirty. To get this mission accomplished I have never had any means of exerting pressure. I am continuing to work on the problem as I have from the beginning — by personal acquaintance and influence, by argument and demonstration. This is a slow process,

[34] Romanus and Sunderland, *Stilwell's Mission to China*, p. 382.
[35] Stilwell, *op. cit.*, p. 119.
[36] *Ibid.*, p. 265.

so slow as to require evaluation from the point of view of time available, and possible results to be obtained.[37]

The Generalissimo's method of dealing with the United States was diametrically opposed to the President's approach to the problem of co-operation. It exploited to the fullest the weakness of the President's method. Chiang's view of the relations between states was totally realistic and unsentimental. He confided to his diary on February 27, 1944:

> Time is the creator of history. Sorrow and joy, success and failure all have a limited duration and all will pass away. . . . Rapprochement and estrangement, gain and loss in diplomatic relations cannot be everlasting and without change. Today's loss may be the foundation of future gain. For love and hate, separation and unity do not depend on sentiments but on power. Given a prolonged period of time and with power in one's grasp, international maneuvering can all be in one's hands. Joy and sorrow, love and hate all depend on me.[38]

Furthermore, Chiang Kai-shek was an ardent nationalist in a land of upsurging nationalism. The emotional intensity of his devotion to the first principle of Sun Yat-sen stood in sharp contrast to his nullification in practice of the other two of Sun's principles, democracy and people's livelihood. Of nationalism, he once wrote: "Of all the common human feelings, the sentiment of nationality is the most worthy one. The Principle of Nationalism is based on this point."[39] In contrast to many Chinese intellectuals and officials of that time, he was anti-Western in his general outlook. In his *China's Destiny*, which was written as a political textbook for the education and training of both Kuomintang officials and the Chinese people alike, he attributed to the Western powers all the present-day ills of China.[40] His nationalism and anti-Western bias were compounded by a mystic sense of identification of his power interests with the interests of China, which impelled him to push those interests as far as he could.

[37] Romanus and Sunderland, *Stilwell's Command Problems*, p. 362.

[38] This passage of Chiang's diary was quoted by his son, Chiang Ching-kuo, in a series of articles eulogizing his statesmanship and character (Chiang Ching-kuo, "Ling-hsiu tsen-yang tu-kuo-liao tsiu hsien-o ti i nien" [How the Leader Passed through a Most Difficult Year"], *Reconstruction in China* [Taiwan, December, 1957], p. 11). This series of articles was apparently extracted from a book entitled *Wo-ti fu-ch'in* ["My Father"], which was written for the specific purpose of celebrating Generalissimo Chiang's 70th birthday and was dedicated to him. This book was printed for private circulation but its existence is widely known.

[39] Chiang Kai-shek, "The San Min Chu I System and Its Method of Application," as quoted in Paul M. A. Linebarger's *The China of Chiang Kai-shek* (New York: World Peace Foundation, 1941), p. 270.

[40] Chiang Kai-shek, *China's Destiny*, translated with notes and commentary by Philip Jaffe (London: Dennis Dobson Ltd., 1947), particularly chap. iii.

In so doing, his diplomatic genius and his aptitude in unadulterated
Realpolitik served him well. In the first Sino-Soviet entente, he used Stalin
and the Chinese Communists for his own purpose, and, after he was well
on his way to hegemony over all China, it was he who "squeezed out" the
Chinese Communists and the Soviet advisers "like a lemon" and then
"threw them away," instead of the other way around as Stalin had
planned.[41] In the process he outwitted such an experienced politician and
revolutionary as Michael Borodin and such a capable soldier, strategist,
and diplomat as General Galen, and succeeded without difficulty in having Andrey S. Bubnov, the chief Soviet military adviser, recalled after
only two months in China.[42]

Later he had the services in an advisory capacity of such outstanding
generals in the Reichswehr as General Hans von Seeckt and General
Alexander von Falkenhausen.[43] After the beginning of the Sino-Japanese
War of 1937, several Soviet loans were made to China, totaling two hundred and fifty million United States dollars, and Soviet military supplies
flowed into China. A group of brilliant army officers was stationed in
China. This included M. Smirnov, deputy commissar of war under Marshal
Klimenti Voroshilov, as the ambassdor to China; Alexander S. Pan-
yushkin, also a professional army man who succeeded Smirnov as ambassador; Georgi Zhukov, later the outstanding Soviet military hero in World
War II, as military attaché; and General Vassily I. Chuikov, later the defender of Stalingrad, as one of Chiang's advisers. The Generalissimo gave
them no opportunity to formulate war strategy. Their influence and their
role were strictly limited.[44] In 1942, when Russia was reeling back on the
Western front, Chiang scored another victory over Stalin by reasserting
the control of the Chinese government over Sinkiang with the assistance
of Governor Shêng Shih-ts'ai, who shifted his allegiance from Moscow to
Chungking. Up to that time Japan was the only antagonist whom Chiang
could neither defeat nor outmaneuver. But even Japan was to lose her
empire in the quagmire of China. Chiang's decisive defeat at the hands
of the Chinese Communists was yet to come.

In dealing with the United States, it was natural for a person of

[41] Stalin was reported to have said in a speech: "Why drive away the Right when we
have the majority and when the Right listens to us. . . . When the Right is of no
more use to us, we will drive it away. At present we need the Right. . . . So they [the
people of the Right] have to be utilized to the end, squeezed like a lemon, and then
thrown away" (quoted in Robert North's *Moscow and the Chinese Communists* [Stan-
ford: Stanford University Press, 1953], p. 96). The best account of how Chiang outmaneuvered Stalin in 1924–27 is given in Conrad Brandt, *Stalin's Failure in China*
(Cambridge, Mass: Harvard University Press, 1958).
[42] F. F. Liu, *A Military History of Modern China* (Princeton, N. J.: Princeton University Press, 1956), p. 29, *passim.*
[43] *Ibid.,* pp. 90–100.
[44] *Ibid.,* pp. 167–70.

Chiang's outlook, background, and experience to push as far as he could what he conceived to be the interests of China. He constantly and persistently demanded a larger role for China in the shaping of global strategy and a larger share of equipment, without committing himself to a greater effort toward the defeat of the common enemy. To the demands or suggestions of the United States for action, he would either turn a deaf ear, or attach conditions, or make a counterdemand, even if the actions and contributions demanded of him were parts of a plan for lifting the siege of China. In his dealings with General Stilwell, it is not improbable that Chiang compared Stilwell unfavorably with his former foreign advisers both in military acumen and political skill. With his rich and varied experience in dealing with Chinese and foreign opponents, he had little difficulty in making Stilwell's position untenable from the start, as Stilwell's diary eloquently testified. In any conflict with the United States or with Stilwell, Chiang did not yield on any point unless he was compelled to do so. In these diplomatic maneuverings, he was given an easy start by President Roosevelt's policy of treating China as a great power and the rejection of the *quid pro quo* policy. But Chiang's apparent success must also be attributed to his political skill in turning his political and military weakness to a diplomatically strong position.

It is true that, as Currie suggested, China was dependent upon the United States for survival, victory, and postwar grandeur. But it was this very dependence which aroused Chiang's resentment and his determination to follow his own course of action. His resentment and his determination found clear expression in an entry of his diary some years later. On July 26, 1948, he wrote:

> If I should make a few requests or show a little dependence on other nations or foreigners, no matter how good and friendly their national character, I would necessarily become their slave and there could not be what is called equality, freedom and justice. Only if a nation can be independent and strengthen itself without asking for help and relying on others, can it exist in the world.[45]

Thus, Chiang used his diplomatic genius to turn this very dependence into a position of political strength by taking advantage of the important role that the United States assigned China in the defeat of Japan and in the postwar world. He seems to have fully realized that the more important the United States considered China, the greater was the American fear of a lowering of Chinese morale, a collapse of the Chinese government, or the conclusion of a separate peace with Japan. Whenever the Generalis-

---

[45] Chiang Ching-kuo, *Wo-ti fu-chin*, chap. ii, p. 17. The reference in this sentence to the United States, although she is not mentioned by name, is obvious.

simo made a demand on the United States, rejected an American proposal, or made a counterdemand, he would point to the military, economic, and political weakness of China and the possibility of a political and military collapse. His pleas were frequently heeded. Whenever he felt ill-used or whenever there was a major clash of policies, the Generalissimo would back up his demands or refusals with a hint or an open threat of a negotiated peace with Japan or a separation from the United States. His hints or threats were generally followed by an American concession.

Furthermore, Chiang was a master of the technique of divide and rule. He skilfully exploited the differences among American officials. Throughout the Pacific war he backed Chennault against General Stilwell. Through Lauchlin Currie and Joseph Alsop and through his own personal emmissaries, including Madame Chiang, he won the support of Harry Hopkins. His personal appeals convinced Vice President Henry Wallace, who visited China in the summer of 1944 as President Roosevelt's representative, that General Wedemeyer should be appointed to take over Stilwell's principal duties in China.[46] Thus, it is not surprising that Stilwell's career in the China-Burma-India theater consisted of a series of crises, temporarily assuaged by one abject apology to the Generalissimo and ending ultimately in his recall.

Chiang's diplomacy revealed itself soon after the beginning of the Pacific war. On December 30, 1941, Chiang Kai-shek asked the American government for a loan of five hundred million dollars to support Chinese currency and ease the Chinese economic situation. Taking advantage of the early Allied reverses in the Pacific and American dependence on China to tie down Japanese forces in China, Chiang maneuvered to nullify all American efforts to attach conditions to the loan or to retain a measure of control over it. Writing to the secretary of the treasury on January 9, Dr. H. H. Kung, the Nationalist Finance Minister, explained:

> Frankly, however, my reason for approaching you is political above all; and the import of a loan of this nature is even more important than the Lend-Lease Bill's import. The essence of such a move is timeliness, so as to demonstrate that China's confidence in the allied powers is matched by equal confidence in China of the allied powers, in the most crucial months of the emergency immediately before us.[47]

The Generalissimo made it clear to the American government through T. V. Soong, the newly appointed minister for foreign affairs, that the loan "should be regarded in the light of an advance to an ally fighting against

[46] Romanus and Sunderland, *Stilwell's Command Problems*, pp. 374–79.
[47] *United States Relations with China*, p. 476. For a detailed account of this episode see Feis, *op. cit.*, pp. 19–23.

a common enemy, thus requiring no security or other pre-arranged terms as to its use and as regards means of repayment."[48] The loan was granted with maximum speed. No strings were attached and no controls retained. As was feared by American officials, the loan was misused by the Nationalist government. It did little to check inflation. Nor did it significantly advance American purposes in China except to pacify the small minority who controlled the Nationalist government and profited from the loan. It did not ease Stilwell's way in his dealing with the Generalissimo. It did not make the Generalissimo more willing to heed American advice. It did not enhance American prestige in China with those Chinese groups whose economic stress was by no means relieved by the generous American aid. This loan provides a good example of what economic aid from one ally to another ought not to be.

In June, 1942, the American government ordered a number of B-17's and transports, originally stationed in the China-Burma-India theater, to be transferred to Egypt and ordered a flight of A-29's en route to China to be held up at Egypt. This diversion of aircraft to the Middle East was made in order to stop the advancing forces under General Rommel.[49] Coming after the failure of Chiang to gain membership in the Combined Chiefs of Staff and the contraction of China's share in lend-lease, it precipitated a crisis in Sino-American relations and elicited a hint by Nationalist leaders at the possibility of a rupture. In a conference with Stilwell, the Generalissimo stated: "The China Theater of War is lightly regarded. Naturally I wish to know whether America and Britain consider it as one of the Allied Theaters."[50] Madame Chiang ended the conference with this ominous note: "The Generalissimo must make a speech at the end of the fifth year [of the Sino-Japanese War] on 7 July. He must tell the Chinese people the truth at that time. The pro-Japanese element is very active. The Generalissimo wants a yes or no answer to whether the Allies consider this theater necessary and will support it."[51] Two days later, on June 28, the Generalissimo in a letter to Stilwell presented the United States the "three minimum requirements essential for the maintenance of the China Theater of War." These were: the assignment of three American divisions to India in the autumn to take part in the campaign to open the Burma road; the maintenance of a 500-plane air force in China; and the increase of the Hump

[48] *United States Relations with China*, p. 478. When Secretary of the Treasury Henry Morgenthau told Maxim Litvinoff, the Soviet Ambassador to Washington, of the Chinese request, Litvinoff commented not once but several times: "It is nothing but blackmail." He advised Morgenthau to drag out the negotiations as long as possible (Feis, *op. cit.*, p. 22).

[49] Romanus and Sunderland, *Stilwell's Mission to China*, p. 169.

[50] Memo of Conference, June 26, 1942, as quoted by Romanus and Sunderland, *ibid.*, p. 171.

[51] *Ibid.*

capacity to 5,000 tons. In a conference between the Generalissimo and Stilwell the next day, the Generalissimo and Madame Chiang made it clear that the June 28 note was an ultimatum. Stilwell and Gauss believed that the talks of a separate peace were simply diplomatic manueverings.[52] Later the Generalissimo scaled down his demands to one American division, 500 planes, and 5,000 tons. Finally, after three months of negotiation, the President granted the Generalissimo his request regarding aircraft in the China theater and on the Hump tonnage but rejected his demand for American combat troops, thus ending the first major crisis.

Though for the time being not totally effective, the Generalissimo's hint of a separation must have left a deep impression on the President. From then on the President seems to have realized that Chiang was difficult to handle, a man whose wishes could not be ignored without bringing about the danger of a separation. Therefore, when the Generalissimo demanded, on February 7, 1943, the establishment of a separate air force under General Chennault, the President overruled Marshall's and Stilwell's objections, telling them in the letter quoted before that their *quid pro quo* approach was entirely wrong and that one could not speak sternly to a man like Chiang. Sherwood considered the fear of a separate peace as the major factor leading the President to support Chennault and reject Stilwell's suggestions.[53]

Madame Chiang's ominous reference to active pro-Japanese elements during the Three Demands crisis was neither the first nor the last time in which the highest leaders of the Nationalist government uttered a hint or made an open threat of a separation. In one of the controversies leading up to the Three Demands, Soong had predicted that inter-Allied cooperation in the form of the China theater would cease if the United States abrogated the 3,500-ton emergency air transport program.[54] Later when the Arnold-Somervell-Dill mission visited Chungking after the Casablanca Conference to enlist Chiang's co-operation in the projected campaign to reopen the Burma road, Chiang presented (on February 7, 1943) to Arnold for approval by the President a new version of the Three Demands: (*a*) an independent air force for the China theater, (*b*) ten thousand tons a month over the Hump, (*c*) five hundred aircraft in China by November, 1943. These demands were again accompanied by hints of a separate peace.[55] As noted, the President ordered the establishment of the Fourteenth Air Force for Chennault. He also granted Chiang's other two requests.

On the eve of the Trident Conference at Washington in May, 1943, the Generalissimo proposed to give first priority in the Hump tonnage to

[52] Stilwell, *op. cit.*, p. 126.
[53] See pp. 99–100, above.
[54] Romanus and Sunderland, *Stilwell's Mission to China*, p. 168.
[55] *Ibid.*, p. 275.

Chennault's air force. Chennault and Stilwell were recalled to Washington to present their cases. As recounted above, the President decided in favor of Chennault's air program. As he told Marshall, one of the reasons he gave for supporting Chennault was that "politically he must support Chiang Kai-shek and that in the state of Chinese morale the air program was therefore of great importance."[56]

But the President's decision was not immediately communicated to the Nationalist government. On May 17, Soong appeared before the Combined Chiefs of Staff and stated that China would make a separate peace with Japan unless the United States began earnestly to undertake operations to effect China's relief and to discharge American commitments made since the Casablanca Conference. The next morning Soong was called to the White House and told that Chennault would have first priority in Hump tonnage and that, starting September 1, ten thousand tons would be flown over the Hump.[57] Thus the Generalissimo's wishes prevailed, and the hints and open threat of a separate peace bore fruit. As Stilwell commented in another context, "Continued concessions have made the Generalissimo believe he has only to insist and we will yield."[58]

C. The President's Changing Approach and His Failure To Carry It Through in the Stilwell Crisis

After the Cairo Conference, the President veered gradually but unmistakably toward the Stilwell-Marshall approach to China. The reasons for this shift may have been as follows: First, the cumulative effects of the Generalissimo's method of making exorbitant demands and counterdemands, of attaching nullifying conditions and high prices to American proposals, of making hints and threats of separation may have finally made itself felt on the President. At Cairo the difficulty in obtaining Chiang's assent to the Allied proposal to retake North Burma in spite of generous political concessions may have driven home to the President the futility of his earlier approach. As Admiral Mountbatten wrote, "They [the Prime Minister and the President] have been driven absolutely mad, and I shall certainly get far more sympathy from the former in the future."[59]

Second, at Teheran, Stalin confirmed his promise given earlier to Hull in Moscow to enter the Pacific war after the defeat of Germany. After Cairo, the emergent shifts in strategic thinking gradually crystallized into a firm plan to attack Japan through the Pacific islands. The military importance of China for the defeat of Japan rapidly diminished. The role of China became the subsidiary one of supporting the Pacific operations, and

[56] *Ibid.*, p. 325.
[57] *Ibid.*, pp. 326–27.
[58] *Ibid.*, p. 282.
[59] Romanus and Sunderland, *Stilwell's Command Problems*, p. 65.

the military value of China was a sort of insurance against the eventuality of a failure of the Soviet Union to honor her promises.

Third, the Chennault-Chiang air program fell far short of its promises, while Stilwell's North Burma campaign seemed to be a tactical success. Thus, the President became increasingly cool and unreceptive to the demands of the Generalissimo and was more and more inclined to exert pressure on the Chinese leader. This changed attitude was revealed (a) in the refusal of Chiang's demand in January, 1944, for a billion-dollar loan or for the United States to finance American military activities at the official rate of twenty to one; (b) in his strong pressure, exerted in April, upon Chiang to take the offensive in Burma; and (c) in his unsuccessful attempt in the summer of 1944 to have Stilwell appointed commander of the Chinese army.

The first two episodes were fully described by Feis and by Romanus and Sunderland.[60] Suffice it to say here that the first incident shows that, in spite of Generalissimo Chiang's virtual ultimatum to back up his request, the President's firm attitude brought about a working compromise on exchange rates and war costs. In the second, a strong message from President Roosevelt, backed up by General Marshall's order to end lend-lease shipments to the Chinese forces designated to launch the Burma offensive, overcame Chiang's reluctance to undertake the military venture. Regardless of the wisdom of the North Burma campaign, the first vigorous application of the *quid pro quo* policy succeeded where persuasion, reasoning, and concessions had failed. For once, a positive American purpose was achieved. If the tactics of pressure had been adopted from the beginning to push Stilwell's army reform program and if all the available resources in the China-Burma-India theater had been concentrated on this program, could Stilwell have created a strong Chinese army to preserve China's internal stability? One does not know, but one wonders.

The adoption by the President of the *quid pro quo* policy and of pressure tactics to counter the use of similar methods by the Generalissimo necessarily meant a contest of wills and of relative political strength. This contest carried with it the possibility of a separation, particularly in view of the Generalissimo's earlier hints and threats of a separate peace. Thus, to carry out successfully the *quid pro quo* policy or the tactics of pressure, the United States had to estimate correctly the seriousness of Chiang's hints and threats if his demands were not satisfied. The answer to this question would hinge largely on an estimation of the relative advantage and disadvantage for Chiang of a separate peace with Japan or a rupture with the United States, as against a continuance of the alliance on American terms. It would also depend on an appreciation of the effects of a rupture with

[60] Feis, *op. cit.*, pp. 121–25; *United States Relations with China*, pp. 492–94, and Romanus and Sunderland, *Stilwell's Command Problems*, pp. 297–301, 304–14.

the United States on Chiang's internal position. The vigorous pursuit of a tactic of pressure made sense only if the United States had been prepared to deal with all foreseeable contigencies. But apparently President Roosevelt adopted Stilwell's approach without providing for its probable consequences and without sharing Stilwell's estimate of Chiang's threats as bluffs or his readiness to back other Nationalist leaders to take Chiang's place. Thus, when the Generalissimo seemingly took a firm stand, President Roosevelt wavered and then backed down. This is what happened in the crisis over the proposal to appoint Stilwell as the commander of all Chinese forces.

The plan for solving the military problems of the China-Burma-India theater by conferring upon Stilwell the unquestioned authority to command Chinese forces was formally suggested by President Roosevelt to Generalissimo Chiang on July 6, 1944, when the Japanese offensive menaced the air bases in "east China" and threatened to knock China out of the war. The initiative in facing squarely the command problem at this time came from the War Department rather than from Stilwell himself,[61] although Stilwell had previously made similar suggestions.[62]

Knowing through bitter experience in the first and the second Burma campaigns that the Generalissimo would use informal channels of communication to circumvent the authority of the field commander, Stilwell demanded an ironclad agreement from Chiang Kai-shek to insure complete authority and freedom from interference.[63] President Roosevelt's message of July 6 proposed that the Generalissimo place Stilwell "directly under you in command of all Chinese and American forces" including the Communist forces, "with the full responsibility and authority for the coordination and direction of the operations required to stem the tide of enemy advances."[64]

The issue between the United States and the Nationalist government was now clearly joined. American officials considered the appointment of Stilwell as commander of all Chinese armies the only way to avert the impending military disaster. To Chiang the American proposal would give the power of command over his armies to his chief critic and the principal advocate of the tactics of pressure. The consequences for Chiang of the acceptance of this proposal are clear. Chiang's secret of staying in power was to give preferential treatment, regardless of their merits, to those commanders who gave him unswerving personal loyalty, and to check and undercut, regardless of their success in battle, the power of those commanders who had once been his political and military rivals and whose

[61] *Ibid.*, pp. 379–85, 418–20.
[62] Romanus and Sunderland, *Stilwell's Mission to China*, pp. 151–54; Romanus and Sunderland, *Stilwell's Command Problems*, pp. 63–64.
[63] *Ibid.*, p. 380.
[64] *Ibid.*, p. 383.

loyalty to him as an individual could not be relied upon. If he was to maintain his personal control over China, there was no alternative policy. For, with the exception of the tenacious defense of the Shanghai-Nanking area in the early days of the war, the armies commanded by the generals of the Whampoa clique, the principal military following of the Generalissimo, did not distinguish themselves on the battlefield. On the contrary, their military achievements compared poorly with those of troops under the command of Li Tsung-jên, who won the victory at Taiêrhchuang, or even with those of the troops under Hsüeh Yüeh who, prior to June, 1944, successfully defended the province of Hunan against Japanese attacks. The relatively well-equipped and well-supplied armies under General Hu Tsung-nan, a top-ranking general of the Whampoa clique, were immobilized throughout the greater part of the war in blockading the Communists and made little positive contribution toward the defense of China. The force of 300,000 men under General T'ang En-po, another Whampoa general, was decisively defeated and scattered within three weeks in April, 1944, by one tank and three infantry divisions and a number of mixed brigades under General Hata. Chiang's identification of his own power interests with the interests of the nation went so far that he refused to send supplies to those Chinese ground forces defending the "east China" airfields whose commanders were suspected of disloyalty toward him.[65]

If Stilwell had been appointed the commander of the Chinese armies with untrammelled authority, he would have substituted military success or failure for Chiang's standard of personal loyalty. The whole basis of Chiang's personal authority would have been undermined. The power and influence of military and political leaders not belonging to the Whampoa faction would have expanded. Chiang and his Whampoa followers would still have been a powerful political force in China but could no longer have been the dominant one. Chiang would probably have remained the most powerful leader in China for a time, but his position would have been constantly challenged by those leaders who had distinguished themselves in the war and who would have had Stilwell's support.

Stilwell had considered General Pai Ch'ung-hsi, the co-leader with Li Tsung-jên of the Kwangsi faction of the Kuomintang, as "the one man best suited to take over" from Chiang.[66] This view could not have been

[65] *Ibid.*, p. 403, and Romanus and Sunderland, *Time Runs Out in CBI* (Washington, D.C.: Government Printing Office, 1959), pp. 4, 9, 71–72.

[66] Romanus and Sunderland, *Stilwell's Command Problems*, p. 411. Hurley testified in the MacArthur Hearings that Stilwell suggested that he "look into the qualifications of General Li Tsung-jen" with a view to ascertaining his capacity for leadership in wartime China as a possible replacement for Chiang (Senate Committee on Armed Services and Committee on Foreign Relations, *Hearings on Military Situation in the Far East*, 82d Cong. 1st sess. [1951], p. 2920 [hereafter cited as *Military Situation in the Far East*]).

unknown to the Generalissimo. Thus, Chiang could not have accepted the probable outcome of Stilwell's appointment with equanimity. It had to be staved off if at all possible. On August 6, he wrote in his diary, "Recently, the pressure from internal and external situations increased daily. . . . If only I can hold military and financial powers in my grasp and do not lose the confidence of the officers, soldiers and the people, . . . then the foundation of the [Nationalist] Revolution will not be shaken and the prospect will remain bright. . . ." [67] Thus, at a time when President Roosevelt was pressing him to appoint Stilwell as commander of the Chinese armies with full authority, Chiang was renewing his determination to hold military and financial power in his own hands.

In retrospect, it would seem that, quite aside from the question of arming the Communists, the threat posed to the personal power of Chiang by the adoption of the American proposal was a sufficient cause for the breakdown of the negotiations over the appointment of Stilwell.[68] This interpretation is supported by two facts which have been ably brought out by Feis and by Romanus and Sunderland. First, contrary to General Hurley's subsequent account,[69] there was no agreement from the beginning to the end of the negotiations on Stilwell's authority as the commander of the Chinese armies. As a matter of fact, the negotiations reached an impasse four or five days after Hurley and Stilwell sent the Generalissimo a draft of an order of appointment and a proposed directive from Chiang to Stilwell, which documents set down in specific terms the proposed authority of Stilwell.[70] One or two days later, on September 16, Hurley and Stilwell held a conference with T. V. Soong. During this conference Stilwell amplified in some detail the specific powers of a field commander as stated in the two papers mentioned above. In Stilwell's own words, he demanded

> nothing less than full power, including the right of reward and punishment — (summary punishment) — and of appointment and relief. He [the Generalissimo] must accept the appointment of foreigners in some positions. The Commander must be allowed to move units from one war zone to another, combine units, inactivate units, activate new units, make drafts from one unit to

[67] Quoted in Chiang Ching-kuo, *Wo-ti fu-ch'in,* chap. iii, 9.

[68] For an interpretation stressing the decisive importance of the Communist issue, see Carsun Chang, *The Third Force* (New York: Bookman Associates, 1952), pp. 122–23.

[69] *Military Situation in the Far East,* p. 2866. In response to Chiang's request, President Roosevelt in August appointed General Patrick J. Hurley as his personal representative in China. Hurley was instructed to promote harmonious relations between Chiang and Stilwell and to facilitate the latter's exercise of command over the Chinese armies placed under his direction (*United States Relations with China,* p. 71). See Feis, *op. cit.,* pp. 172, 178–84.

[70] For these documents, see Romanus and Sunderland, *Stilwell's Command Problems,* pp. 429–30.

another, and change organization as he sees fit. . . . The Generalissimo must refrain from any interference in operations.[71]

Stilwell also proposed the appointment of General Ch'ên Ch'êng as minister of war and General Pai Ch'ung-hsi as chief of staff, replacing General Ho Ying-ch'in, who held the two posts concurrently, and who was universally recognized as second in rank in Chiang's Whampoa hierarchy.[72]

The Hurley-Stilwell drafts and their "plain talk" with Soong brought the basic divergence of purpose into the open, and the clash could no longer be hidden behind generalities. For Stilwell's conception of his power as field commander was totally at variance with that of the Generalissimo. After having remarked, "I know the Generalissimo's mind," Soong went on to tell Stilwell what the Generalissimo's concept was. The basic clash of policies between the two old antagonists was revealed by Stilwell's indignant comment on Chiang's proposal as relayed by Soong: "What the Peanut wants," Stilwell wrote in his undated papers, "is an overall stooge, apparently foisted on him by the United States, with a deputy commander for the Chinese Army! T. V. let that out of the bag."[73]

The open rupture was not long in coming. On September 19, three days after the "plain talk" with Soong, Stilwell, in accordance with recently established practices, delivered in person a forceful and reproving message from the President. In this telegram, Roosevelt urged the Generalissimo to reinforce rather than withdraw the Yunnan forces, warning him that he must "be prepared to accept the consequences and assume the personal responsibility" if the North Burma campaign should fail at the last moment because of his actions. The President also reproached the Generalissimo for his delay in placing Stilwell in command of all forces in China and for "the loss of a critical area in east China with possible catastrophic consequences."[74]

The reproving message created for the Generalissimo the psychological moment for a repudiation of his earlier promise to appoint Stilwell as the commander of Chinese armies. Stilwell's personal delivery of it furnished the pretext. He suspended the talks then and there. He soon decided to reject the President's demand. On September 24, the Generalissimo told Hurley of his decision to demand the recall of Stilwell, placing his stand initially on the insubstantial ground that Stilwell's delivery of the President's message in person made him Stilwell's subordinate. This interpretation was accepted uncritically by Hurley, for he informed the President that "the decision not to appoint General Stilwell was not made by the

[71] Ibid., p. 437.
[72] Stilwell, op. cit., p. 331; Liu, op. cit., pp. 68, 123.
[73] Quoted by Romanus and Sunderland, Stilwell's Command Problems, p. 437.
[74] Ibid., p. 445.

Generalissimo until after General Stilwell, a subordinate, handed the Generalissimo your message of September 18."[75]

But in the *aide-memoirs* given to Hurley by the Generalissimo, Chiang clearly disclosed that there was as yet no agreement on the powers of the field commander. Whereas the Generalissimo put his demand for Stilwell's recall on the basis that he could never "direct General Stilwell" or depend on Stilwell to conform to his direction, Stilwell had specifically stipulated that "the Generalissimo must refrain from any interference in operations," and the President's messages had used such phrases as "full responsibility and authority," "absolute command without any hindrance," and "in unrestricted command."[76] This first series of events suggests that the irreconcilable conflict over the definition of Stilwell's powers as the commander of the Chinese army was the cause of the breakdown of the negotiations.

In contrast, a second series of events revealed by Feis and Romanus and Sunderland shows that the differences over the question of arming the Communists could have been resolved to Chiang's satisfaction if he had desired a compromise. After Stilwell had learned of the impasse in the negotiations, he twice offered concessions on the question of arming the Communists. On September 23, he proposed a scheme for the distribution of lend-lease materials under which they would be turned over to the Generalissimo and distributed according to the following rules: The Ledo and Yunnan forces would have first priority, and then the remainder of the thirty divisions, the Communist troops of five divisions and the second thirty divisions to be organized in "east China" would have equal priority. In other words, Stilwell proposed to arm sixty Nationalist and five Communist divisions, with first priority for the twenty-odd Nationalist divisions fighting in the North Burma campaign.[77] As a further concession, he suggested that the use of Communist forces be confined north of the Yellow River and that he be sent to Yenan to secure a formal acknowledgment by the Communists of Chiang's authority. An agenda for a renewal of talks containing these concessions was taken by Hurley to the Generalissimo on September 24. It cannot be ascertained from Romanus and Sunderland's or Feis's accounts or from published records whether the agenda was submitted to Chiang or whether Chiang studied it. In any case, it was during this conversation with Hurley that Chiang informed Hurley of his decision to request Stilwell's recall, as noted above. Significantly, one of the reasons which Chiang gave to Hurley for his decision was, to use Stilwell's words, that "he [Chiang] is afraid of my [Stilwell's] influence in the Army" and that "he would have a mutiny on his hands!"[78]

[75] *Ibid.*, p. 452.
[76] *Ibid.*, pp. 453–54.
[77] *Ibid.*, pp. 451–52, and Feis, *op. cit.*, p. 192.
[78] Stilwell, *op. cit.*, p. 336, entry for September 25, 1944.

In making these statements, Chiang could not have been referring to the Communist issue, which was never defined in terms of "a mutiny." More probably, he was revealing his concern over Stilwell's influence in the Nationalist forces.

On September 28, Stilwell made his second concession on the Communist issue. To General Ho Ying-ch'in he stated that he was not insisting on the use of the Communists as a condition for agreement and he offered to drop the matter of using the Communists so that "we can proceed advantageously with our other plans."[79] If Chiang had been primarily concerned over the expansion of Communist influence, he could now have reached a compromise with Stilwell. But Stilwell's last offer had no effect on Chiang's adamant stand.

At this point there occurred a dramatic incident whose effect on subsequent developments is still difficult to estimate. On October 1, Generalissimo Chiang received a cable, sent by H. H. Kung, his brother-in-law, from Washington. It stated that Harry Hopkins had told Kung at a dinner party that the President would replace Stilwell if the Generalissimo insisted.[80] Acting on this vital piece of information, Chiang played his usual trump card — a threat of separation. But instead of making it directly to American officials as was the case in 1942 and 1943, when China loomed large in the plans of the United States for the defeat of Japan, Chiang revealed his intention before the Central Executive Committee of the Kuomintang, knowing that this information would find its way to American officials. Instead of threatening a separate peace with Japan, he now stated his determination to fight to the end with or without American aid, knowing that Japan was doomed. Thus the Nationalist leader told his audience that he would insist on the recall of Stilwell and that he was willing to appoint another American to the projected post of field commander, but that the officer would have to be under his orders and empowered to command only such Chinese units as were specifically designated by the Generalissimo. If the United States refused to accept his demands, he would go it alone and fight the war with the means at his disposal.[81] The Generalissimo let the United States guess what the outcome would be if he failed to stand on his feet in the provinces under his control without any American aid. Would there be a separate peace, a total collapse, or a surrender? Once again, the Generalissimo played upon both the fears and sympathies of the United States.

[79] Ibid., p. 337, entry for September 28, 1944.
[80] For a discussion of the facts about this vital episode, see Feis, op. cit., pp. 193–94, n. 20, and Romanus and Sunderland, Stilwell's Command Problems, pp. 456–59.
[81] Ibid., p. 456, and Feis, op. cit., p. 194. Carsun Chang reported a meeting between Chiang and the representatives of the small parties and the leaders of the non-partisans during which Chiang discussed his differences with Stilwell. But no date is given for this meeting. See Chang, op. cit., p. 123.

The Generalissimo's shrewd move was the light touch that tipped the scale and ended a week of indecision in Washington. For now the Generalissimo did insist. Over the objections of Marshall and Stimson, the President yielded to Chiang's rejection of his emergency proposals and was ready to relieve Stilwell as chief of staff to the Generalissimo. But he made a final effort to salvage Stilwell for the Burma campaign by requesting the Generalissimo allow Stilwell to continue to command the Chinese ground forces in Burma and Yunnan. This plea was of no avail. The Generalissimo now wanted total victory and saw it in sight.

Meanwhile, Hurley assumed the role that the Generalissimo apparently had hoped to assign him when the Chinese leader requested the appointment of a special representative. Hurley told the President that the Generalissimo was open to persuasion and leadership and that the present impasse stemmed from the ill-conceived pressure tactics with which Stilwell attempted to subjugate Chiang. In his words, "There is no issue between you and Chiang Kai-shek except Stilwell. . . . My opinion is that if you sustain Stilwell in this controversy, you will lose Chiang Kai-shek and possibly you will lose China with him." [82]

On October 18, the President informed the Generalissimo that Stilwell was to be recalled, the United States was not going to assume the responsibility for the command of ground forces in China, and he would assign General Wedemeyer, one of the three American officers named by Chiang, as chief of staff to the Generalissimo. The China-Burma-India theater was divided into two separate commands: the China theater and the India-Burma theater. Stilwell left China, his mission having been frustrated by Chiang's maneuvers. His bitterness was revealed in the sketch in his notebook of the record of his mission and his view of his recall:

> Given a mission and no means. Hamstrung by "no bargaining."
> Three years of struggle. Secret reports by Chinese, British, and special emissaries — Currie, Willkie, Wallace, Nelson and Hurley.
> . . . Bucked by the British. Bucked by the Chinese.
> In spite of it all, just ready to blossom, and then made whipping dog for Chiang Kai-shek. It was September 19 radio that got Chiang Kai-shek. He blamed it on me — FDR was his great friend. FDR did not stand up to it. I was relieved on the arbitrary and false statements of Chiang Kai-shek.[83]

The critics of Stilwell like to contrast what they call his futile efforts with the easy success of General Wedemeyer. They attribute this dissimilarity in results to Stilwell's *quid pro quo* policy and lack of tact and to

[82] *Military Situation in the Far East*, pp. 2879–81.
[83] As quoted by Romanus and Sunderland, *Stilwell's Command Problems*, p. 470.

Wedemeyer's use of the method of persuasion and his flexible and con-ciliatory approach. Insofar as this explanation refers to Stilwell's lack of political suavity, it is correct. But this is insufficient to account for the intense conflict between Stilwell and Chiang. Perhaps a more important factor was Stilwell's known sympathy for the Chinese Communists. But even these two factors, taken together, do not constitute a full explana-tion. The contrast between Stilwell's failure and Wedemeyer's success stemmed in large part from the fact that by 1945 the situation in China was easing up. Supplies over the Hump were greatly increased. Stilwell's years of effort in reforming the Chinese army were also bearing fruits which Wedemeyer gathered. No longer dependent on China for the defeat of Japan, the United States was not urging China to make a major military effort. There was no major, difficult decision to be made which might engender an intense conflict of purpose. Insofar as military affairs were concerned, pressure was not needed to implement policy, and the method of persuasion and exhortation could be depended upon to produce results.

The critics of Stilwell seldom acknowledge the fact that even Gen-eral Wedemeyer advocated Stilwell's *quid pro quo* approach when the situation demanded it. Less than three years later, in 1947, when Wede-meyer returned to Washington from a mission to China in a critical juncture of the civil war, his report recommended a *quid pro quo* policy, condition-ing American aid upon Chinese reforms. In addressing a gathering of the top officials of the Nationalist government, he found it necessary to speak plain words which caused violent emotional reactions among the Chinese.[84] Similarly, General Chennault, a severe critic of Stilwell, admitted in his memoirs that as a civilian adviser to the Chinese government he had, on occasion, to pretend to be intent on resigning his position.[85]

There was another incident which is a revealing commentary on the correctness of Stilwell's *quid pro quo* policy. When in April of 1949 the total defeat of the Nationalist government by the Chinese Communists appeared imminent, the American minister-counselor at Canton reported the following conversation with Ch'ên Li-fu, the leader of the C.C. clique of the Nationalist party, who had done as much as any other Nationalist leader to frustrate American policies in China. Ch'ên professed to believe that the Nationalist party would close ranks and would be able to prolong the struggle against the Communists until the United States could be per-suaded once again to intervene. "Should that time come," the American minister-counselor reported, "he [Ch'ên] hopes that we will lay our cards frankly on the table and demand a definite *quid pro quo* for anything we

[84] *United States Relations with China*, pp. 257–61.
[85] Claire L. Chennault, *Way of a Fighter* (New York: G. P. Putnam's Sons, 1949), p. 77.

give. This is the only way, he said, we could assure the accomplishment of the ends we desire." [86]

There is profound irony in the fact that the United States received the advice on the soundness of the *quid pro quo* policy from such a man as Mr. Ch'ên, who had done much to defeat American policies, particularly during Marshall's mission to China. The unfortunate thing about Stilwell was that his policy of exacting a *quid pro quo* from the Nationalist government was so closely intertwined with his personal traits that the issue of policy was frequently confounded with the issue of personality. While to this day Americans are still arguing about the correct method of dealing with the Nationalist government, there was little doubt in the mind of such a shrewd Chinese politician as Mr. Ch'ên as to what the United States should do to achieve her purpose.

The initial failure to adopt the tactics of pressure and the subsequent failure to carry them through was undoubtedly related to an exaggerated fear of a separate peace between China and Japan or a diplomatic rupture with China. This fear stemmed partly from the policy of unconditional surrender which President Roosevelt proclaimed at the Casablanca Conference and which was formally reiterated in the Cairo Declaration. The Cairo Declaration also specifically proclaimed the Allies' determination to restore to China all the territories lost to Japan and to expel Japan from "all other territories which she has taken by violence and greed" since 1895. Although the Japanese surrender turned out not to be strictly unconditional, there is little doubt that to American officials a negotiated peace with the enemy would have appeared a compromise with evil itself. All the political and military policies of the United States had one supreme aim: to secure military victory and the unconditional surrender of Japan with the least sacrifice. Throughout the war the United States never once contemplated the possibility of a negotiated peace with Japan, as a tactical maneuver to fend off the pressure of her allies, to meet unforeseen contingencies of the war, or to protect her postwar interests in the Far East. For this reason, no attempt was made to establish contact with the leaders of the so-called peace party of Japan and to secure a Japanese surrender under terms favorable to the United States but short of unconditional surrender. Instead, the announced policy of unconditional surrender and the Cairo Declaration proved to be difficult obstacles for the leaders of the peace group to overcome and discouraged any direct Japanese approach to the United States.[87]

[86] *United States Relations with China*, p. 306.

[87] Robert J. C. Butow, *Japan's Decision to Surrender* (Stanford, Calif.: Stanford University Press, 1954), pp. 39–41, 87–88, 136–41, 231. In the spring of 1945, unauthorized Japanese feelers in Switzerland succeeded in establishing contact with the OSS organization headed by Allen Dulles. Their overtures were given only very

Against this background Japan's efforts to induce the defection of the Chungking government from the Allied cause immensely strengthened Chiang's bargaining position vis-à-vis the United States. The matter was further complicated by rumors of secret contacts between the Japanese and the Nationalists which the Russians and the Chinese Communists spread. Thus, at critical moments in Sino-American relations, the Nationalists' hints and threats of a separation with the United States were accompanied by rumors about Japanese overtures for peace. At the time of the Three Demands crisis in June and July of 1942, Madame Chiang herself warned Stilwell, as noted above, that pro-Japanese elements in Nationalist China were very active.[88] On July 10, Stilwell recorded in his diary the "Russki rumor" that Japan, through a secret agent and a Chinese collaborator, had made a clandestine peace overture to Chungking.[89] During the Cairo Conference, Hull cabled the President in Cairo — on November 29, 1943 — that, according to reports from the American embassy at Chungking, Japan was continuing to make peace offers to the Chinese government but without success.[90] At the time of the Stilwell crisis in September and October, 1944, China's secret agents had been in correspondence with Baron Tadamaro Miyagawa, Konoye's younger brother, and had sent him what were, or were purported to be, Chinese terms for a settlement.[91] Soon after General Wedemeyer took command of American forces in the China theater, Chiang Kai-shek showed him a copy of what was purported to be a Japanese overture for a surrender to China.[92] Thus it appeared that Chiang always had an alternative, whereas a similar option was denied to the United States.

But was a separate peace with Japan or a rupture with the United States a real alternative for Chiang, particularly at the time of Stilwell's recall? In the fall of 1944, the defeat of Japan was certain.[93] The only question was the time of its occurrence and the extent of the sacrifice necessary to obtain it. After the war the United States seemed likely to emerge as the dominant power of the world. Nationalist China would have had much less to gain from a separate peace with Japan than from a total victory in

cursory attention by top American officials (*ibid.*, chap. v). See also F. C. Jones, *Japan's New Order in East Asia* (London: Oxford University Press, 1954), p. 423.

[88] Romanus and Sunderland, *Stilwell's Mission to China*, p. 171.

[89] Stilwell, *op. cit.*, p. 124.

[90] Hull, *op. cit.*, p. 1584.

[91] Wesley R. Fishel, "A Japanese Peace Maneuver in 1944," *Far Eastern Quarterly*, August, 1949, pp. 387–97. For other curious episodes allegedly involving Nationalist officials, see Butow, *op. cit.*, pp. 51–54, and Jones, *op. cit.*, pp. 429–30.

[92] *Military Situation in the Far East*, pp. 2432–33.

[93] In an entry to his diary on October 4, 1944, Stilwell summarized in the following words the information conveyed to him by Major General Frank Merrill, who had just come from Washington: "In general, nothing new. Japan [to go] down eighteen months after Germany" (Stilwell, *op. cit.*, p. 341).

alliance with the United States. It seems unlikely, therefore, that the Generalissimo would have carried out his threat. Even should he have decided upon that course, he would have run a great risk of being repudiated by the Chinese people and replaced by some other leader. As Chiang himself told German Ambassador Trautmann in November, 1937, when the international power configuration was much more favorable to Japan, "He could not accept any Japanese demands so long as the Japanese were not prepared to restore the *status quo ante*." He added confidentially "that the Chinese government would be swept out by the tide of public opinion if he agreed to these demands. There would be a revolution in China." [94] Chiang's estimate of Chinese sentiment agreed with the evaluation of his arch opponents, the Chinese Communists. As a Communist leader told Paul M. A. Linebarger in an interview, "If Chiang made terms with the Japanese, or if he failed to resist, the Communists would need to have nothing to do with him, nor he with them since he would be ruined in any case." [95] In July, 1942, Ambassador Gauss was certain that, in spite of the rumors of Japanese peace overtures, Chiang would have too much to lose to conclude a separate peace with Japan. Stilwell concurred in this judgment. [96]

Similarly, Chiang's expressed determination to carry on the fight, if necessary without American aid, was a bluff. It was unlikely that Chiang's power, dependent as he was on American supplies, would have survived a rupture with the United States. Chiang's demand for Stilwell's recall did not elicit from the Chinese people any outburst of nationalistic sentiment or enthusiastic support. [97] Pro-American sentiment in wartime China was strong. Stilwell was held in high regard by many Chinese outside of the Generalissimo's personal following. There was a common misgiving that Stilwell's recall might entail a reduction of American military commitments in China.

If Chiang had taken the fateful step he threatened, the United States could still have supported Pai Ch'ung-hsi and Chang Fa-kwei in Kwangsi, Hsüeh Yüeh in Hunan, Li Tsung-jên in Honan-Hupeh and Anhwei, Lung Yün in Yunnan, Fu Tso-yi in the Twelfth war area, Li Pin-hsien in the

[94] Trautmann to German Foreign Ministry, in *Documents of German Foreign Policy, 1918–1945,* as quoted in Jones, *op. cit.,* p. 61.

[95] Linebarger, *op. cit.,* p. 267.

[96] Stilwell, *op. cit.,* pp. 125–26.

[97] During the crisis leading to Stilwell's recall, representatives of the small parties and non-partisan leaders advised Chiang to be "cool and level-headed in dealing with the United States" (Chang, *op. cit.,* p. 123). Commenting on the American proposal to place Stilwell in command of all Chinese forces, Carsun Chang, the leader of the National Social party, wrote: "Had this course of action been followed, perhaps things might have turned out differently, because the United States government would then have been more directly responsible for handling the situation in China" (*ibid.*).

Tenth war area, and even the dissident movement of Marshal Li Chi-shên. These military and political leaders would have been more than happy to obtain American aid, of which they received very little, if any, throughout the war. The Generalissimo would be the last man willing to cut himself off from American support only to see it going to his rivals. There was a good chance that a firm American stand would have led to Chiang's retreat. The really tragic thing about the American defeat in the Stilwell crisis is that it was avoidable.

The political and military consequences, had Chiang accepted Stilwell as his field commander, can only be a matter of conjecture. But it seems likely that American purposes would have been more speedily achieved, that the United States would have been more deeply committed to the succour of Nationalist China and would have been more directly responsible for the handling of the situation in China. Chiang's personal power would have been eclipsed, but he would still have been a powerful political figure. The political influence of other Nationalist leaders, long restive under the restraint and repression of the Generalissimo, would have grown. There might have been introduced for the first time a degree of fair competition for political and military power in the Kuomintang on the basis of military success and political competence. The over-all military powers of the Kuomintang might have been increased by a fairer distribution of supplies and by the more rapid realization of Stilwell's army reform program. At the same time, Chiang and other political leaders would have had more respect for the firmness and seriousness of purpose of the United States.

What the recall of Stilwell signified above all was the defeat of the United States in her application of the tactics of pressure, due to a failure of judgment and will rather than the objective weakness of her political position. From this defeat flowed two profound and lasting consequences which poisoned Sino-American relations from then on. The Generalissimo was confirmed in his belief that the United States was so dependent on him to protect her Far Eastern interests and so lacking in firmness of purpose in the pursuit of her policy that she would finally yield to his insistent demands and accept his views, no matter what he did or refused to do. Thus, he was emboldened in his endeavors to push as far as possible what he considered to be the interests of his government and his party. This proved to be a fatal miscalculation and was to become one of the causes of his downfall.

The basic source of this error was the Generalissimo's inability to find and promote the common interests between himself and others or, in other words, his narrow conception of his, his government's, and China's interests. His habit of pushing his interests as far as possible and exacting every ounce of advantage in any situation rendered it difficult for others to work with him. His unbounded confidence in his political and military judgment, his faith in his infallibility, and his mystic sense of identity with the nation made him arrogant and unsusceptible to advice and argument.

Internationally, his attitudes and policies alienated the United States, which alone could have given him the needed support. Within China, they precluded the possibility of building up a regime broadly based on the divergent social and political groups in China, while the Chinese Communists, in spite of an original ideology prescribing a monopoly of power by one social group, confronted him with a policy of developing the "progressive forces," winning over the "middle-of-the-road" forces, and isolating the "die-hards."[98] Thus, the seeds of his downfall were imbedded in the amazing political skill which had given him his earlier successes.

It is doubly unfortunate that the recall of Stilwell inevitably created a deep sense of frustration and defeat on the part of American officials to match the Generalissimo's sense of his indispensability to the United States. From then on, whenever American officials turned their attention to China, they were afflicted by a sense of helplessness. Chiang was not, they felt, willing to help himself. He would not listen to advice and was not susceptible to persuasion. Pressure would not be effective against him. There was a justifiable sense of doubt whether any American purpose could be achieved in China through co-operation with Chiang. Stilwell's recall was accompanied by a presidential decision to reduce American military commitments in China and a renewed confirmation of the strategy for defeating Japan through the Pacific. As noted before, Roosevelt no longer entertained the hope that China would become a great power in the near future. More than ever, he based his plan for postwar stability in the Far East on co-operation with the Soviet Union. At the Yalta Conference, he readily agreed to support Stalin's demands on China. In his conversations with Stalin, he ascribed to the Kuomintang rather than to the Chinese Communists a heavier share of responsibility for the lack of a settlement in China. Thus, Roosevelt tried out the policy of making China a great power for a period of three years, from 1941 to 1944, while experimenting with various military programs. In 1941 and 1942, his chosen means was lend-lease and one of his most influential advisors was Lauchlin Currie, a lend-lease specialist. In 1943, his principal instrument was Chennault's air force. In 1944, he forsook Chennault and experimented with the B-29 Matterhorn project and the Stilwell approach.[99] After Stilwell's recall and

[98] Mao Tse-tung, "Questions of Tactics in the Recent Anti-Japanese United Front," *Selected Works* (London: Lawrence and Wishart, 1954), III, 194, 198. This document is the outline of a report made at a meeting of the senior cadres of the Communist party in March, 1940.

[99] The writer is indebted to Riley Sunderland for this point.

the removal in January, 1945, of the B-29's from Chinese bases to India, he lost much of his interest in China and intensified his search for wartime and postwar co-operation in the Far East with the Soviet Union.

Roosevelt's changed evaluation of the prospect of China's becoming a great power constituted a re-emphasis of the traditional view that American interests in China were not worth a war and that China was not important to the United States, either as an ally or as an enemy. America's wartime and postwar experience suggested to her that it was not within the reasonable limits of her capability to save Chiang from defeat. Gradually, she came to the conclusion that the only rational and feasible policy was to disentangle herself from China, leaving Chiang to his fate, while using her limited resources to defend her interests in Europe. It is not accidental that the man who later took the steps leading to the permanent withdrawal of the United States from China, thus ending an era of one hundred years of friendly Sino-American relations, was none other than General Marshall, who, as Stilwell's immediate superior and close friend, had had intimate knowledge of Stilwell's tribulations and difficulties in dealing with Chiang and whose recommendations for backing Stilwell had not been followed by the President. Thus, the roots of the United States' abandonment of China reached back to the wartime frustrations and defeats symbolized by Stilwell's recall, and the seeds of Chiang's downfall on the mainland of China lay in his apparent triumph over that bitterly disappointed American general.

PART TWO

TO

BRING ABOUT

A UNITED

AND

DEMOCRATIC CHINA

BY

PEACEFUL MEANS

CHAPTER V

THE STRUGGLE

FOR POWER

IN CHINA

AND

THE IMPACT

OF AMERICAN POLICY

A. The Appearance and the Reality of the United Front

The Sino-Japanese War began July 7, 1937. For the purpose of resisting the Japanese attack, a united front between the Kuomintang and the Chinese Communist party was established and was formalized by parallel statements from the two groups. On September 22, 1937, the Central Committee of the Chinese Communist party issued a manifesto in which the Communists proposed as one of the "general objectives for the common struggle of the entire people" the enforcement of "democracy based on people's rights and the convocation of the National People's Congress in order to enact the Constitution and decide upon the plans of national salvation."[1]

On their part, they declared:

(1) The San Min Chu-I (Three People's Principles) enunciated by Dr. Sun Yat-sen is the paramount need of China today. This Party is ready to strive for its enforcement.

(2) This Party abandons its policy of overthrowing the Kuomintang of China by force and the movement of sovietization and discontinues its policy of forcible confiscation of land from landowners.

(3) This Party abolishes the present Soviet Government and

[1] Department of State, *United States Relations with China* (Washington, D.C.: Government Printing Office, 1949), p. 523 (hereafter cited as *United States Relations with China*).

will enforce democracy based on people's rights in order to unify the national political machinery.

(4) This Party abolishes the Red Army, reorganizes it into the National Revolutionary Army, places it under the direct control of the Military Affairs Commission of the National Government, and awaits orders for mobilization to share the responsibility of resisting foreign invasion at the front.[2]

The next day Generalissimo Chiang Kai-shek issued a statement expressing the Nationalist government's approval of the Communists' decisions and accepting their offer of co-operation. In it Chiang declared:

> The various decisions embodied in the Manifesto [of the Chinese Communist Party], such as the abandonment of a policy of violence, the cessation of Communist propaganda, the abolition of the Chinese Soviet Government, and the disbandment of the Red Army are all essential conditions for mobilizing our national strength in order that we may meet the menace from without and guarantee our own national existence.
>
> These decisions agree with the spirit of the Manifesto and resolutions adopted by the Third Plenary Session of the Kuomintang. The Communist Party's Manifesto declares that the Chinese Communists are willing to strive to carry out the Three Principles. This is ample proof that China today has only one objective in its war effort.[3]

Prior to the issuance of these statements, the Red Army had been designated the Eighth Route Army by order of the Nationalist government and was subsequently reorganized into the Eighteenth Group Army. The Communist base area in the Northwest was renamed by the Communists themselves the Shensi-Kansu-Ninghsia border region on September 9. From October, 1937, to January, 1938, the small, isolated guerrilla units in thirteen Communist base areas scattered in Central and South China were reorganized into the New Fourth Army.[4] Thus, on the surface it appeared that the Chinese Communists accepted the Three Principles of the People, had abandoned their policy of overthrowing the Kuomintang gov-

[2] *Ibid.*, p. 524.
[3] *Ibid.*, p. 525.
[4] *K'ang Jih chan-chêng shih-ch'i ti Chung-kuo jên-min chien-fang-chün* ["The Chinese People's Liberation Army during the War of Resistance against Japan"] (Peking: Jên-min ch'u-pan-shê, 1953), pp. 52–55 (hereafter cited as *Chieh-fang-chün*). *K'ang-chan pa-nien lai ti Pa-lu-chün yü Hsin-ssŭ-chün* ["The Eighth Route Army and the New Fourth Army in the Eight Years of War of Resistance against Japan"] (1945), pp. 50–52 (hereafter cited as *Pa-lu-chün*).

ernment by force, and had placed the Red Army under the control of the government.

But the political reality behind the façade of formal statements was quite different. Even before the united front was formalized, the Chinese Communists, at a meeting of party activists in April, 1937, at the national conference of party delegates in May, and especially at the meeting of the Central Political Bureau in August, had already raised the question: "In the united front, is it for the proletariat to lead the bourgeoisie or vice versa?"[5] Three days after the Central Committee had published its manifesto of September 22, it issued a draft resolution which stated, among other things, that "it is necessary to maintain the Communist Party's absolutely independent leadership in what originally was the Red Army as well as all guerrilla units, and Communists are not permitted to show any vacillation in principle on this issue."[6]

Less than two months later, Mao told a meeting of party activists that "we must pointedly raise the question of who is to lead and must resolutely oppose [class] capitulationism."[7] Mao reported that the Chinese Communists had "rejected the Kuomintang's request to appoint its members as cadres of the Eighth Route Army" and had restored the system of political commissars which had been abolished "because of the Kuomintang's intervention."[8] "The principle of the Communist Party's absolute leadership of the Eighth Route Army" had been upheld.[9] Mao also declared proudly that "we have sponsored and resolutely carried out the new strategic principle of 'carrying on independently [of the Nationalist Government] and on our own initiative a guerrilla warfare in the mountain regions,'" and that "in the revolutionary anti-Japanese base areas [i.e., Communist base areas] we have sponsored the principle of 'independence and autonomy in the united front.'"[10]

Mao instructed the Communist leaders that "to explain, to implement and to uphold the principle of 'independence and autonomy in the united front' is the central link in leading the anti-Japanese national revolutionary war to the path of victory."[11] One of the purposes in upholding this principle was "to maintain the foothold we have already gained. . . . this foot-

[5] Mao Tse-tung, *Selected Works*, II (new ed.; London: Lawrence and Wishart, 1958), 65. For an account of the meeting of the Political Bureau held in August, by Chang Kuo-t'ao, a Communist leader who was expelled by the Communists in 1938, see Robert C. North, *Moscow and Chinese Communists* (Stanford, Calif.: Stanford University Press, 1953), p. 180.

[6] Mao Tse-tung, *op. cit.*, 242, n. 5.
[7] *Ibid.*, p. 66.
[8] *Ibid.*, p. 67.
[9] *Ibid.*
[10] *Ibid.*
[11] *Ibid.*, p. 69.

hold is the starting point of our strategy and its loss would mean the end of everything." But the chief purpose of maintaining independence and autonomy was, Mao explained, "to expand our foothold. . . ."[12] To secure it, Mao himself took the trouble to draft an order, issued in May, 1938, "by the Government of the Shensi-Kansu-Ninghsia Border Region and the Rear Headquarters of the Eighth Route Army," to the effect that

> all those who, without securing the approval of this Government or this Headquarters and without obtaining credentials from this Government or this Headquarters, come to reside in the border region and engage in activities must, regardless of the nature of these activities, be proscribed, in order to guard against undesirables in disguise and to keep out traitors and spies."[13]

With this strategy and tactics Mao turned the united front from a possible source of serious restriction on Communist expansion into a means of keeping the Kuomintang in the war against Japan, an instrument to prevent an all-out attack by the Kuomintang, and a shield to protect Communist activities throughout the country. Mao thus placed great value on the maintenance of the united front. He wrote:

> In order to keep up the armed resistance and win the final victory, to turn partial resistance into total resistance, we must uphold the line of the Anti-Japanese National United Front and expand and strengthen this united front. No recommendation for splitting up the united front of the Kuomintang and the Communist Party is to be tolerated.[14]

Chiang had a perfect understanding of the reality behind Mao's policy. Nationalist sources cited a speech supposedly delivered by Mao in the autumn of 1937 in which he said:

> The Sino-Japanese War gives the Chinese Communists an excellent opportunity to grow. Our policy is to devote seventy per cent of our effort to our own expansion, twenty per cent to coping with the government, and ten per cent to fighting the Japanese.
>
> This policy is to be carried out in three stages. During the first stage we are to compromise with [the] Kuomintang in order to ensure our existence and growth. During the second stage we are to achieve a parity in strength with Kuomintang. During the

[12] *Ibid.*
[13] *Ibid.*, p. 74. In a note explaining the origin of the notice, the editor of Mao's *Selected Works* wrote that "this notice was written . . . with a view to counteracting the disruptive activities of the Chiang Kai-shek clique" (*ibid.*, p. 72).
[14] *Ibid.*, p. 68.

third stage we are to penetrate deep into parts of Central China to establish bases for attack on [the] Kuomintang."[15]

The authenticity of this speech cannot be proved or disproved. But the general direction of the policy attributed to the Communists, as distinguished from specific details, was in accord with the strategy and tactics laid down by Mao in his intraparty directives and speeches which have since been made public.

On his part, Mao charged that a scheme was put forward in July, 1937, in the highest Kuomintang training center "to reduce the strength of the Communist Party by two-fifths in the course of the Anti-Japanese War."[16] He also told the Chinese Communists that the Kuomintang's policy toward the isolated Communist guerrilla areas in South China was to eliminate them by surrounding and disarming the Communist forces while local negotiations were going on between the two sides for a reorganization of these units.[17] Regardless of the validity of these charges and counter-charges, there is no doubt that each side planned its policies and strategies on the basis of these analyses of the other's motives.

By the end of August, 1938, it was obvious even to outsiders that relations between the Kuomintang and the Chinese Communists had begun to deteriorate. At that time the defense headquarters at Hankow-Wuchang outlawed three Communist-sponsored mass organizations.[18] This Nationalist move followed by three months the issuance of Mao's notice proscribing the activities of all who entered the Communist area without the permission of Communist authorities. Against this background of open friction, the Chinese Communists convened the sixth plenary session of the Central Committee. At this important meeting the Central Committee indorsed Mao's political-military strategy. In his concluding statement, made on November 6, 1938, Mao declared that "the central task and the supreme form of a revolution is the seizure of political power by force of arms and

[15] Chiang Kai-shek, *Soviet Russia in China* (New York: Farrar, Straus and Cudahy, Inc., 1957), p. 85. See also Tung Hsien-kuang (Hollington K. Tong), *Chiang Tsung-t'ung ch'uan* ["A Biography of President Chiang"], II (Taipei, Taiwan: Chunghua wên-hua ch'u-pan shih-yeh wei-yüan-hui, 1952), 381. Tong is also the author of an authorized biography of Chiang published in 1938: Hollington K. Tong, *Chiang Kai-shek* (London: Hurst and Blackett, 1938). He subsequently served as ambassador to the United States.

The speech attributed to Mao formed a part of a document drafted by the secretariat of the Kuomintang in September, 1943, on the Communist question. See Charles B. McLane, *Soviet Policy and the Chinese Communists* (New York: Columbia University Press, 1958), p. 168, n. 39.

[16] Mao, *op. cit.*, p. 66.

[17] *Ibid.*, p. 68.

[18] *United States Relations with China*, p. 52. See also Chalmers A. Johnson, *Peasant Nationalism and Communist Power* (Stanford, Calif.: Stanford University Press, 1962). pp. 37–38.

the solution of problems by war."[19] He told his comrades that "political power grows out of the barrel of a gun," and that, indeed, "anything can grow out of the barrel of a gun."[20] He further observed that "experience in the class struggle of the era of imperialism teaches us that the working class and the toiling masses cannot defeat the armed bourgeois and landlords except by the power of the gun; in this sense we can even say that the whole world can be remoulded only with the gun."[21] With regard to China, he specifically stated that "the main form of struggle is war and the main form of the organization is the army,"[22] and that "without armed struggle the proletariat and the Communist Party could not win any place for themselves or accomplish any revolutionary task."[23] With regard to the immediate task, "the Party's main fields of work are to be in the war areas and in the enemy's [Japan's] rear."[24] Mao obviously realized that in these areas and behind the Japanese lines, the Communists could exploit the political and military vacuum to expand their political control and their armed forces. It was here that vigorous Communist activities would entail less risk of effective Nationalist counteractions than similar actions elsewhere.

With reference to relations with the Kuomintang, the Central Committee also upheld Mao's views. In his concluding statement, Mao repudiated the view that everything must be done "through the united front," i.e., after having secured the Nationalist government's approval. Again he reaffirmed the principle of independence and autonomy of the Chinese Communist party within the united front.[25] But he also warned that "independence within the united front can only be relative and not absolute; to regard it as absolute would undermine the general policy of unity against the enemy [i.e., Japan]."[26] Thus, his policy was essentially one of expanding his party and army as effectively and quickly as possible short of precipitating an open break with the Kuomintang and bringing about a large-scale Kuomintang attack.[27]

[19] Mao Tse-tung, "Chan-chêng yü chan-lüeh wên-ti" ["Problems of War and Strategy"] in *Mao Tse-tung hsüan-chi* ["The Selected Works of Mao Tse-tung"] (Peking: Jên-min ch'u-pan shê, 1952), II, 505 (hereafter cited as *Hsüan-chi, II*). For some reason, this sentence and the two paragraphs following it were omitted from the English version of Mao's selected works. See Mao Tse-tung, *Selected Works*, II, 223.

[20] *Ibid.*, 228.

[21] *Ibid.*, p. 229.

[22] *Ibid.*, p. 224.

[23] *Ibid.*, p. 225.

[24] *Ibid.*, p. 226.

[25] Mao Tse-tung, "The Question of Independence and Autonomy within the United Front," *ibid.*, p. 220.

[26] Mao Tse-tung, "The Role of the Chinese Communist Party in the National War," *ibid.*, p. 206.

[27] Mao wrote: "[N]either should we break up the united front nor should we bind ourselves hand and foot. . . ." (*ibid.*, p. 221).

Mao distinguished between several categories of possible actions and told the Communists to adopt different tactics in each category. With regard to actions which, in their calculations, the Kuomintang would approve, the Communists were told to ask permission first and implement them afterwards. With regard to actions to which the Kuomintang would not voluntarily grant permission, the Communists would implement them first, confront the Kuomintang with accomplished facts, and then ask for approval. With regard to actions which the Kuomintang would not approve even if confronted with accomplished fact, the Communists were instructed to implement them without asking for approval. With regard to actions which "would jeopardize the whole situation," the Communists would "for the moment neither do nor ask permission to do."[28] This last principle meant that "the Communists should refrain from forming secret groups within the other's party, government or army," and that "so far as we are concerned, . . . we form no secret groups inside the Kuomintang, its government or its army so that the Kuomintang will be easy on this point, and the resistance to Japan will be facilitated."[29] Both Mencius and Lenin were cited to support the self-imposed restraints. On the nature of these restraints, Mao wrote: "Our concession, withdrawal, turning to the defensive or suspending action, whether in dealing with allies or enemies, should always be regarded as part of the entire revolutionary policy, as an indispensable link in the general revolutionary line, as a segment in curvilinear movement. In short, they are positive."[30]

It was therefore not accidental that in December, 1938, one month after Mao delivered his speech, Communist forces under General Ho Lung clashed with Nationalist forces in Hopei under General Chang Yin-wu. In the spring of 1939, Communist forces stepped up their movement into the province of Shantung. In the winter of 1939–40 they defeated, pursued, and decimated Nationalist forces in Hopei. It was a moot question whether the responsibility for initiating these specific clashes fell on the Communists or the Nationalists. But Mao's speech clearly shows that these clashes formed part of his "armed struggle" against the Kuomintang and were in full accord with his policy of expanding his party and army behind the Japanese lines. The Kuomintang acted vigorously to contain the Communist expansion. During 1939 the Nationalist government instituted a rigid military blockade of the Communist areas to prevent Communist infiltration into Nationalist China.[31] Mao reported that the Kuomintang

[28] Mao Tse-tung, "The Question of Independence and Autonomy within the United Front," *ibid.*, p. 221.
[29] *Ibid.*, p. 219.
[30] *Ibid.*, pp. 219–20.
[31] *United States Relations with China*, p. 53.

adopted in March, 1939, measures "to restrict the activities of alien parties" and in October adopted another set of measures to deal with the "Alien-Party Problem."[32] By December, tension between the Kuomintang and the Chinese Communists reached such a height that the Communists charged the Kuomintang with launching a co-ordinated attack on the Shensi-Kansu-Ninghsia border region in what they called the "first anti-Communist upsurge."[33]

Thus, by the spring of 1940, a pattern of limited armed conflict and intensive political struggle characterized the relations between the Kuomintang and the Chinese Communists. In March, 1940, Mao further refined his political-military strategy and fully integrated his military actions with political policy. This political-military strategy took into account the vast inferiority of his military strength vis-à-vis Generalissimo Chiang Kai-shek and the minority status of his party and movement. The political strategy was to develop "the progressive forces," win over the "middle-of-the-road forces," oppose the "die-hards" and force them to recognize the position of the progressive forces."[34] By the term "die-hards," Mao referred, of course, to Generalissimo Chiang and his following. Of the three aspects of this strategy, the chief emphasis and the highest priority were given to developing the "progressive forces" — "the forces of the proletariat, the peasantry and the urban bourgeoisie; the Communist armed forces and base areas, and the organizations of the Communist Party and mass movements throughout the country." But these three phases of Mao's program were inseparable and reinforced each other. The "progressive forces," Mao pointed out, could not be developed without opposing the "die-hards." The task of winning over the middle-of-the-road forces could be accomplished only under three conditions: "(1) that we have sufficient strength; (2) that

[32] Mao Tse-tung, Selected Works, III (London: Lawrence and Wishart, 1954), 170.

[33] Hu Hua, Chung-kuo hsin-min-chu-chu-i kê-ming shih (ch'u-kao) ["A History of the New Democratic Revolution in China (Preliminary Draft)"] (Peking: Hsin-hua ch'u-pan-shê, 1950), p. 159. K'ang Jih chan-chêng shih-ch'i chieh-fang ch'ü kai-k'uang ["General Conditions in the Liberated Areas during the War of Resistance against Japan"] (Peking: Jên-min ch'u-pan-shê, 1953), p. 57 (hereafter cited as Chieh-fang-ch'ü).

[34] Mao Tse-tung, "Questions of Tactics in the Present Anti-Japanese United Front," Selected Works, III, 194, 198. This formulation was an elaboration of an idea which Mao had long entertained. As early as November, 1937, he told a group of party activists that "our task is to oppose national capitulationism resolutely and, in this struggle, expand and consolidate the left-wing bloc and induce the middle-of-the-road bloc to change and become progressive" (Mao, Selected Works, II, p. 71). There is no doubt that the Nationalists knew the substance of this report. A Nationalist pamphlet published in 1942 contained a series of quotations from a directive sent by the Communist party to its cadres which parallel closely Mao's statement. Wu Chung-ti, Tai-ping-yang chan-chêng hou ti Chung-kung yen-lun yü hsing-tung ["The Pronouncements and Actions of the Chinese-Communist Party after the Outbreak of the Pacific War"] (Hsêng-li ch'u-pan-shê, 1942), pp. 33–36.

we treat their interests with due respect; and (3) that we carry on resolute struggles against the die-hards and win victories step by step." [35]

Mao saw no incongruity between waging struggles against the "die-hards" and maintaining the united front with the Kuomintang.[36] On the contrary, he professed to believe that the struggle against the "die-hards" must be waged "as a means to prolong the die-hards' resistance to Japan and their cooperation with us, thereby averting the outbreak of a large-scale civil war." [37] In another directive written two months later, Mao instructed the Communist commanders operating in the lower Yangtze Valley and the East China coast area that it was only by adopting a firm attitude and waging struggles against the "die-hards," "so as *to make them afraid to oppress us*, that we can *reduce the die-hards' sphere of guarding against, containing and opposing communism*, compel the die-hards to recognize our legal status, and furthermore *make them hesitate to engineer a split*." [38] In other words, he relied on the developing strength of the Communists to deter the Kuomintang from launching a large-scale civil war or local attacks rather than on co-operation and concessions to avoid an open break.

Quite probably he realized that waging struggles against the Kuomintang might also increase the chance of an all-out civil war and that the Communists might not be strong enough to deter the Kuomintang from attacking them. But he correctly estimated that the Kuomintang could not launch a nationwide attack against the Communists so long as the war against Japan continued and that at that time the Sino-Japanese War could be concluded only by a Nationalist surrender to Japan. Thus, Mao pointed out to his commanders:

> In appraising the present situation, we ought to understand that, although on the one hand the danger of capitulation [of the Nationalists to Japan] has greatly increased, yet on the other hand there is still a possibility of averting it. *The present military conflicts are local and not nation-wide.* They are merely acts of strategic reconnaisance [sic] on the part of our opponents and are as yet not large-scale actions of annihilating the Communists."[39]

Furthermore, the Communists' experience in the first united front from 1923 to 1927, and their near destruction in 1927, had taught Mao that the danger of a large-scale Nationalist attack could not be averted by what he

[35] Mao Tse-tung, *Selected Works*, III, 197.
[36] *Ibid.*, p. 198.
[37] *Ibid.* Mao characterized the struggle against the Kuomintang as "the most important means for strengthening Kuomintang-Communist cooperation" (*Ibid.*, p. 206).
[38] Mao Tse-tung, "Freely Expand the Anti-Japanese Forces; Resist the Attacks of the Anti-Communist Die-hards," *ibid.*, p. 206. Emphasis added.
[39] *Ibid.*, p. 207. Emphasis added.

called "Right opportunism" on the part of the Communist party. On the contrary, he declared: "In coping with any possible nation-wide emergency, it is also only by adopting a line of struggle that we can enable the whole Party and the whole army to be well prepared psychologically and to have their work well planned. Otherwise the mistake of 1927 will recur."[40]

Thus, Mao devised a set of general rules to govern Communist policy in the local military conflicts which would enable him to push forward his "armed struggle" against the Kuomintang while minimizing the risk of an all-out civil war and gaining time to expand his political and military power. In a highly significant passage, Mao wrote:

> [W]e must pay attention to the following principles in waging struggles against the die-hards. First, the principle of self-defence. We will never attack unless attacked; if attacked, we will certainly counter-attack, that is to say, we must never attack others without provocation; but once we are attacked, we must never fail to return the blow. Herein lies the defensive nature of the struggle. As to the military attacks of the die-hards, we must resolutely, thoroughly, utterly and completely smash them. Secondly, the principle of victory. We do not fight unless we are sure of victory; we must on no account fight without preparation and without certainty of the outcome. We should know how to utilize the contradictions among the die-hards and must not deal blows to many sections of them at the same time; we must pick out the most reactionary section to strike at first. Herein lies the limited nature of the struggle. Thirdly, the principle of truce. After we have repulsed the attack of the die-hards and before they launch a new one, we should stop at the proper moment and bring that particular fight to a close. In the period that follows we should make a truce with them. Then we should on our initiative seek unity with the die-hards and, upon their consent, conclude a peace agreement with them. We must on no account fight on daily and hourly without stopping, nor become dizzy with success. Herein lies the temporary nature of every particular struggle. Only when the die-hards launch a new offensive should we retaliate with a new struggle. In other words, the three principles are "justifiability," "expediency" and "restraint." Persisting in such justifiable, expedient and restrained struggles, we can develop the progressive forces, win over the middle-of-the-road forces, isolate the die-hard forces and make the die-hards chary of heedlessly attack-

[40] *Ibid.* Mao also called for full preparation "for coping with any possible emergency of a local or national character" (*ibid.*, p. 209).

ing us . . . or heedlessly starting a large-scale civil war. And we
can in this way win a favorable turn in the situation.[41]

In these few sentences, Mao laid down the basic principles of limited war
for the side whose over-all military strength was weaker than its adversary's. They were designed to subject the use of force to careful control
and to limit armed clashes to manageable proportions, gaining numerous
local victories without too great a risk of general civil war.

Mao's principle of "justifiability," or "self-defence," did not preclude action to expand freely "our armed forces both independently and on our own
initiative," "disregarding Kuomintang restrictions" and "going beyond
the limits allowed by the Kuomintang."[42] It was also thought to be compatible with actions to "establish our base areas, arouse the masses there
into action and build up there the Communist-led political power of the
anti-Japanese united front independently and on our own initiative."[43] The
expansion of Communist forces, base areas, and local governments was
to be pushed forward in all the territory occupied by Japan. But it was
also to be undertaken at the expense of the political and military power
of the Kuomintang. For Mao specifically envisaged the reduction of "the
die-hards' sphere of guarding against, containing and opposing communism."[44]

In May, 1940, Mao directed the commanders of the New Fourth Army to
expand as rapidly as possible their control "in the area extending from
Nanking in the west to the seacoast in the east, and from Hangchow in the
south to Hsuchow in the north."[45] He criticized them for their lack of vigor
in implementing the party's directive to expand the Communist forces
there to 100,000 men.[46] This directive brought about intensified activities
of the Communist forces. According to both Nationalist and Communist
sources, General Ch'ên Yi, then commander of the First Contingent of
the New Fourth Army and now the foreign minister of China, moved his
forces in July, 1940, to northern Kiangsu and clashed with Nationalist
forces there.[47] In the second half of 1940, several pitched battles took

[41] Mao Tse-tung, "Questions of Tactics in the Present Anti-Japanese United Front,"
ibid., p. 199.
[42] Mao Tse-tung, "Freely Expand the Anti-Japanese Forces; Resist the Attacks of
the Anti-Communist Die-Hards," *ibid.*, p. 204.
[43] *Ibid.*, p. 205.
[44] *Ibid.*, p. 206.
[45] *Ibid.*, p. 205.
[46] *Ibid.*
[47] *Chieh-fang-ch'ü*, p. 113. *Chieh-fang-chün*, pp. 97–100. *Telegram from General
Ho Ying-ch'in and General Pai Ch'ung-hsi to General Chu Teh, General Pang Tê-
huai and General Yeh T'ing*, October 19, 1940 (The General Office of the National
Military Council), p. 2 (hereafter cited as *Telegram*, October 19, 1940). Chiang,
op. cit., p. 93.
The Nationalists charged that General Ch'ên Yi's forces crossed the Yantze River

place in the lower Yangtze Valley. By the end of the year, the New Fourth Army expanded into a force of 100,000 men,[48] thus accomplishing the task assigned to it by Mao.

This expansion of Communist forces occurred in a vital area of China which had been the political center of the Kuomintang before the outbreak of the Sino-Japanese War and in which the Nationalist government still stationed sizable forces. The Kuomintang took action to remove this potentially fatal threat. On July 16, the Nationalist government demanded that both the New Fourth Army and the Eighteenth Group Army withdraw to the north of the Yellow River.[49] In the negotiations on the highest level which accompanied the fighting on the local level, the Communists rejected the demand but offered to withdraw the various units of the New Fourth Army to the north of the Yangtze River. These frictions culminated in the "New Fourth Army Incident" of January, 1941. In this most serious of all wartime clashes between the two sides, the Nationalist armies surrounded and destroyed a Communist force of 9,000 men attached to the headquarters of the New Fourth Army, captured its commander, and killed its deputy commander. On January 17, the Nationalist government ordered the dissolution of the New Fourth Army.

It is not our purpose here to reconstruct the events and to judge the validity of the Communists' and Nationalists' versions of this incident. But it is of interest to note Mao's constant vigilance against the possible outbreak of a large-scale civil war and his determination to carry out his program in spite of this setback. On January 22, a spokesman of the Chinese Communist party issued a statement which, we now know, was drafted personally by Mao. In it, he characterized the "New Fourth Army Incident" as "the beginning of a nation-wide emergency." He charged that the Nationalist government was taking steps to annihilate other units of the New Fourth Army and was preparing to attack the Eighth Route Army, to invade the Shensi-Kansu-Ninghsia border region, and to make wholesale arrests of Communists. He declared that the Kuomintang authorities "must have determined on a complete split."[50] He urged the people throughout the country "to watch the development of events with the utmost vigilance and get ready for coping with any dark reactionary situation."[51] He re-

without authorization from the government and attacked Nationalist forces. The Communists claimed that General Ch'ên sent his forces to northern Kiangsu to relieve other Communist units surrounded by Nationalist troops.

[48] *Chieh-fang-ch'ü*, p. 2; Mao Tse-tung, *Selected Works*, III, 231.

[49] *Telegram*, October 19, 1940, p. 8. For a detailed account, see Johnson, *op. cit.*, pp. 136–40.

[50] Mao Tse-tung, "Order and Statement on the Southern Anhwei Incident," *Selected Works*, III, 228.

[51] *Ibid.*, p. 229.

minded the Kuomintang that the Chinese Communist party was no longer to be so easily deceived and destroyed as in 1927 and that it was now a major party standing firmly on its own feet. He announced to the country that the remaining 90,000 men of the New Fourth Route Army would be put under a new commander and that the Eighth Route Army "will certainly not sit by and watch it [the New Fourth Army] suffer from pincer attacks but will take appropriate steps to render necessary assistance."[52]

Neither Mao nor Chiang, however, wanted a total rupture at this time. Mao subsequently explained that, when the Central Committee of the party ordered its rank and file to get ready to cope with a split which the Kuomintang might bring about, it was preparing for the worst development. The necessity to prepare for the worst did not exclude the chance of avoiding an all-out civil war. "Our preparations are themselves a condition for striving to turn such a possibility into actuality. . . . [A]s we had made sufficient preparations to cope with the Kuomintang's attempt at a split, the Kuomintang dared not bring it about lightly."[53] Seen from this light, the charge made by the spokesman of the Communist party was probably intended as a warning to the Kuomintang and a call for vigilance against Nationalist attacks. Although Mao may have momentarily overestimated the danger immediately after the incident, his considered opinion was that an all-out civil war was possible but not probable. Thus, he characterized as incorrect the appraisal that the incident was a repetition of Chiang's action on April 12, 1927, in suppressing the Communists and Communist-led labor unions in Shanghai. He wrote that "as long as the Sino-Japanese contradiction remains sharp . . . the situation of 1927 can never be brought about, nor can the incident of April 12 . . . be repeated."[54]

On his part Chiang was apparently satisfied with the recent victory. With the war with Japan going on, an all-out attack on the Communist forces and base areas behind Japanese lines was a political and military impossibility. On March 6, 1941, the Generalissimo told the People's Political Council:

> Our government is solely concerned with leading the nation against the Japanese invaders and extirpating the traitors, and is utterly without any notion of again taking up arms to suppress the Communists. . . . I can make myself responsible for the statement that at no future time could there conceivably be another campaign for the suppression of the Communists. . . . Provided unity can be preserved and resistance can be carried on to the end,

[52] *Ibid.*, p. 231.
[53] Mao Tse-tung, "A Review of the Repulse of the Second Anti-Communist Upsurge," *ibid.*, pp. 239–40.
[54] *Ibid.*, pp. 236–37.

the government will be ready to follow your directives in the settlement of all outstanding questions.[55]

This speech was taken by Mao as marking the end of the second anti-
Communist upsurge.[56] But no settlement between the two parties could
be reached, and sporadic local fighting continued. This was the state of
affairs in China when the attack on Pearl Harbor brought about the
Pacific war.

Thus, the situation in China confronting the United States during the
Pacific war was as complex as Chinese politics can be. Present in this
situation was a dimension without precedent elsewhere — a revolutionary
party, organized on Leninist principles, which developed and employed
military power as a principal instrument within a framework of political
policies carefully designed to isolate and defeat its opponent. Its military
power rested squarely on popular support, built up by a program of armed
resistance against Japan and economic, social, and political reforms. In
turn, its military power was used to defend the peasants against the Japanese invaders, to push forward the reforms, and to develop the party organizations and mass movements. It turned the Sino-Japanese War and the
united front with its opponent into a shield to protect itself against possible attack by the Kuomintang armies. Behind this shield it carried out a
rapid all-out expansion of its armed forces and a series of limited, local
clashes with its antagonist.

In the political sphere, it followed a strategy of developing its own forces,
winning over the middle-of-the-road groups, and isolating its irreconcilable
enemies. It utilized the united front to promote this strategy. It practiced
"democracy" in areas under its control to generate popular support and
to win over the middle-of-the-road groups. It demanded the transformation
of the Kuomintang government into a constitutional and democratic regime
as one way to gain influence and power in Nationalist China and as one
of the steps to develop "the progressive forces" and to win over the middle-
of-the-road forces.[57] The lofty pronouncements and widely circulated
treatises such as *On New Democracy* (1940) and *On Coalition Government*
(1945) must be understood in terms of the basic strategy outlined in internal party directives, reports, and speeches — some of which were known
to the Nationalists at the time and many of which have since been pub-

[55] *United States Relations with China*, pp. 529–30, 54.
[56] Mao Tse-tung, *Selected Works*, III, 233.
[57] According to Mao himself, to develop the "progressive forces" means, among
other things, "to extend among the broad masses the movement for constitutionalism
as a fight for democracy" (Mao Tse-tung, *Selected Works*, III, 195). Mao realized
that the middle-bourgeoisie "favors the movement for constitutionalism and attempts
to achieve its objectives by exploiting the contradiction between the progressives and
the die-hards" (*ibid.*, pp. 195–96).

lished. It is against this understanding of Mao's political-military strategy that one must evaluate the American endeavor to bring about a united and democratic China by peaceful means. It is against the record of independent actions taken by the Eighth Route Army and the New Fourth Army, in defiance of the orders of the Nationalist government, that one must judge the reliance on unification of armed forces as a measure for solving the Communist problem in China and for preventing Soviet interference in Chinese affairs. The fact that American officials could not have had comprehensive knowledge of all the plans of the Chinese communist party need not prevent us from undertaking this task. Our purpose is to explain the failure of American policy, not to locate within a vacuum actions which were praiseworthy and actions which were not.

B. The American Policy of Bringing about a United and Democratic China

In the first two-and-a-half years after Pearl Harbor, the United States discouraged the Nationalist government from suppressing the Chinese Communists by force and endeavored to prevent the outbreak of a civil war. After August of 1944, the United States took positive measures to bring the two sides together under a unified command and a coalition government. As Major General Patrick J. Hurley, personal representative of the President at the time of the Stilwell crisis and later ambassador to China, informed the Senate Committee on Foreign Relations in December, 1945: "Our policy in China was clearly defined and could be stated roughly as follows: (1) to unify all anti-Japanese military forces in China, and, (2) to support the aspirations of the Chinese people to establish for themselves a free, unified, democratic government." [58] This was the policy designed to cope with the infinitely complex problems posed by the political-military struggle in China.

In the light of later acrimonious charges over the issues of "forcing a coalition government on Chiang Kai-shek," it is not irrelevant to underscore at the outset that this policy was almost unanimously indorsed at the time and few, if any, dissenting voices were heard. General Hurley was, of course, the most optimistic and indefatigable executor of the policy. While critical of many aspects of Hurley's implementation of the policy, most foreign service officers in China and officials in the State Department agreed with him that the division in China should be ended by creation of a democratic government. In one of the most important reports submitted by John S. Service, a foreign service officer detailed to Stilwell's head-

[58] Senate Committee on Foreign Relations, *Hearings in an Investigation of Far Eastern Policy*, 79th Cong., 1st sess. (December, 1945), p. 32. Excerpts printed in Senate Subcommittee on Internal Security of the Committee on the Judiciary, *Hearings in the Institute of Pacific Relations*, 82d Cong., 1st and 2d sess. (1951–52), p. 1910 (hereafter cited as *Institute of Pacific Relations*).

quarters, it is suggested: "The key to stability [in the Far East] must be a strong, unified China. This can be accomplished only in [sic] a democratic foundation."[59]

Even some of the most forceful critics of the Truman-Marshall policy, which was nothing but an extension of the wartime policy under discussion, seem to have, at this time, approved of that policy. General Claire L. Chennault proposed in a letter to President Roosevelt dated September 21, 1944, that the United States sponsor a new attempt to bring the Nationalists and the Communists together.[60] In response to General Marshall's request for his recommendations on the eve of the Potsdam Conference, General Albert C. Wedemeyer, the commanding general of the United States forces in the China theater, replied on July 9, 1945:

> If Uncle Sugar, Russia, and Britain united strongly in their endeavor to bring about a *coalition of these two* political parties [the Kuomintang and the Chinese Communist Party] in China *by coercing both sides* to make realistic concessions, serious post-war disturbance may be averted and timely effective military employment of all Chinese may be obtained against the Japanese. *I use the term coerce advisedly* because it is my conviction that continued appeals to both sides couched in polite diplomatic terms will not accomplish unification. There must be teeth in Big Three approach.[61]

On December 7, 1945, General Douglas MacArthur, General Albert C. Wedemeyer, and Admiral Raymond T. Spruance laid down in a joint telegram a program for transporting six more Chinese armies with the necessary supplies into North China and Manchuria but suggested that "the U.S. assistance to China, as outlined above, be made available as basis for negotiation by the American Ambassador to bring together and effect a compromise between the major opposing groups in order to promote a united and democratic China." [62] Whatever the private views of the three

---

[59] Report No. 40 submitted by John S. Service, October 10, 1944, "The Need for Greater Realism in Our Relations with Chiang Kai-shek." It is reprinted in whole in Senate Subcommittee of the Committee on Foreign Relations, *Hearings on State Department Employee Loyalty Investigation*, 81st Cong., 2d sess. (March–June, 1950), pp. 1281–83. The quotation was taken from p. 1282 (hereafter cited as *State Department Employee Loyalty Investigation*).

[60] Herbert Feis, *The China Tangle* (Princeton, N.J.: Princeton University Press, 1953), p. 192, n. 14.

[61] Quoted in Charles F. Romanus and Riley Sunderland, *Time Runs Out in CBI* (Washington, D.C.: Government Printing Office, 1959), p. 383. Emphasis added. See also Feis, *op. cit.*, p. 316. For Wedemeyer's own interpretation of this telegram, see General Albert C. Wedemeyer, *Wedemeyer Reports!* (New York: Henry Holt & Co., 1958), pp. 333–34.

[62] This telegram was read in full by Secretary of State Dean Acheson on June 9, 1951, before the Senate Armed Services and Foreign Relations committees during

Far Eastern commanders may have been,[63] the statement quoted, even if made in great haste, indicates the extent to which the policy of effecting a compromise between the two sides was taken for granted at the time

Within the general framework of the policy to bring about a united and democratic China by peaceful means, a significant split over policy occurred between General Hurley and some foreign service officers in China whose views were shared in various degrees by many officials in the State Department and by American men of affairs concerned with China.[64] The most important of these foreign service officers were John P. Davies and John S. Service, who were detailed to Stilwell's headquarters to serve as political advisers to him. This disagreement was related in the first instance to the methods of bringing the two sides together. But beyond the conflicting views on means, there was a more fundamental disagreement arising from divergent estimates of the probable development of Chinese politics and the prospect of the Kuomintang's staying in power. General Hurley believed that a united and democratic China could be

the hearings on the military situation in the Far East which were held as a result of the dismissal of General Douglas MacArthur. Senate Committee on Armed Services and the Committee on Foreign Relations, *Hearings on the Military Situation in the Far East*, 82d Cong., 1st sess. (May–August, 1951), p. 2248 (hereafter cited as *Military Situation in the Far East*).

[63] In a message to Senator William F. Knowland after the above telegram had been made public, General MacArthur characterized as "a prevarication without color or factual support" any inference from the telegram that "he sponsored a compromise which would favor the forces of communism at the expense of the forces of freedom or would effect a political coalition of such diametrically opposed and irreconcilable forces" (*ibid.*, p. 2249). His message was an attempt to explain away his December 7 proposal in two ways: (1) by conveying the impression that the words "major opposing forces" had been intended to denote the many centrifugal forces in China, not necessarily including the Communists, which he now designated variously as only "a nebulous threat at the time" or "a minority faction," and, (2) by emphasizing the desire to strengthen Chiang politically in the process of effecting a unification. The first explanation cannot possibly convince anyone with some knowledge of Chinese affairs at that time. The second explanation suffers from the objection that the use of American assistance as a lever to bring about a compromise could only have resulted in pressure upon the Nationalists and that any attainable "compromise" would inevitably have put the Nationalists in a disadvantageous position.

General Wedemeyer also stated that the language used in the telegram of December 7, 1945, did not fairly represent the views which he consistently held before that time or since. He seems to have forgotten the telegram he sent to General Marshall on July 9, 1945, and also another lengthy message to the War Department dated November 20, 1945. However, under questioning he gave an affirmative answer to the question whether the Nationalists and the Communists were "the two principal groups in China at the time" (*ibid.*, p. 2373). He also conceded that the language used did suggest to the average reader that he favored a coalition government including the Communists (*ibid.*). See also *Institute of Pacific Relations*, p. 747. For a fuller discussion of Wedemeyer's position, see Tang Tsou, "The Historians and the Generals," *The Pacific Historical Review*, February, 1962, pp. 41–48.

[64] For a fuller discussion and documentation of the statements made in this paragraph, see chap. vi, below.

brought about by giving strong support to Generalissimo Chiang, advising him to reach a settlement with the Chinese Communists, but without exerting pressure on him to achieve such a purpose or to undertake necessary reforms. With support from the United States and with the acquiescence of the Soviet Union in the American policy, the Nationalist government would be able to bring the armed forces of the Communist party under a unified command and to take them into the government under terms favorable to the Kuomintang. The result would be a strengthened central government, still controlled by the Kuomintang and capable of maintaining itself in power.

In contrast to Hurley's views, the foreign service officers thought that an American policy of unconditional support for Chiang Kai-shek would only make the Generalissimo more intransigent and prevent a compromise settlement with the Chinese Communists. They believed that a united and democratic China could be brought about only by exerting pressure on the Generalissimo to offer the Communists reasonable terms. Underlying this policy was the assumption that the Nationalist government was not viable even with American support, which in their view could not be very extensive. Consequently, the United States ought not commit herself unalterably to the Nationalist regime but should instead try to maintain an independent position from which she could work with both sides.

Thus Hurley's views and the proposals of the Foreign Service officers can be compared to two intersecting lines. They started from opposite appraisals of the relative strength of the Kuomintang and the Chinese Communists and from disparate views on the methods to bring about a united, democratic China. They met at the common point of the shared intermediate objective of establishing a coalition government. Then they diverged again toward two opposite destinations, with Hurley aiming at the strengthening of the Nationalist government and the two foreign service officers seeking a way to win the Chinese Communists over to the side of the United States or to induce them to follow a policy independent of the Soviet Union.

Ambassador Gauss shared the foreign service officers' views on the necessity of exerting pressure on Generalissimo Chiang to establish a coalition high command or coalition government and to bring about necessary reforms. But it was General Hurley who became the chief executor of American policy after Stilwell's recall and Gauss's resignation. In his conflict with the foreign service officers, Hurley was sustained by President Roosevelt. His understanding of American policy was also supported by President Truman after Roosevelt's untimely death. Hurley resigned in November, 1945, at a time when American policy as interpreted and executed by him had failed to bring about a reconciliation between the two sides and when it was subject to increasing criticism in the United States as a result of that failure. Hurley's resignation and the dispatch of the Marshall mission signified the triumph of those who believed in the necessity of forcing Chiang to offer the Communists better terms in order to obtain a political settlement. The foreign service officers' judgment that the Nationalist regime was not viable found an echo in General Marshall's despair of achieving his objectives through co-operation with the Kuomintang and his ultimate decision to withdraw from China. Their belief in the possibility of winning the friendship of the Chinese Communists survived in a different form in the hope entertained by some people in late 1948 and early 1949 that Mao might become a Chinese Tito.

But in spite of these conflicting views on means and probable outcome, the agreement on the desirability and feasibility of effecting a reconciliation between the two parties was nevertheless significant for the underlying assumptions which it revealed and for the alternative which it excluded. General Hurley's energetic efforts to bring the two sides together reflected his confidence in the political vitality of the Kuomintang, his underestimation of the political strength of the Communists, and his belief in the Soviet ability to control Mao's policy. The advocacy of the same policy by some career officials betrayed a tendency to equate the task of strengthening the Nationalist government with the establishment of a coalition government including the Communists, or else an undue optimism regarding the future political orientation of the Chinese Communist party.

In retrospect, it becomes clear that the consensus of opinion regarding the feasibility of peaceful unification prevented an early realization of the possibility that, in endeavoring to reconcile the irreconcilable and in urging the Nationalist government to do the impossible, the United States would dissipate her influence. More important, the consensus rested on a misjudgment of the nature and intention of the Chinese Communist party and on a failure to comprehend Communist political strategy and tactics.[65] As a result, official opinion ruled out an alternative which might have been tried with greater effectiveness: the use of the immense American influence and prestige to force the Nationalist government to undertake long overdue reforms and to remake itself into the nucleus of a broad anti-Communist front.[66] Under this policy the very possibility of establishing a working relationship with the Chinese Communists could have been used as a most effective lever to exert pressure on Chiang Kai-shek while the prospect of active American support in his fight against Chinese com-

[65] See chap. vi, below.
[66] George E. Taylor, "The Hegemony of the Chinese Communist, 1945–1950," *Annals of the American Academy of Political and Social Science*, September, 1951, pp. 13–21; David Nelson Rowe, "American Policy toward China," *ibid.*, January, 1948, pp. 136–45.

munism could have been held out as an irresistible inducement. Once the
social and political foundations of the Nationalist government had been re-
built by a series of sweeping reforms, there would have existed the indispensable condition for the success of a program of active support to the
government, not excluding possible American participation in a civil war.
This line of action was precluded by the policy of peaceful unification.
Thus, the widespread agreement on the intermediate objective was as significant as the split over means and final ends which has been frequently
stressed.

C. Three Sets of Considerations Contributing to the Consensus

1. Traditional Principles and Sentiments

The policy of bringing about a united and democratic China by peaceful political means was first of all a perfect embodiment of the traditional
attitudes and policies of the United States toward China. Since the dispatch of Secretary Hay's circular of 1900, the policy of the United States
had been to deplore political divisions and civil strife in China, to discourage the powers from interfering in Chinese domestic affairs by supporting
one Chinese faction against another, and to urge the contending Chinese
groups to reconcile their differences. It had always been assumed that
American interest lay in a composition of factional disputes, a cessation
of the perennial civil war, and the establishment of unity in China. In
June, 1917, when the Chinese were divided among themselves on the
question of declaring war against the Central Powers, the Wilson administration appealed to the Chinese government for the re-establishment of
tranquillity and political co-ordination. It informed China that "with [sic]
the maintenance by China of one central, united and responsible Government the United States is deeply interested."[67] Similarly, the United States
followed a policy of strict neutrality between the two sides in the Chinese
revolutions of 1925–27 and successfully discouraged the powers from
adopting forcible measures of reprisal against Nationalists after the Nanking Incident. She also took the lead in granting early recognition and
concessions to the Nationalist government.[68] This principle of American
policy was stated explicitly in Article I of the Nine-Power Treaty which
reads in part: "It is the firm intention of the Powers attending this conference . . . 1. To respect the sovereignty, the independence and the territorial and administrative integrity of China. 2. To provide the fullest and
most unembarrassed opportunity to China to develop and maintain for
herself an effective and stable government."

[67] Department of State, *Foreign Relations of the United States, 1917* (Washington:
Government Printing Office, 1946), p. 49. Emphasis added.
[68] Dorothy Borg, *American Policy and the Chinese Revolution, 1925–1928* (New
York: Macmillan, 1947), chaps. vii, xi, xiv, xvii, xviii, and xix.

The tradition of non-intervention, condemnation of civil war, and advocacy of unity in China — all as a matter of principle — visibly influenced American thinking on Chinese affairs during the period under consideration. In October, 1942, Earl Browder, the secretary general of the American Communist party, charged that the State Department was encouraging the Nationalists to suppress the Communists by force. Undersecretary of State Sumner Welles went out of his way to invite Mr. Browder to see him and handed the American Communist leader a statement reaffirming the desire of the American government for "complete unity" among the Chinese people and all groups or organizations.[69] In connection with this episode, the chief of the Division of Far Eastern Affairs submitted a memorandum to Mr. Welles which was highly revealing of the thinking of American officials concerning China. Referring to the strained relations between the Nationalists and the Communists, this memorandum declared that "the government of the United States has deprecated civil strife in China and has suggested conciliatory attitudes and procedures by and on the part of contending groups or factions among the Chinese."[70] It elucidated the historical foundation of this policy in the following words:

> The American Government has for a hundred years pursued a policy favoring maintenance of the independence and the integrity of China. In pursuing this policy, this government has at all times believed it desirable that the Chinese nation be and continue to be united. It has used its influence in opposition to events, movements and trends directed or leading toward disintegration, partitioning, breakup or subjugation of China. . . . It has been this government's practice not to interfere in China's internal affairs."[71]

Pride in this tradition was shared by many experts on Far Eastern affairs who also insisted on adherence to a policy of impartiality and non-intervention. Professor Owen Lattimore, an outstanding expert on the inner Asian frontiers of China and a prolific writer on American policy toward Asia, concluded, in June, 1945, that American policy under Ambassador Hurley's direction had veered toward all-out support for the Nationalist party. He condemned this policy as, among other things, a departure from traditional principles. In a letter to President Truman recommending

[69] *State Department Employee Loyalty Investigation*, p. 675. Browder's charges were made in an article printed in the *Daily Worker* on October 4, 1942. It was reproduced in *Institute of Pacific Relations*, pp. 595–98. For Undersecretary Welles' statement, see Department of State, *Foreign Relations of the United States, 1942: China* (Washington, D.C.: Government Printing Office, 1956), pp. 248–49.
[70] *Ibid.*, p. 250.
[71] *Ibid.*

a thorough review of American policy as executed by Hurley, he wrote: "In the eyes of many people such a development [America's support for one party] would mean that America itself, long the supporter of China's political and territorial integrity, had initiated a policy identified with the political and territorial division of China."[72] These traditional sentiments were formidable obstacles to the adoption of a policy of active intervention in Chinese political affairs and, from the very beginning, played a part in excluding from serious consideration the idea that America's self-interest might require active American support for one side in the political contest or even direct American participation in a civil war. They further increased the hesitancy of American officials to act resolutely in a situation which permitted only a choice of gross evils.

Not less important in shaping American policy than the intense desire for an unattainable Chinese unity and the specific injunction against active intervention was the profound sympathy for China and deep concern for her welfare which had always been an integral part of the Far Eastern policy of the United States. On the attitude of officials in the State Department and American representatives in China, Herbert Feis observed that they were "moved by a longing that since China was their cause, and it *was* their cause, it should be a worthy cause. They did not think or write solely as American officials who wanted to win a war, indifferent to the plight of the people of China. They wanted China to become a well-governed and well-cared-for country as well as a strong ally."[73] This sentimental concern for China contributed to their natural abhorrence of civil war in that country. John Carter Vincent, counselor of the American Embassy

---

[72] *Institute of Pacific Relations*, p. 3087. The citing of Professor Lattimore's views in this context must not be construed to mean that he exercised any direct influence over the policies of the State Department at any time or that a small group of conspirators guided the China policy of the United States toward a direction and outcome favorable to the Soviet Union. It is far-fetched to claim, as two prominent professors in the Far Eastern field did before the McCarran subcommittee investigating the Institute of Pacific Relations, that Professor Lattimore was "definitely following the Stalinist line," or that he was "the principal agent for the advocacy of Stalinist ideas" (*ibid.*, pp. 1012, 3984, 3985). It cannot be too strongly emphasized that not only is there no proof of the existence of such a conspiracy but, more importantly, the diffuse process of policy formation in the United States precluded the possibility of subverting her foreign policy by a small group in the interest of a foreign power.

The view expressed in these pages is that the collapse of American foreign policy toward China was caused by a set of assumptions, attitudes, and traditions shared by a large number of leaders in the United States. These peculiarly American approaches, shrewdly exploited by Communist policies and propaganda, led to the adoption of unrealistic policies. They also played a part in the faulty execution of inherently unpromising policies which further magnified the consequences of failure. If this analysis is correct, then a basic reorientation of American thinking on Far Eastern policy was needed.

[73] Feis, *op. cit.*, pp. 90–91.

in Chungking in 1942–43, chief of the Division of Chinese Affairs in 1944–45, and director of Far Eastern affairs in 1945–47, recalling his sentiments in those years, has stated, "We were . . . terribly concerned over the result of an outbreak of general civil war in China. I was, particularly. I had been in China and had seen the effect of civil war on the country."[74]

The wish for a worthy cause seems to have contributed to the critical views held by American officials toward the Nationalist government, quite aside from the question of its apparent inability to retain control of China. For the welfare of the Chinese people as such became a significant factor molding American policy. As stated in a memorandum sent in early June, 1944, from the State Department to American embassies at Chungking and Moscow, "The American government was not committed to support the National Government of China in any and all circumstances. It was not concerned with doctrinal questions between contending Chinese groups; it was concerned with the effectuation in China of *a program that would benefit the Chinese people.*"[75]

By projection, this American benevolence toward China was transformed into an exaggerated notion of Chinese friendship for the United States. The extravagant idea of America's popularity in China influenced the estimate of the consequences of a Communist-controlled China for American interests in the Far East. John S. Service told his superiors on April 7, 1944:

> The Communists would undoubtedly plan [play?] an important part in a genuinely unified China — one not unified by the Kuomintang's present policy in practice of military force and threat. But it is most probable that such a democratic and unified China would naturally gravitate toward the United States and that the United States, by virtue of a [sic] sympathy, position, and economic resources, would enjoy a greater influence in China than any other foreign power."[76]

This solicitude for the welfare of the Chinese people was an indispensable basis for American policy toward China, where nothing but a program of social, economic, and political reforms could have removed the conditions exploited by the Chinese Communists and have created the necessary foundation for an effective program of American economic and military assistance, not excluding the use of American forces, to contain

[74] *Institute of Pacific Relations,* p. 1713.
[75] As paraphrased by Feis, *op. cit.,* p. 142. Emphasis added.
[76] Memorandum by John S. Service, entitled "Situation in Sinkiang: Its relation to American Policy vis-à-vis China and the Soviet Union." Excerpts printed in the transcripts of proceedings of the Loyalty Security Board meeting in the case of John S. Service. These transcripts were reproduced as supplements in *State Department Employee Loyalty Investigation,* pp. 1958–2509. The quotation was taken from p. 1979.

Communism. But, unaccompanied by an understanding of the nature and intentions of the Chinese Communist party, it merely raised unwarranted expectations regarding the political orientation of the Chinese Communists and militated against American military action in China.

2. Military Considerations

While traditional principles and attitudes generated a climate of opinion favorable to the policy of striving for an unattainable unity, the paramount wartime objective of a quick victory with the least sacrifice also provided a strong impetus to the mounting efforts to bring about a united and democratic China. Overestimating the military value of China in the war against Japan, American officials and military leaders considered it highly desirable, if not indispensable, to prevent the open outbreak of a Chinese civil war and to unify the Nationalist and Communist armed forces. The various proposals to achieve a political reconciliation between the two sides and to bring them together in a "war council" or a coalition government was at first a political means toward effectively using the reputed military potential of China. Even in the early months of 1945 this military objective was still guiding the recommendations of career officials in the State Department and in China who were ignorant of the abandonment of plans for a landing by American forces on the coast of North and East China. After the course of the war made it apparent that China would no longer play an important part in the defeat of Japan, political considerations elevated the peaceful unification of China into an end to which the unification of the armed forces of the two major political groups became a necessary first step.

In the realm of military calculations, some Americans hoped to accomplish two overlapping purposes by unifying the Chinese armed forces: to remove a major obstacle hampering the war effort of China and to use the strategically placed, well-disciplined, and well-led Communist forces. It was obvious to all observers that the increasing tension between the Kuomintang and the Chinese Communists prevented China from making a maximum effort in the war against Japan. As early as 1939 the Nationalist government had begun a rigid military blockade of Communist areas to prevent the Communists from expanding the territory under their control and infiltrating into Nationalist China.[77] In 1942, sixteen divisions of the best-equipped Nationalist forces under General Hu Tsung-nan were charged with the task of blockading the Communist armies in the Shensi-Kansu-Ninghsia border region to prevent their expansion or infiltration into

[77] United States Relations with China, p. 53. Also, War Department, Military Intelligence Division, "The Chinese Communist Movement," incorporated as Appendix II to Part 7A of Institute of Pacific Relations, p. 2349.

the areas around Sian.[78] In 1943, George Atcheson, chargé d'affaires of the American Embassy, reported that there were possibly 400,000 Nationalist troops blockading the border region.[79]

The mutual antagonism and distrust between the Nationalists and Communists, together with their preoccupation with the struggle for power in China, not only tied down a large number of Nationalist troops but also prevented the effective use against Japan of Communist forces, which had grown rapidly in size since 1937. According to a report sent by the American Embassy in 1942, the strength of the Eighteenth Group Army, the larger and better equipped of the two Communist armies, was estimated at 500,000 to 600,000 by two left-wing informants.[80] According to a United States Army intelligence report, the Communists claimed in 1945 to have an army of 910,000 troops in addition to local militia forces of 2,000,000 men, although it estimated the actual size of the regular Communist forces at 475,000 as of October, 1944.[81] More important than the reputed or actual strength of the Communist forces were the strategic positions they occupied. As the Sino-Japanese War progressed, the Communists greatly expanded the areas under their control in North and East China, where the United States had originally planned to acquire airfields and staging areas for an offensive against Japan.

After the strategy of attacking Japan directly from the Pacific islands had been confirmed at the Cairo Conference, and after the plan for a landing on the China coast was abandoned in 1944, the United States still deemed it important to prevent a collapse of China. It was no accident that the American policy seeking the use of Communist forces and the establishment of some form of coalition high command or government including Communist representatives was crystalized during the military crisis which confronted China in the second half of 1944. While not anxious to use the Communist troops without the assent of the Nationalist government, General Hurley attributed great significance to unifying the Chinese armed forces. He told Secretary of State Edward R. Stettinius on January 31, 1945, that "a unification of the military forces of the Communist Party and the National Government would have a battle effect, equal at least to one fully equipped American army. The result of unification of the Chinese military forces is worth much more consideration than it has hitherto received from Americans."[82]

[78] Charles F. Romanus and Riley Sunderland, *Stilwell's Mission to China* (Washington, D.C.: Government Printing Office, 1952), p. 184; Department of State, *Foreign Relations of the United States, 1942: China*, p. 229.
[79] Department of State, *Foreign Relations of the United States, 1943: China* (Washington, D.C.: Government Printing Office, 1957), p. 284.
[80] *Foreign Relations of the United States, 1942: China*, pp. 207–8.
[81] "Chinese Communist Movement," *Institute of Pacific Relations*, p. 2313.
[82] *Military Situation in the Far East*, p. 3670.

The thinking of many other American officials and military men in China ran along similar lines. They were greatly impressed by the possibility of taking advantage of the strategic location of the Communist forces and their versatility in guerrilla warfare to gain valuable intelligence, to capture at small cost important but lightly guarded objectives in North China, and to disrupt Japanese communications.[83] As the time of an American offensive against Japan drew near, they were keenly aware of the possible help which the Communists could give to American troops landed in China. As John Carter Vincent later testified before the McCarran Committee investigating the *Institute of Pacific Relations*:

> In the late autumn or probably winter of 1944, in December, it was generally understood in the State Department — I was in the State Department then — that there was possibly going to be an American landing on the north coast of China. That area was largely occupied by Chinese Communist guerrillas. It became apparent to us, and by "us" I include Mr. Grew, who himself at the time was anxious that any forces that could aid us in fighting Japan should be utilized and this would. Also, we assumed it would save American lives if we would utilize the Communists.[84]

A State Department paper on American policy toward China dated February 27, 1945, declared that "if the United States was to undertake operations on the China coast, American commanders should be prepared to arm the Communists."[85] At this time, the officials in the State Department did not realize that the Joint Chiefs had already abandoned the plan to make a landing on the China coast.

The importance attributed to the use of Communist forces must be understood in the light of the priority of military considerations in the scheme of national purposes. In their thinking on China policy, American officials in China were dominated by the immediate exigencies of the war. John S. Service and Raymond L. Ludden found the most compelling reason for arming the Chinese Communists in strategic considerations. In a memorandum dated February 14, 1945, they wrote: "American policy in the Far East can have but one immediate objective, the defeat of Japan in the shortest possible time with the least expenditures of American lives. To the attainment of this objective all other considerations should be subordinate."[86] In a telegram dated February 26, 1945,

[83] Feis, *op. cit.*, pp. 205, 268. Romanus and Sunderland, *Time Runs Out in CBI*, pp. 72–75.
[84] *Institute of Pacific Relations*, p. 1793.
[85] Romanus and Sunderland, *Time Runs Out in CBI*, p. 337.
[86] *State Department Employee Loyalty Investigation*, p. 1980.

challenging Hurley's program and recommending the arming of the Communists, George Atcheson urged, with the concurrence of all the political officers on the staff, that "the paramount and immediate consideration of military necessity should be made the basis for a further step in the policy of the United States."[87] It was, thus, military exigency that impelled American officials to stress the importance of using Communist troops and of unifying the Chinese armed forces.

It soon became clear that the unification of the military forces could be brought about only as part of a general accord between the Kuomintang and the Chinese Communist party. As General Hurley reported, "I have persuaded Chiang that in order to unite the military forces in China and prevent civil conflict it will be necessary for him and the Kuomintang and the National Government to make liberal political concessions to the Communist Party and to give them adequate representation in the National Government."[88] Or, as Service and Ludden understood it, "The aim of American policy as indicated clearly by official statements in the United States is the establishment of political unity in China as the indispensable preliminary to Chinese effective military mobilization."[89] Thus the idea of bringing about a political settlement between the two major parties in China was rooted in the desire for the effective prosecution of the war.

3. Considerations Regarding Postwar Political Relations in the Far East

From the very beginning, these military considerations were reinforced by political assumptions which led American officials to follow a policy of unification of China by peaceful means. These political considerations all related in one way or another to the postwar political structure in the Far East. One such consideration sprang from the policy of making China a great power and depending on China to become a stabilizing force in the Far East. Divided and in deep political turmoil, China obviously could not fill the role assigned to her by the United States. As an undated "briefing-book paper" prepared for the Yalta Conference noted: "An unstable, divided, and reactionary China would make stability and progress in the Far East impossible, and would greatly increase the difficult task, which will be largely ours, of maintaining peace in the Western Pacific."[90] In the American view, unity and

[87] United States Relations with China, p. 89.
[88] Ibid., p. 76.
[89] State Department Employee Loyalty Investigation, p. 1980.
[90] Department of State, Foreign Relations of the United States: The Conferences at Malta and Yalta, 1945 (Washington, D.C., Government Printing Office, 1955), p. 353 (hereafter cited as Yalta Papers). See also chap. ii, above.

strength in China could be brought about only by instituting a democratic government. This thought was spelled out in another undated "briefing-book paper."

> The American Government's long-range policy with respect to China is based on the belief that the need for China to be a principal stabilizing factor in the Far East is a fundamental requirement for peace and security in that area. Our policy is accordingly directed toward the following objectives: 1. Political: A strong stable and unified China with a government representative of the wishes of the Chinese people: a. We seek by every proper means to promote establishment of a broadly representative government which will bring about internal unity, including reconcilement of Kuomintang-Communist differences, and which will effectively discharge its internal and international responsibilities.[91]

Since President Roosevelt's grand design for the postwar world envisioned friendly co-operation with the Soviet Union, he dreaded the possibility of a progressive deterioriation of Kuomintang-Communist relations into a civil war, embroiling the United States with Russia. Sumner Welles recalled a conversation with the President in September, 1943, in which Roosevelt expressed his anxiety over the political development in China:

> But what he [the President] feared most of all was the flaring up of civil war after Japan's defeat. The danger there was that the Soviet Union would intervene in behalf of the Communists, and the Western powers would be tempted or forced in their own interest to back the anti-Communist side. We would then see, he said, very much the same situation that we had witnessed in Spain during her civil war, only on a greater scale, and with graver danger inherent in it. It was his thought that no spot was more likely to create difficulties in the postwar years than China. . . .[92]

President Roosevelt's fear of a possible Soviet-American embroilment over the question of China was widely shared by American officials. John S. Service seems to have gone further than most in his desire to avoid offending the Soviet Union for the sake of China. He wrote in a

[91] *Yalta Papers*, p. 356. These "briefing-book papers" were not read by President Roosevelt but the quotations used here did accurately reflect American policies and attitudes at that time.

[92] Sumner Welles, *Seven Decisions That Shaped History* (New York: Harper & Bros, 1950), p. 152.

report dated April 7, 1944: "In determining our policy toward Russia in Asia we should avoid being swayed by China. Neither now, nor in the immediately foreseeable future, does the United States want to find itself in direct opposition to Russia in Asia. . . ." He recommended that in her dealings with China the United States "avoid becoming involved in any way in Sino-Soviet relations; avoid all appearance of [giving] unqualified diplomatic support to China, especially vis-à-vis Russia; and limit American aid to China to direct prosecution of the war against Japan."[93] But even Service's position was not too far from the stand taken at this time by *Life* magazine which reflected the views of Henry Luce, the China-born son of a missionary whose influence on China policy was by no means negligible. An editorial of the May 1, 1944, issue of *Life* reads:

> The United States has no right to tell the Chinese government how to handle its Communists. Neither has Russia, for this is an internal matter. But the United States cannot ignore the fact that if China's government should become a fascistic, power-hungry, repressive, landlords' and usurers' government, it is all too likely to get into trouble with Russia whereas a government which stands for freedom, reform and international cooperation is not. Under no circumstances would the American people ever wish to be embroiled with the Soviet Union in a struggle in which they would feel politically on the wrong side.[94]

This fear of Soviet-American embroilment over China found expression also in a specific concern about the possibility of Russia's supporting the Chinese Communists to establish a separatist regime in North China or Manchuria. As early as January 15, 1944, John P. Davies urged the dispatch of an American military and political observers' mission to Communist China to, among other things, "assess the possibility of North China and Manchuria developing into a separate Chinese state — perhaps even as a Russian satellite."[95] A "briefing-book paper" prepared for the Yalta Conference expressed the fear that "the Russians may utilize the Chinese Communists to establish an independent or autonomous area in North China or Manchuria."[96] This anxiety was heightened by the prospect of Russia's entry into the Pacific war. As another "briefing-book paper" noted:

> It is of course highly desirable that embarrassment and difficulties, political and military, be avoided in the event of Russian

[93] *State Department Employee Loyalty Investigation*, p. 1978.
[94] "News from China," *Life*, May 1, 1944, p. 28.
[95] *United States Relations with China*, p. 564.
[96] *Yalta Papers*, pp. 351–52.

military operations in North China. The obvious and reasonable solution would be a working agreement between the Chinese Government and the Communists which would establish a unified Chinese military command to work with the Russian command.

It urged that the United States "make every effort to bring about cooperation between all Chinese forces and the Russian military command in order to prevent military developments from further widening the gap between the Communists and the Chinese Government and increasing the possibility of a disunited China."[97]

Bringing about a united and democratic China by peaceful means was thought to be the best way of mobilizing China's military power, of making China strong, avoiding embroilment with Russia, and averting a separatist Communist regime. Just as in the case of the policy of making China a great power, traditional principles, military considerations, and political planning for the postwar world appeared to converge perfectly on a program of peaceful unification of China. Peaceful unification was the keystone of the whole structure of American policies. But it was also the weakest point in the entire edifice. For, as we shall see in the next chapter, it rested on an inability to appreciate the deep political chasm dividing the two contending sides in China and on a misjudgment of the nature and intentions of the Chinese Communist party.

D. Implementation of the Policy and Its Results Prior to the Recall of Stilwell

1. American Policy during the Sharpening of Kuomintang-Communist Tension in 1943

American actions to make peace within China and to reconcile the differences between the two sides prior to the recall of Stilwell centered around three developments in this period: the sharpening of tension between the Kuomintang and the Communists in the summer of 1943; the mission of Vice President Henry A. Wallace to China; and Japan's "east China" offensive, which brought on the crisis over Stilwell. The first American endeavor in this period to discourage the Nationalists from suppressing the Communists by force was in response to a new threat of civil war in China and to Soviet expressions of concern over political developments in China. In June, 1943, the intermittent negotiations between the Nationalists and the Communists for a settlement of their differences again reached an impasse. On July 6, the American embassy in Chungking reported that Generalissimo Chiang Kai-shek was asking the Communists

[97] *Ibid.*, p. 352.

to give a conclusive answer to his demands for the relinquishment of their independent government and the incorporation of their forces with those of the Nationalist government. It also reported that Chou En-lai, the Communist representative in Chungking, charged that the Nationalist government had transferred seven more divisions to the Kuomintang-Communist frontier along the border region of Shensi-Kansu-Ninghsia. In September, the embassy reported that an important element in the Kuomintang was urging action against the Communists before the Soviet Union regained sufficient freedom to help them and was endeavoring to push through a resolution during the current session of the Central Executive Committee to force a showdown with the Communists.[98] These developments in Kuomintang-Communist relations took place after the Communist International had been dissolved in May, 1943, and after the Soviet Union had begun the withdrawal of her troops and advisers from Sinkiang in June. The Kuomintang may have been encouraged by Moscow's actions to intensify its pressure on the Chinese Communists. This heightening of tension in what the Communists called "the third anti-Communist upsurge"[99] brought into play both the military and political considerations uppermost in the minds of American officials. For it threatened to interfere with the projected North Burma campaign to open the Ledo Road into China which, in accordance with the decision of the Trident Conference at Washington in May, 1943, was to start the coming November.

Furthermore, a civil war would have greatly complicated Sino-Soviet relations and thus have threatened Soviet-American friendship. For the first time during the Pacific war, the Soviet Union unequivocally voiced

[98] The above passage had been written before the release in March, 1962, of *Foreign Relations of the United States; 1943: China.* It is based mainly on the following two works: Feis, *op. cit.,* pp. 85, 86, 88, and Charles B. McLane, *op. cit.,* p. 168. For the relevant documents, see *Foreign Relations of the United States, 1943: China,* pp. 115–18, 123, 257–58, 275–76, 277–79, 327–28.

[99] Hu Hua, *op. cit.,* pp. 221–22. The first two "anti-Communist upsurges" occurred before the American entry into World War II. According to the Communists, the Nationalist forces launched a large-scale attack against Communist areas in the winter and spring of 1939 and 1940. This is referred to as the first "anti-Communist upsurge." By the "second anti-Communist upsurge," the Communists denote the "New Fourth Army Incident" of January, 1941, in which the headquarter detachment of the Communist New Fourth Army was annihilated by a sudden Nationalist attack and the commander-in-chief of the Communist army was captured and the deputy commander was killed (*ibid.,* pp. 199–201, 206–10). See also Mao Tse-tung, *Selected Works,* III, 141–42.

Shortly after the dissolution of the Comintern in May, 1943, the Kuomintang's Central News Agency circulated a release on June 6 reporting that a cultural group sent a telegram to Mao and requested the latter to take the opportunity to dissolve the Communist party of China and to abolish the government of the border region. This release was taken most seriously by Mao (*ibid.,* pp. 120–25, 136–37).

concern over the increased internal tension in China, both through diplomatic channels and in the press. On the diplomatic front, Soviet representatives in China called at the American embassy and, following the line taken by Chou En-lai, accused the Nationalist government of seeking to impose its terms of settlement on the Communists by threat of force. They also endeavored to find out what the United States would do in the event of an outbreak of civil war, particularly with reference to American aid to the Nationalist government.[100] Meanwhile, there appeared in the Soviet press, for the first time since the outbreak of the Sino-Japanese War, articles which openly championed the cause of the Chinese Communists and criticized the Nationalist government, though refraining from an open attack on Chiang Kai-shek himself. The most important of these was an article by Vladimir Rogov, former Tass representative in China, which appeared in the August 8, 1943, issue of Moscow's *War and the Working Class*.[101] Rogov charged that the "appeasers, the defeatists and capitulators" in Chungking were doing their utmost to "incite the prosecution and rout" of the Communist forces and that the Nationalist government did "not exert firmness in overcoming the activities of the capitulators designed to undermine national unity and weaken China's resistance against Japanese aggression."[102] He praised the Chinese Communist party for its leadership in organizing the broad masses of working people in their struggle for national freedom and independence.

To discourage the Nationalist government from resorting to force, Stanley K. Hornbeck, political adviser on Far Eastern affairs in the State Department, was instructed in August, 1943, to indicate to T. V. Soong the official interest of the United States in the intentions of the Chinese government. Hornbeck informed the Chinese foreign minister that the United States was not urging the Chinese government to take action against the Communists and that, on the contrary, she hoped trouble would be avoided. Falling back on the traditional principle of non-intervention, he told Soong that "we have scrupulously refrained from urging on the Chi-

[100] Feis, *op. cit.*, p. 86; *Foreign Relations of the United States, 1943: China*, pp. 283–84, 314–15; "The Chinese Communist Movement," *Institute of Pacific Relations*, pp. 2382–84.

[101] Louis Budenz, the ex-Communist who was at one time the managing editor of the *Daily Worker*, testified before a Senate subcommittee that Moscow sent this article to the American Communist party in response to the latter's request for instruction on China policy (*State Department Employee Loyalty Investigation*, p. 492). The article was reprinted in full in *Institute of Pacific Relations*, pp. 128–30. But McLane shows conclusively that this article did not represent the beginning of a clear-cut policy of hostility toward Chungking (McLane, *op. cit.*, p. 169). For another article in *Red Star*, see *Foreign Relations of the United States, 1943: China*, pp. 282–83. Cf. David J. Dallin, *Soviet Russia and the Far East* (New Haven: Yale University Press, 1948), pp. 217–19, 220; Henry Wei, *China and Soviet Russia* (Princeton, N.J.: Van Nostrand Co., 1956), pp. 159–61.

[102] *Institute of Pacific Relations*, pp. 129–30.

nese government any particular course of action in regard to matters of Chinese internal politics."[103] George Atcheson of the American embassy in Chungking also told a high Nationalist official that the United States "viewed with concern any serious dissension among the Chinese people which might militate against the establishment and maintenance of a strong, unified China.[104]

For one reason or another, Generalissimo Chiang Kai-shek made a new pledge to follow a moderate policy toward the Chinese Communists. In the Eleventh Plenary Session of the Fifth Central Executive Committee of the Kuomintang, meeting in September, 1943, Chiang Kai-shek intervened to check the impulse of the extreme right wing to solve the Communist problem by force. He told his party: "I am of the opinion that first of all we should clearly recognize that the Chinese Communist problem is a purely political problem and should be solved by political means. Such ought to be the guiding principle of the Plenary Session in its effort to settle this matter."[105] The conclave of Kuomintang dignitaries duly obeyed the instruction of the party leader who in any case held an absolute veto over the decisions of the Central Executive Committee and a suspensive veto over those of the party Congress itself.[106]

It cannot be ascertained from available materials what weight Generalissimo Chiang gave to American advice in making this declaration. One also wonders whether the Nationalist government would have launched a large-scale attack if the United States had not made her position clear. But it would seem that, as long as the Sino-Japanese War continued, the outbreak of an all-out civil war was improbable. In most places the main Nationalist forces were separated from the Communist base areas by Japanese troops. The principal exception was the Shensi-Kansu-Ninghsia border region which had been rapidly losing its military importance in relation to the other Communist bases in North and East China, though it remained the political center of the Communist movement. An attack, even if successful, would not have given the Nationalists much military advantage. On the other hand, by totally dividing the nation in the midst of a life-and-death struggle against foreign invaders, the Nationalists would have incurred a heavy political liability. Thus, American advice may have increased the Nationalists' awareness of the political implications of an all-out civil war. But Generalissimo Chiang's habit of ignoring

[103] Feis, op. cit., pp. 87–88. Foreign Relations of the United States, 1943: China, pp. 97–98.

[104] Ibid., pp. 334–35.

[105] Ibid., p. 54.

[106] Professor Tuan-sheng Ch'ien used the term "party leader" to translate the Chinese term "tsung-ts'ai." See Government and Politics of China (Cambridge: Harvard University Press, 1950), pp. 121–23.

or evading American advice suggests that America's attitude could not have been a decisive factor in not launching a large-scale attack at this time.

Whatever the reasons, no serious armed clash ensued. Even the semi-official Communist histories of that period report only bombardment of frontier outposts and forays by Nationalist forces.[107] The failure of the Nationalists to attack on a large scale was attributed by the Communists to the mobilization in the Communist region, the power and prestige of the Communist armed forces,[108] and the timely exposure of the Nationalist plot by the Communists.[109] The single reason given in one of the earlier semi-official histories was "the aroused public opinion at home and abroad," which condemned the reactionary policy of the Nationalists.[110] This analysis followed the line laid down in an editorial dated October 5, 1943, in the Communist official organ, the *Liberation Daily*.[111]

On the surface, the first serious move made by the United States to alleviate Kuomintang-Communist tension seemed to have produced its intended effect. Indeed, the American government later interpreted Chiang's instruction to his party as an unalterable policy of the Kuomintang and on the basis of this remark and similar pronouncements attributed the American policy of peaceful unification to Chiang Kai-shek.[112] In this case, the propensity of some American officials to take Chinese pronouncements at face value and the needs of the United States policy, reinforced each other and strengthened the will to believe. But, as a matter of fact, the terms "political problem" and "solution by political means" had an entirely different meaning for Generalissimo Chiang. In its essence, to solve a problem by political means signified to him the use of military pressure to induce his opponents to accept demands made on the basis of his estimate of his military strength.[113] In any case, the nature of Chinese politics pro-

[107] *Chieh-fang-ch'ü*, p. 22.
[108] Hu Hua, *op. cit.*, p. 222.
[109] *Chieh-fang-chün*, p. 175.
[110] *Pa-lu-chün*, p. 107.
[111] Mao, *Selected Works*, III, 131–47. This editorial was written by Mao himself.
[112] *United States Relations with China*, pp. 54–55, 134–36.
[113] In September, 1949, Generalissimo Chiang feared that the governor of Yunnan, General Lu Han, would go over to the rapidly advancing Communist forces. His plan to head off this impending defection was based on the decision that, to use his words as quoted by his son, "the principle for the solution of the problem of Yunnan should be to rely primarily on politics and to avoid bloodshed." His son, Chiang Ching-kuo, explained that the Generalissimo wanted to avoid a military solution so as not to weaken further the defense against Communist forces. Chiang Ching-kuo also noted that General Lu suddenly changed his mind and agreed to come to Chungking to report to the Generalissimo because Yunnan was now surrounded by Chiang's troops and by his visit General Lu hoped to ease the military pressure against him (Chiang Ching-kuo, *Fu-chung chih-yüan* ["Carrying a Heavy Burden To Reach a Great Distance"] [1960]).

vided no other internal basis for a negotiated settlement except the balance of military forces. To seek a political solution in this sense would inevitably lead to the outbreak of a civil war when the two sides had different estimates of their own strength and when the demands of one side were not acceptable to the other.

Ambassador Gauss was under no illusion about the future of Kuomintang-Communist relations. He reported to Washington in October, 1943, that all the political factors in China pointed to but one conclusion, "the continued struggle between the two rival parties — civil war at some undetermined future date."[114] He observed that whether the civil war "will come prior to the conclusion of the war against Japan or after that date would seem to depend largely upon the Kuomintang's estimate of the possibilities of success." The Chinese Communists also arrived at the same conclusion. Analyzing Chiang's remarks, an editorial of the official organ of the Communist party suggested that the Kuomintang leaders were probably "stalling for the time being and fighting the Communists in the future."[115] They were forced, it continued, to postpone the civil war for the following reason: "Civil war means capitulation [to Japan]. . . . the Chinese people support Resistance [against Japan] and oppose civil war. . . . they [the Kuomintang leaders] are facing the grave crisis of being isolated as never before because the Kuomintang has severed itself from the masses and lost the allegiance of the people; and the United States, Great Britain and the Soviet Union are at one in opposing the Chinese government's attempt to start civil war."[116]

Meanwhile, after 1943 the influence of the Chinese Communists spread and the size of their armed forces increased by leaps and bounds. Information to this effect was conveyed to Washington by American observers in China.[117] These reports have since been confirmed by semi-official Communist histories. According to these, the year of 1943 was a turning point in the fortunes of the Communist party. It marked the beginning of a new phase of expansion, reversing the downward trend of the previous two years. In 1941 and 1942, the annihilation campaigns of the Japanese armies had pressed the Communists hard. The size of the Eighth Route Army had decreased from 540,000 to 300,000 [118] and the population in the "liberated areas" had contracted to less than 50,000,000. The loss of Communist cadres was reported as "high" and the financial and economic condition

[114] Foreign Relations of the United States, 1943: China, p. 357.
[115] Mao Tse-tung, Selected Works, IV (London: Lawrence and Wishart, 1956), 135.
[116] Ibid., pp. 135–36.
[117] Feis, op. cit., p. 91.
[118] Chu Teh, On the Battlefronts of the Liberated Areas (Peking: Foreign Language Press, 1952). This is an English translation of General Chu's military report made on April 25, 1945, at the Seventh Congress of the Chinese Communist party.

"extremely difficult."[119] The serious famine in North China compelled the soldiers and people in hard-hit areas to eat grass roots and tree bark. In contrast to this low ebb, the new phase from 1943 to 1945 saw a rapid expansion of Communist forces, a sharp increase of population under their control, and a new growth of the militia.[120] This period of Communist expansion coincided with Japan's "east China" offensive and with intensified American efforts to check Nationalist attempts to suppress the Communists and to bring the two sides together.

2. The Wallace Mission

The Wallace mission to China in June, 1944, the second move by the United States to compose Kuomintang-Communist differences, had its origins in the same set of considerations that governed American policy throughout the war: to enable China to make a greater military effort and to help harmonize Sino-Soviet relations. Characteristically, it was conceived at a time when the war in the China-Burma-India theater was not going well and Sino-Soviet relations showed new signs of strain. In North Burma, the Chinese-American offensive to open the Ledo Road was stalled after the capture of the Myitkyina airfield in May, 1944, and the Chinese offensive west of the Salween River was contained by the Japanese. In "east China," the Japanese armies launched a powerful offensive in April to capture the American airfields and to open secure land communications from Peiping to Canton and Indochina. By the end of June, when Wallace arrived in China, the Chinese armies in the province of Hunan had been routed and the capital of Hunan had been captured.

In the same period, border incidents occurred between the Chinese province of Sinkiang and Soviet-controlled Outer Mongolia. The Soviet government also showed its antipathy toward the Nationalist government by rejecting an American request to send supplies to American air forces in China over the land route through Russian Turkestan. On his part, Chiang complained to the United States that the Communists were making preparations for an attack on Sian, a Nationalist stronghold blockading the Communist border region of Shensi-Kansu-Ninghsia. He expressed his belief that they were emboldened by a secret understanding with the Soviet Union. In contrast to the steady deterioration in Sino-Soviet relations, Russia concluded in March, 1944, an agreement with Japan, settling the long unsolved questions of the Siberian fisheries and the oil and coal concessions in northern Sakhalin. This action further aroused the anxiety of Chiang. Against this background, Wallace was told to do what he

[119] Lo Chia, *Chung-kuo kê-ming chung ti wu-chuang tou-chêng* ["The Armed Struggle in the Chinese Revolution"] (Shanghai: Hua-tung jên-min ch'u-pan-shê, 1954), pp. 40–41. Also, *Chieh-fang chün*, p. 175; *Pa-lu-chün*, pp. 167–68.
[120] Lo Chia, *op. cit.*, p. 42.

could to bring the Chinese Nationalists and Communists together and to restore mutual trust between the Soviet Union and China.[121]

The Wallace mission is significant, not because of its results, but because of the materials which it provides for an understanding of the complex relationship between the United States, the Soviet Union, the Nationalist government, and the Chinese Communists. Shortly before Wallace arrived in China, Ambassador W. Averell Harriman was instructed by President Roosevelt to discuss the question of China with Soviet leaders with a view to enlisting their support for reconciling the two sides. In his response to Harriman's remarks and questions, Stalin appeared to give complete indorsement to American policy in China and to American leadership in Chinese affairs. Stalin reaffirmed his opinion, expressed once before at the Teheran Conference, that Chiang was the best man available in China and should be supported. He criticized Chiang only for the latter's failure to use the Chinese Communists in the fight against Japan. He thought Chiang foolish in quarreling with the Communists on ideological grounds. He said with a laugh: "The Chinese Communists are not real Communists. They are 'margarine' Communists. Nevertheless, they are real patriots and they want to fight Japan."[122]

After Wallace arrived at Chungking, he conveyed to Generalissimo Chiang President Roosevelt's wish that the Nationalists and the Communists should compose their differences. The American motives in urging a reconciliation between the two warring Chinese parties were made clear in Wallace's remarks that "we are not interested in 'Chinese Communists' but are interested in the prosecution of the war"[123] and that "there should not be left pending any question which might result in conflict between China and the U.S.S.R."[124] He told the leader of the Kuomintang that the President felt that, inasmuch as the Communists and the Nationalists were all Chinese, they were basically friends and that "nothing should be final between friends." He informed Chiang of Roosevelt's willingness to be called in as "a friend" to mediate the differences between the two Chinese parties.[125] To convince Chiang of the soundness of the American policy, Wallace mentioned to him Ambassador Harriman's conversation with Stalin. In a separate talk, John Carter Vincent, who accompanied Wallace on his visit to China, told T. V. Soong of the gist of the same conversation.

In response to Wallace's suggestion of a reconciliation with the Communists, Chiang at the next two meetings made a somewhat lengthy ap-

[121] Feis, *op. cit.*, pp. 136–40, 145. Also, *United States Relations with China*, pp. 55–56; Wei, *op. cit.*, pp. 158–61, 164–66.

[122] Feis, *op. cit.*, pp. 140–41. Also, Herbert Feis, *Churchill-Roosevelt-Stalin* (Princeton, N.J.: Princeton University Press, 1957), pp. 407–8.

[123] *United States Relations with China*, p. 555.

[124] *Ibid.*, p. 550.

[125] *Ibid.*, p. 549.

praisal of the nature and intentions of the Chinese Communist party and American policy. He tried his best to convince Wallace and Vincent that the Chinese Communist party was part of the international Communist movement. According to Vincent's notes, Chiang said that "the Chinese people did not regard the Communists as Chinese, but regard them as 'internationalists,' subject to the orders of the Third International," notwithstanding the dissolution of the latter organization. The view that the Chinese Communists were not tied to the Soviet Union and were in fact nothing more than "agrarian democrats" was, in Chiang's opinion, "clever Communist propaganda." Somewhat jokingly he remarked that "the Chinese Communists were more communistic than the Russian Communists." Chiang also endeavored to persuade Wallace that the aim of the Communists was to capture power in China. According to Chiang, the Communists were now convinced that the defeat of Japan was certain and thus hoped for the collapse of the Kuomintang prior to the end of the war, which would "enable them to seize power." Their propaganda and subversive actions had lowered the morale of the Chinese people and the army.[126] But Chiang made a renewed pledge to solve the Communist problems by political means. He also expressed his willingness to let President Roosevelt mediate the Kuomintang-Communist conflict.[127]

Chiang also attempted to delineate for his American audience the international complications confronting him in dealing with the Communists. This analysis can be reconstructed as follows: The Nationalist government could not openly criticize the Communists for their connection with the Third International because it was afraid of offending the Soviet Union. This handicap was counterbalanced by the fact that the Communists could not openly use the Soviet Union for support. But the Communists gained an advantage when they succeeded in using the United States and American opinion to force the Kuomintang to accede to their demands. For the American government had put much pressure on the Nationalist government to reach an agreement with the Communists, but not on the Communists. This attitude arose from a basic misunderstanding of the Chinese situation due to the influence of Communist propaganda, a failure to realize "the threat which the Communists constituted to the Chinese government," and an overestimation of the "utility of the Communists against the Japanese." Chiang suggested that the United States adopt an attitude of "coolness" toward the Communists and issue a statement that the Communists should come to terms with the Chinese government.[128]

It is interesting to note that, as late as the Wallace mission, the idea of establishing a coalition command or government including the Chinese

[126] Ibid., pp. 552–53.
[127] Ibid., p. 559.
[128] Ibid., pp. 553–54.

Communists was not unequivocally an element of American policy. During his conversations with Chiang, Wallace merely stressed the need for working out a settlement with the Communists but did not suggest any specific solution. Both Wallace and Vincent urged on Chiang the importance of taking measures to improve the economic lot of the Chinese people. Vincent specifically stated that the best defense against communism in China was agrarian reform.[129]

After Wallace left Chungking, he recommended in a telegram sent from Kunming on June 26 that President Roosevelt accept Chiang's proposal to appoint a personal representative to work with Chiang on both military and political matters, to command all American forces in China, and to bring about full co-ordination of American and Chinese military efforts.[130] He told the President that Stilwell did not enjoy the confidence of Chiang and could not serve in that capacity. Wallace's first thought was to recommend the appointment of General Chennault whose name was suggested by Vincent.[131] But Joseph Alsop, who was sent by General Chennault to act as Wallace's escort, pointed out that the War Department would oppose Chennault's appointment. Then Wallace recommended in his cable that Wedemeyer, for whom Chiang had expressed admiration, be selected.[132] In a final report submitted to President Roosevelt on July 10, Wallace proposed that American policy "should not be limited to support of the government" which was, in essence, "a coalition headed by Chiang and supported by the landlords, the warlord group most closely associated with landlords, and the Chiang group of bankers."[133] Instead, Wallace recommended that the United States support "a new coalition" consisting of progressive banking and commercial leaders, the large group of Western-trained men, and "the considerable group of generals and other officers who are neither subservient to the landlords nor afraid of the peasantry."[134] As persons falling into the last group he named Generals Ch'ên Chêng, at present the Vice President of the Republic and President of the Executive Yüan on Taiwan, Chang Fa-kwei, and Pai Ch'ung-hsi.[135] He envisaged the use of American military and economic aid as a lever to help build this new coalition. As to the role to be played by Chiang, Wallace stated that "if he retains the political sensitivity and ability to call the

[129] *Ibid.*, p. 556.
[130] *Institute of Pacific Relations*, p. 1371.
[131] Vincent's testimony, *ibid.*, pp. 1812–13.
[132] Wallace's testimony, *ibid.*, pp. 1365–71; Alsop's testimony, *ibid.*, pp. 1447–48. See also Joseph Alsop, "The Strange Case of Louis Budenz," *Atlantic Monthly*, April, 1952, pp. 29–33.
[133] *Institute of Pacific Relations*, p. 1384.
[134] *Ibid.*
[135] *Ibid.*, p. 1368. General Stilwell also believed that Pai Ch'ung-hsi was a possible successor to Chiang (Charles F. Romanus and Riley Sunderland, *Stilwell's Command Problem* [Washington, D.C.: Government Printing Office, 1956], p. 444).

turn . . . he will swing over to the new coalition and head it," and that "if not, the new coalition, in the natural course of events will produce its own leader."[136] In Wallace's suggestion of economic reforms and the use of American assistance to help build a new political coalition, the American government had a program which, if it had been adopted and given priority over the effort to seek a settlement with the Communists, might have altered the political alignment in Nationalist China and brought about a new non-Communist coalition as a counterweight to the growing power of the Communists. But the President's policy laid the stress on reaching a settlement with the Communists. Soon the acute military crisis created by Japan's "east China" offensive led President Roosevelt and the State Department to seek actively military co-operation from the Communists and, for this purpose, to persuade Chiang to set up a coalition command and a coalition government.

It seems clear that the effect of Chiang's assurances to Wallace was to strengthen President Roosevelt's conviction of the feasibility of a settlement between the Kuomintang and the Communists. As President Roosevelt's message to Chiang after Wallace's return suggested, Chiang's pledges stood for nothing less than a prelude to the effective prosecution of the war on the part of China, an improvement in Sino-Soviet relations, and and early implementation of a "democratic program" in China.[137] But as the negotiations between the Kuomintang and the Communists showed, Chiang wished to impose a political settlement which would insure the ultimate destruction of the Communists. Gauss told Washington shortly after the Wallace mission: "In its essence the struggle [between the Kuomintang and the Chinese Communist party] is one in which the Central government is apparently seeking by political means to encompass the destruction of the Communists, while the latter are by the same means struggling to insure their survival."[138] This basic divergence in the American and Nationalist approaches to the Communist question rendered valueless Chiang's expression of his willingness to let the United States act as a mediator. Chiang would have sincerely welcomed American mediation only if he could have persuaded the United States to support his political program or maneuvered her into accepting it. But this proved to be impossible, and General Marshall was to find that the Nationalists were as much responsible as the Communists for the breakdown of his attempts to solve the Communist question by political means in accordance with America's conceptions.

The Wallace mission did not have its intended moderating effect on the negotiations then going on between the Kuomintang and the Chinese

[136] Institute of Pacific Relations, p. 1384.
[137] United States Relations with China, p. 360.
[138] Feis, The China Tangle, p. 164.

Communist party. As indicated by Chiang's remarks to Wallace, the terms of the Nationalist government remained the incorporation of the Communist forces within the army of the central government and the reincorporation of territory then under Communist control as "an integral part of China administratively." In return, the Communists would be granted the uncertain privilege of becoming a legal political party and the precarious freedoms of assembly and discussion.[139] As the government's proposal of June 5, 1944, showed, Chiang was willing to allow the Communists to keep ten divisions of their armed forces, out of a regular force of 470,000 men and a "people's militia corps" of 2,000,000 men which the Communists claimed to have.[140] The rest were to be disbanded by a specific date set by the Nationalist government. More important, the ten divisions of Communist forces "must be concentrated for service within a certain specified period" and they "must obey the orders" of the Nationalist government.[141] The Nationalist government also wanted the power to appoint or remove the highest official in the Communist area.[142] The Communists objected as vehemently to the provision regarding the concentration of their forces for service within a specified period as to that concerning the disbandment of the rest of their troops. If actually carried out, the "concentration of their forces for service" might very well have meant a rapid contraction of the areas under the control of these forces and was probably designed by the Nationalists to have that effect. In other words, what the government demanded from the Communists was a first step in self-destruction, dressed up by attractive legalistic formulas about constitutional guarantees and the administrative integrity of the government.

At the same time, the Wallace mission did not restrain the Communists from pushing their claims. On the contrary, it resulted in the dispatch of the American army observer mission to Yenan, which Mao welcomed because of "its political effect upon the Kuomintang." [143] The terms proposed by the Communists for a settlement were at the opposite pole from Chiang's. What they wanted from the government was, on the one hand, recognition of the Communist-controlled governments in North China and provision by the government of material aid and lend-lease supply to the Communist forces and, on the other hand, an opportunity to extend their influence in Nationalist China as a legal political party enjoying the freedoms of speech, the press, assembly, and association.[144] These de-

[139] *United States Relations with China*, pp. 553–54.
[140] *Ibid.*, pp. 534, 545, 546.
[141] *Ibid.*, p. 534.
[142] *Ibid.*
[143] Mao's remark to Service as quoted in Feis, *The China Tangle*, p. 162.
[144] *United States Relations with China*, pp. 535–36.

mands had been presented by the Communists before Wallace arrived in China. Naturally, the Wallace mission did nothing to cause the Communists to lower their demands. As a matter of fact, the Communists steadily raised their price for a settlement as their power grew and the influence of the government declined. This was vividly portrayed in a letter sent by the Nationalist negotiators to the Communist representative:

> But the real reason for the divergence [of views between the two sides] is the steady increase in the number of requests of the Chinese Communist Party. What you asked at Sian [in early May, 1944] was more than what Divisional Commander Lin [Lin Piao of the Communist army] asked for last year. The 12 points raised by the Chinese Communist Party [in early June, 1944] outnumber the requests you made at Sian. The present letter [of the Communist representative dated August 30, 1944] adds the eight so-called verbal requests to the 12 points. Since requests increase with time, the divergence of views naturally widens. Take for instance the question of North Shensi Border Area and other anti-Japanese bases.[145] Divisional Commander Lin requested that the *North Shensi Border Area* be turned into an administrative area within the original area, and all the other areas be reorganized and obey the laws and orders of the National government. The document you signed at Sian did not contain [mention?] other anti-Japanese bases. The 12-point proposal of the Chinese Communist Party asks for the recognition of Shensi-Kansu-Ningsia Border Area and the Anti-Japanese Governments elected by the People in *North China Bases*. Your letter now seeks the recognition of Shensi-Kansu-Ningsia Border Area and the Anti-Japanese Governments elected by the people in Anti-Japanese Bases behind the enemy lines in *North, Central, and South China*. Under such conditions of steady changes and gradual expansion of requests, which side should be responsible if the conversations cannot be brought to a successful conclusion?[146]

Furthermore, the Communists declared that they would certainly demand that the government recognize the legitimacy of all the armies and governments in the "liberated areas" and that these armies and governments would surely expand with time. They justified their increased demands on the basis of their "achievements" in the anti-Japanese war and the need for building up their armies to fight the common enemy. Sarcastically, they asked the Nationalists: Why did the government want to disband the

---

[145] These are euphemisms for territories under Communist control.
[146] *United States Relations with China*, p. 542. Emphasis added.

military forces which had won battles (meaning, of course, the Communist forces)? Why did the government refuse to grant formal recognition to areas liberated from the Japanese (meaning, the Communist bases)? [147] In other words, in the name of the "needs of resistance against Japan," the Communists demanded government recognition of what they had already gained; and in the name of "democracy" they asked the Nationalist government to allow them to expand their power in areas still under government control.[148]

Wallace's and Vincent's advice on the need for economic reforms went unheeded by the Nationalist government. At this time, Chiang still did not realize the significance of agrarian reform for the stability of his regime, because he made a fundamentally erroneous appraisal of the factors contributing to the spread of Communist influence. He wrote in his diary on October 21, 1944:

> The essentials of the organization of the Communist Party are: (1) violence (i.e., oppression) and ruthless killing; (2) special agents (i.e., control and surveillance) and repression. The purposes of its training are: (1) elimination of nationalistic spirit and development of internationalist spirit (destruction of the nation's history and ethics), (2) elimination of human nature and development of animal nature (arbitrarily dividing the society into classes and causing hatred and struggle). . . .[149]

In an entry in his diary a day before, he conceded that the Chinese Communists achieved a certain amount of success in establishing a dictatorship, in controlling the society ,and in increasing production in Northern Shensi. But he believed that in the areas behind the Japanese lines they could only develop their secret organizations and that their control over the people could not last long. These appraisals emphasized the Communist apparatus of control, which was only one reason for Communist success. They failed to note the popular support enjoyed by the Communists, which the United States army intelligence report so vividly described.[150] He apparently felt that, once their military power was broken, the Communists would be destroyed. Thus, he concluded that "only if our armies reach these areas, the

---

[147] Letter dated October 13, 1944, from Mr. Lin Tsu-han of the Chinese Communist party to Mr. Wang Shih-chieh and General Chang Chih-chung, representatives of the Nationalist government in the Kuomintang-Communist negotiations (*Kuo Kung t'an-p'an chên-hsiang* ["The Real Facts of the Kuomintang-Communist Negotiations"] Hsin-hua shu-tien, pp. 5–6). Each document in this collection is numbered separately.

[148] *United States Relations with China*, pp. 536–46.

[149] Quoted in Chiang Ching-kuo, *Wo-ti fu-ch'in* ["My Father"] (Taipei, Taiwan, 1956), printed for private circulation, chap. iii, p. 2.

[150] "The Chinese Communist Movement," *Institute of Pacific Relations*, pp. 2336–37.

people will welcome our liberating them." He even believed that, when they had an opportunity, many Communist party members and cadres would come over to his side.[151] Thus, he placed his hopes exclusively on a successful military campaign while he professed to seek a political solution. It was only in May, 1949, when the Communist forces had already crossed the Yangtze River, that Chiang made plans to implement a program of agrarian reform in Taiwan.[152] Thus, Chiang did not see the urgency of reforms until time had run out. As a result, the Nationalists could not win either in the sphere of political competition or on the battlefield.

3. The Intensified Effort during the "East China" Crisis of 1944

The third round of American efforts to make peace within China was an integral part of the American program to deal with the deepening military crisis in "east China," brought about by the Japanese offensive. The first phase of this offensive was started by the Japanese on April 19 to clear the Chinese off the section of the Peiping-Hankow railway south of the Yellow River. The second phase of the offensive began on May 27 with a drive on Changsha.[153] On June 28, 1944, four days after Wallace left Chungking, the Japanese armies opened an attack on Hengyang, the gateway stronghold to Kweilin, the principal air base in "east China." [154] The military crisis deepened as the Japanese marched toward Kweilin and appeared to pose a serious threat to the wartime capital at Chungking and the Hump terminal at Kunming. This critical situation led to increasingly active efforts on the part of the United States to bring the Nationalists and the Communists together.

On July 1, General Marshall asked Stilwell what the latter would think of transferring his principal efforts from Burma to "the rehabilitation and in effect the direction of the leadership of the Chinese forces in China proper." [155] Marshall's term "Chinese forces" meant both the Nationalist and Communist forces and was so understood by Stilwell.[156] In asking Stilwell for his reaction to this proposal, Marshall adopted the recommendation made on June 30 by the Operations Division of the War Department General Staff that Stilwell be promoted from lieutenant general to full general and put in command of all Chinese forces. Thus, the initiative

---

[151] Quoted in Chiang Ching-kuo, Wo-ti fu-ch'in, chap. iii, p. 1.

[152] Chiang Ching-kuo, Fu-chung chih-yüan, p. 110. In the China Aid Act of 1948, the United States set aside 10 per cent of the money authorized for the purpose of starting an agrarian reform program in China.

[153] Romanus and Sunderland, Stilwell's Command Problems, pp. 319, 322, 372.

[154] Ibid., p. 399.

[155] Ibid., p. 380.

[156] Letter from Riley Sunderland, dated January 8, 1962.

for using the Communist forces under the command of Stilwell came from the Operations Division via Marshall.

Stilwell was not averse to the idea of using the Communist forces. Twice before, when the military prospect looked bleak, he had turned to this notion as a possible solution of his troubles. When in April, 1942, there was no hope of having an American division assigned to him to strengthen his hand in Burma, he made the casual remark to his staff that he wished he had some Chinese Communist troops in Burma and that he was sure they would accept orders from him.[157] Again in September, 1943, when the Japanese armies were increasing their pressure in the Yangtze Valley, General Stilwell submitted a detailed plan to the Generalissimo to forestall a Japanese drive, a plan which included the use of Communist troops to execute a diversionary attack in Northwest China. For this purpose, he proposed that the Communists be given supplies from the stocks of arms and ammunition in the possession of the Nationalist government.[158] This proposal for the use of Communist forces was made at a time when the tension between the two parties reached a high point and when an important faction in the Kuomintang was urging the party to use force to suppress the Chinese Communists.[159] Needless to say, Stilwell's suggestion was rejected by the Generalissimo. Whether by coincidence or not, a serious move to have Stilwell recalled started shortly afterward.[160]

Now the "east China" crisis led the Operations Division and General Marshall to adopt the idea of using Communist forces without any prompting by Stilwell or any of his associates.[161] In response to Marshall's proposal, Stilwell told his superior:

> [E]ven with complete authority [to be conferred upon Stilwell over the Chinese armies], the damage done [in "east China"] is so tremendous that I see only one chance to repair it. This is to stage a counteroffensive from Shansi, and attacking through Loyang toward Chengchow and Hankow. . . . The Communists should also participate in Shansi, but unless the Generalissimo makes an agreement with them, they won't. Two years ago, they offered to fight with me. They might listen now.[162]

On the recommendation of the Joint Chiefs of Staff, President Roosevelt told the Generalissimo, in a message dated July 6, to place Stilwell in command of all Chinese forces.[163] This proposal meant that lend-lease

---

[157] Romanus and Sunderland, *Stilwell's Mission to China*, p. 121.
[158] *Ibid.*, pp. 367–69.
[159] See pp. 157–59, above.
[160] Romanus and Sunderland, *Stilwell's Mission to China*, pp. 371–72, 374–76.
[161] Romanus and Sunderland, *Stilwell's Command Problems*, p. 420.
[162] *Ibid.*, p. 380.
[163] *Ibid.*, p. 383. See also Feis, *The China Tangle*, p. 170.

supplies would go to the Communist forces once they formed part of Stilwell's command.[164] As the President explained in another message, "When the enemy is pressing us toward possible disaster, it appears unsound to refuse the aid of anyone who will kill Japanese."[165]

Thus a complicating factor was injected into the already extremely difficult task of negotiating with the Generalissimo. While initially Chiang professed to agree "in principle" with the President's demand for the appointment of Stilwell, he made it clear almost from the beginning that he would not consent to the use of Communist forces.[166] On a later occasion he pleaded with Ambassador Gauss that the United States should not stress the need for Communist forces to defeat Japan, for "the Chinese Communists are under the influence of a foreign power." He indicated to Gauss his belief that the problem of Communist co-operation would not be solved by the appointment of a foreign commander of Chinese armies.[167]

But in spite of these facts, it was not the proposal to use Communist forces that was the primary cause of the breakdown of negotiations over Stilwell's appointment, as our analysis in Part I, chapter iv, tries to show. The crucial effect of the intensified effort to push through the plan to use Communist forces lay rather in the political sphere. This was the strong impetus given to the idea of granting the Communists participation in some responsible organ with real authority in the central government. Clearly, the use of Communist forces would be impossible without some sort of political agreement between the two sides, giving the Communists a voice in making decisions regarding the prosecution of the war. Stilwell recognized this and told Marshall that, unless the Generalissimo reached some sort of agreement with the Communists, they would not participate in a counterattack to relieve the critical situation in "east China."[168] On July 14, a week after he had proposed the use of Communist forces, President Roosevelt appealed to Generalissimo Chiang to reach a "working agreement" with the Communists.[169]

[164] Ibid., p. 171, n. 12. On August 31 and September 4, the War Department told Stilwell that it was prepared to give lend-lease supplies to a Chinese army which might include Communists (Romanus and Sunderland, Stilwell's Command Problems, pp. 420, 423).

[165] United States Relations with China, p. 67.

[166] Feis, The China Tangle, p. 172.

[167] United States Relations with China, p. 561. In summarizing Ambassador Gauss' report of Generalissimo Chiang's conversation, Feis represented Chiang as having indicated to Gauss that "it would be useless if — in order to fight the Japanese — China were turned over to the Communists" (Feis, The China Tangle, p. 176). Though no statement in the paraphrased version of Gauss' report as printed in the United States Relations with China corresponds exactly to the sentence quoted by Feis, this latter observation was certainly implicit in all the arguments made by Chiang.

[168] Romanus and Sunderland, Stilwell's Command Problems, p. 380.

[169] United States Relations with China, p. 560.

The wide gap between Roosevelt's advice and Chiang's inclinations is vividly revealed in the following entry in Chiang's diary in August:

> So long as I am alive and healthy, the nation will have a future. Although the Communist party has an international background and mysterious plots, one day it will ultimately come to a dead end. There is no need to be unduly anxious, if only I can bear the abuses and wait for the opportune moment. If the time comes when there is no other alternative, then the only way to deal with the situation is to cut the entangled hemp with a sharp knife. At this time, all sacrifices will not be begrudged, even if there is the danger of destroying the nation and ruining the family.[170]

In a conversation with the Generalissimo on August 30, Ambassador Gauss informed the Nationalist leader that the American government was "interested in seeing a prompt solution of a Chinese internal problem which finds the Chinese armed forces facing each other instead of facing and making war on Japan." He suggested that as a first step toward the unification of China "some form of responsible war council" be established to give representation and a share of responsibility to various parties and groups.[171] In response to Ambassador Gauss' report and after consulting the President, Secretary Hull told the ambassador to inform Generalissimo Chiang that the President and the Secretary thought Mr. Gauss' suggestion of a coalition council "timely as well as practical and worthy of careful consideration."[172] Acting on this instruction, Gauss made on September 15 another attempt to persuade the Generalissimo to form a "united council of all Chinese parties" for joint conduct of the war.[173]

Meanwhile, the Communists raised their political price for a settlement in proportion as their power increased and the "east China" crisis deepened. In November, 1943, the Chinese Communist party asked, in the realm of political affairs, only for "a legitimate status under the *Program of Armed Resistance and National Reconstruction*" and the enforcement of the Three Principles of the People.[174] This "Program" was the wartime declaration of policy adopted by the Kuomintang congress in 1938. It did no more than grant to the people the freedoms of speech, the press, and assembly "within the limits of Dr. Sun Yat-sen's revolutionary principles or the provisions of the law," while placing all wartime power "under the control

---

[170] Quoted in Chiang Ching-kuo, *Wo-ti fu-ch'in*, chap. iii, pp. 4–5. The Chinese phrase translated here "to cut the entangled hemp with a sharp knife" is very commonly used to denote drastic action and has a meaning somewhat similar to the phrase "cutting the Gordian knot."

[171] *United States Relations with China*, p. 562.

[172] *Ibid.*, p. 563.

[173] Feis, *The China Tangle*, p. 187.

[174] *United States Relations with China*, p. 533.

of the Kuomintang and of General Chiang Kai-shek." [175] In other words, the Communists were merely asking for the enforcement of the limited, vague guaranties of freedom promised by the Kuomintang to the Chinese people and a legal status under Nationalist rule. In contrast to this mild request, the Communists asked, on June 6, 1944, the government "to adopt democracy and safeguard the freedoms of speech, the press, assembly, association, and person . . . to recognize the legal status of the Chinese Communist Party . . . to set free political offenders," and "to permit the people to enforce local self government." [176] Not only were a number of important demands added, but the freedoms and the legal status of the party, as well as other things, were demanded as a matter of right and no longer on the basis of the Kuomintang "Program." Then, in the wake of American advice to Chiang to broaden the base of his government, the Communists also called for a reorganization of the government. While it cannot be ascertained whether or to what extent the Communists were emboldened by the American stand, there is no doubt that the United States and the Chinese Communist party, each for its own reasons, suggested quite similar concrete programs to ward off the crisis confronting China.

Only half a month after Gauss had first urged Chiang to establish "some form of war council" to give representation to various parties, Mr. Lin Tsu-han, one of the chief Communist representatives in Chungking, expressed his hope in the People's Political Council on September 15 that the Kuomintang immediately relinquish one-party rule and organize a coalition government composed of representatives of all anti-Japanese parties.[177] Subsequently, Mao and the party historians following him traced the Communists' formal demand for the establishment of a coalition government to Lin's speech.[178] But at the time the Communists' policy on the question of coalition government was not so definite as it appears in Mao's

[175] *The China Year Book, 1938–1939* (Chungking: Commercial Press, 1939), pp. 337–38.

[176] *United States Relations with China*, p. 535.

[177] "Report by Comrade Lin Tsu-han concerning the negotiations between the Kuomintang and the Chinese Communist Party to the Peoples' Political Council," *Kuo Kung t'an-p'an chên-hsiang*, p. 11. This part of the speech does not appear in the translation of Mr. Lin's report as published on pp. 544–48 of the *United States Relations with China*, which took it from *China Handbook 1937–1945*, a government publication.

[178] Mao, *Selected Works*, IV, 267. A Communist history of the period, written after the event, stated that Lin Po-chu (Lin Tsu-han) demanded in September, 1944, at a meeting of the Peoples' Political Council, the establishment of "a coalition government." Another Communist history also said that in September, 1944, the Chinese Communist party called for "the reorganization of the National Government and the High Command and the establishment of a coalition government." See Hu Chiao-mo, *Chung-kuo Kung-ch'an-tang t'i san-shih nien* ["The Thirty Years of the Chinese Communist Party"] (Peking: Jên-min ch'u-pan-shê, 1951), p. 48; Hu Hua, *op. cit.*, p. 229.

and the party historians' version of history. The comments of an "observer" in Yenan and the editorial of the Communist official organ there did not put forward the slogan of coalition government. They merely demanded the convening of an emergency conference on national affairs, the abolition of the oligarchic rule "of the Kuomintang and a thorough reorganization of the National government and high command."[179] It would seem that the slogan of coalition government was first raised by Communist representatives in Chungking on their own initiative. They were on the scene, maintained close liaison with the small parties and groups, and were in a better position to detect any developments in Chinese sentiments and American policy. It was only after Lin's speech had elicited positive response from the small parties and groups and approximately one month after Gauss had advised Chiang on September 15 to form a "united council of all Chinese parties" that Chou En-lai, in a speech on October 10, called for the end of the "one-party dictatorship" and the establishment of a "coalition government" which was to be empowered to reorganize the high command, to invite the representatives of all principal armed forces to participate in it, and, thus, to organize a "coalition high command."[180] On October 13, Mr. Lin Tsu-han, who was the chief Communist representative in the negotiations with the Kuomintang, formally demanded the establishment of a coalition government in a letter to the Nationalist negotiators.[181] Chou's speech and Lin's formal demand were made at a time when the military crisis in China was heightened by the rapid Japanese advance toward Kweilin, the principal American air base and the military and political center in "east China." Thus, the demand for establishment of a coalition government made its first official appearance as an item in the Kuomintang-Communist negotiations.

[179] "The Comments of an Observer in Yenan on the Military Situation in China," September 21, 1944, dispatch of the Hsin-hua News Agency, *Kuo Kung t'an-p'an chên-hsiang*, p. 4. Editorial of the Chieh-fang jih-pao, September 24, 1944, *ibid.*, p. 7. The "observer" is quite possibly Mao or some other highly placed Communist.
[180] Chou En-lai, "What Are the Solutions?" a speech commemorating the Double Ten Day, 1944 (*ibid.*, p. 8).
[181] Letter from Lin Po-chu to General Chang and Mr. Wang, October 13, 1944, *ibid.*, p. 3.

CHAPTER VI

THE

AMERICAN

IMAGE OF

CHINESE

COMMUNISM

AND

THE

AMERICAN

POLITICAL

TRADITION

A. Hurley's Optimism and His Program of Seeking a Political Settlement Favorable to the Nationalists

The recall of Stilwell meant a defeat of the Stilwell-Marshall tactics of pressure.[1] It entailed no change in the American policy of peaceful unification of China. As a matter of fact, General Hurley, in his capacity first as Roosevelt's special representative and later as American ambassador to China, pursued that policy vigorously. In Hurley's scheme of priorities, political unification of China was subordinate to the over-all objective of sustaining the Nationalist government. To him the American policy was, to use his own formulation:

(1) to prevent the collapse of the National Government; (2) to sustain Chiang Kai-shek as President of the Republic and Generalissimo of the Armies; (3) to harmonize relations between the Generalissimo and the American commander; (4) to promote pro-

[1] See chap. iv, above.

duction of war supplies in China and prevent economic collapse; and (5) to unify all the military forces of China for the purpose of defeating Japan.[2]

This understanding of American policy was accepted as "sound" by Secretary of State Edward Stettinius who told Hurley that the latter's information and comments had given him "a valuable insight into the problems" of China.[3] In February, 1945, Hurley reported to Washington: "I am convinced that our government was right in its decision to support the National Government of China and the leadership of Chiang Kai-shek. I have not agreed to any principles or supported any method that in my opinion would weaken the National Government or the leadership of Chiang Kai-shek."[4] Hurley's program was sustained by both Roosevelt and Truman. Hurley's scheme of priorities was apparently related to the thought that, as he had told Roosevelt in November, 1943, "it is advisable . . . to give consideration to the relative importance placed by the Chinese Central Government upon conserving its strength for maintenance of its postwar internal supremacy as against the more immediate objective of defeating Japan."[5]

As a means of sustaining the leadership of Chiang Kai-shek, Hurley's plan consisted of two essential elements. First, he would supply the Communist forces only after conclusion of an agreement between the two parties to which Chiang would freely assent. As he reported to the secretary of state on January 31, 1945: "In all my negotiations with the Communists, I have insisted that the United States will not supply or otherwise aid the Chinese Communists as a political party or as an insurrection against the National Government. Any aid to the Communist Party from the United States must go to that Party through the National Government of China."[6] Or as he stated his position at a press conference in Chungking on February 15, 1945: "My policy is this, that we would not give assistance to any individual, to any activity or any organization within the China Theatre.

[2] Cable from Hurley to Secretary Stettinius, December 23, 1944, Senate Committee on Armed Services and Committee on Foreign Relations, Hearings on the Military Situation in the Far East, 81st Cong., 2d sess. (1951), pp. 2908–09 (hereafter cited as Military Situation in the Far East).

[3] Ibid., p. 2908.

[4] Department of State, United States Relations with China (Washington, D. C.: Government Printing Office, 1949), p. 62 (hereafter cited as United States Relations with China).

[5] Hurley to the President, November 20, 1943. At this time, Hurley went to China to make arrangements for the Cairo Conference and held two conferences with Chiang (Department of State, The Foreign Relations of the United States: The Conferences at Cairo and Teheran, 1943 [Washington, D.C.: Government Printing Office], p. 263 [hereafter cited as Cairo Papers]). This dispatch appears also in Department of State, Foreign Relations of the United States, 1943: China (Washington, D.C.: Government Printing Office, 1957), pp. 163–66. This volume was released in March, 1962.

[6] Military Situation in the Far East, p. 3672.

. . . I am ordered to support the Central Government and I am going to do that to the best of my ability."[7]

It was on the basis of this conception of American policy that Hurley took steps in January, 1945, to defeat a plan, worked out by Wedemeyer's chief of staff and approved by Wedemeyer, for the operation of 4,000 to 5,000 American paratroops and technicians under American officers in Communist territories.[8] In February, 1945, he also refused a request made by General Chu Teh, the commander-in-chief of the Communist forces, for a loan of twenty million dollars to be used to induce the defection of Chinese puppet troops from the Japanese-sponsored government at Nanking. In rejecting the Communist plan, Hurley wrote:

> The established policy of the United States to sustain Chiang Kai-shek as Generalissimo of the Armies and as President of the Government and to prevent the collapse of the National Government would be defeated by the acceptance of the Communist Party's plan or by granting the Lend-lease and monetary assistance requested by Chu Teh. Although financial assistance of the type requested by General Chu might in the end prove to be more economical than importing a similar quantity of arms and ammunition from the United states for use against Japan, I am of the firm opinion that such help would be identical to supplying arms to the Communist armed party and would therefore be a dangerous precedent.[9]

The second element in Hurley's program to implement the policy of peaceful unification was to refrain from applying pressure on Generalissimo Chiang either to compel him to offer the Communists better terms than he was willing to grant or to effect basic changes in his regime or his policies. As his handling of the Stilwell crisis shows, Hurley disapproved of the Stilwell-Marshall tactics of pressure. He stated in his telegram to the

---

[7] Quoted in Herbert Feis, *The China Tangle* (Princeton, N. J.: Princeton University Press, 1953), p. 266.

[8] *Ibid.*, pp. 205–6. See also Department of State, *Foreign Relations of the United States: The Conferences at Malta and Yalta, 1945* (Washington, D.C.: Government Printing Office, 1955), pp. 349–50 (hereafter cited as *Yalta Papers*).

The Office of Strategic Services in China also put its weight behind the project. Lt. Colonel Willis H. Bird of that organization entered into negotiations with the Communists in Yenan without the knowledge of Wedemeyer's headquarters. In an afternoon, he arrived at an agreement with the Communists under which the United States would place special operations men with Communist units and would provide complete equipment for up to twenty-five thousand Communist guerrillas (Charles F. Romanus and Riley Sunderland, *Time Runs Out in CBI* [Washington, D.C.: Government Printing Office, 1959], pp. 251–52). Hurley thought that this plan encouraged the Communists to take an intransigent position and cause a breakdown in the Kuomintang-Communist negotiations.

[9] *Military Situation in the Far East*, p. 3676.

President on October 13, 1944, recommending Stilwell's recall, that "Stilwell's fundamental mistake is in the idea that he can subjugate a man who has led a nation in revolution and who has led an ill-fed, poorly equipped, practically unorganized army against an overwhelming foe for 7 years." On the contrary, he believed that "the Generalissimo reacts favorably to logical persuasion and leadership and the American government can do business with him." He was optimistic from the very beginning that a solution of the "so-called Communist" question could be found.[10]

Hurley believed that an agreement between the Communists and the Nationalists would strengthen the Nationalist government both morally and politically. The policy of peaceful unification was initially for Hurley a program under which the Nationalist government would obtain control over the Communist forces in exchange for Communist participation in a coalition government and the recognition of the Chinese Communists as a legal party, entitled to enjoy all political and civic freedoms under a democratic system of government. This was the meaning of a five-point draft agreement between the Nationalists and the Communists which he worked out in November, 1944. It was accepted by the Communists but rejected by Chiang.[11] On at least two later occasions, Hurley tried without success to convince the Generalissimo of the advantage of acceding to his proposals, arguing that his five-point program was the only one in which the Communists had agreed to submit control of their armed forces to the Nationalist government.[12]

As General Hurley's program did not envisage the use of American pressure to force Chiang to accept his ideas or to offer the Communists better terms to get an agreement, he moved steadily toward support for the Generalissimo's plan to solve the Communist question. Stripped of all verbiage, the Generalissimo's scheme aimed at the actual incorporation of Communist forces in return for the establishment of a "constitutional" rule which would not really alter the power position of the Kuomintang or change political life under the Nationalist regime. At the time many career

[10] *Ibid.*, pp. 2879–80. In one of his reports in July, 1945, there appears a statement which indicates that Hurley at one time did favor forcing Chiang to offer the Communists more favorable terms than he was willing to grant voluntarily. Hurley wrote: "Before the Yalta Conference, I suggested to President Roosevelt a plan to force the National Government to make more liberal political concessions in order to make possible a settlement with the Communists. The President did not approve the suggestion" (*United States Relations with China*, p. 99). This suggestion almost certainly reflected a fleeting thought of Hurley's rather than his settled policy. Only a sentence in Hurley's telegram to Roosevelt dated January 14, 1945, comes close to a suggestion of using pressure on Chiang: "I am still in favor of every concession that we can get from the National government for the participation in that government by the Communists" (*Yalta Papers*, p. 350).

[11] See chap. vii, below.

[12] *Military Situation in the Far East*, pp. 3673, 3678.

officials in China and in the State Department pointed out that this plan would not be acceptable to the Communists. Yet once Hurley abandoned his own blueprint, he bent his efforts toward achieving the peaceful unification of China on Chiang's terms, or at least on terms which Chiang would willingly accept.

Hurley's key assumption was that since the Soviet Union would support America's policy of sustaining Chiang, the Chinese Communists would eventually have to accept Chiang's terms. This optimistic assumption stemmed from three beliefs. First, he remained of the opinion at least up to January, 1946, that the Soviet Union would wholeheartedly follow American policy in China.[13] Second, he reached the conclusion at the very beginning that the Chinese Communists were not dedicated Communists and that the two Chinese parties were sufficiently agreed on the basic principles of government to compose their differences within a democratic framework. Finally, and perhaps most importantly, he doubted that the Chinese Communists had real strength and genuine popular support. He felt that the Communists would be content to become a minority party in a unified and democratized government if they knew that the Soviet Union would not support them and if the United States refused to aid them while maintaining friendly relations with them. At the same time he was confident that the Nationalist government would of its own volition take the necessary measures to strengthen itself if it was given American support and advice.[14] He took an optimistic view of the Kuomintang's ability to remain in control in a coalition government. Therefore, he believed that the policy of peaceful unification would effectively sustain the Nationalist government. In the initial phase of his mediation, he did not realize that the Kuomintang could not accept a genuine coalition government including the Communists without incurring a grave risk of losing its control before long. In the later phase of his activities, he clung tenaciously to the belief that a political settlement on Nationalist terms was possible. When his optimism was disproved by events, his whole program collapsed. At the time of his resignation in November, 1945, there was no settlement between the two warring parties. The Chinese Communists were stronger than ever, and the Russians were obstructing the Nationalist efforts to take over Manchuria and were helping the Communists there while the United

[13] Harry S. Truman, *Years of Trial and Hope* (Garden City, N.Y.: Doubleday, 1956), p. 66. See also ch. viii, below.
[14] In his telegram to Roosevelt dated January 14, 1945, Hurley told the President of Chiang's plan to form a war cabinet and commented as follows: "By means of the war cabinet he [Chiang] intends to start liberalizing and cleansing the government even before the convocation of the National Assembly and the adoption of a constitution, a measure which I consider a substantial step forward in the organization of a stable, unified and democratic government in China" (*Yalta Papers*, p. 348).

States was resolved not to intervene militarily in China. In spite of Hurley's policy of sustaining the Nationalist government, Chiang's regime had not been strengthened either by obtaining control over Communist forces or by adopting sweeping reforms. In spite of his program of peaceful unification, civil war was imminent in China. In spite of his success in gaining verbal assurances from the Soviet leaders, Russian policy had undergone a visible change which he did not then or later discern.

1. Hurley's Trust in the Ultimate Intention of the Soviet Union

Hurley's trust in Soviet good will and excessive reliance on Soviet assurances apparently took shape in November, 1942, when, carrying a letter of introduction from Roosevelt, he visited the Soviet Union, had a seven-hour conference with Stalin, and was taken on a tour of the Stalingrad battlefront.[15] In November, 1943, Hurley, who was then serving as Roosevelt's personal representative in the Middle East, was sent by the President to Chungking to sound out Chiang on his attitude toward a meeting with Roosevelt, Churchill, and Stalin. When Chiang told Hurley of his suspicions concerning Russia's desires to communize China and perhaps to annex a part of China, Hurley "recalled to him Stalin's renunciation of world conquest as a fundamental policy of Communism."[16] Hurley tried to impress upon Chiang his belief that "Stalin is now committed to the proposition that Communism could succeed in Russia alone without an attempt being made to force it on the rest of the world." He informed Chiang of his opinion that "Russia is no longer subsidizing or directing Communist activities in other nations." He suggested that Russia's own experience with communism "is to some extent neutralizing the harsher elements of the Communistic ideology." As evidence to support his judgments, he pointed to the recently signed Moscow Declaration of the four powers on their agreement to establish an international organization to maintain peace.

After Hurley was appointed personal representative of the President to Chiang Kai-shek, in August, 1944, he went to Moscow on his way to China with the purpose of securing a definition of Soviet policy toward China and thus laying the groundwork for his China policy. In a conference on August 31, Molotov told Hurley that the Soviet Union was glad to see the United States "taking the lead economically, politically and militarily in

[15] Don Lohbeck, *Patrick J. Hurley* (Chicago: Henry Regnery Co., 1956), pp. 173–83. Feis, *op. cit.*, p. 179.

[16] The quotations in this paragraph were taken from Hurley's message to Roosevelt, November 20, 1943, printed in *Cairo Papers*, pp. 102–3. This dispatch also appears on pp. 163–66 of the Department of State, *Foreign Relations of the United States, 1943: China.*

Chinese affairs,"[17] and aiding the Chinese to unify their country. Minimizing the ideological tie between the Chinese Communists and the Soviet Union, Molotov asserted that some of the people in China "called themselves Communists" merely as "a way of expressing dissatisfaction with their wretched economic condition." They were "related to Communism in no way at all." The Soviet government, he continued, "should not be associated with these Communist elements." He suggested that, if the Chinese government could be persuaded to work in the common interest and improve economic conditions, these Communist elements "would forget this political association [with Communism]." He phrased his disclaimer of any interest in Chinese affairs in such a way as to leave the implication that, if Generalissimo Chiang took steps to improve Sino-Soviet relations, the Soviet Union might show a greater interest in China and this interest could be of help to the Nationalist government. Molotov's assurances fit very well with Roosevelt's grand design of postwar co-operation with the Soviet Union and his policy of unification of China. They were accepted by Hurley as the basis for his program to implement Roosevelt's policy. Soon after he arrived in Chungking, he imparted this presumably vital piece of information to Generalissimo Chiang. Indeed, he thought that he had persuaded Chiang to accept Molotov's assurances at their face value. This he indicated in his report to the secretary of state on December 23, 1944:

> At the time I came here Chiang Kai-shek believed that the Communist Party in China was the instrument of the Soviet Government of Russia. He is now convinced that the Russian government does not recognize the Chinese Communist Party as Communists at all and that (1) Russia is not supporting the Communist Party in China; (2) Russia does not repeat nor [not?] want dissensions or civil war in China; and (3) Russia desires more harmonious relations with China. These facts have gone far toward convincing Chiang Kai-shek that the Communist Party in China is not an agency of the Soviet. He now feels that he can reach a settlement with the Communist Party as a Chinese political party without foreign entanglement.[18]

In the light of Chiang's deep convictions about the nature and intentions of the Chinese Communist party both before and since that time, it would seem that Hurley's conclusions about Chiang's easy conversion to his views were overstated, if not entirely mistaken. It seems probable that Chiang took Hurley's résumé of his talk with Molotov to mean that the Soviet

---

[17] The quotations in this paragraph are taken from *United States Relations with China*, p. 72.

[18] *Military Situation in the Far East*, p. 2909.

Union could be dissuaded from actively supporting the Chinese Communists by diplomatic concessions on the part of the Nationalist government. Such a view of Soviet intentions seemed to find warrant in Soviet policy toward China between the outbreak of the Sino-Japanese War and the German invasion of Russia.

In order to keep Japan entangled in China, the Soviet Union had granted the Nationalist government three loans totaling $250,000,000 to buy arms and ammunitions, all of which went to the central government alone.[19] In Chiang's calculations, the Chinese Communists' political position would be gravely weakened if they were deprived of Soviet support. Thus, Hurley's assurances probably had a triple effect. They may have intensified Chiang's desire to detach the Soviet Union from the Chinese Communists by diplomatic concessions. They may have persuaded Chiang to continue negotiations with the Chinese Communists, seeking to destroy them by political means. They may also have strengthened his predisposition to refuse his antagonists better terms, while lessening his sense of urgency to reinvigorate his regime. An appraisal of Hurley's judgment on Soviet policy and intentions will be made later; suffice it here to note that Molotov's characterization of the Chinese Communists exercised a perceptible influence on Hurley's understanding of the Chinese Communist party.

2. Hurley's Misunderstanding of the Nature of Chinese Communism

Shortly after his arrival in China, Hurley reached the conclusion that the Chinese Communists were not dedicated Communists. Like some officials in the State Department,[20] he used time and again the phrase "so-called Communists" in his reports to President Roosevelt.[21] This initial susceptibility was further strengthened by his superficial impressions of the Chinese scene and his erroneous interpretation of Chinese Communist pronouncements using democratic slogans and designed for popular consumption. When in November, 1944, he was at Yenan to negotiate with the Communists, he was greatly impressed by the contrast between the state-controlled economy of Russia and the free economy of the Chinese Communist region. As Hurley told the senators during the MacArthur hearings,

[19] Tien-fong Cheng, A History of Sino-Soviet Relations (Washington, D.C.: Public Affairs Press, 1957), pp. 211–15. See also, Henry Wei, China and Soviet Russia (Princeton, N.J.: D. Van Nostrand Co., 1956), pp. 139–48, and Max Beloff, The Foreign Policy of Soviet Russia (London: Oxford University Press, 1949), II, 184–85.
[20] Foreign Relations of the United States, 1943: China, pp. 317, 324.
[21] See his report dated September 23, 1944, quoted in Charles F. Romanus and Riley Sunderland, Stilwell's Command Problems (Washington, D.C.: Government Printing Office, 1956), p. 450. See also his report dated October 13, 1944, as printed in Military Situation in the Far East, pp. 2879–87.

I knew communism as it existed in Russia. I couldn't buy a nickel's worth of anything, any place, except from the Soviet Government. Now I go up into the Communist area of China. . . . I find the stores open, the stock market open, the highest bidder getting the property, money being exchanged, the profit motive in operation. Now, when anybody tells me that this is communism, I know that they are mistaken.[22]

Hurley's observations about economic life in Yenan were not wrong and his conclusion that the economy in Communist areas did not represent communism was correct. But the Chinese Communists themselves would have wholeheartedly agreed with him on this point. For Mao Tse-tung had defined the Chinese society during the Sino-Japanese War as "a colonial, semi-colonial and semi-feudal society."[23] The Communist revolution in such a society must go through two stages: first, the bourgeois-democratic revolution and, second, the socialist revolution. The objective of the bourgeois-democratic revolution was "to clear the paths for the development of capitalism."[24] During this stage of their revolution, the Communists did not "forbid the development of capitalist production that 'cannot dominate the livelihood of the people,' for China's economy is still very backward."[25]

What Mao insisted on in his writings and what Hurley overlooked was that the Chinese revolution belonged to "the category of the *new* bourgeois-democratic revolution and formed part of the proletarian-socialist world revolution."[26] By the term "new bourgeois-democratic revolution" Mao referred to a revolution "under the leadership of the proletariat or a leadership in which the proletariat participates."[27] Mao's assertions were merely a restatement of old-fashioned Marxism-Leninism. They rested on the Leninist distinction between the content and the class force of a revolution.[28]

[22] *Ibid.*, p. 2903.
[23] Mao Tse-tung, "On New Democracy," *Selected Works of Mao Tse-tung*, III, (London: Lawrence and Wishart, 1954), 108 (hereafter cited as *Selected Works*, III).
[24] *Ibid.*, p. 111.
[25] *Ibid.*, p. 122.
[26] *Ibid.*, p. 111. Emphasis added.
[27] Mao Tse-tung, *Hsin-min-chu-chu-i lun* ["On New Democracy"] (San Francisco, Calif.: Cooperative Publishers, 1945), p. 8. In the *Selected Works*, there is a significant change in phraseology. The new bourgeois-democratic revolution is characterized as "led by proletariat" and the phrase which weakens the Communists' claim to exclusive leadership is eliminated (*Selected Works*, III, 112).
[28] For an able discussion of this distinction, see Benjamin Schwartz, *Chinese Communism and the Rise of Mao* (Cambridge, Mass.: Harvard University Press, 1952), pp. 58, 78, and Alfred G. Meyer, *Leninism* (Cambridge, Mass.: Harvard University Press, 1959), chap. vi, See also Morris Watnick, "Continuity and Innovation in Chinese Communism," *World Politics*, October, 1953, pp. 84–105; Franz Borkenau, "Mao Tse-tung," *Twentieth Century*, August, 1952, pp. 139, 144; Lucian W. Pye, *Guerrilla Communism*

While the content of the revolution was bourgeois-democratic in nature, the class force leading the revolution was to be the proletariat or an alliance of classes of which the proletariat was a major element. When Hurley judged the nature of the Communist party by the nature of the economy in Yenan, he betrayed a total ignorance of Communist theory and practice.

Hurley's ignorance of communism was apparently both a cause and an effect of the insufficient attention given to Communist theoretical and polemical literature, particularly that written for the instruction of the faithful, and a corresponding over-reliance on what was told to people outside the party, especially to foreign visitors and journalists. At that time the Chinese Communists freely gave verbal indorsement to democratic principles and the principles of Sun Yat-sen, the founder and the first director-general of the Kuomintang. These transient slogans and policies were taken by Hurley as fundamental aims and principles.

On April 2, 1945, he told a news conference in Washington:

> You gentlemen should know, though — I believe you all do know that it is a matter of common knowledge that the Communist Party of China supports the principles of Dr. Sun Yat-sen. That was generally referred to as the people's three principles of China. The three principles are government of the people, by the people, and for the people. All the demands that the Communist Party has been making have been on a democratic basis. That has led to the statement that the Communist Party [sic] in China are not, in fact, real Communists. The Communist Party of China is supporting exactly the same principles as those promulgated by the National Government of China and conceded to be objectives also of the National Government. . . . Well, as a matter of fact, the divergence between the parties in China seems to be not in the objective desired because they both assert that they are for the establishment of a government in China that will decentralize authority and conduct itself along democratic lines, employing democratic processes. The˗divergence between them is the procedure by which they can be achieved.[29]

Subsequently, in the MacArthur hearings, Hurley explained that in making this statement, he was influenced by President Roosevelt's suggestion that he say something favorable about the Communists so as to maintain a basis for unification.[30] But he he did not try very hard to rest his defense on this explanation. Instead he readily admitted that "it does look . . .

in Malaya (Princeton, N.J.: Princeton University Press, 1956), pp. 17, 37, 39, 41; and Franz Borkenau, European Communism (New York: Harper & Bros., 1953).

[29] Reproduced in Military Situation in the Far East, p. 2896.

[30] Ibid., p. 2906.

as if I had lost my perspective and didn't know very well what I was talking about; and if that's what Senator McMahon is trying to prove and it will make for friendship between the Senator and myself for the sake of argument I will admit — I don't care what they say about me."[31] Furthermore, in a report to Washington in early 1945, Hurley observed that "the Communists are not in fact Communists, they are striving for democratic principles."[32] It is reasonable to conclude that Hurley's characterization of Chinese Communists as not dedicated Communists reflected his belief.

Hurley obviously did not realize that Mao had written that the establishment of a "new-democratic" society and a state under the "joint dictatorship of all the revolutionary classes" was merely the aim of his revolution in "its first stage."[33] Mao had declared without equivocation:

> Everybody knows that, as regards the social system or program of action, the Communist Party has its present program and its future program, or its minimum program and maximum program. For the present, New Democracy; and for the future, Socialism — these are two parts of an organic whole, guided by one and the same Communist ideology.[34]

The idea of joint dictatorship of all revolutionary classes was a development of the notion of a "democratic dictatorship of the proletariat and peasantry" which was incorporated in the 1931 constitution of the Chinese Soviet Republic, the Political Resolution of the Sixth National Congress of

[31] *Ibid.* Hurley also said that "most of the Communists were just reformers, outs, who wanted to be the ins and that the only difference between Oklahoma Republicans and the Chinese Communists was that the Oklahoma Republicans were not armed" (*ibid.*, pp. 2420–21).

[32] *United States Relations with China*, p. 86. For a description of the circumstances leading to the dispatch of this report, see Feis, *op. cit.*, pp. 220–22.

[33] Mao, *Hsing-min-chu-chu-i lun* ("On New Democracy"), p. 8. In this Chinese version, Mao stated in another context, "The democratic republic of China which we now want to establish can only be a democratic republic under the *joint dictatorship of all parties and all factions*" (*ibid.*, p. 16: Emphasis added). This sentence appears in the version cited by Brandt, Schwartz, and Fairbank in the following form: "The democratic republic of China which we are aiming to construct now can only take the form of dictatorship of all *anti-imperialist and anti-feudal people*, i.e., a new democratic republic" (Conrad Brandt, Benjamin Schwartz, and John K. Fairbank, *A Documentary History of Chinese Communism* [Cambridge, Mass.: Harvard University Press, 1952], p. 266: Emphasis added). In the *Selected Works*, there is the following sentence in its place: "The democratic republic of China which we now want to establish can only be a democratic republic under the *joint dictatorship of all anti-imperialist and anti-feudal people led by the proletariat*, that is, a new-democratic republic" (Mao Tse-tung, *Selected Works*, III, 118. Emphasis added). The Chinese version cited fitted the Communist demand for setting up a coalition government better than the other two versions, while the latest phraseology, stating explicitly that the joint dictatorship was to be "led by the proletariat," i.e., the Chinese Communist party, probably reflected more faithfully their real aim at that time.

[34] Mao, *Selected Works*, III, 131.

1928, and the Manifesto of the Second National Congress of 1922. This latter strategic concept originated in 1905 with Lenin's *Two Tactics*.[35] Lenin made clear that it was the proletariat which must lead the bourgeois-democratic revolution, that the revolutionary democratic dictatorship of the proletariat and peasantry would be provisional only, and that the proletariat would seek at the earliest opportunity to convert the revolution from the bourgeois-democratic to the final proletarian stage.[36] For Lenin, as for Mao, behind the minimum program of the bourgeois-democratic revolution stood the maximum program of the proletarian class struggle and proletarian revolution.[37]

Similar statements by Communist leaders during Hurley's ambassadorship underscored this point. In his political report entitled *On Coalition Government*, made at the Seventh National Congress of the Chinese Communist party on April 24, 1945, Mao emphatically declared: "We Communists never conceal our political stand. It is definite and beyond any doubt that our future or maximum programme is to head China for socialism or communism. Both the name of our Party and our Marxist worldview unequivocally point to this ultimate ideal of the future, a future of incomparable brightness and beauty."[38] Not long after Mao's report, General Wang Yo-fei, the ranking Chinese Communist in Chungking at the time, stated frankly to Hurley that "the [Communist] Party now supported democratic principles but only as a stepping stone to a future Communist state."[39]

To be quite fair, Mao did disclaim the intention of setting up a proletarian dictatorship and a one-party government if the Communists should come to power.[40] But even so the "democratic dictatorship of the proletariat and peasantry" under the Soviet Republic in the early thirties and the monolithic structure of the party should have raised serious questions as to whether the joint dictatorship of several revolutionary classes, "led wholly or partly by the proletariat," would culminate in a Communist-controlled dictatorship. Perhaps the nature of the "New Democracy" of Mao was more correctly portrayed by him in other less widely known but far more revealing statements. In 1941, Mao said:

> In judging whether an area is new-democratic in social character, the main criterion is whether the representatives of the

[35] Karl A. Wittfogel, "The Influence of Leninism-Stalinism in China," *Annals of the American Academy of Political and Social Science*, September, 1951, pp. 24–25.
[36] R. N. Carew Hunt, *The Theory and Practice of Communism* (rev. ed.; London: Geoffrey Books, 1957), p. 153.
[37] Meyer, *op. cit.*, pp. 122, 128.
[38] Mao Tse-tung, *Selected Works*, IV (London: Lawrence and Wishart, 1956), 274.
[39] *United States Relations with China*, pp. 103–4.
[40] Mao, *Selected Works*, IV, 277.

broad masses of the people participate in the political power and whether the Communist Party assumes leadership in it. Therefore the united front political power under Communist leadership serves as the chief sign of a new-democratic society.[41]

He also stated that "when the example of the anti-Japanese base areas [i.e., Communist areas] is followed throughout the country, then the whole of China will become a new-democratic republic."[42] As the Communists exercised unchallenged control over these "bases" and the active opponents of the regime were eliminated either as the "special agents" of the Kuomintang or as "Trotskyites," these remarks were hardly reassuring.

As for Sun Yat-sen's Three Principles of the People, the Communists supported them merely for the bourgeois-democratic stage of their revolution and, even for this period, they supported only their own version. In *On New Democracy*, Mao took special care to preserve the ideological identity and purity of the communist party. While admitting that the Three Principles of the People "basically agree with the Communists' political programme for the stage of democratic revolution in China," Mao hastened to point out:

> Besides the stage of democratic revolution communism envisages a stage of socialist revolution; hence besides the minimum programme it has its maximum programme, i.e., the programme for the realisation of the social system of socialism and communism. The Three People's Principles include only the stage of democratic revolution, but not the stage of socialist revolution; therefore they contain only a minimum programme, i.e., no programme for building up a social system of socialism and communism.[43]

Mao himself pointed out that Sun Yat-senism and communism differed also in their programs for the democratic revolution, world outlook, and revolutionary thoroughness. He made it clear that the Three Principles of the People of which he was speaking were the Communist interpretation of Sun Yat-senism. He maintained that Sun reinterpreted his Three Principles of the People in the Manifesto of the First National Congress of the Kuomintang,[44] issued in 1924 at the height of Communist influence

[41] Mao, *Selected Works*, III, 241. See also K'ang Jih chang-chêng shih-ch'i chieh-fang-ch'ü kai-k'uang ["The General Conditions of the Liberated Areas during the Anti-Japanese War"] (Peking: Jên-min ch'u-pan-shê, 1953), p. 23.

[42] Mao, *Selected Works*, III, 241.

[43] Mao, *Hsin-min-chu-chu-i lun* ["On New Democracy"], p. 31. The translation of this passage was taken from the *Selected Works of Mao Tse-tung*, III, 133, there being no disparity between the two versions.

[44] Mao, *Hsin-min-chu-chu-i lun* ["On New Democracy"], p. 32.

in the Kuomintang. What marked off the "new," "revolutionary," and "genuine" Three Principles of the People from the "old" and "reactionary" Three Principles was that the former contained "the three cardinal policies of alliance with Russia, cooperation with the Communists and assistance to the peasants and workers."[45] To quote Mao, "It is only such Three People's Principles that basically agree with the Communist Party's political programme for the stage of democratic revolution or its minimum programme."[46] He clearly stated, too, that "there is no basic agreement between the Three People's Principles of the old category and the Communist Party's minimum programme because the former fitted in with the old period and are now obsolete."[47] These same points were repeated more forcefully and more concisely in his On Coalition Government (1945).[48] This interpretation ran directly counter to the opinion predominant in Kuomintang circles that the adoption of the so-called "three policies" by Sun was merely a matter of political maneuver and did not involve a change in Sun's ideological orientation.[49] There is no evidence that Sun ever used the term "three cardinal policies" or "three policies" to distinguish his pro-Russian and pro-Communist policies from other policies adopted in the period 1924–25. The very term "three policies" was a Communist creation.[50]

Actually, in the several years preceding Hurley's remarks about the similarity between the basic principles of the two parties, the ideological differences between the Communists and the Kuomintang had been progressively sharpened as the political and military conflicts became increasingly acute. Mao's On New Democracy represented an attempt to provide a theoretical basis for the policy of competing with the Nationalist party for leadership, to emphasize the distinction between the programs and aims of the Communist party and those of other groups, to restore ideological purity and doctrinal unity to the movement, and to formulate a clear-cut party line in the process of consolidating the Communist

[45] Ibid., p. 33.

[46] Ibid., p. 37. The translation was taken from Mao, Selected Works, III, 139.

[47] Ibid., p. 140.

[48] Mao, Selected Works, IV, 276–77.

[49] Shu-ch'in Tsui, "The Influence of the Canton-Moscow Entente upon Sun Yat-sen's Political Philosophy," Chinese Social and Political Science Review, April, 1934, pp. 96–145; July, 1934, pp. 177–209; October, 1934, pp. 341–88; and his "The Influence of the Canton-Moscow Entente upon Sun Yat-sen's Revolutionary Tactics," ibid., April, 1936, pp. 101–39. See also Tsui Shu-ch'in, Sun Chung-shan yü kung-ch'an-chu-i ["Sun Yet-sen and Communism"] (Hongkong: Ya-chou ch'u-pan-shê, 1954). For a recent study, see Shao Chuan Leng and Norman D. Palmer, Sun Yat-sen and Communism (New York: Frederick A. Praeger, 1960).

[50] Martin Wilbur and Julie How (eds.) Documents on Communism, Nationalism, and Soviet Advisers in China (New York: Columbia University Press, 1956), pp. 392–3. See also Harold Schiffrin and Chao-ying Fang, review of Sun Chung-shan hsüan-chi, Journal of Asian Studies, February, 1958, pp. 262–65.

forces.[51] It was published in January, 1940, at the time of what the Communists called "the first anti-Communist upsurge," during which Nationalist forces allegedly launched a co-ordinated attack on the Communist areas.[52]

On their part, the Nationalists had been seeking to combat the ideology of communism by advocating a return to traditional values and a revival of neo-Confucianism. To the doctrine of class struggle, the Kuomintang opposed the doctrine of universal harmony. To the specific programs of social and economic reforms adopted and advocated by the Communists, the Nationalists opposed the traditional rules of conduct — the "Four Cardinal Principles" of Propriety, Righteousness, Integrity, and Honor, and the "Eight Virtues" of Loyalty, Filial Devotion, Kindness, Love, Faithfulness, Justice, Harmony, and Equity. To the Communist program of rapid modernization, the Nationalists opposed rebuilding a national culture on the foundation of the basic elements of China's own civilization. While the Communists disseminated works on dialectical materialism, Bolshevik principles of organization, and Communist strategy and tactics, the Nationalists advocated the study of Chinese classics.[53]

The clash in ideologies reached a new height with the publication on March 10, 1943, of Chiang Kai-shek's *China's Destiny*, which was intended to be a political textbook for Nationalist officials and the Chinese people alike. In this political tract Chiang denounced the Communists for appealing "to the youth to forsake our traditional values." Lumping Communism and liberalism together, Chiang commented:

> As for the struggle between Liberalism and Communism, it was merely a reflection of the opposition of Anglo-American theories to those of Soviet Russia. Not only were such theories unsuited to the needs of China's national life, but they were also opposed to the spirit of China's own civilization. The people who promoted them forgot completely that they were Chinese and missed completely the object of learning which was to study and to apply the acquired knowledge for the benefit of China.[54]

[51] Brandt, Schwartz, and Fairbank, *op. cit.*, p. 260; Hu Chiao-mu, *Chung-kuo Kung-ch'an-tang t'i san-shih nien* ["Thirty Years of the Chinese Communist Party"] (Peking: Jên-min ch'u-pan-shê, 1951), pp. 43–44.

[52] Hu Hua, *Chung-kuo hsin-min-chu-chu-i kê-ming shih* (ch'u-kao) ["A History of the New Democratic Revolution in China (Preliminary Draft)"] (Peking: Hsin-hua ch'u-pan-shê, 1950), pp. 199-200.

[53] Mary C. Wright, "From Revolution to Restoration: The Transformation of Kuomintang Ideology," *Far Eastern Quarterly*, August, 1955, pp. 515–32. See also Arthur F. Wright, "Struggle vs. Harmony: Symbols of Competing Values in Modern China," *World Politics*, October, 1953, pp. 31–44, and John K. Fairbank, *The United States and China* (new ed.; Cambridge, Mass.: Harvard University Press, 1958), pp. 190–96.

[54] Chiang Chung-chêng, *Chung-kuo chih ming-yün* ["China's Destiny"] (Changsha:

Without naming the Chinese Communists, the leader of the Kuomintang condemned their maintenance of separate armed forces and their assertion of regional control as a "new type of feudalism," a "new form of warlordism." [55] The government, he averred, would try to deal with this problem of armed regional domination "in a magnanimous spirit" and seek "a solution by rational means." But he warned that unless the Communists were willing to abandon their feudal and warlord-like ways of doing things, the magnanimous policy of the government would be of no avail.[56] Clearly, Chiang was not optimistic about a peaceful solution of the Communist problem.

The publication of Chiang's *China's Destiny* drew forth a vehement counterattack from the Chinese Communists who had allowed to go unanswered many Nationalist criticisms of Mao's *On New Democracy*. In a pamphlet, *A Critique of 'China's Destiny,'* published on July 20, 1943, Ch'ên Po-ta, a leading Communist theoretician, condemned Chiang's ideas as "compradore-feudalist fascism or new despotism (though still preserving the façade of the Three Principles of the People as a matter of form)."[57] He implied that the publication of Chiang's political treatise was a "war proclamation to the Chinese people [i.e., the Chinese Communists] and a preparation in the realm of thought and public opinion for the launching of a civil war to decide the fate of Kuomintang in two years."[58] At the time, Ambassador Gauss reported to Washington the political significance of Chiang's *China's Destiny* and the Chinese Communists' counterattack.[59] If Hurley had devoted some of his attention to the study of the development of Kuomintang-Communist relations and the accompanying ideological controversy, he could easily have discovered the deep gulf separating the two sides.

It must not be overlooked, however, that, despite his belief that the

Chung-kuo wên-hua fu-wu shê, 1943), p .52. In translating this passage, the writer used freely the translation of this work by Philip Jaffe and the authorized translation by Wang Chung-hui. Jaffe's translation of this passage is closer to the original Chinese version of the *China's Destiny* than Wang's translation. The latter came out after Chiang's work had stirred up adverse criticism in the United States. In the passage quoted, it was altered to tone down the anti-Western flavor of the Chinese version and thus altered the original meaning. Jaffe's translation was more accurate in this respect but was obviously a more hasty piece of work. See Chiang Kai-shek, *China's Destiny and Chinese Economic Theory*, translated and edited with notes and commentary by Philip Jaffe (New York: Roy Publisher, 1947), p. 100; and Chiang Kai-shek, *China's Destiny*, authorized translation by Wang Chung-hui (New York: Macmillan Co., 1947), p. 83.

[55] *Ibid.*, p. 223.

[56] *Ibid.*, p. 224.

[57] Ch'ên Po-ta, P'ing "Chung-kuo chih ming-yün" ["A Critique of 'China's Destiny'"] (Hsin-hua shu-tien, 1949), pp. 2, 53. For a slightly different translation, see Ch'ên Po-ta "Chiang Kai-shek's 'China's Destiny'" in *The Chinese Comments*, ed. Stuart Gelder (London: Gollancz, 1946), p. 257.

[58] Ch'ên, P'ing "Chung-kuo chih ming-yün" p. 49. Cf. Gelder, *op. cit.*, p. 280.

[59] *Foreign Relations of the United States, 1943: China*, pp. 347–48.

Chinese Communists were not dedicated Communists, Hurley staunchly supported the Nationalists and steadfastly refused to arm the Communists unless they came to an agreement with the government. The Chinese Communists themselves focused their attention on his actions and refused to be reassured by his nice words. Commenting on Hurley's April 2 press interview, the Communist Hsin-hua News Agency commented: "From the lips of a selfsame Hurley [who had earlier proposed the establishment of a coalition government on terms acceptable to the Communists] the Kuomintang suddenly became a Beauty while the Chinese Communist Party was a Monster; he bluntly declared that the United States would cooperate only with Chiang Kai-shek but not with the Chinese Communist Party." [60] It now transpires that this comment was written by Mao himself. But Hurley's program of negotiations, particularly his five-point draft, shows that his misunderstanding of the nature of the Chinese Communist party prevented him from gauging correctly the trend toward an intensification of the political conflict, led him to underestimate the determination of the Chinese Communists to achieve total power, and caused him to exaggerate the possibility of a settlement.

3. Hurley's Low Estimate of Communist Strength

Insofar as Hurley's own policy was concerned, the most consequential of his three beliefs was probably his low estimate of the political and military strength of the Communists. This appraisal led him to the firmly held conviction that without Soviet support the Chinese Communists could not successfully compete with the Nationalists for control of China, that the influence of the Soviet Union would dominate their policy, and that once Russia concluded a treaty with the Nationalist government in which Russia pledged her support to the Nationalists, the Communists would come to terms with the latter. Insofar as Hurley and Chiang were concerned, this seems to have been the decisive reason for reaching an accord with the Soviet Union to implement the Yalta Agreement. One of Hurley's reports sent in early July, 1945, stated these views so explicitly and forcefully that it deserves lengthy quotation:

> We are convinced that the influence of the Soviet will control the action of the Chinese Communist Party. The Chinese Communists do not believe that Stalin has agreed or will agree to support the National Government of China under the leadership of Chiang Kai-shek. The Chinese Communists still fully expect the Soviet to support the Chinese Communists against the National Government. Nothing short of the Soviet's public com-

[60] Mao Tse-tung, *Selected Works*, IV, 328–29.

mitment will change the Chinese Communists' opinion on this subject. . . .

I believe the Soviet's attitude toward the Chinese Communists is as I related it to the President in September last year and have reported many times since. . . . Notwithstanding all this the Chinese Communists still believe that they have the support of the Soviet. Nothing will change their opinion on this subject until a treaty has been signed between the Soviet and China in which the Soviet agrees to support the National Government. When the Chinese Communists are convinced that the Soviet is not supporting them, they will settle with the National Government if the National Government is realistic enough to make generous political settlements. The negotiations between the National Government and the Communist Party at this time are merely marking time pending the result of the conference at Moscow.[61]

The leadership of the Communist Party is intelligent. When the handwriting is on the wall, they will be able to read. No amount of argument will change their position. Their attitude will be changed only by inexorable logic of events. The strength of the armed forces of Chinese Communists has been exaggerated. The area of territory controlled by the Communists has been exaggerated. The number of Chinese people who adhere to the Chinese Communist Party has been exaggerated. State Department officials, Army officials, newspaper and radio publicity have in large measure accepted the Communist leaders' statements in regard to the military and political strength of the Communist party in China. Nevertheless, with the support of the Soviet the Chinese Communist could bring about civil war in China. Without the support of the Soviet the Chinese Communist Party will eventually participate as a political party in the National Government.[62]

Thus, General Hurley's estimate of Communist strength, reinforced by his appraisal of Soviet policies and intentions, led him to place all his hopes for a political solution of the Communist issue on his and Chiang's plan to come to an agreement with the Soviet Union, exchanging Chinese diplomatic concessions for a formal pledge of Soviet support.

[61] This refers to the negotiations between T. V. Soong and Stalin and Molotov to reach an agreement to implement the Yalta accord. They started on June 30 and culminated in the Sino-Soviet Treaty of Friendship and Alliance of August 14, 1945.

[62] *United States Relations with China*, pp. 99–100. In the spring of 1945, General Wedemeyer believed that the Chinese Communists could be defeated by comparatively small assistance to the national government (Admiral William Leahy, *I Was There* [New York: Whittlesey House, 1950], p. 337).

Hurley was, of course, correct in refusing to accept the Chinese Communists' statements of their own strength at face value. But his rejection of the Communist claims was not based on a careful evaluation of the actual strength of the Chinese Communists. Insofar as one can ascertain from published materials, Hurley made no systematic effort to seek the information necessary to arrive at the best possible estimate. In contrast to Hurley, the foreign service officers did endeavor to collect first-hand information and they arrived at estimates quite different from Hurley's. They did not share Hurley's reliance on Soviet ability to control the domestic policies of the Chinese Communists. In retrospect, it becomes clear that the Chinese Communist movement though inspired from abroad and completely dominated by Soviet agents in its formative years, had now gained widespread popular support through providing leadership in the guerrilla war and taken deep roots in the tenant-cultivated soils of earth-bound China. The Chinese Communist party might be influenced but could not be "controlled" by the Soviet Union, and even without foreign support it would still be a formidable adversary. The solution of the Communist problem had, first of all, to be sought within China, not from the Soviet Union.

The obverse of Hurley's low estimate of Communist strength was his optimism about the political future of the Kuomintang. His replacement of Gauss as ambassador coincided with a reorganization of the Nationalist government, under which T. V. Soong became the acting president of the Executive Yüan, Ch'ên Chêng was appointed minister of war, and O. K. Yü replaced H. H. Kung as minister of finance.[63] These changes looked promising. Furthermore, Hurley was satisfied that Chiang was the best man in Asia for the United States to support. To use his subsequent words, Chiang was "a Christian and anti-Communist" who "had fought nearly 30 years of civil war in China and 8 years against Japan, part of it as our ally." [64] Up to the time of Japan's surrender, the United States was training and equipping thirty-nine Nationalist divisions. American liaison teams were placed in these Nationalist divisions and in that part of the Chinese services of supply which supported them. American forces in the Pacific were moving steadily closer to China.[65] Hurley was satisfied that the Nationalist government would continue to develop its strength and that American influence in China would increase with time. This conviction, in conjunction with the traditional policy of non-intervention and his view of the futility of using pressure on Chiang, ruled out aggressive action on the part of the United States to rebuild the Nationalist government into the

[63] Feis, op. cit., p. 221, n. 25.
[64] Military Situation in the Far East, p. 2919.
[65] Romanus and Sunderland, Time Runs Out in CBI, p. 338.

nucleus of a broad anti-Communist front. Thus, Hurley hopefully proceeded with his policy of bringing about a political settlement on Chiang's terms, neglecting other more urgent steps which the United States could profitably have taken.

Events in China after the surrender of Japan were to show that the reorganization of the Executive Yüan had not brought into being a government with even a minimum degree of efficiency and honesty, not to say a capability of performing effectively the tremendous task of taking over occupied China and rehabilitating a war-torn country. At the same time, the withdrawal of the American liaison teams was to leave the American-trained divisions and the Chinese services of supplies without indispensable advice. Once more, American hopes for reform and progress in China were to be disappointed.

B. Davies' and Service's Hope of Winning the Chinese Communists from Moscow

1. Davies' and Service's Realistic Estimates of the Relative Strength of the Kuomintang and the Chinese Communist Party

The lack of reliable source materials prevents us from determining with any precision the political and military strength of the Chinese Communists. But the significant fact was that Hurley's estimate of the relative strength of the Nationalist government and the Chinese Communist party ran directly counter to the appraisal of the career officers in China whose knowledge of the Chinese language and close contact with Chinese affairs enabled them to base their reports on personal observations and experiences. The most systematic and extensive analysis of the weaknesses of the Nationalist government was made by John S. Service in a memorandum of June 20, 1944, entitled "The Situation in China and Suggestions regarding American Policy." [66] Service told his superiors that the

[66] This is the longest and one of the best reports written by John S. Service which have been printed in public records (Senate Committee on Foreign Relations, *Hearings on State Department Employee Loyalty Investigation*, 81st Cong., 2d sess. (1950), pp. 2035–46 [hereafter cited as *State Department Employee Loyalty Investigation*]). It reveals his power for keen observation and penetrating analysis. Particularly interesting are his concrete proposals which looked toward active but tactful intervention by the United States in Chinese affairs in order to bring about democratic reforms and to build up the "liberal and progressive forces within China" (*ibid.*, p. 2045). Unfortunately, his otherwise correct approach was vitiated by his undue optimism regarding the nature and intentions of the Chinese Communist party. He left the clear implication that the Chinese Communists should also be supported by the United States against the existing regime. "We should maintain friendly relations with liberal elements in the Kuomintang, the minor parties, and the Communists. . . . We should continue to show an interest in the Chinese Communists. This includes contact with the Communist representatives in Chungking, publicity of the blockade and the situation be-

position of the Kuomintang and the Generalissimo was weaker than it had been for the past ten years. This gradual disintegration of the authority of the government was due to the threat of an economic collapse, the demoralization of the army and the bureaucracy, the disaffection of the intellectual and salaried classes, the growing resentment among the peasants against all kinds of abuses, the resurgence of centrifugal forces in Chinese politics, mounting tension between the Kuomintang and the Chinese Communist party, and the rigid, repressive policies of the government.[67] Service maintained that the Kuomintang was not only incapable of averting a disaster by its own initiative but its policies were precipitating the crisis. For it was unwilling to undertake necessary reforms which would injure the vested interests of the small and shrinking group of its supporters. Instead, it intensified its totalitarian control in order to perpetuate its power. Furthermore, these suicidal policies were rooted in the composition and nature of the party. The Kuomintang was a "congerie of conservative political cliques interested primarily in the preservation of their own power against all outsiders and jockeying for position among themselves."[68] Its social foundation had been eroded by the war.. It now rested "on the narrow base of the rural gentry landlords, the militarists, the higher ranks of the government bureaucracy, and merchant bankers having intimate connections with the government bureaucrats."[69] Service warned that this process of disintegration might end in a collapse.[70]

In contrast to this continuous decline of the authority of the Kuomintang, the Chinese Communists expanded and consolidated their power over a wide stretch of Chinese territory. The appraisals made by the foreign service officers of the strength of the Communists also contradicted

tween the two parties . . ." (*ibid.*, p. 2045). But to read this dispatch in a proper perspective, it should be remembered that the American government had been pursuing a policy of discouraging the Nationalists from suppressing the Communists by force and that President Roosevelt was soon to urge Generalissimo Chiang to permit the use of the Communist forces against Japan.

On this report, Herbert Feis noted: "There are two reasons for believing that the views represented in this memorandum of June 20, 1944, were widely held: (1) American policy during the summer of 1944 followed the suggested lines, (2) the memo was given exceptional attention and praise. It was approved by Gauss in the dispatch with which he transmitted it to the State Department. The Division of Chinese Affairs found it to be a timely and valuable discussion. The State Department sent Service a special letter of commendation for his 'timely and able analysis' and 'constructive suggestions'" (Feis, *op. cit.*, p. 164, n. 9).

[67] Commenting on this section of Service's report, Carsun Chang wrote: "I do not think that the most fervent supporters of Chiang Kai-shek can take exception to this able analysis of the pathological political condition of China during the war" (Carsun Chang, *The Third Force in China* [New York: Bookman Associates, 1952], p. 100).

[68] *State Department Employee Loyalty Investigation*, p. 2039.

[69] *Ibid.*

[70] *Ibid.*, pp. 2036–40.

the views of Ambassador Hurley. As early as November 7, 1944, John P. Davies reported to Washington:

> The Chinese Communists are so strong between the Great Wall and Yangtze that they can now look forward to the postwar control of at least North China. They may also continue to hold not only those parts of the Yangtze valley which they now dominate but also new areas in Central and South China. . . .
>
> The Communists have survived ten years of civil war and seven years of Japanese offensives. They have survived not only more sustained enemy pressure than the Chinese Central Government forces have been subjected to, but also a severe blockade imposed by Chiang.
>
> They have survived and they have grown. . . . And they will continue to grow.
>
> The reason for this phenomenal vitality and strength is simple and fundamental. It is mass support, mass participation. The Communist governments and armies are the first governments and armies in modern Chinese history to have positive and widespread popular support.[71]

The contrast between the gradual disintegration in Nationalist China and the political dynamism in Communist China alerted both Davies and Service to the possibility that the Communists would be victorious in a civil war, if the Nationalists resorted to force. Davies reported from Yenan on November 7, 1944:

> Relying upon his dispirited shambling legions, his decadent bureaucracy, his sterile political moralisms, and such nervous foreign support as he can muster, the generalissimo may nevertheless plunge China into civil war. He cannot succeed, however, where the Japanese in more than 7 years of determined striving had failed. The Communists are already too strong for him.
>
> Civil war would probably end in a mutually exhausted stalemate. China would be divided into at least two camps with Chiang reduced to the position of a regional warlord. The possibility should not be overlooked of the Communists — certainly if they receive foreign aid — emerging from a civil war swiftly and decisively victorious, in control of all China.[72]

Service also held the view that the Communists could not be eliminated by force because of the popular support they enjoyed and that, if the Na-

[71] *United States Relations with China,* pp. 566–67.
[72] Memo by John P. Davies, "Will the Communists Take Over China?" *State Department Employee Loyalty Investigation,* pp. 1436–37.

tionalist government started a civil war, "a Communist victory will be inevitable."[73]

Both Davies and Service based their forecasts on the assumption that the United States would not actively intervene on the side of the Nationalists, at least not to such an extent as would tip the balance. Davies thought at the time that, only if Chiang was able to enlist foreign military intervention on a scale equal to the Japanese invasion of China, would he be able to crush the Communists. But he thought that "foreign intervention on such a scale would seem to be unlikely."[74] In his testimony before the Tydings Committee investigating Senator Joseph McCarthy's charge of subversive influence in the State Department, Service emphasized that American military support for the Nationalist government in a civil war would have involved a huge and incalculable commitment, and that "almost certainly it would have involved large American forces — a sacrifice which the American people have not even yet shown an indication of willingness to accept."[75] He also thought that American aid would not be effective unless the Nationalist government reformed sufficiently to recapture popular support — an unlikely contingency, according to Service.

Thus, to Davies and Service, active American support for the Nationalist government to suppress or contain the Chinese Communists by force was never a feasible alternative. Instead, they placed their hopes on a political settlement bringing the two parties together under a coalition government. In this their position was the same as Hurley's. But, starting from diametrically opposite estimates of the relative strength of the Kuomintang and the Chinese Communists, the foreign service officers and Hurley entertained totally different ideas as to how such a coalition government could be established. Whereas Hurley believed that the Chinese Communists would accept Generalissimo Chiang's terms for a settlement once the Soviet Union concluded a political accord with the Nationalist government, the foreign service officers were convinced that unification could be achieved only if the United States applied pressure on the Nationalists. They urged that the American government co-operate with and aid the Communists partly as a military move in the war against Japan and partly as a measure to induce the Kuomintang to come to terms with the Communists.[76]

[73] Memo by John S. Service, "The Present and Future Strength of the Chinese Communists," dated October 9, 1944, *ibid.*, p. 1979.

[74] Davies' dispatch from Yenan, dated November 7, 1944, *ibid.*, p. 1437.

[75] *Ibid.*, p. 1264.

[76] In a memorandum entitled, "Military Weakness [*sic*] of Our Far Eastern Policy," dated February 14, 1945, Service and Ludden recommended the issuance of a public statement by the President, declaring America's intention to use the Communists in the war against Japan. They averred that such a declaration would have such profound

The conflicting estimates of relative strength, the divergent views over procedures, and the differing opinions regarding the terms of a Kuomintang-Communist rapprochement led naturally to entirely opposite judgments on the probable outcome of a political settlement. Whereas Hurley believed that the establishment of a coalition government would strengthen the Nationalists, Davies and Service saw clearly that it would mean the emergence of the Communists as the dominant political force in China.[77] Davies reported on December 9, 1944, that "the Generalissimo realizes that if he accedes to the Communist terms for a coalition government, they will sooner or later dispossess him and his Kuomintang of power."[78] Davies obviously concurred in this estimate of Chiang. The reasons for his belief can be found in his dispatch of November 7, 1944, which deserves to be quoted at length.

> Should the Generalissimo accept this compromise proposal [of the Communists] and a coalition government be formed with Chiang at the head, the Communists may be expected to continue effective control over the areas which they now hold. They will also probably extend their political influence throughout the rest of the country, for they are the only group in China possessing a program with positive appeal to the people.
>
> If the Generalissimo neither precipitates a civil war nor reaches an understanding with the Communists, he is still confronted with defeat. . . . Chiang's feudal China cannot long exist alongside a modern dynamic popular government in north China.
>
> The Communists are in China to stay. And China's destiny is not Chiang's but theirs.[79]

internal effects that "the Generalissimo would be forced to make concessions of power and permit united front coalition" (*ibid.*, p. 1981). In a telegram sent on February 26, 1945, George Atcheson, with the approval of all the political officers in the embassy, also expressed the idea that American aid to the Communists would strengthen the internal forces in China favorable to unity and thus "compel Chiang Kai-shek to make the concessions required for unity and to put his own house in order" (*ibid.*, p. 2014).

[77] It would seem that there was a shift in Service's position after he went to Yenan. In June, 1944, he believed that "it is almost certain that the Generalissimo and the Kuomintang would continue to play a dominant part in such a [multiparty united front] government" (*United States Relations with China*, p. 573). The excerpts from Service's reports under the dateline of June 20, 1944, as printed in *United States Relations with China*, present something of a puzzle to the researcher who is without access to State Department files. Two of the four paragraphs are taken from Service's report, "The Situation in China and Suggestions regarding American Policy," but with their order of appearance reversed. The quotation which is cited here in the footnote cannot be found in the report as printed in the *State Department Employee Loyalty Investigation*, pp. 2035–46. Yet the list of Service's reports shows that there was only one report sent by Service on June 20, 1944 (*ibid.*, p. 2485).

[78] *United States Relations with China*, p. 572.

[79] *State Department Employee Loyalty Investigation*, p. 1437.

Service thought so too. As Service himself told the Loyalty Security Board of the Department of State in May, 1950, "I believe that it is correct to say that we anticipated that, as the dominant and most dynamic force, the Communists would substantially be the strongest force, [or?] evenually [sic] become the strongest force in a coalition government. . . ."[80] Subsequent events and the Generalissimo's strenuous attempts to avoid arriving at a settlement with Communists except on his own terms suggest that Davies' and Service's appraisals of the relative strength of the Nationalists and Communists were much more accurate than Hurley's.

Given the actual and potential relative strength of the two parties, the supply of lend-lease arms to the Communists and the establishment of a coalition government including them would certainly have facilitated their ascendancy to total power in China. This Davies and Service undoubtedly knew.[81] Clearly, the fundamental assumption of their policy recommendations was that the Chinese Communists could be weaned from Moscow or at least encouraged to follow an independent and nationalistic policy. For them, the establishment of a coalition government, as well as the supply of arms to the Communists, was one way to establish a working relationship with the Communist party and to free the United States from her total commitment to a decadent regime. Service was optimistic about the possibility that a coalition government, with the Communists playing an important role, would serve American interests better than the existing regime. Part of his optimism was the obverse of his disgust with Chiang's government. He wrote a report dated October 10, 1944, that "any new Chinese government under any other than the present reactionary control will be more co-operative [with the United States] and better able to mobilize the country."[82] But basically he felt, as he told the Loyalty Security Board, that "there was a good chance" that a coalition government with the Communists as the strongest force would be "the kind of government that we might be able to work with, that would not swing over completely to the other side."[83]

Davies' contemporary reports were more guarded and more specific as to the possibilities and limitations of his recommendations. In a memo dated November 15, 1944, Davies wrote:

> But we must be realistic. We must not indefinitely underwrite a politically bankrupt regime. And if the Russians are going to

[80] *Ibid.*, p. 2024.

[81] In a report dated September 28, 1944, Service wrote: "And by improving the military effectiveness of the Communist forces, it [American military aid to the Communists] would increase their claimable share in winning the war. Both of these factors would raise the prestige of the Communist Party and ultimately its influence in China" (*ibid.*, p. 1327).

[82] *Ibid.*, p. 1988.

[83] *Ibid.*, p. 2024.

enter the Pacific War, we must make a determined effort to capture politically the Chinese Communists rather than allow them to
go by default wholly to the Russians. Furthermore, we must fully
understand that by reason of our recognition of the Chiang Kai-
shek Government as now constituted we are commited to a
steadily decaying regime and severely restricted in working out
military and political cooperation with the Chinese Communists.

A coalition Chinese Government in which the Communists find
a satisfactory place is the solution of this impasse most desirable
to us. It provides our greatest assurance of a strong, united, democratic, independent and friendly China — our basic strategic aim
in Asia and the Pacific. . . .

In seeking to determine which faction we should support we
must keep in mind these basic considerations: Power in China is
on the verge of shifting from Chiang to the Communists.[84]

Davies was realistic enough to recognize that, if the Russians were to
enter North China and Manchuria, it would be impossible for the United
States to win the Communists over entirely. But he was hopeful that
through control of supplies and postwar aid the United States could exert
considerable influence in the direction of Chinese nationalism and independence from Soviet control.[85]

Service's and Davies' hopes were shared by most of the foreign service
officers in China. This was shown by a report sent on February 26, 1945,
by George Atcheson, in charge of the embassy during Hurley's trip back
to the United States. It was drafted with the assistance and agreement of
all the political officers on the staff of the embassy at Chungking and indorsed by Brigadier General Mervin E. Gross, Wedemeyer's acting chief
of staff, then in acting command.[86] Among other things, this controversial
telegram suggested that by sending American aid to the Communists and
by urging the formation of "a war cabinet" including them, the United
States "could expect" to hold the Communists "to our side instead of throwing them into the arms of the Soviet Union, which is inevitable otherwise
in the event the U.S.S.R. enters the war against Japan."[87]

2. Davies' Conception of the Communists as "Backsliders"

In retrospect, it is clear that Service was clearly too optimistic about
the political orientation of a Communist-dominated coalition government.

[84] *United States Relations with China*, p. 574.
[85] *Ibid.*
[86] Feis, *op. cit.*, p. 268, n. 4.
[87] *United States Relations with China*, p. 92.

This misjudgment will be examined shortly. Davies' more guarded appraisals were linked to his more cautious judgments on the character of Chinese communism. Measured against the general understanding of the Chinese Communist movement at the time, his analysis, as far as this can be ascertained from published records, seems to have been among the more sophisticated views on the subject.[88] As early as June 24, 1943, Davies reported to his superiors the general suspicion that the leaders of the Chinese Communist party retained their pro-Russian orientation and were likely to be susceptible to Moscow's direction, notwithstanding the dissolution of the Comintern.[89] In a report on January 4, 1945, he clearly revealed his skepticism about the benevolent remarks of the Russian leaders which so greatly impressed Hurley. He wrote:

> The current situation in China must afford the Kremlin a certain sardonic satisfaction. . . . They observe the Chinese Communists consolidating in North China, expanding southward in the wake of Chiang's military debacles and now preparing for the formal establishment of a separatist administration. . . . However Marshal Stalin may describe the Chinese Communists to his American visitors, he can scarcely be unaware of the fact that the Communists are a considerably more stalwart and self-sufficient force than any European underground or partisan movement.[90]

But it is obvious today that even Davies tended to confuse the Communists' realistic adjustment to the Chinese environment with abandonment of their ultimate goals and to identify tactical moves with permanent change. In a memo entitled, "How Red Are the Chinese Communists?," Davies reported from Yenan on November 7, 1944:

> The Chinese Communists are backsliders. . . . Like the other eminent backslider, Ramsey MacDonald, they have come to accept the inevitability of gradualness. . . . Yenan is no Marxist New Jerusalem. The saints and prophets of Chinese Communism . . . lust after the strange gods of class compromise and party coalition, rather shamefacedly worship the golden calf of foreign

---

[88] Perhaps the only correct official appraisal of the nature and intentions of the Chinese Communists in this period was made in a military intelligence report entitled "The Chinese Communist Movement." See Senate Committee on the Judiciary, Subcommittee To Investigate the Administration of the Internal Security Act and Other Internal Security Laws, *Hearings on the Institute of Pacific Relations*, 82d Cong., 1st and 2d sess. (1951–52), pp. 2305–2447 (hereafter cited as *Institute of Pacific Relations*).

[89] *United States Relations with China*, p. 565.

[90] *Ibid.*, p. 567.

investments and yearn to be considered respectable by worldly standards. All this is more than scheming Communist opportunism.[91]

He also thought that the trend toward nationalism which he believed to be strong among the rank and file might conflict with the pro-Russian orientation of the leaders and thus produce a schism within the party.[92] It now appears clear that Davies did not see the possibility that Chinese nationalism might find its place within a framework of foreign policy derived from ideological considerations. He did not realize that in a party organized along Leninist lines, particularly in a group as unified as the Chinese Communist party, a schism can be produced only if the group is confronted with a dire dilemma, such as a choice between certain defeat and relinquishment of its fundamental principles (for instance, its internationalist orientation). This means that in the Chinese setting a schism would not have taken place unless the United States and her Chinese allies had brought overwhelming power to bear upon the Chinese Communists.

3. Service's Conceptions of the Communists as "a Party Seeking Orderly Democratic Growth toward Socialism" and the Sources of this Error

Service's views on the nature and intentions of the Chinese Communists deserve more detailed analysis because they reflected more accurately the thinking of many men of affairs and the general climate of opinion at the time. Although Service never characterized the Chinese Communists as "agrarian reformers" or used the generally accepted term "so-called Communists," [93] his reports, particularly those sent shortly after his arrival in Yenan, betrayed a profound misconception of the nature and intentions of the Chinese Communists. In a report sent from Yenan on September 8, 1944, Service wrote:

> [T]he Communist Party becomes *a party seeking orderly democratic growth toward socialism,* as is being attempted for instance, in a country like England, rather than a party fomenting immediate and violent revolution. It becomes a party which is *not seeking*

[91] *State Department Employee Loyalty Investigation,* p. 1436.
[92] *United States Relations with China,* p. 565.
[93] *State Department Employee Loyalty Investigation,* pp. 1373, 1332, 2021. In carefully scrutinizing all of Service's reports at the request of the Loyalty Security Board of the State Department, George Kennan, counselor of the Department, wrote in his notes: "Should be noted the CA's [i.e., The Division of Chinese Affairs] comments in the Department of Service's reporting consistently put Communist in quotation marks, implying something distinct from the Soviet brand. No evidence of this attitude has yet appeared in any of Service's work" (*ibid.,* p. 2488).

an early monopoly of political power but pursuing what it considers the long-term interests in [*sic*] China.[94]

This misconception of the nature of the Chinese Communist party stemmed from several sources. The most obvious one was ignorance of the inner dynamics of the movement — the fact that its totalitarian character is inherent in the Leninist principles of organization and in its aspiration for total power as an indispensable means to effect rapid and profound changes in the social order.[95] This led him to take at face value the "democratic" paraphernalia in Communist areas. In one of his most unguarded statements, Service wrote: "The Communist political program is democracy — advancing from the field of theory to that of practice, the Communist political program is simply democracy. This is much more American than Soviet in form and spirit."[96]

This judgment of the nature of the Chinese Communist party arose also from a misunderstanding of democracy. In Service's mind, a government which enjoyed popular support and promoted the interests of the majority was a democracy. Since the Communists enjoyed popular support and were apparently looking after the interest of the majority, there was democracy, or at least a tendency toward democracy in the Communist areas. Of democracy and popular support, Service wrote: "This widespread popular support enjoyed by the Communists must, under the circumstances in

[94] *Ibid.*, p. 2127. Emphasis added.

[95] After examining all the reports written by Service, George Kennan drew the following conclusion: "[T]here was in them [Service's reports] and in certain places a certain naïveté with respect to the Soviet Union, and perhaps with respect to the forces which were already at work though not on the surface within the International Communist movement and within the Chinese Communist movement in particular. . . . In the Russian Communist movement, all of us are convinced that the factors which have forced this movement to be more and more ruthless, more dictatorial, more addicted to a monopoly of power, more intolerant of any rival opinion, that those factors were planted in it at a very early date, actually at the time of the split between Bolsheviks and Mensheviks in 1904 and 1905, and that the principles of party organization and of methods which were adopted at that time by Lenin were ones which carried with them a sort of logical compulsion toward a greater and greater concentration of power, toward greater and greater excess on the part of the regime toward its enemies and toward the situation we have got today. Now it may be that the same is operable [*sic*] in the Chinese Communist movement to the extent that those Chinese Communists did have their ideological origin in Moscow; that they, in other words, had been infected by some of those same things. You don't see in the earlier ones of these reports from Yenan any recognition of that possibility" (*ibid.*, p. 2118).

It is to be noted that Davies and Service were trained as specialists in Chinese language and history and that their training as foreign service officers did not include an intensive study of Marxism-Leninism and the Communist movement.

[96] *Ibid.*, p. 1365. He also wrote: "The Communists have used their influence in a democratic way to further democratic ends" (*ibid.*, p. 2080). "The policies of the Communist Party have been democratic and there is little which under the circumstances can be called undemocratic" (*ibid.*, p. 2085).

which it has occurred, be considered a practical indication that the policies and methods of the Chinese Communists have a democratic character."[97]

On democracy and promotion of the interests of the people, Service stated:

> The conclusion therefore seems justified that the peasants support, join and fight with the Communist armies because they have been convinced that, the Communists are fighting for their interests, and because the Communists have created this conviction by producing some tangible benefits for the peasants.
>
> These benefits must be improvement of the social, political and economic condition of the peasants. Whatever the exact nature of this improvement, it must be — *in the broadest sense of the term as serving the interests of the people — toward democracy.*[98]

It is clear that Service failed to see that a totalitarian movement or government can sometimes stir up intense popular enthusiasm and serve the interests of the majority and that a system of elections can be nothing more than a tool to foster a sense of participation among the masses. Modern totalitarianism differs from traditional absolutism in placing a high value on widespread popular support which it often succeeds in obtaining.[99] What distinguishes the popular support for a totalitarian government from that for a democracy is the different manner in which they are created — in one case there is a monopolistic control by one party over all effective levers of power and, in the other, there is more than one center of power competing for the consent and support of the governed through constitutional processes.

No one can deny that in 1944 and 1945 when Service wrote the bulk of his reports the Communists enjoyed widespread popular support in the border regions and guerrilla bases. Only popular support enabled them to survive Japanese attacks and to contest the control of the Nationalist government. In order to generate this backing, it was imperative for them to

[97] *Ibid.*, p. 1328.

[98] *Ibid.*, p. 1361. Emphasis added. On elections and democracy, Service still held in 1950 when he testified before the Tydings Committee that "the fact that they [the Communists] did hold any form of village elections is a measure of democracy which China up to that time had not known" (*ibid.*, p. 1312).

[99] Hans J. Morgenthau, "The Dilemmas of Freedom," *American Political Science Review*, September, 1957, pp. 717–18; Carl J. Friedrich and Zbigniew K. Brzezinski, *Totalitarian Dictatorship and Autocracy* (Cambridge, Mass.: Harvard University Press, 1956). Since Service failed to understand this particular feature of modern totalitarianism, he could not explain the popular support enjoyed by the Communists except by attributing to them a democratic orientation. "We cannot yet say with certainty that the Communist claims of democratic politics are true, but that they are at least partially true is the only reasonable explanation of the popular appeal which the Communist armies have shown" (*State Department Employee Loyalty Investigation*, p. 1372).

adopt policies that actually promoted the interests of the people and secured their unswerving loyalty. The more hard-pressed the Communists
were, the more assiduously they had to court the people. It is therefore not
without reason that the efficiency and general standard of government
were lower in Yenan, a relatively safe base, than in the front-line areas.[100] It
was also not accidental that many of the policies, which were to win the
praise of American observers were either inaugurated or effectively implemented during the period of 1941–42 when the Japanese "mopping-up"
campaigns confronted the Communists with the gravest crisis in all the
years of the Sino-Japanese War.

In 1941 the Communists began seriously to reorganize the governments in the border regions and guerrilla bases in accordance with the so-
called "three-thirds system" under which the Communists would occupy
no more than one-third of the positions in governmental organs and elec-
tive bodies on all levels, the other two thirds being divided between "Kuomintang" members and other political elements. In the period 1941–42, the
Communists also implemented more effectively than before their policy
of rent and interest-rate reduction, set up a unified system of progressive
taxes, lowered the amount of grain collection from the peasants, reduced
the number of government employees, removed incompetent cadres from
office through elections, and generally improved the administrative efficiency of their governments.[101] The true nature of the elections in Com-
unist areas is revealed in a Communist history of this period: "The elections
in the guerrilla bases became a mass movement to unite all anti-Japanese
people."[102] The intraparty movement for the "rectification of the style of
work" was also part and parcel of the Communist response to the grave
challenge. It had two features which at first glance appeared to conflict with
each other: the emphasis on the necessity of adapting Marxist-Leninist
theory to Chinese conditions and the rigorous application of the Leninist concept of the Party as a highly centralized, highly disciplined elite.[103]
American observers generally directed their attention toward the former
characteristic, which the Communists themselves stressed in their talks
with outsiders. These observers were quite unaware of the second feature
which was hidden to untrained eyes.[104]

[100] Affidavit of Lord Lindsay of Birker (Michael Lindsay), *Institute of Pacific Relations*, p. 5372.
[101] *K'ang Jih chan-chêng shih-ch'i chieh-fang-chü kai-k'uang*, pp. 3, 11, 12, 31–33,
62–65, 103–4. See also Hu Hua, *op. cit.*, p. 223, Hu Ch'iao-mu, *op. cit.*, p. 46.
[102] *K'ang Jih chan-chêng shih-ch'i chien-fang ch'ü kai-k'uang*, p. 32.
[103] Brandt *et al.*, *op. cit.*, pp. 372–419. See also Boyd Compton, *Mao's China: Party
Reform Documents, 1942–1944* (Seattle: University of Washington Press, 1952).
[104] See, for example, Service Report No. 34, "The Orientation of the Chinese Communists toward the Soviet Union and the United States," dated September 28, 1944,
Institute of Pacific Relations, pp. 5419–24.

By 1944 when American correspondents and the Army Observer mission, which Service accompanied, visited the Communist areas, these reforms had been pushed forward for two years and the Communists had entered another new phase of expansion. Consequently, the dynamism, hopefulness, self-reliance, and dedication in the Communist areas contrasted sharply with the gloom, stagnation, despair, and selfishness in Nationalist China. Against this background, it is understandable that American observers were enchanted by the political atmosphere of Yenan. Furthermore, in the special circumstances under which the Communists extended and consolidated their authority, their monopolistic hold on all effective levers of power appeared natural to many American observers. In most instances in the early years of the Sino-Japanese War, the Communist armies flowed into the political void created by the defeat of the Nationalist troops at the hands of the Japanese. In the border regions and guerrilla bases there was no organized political opposition and only in the Shansi-Hopei-Chahar border region was there a nominal Kuomintang organization, which in fact collaborated with the Communists in an area under their indisputable control. Those opposed to the Communists found refuge in the Japanese-held cities and towns. Those who remained in the Communist areas or went back voluntarily were ready to co-operate with them.

Service himself vividly portrayed the political success of the Communists in his report entitled "The Development of Communist Political Control in the Guerrilla Bases," which even today makes fascinating reading. Service recognized that "the actual situation, therefore, is that no strong opposition has developed to the Communists and they have remained the undisputably [sic] dominant political factor."[105] In this report and elsewhere, he pointed out that popular support was indispensable to the Communists in their fight for survival against Japanese assaults and in their struggle for control over all China.[106] Service wrote:

> The Communist leaders stress the importance and precedence of these measures: *first and basic*, limited rent-interest reduction to win the active support of the peasants, who are the bulk of the population; *second*, democratic self-government to bring all classes, particularly the landlord-merchants into active participation and hence support of the government. This conception of importance of *democracy as a means of obtaining the participation and support of the capitalist groups* is interesting and signifi-

[105] Service memo dated September 10, 1944, "The Development of Communist Political Control in the Guerrilla Bases," *State Department Employee Loyalty Investigation*, pp. 2080–85. The quotation is taken from p. 2083.
[106] *Ibid.*, p. 1362. See also *United States Relations with China*, p. 566.

cant in the study of present and probable future Communist policies. They have no illusions that China can hope to build a proletarian state in anything like the near future.[107]

But Service's insufficient grasp of the distinction between democracy in the West and "democracy" as a means to obtain popular support prevented him from drawing the proper conclusion from his valid observations. Service also did not lay sufficient stress on the commonplace that modern democracy cannot exist without more than one party or without those conditions which make possible the development of an effective opposition party. Hence the following somewhat self-contradictory statement appeared in his report: "This institution of political democracy [in the Communist areas] has not, however, been accompanied by political development along definite party forms."[108]

4. Service's Trust in Communist Professions of Friendship for the United States

Even before he visited Yenan in the company of the Army Observer Group in the summer of 1944, Service believed that the Chinese Communists were friendly to the United States. In a report dated April 21, 1944, he stated: "The Communists, from what little we know of them, also are friendly toward America, believe that democracy must be the next step in China, and take the view that economic collaboration with the United States is the only hope for speedy postwar rehabilitation and development. It is vital that we do not lose this good will and influence."[109] This belief was further strengthened by his initial contacts with the Chinese Communist leader in Yenan. Shortly after he arrived in Yenan, he concluded that "politically, any orientation which the Chinese Communists may once have had toward the Soviet Union seems a thing of the past."[110] He reported that the Chinese Communists believed that the United States rather than the Soviet Union would be the only country able to give economic assistance to China. He further stated that they concluded that "American friendship and support is more important to China than Russia [Russian support?]"[111] He himself obviously did not doubt the sincerity of their beliefs.[112]

These conclusions were based primarily upon personal remarks of Chi-

[107] *State Department Employee Loyalty Investigation*, p. 2082. Emphasis added.
[108] *Ibid.*, p. 2083.
[109] *Ibid.*, p. 1978.
[110] Report by Service, dated September 28, 1944, *Institute of Pacific Relations*, p. 5419.
[111] *Ibid.*
[112] *Ibid.*, pp. 5419–20.

nese Communist leaders who in their talks with Service stressed the importance of American economic aid to China's reconstruction and Chinese good will toward America. According to Service's summary of his interviews with Po Ku, a member of the Politbureau, Mao Tse-tung, and Liu Shao-ch'i, the Chinese Communist leaders believed that the Soviet Union would be unable to provide the needed large-scale economic assistance to China, that the United States was the only country in a position to do so, that "America has all of China's good will," and that China should make investment attractive to foreign capital.[113]

These professions of friendship for the United States and the belittling of the future role of the Soviet Union stood in sharp contrast to the Chinese Communists' orientation toward the Soviet Union in the earlier days, which Service dismissed as "a thing of the past." The Chinese Communist leaders had never failed to acknowledge the Soviet source of their aspirations.[114] They had seldom deviated from Marxist-Leninist conceptions on international affairs. As far back as 1926, Mao Tse-tung had subscribed to the theory of the two camps. In an article entitled "Analysis of the Classes in Chinese Society," he wrote that "the present world situation is one in which the two big forces, revolution and counter-revolution, are engaged in the final struggle." The forces of revolution rallied around the Third International and the counterrevolutionary elements were grouped around the League of Nations. Sooner or later, the intermediate class would either turn left and join the ranks of revolution or turn right and join the counter-revolution. "There is no room for any to remain 'independent.' " [115] Mao made it clear in which camp he stood. The Communist determination to advance Communism throughout the world was again attested to by a proclamation issued by the Chinese Communist party in the winter of 1931 at the time of the establishment of the so-called Provisional Central Government of the Chinese Soviet Republic. It reads in part:

> . . . the provisional government of the Soviet Republic of China declared that it will, under no condition, remain content with the overthrow of imperialism in China, but, on the contrary, will aim as its ultimate objective in waging a war against world imperialism until the latter is all blown up.[116]

[113] *Ibid.*, p. 5423–24.

[114] For a general discussion of the ideological basis of the view of the Chinese Communists on international affairs, see H. Arthur Steiner, "Mainsprings of Chinese Communist Foreign Policy," *American Journal of International Law*, January, 1950, pp. 69–99. See also I-kua Chou, "Communist China's Foreign Policy," *American Scholar*, Spring, 1955, pp. 137–57.

[115] Mao Tse-tung, *Selected Works*, I (London: Lawrence and Wishart, 1954), 14–15.

[116] Quoted by O. Edmund Clubb in "Chinese Communist Strategy in Foreign Relations," *Annals of the American Academy of Political and Social Science*, September, 1951, p. 157.

The theory of the two camps again found forceful expression in his *On New Democracy*. In this now famous work, he asserted that the Chinese Revolution is part of the world revolution and that China could never attain independence "without the assistance of the Soviet Union" and "the international proletariat." "Refuse Soviet aid and the revolution will fail," [117] he asserted. On the present and future of the capitalist countries, he wrote: "Today, after the outbreak of the second imperialist war, there is no longer even a dash of democratic flavoring in *all* of the capitalist countries. *All of them* have already been transformed or will shortly be transformed into bloody military dictatorships of the bourgeoisie." [118] Anticipating his famous statement of "leaning to one side," [119] he wrote:

> As the conflict between the socialist Soviet Union and the *imperialist Great Britain and the United States* becomes further intensified, it is inevitable that China must stand either on one side or on the other. Is it possible to incline to neither side? No, this is an illusion. All the countries in the world will be swept into one or the other of these two camps, and in the world today "neutrality" is becoming merely a deceptive phrase. [120]

In reaffirming the theory of the two camps in this political tract written in the period of German-Soviet pact, Mao even refused to draw a basic distinction between Japan, with whom China was at war, and the United States and Great Britain, from whom China had obtained and continued to expect financial, moral, and diplomatic support. He used the term "Eastern imperialism" to refer to Japan and the term "Western imperialism" to indicate the Western power. He rejected the idea of establishing an alliance with Great Britain and the United States to oppose Japan on the ground that such an alliance would inevitably involve China in a war with the Soviet Union. Mao wrote:

> Eastern and Western imperialisms, being different, suppose we, unlike he [i.e., Wang Ching-wei] who allies himself with the

[117] Mao, *Selected Works*, III, 109–15, 124.

[118] Mao, *Hsin-min-chu-chu-i lun* ["On New Democracy"], pp. 16–17. Emphasis added. In the *Selected Works*, this passage is rendered in such a way as to tone down his attack on the capitalist countries: "Today, after the outbreak of the second imperialist war, there is no longer even a dash of democratic flavoring in *many* of the capitalist countries, *which* have come under or are coming under the bloody military dictatorship of the bourgeoisie" (Mao, *Selected Works*, III, 119. Emphasis added).

[119] Mao Tse-tung, *On People's Democratic Dictatorship* (Peking: Foreign Languages Press, 1952), p. 10.

[120] Mao, *Hsin-min-chu-chu-i lun* ["On New Democracy"], p. 34. Emphasis added. In the *Selected Works*, the crucial sentence is rendered thus: "As the conflict between the socialist Soviet Union and *the imperialist powers* becomes intensified. . . ." The specific reference to Great Britain and the United States is omitted (Mao, *Selected Works*, III, 135. Emphasis added).

Eastern imperialism, ally ourselves with a group of *ta-ma* Western imperialists and then march eastward and attack, would not that be quite revolutionary? But unfortunately, the Western imperialists want to oppose the Soviet Union and communism, so if you are allied with them they will request you to march northward and attack, and your revolution will come to nothing.[121]

Perhaps of more immediate importance than the espousal of the theory of the two camps and the castigation of the United States as one of the imperialist powers was the compulsion on the part of the Chinese Communists to express approval of the zigzags in Soviet foreign policy. Obviously, they considered it their duty to align their policy with that of the Soviet Union, even at the cost of their own political influence in China. One glaring example was their justification of the German-Soviet Non-aggression Pact of August, 1939. The German-Soviet pact was far from popular in China, particularly among the influential group of intellectuals, because it disappointed them in their hope that a world-wide alliance between the democracies and the Soviet Union would be established to oppose Germany, Japan, and Italy. It also stirred up fears of a Russo-Japanese rapprochement which would isolate China diplomatically. In an interview on September 1, 1939, with the correspondent of a Communist newspaper, Mao expressed unqualified approval of the German-Soviet pact.[122] Mao's views on the subject were further elaborated in an interview with Edgar Snow on September 26, 1939. Mao characterized the European war as "an imperialist war" and "simply a robber war with justice on neither side." Indeed, according to him, "the so-called democratic countries began to utilize war to bring an end to democracy" and "became the center of anti-Soviet, anti-Communist, anti-democratic and anti-popular movements and the enemy of the colonial and semi-colonial people's movement." He indicated that the policy of the Communist parties in different countries must be changed in the light of the new international situation.[123] Two days later, he justified the Soviet invasion of Poland as an act to recover "the Soviet Union's own territory," "to liberate the small nations," "to check the eastward expansion of the German aggressive forces and to smash Chamberlain's intrigue."[124]

[121] Mao, *Hsin-min-chu-chu-i lun*, ["On New Democracy"], p. 34. In the *Selected Works*, the words "ta-ma" are omitted. The translation is taken from the *Selected Works* with the omitted words reinserted to bring out the flavor of the original version (*Selected Works*, III, 136). The two Chinese words were used by members of lower classes to insult others. They cannot be translated and printed.

[122] *Ibid.*, pp. 31–37.

[123] Edgar Snow, "Interviews with Mao Tse-tung," *China Weekly Review*, January 13, 1940, pp. 244–46, and January 20, 1940, pp. 277–80. The quotations are taken from pp. 277, 278, 279.

[124] Mao, "Soviet Union and Mankind," in *Selected Works*, III, 50.

This view of the nature of the international alignment represented a complete reversal of the position of the Chinese Communists. Earlier, the editorials of the official Communist newspaper had characterized Great Britain, the United States, France, and the Soviet Union as friends of China whereas Germany and Italy were referred to as supporters of Japan. Under the slogan "Fascism is war," the democracies were urged to unite quickly and deal the Fascists heavy blows. The democracies and the Soviet Union were mentioned in one breath as the nations from which China should ask material support and sanctions against Japan.[125]

Another conspicuous example of the compulsion of the Chinese Communists to express approval of Soviet policy was their pronouncement on the Soviet-Japanese Neutrality Pact of April, 1941, and the accompanying Frontier Declaration under which "the U.S.S.R. pledges to respect the territorial integrity and inviolability of Manchoukuo, and Japan pledges to respect the territorial integrity and inviolability of the Mongolian People's Republic." [126] The pact aroused apprehension in China that the Soviet Union would discontinue the shipment of war supplies to China. It stirred up fear that the easing of tension between the two countries would enable Japan to shift part of her seasoned troops from Manchuria to eastern and central China. The Frontier Declaration seemed to indicate Russia's willingness to recognize Manchoukuo. It ran counter to the Sino-Soviet Treaty of 1924 in which the Soviet government recognized "the sovereignty" of China over Outer Mongolia. The Nationalist government protested against the Frontier Declaration and the leading independent newspaper in China called the agreement "regrettable." Even after the Soviet government reassured China that Sino-Soviet relations would not be altered by the pact, public opinion in China was still dissatisfied with the declaration regarding Manchoukuo and Mongolia, though it took comfort in the fact that trade with Russia would not be interrupted.[127]

Against this background the endeavor on the part of the Chinese Com-

[125] *Hsin-hua jih-pao shê-lun* ["The Editorials of the New China Daily"] (Chungking: Hsin-hua jih-pao-shê, 1938), pp. 16, 881, 928, 158. See also Mao, "On Protracted War," *Selected Works*, II, 198.

[126] For the full text of the Neutrality Pact and Frontier Declaration, see *Amerasia*, May, 1941, pp. 109–10.

[127] Beloff, *op. cit.*, pp. 374–75. See also Philip J. Jaffe, "The Soviet-Japanese Neutrality Pact," *Amerasia*, May, 1941, pp. 109–14.

Several works written from the Nationalist point of view suggested that shipments of war supplies from the Soviet Union were discontinued or reduced as a result of the Soviet-Japanese Pact (Wei, *op. cit.*, p. 153; Cheng, *op. cit.*, p. 220). On the other hand, Beloff indicated that the subsequent course of trade relations bore out the Soviet assurance that Russian policy toward China remained unchanged. Soviet deliveries to China stopped only after the Nazi attack on Russia. For a discussion of the pact see David J. Lu, *From the Marco Polo Bridge to Pearl Harbor* (Washington, D.C.: Public Affairs Press, 1961), pp. 136–40.

munists to justify this new turn in Soviet policy was a measure of their subservience to the Soviet Union in international affairs. In a statement published shortly after the signing of the Soviet-Japanese Neutrality Pact, the Chinese Communists asserted that in strengthening the international position of the U.S.S.R. the pact "benefits the peace-loving persons and oppressed peoples of the world and not reactionary groups." On the Frontier Declaration on Manchoukuo and Outer Mongolia, they commented that in guaranteeing the security of Outer Mongolia it "is not only of positive significance for Outer Mongolia" but "will also benefit the liberation cause of the whole of China." As to the Soviet pledge "to respect the territorial integrity and inviolability of Manchoukuo," they took the position that "the return of the four Northeastern provinces of China is our personal affair. Under no circumstances can we entertain a hope, as certain speculators do, that the U.S.S.R. will start a war with Japan and we shall be able to take advantage of this."[128]

Another twist took place two months later when Germany invaded the Soviet Union. The Chinese Communist organs echoed an inner-party directive written by Mao himself, calling for unity "against the common foe with all the people in Britain, the United States and other countries who are opposed to the fascist rulers of Germany, Italy and Japan."[129] Thus, like Communists all over the world, the Chinese Communists traveled full circle and reverted to the party line of "the anti-Fascist international front." Whatever might be said about the uniqueness of the domestic program of the Chinese Communists, there could scarcely be any doubt that in international affairs their attitudes were precisely the same as those of other Communist parties.

This practice of following the twists and turns in Soviet policy, the espousal of the theory of the two camps, the adherence to the cause of advancing communism throughout the world, and the glorification of the role of the Soviet Union in the Chinese revolution — all reflected the Chinese Communist party's ideological and organizational ties with the Soviet Union and its hope for eventual Soviet support. They suggest to us now that its profession of friendship for the United States had only a tactical significance. Why, then, was Service so optimistic about its present and future orientation in international affairs? One factor was obviously his belief in the democratic character of the Communist regime and his approval of its program of seeking Chinese unity which paralleled the American policy of peaceful unification. Another factor was his misjudgment of the role of ideology in Communist behavior. To Service, the Marxism of the Chinese Communists was "chiefly an attitude and

[128] This statement was reproduced in *Amerasia*, May, 1941, pp. 113–14.
[129] Mao, *Selected Works*, IV, 23.

approach to problems."[130] His conclusion about the diplomatic orientation of the Chinese Communists rested on the assumption that such an approach to problems would not lead them to misjudge the intentions of a capitalistic United States and to repose greater trust in the Soviet Union. Another related assumption was that ideology would not influence their choice of long-term objectives in international affairs. This underestimation of the importance of ideology led Service and other American observers to overestimate the immediate, as distinguished from the long-term, significance for the Chinese Communists' international orientation of several undeniable factors: their ability to survive and grow without any direct assistance from the Soviet Union, their possession of an indigenous political base, and the existence of a leadership which did not owe its power in party councils to Stalin's support.

Furthermore, insofar as Service saw the importance of ideology, he was misled, as noted above, by the chêng-fêng movement of the Chinese Communists, which, among other things, stressed the need to apply Marxism-Leninism in the light of the specific conditions in China. Thus, he reported that "the Communists have worked to make their thinking and program realistically Chinese and they are carrying out democratic policies which they expect the United States to approve and sympathetically support."[131] He overlooked the other equally important aspect of the chêng-fêng movement, which was the strengthening of the party by the rigorous application of the Leninist principles of organization. Service's affirmation of the one aspect and neglect of the other was consistent with his basic view that, to the Chinese Communists, Marxism-Leninism was chiefly an attitude and an approach rather than a program with specific content. Service recognized the power-political considerations underlying the Communists' "friendship" for the United States. But his underestimation of the importance of Marxism-Leninism as a framework within which Yenan's specific policies took their place led him to stress the sincerity of the Chinese Communists. Thus he concluded:

> This apparently strong orientation of the Chinese Communists toward the United States may be contrary to general expectation — which may be too ready to emphasize the Communist name of the party. Apart from what may be called the practical considerations that the United States will be the strongest power in the Pacific area and America the country best able to give economic assistance to China, it is also based on the strong Communist emotion that China cannot remain divided. I believe that

[130] Report by Service, August 3, 1944, *United States Relations with China*, p. 565.
[131] Service's Report, September 28, 1944, *Institute of Pacific Relations*, p. 5419.

the Chinese Communists are at present sincere in seeking Chinese
unity on the basis of American support.[132]

Service foresaw that the Chinese Communists would turn to the Soviet
Union for support in order to survive an American-supported Kuomintang
attack.[133] After he had been in Yenan for over six months, he was observ-
ant enough to find out that, despite Communist denials, there was contact
between the Chinese Communists and Moscow through party channels,
though not on the government level.[134] But these observations seem to
have strengthened his view that the American government should take
active steps to wean the Chinese Communists from Moscow.

In retrospect, it seems clear that the Communists' professions of friendship for the United States in 1944–45 represented a tactical adjustment to
the power-political situation in the Far East at that time and in the near
future on the basis of their estimates. This tactical adjustment was a product of a curious mixture of fears and hopes. It stands to reason that, on the
one hand, the Chinese Communists were impressed with the tremendous
power which the United States could bring to bear in China and, on the
other, they were uncertain of Soviet intentions toward them and of Soviet
ability to help them.[135] Their belief in the aggressive nature of all capitalist
countries may have inclined them to think that American power would
be used to the limit to further American interests. But, for the moment,
the American policy of peaceful unification of China was in accord with
their political strategy and would most likely help increase their influence.
By their professions of friendship for the United States and their stress

[132] Ibid., pp. 5419–20.
[133] Ibid., p. 5420.
[134] Report by Service, March 23, 1945, State Department Employee Loyalty Investigation, p. 2020.
[135] Service reported that the Chinese Communists "complain they knew less than
anyone else about such subjects as what the Soviet Union will do" (ibid.).
Testifying before the Security Loyalty Board, George Kennan stated: "Throughout
a large part of this period I am quite convinced that the Soviet Government was not
able to give very much attention to the Chinese Communists, that it was not giving
them any aid. On the contrary, if it was giving any aid to China it was going certainly
primarily to the Chinese Central Government, and it was simply too preoccupied with
the tremendous pressure of its own war effort and the resistance of the German attack
to bother about these fellows out there at all. I think it entirely plausible . . . that the
Communists felt themselves on their own and were themselves uncertain how their
relationship with the Soviet Government was going to shape up when the war was over.
Now that being the case, I think it is quite plausible that during those years they
wandered further from the typical Comintern outlook of affiliation with the Soviet
Government than perhaps any Communist Party in good standing has ever wandered,
and they were also at that time engaged in the war with the Japanese and in the Far
East a very considerable battle threatened their own power in China against [sic] the
Chinese Central Government. For that reason I think it is no wonder that they gave an
impression of sincerity and of concentration on purposes which are not normally associated with the Communist movement throughout those years" (ibid., pp. 2120–21).

on the importance of American economic assistance and foreign investment, they hoped to deflect the United States from actively intervening
on the side of the Nationalists and to encourage her to act vigorously in
her policy of bringing about a coalition government.[136]

It is easy to see that such a balance between hopes and fears was essentially unstable and Communist "friendship" for the United States had
a precarious foundation. Any move made by the United States to strengthen
the military and political position of the Nationalist government would
arouse resentment on the part of the Communists. This resentment could
be kept from erupting into openly anti-American attitude and action
only when it could be offset by a greater fear of American might. Reflecting Hurley's program of supporting Chiang, the imminent end of the European war, and the impending recovery by the Soviet Union of freedom of
action in the Far East, Mao's public pronouncement in 1945 gave evidence of a slight shift toward a greater partiality for the Soviet Union. In
his famous political report to the Seventh National Congress, "On Coalition Government," Mao called on the Nationalist government to desist
from taking a hostile attitude toward the Soviet Union and to improve
Sino-Soviet relations, while warning the American and British governments not to help "the Chinese reactionaries to stop the Chinese people's
pursuit of democracy." After expressing the gratitude of the Chinese
people to the Soviet government for its assistance in the war, he asserted
that "the final, thorough solution of the Pacific problem is impossible without the participation of the Soviet Union."[137] But Mao still professed to
steer a middle course in foreign affairs. To balance his tribute to the
Soviet Union, he expressed appreciation toward the United States and
a feeling of neighborliness for the American people.[138]

[136] In conversations with American foreign service officers, Chinese Communist
leaders urged, as early as November, 1942, that the American government use its immense influence to restrain the Kuomintang, to end the Nationalist blockade, and to
recognize the Communist army as "a participant in the war" "of democracy against
fascism." See memorandum by Service dated January 23, 1943, "Kuomintang-Communist Situation," *ibid.*, pp. 1974–77; see especially p. 1977.

[137] Mao Tse-tung, "On Coalition Government," Gelder, *op. cit.*, p. 50.

[138] Mao wrote: "We are also grateful to Britain and the United States, particularly
the latter, for their immense contribution to the common cause — the defeat of the
Japanese aggressors, and for their sympathy with the Chinese people and their help."
After referring to a statement made by the late President Roosevelt, he stated that "in
fact, the American people, once thought by the Chinese people to be living very far
away, are now our next door neighbors. Together with the British, American, Soviet,
French and other peoples of the world, the Chinese people will build up a firm and
durable world peace" (*ibid.*, pp. 50–51). These two paragraphs are retained in the
Chinese version of the work published in January, 1950 (Mao Tse-tung, *Lun lien-ho
chêng-fu* ["On Coalition Government"] [Tientsin: Hsin-hua shu-tien, 1950], pp. 78–
80). They are omitted in both the Chinese and English versions of Mao's *Selected
Works*, published in 1953 and 1956, respectively. In the Chinese version of 1950, there

If the above analysis is correct, Communist friendship could not have been permanently secured for the United States through the course of action recommended by Davies and Service. The Communists might have maintained their friendly posture so long as American actions and policy facilitated the expansion of their power and influence. But once they had come into power or felt strong enough to defy the United States with impunity, the power-political calculations from which professions of friendship for the United States apparently stemmed would have lost much of their weight. Correspondingly, ideological considerations and the organizational ties with the international Communist movement would have exercised greater influence. The likely outcome would have been the adoption of an increasingly pro-Soviet policy, particularly when the Soviet Union was in a position to lend them the necessary support.[139]

It would seem that the Chinese Communists would have maintained a "friendly" attitude toward the United States only under two circumstances. The first would have been an irreconcilable conflict of interests between the Soviet Union and the Chinese Communist party, developing into an open rupture. There was very little the United States could have done positively to bring about such a discord. Second, the Chinese Communists would have continued to adopt an outwardly friendly attitude toward the United States or a relatively independent policy only if the United States had confronted them with overwhelming power and the Soviet Union had not been in a position to render them any effective help: that is to say, when accommodation to American policy and co-operation with the United States would have constituted the only alternative to total defeat or destruction. Such a position of overwhelming strength could have been created only under the following conditions: (a) had the United States been willing and able to intervene in the Chinese political-military struggle on a large scale; (b) had the Pacific war terminated before or at the end of the war in Europe by an early modification of the policy of unconditional surrender and thus before the Soviet Union could exploit the fluid situation in the Far East; (c) had American power been maintained in such overwhelming proportions as to dissuade any Soviet attempt to challenge it.

But the very assumption on which Service and Davies based their recommendations ran counter to these prerequisites for the success of

is a lengthy discussion of the Yalta Conference which is omitted from both the 1953 Chinese edition and the 1956 English edition.

[139] This analysis rejects by implication the widely held view that if the United States had not helped the Nationalist government against the Communists, the latter would have remained friendly to the United States when they came to power in China. The foreign policy of Marshall Tito after his ascension to power but before his break with Moscow seems to support the judgment expressed here.

their policy to detach the Chinese Communists from the Soviet Union. First and foremost, they assumed that the United States could not and would not intervene militarily in the Chinese civil war on a scale necessary to defeat the Communists or to contain them in a part of China. Second, they, like most of the other American officials, assumed that it was to the advantage of the United States to bring the Soviet Union into the Pacific war. Once Soviet military and political power re-entered the Far East, the Russian Communists would be in a position to give considerable help to their Chinese comrades. Thus, the thinking of Davies and Service was involved in a paradox. Having assumed that the United States could not and would not intervene in China on a large scale, they gambled on the chance of retaining the friendship of the Chinese Communists. Yet the Communists would have remained "friendly" only if the United States had been willing and able, on the one hand, to undertake eventually all necessary measures, including military intervention, to effect the outcome of the political and military struggle in China and, on the other hand, to pursue a policy which would not immediately jeopardize their existence. Any policy based upon a refusal to intervene militarily in the Chinese civil war would have been doomed to failure. Service's and Davies' misunderstanding of the nature and intentions of the Chinese Communist party prevented them from seeing all the implications of their recommendations. This misjudgment stemmed ultimately from an underestimation of the role of ideology in Chinese Communist affairs.

It is beyond the scope of this study to discuss systematically the role of ideology in human affairs. But the international orientation of the Chinese Communist party, together with the foreign policies of the Peking regime, seems to suggest that ideology provides a broad framework within which other political forces, such as nationalism and national interest, may find expression. It may determine the form and direction which these other political forces take. As for the interaction between ideology and reality, the process can be very complex. Composed of a series of assumptions of various degrees of abstraction, ideology can be "creatively" applied to unforeseen situations without losing its vitality. It is not incompatible with tactical adjustments to power reality, even with those expediencies which apparently run counter to a fundamentalist interpretation of its meaning, for tactical expediency is nothing more than a means with which the power reality necessitating the tactical maneuver can later be changed. Only when confronted by stubborn reality which the elite endeavors and fails, over a long period of time, to change, will ideology be eroded. The willingness and ability of the ideology's opponents to create positions of strength constitute one element of the political reality which will lead either to ideological adaptation or to ideological erosion.

C. The Source of the General Misunderstandings of the Nature and
Intentions of the Chinese Communist Party

In order to put the views of Service and Davies in proper perspective, one must underscore the fact that their assumptions were widely shared by other American officials and men of affairs and that, in particular, their misunderstanding of the nature and intentions of the Chinese Communist party was simply a reflection of the climate of opinion at the time. Such a widespread misjudgment could not have been the product of a conspiracy. Its source must be sought in a social and political fact which was as ubiquitous as the misjudgment. This seems to have been none other than the American political tradition itself. This interpretation emerges clearly when one broadens an analysis of the views of Service and Davies into an examination of the prevailing opinions of other officials, scholars, writers, and men of affairs and when one undertakes this task in the light of the American political tradition in which American liberalism forms a predominant part.

1. The American Political Tradition

The American polity was, and perhaps still is, unique in that it was blessed with a high degree of moral unity. It was a society in which basic values were "taken for granted" and all problems emerged as problems of techniques to be solved "on the basis of a submerged and absolute liberal faith."[140] There was a belief that "values in America are in some way or other automatically defined: given by certain facts of geography and history peculiar to us."[141] This "giveness" of her values concealed the importance of the agreement on basic principles to which America owed

[140] Louis Hartz, *The Liberal Tradition in America* (New York: Harcourt, Brace & Co., 1955), p. 10.

[141] Daniel J. Boorstin, *The Genius of American Politics* (Chicago: University of Chicago Press, 1953), pp. 8–9.
This prevailing interpretation of the American political tradition has recently been challenged by implication in Harry V. Jaffa's study of the Lincoln-Douglas Debate, *Crisis of the House Divided* (Garden City, N.Y.: Doubleday & Co., 1959). Jaffa argues that basic disagreement over political values, principles, and philosophies were not only involved in the issues leading to the Civil War but also clearly expounded by the two great debaters themselves. For our purpose, it is not necessary to decide which of the two views of the Civil War and, consequently, the two interpretations of the American political tradition is correct. It is sufficient to take as our point of departure that in the twentieth century scholars generally believed or assumed that a basic automatic agreement on values characterized the American polity. Whether it was real or assumed, this moral unity which at once found expression and was stressed in American historiography was in itself the decisive fact in contemporary American politics and policies. It explains why in the twentieth century the theoretical differences between Lincoln and Douglas have been minimized or overlooked. By questioning this prevailing interpretation and stressing the moral cleavage preceding the Civil War, Jaffa blazed a new trail.

the amazing vitality of her institutions. The marvelous success of her democracy drew attention to the specific details and performance of her governmental system. There was a lack of interest in political theory, particularly theory concerning basic political values and assumptions, which seemed to be superfluous to American life. Taken for granted, this moral unity retarded the development of knowledge of the strength and weakness of the American political tradition and hindered the evolution of a conscious national purpose.

This general political tradition affected the development of academic studies which furnished intellectual leadership for the nation. By drawing a distinction between fact and value, science and philosophy, many leaders in the profession of political science relinquished, beginning in the twenties, their traditional role as interpreters of the meaning of political developments and political doctrines for their age. Instead, they considered as their primary task the meticulous verification of factual propositions or the construction of scientific theories on the model of the natural sciences.[142] This development left the average American without adequate guidance in the meaning and doctrinal basis of American democracy. But since political problems are inextricably intertwined with deeper questions of values, even political scientists could not avoid speculating on such questions of political philosophy as the definition of democracy. When they did, "one of the consequences of the belief in the unity and clarity of American thought," in the words of Bernard Crick, "is a great closeness of academic speculation to popular thought."[143]

The moral unity and uniformity in American life accentuated the natural tendency to view alien things in terms of an image of one's self and to judge foreign life in terms of one's own assumptions.[144] Since the "giveness" of American values obscured the importance for American politics of the common, implicit acceptance of liberalism as the American creed, Americans tended to belittle the role of political doctrine or ideology in the political life of other societies. The lack of interest in the deeper philosophical questions of their own society was matched by a profound ignorance of political doctrines and ideologies abroad. Thus, at a time when

[142] Bernard Crick, *The American Science of Politics* (Berkeley and Los Angeles: University of California Press, 1959), Parts III and IV, and "The Science of Politics in the United States," *Canadian Journal of Economics and Political Science*, August, 1954, pp. 308–20; Tang Tsou, "Fact and Value in Charles E. Merriam," *Southwestern Social Science Quarterly*, June, 1955, pp. 9–26, and "A Study of the Development of the Scientific Approach in Political Studies in the United States — with Particular Emphasis in the Methodological Aspects of the Works of Charles E. Merriam and Harold D. Lasswell" (Ph.D. thesis, University of Chicago, 1951).

[143] Crick, *The American Science of Politics*, p. 257.

[144] Louis Hartz wrote: "It is peculiarly easy for us to judge others by ourselves because especially since the Jacksonian upheaval we have been so much alike" (Hartz, *op. cit.*, p. 302; see also p. 297).

the United States was highly confident of her political strength and influence, American confrontation with revolutionary movements and regimes did not alert Americans to the contrast between the revolutionaries' seriousness of purpose and their own insufficient awareness of a national aim. Instead, many American officials during World War II underestimated the personal and group commitments to ideology in the case of revolutionary movements and underrated the institutional and social commitments in the case of established regimes. They were ready to grasp at any slight departure from orthodoxy or any tactical adjustment to reality as an indication of "backsliding" or apostasy. Furthermore, political influence in the United States frequently stemmed from economic power and assumed the form of economic relationships. This fact reinforced the depreciation of ideology in leading Americans to overestimate the efficacy of economic power, in the specific form of American economic aid, to change the political orientation of revolutionary groups.

Under these circumstances, Americans were easily influenced by verbal professions of leaders of other countries or by writings of those fellow countrymen who had an ax to grind. Thus, it was the American political tradition rather than the influence of a group of conspirators which was the ultimate source of the American notion that the Chinese Communists were not "real Communists," but rather "backsliders," "agrarian reformers," and advocates of democracy of the American type. To the extent that American policy and opinion were influenced by the works of those who had an ulterior motive, it was the American political tradition which rendered American officials and scholars susceptible to this influence.

2. The General Ignorance of Communism

Seen from this point of view, it comes as no surprise that Hurley's ignorance of communism and Davies' and Service's underestimation of the importance of ideology were not isolated phenomena. This general ignorance was brought out dramatically in 1952 in the hearings on the Institute of Pacific Relations. John Carter Vincent, who served as counselor in the embassy at Chungking in 1942 and 1943, chief of the Division of Chinese Affairs in 1944, and director of the Office of Far Eastern Affairs in 1945–47, told the McCarran Committee that he had not read any works of Mao Tse-tung or any other Chinese Communist leaders.[145] Nor had he read *The Communist Manifesto* by Marx and Engels, *State and Revolution* by Lenin, *Program of the Communist International and Its Constitution*, and *The Revolutionary Movement in the Colonies and Semi-Colonies, a Resolution of the Sixth World Congress of the Comintern*. He had never heard of Lenin's *Left Wing Communism: An Infantile Disorder* or Stalin's

---

[145] *Institute of Pacific Relations*, pp. 1745–83.

Foundations of Leninism and *Problems of Leninism*.[146] He could not identify Georgi Dimitrov, the veteran leader of the Comintern and once its head, and he thought that the Bulgarian Communist might have been a "Russian official." [147] Naturally, it was only, according to his own testimony, sometime during the Marshall mission to China in 1946 that he came to the definite conclusion that the Chinese Communists were dedicated Communists and were part of the international Communist movement.[148]

[146] *Ibid.*, pp. 1689–90, 1705. On April 18, 1947, Acting Secretary of State Dean G. Acheson informed Senator Walter George: "Vincent advised me that he has never even read the two documents under reference [i.e., (1) *The Program of the Communist International and Its Constitution*, and (2) *The Revolutionary Movement in the Colonies and Semi-Colonies, Adopted as a Resolution by the Sixth World Congress of the Comintern in 1928*]. I have never read them myself" (*ibid.*, p. 4541).

[147] *Ibid.*, p. 1957.

[148] *Ibid.*, p. 1708. The question whether Professor Owen Lattimore, a distinguished scholar in the Far Eastern field, was ignorant of communism is very difficult to answer. Lattimore told the MacCarran Committee that "I was not an expert on Communism, even Chinese Communism." According to his wife, he was "not interested in anything political until the Japanese invasion of China in 1937 and, even after that, he was woefully ignorant of Communism" (Owen Lattimore, *Ordeal by Slander* [Boston: Little, Brown & Co., 1950], p. 53).

Several commentators expressed disbelief in Lattimore's profession of ignorance on communism. They thought that it was a way of wriggling out of the charges made against him for his allegedly "pro-Communist" activities and opinion. See editorial, "Owen Lattimore: Whose Ordeal?" *New Leader*, March 17, 1952, pp. 30–31; William H. Chamberlain, "Owen Lattimore – On the Record," *ibid.*, p. 21. Another writer pointed out that as the editor of *Pacific Affairs*, Lattimore assigned himself the task of reviewing six books dealing specifically with the Soviet Union and communism before, according to his own testimony, he had had contact with Marxist political thinking. A majority of the twenty-one books which he reviewed in 1934–36 deal in some way with the Soviet Union, Soviet policy in the Far East, or communism (Richard Walker, "Lattimore and the IPR," *New Leader*, March 31, 1952, p. 511). For a hostile appraisal of his activities and opinions, see also Irving Kristol, "Civil Liberties: 1952 – A Study in Confusion," *Commentary*, March, 1952, pp. 228–36. One passage in the account written by Lattimore on his tribulations when he was being persecuted for his views and activities tends to support, to some extent, the judgment rendered in the editorial of the *New Leader* mentioned above. "Then he [the counsel of the Tydings Committee] moved on to one of [Senator] Hickenlooper's favorite approaches – questions that would make it easy for me to set myself up as more of an expert on Russia than I am. If I had done so, I should of course have put myself in a weak position. This trap was so obvious, and I declined to walk into it" (Lattimore, *op. cit.*, p. 184).

The only thing one can say, without great risk, is that Lattimore's naïveté about the Soviet Union led him sometimes to hold unduly favorable views of Soviet life and to tolerate pro-Communist views. In this sense, he was ignorant of communism. This combination of a tolerant, indulgent, or sometimes sympathetic view toward communism and a profound ignorance of the realities of communism was, to use George Kennan's phrase, "the danger of the times," which found particularly strong expression in left-wing non-Communist groups in the Western world. Sometimes, it led to defeatism in foreign policy on the one hand and an underestimation of the Communist menace on the other. This general political and intellectual orientation and attitude seems to be a more plausible explanation of the opinion and activities of a group of people concerned with Chinese affairs than the theory of conspiracy which is most forcefully expounded by Freda Utley in *The China Story* (Chicago: Henry Regnery Co., 1951).

3. The Tendency To Understand the Chinese
Struggle for Power in American Terms

American officials and writers were confronted with a sociopolitical revolution in China which had already assumed the form of local, limited military conflict. But they were the heirs of a political tradition which had been insulated from conscious experience of social revolution and continuous, deep social cleavages.[149] The American Civil War was considered to be "a sectional struggle" and "a struggle within a well-established working federal scheme."[150] Whatever its deeper causes, it did not interrupt the American political tradition or the continuity of American thinking about institutions. Whatever may have been the real nature of the issues leading to its eruption, the controversy has generally been interpreted as one which assumed, rather than call into question, the basic moral and political values. Such protest movements in the United States as American Progressivism were, to use the words of Richard Hofstadter, "not nearly so much the movement of any social class, or coalition of classes, against a particular class or group as it was a rather widespread and remarkably good-natured effort on the greater part of society to achieve some not very specified self-reformation."[151] This lack of a conscious experience of social revolution and the absence of deep social cleavage further obscured the tacit agreement on basic principles which underlay the tremendous success of American democracy. It gave currency to the idea that "compromise is not only a self-sufficient political ideal but the distinguishing and essential characteristic of democracy as a form of government."[152] It also tended to lead Americans to forget that a constitutional political life can only flourish after the irreconcilable conflicts of principles and the life-and-death struggle for domination have been settled by force and after the resort to violence is no longer equally open to both sides.

With these predispositions American observers and commentators looked at China, a country which is particularly difficult for Westerners to understand precisely because of her rich cultural heritage and long history. They tended to view Chinese things in terms of an American image and to judge Chinese affairs by American standards — a natural tendency of all peoples aggravated in the United States by the moral unanimity and uniformity of the American society.[153] Applying the liberal and progressive standards of a thoroughly patriotic American to the

[149] Hartz, op. cit., pp. 305–6.
[150] Boorstin, op. cit., pp. 100–1.
[151] Richard Hofstadter, The Age of Reform (New York: A. A. Knopf, Inc., 1955), p. 5.
[152] John H. Hallowell, The Moral Foundation of Democracy (Chicago: University of Chicago Press, 1954), p. 27.
[153] Hartz, op. cit., p. 302. See also p. 297.

Chinese scene, Raymond Gram Swing told his listeners in a broadcast on May 11, 1943:

> [T]hese [the Chinese Communists] are not *Marxist Proletarians*, these so-called Communists, they are *agrarian radicals*, trying to establish democratic practices and particularly to break up the great estates, so that the farm worker can have individual status and now own property. A word is in order about *these agrarian radicals*. They should not be called Communists, whatever their origin may be.[154]

Another liberal, Maxwell S. Stewart, an associate editor of the *Nation* who had lived in China for seven years, realized that "you can find in it [the Chinese Communist movement] resemblances to Communist movements in other countries." But significantly, he stated: "You can also find resemblances to the grass-roots populist movements that have figured in American history." [155] After having visited Yenan and talked with Mao Tsetung in 1944, Harrison Forman, correspondent for the *New York Herald Tribune* and representative of the National Broadcasting Company in the Far East, concluded: "The Chinese Communists are not Communists — not according to the Russian definition of the term . . . the Chinese Communists are no more Communistic than we Americans are."[156] An editorial in the March 13, 1944, issue of the *New Republic* reads: "They [the Chinese Communists] could more appropriately call themselves the Chinese democrats. . . . Their main political objectives are: putting an end to landlordism and aiding education and industrialization."[157] In an editorial commenting on the recall of Stilwell, the *New York Times* said that the Chinese Communists "are in fact peasant agrarians."[158] Thus, from the American liberal perspective, the Chinese Communist movement was simply the Chinese counterpart of the populist movement, a good-natured effort to achieve certain highly desirable reforms.

Given this understanding of the nature of Chinese Communism, it was not difficult for most American observers and officials to believe that the two sides could be brought together under constitutional rule. Many of these observers knew, of course, that there were ideological and political

[154] "An Appraisal of Conditions in China by Raymond Gram Swing," *Amerasia*, September, 1943, pp. 287–89. The whole script is reprinted in *Institute of Pacific Relations*, pp. 4286–88. The quotation is taken from p. 4287. Emphasis added.

[155] Maxwell S. Stewart, *Wartime China* (New York: Institute of Pacific Relations, 1944), p. 45. According to *Who's Who in America*, Stewart lived in Shanghai from 1923 to 1925 and served as an instructor in Yenching University from 1926 to 1930.

[156] Harrison Forman, *Report from Red China* (New York: Henry Holt & Co., 1945), p. 177.

[157] *New Republic*, March 13, 1944, p. 335. See also *ibid.*, November 13, 1944, p. 616.

[158] *New York Times*, November 1, 1944, p. 22.

differences between the Kuomintang and the Communists. But their conception of democracy did not rule out the possibility of bridging these differences by the establishment of a coalition government and constitutional rule. For is not democracy simply "the process of clearing collective conflicts through a legislature," as one American philosopher suggested?[159] Had not the Chinese Communists "become versed in the democratic art of compromise," as Raymond Gram Swing said?[160] Underlying this trend of thought was the implicit belief that the liberal values of America were shared by men everywhere and the liberal principles taken for granted in the United States were of universal applicability.

4. Misunderstanding of Chinese Political Tradition and Chinese Character

Traditionally, the United States entertained benevolent sentiments toward China, held great hope for her progress, and took pride in America's moral influence.[161] These sympathetic attitudes facilitated the attribution to China of those favorable traits which the American people found in themselves. Individualism, moderation, and an inclination toward democracy were thought to be predominant features of Chinese culture which would either prevent the spread of communism in China or change its nature. According to Secretary of State Hull, President Roosevelt, on March 14, 1941, told Admiral Nomura, the Japanese ambassador, that "the people of China were constituted very differently from those of Russia and had a philosophy that stabilized and guided them along much broader lines." He reassured the Japanese ambassador that, to use Hull's words again, "China [Chinese communism?] was not really communistic in the same sense as Russia, and Japan had an undue fear of Communism in China."[162]

Dr. Walter Judd, who later became one of the most outspoken Republican critics of the Truman-Marshall policy, wrote in September, 1942:

> You could persuade Herbert Hoover, J. P. Morgan, and Winston Churchill to be Communists as easily as you could persuade a land-owning Chinese peasant, whose ancestors have lived on one piece of land for centuries, to take the only tangible thing he has and dump it into a common pot just on the promise that around the corner will be something better.[163]

[159] T. V. Smith, *The Legislature of Life* (Chicago: University of Chicago Press, 1940), p. 1.

[160] Raymond Gram Swing, "An Appraisal of Conditions in China," *Institute of Pacific Relations*, p. 4287.

[161] Harold Isaacs, *Scratches on Our Mind* (New York: John Day Co., 1958).

[162] Cordell Hull, *Memoirs*, II (New York: Macmillan Co., 1948), 990.

[163] Walter Judd, "Behind the Conflict in the Pacific," *Journal of National Education Association*, September, 1942, p. 169. In order to put President Roosevelt's and Dr.

Even in 1950, Professor Owen Lattimore told the Tydings Committee that he did not despair of the possibility of "a democratic success in China." For "despite the relatively backward state of their country, the Chinese people have a strong and rugged sense of individualism and democracy." [164] In 1951, General Wedemeyer still found it possible to express agreement with the view that the Chinese are individualists and "do not lend themselves, in a philosophic way, to the ideals or ideas of Marxism."[165] As late as 1957, Dr. John Leighton Stuart, the leading missionary educator in China and subsequently American ambassador to China, who as president of Yenching University, was beloved and respected by his Nationalist and Communist students alike, still found it hard to believe that "China with so rich a cultural heritage could be ruled by Bolshevism too long." He still had faith in the idea that the mainland of China was not irretrievably lost.[166]

It is perhaps not inappropriate to note that both Judd and Stuart had served as missionaries in China and that many foreign service officers and scholars in the China field had missionary background. The missionary movement since the First World War derived its strength from the Christian liberals' "firm faith that a new social order based on the ethical teachings of Jesus could be realized." [167] Most missionaries "viewed the China

Judd's remarks in the proper historical context, one must point out that Roosevelt was trying to refute Japan's argument that her actions in China were motivated by a desire to check the spread of communism in East Asia and that Judd was endeavoring to show that American support for China against Japan would not lead to a Communist China after the war. But judging from the climate of opinion at the time, it is reasonable to believe that their remarks also represented their genuine conviction.

[164] *State Department Employee Loyalty Investigation*, p. 440.

[165] *Military Situation in the Far East*, p. 2364.

[166] John Leighton Stuart, "Introduction," to Tien-fong Cheng, *op. cit.*, p. 5. In contrast to this line of thinking, Professor John K. Fairbank of Harvard indicated in an article published in the September, 1946, issue of the *Atlantic Monthly* that the Chinese political tradition was authoritarian and that the totalitarian nature of Communism was no bar to its success in China (John K. Fairbank, "Our Chances in China," *Atlantic Monthly*, September, 1946, pp. 37–50). Prior to the appearance of this article, Karl A. Wittfogel had raised some very poignant questions about the nature of Chinese society in his pamphlet, *New Light on Chinese Society* (New York: Institute of Pacific Relations, 1938). This point of view has since been carried much further. Many writers have stressed elements in the traditional culture of China which facilitated the ascension to power by the Chinese Communists. See, for example, Brandt *et al.*, *op. cit.*, "Introduction," pp. 11–27; Charles P. Fitzgerald, *Revolution in China* (New York: Praeger, 1952); Fairbank, *The United States and China*; Franz Michael, "State and Society in Nineteenth Century China, *World Politics*, April, 1955, pp. 417–33; and Schwartz, *op. cit.* This trend of thought has reached an extreme in Karl A. Wittfogel, *Oriental Despotism* (New Haven: Yale University Press, 1957); see also Karl A. Wittfogel, "Chinese Society: A Historical Survey," *Journal of Asian Studies*, May, 1957, pp. 343–64. Social scientists in the United States, particularly political scientists, are confronted with a very interesting theoretical problem with tremendous practical implications.

[167] Paul A. Varg, *Missionaries, Chinese, and Diplomats* (Princeton, N.J.: Princeton University Press, 1958), p. 152.

scene against the background of their own political outlook — an outlook they shared with the followers of Woodrow Wilson . . . and the virile tradition of what they would have called Christian humanism." [168] They cultivated a moral approach to China, treating her as a country "to be encouraged to adopt Christian values, technology, popular education and constitutionalism." [169] Protestant Christianity and the liberal tradition thus reinforced each other to foster an illusive view of China.

5. The Immaturity of the Writings of Some of the Experts

The general misconceptions about the nature and intentions of the Chinese Communists were not challenged by experts in the Far Eastern field. As a matter of fact, some of the most influential scholars in the field shared and promoted many of these misunderstandings. The writings of T. A. Bisson and Owen Lattimore on policy questions can be taken as conspicuous examples. These two influential authors were specialists on the Far East. In one sense, their misconceptions cannot be attributed to the tendency to understand Chinese politics in terms of an American image.[170] In their case, ignorance and naïveté about international communism were reinforced by their lack of adequate conceptual tools for the analysis of the general situation in China and the issues confronting the United States. It is true that within the areas of their specialization, they had mastered their problems. T. A. Bisson's study, *Japan in China*, is an able piece of work. In his *Inner Asian Frontier of China*, Lattimore applied a set of fairly interesting concepts to analyze a wealth of empirical data. But, unfortunately, when they reached out into the general area of Chinese affairs and American foreign policy, their writings were

[168] *Ibid.*, p. 293.

[169] *Ibid.*, p. 324.

[170] Mr. Lattimore prided himself on his deliberate efforts to understand political questions in other countries in the light of their specific conditions and from the point of view of the peoples there. Testifying before the Tydings Committee, he stated: "When I have dealt with, analyzed and discussed political questions in China, Mongolia, et cetera, I have always started, tried to start from the base line, what is this country, what are these people; second, what is going on in this country; third is tendency A or tendency B the stronger one in this country" (*State Department Employee Loyalty Investigation*, p. 849).

In his *The Making of Modern China*, he wrote: "When we want to make up our minds whether we ought to call another country 'democratic,' we quite naturally begin by comparing it with our own democratic country. Has it got the same institutions that exist in our own country? Has it got the same kind of procedure for seeing that the will of the majority is carried out, and the same safeguards for seeing that the rights of minorities are protected? If it has not, we hesitate to call it a democracy.

"This way of looking at things can often lead to misunderstandings" (Owen and Eleanore Lattimore, *The Making of Modern China* [New York: W. W. Norton & Co., 1944], p. 183).

not characterized by the same level of competence. Lacking a firmly rooted intellectual orientation and a tight grasp of the essentials of foreign policy, they were, in their semischolarly writings, influenced more by the changing political currents at the time than by a determination to reach an independent judgment.

In his controversial article, "China's Part in a Coalition War," T. A. Bisson dismissed the generally used terms "Kuomintang China" and "Communist China" as "only party labels." He averred that "to be more descriptive, the one [Kuomintang China] might be called *feudal* China; the other, *democratic* China. These terms expressed the actualities as they exist today, the real institutional distinctions between the two Chinas." [171] After a description of the various social, economic, and political reforms in Communist areas, he concluded: "By no stretch of the imagination can this be termed Communism; it is, in fact, the essence of *bourgeois* democracy, applied mainly to agrarian conditions." [172] Commenting on Bisson's concepts of "feudal China" and "democratic China," Professor John K. Fairbank told the McCarran Committee: "Now in retrospect I do not support his [Bisson's] use of these terms, 'democratic' and 'feudal.' Those are cliché terms. He may have picked them up from Communist inspiration or stimulus to him." [173]

Mr. Lattimore's writings on the current problems of China and American policy toward Asia betrayed the same disconcerting lack of theoretical insight. Although he never called the Chinese Communists "agrarian reformers," his discussion of the nature of the Chinese Communist movement was misleading. He confused the exploitation of wartime patriotism and rural discontent by a tightly organized elite with a peasants' movement. He wrote: "During the ten years of civil war the Communists, cut off from city and urban workers, had become a peasant party." [174] He mistook the popular support given by the various social strata to the Communists for the sharing of control of the party by these interest groups. He concluded: "From being a one-doctrine party, they were tending to become a coalition party." [175] He equated measures taken by the Communists to promote popular participation in governmental work with democracy; he praised the Communist three-thirds system of limiting membership in vari-

[171] T. A. Bisson, "China's Part in a Coalition War," *Far Eastern Survey*, July 14, 1943, p. 138.

[172] *Ibid.*, p. 139.

[173] *Institute of Pacific Relations*, p. 3801. For a good brief survey of the use of the "feudal" concept by Chinese Marxists, see Benjamin Schwartz, "A Marxist Controversy of China," *Far Eastern Survey*, February, 1954, pp. 143–53. See also Karl A. Wittfogel, "The Influence of Leninism-Stalinism on China," *Annals of the American Academy of Political and Social Science*, September, 1951, pp. 23–24; and Wittfogel, *Oriental Despotism*, pp. 409–10, p. 410 n. *h.*

[174] Owen Lattimore, *Solution in Asia* (Boston: Little, Brown & Co., 1945), p. 108.

[175] *Ibid.*

ous governmental organs as "the most positive step yet taken in China by any party away from dictatorship and toward democracy." [176] This adulation was perfectly consistent with his concept of democracy. For he condemned the "habit of taking a narrow view of foreign claimants to the status of democracy." [177] To him, "What moves people to act, to try to line up with one party or country and not with another, is the difference between what is more democratic and less democratic in practice." [178] In other words, democracy was identical with popular support enjoyed by a party or nation.[179] According to this logic, the Chinese Communist party could be the creator of a system of democracy and the Soviet Union could be called a democratic nation.

For one reason or another, Mr. Lattimore's writings betray an instability in judgment. In *The Making of Modern China,* published in 1944, he obviously still considered Nationalist China "democratic" in the sense that "the party [the Kuomintang] and the government [the Nationalist government] represent what the vast majority of the people want." [180] He praised the beginnings made by the Kuomintang "to permit political expression through channels other than those of the Kuomintang itself" and the mitigation of the Kuomintang "monopoly of political action and political expression" by various measures taken by the government. Yet in his *Solution in Asia,* published in 1945, he made an entirely different appraisal of the Kuomintang and of the Chinese Communist party. Now he said that the Kuomintang had been transformed "from a coalition of interests toward a monopoly of one interest," from "a coalition party" to a "landlord party." [181] Instead of Nationalist China or China as such, it was now the Communist party that moved "toward democracy." [182] Actually, Nationalist domination and inflexibility increased steadily after 1939, five years before Lattimore published his *The Making of Modern China.* There may have been an intensification of Nationalist control in 1944 and 1945, but there was no reversal of political trend in these two years which correspond to the change in Lattimore's judgments.

[176] *Ibid.,* p. 109.

[177] *Ibid.,* p. 139.

[178] *Ibid.,* pp. 139–40.

[179] This interpretation of Mr. Lattimore's concept of democracy is supported by another passage in *The Making of Modern China*: "China is a democratic country in the sense that the Party and the government represent what the vast majority of the people want" (Owen and Eleanor Lattimore, *op. cit.,* pp. 182–93).

[180] *Ibid.* Freda Utley asserted that this book was written in 1942 and published in early 1943 (Freda Utley, *op. cit.,* p. 192). The date of publication is crucial to her purpose of proving that Lattimore followed the party line toward the Kuomintang which was said to have changed in the summer of 1943. She may have other evidence to support her contention but a check of the Library of Congress Catalogue shows that the first edition was published in 1944.

[181] Lattimore, *Solution in Asia,* pp. 107–8.

[182] *Ibid.,* p. 109.

Lattimore's use of the term "peasant party," "landlord party," and "co-alition party" reflected a widespread approach in American political science which emphasized the study of interest groups as the most dynamic forces in politics, treated the government and the party as organs mainly responding to their activities, and analyzed party programs and governmental policies as the resultant of conflicting or parallel pressures. Whatever merits this approach had for a study of American politics, it could not be applied to modern China, where, so far as "interest groups" existed, they owed their political organization and cohesiveness largely to the leadership of the political parties and government, and where, after the breakdown of the traditional social structure, the "gentry" had lost their former political functions and the peasantry had become a social force to be exploited and manipulated by political groups and individual leaders. Thus, basically, Lattimore was still trying to analyze Chinese politics in American terms, in spite of his avowed intention to understand political questions in other countries from the point of view of the peoples there.

In the writings about Chinese politics at this time, one searches in vain for the view that a Communist party based on Leninist principles is a tightly organized and highly disciplined group of professional revolutionaries, aiming at the seizure of power whenever possible, exploiting mass discontent from whatever sources are at hand, and employing a multiplicity of means and a variety of institutional forms to achieve its purpose. It was not widely understood that the totalitarian character of the party arises both from its aspiration for total power, so necessary for the realization of its highly ambitious program of drastic institutional change, and from its organizational principles which make it a force altogether outside the interest groups, manipulating them without being dominated by them. The ability of a tightly organized and rigorously disciplined elite under able leadership to make a flexible choice of slogans and means in its endeavors to capture power was a political fact which American specialists, trained and immersed in the liberal, democratic environment of a free society, failed to take adequately into account.

6. The Influence of a Group of Writings which Showed a Similar Underlying Pattern

When the scholars failed to discharge their function of providing intellectual leadership and when the political tradition fostered certain erroneous assumptions about the nature of politics, American officials and men of affairs became susceptible to the influence of the writings of a number of authors who had different kinds of axes to grind. The reports and works of Edgar Snow, Gunther Stein, and Lawrence K. Rosinger can be taken as examples. In the case of Snow a distinction must be made between his earlier reports and his articles published in 1944 and 1945. His *Red Star over China,* the first book written by a foreign correspondent who visited Communist territory, was a sympathetic but generally accurate account of the Soviet area in late 1936. His reports of the absence at that time of *direct* Russian participation on any significant scale in the development of the Chinese Soviet movement seem to be credible. He further balanced these denials by stressing the spiritual and ideological influence of the Soviet Union, her role as the "mighty fatherland" of the Chinese Communists, and their hope of having her as a great ally of their cause. He quoted the Constitution of Soviet China to the effect: "That the Soviet Government in China declares its readiness to form a revolutionary united front with the world proletariat and all oppressed nations, and proclaims the Soviet Union, the land of proletarian dictatorship, to be its loyal ally." [183] Finally, he concluded:

> Of course, the political ideology, tactical line, and the theoretical leadership of the Chinese Communists have been under the close guidance, if not positive detailed direction, of the Communist International which during the past decade has become virtually a bureau of the Russian Communist Party. In the final analysis this means that, for better or worse, the policies of the Chinese Communists, like Communists in every other country, have had to fall in line with, and usually subordinate themselves to, the broad strategic requirements of Soviet Russia, under the dictatorship of Stalin.[184]

He accurately characterized the land redistribution program of the Chinese Communists as nothing "more than a phase in the building of a mass base, a tactic enabling them to develop the revolutionary struggle towards the conquest of power and the ultimate realization of thoroughgoing Socialist changes in which collectivization would be inevitable." [185] In other words, it was merely a maneuver to gain power in order to achieve the ultimate aim of "a true and complete Socialist State of the Marx-Leninist conception." [186]

After the conclusion of the Soviet-German pact of August, 1939, some of Snow's questions put to Mao Tse-tung in an interview were embar-

[183] Edgar Snow, *Red Star over China* (New York: Random House, 1938), pp. 370–71.
[184] *Ibid.,* p. 374.
[185] *Ibid.,* p. 212.
[186] *Ibid.* For the interpretation of Snow's work, compare Harold Isaacs, *op. cit.,* and Captain Malcolm Kennedy, *A Short History of Communism in Asia* (London: Weidenfeld & Nicolson, 1957).

rassing.[187] As late as 1941 in his *The Battle for Asia*, he still emphasized that the goal of the Chinese Communists remained "international socialism" and that they would use whatever methods they believed necessary to attain that end. As a matter of fact, he ridiculed the already current notion that the Chinese Communists were not real Communists and were "only a peasant reform party." In his view that notion arose out of an attempt to reconcile the contradiction in the sentiments of many liberals who wanted to be known as pro-China but anti-Stalin. The hopes that the Chinese Communists were "different" and "only reformers" and had abandoned revolutionary methods to achieve their program were doomed, he prophesized, to ultimate disappointment.[188] He quoted Mao's answer to his written question: "We are always social revolutionaries and we are never reformists." [189]

The change in Snow's characterization of the Chinese Communists came in an article entitled "Sixty Million Lost Allies," published on June 10, 1944. In it he deplored the absence of official ties with the Communists and the consequent inability to utilize them and their bases for the war against Japan. He justified his advocacy of a program of utilizing the military potential of the Chinese Communists partly on the ground that they were not really Communists. In contrast to his own statements in *Red Star over China*, he wrote:

> For Americans with little background on China, the term "Communist" may here be misleading. The fact is there never has been any Communism in China, even in Communist areas. Long before it became defunct, the Comintern ceased to have much direct contact with the Chinese Communist Party. It [the Chinese Communist party] became a *purely Chinese offspring* of Marxism, and in practice won its following, chiefly among the peasants, by working out a program of *agrarian democracy*, with socialism, as an ultimate, but, admittedly, quite distant goal.[190]

[187] At one point, Snow asked Mao: "Why, if Germany was imperialist and no different from Britain and France, the Soviet Union should participate in Germany's imperialist adventure to the extent of making available to Germany Russia's great reserves of wheat, oil, and other war materials? Why, incidentally, did Russia continue to lease oil lands to Japan in Sakhalin, or to give Japan fishing rights? The latter were of great value in enabling Japan to export large quantities of fish, and thus establish foreign credits with which to buy munitions and carry on a robber imperialist war against the 'national liberation movement' of 'semi-colonial China'" (Snow, "Interviews with Mao Tse-tung," *China Weekly Review*, January 20, 1940, p. 279).

[188] Edgar Snow, *The Battle for Asia* (Cleveland: World Publishing Co., 1941), pp. 290–91.

[189] *Ibid.*, p. 292.

[190] Edgar Snow, "Sixty Million Lost Allies," *Saturday Evening Post*, June 10, 1944, p. 44. Emphasis added.

The increasing confusion in the United States over the nature of Chinese communism was reflected in another article by Snow published on May 12, 1945. In it Snow flatly contradicted himself within a single page. On the one hand, he characterized Chinese communism as the "Chinese agrarian reform movement." In so doing, he committed the error of translating the Chinese name of the party, "Kungchantang," into "share-in-production party," [191] whereas it actually means "share-in-property party." On the other hand, he pointed out that the Chinese Communists did "aspire to ultimate complete power," that they would not "establish a liberal democracy in the American sense," and that they were "Marxists" and real Communists and "very close to the Soviet Union in their sympathies." [192] But for Snow, these diametrically opposed judgments on the nature of Chinese communism led to the same practical conclusion. Since the Chinese Communist party represented nothing more than a moderate agrarian reform movement, it was possible for the United States to work with the Chinese Communists and to bring them and the Kuomintang together in a coalition government. On the other hand, even if they were real Communists and were closely tied to the Soviet Union, they were nevertheless Chinese nationalists. They would have to depend on American economic help if they should come into power. In any case, helping the Chinese Communists would not tend to promote the cause of communism any more than America's present and future aid to the Soviet Union.[193]

On the subject of the nature and intentions of the Chinese Communists, the writings of Gunther Stein and Lawrence K. Rosinger show a similar pattern, though without the glaring contradictions of Snow's articles. In his *The Challenge of Red China*, Stein flatly stated that the Chinese Communists "are and intend to remain Communists." [194] He even criticized the Chinese Communists for their denunciation, in September, 1939, of the European war as an "imperialist war." This move had been made, in his view, as a step in "ideological publicity" rather than "practical politics." He reported that he confronted Po Ku, a member of the politbureau of the Communist party, with this criticism and that the latter "only smiled." [195] But Stein played down the revolutionary and anti-Western components of communism. He accepted and promoted the Communist claim that "being Communist means no more than to accept the Marxist methods of thinking and of solving problems." [196] A political philosophy of violent, revolutionary action was thus reduced to an innocuous tool of

[191] Edgar Snow, "Must China Go Red?" *Saturday Evening Post*, May 12, 1945, p. 67.
[192] *Ibid.*
[193] *Ibid.*, p. 68.
[194] Gunther Stein, *The Challenge of Red China* (New York: McGraw-Hill Book Co., 1945), p. 106.
[195] *Ibid.*, p. 446.
[196] *Ibid.*, p. 106.

intellectual analysis. Through his description of the "three-thirds system of democratic representation," the village meetings, and the New Democracy, he helped propagate the Communist argument that "a convinced Communist" was also "a convinced democrat."[197] He averred that the "new political system [New Democracy] . . . democratized the minds of the Communists to a considerable extent. It made them think less in the old class term of the Communist party and more in terms of the Chinese nation as a whole."[198] His underestimation of the role of Marxism-Leninism created a lopsided emphasis on nationalism as a component in communist attitudes, thinking, and policies.

Rosinger's analysis of the Chinese Communists followed almost exactly the same pattern as Stein's. He stated that "they [the Chinese Communists] regard themselves as Communists both in political theory and outlook" and that "many of the leaders [in the Communist areas] as well as ordinary citizens, are actually Communists."[199] But somehow in his description of the Communist program, he conveyed the idea that the Communists desired to share their power with other elements and were striving for democracy.[200] His conclusion was that the United States had a community of interests with "the democratic forces in China," and only "a progressive China" could serve the interests of this country.[201] He left no doubt in the minds of his readers that these laudatory terms referred to the Communists.

But in order to remind ourselves of the climate of opinion at the time, it must be pointed out that even some of the staunchest advocates of the Nationalist cause in later years were under similar illusions about the Chinese Communists, at least for a time. If any Western observer in China could have detected the true nature of the Chinese Communist movement at the time, such a person would have been Freda Utley. She had been a member of the British Communist party, married a Russian citizen, lived for six years in Moscow, worked in a research agency of the Soviet government, and had become completely disillusioned with communism.[202] Later, she was to write the most forceful and systematic book justifying Senator Joseph McCarthy's crusade against the State Department and Owen Lattimore on the question of China policy. Yet in her book *China at War*, published in 1939, she characterized the Chinese Communist party as "a party of social reformers and patriots"[203] and Chinese communism as "a move-

---

[197] *Ibid.*, pp. 106, 107.
[198] *Ibid.*
[199] Lawrence K. Rosinger, *China's Crisis* (New York: Alfred A. Knopf, Inc., 1945), p. 92.
[200] *Ibid.*, pp. 83, 87, 95.
[201] *Ibid.*, p. 259.
[202] Utley, *The China Story*, p. 210.
[203] Freda Utley, *China at War* (London: Faber and Faber, 1939), p. 251.

ment of peasant emancipation." [204] According to her, the aim of the Chinese Communists "has genuinely become social and political reform along capitalist and democratic lines," [205] and they had become "radicals in the English nineteenth century meaning of the word." [206] Representative Walter Judd, once a medical missionary in China and a most influential supporter of the Nationalist government, obviously shared similar misconceptions at one time. As he admitted in a speech in the House on March 15, 1945, "I, too, was taken in for a time by the talk of their being just agrarian reformers, just Chinese patriots struggling only for freedom of China and for democracy." [207] Thus, very few persons were right on the nature and intentions of the Chinese Communist party, although in the political arena many were later willing to throw the first stone.

7. The Harmony between the American Image of Chinese Communism and the Widely Shared Practical Considerations and Predispositions

After the collapse of the Nationalist government in China, the discussion of China policy has been thrown into confusion by the attempt to hunt out American conspirators in China and in the United States who had supposedly misled the United States in order to serve their foreign masters. This has proved to be a most hazardous, fruitless, and harmful endeavor. Actually, such a widely accepted misconception could not have been the product of a group of conspirators and agents, however clever they may have been. Instead, the misunderstanding of the nature and intentions of the Chinese Communist party had its roots in widely shared considerations and predispositions. It is easy to see that the comfortable notion of the Chinese Communists as agrarian reformers, sincere democrats, and the like fitted perfectly well with the political and military considerations dominating the mind of American officials and opinion leaders in these years: the desire to utilize the military potential of the Chinese Communists, the hope of avoiding entanglement with Russia over China, and the wish to bring about a unified and democratic China as the stabilizing force in the Far East. These considerations were in harmony with the American aversion to engaging in a rough political and military contest with other powers in continental Asia. The wish was thus the father to the thought. Likewise, it is not difficult to understand that the American image of Chinese communism and the accompanying program to bring about a coalition government were rooted in the American politi-

[204] *Ibid.*, p. 252.
[205] *Ibid.*, p. 254.
[206] *Ibid.*
[207] *Congressional Record*, XCI, 79th Cong., 1st sess., (1945), p. 2298.

cal tradition, which rested upon a unique consensus on basic values, tended to gloss over social cleavages, and strengthened the natural tendency to look at alien things in one's own image. This American political tradition also led to a lack of interest in political theory and an ignorance about communism, which in turn contributed to the spread of the misconception. But the optimistic expectations of postwar Soviet co-operation, the naïve view about the nature of Chinese communism, and the hope for establishment of a coalition government in China had no basis in reality. Actions taken in accordance with these miscalculations could only bring about frustration or create situations inimical to American interests.

CHAPTER VII

THE

YALTA

AGREEMENT

AND

THE

POLICY OF

PEACEFUL

UNIFICATION

OF CHINA

A. The Yalta Agreement and the Structure of American Policies

The Yalta Agreement of February, 1945, was a major link in the structure of American policies in the Far East. It was a supplement to the Cairo Declaration which reaffirmed the principle of unconditional surrender of Japan and provided the basic outline of the postwar structure of power in the Far East. Insofar as the Yalta Agreement was designed to assure Soviet participation in the Pacific war, it was an expression of the policy of securing the unconditional surrender of Japan. Insofar as it was aimed at obtaining Soviet co-operation with the Nationalist government, it was an indispensable means to promote the American policy of peaceful unification of China. The immediate and primary considerations impelling American officials to conclude and implement it were undoubtedly military in nature. But their deeper thoughts centered on its political effects on the internal situation in China. Both the military considerations and political calculations reflected the powerful position of the Soviet Union in the Far East in the last year of the Pacific war and the inability of the United States to implement her policies without Soviet co-operation. The Yalta Agreement was the price paid for this co-operation.

237

When viewed from the long perspective of history, the Yalta Agreement, which compromised the territorial and administrative integrity of China and the principle of equal opportunity, represented a recurrence of the persistent pattern of the policy of the United States toward China. It was a new retreat from the principles of the Open Door soon after the latest advance in which these principles culminated in the policy of making China a great power and in the relinquishment by the United States and Great Britain of their extraterritorial rights in China. Its two antecedents were: first, the Root-Takahira Agreement of 1908 under which, according to one interpretation, the United States gave Japan a free hand in Manchuria in return for a Japanese pledge to respect the security of the Philippines;[1] and second, the Lansing-Ishii Agreement of 1917 in which the United States recognized that Japan had special interests in China, particularly in the part to which her possessions were contiguous. But the contrast between the retreat and the preceding advance was immeasurably sharper in 1945. The latest retreat came after the United States had refused to sacrifice China for the purpose of reaching a modus vivendi with Japan. It took place at a time when China was supposed to be one of the four great powers. In contrast to the Root-Takahira and Lansing-Ishii agreements, the Yalta Agreement was unadorned by written affirmation of the integrity of China and the Open Door, and, therefore, could not be interpreted through a strict, legalistic construction or, indeed, by any stretch of the imagination, as something other than a compromise with principles.

In retrospect, it seems clear that the Yalta Agreement foreshadowed a fundamental change in the Far Eastern balance of power. From the dispatch of the Open Door notes to the First World War, the balance of power in the Far East was maintained by a shifting equilibrium among the conflicting policies and interests of the powers.[2] The four years of the war marked a transitional period during which Japan, in alliance with Great Britain and supported by other nations in the Entente, emerged as the strongest power in the Far East. Even during the Paris Peace Conference, the United States could do nothing to promote the principles of her Far Eastern policy. The Root-Takahira and the Lansing-Ishii agreements were expressions of this political reality. From the Washington Conference to the surrender of Germany in the Second World War, the Far Eastern structure of power rested on American-Japanese antagonism. In the ten years preceding 1941, this balance was progressively upset because of the unwillingness and inability of the United States to use her military power to counter Japan's actions in China. The effective use of American naval and air power in the Pacific war gradually restored the balance in favor of

[1] A. Whitney Griswold, *The Far Eastern Policy of the United States* (New York: Harcourt, Brace & Co., 1938), p. 129.
[2] See chap. i., above.

the United States and presaged the defeat of Japan. The end of the war in Europe enabled Russia to re-enter the Far Eastern scene as one of the two superpowers. The confrontation between the Soviet Union and the United States constituted the essence of a new bipolar international system, and strife-ridden China became the immediate object of contention. This new structure of power set a more narrow limit than the two previous ones on what the United States could do or could have done to defend her interests in China. For the United States was now confronted by a rising land power with a common border with China, a superpower which was also the center of a revolutionary movement having powerful Chinese adherents. The concessions made in the Yalta Agreement to the Soviet Union were an expression of this emergent political reality.

Seen from this perspective, the Yalta Agreement can be interpreted as an attempt to prevent the balance of power from being totally upset by a resurgent Soviet Union working in co-ordination with the Chinese Communists.[3] According to Ambassador Harriman, President Roosevelt sought by the Yalta agreement "to limit Soviet expansion in the East and to gain Soviet support for the Nationalist government."[4] The Yalta Agreement was also a price paid by the United States to insure Soviet entry into the Pacific war at such a moment as to save American lives. Many persons have come to doubt whether Soviet participation was necessary to secure the surrender of an already defeated Japan. But what cannot be denied is that with or without American agreement the Soviet Union could have, in one way or another, acquired greater gains than those conceded her at Yalta. Judged in terms of the emergent power configuration, the price paid by the United States for Soviet co-operation was not excessive, if the Yalta Agreement could limit Soviet expansion.

For two reasons, however, the Yalta Agreement was destined to be unsuccessful in limiting Soviet ambitions. First, it was intended to support the policy of peaceful unification, which had no basis in Chinese politics. The Chinese Communists had by the end of the Pacific war developed such a strong position in China that the Soviet assurances in the Sino-Soviet treaty of August, 1945, to support the Nationalist government only

[3] George F. Kennan, *Russia and the West under Lenin and Stalin* (Boston: Little, Brown & Co., 1960), pp. 349–69; George A. Lensen, "Yalta and the Far East," and Forrest C. Pogue, "Yalta in Retrospect," in John L. Snell (ed.), *The Meaning of Yalta* (Baton Rouge: Louisiana State University Press, 1956), pp. 127–66, 180–208; Oscar J. Hammen, "The 'Ashes' of Yalta," *South Atlantic Quarterly*, October, 1954, pp. 477–84; Raymond J. Sontag, "Reflections on the Yalta Papers," *Foreign Affairs* (July, 1955), pp. 615–32; Rudolph A. Winnacker, "Yalta — Another Munich?" *Virginia Quarterly Review*, Autumn, 1948, pp. 521–37.

[4] Statement of W. Averell Harriman, Senate Committee on Armed Services and Committee on Foreign Relations, *Hearings of Military Situation in the Far East*, 82d Cong., 1st. sess. (1951), p. 3332 (hereafter cited as *Military Situation in the Far East*).

temporarily weakened their bargaining position and did not bring about a settlement on Nationalist terms. Even if the Soviet Union had wanted to do so, she could not have imposed a settlement on the Chinese Communists. Just as the United States found it necessary to grant limited aid to the Nationalist government and could not prevent it from waging a large-scale civil war, the Soviet Union could not but lend a helping hand to the Chinese Communists in Manchuria. Once Moscow had reached a new estimate of the military and revolutionary potentiality of the Chinese Communists and once the American program of seeking a settlement between the Nationalists and the Communists had completely broken down, she gave open diplomatic support to the Chinese Communists. The breakdown of the Yalta Agreement was at once both cause and effect of the collapse of the policy of peaceful unification.

The second factor leading to the failure of the Yalta Agreement was the unwillingness and inability of the United States to use her ground forces in China for the purpose of establishing and maintaining a structure of power within which the Yalta Agreement might have found its place. As we shall see, the American government rejected China's proposal to turn the projected Sino-Soviet treaty implementing the Yalta Agreement into a four-power treaty of which the United States and Great Britain would be signatories. It did not inject its military power into Manchuria. Its deployment of American marines in the principal ports and lines of communication in North China proved to be a temporary measure. Stalin's violation of the Sino-Soviet treaty and agreements, the ill-advised attempt of Chiang to occupy the larger part of Manchuria without firm American military support, the triumph of the Chinese Communists in the all-out civil war, and the conclusion of the Sino-Soviet Treaty of Friendship, Alliance and Mutual Assistance of February, 1950, led step by step to the new balance of power in the Far East, characterized by the confrontation between the ground forces of the Sino-Soviet bloc on the Asiatic mainland and the naval and air power of the United States based on the island-perimeter.

The Yalta Agreement has come to symbolize the "betrayal" of China, the "appeasement" of communism, and immoral secret diplomacy. In terms of the abstract American principle of the integrity of China and the Wilsonian rule of open covenants openly arrived at, the Yalta Agreement is clearly indefensible. But condemnation of the Yalta Agreement merely obscures the power-political issues confronting the United States toward the end of the Pacific war. To understand the Yalta Agreement and to appraise American policy, it is necessary, first of all, to see how the Soviet Union came to occupy a powerful position in the Far East toward the end of the Pacific war, how American policy contributed to this development, and how the Soviet leaders skilfully exploited their advantageous position.

B. The Re-emergence of the Soviet Union as a Far Eastern Power

Stalin wrote in 1925:

> If war breaks out we shall not be able to sit with folded arms. We shall have to take action, but we shall be the last to do so. And we shall do so in order to throw the decisive weight on the scales, the weight that will tip the balance.[5]

In Europe, Hitler's attack in 1941 deprived Stalin of the chance to follow his own prescription. But he was given a second opportunity in the Far East which he skilfully exploited. During the Pacific war, up to October, 1944, Stalin pursued a dual course to preserve and develop his advantageous position as a neutral in a war between a progressively weakened Japan, bent on preserving her imperial institution, and a gradually victorious United States, clinging to her formula of unconditional surrender. On the one hand, he calmly resisted all attempts to draw Russia into the war against Japan and refrained from any actions which would arouse Japan's suspicion of his intentions. On the other hand, he and his aides stated repeatedly that the Soviet Union would eventually fight Japan. After he agreed in October, 1944, to undertake joint planning with the United States in the Pacific war and, in February, 1945, gave promise in writing to enter the war against Japan, he preserved his strong position by utmost secrecy, which prevented Japan from learning his true intentions.

Within a few days after Pearl Harbor, Soviet officials, in response to American and Chinese soundings, made clear that she was not then ready to enter the Pacific war.[6] In January, 1943, Stalin rejected President Roosevelt's offer to send one hundred American bombers in organized units to the Maritime Provinces in case of a Japanese attack.[7] But at the same time, he told Chiang in December, 1941,[8] Harriman in August, 1942,[9] and Hull in October, 1943, that the Soviet Union would eventually take part in the Pacific war. His statement to Hull was, to use Hull's own word, "forthright." "He made it emphatically, it was entirely unsolicited, and he asked nothing in return."[10]

[5] Quoted in Elliot R. Goodman, *The Soviet Design for a World State* (New York: Columbia University Press, 1960), p. 298.
[6] Department of Defense, "The Entry of the Soviet Union in the War against Japan: Military Plans, 1941–1945" (mimeographed; September, 1955), pp. 1–10 (hereafter cited as "The Entry of the Soviet Union"); Herbert Feis, *The China Tangle* (Princeton, N.J.: Princeton University Press, 1953), pp. 5–8; Charles F. Romanus and Riley Sunderland, *Stilwell's Mission to China* (Washington, D.C.: Government Printing Office, 1953), pp. 51–52; Cordell Hull, *Memoirs* (New York: Macmillan Co., 1948), II, 1111.
[7] "The Entry of the Soviet Union," pp. 13–16.
[8] Romanus and Sunderland, *op. cit.*, pp. 51–52; Feis, *op. cit.*, pp. 7–8.
[9] Statement by W. Averell Harriman, *Military Situation in the Far East*, p. 3329.
[10] Hull, *op. cit.*, p. 1310.

The fierce fighting with Germany was, of course, the compelling reason for the Soviet refusal to act in the Far East. But it is most unlikely that Stalin failed to see the political advantage of staying out of the Pacific war for the time being, so that he could select the best time to intervene. As the Joint Chiefs of Staff wrote in August, 1943, in an estimate of the situation:

> Russia is likely to intervene in the war against Japan at some stage, but not before the German threat to her has been removed. After that, she will make a decision in the light of her own interests and will intervene only when she reckons that Japan can be defeated at a small cost to her.[11]

At the Teheran Conference in November-December, 1943, Stalin continued to follow his dual course. On the one hand, he evaded American requests to establish air bases in the Maritime Provinces and to undertake advance planning for the initiation of air operations against Japan.[12] Compliance with these requests might have revealed to Japan his intentions, prematurely involved the Soviet Union in the Pacific war, and destroyed his bargaining position vis-à-vis the United States. On the other hand, Stalin reaffirmed his pledge to enter the war against Japan after the defeat of Germany. In response to Churchill's question, he made it plain that the Soviet Union had certain political claims in the Far East. But, at his suggestion, decision on them was deferred. In disclosing his political claims for the first time, he couched them in innocuous terms. He gave President Roosevelt the impression that he approved of making Dairen an international free port and that his claims over the Chinese Eastern and the South Manchurian railroads did not extend beyond the privilege of moving Russian trade over them to and from Dairen in bond.[13] The lease of Port Arthur as a naval base, the recognition of the status quo in Outer Mongolia, joint ownership of the railways, and the safeguarding of the "pre-eminent interests" of the Soviet Union in Dairen and in the Manchurian railways — all of which were later provided in the Yalta Agreement — were not mentioned.

After 1944, the success of the Red armies in Europe enabled the Soviet Union to turn her attention to the Far East. It was also in that year that

[11] "The Entry of the Soviet Union," p. 20.

[12] Ibid., pp. 23–27; Feis, op. cit., pp. 107–8; General John R. Deane, The Strange Alliance (New York: Viking Press, Inc., 1946), pp. 226–27.

[13] Roosevelt-Churchill-Stalin luncheon meeting, November 30, 1943, Department of State, Foreign Relations of the United States: The Conferences at Cairo and Teheran, 1943 (Washington, D.C.: Government Printing Office, 1961), p. 567 (hereafter cited as Cairo Papers); Minutes of a meeting of the Pacific Council, January 12, 1944, ibid., p. 869; Feis, op. cit., pp. 110–13; Herbert Feis, Churchill, Roosevelt and Stalin (Princeton, N.J.: Princeton University Press, 1957), pp. 254–57; Max Beloff, Soviet Policy in the Far East, 1944–1951 (London: Oxford University Press, 1953), pp. 21–23.

the Allies gradually abandoned the idea of using China as an essential base of operation. Since the main American effort would be made in the Pacific, the problem of dealing with Japanese forces on the Chinese mainland remained unresolved. In July, 1944, the Joint Chiefs of Staff approved a plan which called for an invasion of Japan's home islands. A landing on Kyushu was tentatively scheduled to begin on October 1, 1945, and an assault on the Tokyo region on Honshu was to take place at the end of December, 1945.[14] At the Quebec Conference in September, 1944, the plan for an invasion of Japan was approved by Roosevelt and Churchill. The target date for the surrender of Japan was put at eighteen months after the end of the war in Europe.[15] At this time the plans formulated by the Joint Chiefs did not take into account Russian participation. But as a result of Stalin's show of sensitivity about what he considered to be America's reluctance to ask for Soviet help, all later American plans included specific missions for the Soviet forces to perform.[16]

What the Soviet Union planned to do with her military power in the Far East was revealed to American officials in October, 1944. In outlining his plan for vast land operations in China, Stalin said:

> If we are thinking seriously about defeating the Japanese, we cannot be limited to the Manchurian region. We shall strike direct blows from different directions in Manchuria. But to have real results we must develop outflanking movements — blows at Kalgan and Peking. . . . I do not believe that the major battles will be so much in Manchuria as in the south where Japanese troops are to be expected to be found when they withdraw from China.[17]

Such a ground campaign would carry the Soviet forces into North China where Chinese Communist forces were operating. In contrast, the United States did not plan landing operations in China except for some landing on the coast to take airfields. In response to Stalin's question, Harriman informed him that only Soviet forces would be used in Manchuria. Stalin expressed agreement with the American plan. He observed: "The Americans would cut off the Japanese garrisons on the southern islands and the Russians would cut off the Japanese land forces in China."[18]

[14] "The Entry of the Soviet Union," p. 29.
[15] Ibid., p. 31.
[16] Ibid., pp. 34–36; Deane, op. cit., p. 240. For two interesting comments on this episode, see Kennan, op. cit., p. 380; and Beloff, op. cit., p. 22.
[17] Feis, The China Tangle, p. 230; Feis, Churchill, Roosevelt and Stalin, pp. 454–55. This quotation from Feis is the most revealing and least ambiguous of all published accounts. See the reports of Harriman and General John R. Deane as printed in Department of State, Foreign Relations of the United States: The Conferences at Malta and Yalta, 1945 (Washington, D.C.: Government Printing Office, 1955), pp. 370–71 (hereafter cited as Yalta Papers). See also Deane, op. cit., p. 249.
[18] Feis, Churchill, Roosevelt and Stalin, p. 465.

Stalin's bargaining position was strong not only because of his military capabilities but also because of his freedom of choice in deciding the time of his entry into the war. As General John R. Deane, the head of the United States military mission to the Soviet Union, observed, "Time and timing were the essential elements of the situation with regard to Russian's participation in the Pacific War."[19] The Joint Staff Planners told the Joint Chiefs that in order to provide maximum support to America's attack on Japan, the Russian offensive into Manchuria should be launched at least three months before the projected invasion of Kyushu, while the maximum military advantage would accrue to the Russians if they attacked after American forces had effected an initial lodgement on Kyushu and Japanese forces in Manchuria had begun to move to reinforce Japan.[20] Just before the Yalta Conference, the Joint Chiefs advised the President that "Russia's entry [into the Pacific war] at as early a day as possible consistent with her ability to engage in offensive operations is necessary to provide maximum assistance to our Pacific operations."[21] After General MacArthur learned about the prospective Russian participation, he told Brigadier General George A. Lincoln, in February, 1945, that he "considers it essential that maximum number of Jap[anese] divisions be engaged and pinned down on the Asiatic mainland, before United States forces strike Japan proper."[22] He also said that "from the military standpoint we should make every effort to get Russia into the Japanese war before we go into Japan, otherwise we will take the impact of the Jap[anese] divisions and reap the losses, while the Russians in due time advance into an area free of major resistance."[23]

The bargaining position of the Soviet Union appeared to the United States stronger than it actually was because of an erroneous American intelligence estimate. In the fall of 1944, the intelligence section of the War Department general staff estimated the total strength of the Japanese army at about five million officers and men. Of these, slightly less than two million were reported to be in Japan proper; a little more than two million in Manchuria, Korea, China, and Formosa. Japan's Kwantung Army in Manchuria was put at more than one million combatants. It was said to be the cream of the Japanese army.[24] This estimate governed American planning up to the end of the war.[25] It was accepted in preference to another

[19] Deane, op. cit., p. 223.
[20] "The Entry of the Soviet Union," pp. 40–41.
[21] Yalta Papers, p. 396.
[22] "The Entry of the Soviet Union," p. 50. See also Walter Millis (ed.), The Forrestal Diaries (New York: Viking Press, Inc., 1951), p. 31.
[23] "The Entry of the Soviet Union," p. 51.
[24] Rear Admiral Ellis M. Zacharias, "The Inside Story of Yalta," United Nations World, January, 1949, pp. 14–16.
[25] Henry L. Stimson and McGeorge Bundy, On Active Service in Peace and War (New York: Harper & Bros., 1947), p. 618; "The Entry of the Soviet Union," pp. 85–86.

estimate which put the upper limit of high quality first-line troops available to Japan at two million. According to this appraisal, the Japanese soldiers defeated in the southwest and central Pacific campaigns represented the cream of the Japanese army; the Kwantung Army was only a shadow of its former self and no sustained difficulties would be expected in Manchuria.[26]

The prospective land operations undertaken by the Red Army would put Stalin in a position to take what he wanted in Manchuria with or without American agreement. Few American officials made this point as forcefully as General MacArthur. He was reported to have said:

> He understands Russia's aims; . . . they would want all of Manchuria, Korea and possibly part of Nationalist China. This seizure of territory was inevitable; but the United States must insist that Russia pay her way by invading Manchuria at the earliest possible date after the defeat of Germany.[27]

In addition, the presence of the Red Armies in China would give Stalin tremendous leverage in China's internal politics. He could lend his support to the Chinese Communists in North China and Manchuria either to set up a separate state or to establish regional domination in the most important part of China. As noted in chapter v, Davies recognized as early as January, 1944, the possibility of North China and Manchuria developing into a separate state — perhaps even a Russian satellite.[28] On December 15, 1944, Harriman told the President that, to use Feis's words, "if there was no arrangement between the Soviet and Chinese governments before the Soviet Union entered the Pacific War, the Soviet forces would back the Communists in the North and turn over to them the administration of the Chinese territories which the Red Army would liberate."[29] Alternatively, Stalin could support Chiang's leadership and American policy in China in return for American and Chinese acceptance of his terms. Between these two extremes there was a wide range of other possibilities.

Stalin appeared to be accommodating. In spite of his potential power to grasp what he wanted, he made only limited demands. In exchange, he promised to enter the Pacific war and to support American policy in China. In retrospect, it appears that of all the possible alternatives, Stalin chose the least ambitious one which, in the end, served him better than any other.

[26] Zacharias, loc. cit.

[27] "The Entry of the Soviet Union," pp. 51–52, n. 4.

[28] Department of State, United States Relations with China (Washington, D.C.: Government Printing Office, 1949), p. 564 (hereafter cited as United States Relations with China).

[29] Feis, The China Tangle, p. 233. This statement does not appear in the only report dealing with the Soviet entry into the war, dated December 15, 1944, from Harriman to Roosevelt, which is printed in the Yalta Papers. See Yalta Papers, pp. 378–79.

Apparently, his experiences in dealing with Chinese affairs in the twenties led him to underestimate the revolutionary potential of the Chinese Communists and exaggerate the military strength of the Kuomintang. He may also have been uncertain about American intentions and capabilities. In any case, he could afford to wait and to watch developments in China while pursuing a course of action which would not arouse American suspicion and Nationalist hostility.

Whatever the reasons, Stalin's demands seemed reasonable,[30] and his policy moderate. President Roosevelt was ready to meet his demands in order to insure Soviet entry into the Pacific war, to bring about a Sino-Soviet rapprochement, to obtain Soviet support for the Nationalist government, and to ward off Soviet interference in Chinese politics. He also hoped to minimize the danger of Soviet support for the Chinese Communists by rapidly pushing forward the unification of China.[31]

Chiang, of course, acutely realized the danger of open Soviet support for the Chinese Communists. But a settlement with the Chinese Communists was not his solution to the complications which would follow the entry of the Soviet Union in the Pacific war, except as this settlement could be obtained on his own terms. Only in November, 1944, he had rejected the proposed agreement with the Chinese Communists drafted by Hurley.[32] Instead, he endeavored to weaken the Communist position by winning Soviet support for himself through diplomatic concessions, with the United States serving as mediator. In June, 1944, he had suggested to Wallace

[30] In a speech delivered in March, 1951, before the National War College, Vice-Admiral Oscar C. Badger, one of the ranking naval commanders in the Pacific war, told his audience: "During the war a great many people were trying to predict the price that the Soviet Union would demand at the end of the war for her participation. In general, those predictions were limited to three. All pointed toward the acquisition of warm-water ports as outlets for Soviet world trade. I think the general consensus of opinion pointed toward the possibility that Stalin might demand all three, but if not, they would be made in the following order of importance:

"First, Soviet control of a belt extending to the Persian Gulf.

"Second, Soviet control [of] and access to the Dardanelles with definite rights to adjacent territory, and

"Third, Soviet commercial and military rights in the ports of Port Arthur and Dairen with commanding control of those ports and the land approaches to them, including the Manchurian railway.

"To many, it was a considerable surprise when Soviet demands pointed merely to the third or Manchurian factor. On the other hand, I think that, among western powers, this demand was received with considerable relief as being the lesser of three evils" (*Military Situation in the Far East*, p. 2731).

At the Teheran Conference in late 1943, in his conversations with Churchill in October, 1944, and at the Yalta Conference, Stalin did raise the question of the Dardanelles but did not press the issue (*Yalta Papers*, pp. 903–4; Feis, *Churchill, Roosevelt and Stalin*, p. 254). In June, 1945, however, Moscow pressed her claims on Turkey (Herbert Feis, *Between War and Peace: The Potsdam Conference* [Princeton, N.J.: Princeton University Press, 1960], pp. 291–95).

[31] Feis, *Churchill, Roosevelt and Stalin*, pp. 509–10.

[32] Feis, *The China Tangle*, p. 232.

that Roosevelt might act as "an arbiter or middleman" between China and the Soviet Union.[33] Apparently, he hoped that American mediation would soften Soviet demands and that American influence would counterbalance Soviet power. To guard against all possible contingencies, he had, even before the spring of 1944, prepared plans to prevent contact between Russian troops and Chinese Communist forces in the event that the Red Army attacked Japan through North China.[34] After having received in November a message from Roosevelt with a hint that the Soviet Union would soon enter the war, he asked Stalin to receive Foreign Minister Soong. In adopting this course of action, Chiang was probably encouraged by Stalin's avowed policy of supporting him as the best man available in China and of allowing the United States to play the leading role in Chinese affairs. He probably remembered that the Soviet Union had sent all her aid to his government between 1937 and 1941 and had adopted an officially correct attitude toward the internal affairs of China. Thus, Chiang was ready to offer diplomatic concessions to Stalin to make certain that Stalin meant what he said to Harriman and what Molotov told Hurley.[35]

At the end of December, 1944, the top leaders of the United States were reasonably certain that a new weapon, the atomic bomb, would be ready by August, 1945. General Leslie R. Groves, commanding general of the Manhattan District Project, told Marshall on December 30 that the first "gun type bomb" should be ready about August 1, 1945, and the second one by the end of the year. The first would have the effect equivalent to about ten thousand tons of TNT.[36] Groves also reported that more material would have to be developed before a second type of atomic bomb, the implosion type bomb, could be successfully made, but that there should be sufficient material for making the first implosion type bomb sometime in the latter part of July. He estimated that the first implosion type bomb would have the explosive force equivalent to about five thousand tons of TNT.[37] As it later turned out, both the first implosion type bomb, which was tested in July in New Mexico, and the first gun type bomb, which was dropped on Hiroshima, had the explosive power of about twenty thousand tons of TNT.[38] This knowledge about the probability of the successful de-

[33] *United States Relations with China*, p. 550.

[34] This information was given by the Chinese ambassador to John Carter Vincent of the State Department when the former returned to Washington from Chungking in the spring of 1944 (*Yalta Papers*, p. 351).

[35] On February 4, 1945, Hurley reported that the Chinese government contemplated sending Soong to Moscow and added that "the Chinese are anxious to ascertain if the Soviet attitude continues as outlined last September by Molotov" (*United States Relations with China*, pp. 92–93).

[36] *Yalta Papers*, pp. 383–84.

[37] *Ibid.*

[38] Herbert Feis, *Japan Subdued: The Atomic Bomb and the End of the War in the Pacific* (Princeton, N.J.: Princeton University Press, 1961), pp. 60, 72, 110–11.

velopment of atomic bombs did not change the view of Roosevelt and Truman on the desirability of participation of the Soviet Union in the Pacific war as soon as possible. The dominant trend of thought among top American officials was to count on "Soviet entry into the war to supplement the impact of the atomic bomb."[39] Or, as Louis Morton conclusively demonstrated, a desire to forestall Soviet intervention in the Far Eastern war did not govern the use of the atomic bomb and its timing.[40] The use of the atomic bomb had one purpose: the defeat of the enemy. If it was influenced at all by political considerations which individual officials may have entertained, these influences were remote, indirect, and not apparent in published records and accounts. Only if a different approach toward the problem of war and peace had obtained in the United States, or, more precisely, only if the United States had been accustomed to the use of military power for political purposes, would American officials have considered the probable use of the atomic bomb as a substitute for Soviet entry into the war.

C. The Yalta Agreement

Geopolitical factors decreed that any Soviet advance in the Far East would have to be accomplished at the expense of China. Given the weakness of the Nationalist government, Soviet claims could be limited only by American power rather than by China's legal rights. Since effective resistance could come from the United States rather than China, the fulfilment of Soviet claims would depend more heavily on American acquiescence than on Chinese agreement. To secure a firm position in China, the Soviet Union would have to avoid the danger that following the precedents of Secretary Bryan's *caveat* and Secretary Stimson's non-recognition doctrine, the United States would refuse to recognize any treaty or agreement between the Soviet Union and China which impaired the territorial and administrative integrity of China or ran counter to the Open Door policy. Thus, Stalin's tactic was apparently to gain American acceptance of his demands before pressing them on China. For the United States, his *quid pro quo* was primarily Soviet participation in the Pacific war; for China, it was primarily an assurance to support the Nationalist government. To both the United States and China, his promises weighed more heavily than his demands; his capability to do good or evil appeared formidable. In the negotiations, neither the United States nor Nationalist China found it desirable or possible to deny his claims. The United States tried only to make it difficult for him to increase his demands, and China endeavored

[39] *Ibid.*, p. 38.
[40] Louis Morton, "The Decision To Use the Atomic Bomb," in *Command Decisions*, prepared by the Office of the Chief of Military History, Department of the Army (New York: Harcourt, Brace & Co., 1959), pp. 407–8.

merely to obtain a softening of his terms and to secure a firmer assurance of his intentions.

In his conferences with Harriman in October, 1944, Stalin promised to enter the war two or three months after the defeat of Germany.[41] But he made it clear for the first time that before entering the war he would want to have a precise understanding regarding his political claims. On December 14, 1944, Harriman asked Stalin what political questions should be clarified in connection with Russia's entry into the war against Japan. Stalin said that the Kurile Islands and the lower Sakhalin should be returned to Russia. He wanted to lease Port Arthur and Dairen and the surrounding area. He wished to lease the Chinese Eastern Railway. He demanded "the recognition of the *status quo* in Outer Mongolia — the maintenance of the Republic of Outer Mongolia as an independent identity."[42]

In a meeting with Roosevelt on February 8, during the Yalta Conference, Stalin said that he would like to discuss the political conditions under which the Soviet Union would enter the war against Japan. Then he referred to his conversation with Harriman.[43] Roosevelt endeavored to modify these claims by indicating his preference for making Dairen an internationalized free port, and by suggesting a joint Sino-Soviet commission to manage the Manchurian railways.[44] Two days later, Molotov submitted to Harriman a draft agreement which embodied Stalin's proposals rather than Roosevelt's preferences for dealing with the ports and the railways.[45] The same afternoon, Stalin worked out with Roosevelt a compromise under which Port Arthur would be leased to the Soviet Union, Dairen would be made a free port under international control, and the Manchurian railways would be put under a joint Sino-Soviet commission. But in drawing up the final text, Soviet officials sought a special status for Russia in the port of Dairen and the railways by inserting two phrases providing that the "pre-eminent interests" of the Soviet Union in the port and the railways be safeguarded. Roosevelt accepted these changes without further discussion with Stalin.[46] These two phrases were to furnish Stalin with a pretext for making greater claims on China than those which Roosevelt thought he agreed to support.

In the Yalta Agreement of February 11, 1945, Stalin also succeeded in obtaining a pledge from Roosevelt that the Soviet claims "shall be un-

[41] Feis, *Churchill, Roosevelt and Stalin*, p. 466; *Yalta Papers*, p. 369; Feis, *The China Tangle*, pp. 230–31.
[42] *Yalta Papers*, p. 379. Stalin's demand covered the South Manchurian Railway.
[43] *Ibid.*, p. 768.
[44] *Ibid.*, p. 769. The Manchurian railways referred to here consist of the Chinese Eastern Railway and the South Manchurian Railroad.
[45] *Ibid.*, pp. 894–96.
[46] Feis, *The China Tangle*, p. 247.

questionably fulfilled."[47] This provision obligated the United States to gain Chinese acceptance of the Soviet terms. Roosevelt endeavored to modify this obligation only to the extent of proposing the insertion of a statement that "it is understood that the agreement concerning the ports and the railways referred to above requires the concurrence of Generalissimo Chiang Kai-shek."[48] Stalin agreed to the need for the concurrence of the Generalissimo on these matters and extended it to cover his demand concerning Outer Mongolia. In return, he obtained from Roosevelt a commitment to "take measures to obtain Chiang's concurrence."[49]

President Roosevelt had not consulted Generalissimo Chiang about the concessions made to the Russians, although during the Cairo Conference he had discussed with Chiang the possibility of making Dairen a free port at the end of the war.[50] In explaining this omission to Stalin, Roosevelt made the unfortunate remark that "he had not had an opportunity to talk to Marshall [sic] Chiang Kai-shek and he felt that one of the diffi-

[47] *Yalta Papers*, p. 984.

[48] Feis, *The China Tangle*, p. 240. For the text of the Yalta Agreement, see n. 49, below.

[49] *Yalta Papers*, pp. 895, 984. As finally worded, the Yalta Agreement, with the title of "Agreement regarding Entry of the Soviet Union into the War against Japan," read as follows:

"The leaders of the three Great Powers — the Soviet Union, the United States of America and Great Britain — have agreed that in two or three months after Germany has surrendered and the war in Europe has terminated the Soviet Union shall enter into the war against Japan on the side of the Allies on condition that:

"1. The *status quo* in Outer-Mongolia (The Mongolian People's Republic) shall be preserved;

"2. The former rights of Russia violated by the treacherous attack of Japan in 1904 shall be restored; viz:

"(a) the southern part of Sakhalin as well as all the islands adjacent to it shall be returned to the Soviet Union,

"(b) the commercial port of Dairen shall be internationalized, the preeminent interests of the Soviet Union in this port being safeguarded and the lease of Port Arthur as a naval base of the U.S.S.R. restored,

"(c) the Chinese-Eastern Railroad and the South-Manchurian Railroad which provide an outlet to Dairen shall be jointly operated by the establishment of a joint Soviet-Chinese Company it being understood that the preeminent interests of the Soviet Union shall be safeguarded and that China shall retain full sovereignty in Manchuria;

"3. The Kuril[e] islands shall be handed over to the Soviet Union.

"It is understood, that the agreement concerning Outer-Mongolia and the ports and railroads referred to above will require concurrence of Generalissimo Chiang Kai-shek. The President will take measures in order to obtain this concurrence on advice from Marshal Stalin.

"The Heads of the three Great Powers have agreed that these claims of the Soviet Union shall be unquestionably fulfilled after Japan has been defeated.

"For its part the Soviet Union expresses its readiness to conclude with the National Government of China a pact of friendship and alliance between the USSR and China in order to render assistance to China with its armed forces for the purpose of liberating China from the Japanese yoke" (*ibid.*, p. 984).

[50] *Cairo Papers*, p. 891; Feis, *The China Tangle*, p. 112, n. 14.

culties in speaking to the Chinese was that anything said to them was known to the whole world in twenty-four hours."[51] Stalin readily expressed his agreement and said that when it was possible to free a number of Soviet troops in the west and move twenty-five divisions to the Far East, it would be possible to speak to Chiang Kai-shek about these matters.[52] Thus, the Yalta Agreement was not disclosed to the Chinese until June, when Stalin thought the time had come to do so.

The deep secrecy shrouding the Yalta Agreement rested on firm military grounds. As the Joint Staff Planners pointed out in November, 1944, a Japanese attack to cut the Trans-Siberian Railway before the Russians were ready to launch a strong offensive might throw them off balance and could conceivably result in a serious defeat of the Soviet Far Eastern forces.[53] Since a quick victory over Japan rather than a postwar balance of power was the supreme objective of the United States, the American government thought that it had as much stake in maintaining secrecy as the Russians, even to the extent of denying knowledge of the Yalta Agreement to the Chinese government. It turned out that this secrecy had political as well as military effects. Secrecy enabled Stalin to deploy his forces from Europe to the Far East for a strong offensive and thus to influence political developments in the Far East. It kept Japan from having definite knowledge of the Soviet intention to enter the war. The lack of concrete evidence of Soviet intentions prolonged Japan's illusion that she could obtain a peace settlement with the Allies through Soviet mediation. This illusion prevented Japan from approaching the Allies directly to seek peace. Thus, whether or not Stalin realized it, the chief political effect of his insistence on secrecy was to preserve his power to influence the timing of the end of the Pacific war and to shape the postwar political configuration in the Far East. For the United States, failure either to consult China beforehand or to communicate the Yalta Agreement immediately after its conclusion was to become a source of friction in her relations with China. It was to incur for the administration the moral reproach of its critics. It deviated so sharply from the American style of diplomacy that few American officials ventured to defend this aspect of the Yalta Agreement.[54]

[51] *Yalta Papers*, p. 769.
[52] *Ibid.*, pp. 769–70.
[53] "The Entry of the Soviet Union," p. 40.
[54] Commenting on the Yalta Agreement in the hearings on his nomination as ambassador to the Soviet Union, Charles E. Bohlen testified on March 2, 1953, before the Senate Committee on Foreign Relations, as follows: "I think that, in general, it is distasteful, to put it mildly, to do things involving another country without the representative of that country present; but there the major considerations were secrecy and security" (Senate Committee on Foreign Relations, *Hearings on the Nomination of Charles E. Bohlen*, 83d Cong., 1st sess. [1953], p. 21). In another context, Bohlen said: "Another feature [of the Yalta Agreement] which, I think, no one would undertake to

Roosevelt, curiously enough, did not try to obtain a definite commitment from Stalin that he would support the Nationalist government in its internal conflict. The only commitment assumed by the Soviet Union in this respect was that "For its part the Soviet Union expresses its readiness to conclude with the National Government of China a pact of friendship and alliance between the USSR and China in order to render assistance to China with its armed forces for the purpose of liberating China from the Japanese yoke." [55] This envisaged a military alliance in the war against Japan rather than support for the Nationalist government to maintain its authority within China.[56] Perhaps the reason for Roosevelt's omission can be found in a conversation between him and Stalin. In this brief and only discussion on record of conditions in China, Roosevelt referred to the slow progress in bringing the Communists and the Chungking government together, and said that the fault lay more with the Kuomintang and the Chungking government than with the so-called Communists.[57] Stalin expressed the thought that for the purpose of building a united front against the Japanese, Chiang Kai-shek should assume leadership.[58] It must also be remembered that the Yalta Conference took place four months after the recall of Stilwell and at a time when President Roosevelt became very dubious of his own notion of China as a great power.

defend politically, as it were, was the fact that it was done behind the back of the Chinese. My understanding then was that the reason for that was grounds of military security" (*ibid.*, p. 8).

[55] *Yalta Papers*, p. 984.

[56] The language used enabled the Soviet government to claim that it had fulfilled the Yalta Agreement. Mr. Y. Malik of the Soviet delegation to the United Nations General Assembly stated in 1952: "Indeed, it was in pursuance of the Yalta Agreement that the U.S.S.R. had agreed to enter the war against Japan on the side of the Allies three months after the surrender of Germany, to conclude a treaty of friendship and alliance with the Chinese Government and to help in liberating China from Japanese occupation. It was of course not true to say that the U.S.S.R. had pledged itself to help the Chinese Nationalist Government in the civil war which it was then fighting against the army of national liberation, for the U.S.S.R. always abstained from intervening in the domestic affairs of other states. In accordance with the Yalta Agreement, the U.S.S.R. had declared war on Japan within the prescribed time. It had launched an offensive against first-rate Japanese troops in Kwantung. After the capitulation, the Soviet forces had continued to fight against those Japanese troops which had not surrendered. Thus the U.S.S.R. had fought until victory was won and granted all necessary assistance to the Chinese Government. At the time the Governments of the United Kingdom and the United States had welcomed the U.S.S.R.'s entry into the war. It was therefore false to claim that the Soviet Union had not fulfilled its obligations under the Yalta Agreement or under the Treaty of Friendship and Alliance of 14 August 1945" (United Nations, *Official Records of the Sixth Session of the General Assembly, First Committee, 1951–1952*, pp. 273–74). From a legalistic point of view, Malik's assertion that the Soviet Union had fulfilled her obligations under the Yalta Agreement is entirely correct, although it is false to make the same claim with regard to the Sino-Soviet Treaty of Friendship and Alliance.

[57] *Yalta Papers*, p. 771.

[58] *Ibid.*

D. The Growing Apprehension about Soviet Intentions and the Review of the Yalta Agreement

Within a few months after the Yalta Conference, Soviet actions in eastern Europe, particularly in Poland, deeply disturbed American officials. Some of them began to entertain serious doubts about Stalin's intentions and to question, by implication, Roosevelt's policy of co-operation with the Soviet Union. On April 4, Ambassador Harriman told Washington that "the Soviet government views all matters from the standpoint of their own selfish interests" and that "the Soviet program is the establishment of totalitarianism."[59] He concluded that, unless the United States and Great Britain now adopted an "independent line," the chances of Soviet domination in Europe would be enhanced. Two days later he reported that the continued generous and considerate attitude adopted by the United States was regarded in Russia only as a sign of weakness. He urged effective reprisals, selecting "one or two cases where their [the Russians'] actions are intolerable and make them realize that they cannot continue their present attitude except at great cost to themselves."[60] President Roosevelt's death on April 12 removed from the scene the chief advocate of continued co-operation with Russia.

Harriman's reports marked the beginning of a reappraisal of Soviet intentions and American policies. From this time on, the misjudgment of Soviet intentions was a factor of rapidly diminishing importance in determining American policy in the Far East. But so long as the United States had to rely on the help of the Soviet Union to defeat Japan, and so long as she did not plan to use her troops in Manchuria and North China, it was still necessary for her to gamble on Soviet good will. So long as she could not bring the Pacific war to an end before Soviet troops could be deployed from Europe to the Far East, it was not within the capability of her ground forces to gain a prior entry to Manchuria, and it was not possible for her to prevent the Soviet government from entering the war at a time of its own choosing and from seizing what it claimed. None of these conditions could have been changed, unless the United States had abandoned her policy of unconditional surrender at an early date and brought the Pacific war to a close before, or at least shortly after the surrender of Germany. Thus, the growing apprehensions about Soviet intentions led to no major change in America's policy in the Far East.

This was so, in spite of the fact that the developing doubts about Soviet intentions were paralleled by the crystallization of a sophisticated view of Stalin's professions of support for the Nationalist government and American policy in China. This more accurate appraisal emerged in connection

---

[59] Millis, *op. cit.*, p. 39.
[60] *Ibid.*, p. 41.

with Ambassador Hurley's visit to Moscow in April, 1945, on his way from Washington back to his post at Chungking. It took the form of comments on Hurley's optimistic views. After a conference with Stalin and Molotov on April 15, Hurley reported to Washington: Stalin "stated frankly" that the the Soviet government would support the American policy of "upholding the National government under the leadership of Chiang and of endorsing the Chinese aspirations to establish a united, free, and democratic government." Stalin added, according to Hurley, that he would be glad to co-operate with the United States in achieving unification of the military forces in China. He wished the American government to know that it would have "his complete support in immediate action for the unification of the armed forces of China with full recognition of the National Government under the leadership of Chiang Kai-shek." Hurley concluded that "Stalin agreed unqualifiedly to America's policy in China."[61]

Hurley's judgment that Stalin wanted military and political unification in China seems to be correct. As Charles B. McLane observes, Soviet policy at this time was "to urge greater collaboration between the Communists and the Kuomintang for the remainder of the war and to recommend that immediate preparations be made for establishing a coalition government as soon as the war was over."[62] Moscow adopted this policy so that its gains as envisaged in the Yalta Agreement would not be put into jeopardy by an outbreak of full-scale civil war. But what Hurley overlooked was the possibility that Soviet support for military and political unity in China could not, in itself, bring about a settlement in China on Nationalist terms. Nor did he realize that the Soviet policy of co-operating with Chiang was merely one tactical move in a broad and flexible pattern of policies which could be modified or discarded in the light of the developing situation.

These possibilities were clearly foreseen by American officials at the time. On April 19, Ambassador Harriman, back in Washington for a visit, indicated to an official in the State Department his feeling that Hurley's report, while factually accurate, gave a "too optimistic impression of Marshal Stalin's reactions." He was certain that if and when Russia entered the conflict in the Far East she would make full use of and would support the Chinese Communists even to the extent of setting up a puppet government in Manchuria and possibly in North China if Kuomintang-Communist differences had not been resolved by that time.[63] He observed that statements made by Stalin indorsing American efforts in China did not

[61] *United States Relations with China*, p. 86. Excerpts from Hurley's message to Secretary Stettinius are reproduced in Don Lohbeck, *Patrick J. Hurley* (Chicago: Henry Regnery Co., 1956), pp. 371–72.

[62] Charles B. McLane, *Soviet Policy and the Chinese Communists, 1931–1948* (New York: Columbia University Press, 1958), p. 181.

[63] *United States Relations with China*, pp. 98–99.

necessarily mean that the Russians would not pursue whatever course of action they wished to serve their interests.

On April 23, George Kennan, the chargé d'affaires in Moscow, sent a telegram to Harriman commenting on Hurley's report. Kennan pointed out that Stalin knew that unification of the armed forces was "feasible in a practical sense only on conditions which are acceptable to the Chinese Communist Party."[64] He predicted that "in the future Soviet policy respecting China will continue what it has been in the recent past: a fluid, resilient policy directed at the achievement of maximum power with minimum responsibility on portions of the Asiatic continent lying beyond the Soviet border" and that, within this framework, one of the specific aims of the Soviet Union would be the acquisition of sufficient control in all areas of North China to prevent penetration in that area by outside power including America and Britain. . . ." He warned that "it would be tragic if our natural anxiety for the support of the Soviet Union at this juncture, coupled with Stalin's use of words which mean all things to all people and his cautious affability, were to lead us into an undue reliance on Soviet aid or even Soviet acquiescence in the achievement of our long term objectives in China." But these realistic appraisals of Soviet intentions brought no change in American policy. They merely led the Department of State to take steps to impress on Generalissimo Chiang the urgency of achieving early military and political unification in China as a basis for improving Sino-Soviet relations. A telegram in this sense was dispatched to Hurley on April 23.[65]

One need not go far to seek the reasons why the reappraisal of Soviet intentions merely sharpened the dilemma confronting the United States without leading to any change in policy. On April 23, the question of Soviet intentions in eastern Europe and the appropriate American response was discussed at a White House meeting in what Walter Millis calls the first crisis of policy under the Truman administration. According to Forrestal's diary, Truman remarked that "if one part of the agreements which they [the Russians] had entered with President Roosevelt at Yalta were breached he [Truman] would consider that the entire Yalta agreement was no longer binding on any of the parties interested."[66] But General Marshall argued for a cautious approach. He said that he "hoped for Soviet participation in the war against Japan at a time when it would be useful to us" and that the Russians had it within their power to delay their entry into the Far Eastern war until "we had done all the dirty work."[67] Thus, the need for Soviet help in the Pacific war slowed down the process of

[64] The quotations in this paragraph are drawn from *ibid.*, pp. 96–97.
[65] *Ibid.*, p. 98.
[66] Millis, *op. cit.*, p. 50.
[67] *Ibid.*, p. 51.

evolving a new policy toward the Soviet Union in both Europe and the Far East. Soon some officials began to question whether Russian co-operation was necessary for the defeat of Japan, whether it was in the interest of the United States, or whether the Soviet Union needed American inducements to enter the war.[68] The Joint Staff Planners raised the question whether or not at least token forces should be introduced into China in light of the probability that Russian forces would be the first to enter Manchuria. However, this line of thought was not accepted widely enough to become the basis of American policy. Up to the end of the Pacific war, both President Truman and General Marshall believed that Soviet participation was highly desirable, if not absolutely necessary. Furthermore, there was no way to keep the Russians out of the Pacific war and out of Manchuria and parts of North China. These considerations continued to set a limit to any endeavor to revise American policy.

On May 12, Acting Secretary of State Joseph C. Grew sent a memorandum to Stimson and Secretary of the Navy James Forrestal. In it, Grew asked the following two questions relating to China policy:

> Is the entry of the Soviet Union into the Pacific war at the earliest possible moment of such vital interest to the United States as to preclude any attempt by the United States government to obtain Soviet agreements to certain desirable political objectives in the Far East prior to such entry? Should the Yalta decision in regard to Soviet political desires in the Far East be reconsidered or carried into effect in whole or in part?[69]

Grew suggested that the Soviet government should agree to use its influence with the Chinese Communists to assist the American government in the latter's endeavors to bring about the unification of China under the national government headed by Chiang Kai-shek, and that the achievement of Chinese unity on the basis considered most desirable by the United States should be agreed to by the Soviet Union before the United States government made any approach to the Chinese government on the basis of the Yalta Agreement. By this time Grew had begun to entertain profound apprehension about Soviet intentions.[70]

In response to Grew's questions, the War Department set down, in a memorandum dated May 21, the following evaluations of the Soviet role in the Pacific war: Russian entry would have a profound military effect and would materially shorten the war and thus save American lives. The

---

[68] "The Entry of the Soviet Union," pp. 60–61, 67; Deane, *op. cit.*, pp 261–66. For Harriman's view, see Millis, *op. cit.*, p. 55.

[69] "The Entry of the Soviet Union," p. 69; see also Joseph Grew, *The Turbulent Era* (Boston: Houghton Mifflin Co., 1952), II, 1456–57.

[70] *Ibid.*, p. 1446.

Soviet Union's decision to enter the war and the timing of the entry would be made on the basis of military and political considerations with little regard to any political actions taken by the United States. The concessions to Russia contained in the Yalta Agreement were "generally matters which are within the military power of Russia to obtain regardless of United States military action short of war."[71] Russia was militarily capable of defeating the Japanese and occupying Karafuto, Manchuria, Korea, and northern China before it would be possible for the United States military forces to occupy these areas. Furthermore, Russia could, if she chose, await the time when American effort had practically completed the destruction of Japanese military power and could, then, seize her objectives at a lesser cost to herself than would have been occasioned by her entry into the war at an earlier date. The United States could bring little, if any, military leverage to bear on Russia insofar as the Far East was concerned unless America chose to use force. On the basis of this evaluation, the War Department reached an ambiguous conclusion. On the one hand, it stated that military considerations did not preclude an attempt by the American government to obtain Soviet agreement to desirable political objectives in the Far East prior to the entry of the Soviet Union in the Pacific war. It concurred in the desirability of obtaining Soviet commitments and clarifications which the State Department sought. On the other hand, it observed that from the military point of view it would be desirable to have a complete understanding and agreement with the Soviet Union concerning the Far East. It expressed the belief that not much good would come of a rediscussion of the Yalta Agreement at this time.

On one point the War Department was not equivocal. It clearly stated its view that unless the Nationalist government reached a satisfactory understanding with the Soviet Union, Soviet entry into the war and the prospective contact between the Red Army and the Chinese Communist forces would make American problems in China even more complicated than they already were. It suggested that, as a preliminary step to a Sino-Soviet rapprochement, "some sort of understanding between the Chinese Communists and the Generalissimo seems to rank in order *as of first importance*."[72] For our purpose, the most important point in this memorandum is that it establishes clearly the connection between America's lack of military power to prevent the Soviet Union from influencing the Chinese situation and the policy of seeking military and political unity in China. It shows that the hope of limiting Soviet influence in China depended, just as the policy of making China a great power, on the success of the policy of peaceful unification. This latter policy became the arch of all other pol-

[71] "The Entry of the Soviet Union," p. 70.
[72] *Ibid.*, pp. 70–71 (emphasis added); see also Grew, *op. cit.*, pp. 1457–59.

icies in China. When it collapsed the whole structure of American policies crumbled.

At this point one can detect some subtle but significant differences between Hurley's policy, Chiang's program, and the outlook of some American officials in Washington and Moscow. Hurley's policy rested on the assumption that the Chinese Communists would have to come to terms with the Kuomintang because the Soviet Union would support the Nationalist government and American policy in China. To secure from the Soviet government a public promise of support for the Nationalist government, to be embodied in a treaty implementing the Yalta Agreement, was seen by him as the key to obtaining a satisfactory settlement between the two Chinese parties and to the solution of the Communist problem in China. Chiang also placed a high value on Soviet support. But recognizing that ultimate Soviet intentions were hostile, he sought to balance Soviet power by American might. Increasingly aware of the same fact, American officials in the State and War Departments hoped that Soviet influence on Chinese affairs could be contained and neutralized by the establishment of political and military unity in China. These three approaches gave the highest priority to three different factors. But in all three, there was missing a clear emphasis on what in retrospect seems to have been the most significant, possibly the decisive, element in the situation, which might have given American policy a greater chance of success. This was the need for the Nationalist government and the United States to co-operate with each other to create such a position of strength that the Soviet Union would find it in her interest to ignore the Chinese Communists and to deal with the Kuomintang, and that the Chinese Communists would consider it more desirable to accept the status of a minority party over a fairly long period of time than to risk an immediate civil war.

But it is easy to see why American policy did not develop in the direction of giving highest priority to the building of a Sino-American position of strength in China. Chiang's vested interests, his failure to see the need for reforms, and his resistance to American advice rendered Sino-American co-operation for such a purpose difficult. Hurley's low estimate of the strength of the Chinese Communists, his optimism about the viability of the Nationalist regime, and his disbelief in the tactics of pressure militated against a policy of forcing Chiang to undertake necessary reforms or creating a new non-Communist coalition of political groups to serve as a more solid foundation of the central government. After the summer of 1944, the policy of seeking to establish a coalition government in China became a settled program. By this' time, military planners in Washington had ruled out the idea of using American ground forces in China and rejected Stilwell's proposals to re-equip and retrain sixty and later ninety

Chinese divisions. ℰ·· long as the war against Japan continued, there was a limit to what American armed forces could do in China to counter Soviet actions. Few officials saw the necessity or feasibility of deploying on the Chinese mainland whatever military power the United States could send there.

Thus, the United States had no alternative but to rely on the good faith of the Soviet Union and to place her hope for political stability in the Far East on achieving political and military unity in China. The outcome of the review of American policy in mid-May was the decision not to ask for a revision of the Yalta Agreement but to ask Stalin to clarify his position regarding Chinese sovereignty in Manchuria and regarding the American effort to bring about unity in China.[73] This task was undertaken by Harry Hopkins with the help of Ambassador Harriman. Before Hopkins left for Moscow, Truman impressed upon him the need for getting as early a date as possible for Russia's entry into the Pacific war.[74] In his talk with Hopkins and Harriman on May 28, Stalin reaffirmed his promises to enter the war in early August, provided that China had, by that time, accepted the terms of the Yalta Agreement. Stalin made a categorical statement that he would do everything he could to promote unification of China under the leadership of Chiang. He further stated that Chiang's leadership should continue after the war because no one else and, specifically, no Communist leader, was strong enough to unify China. He said that he wanted China to control all of Manchuria as part of a unified China, that he would respect Chinese sovereignty in all areas his troops entered to fight the Japanese, and that he would welcome representatives of the Generalissimo to be with his troops entering Manchuria in order to facilitate the organization of a Chinese administration in Manchuria. He added that he desired an understanding with the Allies on areas of operation in Manchuria and China.[75]

Given the military situation and the strong bargaining position of the Soviet Union, Stalin's sweeping promises were the best results which the United States could have hoped for. Thus, Hopkins concluded in his report to Truman that "we were very encouraged by the conference on the Far East."[76] Truman has since written in his memoirs that he was reassured to learn of Stalin's confirmation of the promise to enter the Pacific war, because American military experts had estimated that an invasion of Japan would cost at least five hundred thousand American casualties

[73] Feis, *The China Tangle*, p. 308.
[74] Harry Truman, *Year of Decisions* (New York: Doubleday & Co., 1955), p. 264.
[75] "The Entry of the Soviet Union," pp. 42–44; Robert E. Sherwood, *Roosevelt and Hopkins* (New York: Harper & Bros., 1948), pp. 902–3; Truman, *op. cit.*, pp. 264–65; Statement of W. Averell Harriman, *Military Situation in the Far East*, p. 3338.
[76] "The Entry of the Soviet Union," p. 73; Sherwood, *op. cit.*, p. 903.

even if the Japanese forces in Asia were contained by the Russians on the Chinese mainland.[77] According to Feis, Stimson had, in mid-May during the review of the Yalta Agreement, entertained the thought that the time for serious discussion with the Soviet government about questions relating to Manchuria and China would be after the United States had successfully tested the atomic bomb and the world knew it.[78] After Stalin had given his assurances to Hopkins, this thought was abandoned and the American government took steps to implement the Yalta Agreement. In the last section of this chapter, we shall discuss the negotiations leading to the conclusion of the Sino-Soviet treaty. Since the crucial factor throughout this period was the capability of the Soviet Union to influence events in the Far East, we shall try to show first how the policy of unconditional surrender contributed to the Soviet ability to maintain a strong bargaining position vis-à-vis the United States up to the very end of the war.

E. The American Principle of Unconditional Surrender and the Soviet Ability to Manipulate Events in the Far East

The analysis has shown that the growing apprehensions about Soviet intentions were counterbalanced by the lack of military capability to prevent Stalin from taking what he wanted. Unless the Pacific war ended before or shortly after the surrender of Germany, there was no feasible alternative to reliance on Stalin's good faith short of the drastic and inconceivable step of threatening or fighting a war with Russia. But the Japanese would not give up their struggle so long as the United States insisted on unconditional surrender and, in particular, so long as the Japanese did not have any reason to believe that unconditional surrender did not involve the destruction of the imperial system. On their part, the American public and many American officials mistakenly believed that the Emperor was instrumental in bringing about the rise of militarism in Japan and the adoption of an aggressive policy abroad. This widespread misconception limited the freedom of action on the part of those who knew better. The American government was slow in accepting and implementing the view of those who recognized the role which the Emperor could play in securing Japan's surrender. Consequently, it did not clarify the formula of unconditional surrender to indicate a willingness to permit the retention of the imperial system until three months after Germany's surrender. By that time the Soviet Union had already declared war against Japan; Soviet forces were fully prepared for their advance into Manchuria, North China, and Korea; and the Soviet government was in a position to exploit the fluid situation to maximum advantage.

[77] Truman, *op. cit.*, p. 265.
[78] Feis, *The China Tangle*, pp. 307, 311–12.

Meanwhile, the Japanese government lacked definite evidence of the Soviet intention to enter the war. It approached the Soviet Union for help, at first to enable it to continue the war and later to end the war short of unconditional surrender. On its part, the American government was prevented by its principle of unconditional surrender from taking the initiative to establish direct contact and communication with either the Japanese government or what Robert J. C. Butow calls the "end-the-war" faction in Japan. Japan's illusions about the Soviet Union, partly the product of American policy, further strengthened the bargaining position of the Soviet Union vis-à-vis the United States. Under these circumstances, Stalin's maneuvers to make the Soviet Union a decisive factor in ending the war and to reap maximum benefits with minimum sacrifice succeeded. If a modification of the formula of unconditional surrender had not been made at the last moment, and if the United States had not possessed the atomic bomb, Russia might have made even greater gains.

Joseph C. Grew, Undersecretary of State from December, 1944, to August, 1945, was one of the first American officials to recognize the role which the Emperor might play in bringing about the surrender of Japan.[79] But, probably because of the American people's dislike of the Japanese Emperor and the popular attachment to the principle of unconditional surrender, he was slow in proposing a public clarification of America's position on the imperial system as a step to secure Japan's surrender.[80] As late as May 1, 1945, his suggestions did not go further than deferring the decision on the question of the Japanese Emperor until the United States had effected a military occupation.[81] This was a view which he had consistently held from April, 1944, up to that time.[82]

Meanwhile, the initiative in making a public clarification of the principle of unconditional surrender was taken by Ellis M. Zacharias, deputy director of Naval Intelligence, and the Joint Staff Planners.[83] On May 8, the date on which Germany formally surrendered, President Truman issued a statement on Japan to the press. In it he declared that "our blows will not cease until the Japanese military and naval forces lay down their arms in unconditional surrender" but "unconditional surrender does not mean the extermination or enslavement of the Japanese People."[84] The proclamation said nothing about the Emperor.

This first minor and all too obscure breach in the formula of uncondi-

[79] Grew, op. cit., p. 1406.
[80] For Ellis M. Zacharias's impression of Grew's and his advisers' hesitations, see Ellis M. Zacharias, Secret Missions (New York: G. P. Putnam's Sons, 1946) pp. 333–4.
[81] Millis, op. cit., pp. 53–54.
[82] Grew, op. cit., pp. 1408–21.
[83] Zacharias, Secret Missions, p. 342; "The Entry of the Soviet Union," p. 63.
[84] Department of State, Bulletin, May 13, 1945, p. 886.

tional surrender was followed by a proposal, made by Grew on May 28, that the President make a public undertaking that unconditional surrender would not mean the elimination of the present dynasty if the Japanese people desired its retention.[85] Stimson, Marshall, and Forrestal favored the principle of the proposal. But they feared that the statement, if issued at the time, would be considered by the Japanese as a sign of weakness, since the battle of Okinawa was proceeding slowly and with heavy losses.[86] Grew's proposal was shelved.

Grew has since argued, in a letter to Stimson in February, 1947, that if the President had made such a categorical public statement about the dynasty as he had proposed, the surrender of Japan could have been hastened. He wrote that "if surrender could have been brought about in May, 1945, or even in June or July, before the entrance of Soviet Russia into the war and the use of the atomic bomb, the world would have been the gainer."[87] Grew's letter poses a question which is not easy to answer even now.[88] There is very little doubt that such a modification of the formula of unconditional surrender was a necessary condition for Japan's surrender. But the real problem was twofold. First, could a categorical promise, made in May, 1945, on the retention of the Emperor have changed Japan's policies rapidly enough and the balance of power between the militarists and the "end-the-war" faction drastically enough to bring about a surrender in June or July? Second, was it the sufficient condition for Japan's surrender? Was it the only modification in the policy of unconditional surrender which would have been necessary to achieve an early termination of the war? To both of these questions, the answer seems to be negative. Seventeen months before Grew made his proposal, the Cairo Declaration had reaffirmed that Japan would be deprived of her territorial acquisitions since 1895. Its contents and its attribution to Japan of the crime of aggression had seriously hindered the development of any positive program on the part of those Japanese who wished to end the war

[85] Grew, op. cit., p. 1421.
[86] Stimson and Bundy, op. cit., p. 628; Grew, op. cit., p. 1424.
[87] Ibid., pp. 1425–26.
[88] In his memoirs, Stimson indorsed Grew's retrospective estimate of the probability of an early surrender of Japan (Stimson and Bundy, op. cit., p. 629). Robert J. C. Butow, in his thorough study of Japan's decision to surrender, took the same position (Robert J. C. Butow, Japan's Decision to Surrender [Stanford, Calif.: Stanford University Press, 1954], pp. 131–41). But this view is by no means shared by other authorities. In his detailed study of American policy at the last months of the war, Herbert Feis concluded that "if the American government had made known [in May] that it would not insist upon removing the Emperor, the first Japanese response would have been only a preface to an effort to negotiate over other conditions" (Feis, Japan Subdued, p. 175). Samuel Eliot Morison expressed the view that the atomic bomb was instrumental in bringing about Japan's surrender (Samuel Eliot Morison, "Why Japan Surrendered," Atlantic Monthly, October, 1960, pp. 41–47).

at an early date.[89] As a result, the pro-peace faction had only embryonic ideas of what to do at the time of Germany's surrender.[90]

More important, so long as the Japanese government had an alternative to a direct approach to the United States, it would not at once have accepted surrender on Allied terms even if they had included an acceptable promise on the imperial system. This alternative was to seek a rapprochement with the Soviet Union so that Japan could either fight the war with greater success or obtain better terms through Soviet mediation.[91] It is true that in November, 1944, Stalin had publicly denounced Japan as an aggressor. On April 5, Moscow had declared that the Soviet-Japanese Neutrality Pact would not be renewed after its term expired. But the pact would still be valid for another year. Foreign Minister Shigenori Tōgō suspected that the Soviet Union might already have reached some type of agreement with the United States and Great Britain for the division of spoils after Japan's defeat.[92] But the secrecy veiling the Yalta Agreement prevented his having concrete evidence to support his judgment.

Thus, to continue the war rather than to submit to unconditional surrender, Japan turned to the Soviet Union for help. The objective of Japan's diplomacy in mid-May was to prevent the Soviet Union from entering the war and to entice her into an attitude of friendliness.[93] Japan's military plan in early June was to seek a victory in the decisive battle for the homeland.[94] Throughout May and the greater part of June, Japan's policy was to effect a rapprochement with the Soviet Union for the purpose of continuing the war. In return for Soviet abstention from the war and assistance to Japan, Tōgō was willing to give back to Russia what the latter had lost as a result of the Russo-Japanese War of 1904–5.[95] The Japanese government would probably have offered much more extensive concessions than Tōgō contemplated had the Soviet Union indicated any positive interest in Japan's overtures.[96] In Switzerland, two Japanese officials, separately and on their own responsibility, established contact in April and May with the American OSS organization. Both of them proposed peace terms which, besides the preservation of the imperial system, included the re-

[89] Butow, op. cit., p. 40.
[90] Ibid., pp. 78–79.
[91] "The war would have been prolonged until Soviet Russia's entry into it even if the American concession [regarding the Emperor] had been formulated unequivocally earlier, since the Japanese were angling for still better terms as long as the illusory Moscow channel was open" (Paul Kecskemeti, Strategic Surrender [Stanford, Calif.: Stanford University Press, 1958] p. 206).
[92] Butow, op. cit., pp. 77–78.
[93] Ibid., pp. 84–85.
[94] Ibid., pp. 93–102.
[95] Ibid., p. 84.
[96] Ibid., pp. 88–90.

tention by Japan of Korea and Formosa.[97] Neither succeeded in persuading his superiors in Tokyo to support his efforts. So long as hope for Soviet assistance remained alive, the Japanese government was unwilling to approach the United States directly.

When the attempt to enlist Soviet help to continue the war got nowhere, the Japanese government decided on June 22 to approach the Soviet Union with a view to obtaining Soviet mediation for a negotiated peace.[98] In early July, it proposed to send Prince Konoye to Moscow, seeking to end the war short of unconditional surrender. On July 13, at the instruction of Tōgō, Naotake Satō, Japan's ambassador to Moscow, saw Solomon Abramovich Lozovsky, the acting People's Commissar for Foreign Affairs, and asked the Soviet government to receive Prince Konoye as the Emperor's special envoy bearing his personal letter.[99] The Japanese message of July 12 stated that "as long as America and England insist on unconditional surrender, our country has no alternative but to see it through in an all-out effort for the survival and the honor of the homeland."[100]

In the negotiations with the Japanese both before and after this time, the Soviet government neither flatly rejected Japan's overtures nor made any positive response, on the ground that the Japanese proposals were not specific enough to justify an answer. Thus, on July 18, Lozovsky informed Satō in a note that the Japanese message of July 12 was general in form and contained no concrete proposals, that the mission of Konoye was also not clear, and that the Soviet government was unable to give a definite reply.[101] Apparently, Moscow was in no haste to put an end to Japan's illusory hope for Soviet mediation; she was careful not to take any step which would lead the Japanese to approach the Allies directly. She confronted the Japanese government with the choice of either proposing specific concessions or obtaining no definite answer. Had Japan made explicit promises to grant extensive concessions, the bargaining position of the Soviet government vis-à-vis the United States and China would have been further strengthened.

The slow progress made in Japan by the "end-the-war" party and the active measures taken by the Japanese government to seek Soviet help tend to show that such a clarification in late May, 1945, as proposed by Grew would not have produced a quick result. Even if an early implemen-

[97] *Ibid.*, pp. 108–10.

[98] *Ibid.*, pp. 118–20.

[99] Department of State, *Foreign Relations of the United States: The Conference of Berlin (The Potsdam Conference), 1945*, I (Washington, D.C.: Government Printing Office, 1960), 875 (hereafter cited as *Potsdam Papers*, I).

[100] *Ibid.*, p. 876.

[101] Department of State, *Foreign Relations of the United States: The Conference of Berlin (The Potsdam Conference), 1945*, II (Washington, D.C. Government Printing Office, 1960), 1250–51, 1262–64 (hereafter cited as *Potsdam Papers*, II).

tation of Grew's proposal had led to Japan's surrender shortly before the dropping of the atomic bomb on August 6 and the Soviet declaration of war on August 8, the political situation in the Far East would not have been very much different from what it was. For the redeployment of the Red Army would still have been substantially completed and the Soviet Union would still have been in a position to do what she in fact did.

It is an unprofitable task to speculate on whether the relationship between Japan, the United States, and the Soviet Union could have been fundamentally different if the United States had not proclaimed the principle of unconditional surrender, if she had refrained from issuing the Cairo Declaration, or if she had modified the policy of unconditional surrender at the time of the fall of the Tōjō cabinet in July, 1944, and established confidential contact with the Japanese "peace" faction at that time.[102] For in June, 1945, the United States was still finding it difficult to modify the formula of unconditional surrender. She continued to seek Soviet entry into the war. On June 18, President Truman met with the Joint Chiefs of Staff in an important conference to discuss strategy in the war against Japan. This was the first time since 1942 that such a meeting included civilian officials.[103] General Marshall reported that General MacArthur and Admiral Nimitz were in agreement with the Chiefs of Staff in selecting November 1 as the target date to invade Kyushu.[104] With reference to the Asiatic mainland, Marshall said that "our objective should be to get the Russians to deal with the Japs in Manchuria (and Korea if necessary) and to vitalize the Chinese to a point where, with assistance of American air power and some supplies, they can mop-out [sic] their own country."[105] The President said that one of his objectives in the impending conference at Potsdam would be to get from the Russians all possible assistance in the war.[106]

During this meeting on June 18, Stimson and Assistant Secretary of War John McCloy raised the question of an alternative to invasion of Japan as a means to end the war. Leahy questioned the wisdom of insisting on unconditional surrender, which would merely make the Japa-

[102] Professor F. C. Jones wrote that "the fall of Tōjō might have been followed by peace, but for the Allied demand for unconditional surrender" (F. C. Jones, "The Military Domination of Japanese Policy," in Soldiers and Governments, Michael Howard (ed). [London: Eyre and Spottiswoode, 1957], p. 130).

[103] Stimson and Bundy, op. cit., p. 620.

[104] Potsdam Papers, I, 904.

[105] Ibid., p. 905.

[106] Ibid., p. 909. The Joint Chiefs' target date for the invasion of the Tokyo Plain was March 1, 1946 (ibid., p. 911). In his memoirs, Truman writes: "There were many reasons for my going to Potsdam, but the most urgent, to my mind, was to get from Stalin a personal reaffirmation of Russia's entry into the war against Japan, a matter which our military chiefs were most anxious to clinch" (Truman, op. cit., p. 411). Emphasis added.

nese desperate and increase American casualties. Truman responded by saying that it was primarily for that reason he had left the door open for Congress to take appropriate action with reference to unconditional surrender. But he did not feel, he said, that he could take any action at this time to change public opinion on the matter.[107] For the first time, the suggestion was made at this meeting that the Japanese should be given a warning before the United States dropped an atomic bomb. McCloy has since noted that "at that time everyone was so intent on winning the war by military means that the introduction of political considerations was almost accidental."[108]

On July 2, Stimson proposed in a lengthy memorandum to the President that the United States, Great Britain, and China, and, if by then a belligerent, Russia, issue a statement, warning Japan of what was to come and giving her a definite opportunity to capitulate. Stimson suggested that if in this warning "we should add that we do not exclude a constitutional monarchy under her present dynasty, it would substantially add to the chances of acceptance."[109] Although Stimson did not mention the atomic bomb, it was understood by him and others concerned that the atomic bomb would be dropped if the warning elicited no positive response.[110] Stimson did not believe that use of the atomic bomb would obviate the need for Soviet participation in the Pacific war. But he proposed that the warning to Japan be issued before the Russian attack had "progressed too far," if the Soviet Union was already a belligerent.[111] Stimson prepared a draft declaration by the heads of state. It included a statement that the future form of government in Japan "may include a constitutional monarchy under the present dynasty. . . ."[112] On July 3, the State Department expressed its concurrence in Stimson's draft, proposing a minor change in the key sentence regarding the retention of the Emperor.[113]

On the same day, James Byrnes was sworn in as secretary of state to succeed Stettinius. Just before he left for the Potsdam Conference two or three days later, he told former Secretary of State Hull of the content of the draft declaration. Hull objected to the statement about the Emperor because it "seemed too much like appeasement of Japan" and "seemed to guarantee continuance not only of the Emperor but also of the feudal privileges of a ruling caste under the Emperor."[114] He elaborated his views

[107] *Potsdam Papers*, I, 909.
[108] John J. McCloy, *The Challenge to American Foreign Policy* (Cambridge, Mass.: Harvard University Press, 1955), p. 42.
[109] Stimson and Bundy, *op. cit.*, p. 623.
[110] Louis Morton, "The Decision To Use the Atomic Bomb," in *Command Decisions*, p. 401.
[111] Stimson and Bundy, *op. cit.*, p. 624.
[112] *Potsdam Papers*, I, 893-94.
[113] *Ibid.*, p. 893, n. 4.
[114] Hull, *Memoirs*, II, 1594.

in a telegram sent on July 16 through the Department of State to Byrnes at Potsdam. He warned that if the statement should fail to bring about a surrender, "terrible political repercussions would follow in the United States."[115] In reply, Byrnes told Hull in a telegram on July 17 that "I agree that the issuance of statement should be delayed and, when made, should not contain commitment to which you refer."[116] Thus, when Stimson saw Byrnes on the same day, he found Byrnes opposed to his suggestion of assuring the Japanese on the imperial system.

The draft proclamation sent on July 24 by the American government to the British prime minister and Generalissimo Chiang for approval omitted any reference to the imperial institution.[117] On the same day, Stimson again impressed on Truman the importance of reassuring the Japanese on the continuance of their dynasty. He said that the insertion of such an assurance in the warning "was important and might be just the thing that would make or mar their acceptance."[118] He expressed to Truman his hope that "the President would watch [the situation] carefully so that the Japanese might be reassured verbally through diplomatic channels if it was found that they were hanging fire on that one point."[119] For the first time, an American official proposed that the American government approach the Japanese government through confidential channels and thus take an action which had been ruled out by the policy of unconditional surrender.

While these deliberations were taking place, Stalin informed the successful bidders for his co-operation of the proposals of the loser. During the early days of the Potsdam Conference, he told Churchill of the Japanese overtures and the Russian reply.[120] Apparently Stalin's tactic was to strengthen his bargaining position by informing British and American officials of the Japanese moves. In spite of the fact that he had told Churchill of his reluctance to inform Truman directly about Japan's overtures, he handed Truman and Byrnes, in a personal meeting on June 18, the note from Ambassador Satō and the imperial message of July 12.[121] Stalin observed that it might be desirable for him to lull the Japanese to sleep and he might return a general and non-specific answer, pointing out that the exact character of the proposed Konoye mission was not clear. Actually, Truman had learned of the Japanese overtures through inter-

[115] For the text of Hull's telegram to Byrnes, see *Potsdam Papers*, II, 1267.
[116] *Ibid.*, p. 1268.
[117] *Ibid.*, pp. 1275–76.
[118] Stimson Diary, entry on July 24, quoted in *ibid.*, p. 1272, n. 3.
[119] *Ibid.*
[120] Winston Churchill, *The Second World War*, Volume VI; *Triumph and Tragedy* (London: Cassell, 1954), p. 555.
[121] *Potsdam Papers*, II, 87, 1587–88; James Byrnes, *Speaking Frankly* (New York: Harper & Bros., 1947), p. 205.

cepted and decoded Japanese messages.[122] He replied that such an answer was satisfactory. But neither the knowledge of Japan's peace feeler nor its disclosure by Stalin led to any American attempt to modify the formula of unconditional surrender or to establish direct contact with Japan. Had direct and confidential channels of communication been established with the Japanese or had Washington seen fit to use the contact already established between the Japanese in Switzerland and the OSS, it might have been possible to disabuse them of their illusions about the Soviet Union, to discourage them from seeking Soviet mediation, and to clarify the American position on unconditional surrender.[123]

As it was issued by the United States, China, and Great Britain, the Potsdam Declaration did not mention the Emperor. It called on the Japanese government to proclaim now the unconditional surrender of all Japanese armed forces in order to avoid prompt and utter destruction.[124] On July 28, the Japanese prime minister announced that "the government did not find any important value in the Allied proclamation" and that "there is no other recourse but to ignore it entirely." [125] At the same time, Tōgō urged Ambassador Satō to meet Molotov without delay and endeavor to find out the Soviet Union's attitude regarding the joint declaration.[126] On the same day, Stalin told Truman and Attlee in a plenary meeting that the Soviet government had received a new proposal from Japan. He observed that Japan would receive a more definite answer and that the answer would be negative.[127] Having strengthened the Soviet position once more by revealing a new Japanese approach, Molotov proposed the next day to Truman and Byrnes that the Allies address a formal request to the Soviet government for its entry into the war.[128] Truman accepted this suggestion and sent Stalin a letter, drafted by Byrnes, to that effect, justifying Soviet entry on the basis of the Moscow Declaration of October, 1943, and the United Nations Charter which at that time had not been formally ratified.[129]

After the Japanese government rejected the Potsdam Declaration, the United States proceeded to back up her ultimatum with the full applica-

[122] Truman told the historians of the Department of State in January, 1956, that he was familiar with the contents of the first Japanese peace feeler before Stalin mentioned it to him (*Potsdam Papers*, I, 873). Secretary of the Navy Forrestal recorded the content of these messages in his diary on July 13, July 15, and July 27 (Millis, *op. cit.*, pp. 74–76). See also James F. Byrnes, *All in One Lifetime* (New York: Harper & Bros., 1958), p. 292.

[123] Kecskemeti, *op. cit.*, pp. 206–7; Butow, *op. cit.*, pp. 134–35.

[124] For the text, see *Potsdam Papers*, II, 1474–76.

[125] *Ibid.*, p. 1293.

[126] *Ibid.*, pp. 1292–93.

[127] *Ibid.*, p. 460.

[128] *Ibid.*, p. 476.

[129] *Ibid.*, pp. 1333–34; Byrnes, *Speaking Frankly*, pp. 207–8.

tion of her military power. On August 6, an atomic bomb struck Hiroshima and destroyed it at one stroke. It did not immediately bring about a Japanese appeal for surrender. But it did force the hand of the Soviet Union. On August 8, the Soviet government declared war on Japan, despite the fact that there was still no treaty between China and Russia to implement the Yalta Agreement, which Soviet officials had declared repeatedly to be the precondition for Soviet participation in the war. The Soviet declaration of war finally dashed Japan's hope of obtaining Soviet mediation to end the war on acceptable terms. Japan now had to approach the Allies directly. On the day of the Soviet declaration of war, a second bomb was dropped on Nagasaki. When the heated debates among the opposing factions of Japanese officials reached a deadlock, the Emperor made known his wishes, in the imperial conference of August 9, that the Potsdam Declaration be accepted with a reservation regarding the Emperor.[130] On August 10, the Japanese government dispatched identical notes to the Allied powers, announcing the acceptance of the Potsdam ultimatum "with the understanding that the said Declaration does not comprise any demand which prejudices the prerogative of his majesty as a Sovereign Ruler." On August 11, the Allies sent to Japan a reply, drafted by Byrnes. It stated:

> From the moment of surrender, the authority of the Emperor and the Japanese Government to rule the state shall be subject to the Supreme Commander of the Allied Powers who will take such steps as he deems proper to effectuate the surrender terms. . . . The ultimate form of government of Japan shall, in accordance with the Potsdam Declaration, be established by the freely expressed will of the people." [131]

By implication, the note allowed the imperial system to continue and thus qualified the principle of unconditional surrender. The Byrnes note provoked another deadlock among Japanese leaders over the question of whether it was acceptable from the standpoint of maintaining the national polity. Once more, the personal intervention of the Emperor was required to decide the issue in favor of acceptance. On August 14, the Emperor issued an Imperial Rescript ending the war.

By this time, the Soviet Union had already declared war and was in a position to claim the spoils. Her armies were advancing rapidly in Manchuria, crushing the already seriously weakened Kwantung Army. There was not much the United States could do to check Soviet occupation of the whole of Manchuria, short of the inconceivable move of threatening

---

[130] Butow, op. cit., pp. 158–76.
[131] For Byrnes' account of the drafting of this note, see Byrnes, Speaking Frankly, pp. 209–10.

atomic war with Russia. In Potsdam, the American and Soviet chiefs of staff reached an agreement on the boundary line between operational zones of air forces of the two nations in Korea and Manchuria. This ran through Cape Boltina, Changchun, Liaoyuan, Kailu, Chihfeng, Peiping, Tatung, and then along the southern boundary of Inner Mongolia. The American air force would operate south of this line, including all the points named. The Soviet air force would operate north of this line.[132] No agreement was reached on the operational zones of the ground forces in China. There was a proposal to land American troops in South Manchuria at Dairen. But after being carefully considered, it was rejected.[133] Thus, General Order Number 1, which was drafted in Washington to be issued by the Emperor, directed all Japanese forces in Manchuria to surrender to the Russian commander and those in China, outside of Manchuria, to surrender to Generalissimo Chiang.[134] Having been informed of this arrangement, Stalin expressed approval of the provision regarding the Soviet's role in Manchuria but took care to point out that "the Liaotung Peninsula is a composite part of Manchuria."[135]

At this point, the basic dilemma confronting the United States again emerged. It was not within her military capability to prevent the expansion of Soviet influence in China. She had to rely on purely political means to gain Soviet co-operation and to preserve her political position in China. One of these political measures was a Sino-Soviet rapprochement to be formalized in a treaty implementing the Yalta Agreement. For the conclusion of such a treaty the Soviet government and Chinese officials had started negotiations in Moscow in July. It is to the steps leading to the conclusion of the Sino-Soviet treaty that we now turn.

F. The Implementation of the Yalta Agreement

The diplomatic and military developments discussed above furnished the background for the negotiations between China and the Soviet Union to implement the Yalta Agreement. As will be recalled, Stalin, in his conference with Hopkins on May 28, reaffirmed his pledge to enter the Pacific war in early August, and gave specific and firm promises to support Chiang

---

[132] *Potsdam Papers*, II, 411, 1327–32.

[133] Feis, *The China Tangle*, pp. 339–40. At the Potsdam Conference, General Marshall and Admiral King told Harriman of a proposal that American troops land in Korea and Dairen if the Japanese gave in prior to the occupation by Soviet troops of these areas. Later, Harriman urged that these landings be carried out to accept the surrender of Japanese troops at least on the Kwantung Peninsula and in Korea (Truman, *op. cit.*, pp. 433–34). Edwin W. Pauley, Truman's representative on reparations, made a similar suggestion (*ibid.*, p. 433). See also p. 283, below.

[134] Truman, *op. cit.*, p. 440.

[135] *Ibid.*

as the leader of China and to respect Chinese sovereignty and territorial and administrative integrity, particularly in Manchuria. He repeated his statement made at Yalta that the Russian people must have a good reason for going to war and the fulfillment of this condition depended on China's willingness to agree to the proposals made at Yalta. He told Hopkins that he wanted to see T. V. Soong, the foreign minister of China, not later than July 1, to discuss these proposals. He expected the American government to take the matter up with Chiang at the same time.[136]

On June 9, President Truman personally told Soong about Stalin's assurances and the Yalta Agreement. Acting on Truman's instruction, Ambassador Hurley informed Chiang about the same matters a few days later. Truman made it clear to Chiang and Soong that President Roosevelt at Yalta agreed to support the Soviet claims upon the entry of Russia in the war against Japan and that he was also in agreement.[137] Soong had apparently few illusions about Soviet intentions. As he privately told Admiral William D. Leahy, the President's chief of staff, his long-range view was that China could not agree to permit Russia to exercise the degree of control in Manchuria that was possible under the Yalta Agreement and that China would prefer to settle the controversy by military action when forces should become available, any time in the next five hundred years.[138] Both Soong and Chiang were concerned about the meaning of the term "pre-eminent interests" as used in the Yalta Agreement.[139] But they were interested in Stalin's promises of support for Chiang and his assurances regarding Manchuria. They also realized that China alone could not stand up to the Soviet Union and that she needed the United States as a counterweight and as a defender of Chinese interests. As Soong told Secretary Stettinius on June 5, China's only chance of keeping out of the Soviet orbit was a strong connection with the United States.[140]

Thus, Soong sought to obtain from Grew a clarification of the term "pre-eminent interests" and an interpretation of the Yalta Agreement. When Hurley informed Chiang of the Yalta Agreement, Chiang proposed that the United States and Great Britain become parties to whatever agreement China might sign with the Soviet Union. He observed that a multilateral agreement would make it more certain that the Soviet Union

[136] Sherwood, *op. cit.*, pp. 902–3; "The Entry of the Soviet Union," pp. 72–74; Truman, *op. cit.*, pp. 264–65.

[137] For the text of the cable sent by the State Department to Hurley at Truman's instruction, see *ibid.*, pp. 268–69. For Acting Secretary of State Grew's memo of the talk between Truman and Soong, see Grew, *op. cit.*, pp. 1465–66.

[138] Admiral William D. Leahy, *I Was There* (New York: New York: Whittlesey House, 1950), p. 381.

[139] For Chiang's view, see Hurley's telegram to Truman, May 10, 1945, reprinted in statement by W. Averell Harriman, *Military Situation in the Far East*, p. 3337.

[140] Feis, *The China Tangle*, p. 312.

would comply with its terms.[141] He also suggested that Port Arthur be designated as a joint naval base for the four great powers: China, the United States, the Soviet Union, and Great Britain. These suggestions were flatly turned down by the American government.[142]

Under these unfavorable circumstances, Soong arrived in Moscow on June 30 to negotiate with Stalin. Stalin made clear to Soong at the outset and several times afterward that all outstanding issues would have to be settled in advance before the Soviet Union would enter into a pact of friendship with the Chinese government.[143] He began the conversations by insisting that China recognize the independence of Outer Mongolia.[144] According to the Soviet view, the insertion of the words "the Mongolian People's Republic" in parenthesis after the phrase "the *status quo* in Outer Mongolia" in the Yalta Agreement indicated that the provision meant the independence of Outer Mongolia.[145] Soong replied that China could not agree to the cession of territory, that recognition of the independence of Outer Mongolia would complicate the question of Tibet, and that the Chinese government might fall. He stated that the Chinese Communists would be among its most active critics if it ceded Outer Mongolia.[146] Stalin reassured Soong that there would be nothing to fear if the Chinese and Soviet governments stood together. He suggested a secret agreement on the independence of Outer Mongolia which might be published after the defeat of Japan.

Stalin asked from Soong rights and privileges in Manchuria which went far beyond the specific provisions of the Yalta Agreement. The Yalta Agreement made no mention of establishing a military zone on the southern part of the Liaotung Peninsula. Stalin now demanded the creation of a naval base area surrounding Port Arthur and Dairen which followed the general boundaries of the former czarist lease. He wanted the right to station naval and air forces in this zone, authority over the civil affairs of the whole area, exclusive control over military affairs in Port Arthur, and the renunciation by the Chinese government of its right to fortify the islands within a radius of one hundred kilometers from the naval base. The Yalta provision regarding the "internationalization of Dairen" was interpreted by Stalin as meaning joint Sino-Soviet control, with no other country involved. Specifically, he wanted joint Sino-Soviet administration of

[141] Excerpts from memo from Dr. Wang to Hurley, June 15, 1945, in Lohbeck, *op. cit.*, pp. 396–97. Feis, *The China Tangle*, pp. 314–15.
[142] *Ibid.*, p. 315.
[143] Chiang Chün-chang, "Sung Tzŭ-wen Mo-ssŭ-k'o t'an-p'an chui-chi," ["An Account of T. V. Soong's Negotiations in Moscow"], *Chung-kuo i-chou* ["Chinese Newsweek"] March 24, 1952, pp. 14–16; Feis, *The China Tangle*, p. 317.
[144] Truman, *op. cit.*, p. 315.
[145] *United States Relations with China*, p. 113, n. 2.
[146] Truman, *op. cit.*, p. 315; Feis, *The China Tangle*, p. 317.

Dairen, the right of the Soviet police to exercise security control, and an equal share in the surplus of customs duties collected there. He also demanded the establishment of a naval base in one of the inner bays of Dairen for exclusive use of the Chinese and Soviet navies.

The Yalta Agreement had provided for the joint operation of the Chinese Eastern and South Manchurian railroads. Stalin now demanded exclusive ownership not only of the railroads but connected enterprises (factories, workshops, lands, coal mines, and timber tracts), a governing voice in their management and operations, joint responsibility for their protection, and the right to use them to transport Soviet troops in war and peace.[147]

Obviously, the Yalta Agreement was not intended by President Roosevelt to permit the Soviet Union to make these extensive claims against China. But most if not all of them could be easily subsumed and justified under the general provision that "the former rights of Russia violated by the treacherous attack of Japan in 1904 should be restored." The sweeping nature of this general provision was recognized by the State Department in a memorandum dated July 13 giving the American interpretation of the Yalta Agreement. The question in interpreting the Yalta Agreement was whether the general provision or the specific provisions following it should be considered as controlling. As the State Department memorandum pointed out, "It is not clear to what extent the specific provisions are to be construed as explanatory to the main provision and to what extent they represented modifications of or limitations on the main provisions."[148] Even the specific provisions regarding Dairen and the Chinese Eastern and South Manchurian railroads contained the ambiguous phrase providing that "the pre-eminent interests" of the Soviet Union should be safeguarded. Furthermore, in contrast to American hesitations, Stalin, from the very beginning, usurped for himself the right to interpret the Yalta Agreement. According to a Chinese source, Stalin told Soong that "the [Yalta] Agreement was suggested by the Soviet Union and drafted by Molotov. They [Roosevelt and Churchill] merely attached their signatures to it. I can make this statement again in front of Churchill."[149] The very ambiguity

[147] Pu Tao-ming, "Chung Su t'iao-yüeh" ["The Sino-Soviet Treaty"], in *Wo-mên ti ti-kuo* ["Our Enemy Nation"] (Taipei, Formosa: Chung-yang jih-pao-shê, 1952), pp. 127–131. In his capacity as director of the Western Asia department in the Chinese foreign ministry, Mr. Pu served as a member of the delegation negotiating with the Soviet Union to conclude the Sino-Soviet Treaty of 1945. See Aitchen K. Wu, *China and the Soviet Union* (New York: John Day Co., 1950), p. 287. The article by Pu was written under the guidance of Wang Shih-chieh, who succeeded Soong as foreign minister of China, participated in the negotiations in August, 1945, and signed the treaty on behalf of China (*Wo-mên ti ti-kuo*, p. 2; Feis, *The China Tangle*, pp. 317, 342; Truman *op. cit.*, pp. 315–17).

[148] *Potsdam Papers*, I, 868.

[149] Chiang Chün-chang, *op. cit.*, p. 14. Stalin's statement was highly misleading. It is true that Molotov prepared the first and the final drafts of the Yalta Agreement

of the Yalta Agreement must be considered an indication of the skill of Soviet officials in drafting the document. For the loose wording made it easy for President Roosevelt to accept the agreement at a time when the power of the Soviet Union in the Far East was not yet fully developed and enabled Stalin to make extensive claims when the Red Army was in a position to back them up.

Soong asked Ambassador Harriman to ascertain from Truman the American government's interpretation of the provision regarding Outer Mongolia in the Yalta Agreement.[150] On July 4, Truman instructed Secretary Byrnes to inform Harriman that at the present time the United States did not want to act as interpreter on any point in the Yalta Agreement.[151] But Harriman was authorized to tell Soong informally that the accepted meaning of the provision would be that the present factual and juridical status of Outer Mongolia was to be preserved. Then Truman told Harriman, for the latter's information only, what, as the American government understood it, the status quo was: "While the *de jure* sovereignty of Outer Mongolia remains vested in China, *de facto* this sovereignty is not exercised."[152]

In the third meeting, Soong, on Generalissimo Chiang's instruction, offered to grant Outer Mongolia the highest degree of autonomy. In response to Stalin's question, Soong explained that Outer Mongolia would be independent in regard to internal administration, foreign relations, and military affairs, and that she could enter into agreement with the Soviet Union, but that China would retain sovereignty over that region. Stalin insisted on outright independence and ended the talk by saying that unless this issue were settled no agreement would be possible.[153]

Soong cabled Chungking for instructions, saying that the negotiations were at a deadlock. At this point, Chiang sent a significant instruction to Soong. In this message, Chiang clearly revealed the decisive consideration leading him to seek an agreement with the Soviet Union. Chiang told Stalin through Soong that, for the sake of promoting the common interests of the two countries and permanent peace, China would permit the independence of Outer Mongolia after a plebiscite, provided the Soviet government gave concrete and firm answers to three questions. First, the sovereignty and territorial and administrative integrity of China over Manchuria should be preserved. Second, the Soviet Union should abide by her former promises to assist the Chinese government in suppressing the local rebellions

It is also true that Churchill's role in the Far Eastern accord was minor. But Roosevelt did attempt to modify Stalin's terms and certainly had his own interpretation of the Yalta Agreement.

[150] Truman, *op. cit.*, pp. 315–16.
[151] *Ibid.*, p. 317.
[152] *Ibid.*
[153] Chiang Chün-chang, *op. cit.*, p. 14–15.

in Sinkiang. Chiang stated his third and certainly his most important condition in the following words:

> The Chinese Communist Party, with its own military and political organizations, makes impossible complete unity in military command and political control. The Chinese government sincerely hopes that the Soviet government will give all its material and moral support to the central government and that any assistance given to China should be confined to the central government.[154]

At the conference on July 11, Soong first dwelt on the tremendous sacrifice China would have to incur in ceding a part of her territory. He said that, unless there were to be adequate compensations, it would be difficult to justify this sacrifice to the nation. Then he proceeded to translate Chiang's message. Stalin accepted Chiang's proposal on Outer Mongolia. He denied that the Soviet Union had supported the Chinese Communists in the past. He assured Soong that he would withhold support from the insurgents in Sinkiang and the Chinese Communist party. He stated categorically that he would support only the National Government of China and that all the military forces of China must come under the government's control. If the Chinese government needed Soviet aid, assistance would be given to the central government under the leadership of Generalissimo Chiang, as it had been in the past.[155] Stalin stated that the Soviet forces would begin to withdraw from Manchuria within three weeks after the defeat of Japan, although he declined to include this promise in the proposed agreement on the entry of Soviet forces into the territory of the Three Eastern Provinces.[156] In response to Soong's question, Stalin answered that in his opinion the evacuation of Soviet troops would be completed within a period of not more than two months. Soong asked again whether the evacuation would really be completed within three months. Stalin stated that three months would be a maximum period sufficient for the completion of the withdrawal of troops.[157] This was probably the most important conference in the negotiations. In this talk, the two sides agreed on the principles which underlay the subsequent Sino-Soviet treaty and the related agreements and exchanges of notes. As recounted by a Chinese

[154] The Chinese text of this instruction is printed in *ibid.*, p. 15. In a message to Stalin which Chiang passed on to Truman on July 20, 1945, Chiang made substantially the same points (*Potsdam Papers*, II, 1225–27). See the summary given in Truman, *op. cit.*, p. 318; Feis, *The China Tangle*, pp. 318–19.

[155] Truman, *op. cit.*, p. 319; Harriman to Truman, July 12, 1945, *Potsdam Papers*, I, 862; Feis, *The China Tangle*, p. 319; Chiang Chün-chang, *op. cit.*, pp. 15–16.

[156] Minutes of the fifth meeting between Stalin and Soong, July 11, 1945, *China Handbook, 1945* (New York: Rockport Press, 1950), p. 331.

[157] Earlier, Stalin had agreed that representatives of the Nationalist government should accompany the Red Army to organize the civil administration of Manchuria when the Soviet forces advanced into that region (Truman, *op. cit.*, p. 316).

diplomat stationed in the Soviet Union during this period "The meeting lasted two hours and rapid progress was made. . . . The atmosphere of the meeting was cheerful and friendly."[158]

The issue of Outer Mongolia was the most hotly debated question in the negotiations at this time. Soong's spirited defense of China's legal title to Outer Mongolia has elicited the following comment in the State Department's White Paper on China: "One of the main preoccupations of Dr. Soong during the negotiations was to secure Soviet recognition of Chinese sovereignty in Outer Mongolia. . . . Dr. Soong was apparently willing to agree to other significant and important concessions in return for Outer Mongolia and it was with some difficulty that he was persuaded by Mr. Harriman to accept substance in place of form."[159] This interpretation gave too little credit to Soong's and Chiang's diplomatic skill. It is of course true that to relinquish the legal title to a large piece of territory was unpalatable to Soong, Chiang, or any other Chinese who had been inculcated in the past fifty years with a deep sense of national humiliation over China's loss of territory and rights to the powers. But the Chinese were also realistic enough to recognize the inevitable and to try to gain the best advantage from it. The actual control of Outer Mongolia had been in the hands of the Soviet government since 1921, when the Red Army marched into that region and defeated the Russian White Guards of Ungern Sternberg, who had shortly before established a puppet Mongolian regime there.[160] The Sino-Soviet treaty of 1924 reaffirmed Chinese sovereignty over Outer Mongolia but did not change the reality of actual Soviet control.[161] The Chinese government never failed to register its legal claims to Outer Mongolia and Chinese writers continued to regard Outer Mongolia as an integral part of China.[162]

By 1945, however, Chinese opinion gave signs of readiness to abandon the legal fiction for the sake of a Sino-Soviet rapprochement. Early in 1945, two Chinese delegates to the Hot Springs Conference of the Institute of Pacific Relations expressed their personal opinion that they saw no objections to independent membership of Outer Mongolia in a future world security organization, "provided that the people in that region were capable of growth and self-government."[163] At the time of the San Francisco Conference, *Ta-kung pao*, the leading newspaper in Chungking, suggested in an editorial that Outer Mongolia be accorded a supreme measure of

[158] Wu, *op. cit.*, p. 287.

[159] *United States Relations with China*, p. 117, n. 7.

[160] Gerald M. Friters, *Outer Mongolia* (Baltimore: Johns Hopkins Press, 1949), p. 193; Allen S. Whiting, *Soviet Policy in China* (New York: Columbia University Press, 1954), pp. 161–63.

[161] *Ibid.*, pp. 221–22, 229–30.

[162] Friters, *op. cit.*, pp. 193–209.

[163] Quoted in *ibid.*, p. 209.

autonomy or alternatively might be recognized as an independent state and that simultaneously a Sino-Soviet pact should be concluded on a friendly basis.[164] Subsequently, in justifying the Sino-Soviet treaty, Chiang told a joint session of the Supreme National Defense Council and the Central Executive Committee of the Kuomintang that "the racial group in Outer Mongolia had, in effect, declared its independence from the mother country as early as 1922 when the Peking government was in existence. This was almost a quarter of a century ago."[165]

In the light of these facts, it would seem that Soong's spirited defense of China's legal title was undertaken, on the one hand, to minimize China's loss, and, on the other, to strengthen her bargaining position and to gain the maximum advantage in return for her concession. Chiang fully recognized the importance that Stalin attributed to Outer Mongolia. After the negotiations were deadlocked over Outer Mongolia, Chiang instructed his son, Chiang Ching-kuo, to see Stalin in a private capacity. In their informal talk, Stalin stressed the strategic importance of Outer Mongolia in the defense of Siberia and expressed his fear of a revived Japan.[166] He insisted on the independence of Outer Mongolia. Shortly afterward, Generalissimo Chiang offered his compromise solution. It is obvious that Chiang would have gained much and lost little from the compromise if Stalin had strictly fulfilled all his promises.

As for the Manchurian railroads and ports, both Soong and Stalin made some concessions, but their positions remained far apart. On the railroads, Stalin agreed that they be equally owned by a joint Sino-Soviet company, that the railroad guards should be Chinese, and that the Soviet government should not have the privilege of moving troops through Manchuria except in time of war or in the event of a threat of war. But he demanded a majority in the board of directors of the railroad. Soong offered joint operation with equal participation in the board and management. Stalin insisted that the military zone under Russian control include Dairen and that there should be a naval base within Dairen. Soong offered the area south of Dairen as a military zone, with Dairen a free port under Chinese administration.[167]

[164] Wu, op. cit., pp. 286–87.
[165] The Collected Messages of Generalissimo Chiang Kai-shek, 1937–1945, II, (New York: John Day Co., 1946), 856.
[166] Chiang Ching-kuo, "Wo-ti fu-ch'in fan Kung fên-tou san-shih nien" ["My Father's Thirty-Year Struggle against Communism"] Chung-kuo chien-shê ["China's Reconstruction"], November, 1957, pp. 4–5. See also Chiang Ching-kuo, Wo-ti fu-ch'in ["My Father"] (Taipei, 1956), chap. v, pp. 6–9. There are considerable differences in these two accounts by Chiang Ching-kuo of his talk with Stalin.
[167] Harriman to Truman and Byrnes, July 12, 1945, Potsdam Papers, I, 862. See also Harriman's memorandum, July 18, 1945, for a summary of the differences between Soong's and Stalin's proposals (ibid., II, 1237–41).

Soong suggested to Stalin that he return to Chungking to consult the Generalissimo,[168] apparently in an attempt to see if Stalin would relax his conditions. Stalin pressed for acceptance of his demands, saying that it was better to come to agreement before he met Truman at the Potsdam Conference as he wished to decide with Truman the date of his entry into the war. Soong expressed to Harriman the hope that Truman in his meeting with Stalin would obtain Stalin's acceptance of the Chinese position or work out a compromise which Chiang could accept.[169] Both sides endeavored to gain American support to strengthen their bargaining positions. The negotiations would have to wait. Soong left Moscow on July 14, after having told Stalin that he would be prepared to come to Moscow again at any time Stalin wished.

At the Potsdam Conference, Stalin presented his case to Truman in a meeting on July 17. He complained that the Chinese did not recognize "the Soviet pre-eminent interest" and attempted to get around it.[170] When Truman questioned him on the effect on American rights of his proposed arrangement for Dairen, Stalin answered that Dairen would be a free port open to the commerce of all nations. Truman observed that "the arrangement would follow, therefore, the Open Door policy."[171] Secretary Byrnes observed that any arrangements which were in excess of the Yalta Agreement would cause difficulties. Stalin replied that his terms were more "liberal than the Yalta agreement, which had provided for the restoration of Russian rights [as they had existed prior to 1905]."[172] Stalin continued that "this would have entitled them to station troops and to have the railroads run for 80 years exclusively by Russians," but that he had not insisted on these former rights. "He did not wish," he explained, "to add in any respect to the Yalta agreement or to deceive the Chinese."[173] Truman and Byrnes both indicated that the main interest of the United States was in a free port. At dinner that evening, Truman told Stimson that he thought he had clinched the Open Door in Manchuria.[174]

Three days later, Chiang appealed to Truman for help. He sent the President a copy of his telegram to Stalin in which he outlined his concessions. He informed Truman that the Chinese government had gone the limit to fulfil the Yalta Agreement, that it had even gone beyond it in the case of Outer Mongolia, and that it had gone as far as public opinion in China would permit. He urged Truman to impress on Stalin his eminently rea-

---

[168] Ibid., I, 862.
[169] Ibid., pp. 863–64.
[170] Ibid., II, 1586.
[171] Ibid.
[172] Ibid.
[173] Ibid.
[174] Feis, The China Tangle, p. 329.

sonable stand so that Stalin would not insist on the impossible.[175] On July 23, Truman sent Chiang the following brief reply:

> I asked that you carry out the Yalta agreement but I had not asked that you make any concession in excess of that agreement. If you and Generalissimo Stalin differ as to the correct interpretation of the Yalta agreement, I hope you will arrange for Soong to return to Moscow and continue your effort to reach complete understanding.[176]

In effect, Truman declined Chiang's request. On July 28, Byrnes sent a cable to Hurley for Soong, urging him to communicate with Stalin before July 30 or 31 and to request an opportunity to return to Moscow for a discussion of unsettled issues.[177]

Ambassador Harriman and officials in the State Department took a much more serious view of Stalin's demands and the status of Sino-Soviet negotiations than Truman and Byrnes. As early as July 9, Harriman recommended to the President and Secretary Byrnes that immediate steps be taken to prepare for use at the forthcoming conference at Potsdam a study of the United States' interpretation of the Yalta Agreement, specifically the terms which China should grant the Soviet government. In pursuance of this suggestion, the State Department drew up a memorandum in which it rendered its interpretation on the basis of "a normal construction, taken by themselves, of the somewhat ambiguous and vaguely worded terms of the specific sub-headings of the main provision calling for the recovery by the Soviet Union of its former rights in Manchuria."[178] Referring to Stalin's terms, the State Department pointed out that the acceptance and implementation of Soviet proposals for the railroads and Dairen "would represent a reversion to a situation which was one of the most pernicious foci of imperialism."[179] It proposed that the American government make an effort to influence the Soviet government toward a modification in favor of China. Stalin's slight concessions, made toward the end of his negotiations with Soong, were not considered satisfactory by many American officials. On July 16, Stimson urged Truman to support Soong's position on the ground that any other course would constitute an abandonment of the Open Door policy.[180]

During the Potsdam Conference, John Carter Vincent, chief of the Division of Chinese Affairs, drafted six memoranda concerning the Sino-Soviet

[175] *Potsdam Papers*, II, 1225–27.
[176] *Ibid.*, p. 1241.
[177] *Ibid.*, p. 1245.
[178] *Ibid.*, I, 870.
[179] *Ibid.*
[180] *Ibid.*, II, 1224.

negotiations.[181] These documents are particularly interesting in view of the fact that he was to become a major target of attack by the "China bloc" in Congress and Senator Joseph McCarthy for his role in advocating the establishment of a coalition government in China including the Communists. Vincent fully realized the incompatibility between Stalin's proposals and the traditional policy of the United States. His reasoning, appraisals, and recommendations can be reconstructed as follows: The Russians were asking for a special position in Manchuria to the detriment of Chinese sovereignty and political unity, notwithstanding Stalin's avowals to the contrary.[182] The American government was committed to the respect of Chinese sovereignty and the promotion of political unity. A foreign power established in China, or in portions of China, on a preferential military and economic basis would be inimical to American interests and security. The Soviet proposals might adversely affect America's traditional and present policies and objectives: observance of the Open Door and equality of opportunity; respect for the territorial and administrative integrity of China; and opposition to the growth of political and economic spheres of influence.[183] Agreements based on these proposals would be, in the main, retrogressive. They would be measures of expediency and should be liquidated as soon as possible in the interest of a sovereign and united China.[184]

Vincent wrote:

Let us face these facts. A bargain is being made on the basis of a bargain made at Yalta. We should live up to our commitments at Yalta. But we should stand firm and counsel China to stand firm against any concessions which go beyond the Yalta commitments.[185]

Specifically, he recommended that the American government support Soong's proposal concerning the Manchurian railroads, Dairen, and the boundary of the Port Arthur base area.[186] If necessary, an international administration composed of a Chinese, a Russian, an Englishman, and an American might be established to supervise the administration of Dairen. He suggested that the American government seek an early opportunity for discussion with Stalin and Molotov and that, if they agreed, Soong might be invited to come to Potsdam to join in the discussions.[187]

On July 23, Vincent suggested in the last of his six memoranda that the

---

[181] A footnote in the *Potsdam Papers* indicates that the three unsigned memoranda were drafted by Vincent (*ibid.*, 1228, n. 3).

[182] *Ibid.*, 1234.

[183] *Ibid.*, p. 1229.

[184] *Ibid.*, p. 1234.

[185] *Ibid.*, p. 1230.

[186] *Ibid.*, p. 1233.

[187] *Ibid.*, p. 1229.

United States seek a written understanding with the Soviet Union and China to reserve America's historic position regarding the Open Door and the sovereignty of China in Manchuria in the face of potential encroachment as the result of the Sino-Soviet negotiations. He observed that a large segment of the American public was profoundly interested in China and in safeguarding the American position in China. He prophesied that they would be critical of the Yalta commitments and even more so of any concessions beyond the Yalta commitments, and that they would expect reservations safeguarding American interests in the face of these commitments.[188] He expressed the view that American commitments at Yalta, and the promise to obtain Chinese acceptance of those commitments, placed the United States squarely in a position of responsibility which the American government could not transfer to the Chinese on the theory that the negotiations were bilateral and that the Chinese should get as good terms as they could from the Russians. He recognized that the Chinese were in no position to bargain and American interpretation of the Yalta Agreement was for them controlling. He even went so far as to argue:

> Should the Chinese supported by us take a firm stand against concessions beyond the Yalta commitments, and as a result agreements not be consummated, in the final settlements regarding Manchuria we would be in as strong a position to safeguard American interests as we are now — conceivably with the backing of public opinion, in a stronger position than we are now.[189]

In Vincent's memoranda and recommendations, the spirit and the pattern of the traditional policy of the United States toward China are clearly discernible. The traditional policy required giving moral and diplomatic support to China. This Vincent recommended. It did not envisage the use of military power to enforce America's position. This he did not suggest. It called for a diplomatic document to reserve American rights, protect American interests, and reaffirm the Open Door policy when the United States was compelled by circumstances to retreat in fact from the principles of the Open Door. This he proposed. The traditional policy developed out of efforts to check encroachments on China which the powers undertook to accomplish by conventional diplomatic and military pressures. For the key problem confronting the United States in the forties, i.e., how to deal with the Chinese Communist movement, it offered the principle of non-intervention and the promotion of Chinese unity. This principle and this aim Vincent also espoused. Vincent's deep solicitude for the welfare of the Chinese people, his profound concern for political unity in China,

[188] *Ibid.*, p. 1242.
[189] *Ibid.*

his refusal to contemplate armed intervention in the Chinese civil war, and his advocacy of a coalition government stood in juxtaposition to his opposition to Russian imperialism. All this made him the embodiment of the traditional attitude toward China. If any one element in Vincent's outlook can be said to have influenced his thinking and policy recommendations more than any other, it was the traditional policy of the United States. His merits and shortcomings were also its merits and shortcomings. It was no accident that he served as the top official handling Chinese affairs in the State Department from 1944 to 1947. His promising career was later cut short by the collapse of American policy in China. His personal misfortune symbolized the misfortune which had befallen that policy.

From the perspective of a person who assisted President Roosevelt in the negotiation of the Yalta Agreement, Ambassador Harriman came to the same conclusions as Vincent. He believed that the Soviet demands were not in accord with Roosevelt's intentions. He urged President Truman to give his interpretation of the Yalta Agreement specifically in connection with the differences over the arrangements for the port of Dairen and the operation of the railroads. Like Vincent, he recommended that, if Stalin did not agree to Soong's proposal for a free port under Chinese administration, the American government propose the creation of an international commission consisting of representatives of China, the Soviet Union, the United States, and possibly Great Britain to supervise the operation of Dairen as a free port. He stressed the importance of obtaining from the Soviet government reaffirmation in writing of the oral assurances of Stalin to support the Open Door policy in Manchuria. Finally, on July 31, he sought instructions from Secretary Byrnes to authorize him to inform Stalin of the American views regarding Dairen and to obtain Stalin's reaffirmation of the Open Door policy in writing.[190] On August 5, Byrnes accepted Harriman's recommendations and authorized him to take up these matters with Stalin.[191]

Soong returned to Moscow to reopen negotiations with Stalin. In the renewed talks, which lasted from August 7 to August 14, Soong's hand was strengthened by American support. Ambassador Harriman protested to Stalin against Soviet claims and sent to Molotov a written restatement of America's position. On the instruction of Byrnes, he wrote a letter to Molotov, suggesting that the language of the proposed Soviet promise to refrain from helping dissident elements in China and to support the national government be so explicit that there could be no future misunderstanding.[192] Harriman informed Soong of Washington's view that if Soong

[190] *Ibid.*, 1237–44, 1246–47.
[191] Feis, *The China Tangle*, p. 330.
[192] *Ibid.*, pp. 342–44.

made any concessions which went beyond its interpretation of the Yalta Agreement, his reason for doing so would be that these concessions would be of value in obtaining Soviet support for the national government.[193] But the United States was not in a position to take military measures to back up her diplomatic support. Harriman, who was deeply disturbed by the intransigent attitude of Stalin in dealing with Soong, proposed that American forces land at least on the Kwantung Peninsula and in Korea to accept surrender of Japanese troops.[194] Ambassador Edwin Pauley, the President's representative on reparations, suggested that American forces "should occupy quickly as much of the industrial areas of Korea and Manchuria as we can, starting at the southerly tip and progressing northward."[195] But nothing came out of these recommendations.

Furthermore, the rapidly developing events made an immediate agreement with the Soviet Union imperative for China. One day before the resumption of negotiations, the first atomic bomb was dropped on Hiroshima. Two days later, the Soviet Union declared war on Japan and the Red Army advanced rapidly into Manchuria. On August 10, Stalin warned Soong against further delay, saying that otherwise the Chinese Communists would get into Manchuria. From August 11 to 14, Soong took several steps to win a quick agreement. He agreed to Stalin's original demand for a military zone on the Kwantung Peninsula along the line of the former czarist lease, in exchange for a provision excluding Dairen, a part of the zone, from military supervision or control in times of peace. He yielded on details of the management of the railroads. Both before and after the conclusion of the treaty, Harriman endeavored to obtain from Stalin a written statement affirming his oral assurances on the Open Door policy in Manchuria. But in September the project was dropped without having achieved any concrete result.[196]

Subsequently, in explaining the Chinese government's decision to sign the treaty, a member of the Chinese delegation wrote as follows:

> On August 14, 1945, when our government decided to sign the treaty, we did not have in the Northeast [Manchuria] a single soldier while hundreds of thousands of Soviet troops had already marched into that region. If we had refused to conclude the treaty, we could not have recovered the Northeast, unless we would use force to expel the Soviet armies and to prevent the Soviet Union and the Chinese Communist Party from joining forces.[197]

[193] Statement of W. Averell Harriman, *Military Situation in the Far East*, p. 3339.
[194] Truman, *op. cit.*, p. 434.
[195] *Ibid.*, p. 433.
[196] Feis, *The China Tangle*, p. 350.
[197] Pu, "Chung Su tiao-yüeh," *loc. cit.*, p. 122.

In another context he pointed out that it was out of the question for the Chinese government to use force. In other words, the only possible policy for China was to rely on the good faith of the Soviet Union for keeping the promises which she was willing enough to give. Indeed, as Soong said to Harriman, "it was after all a matter of good faith."[198] There was also the hope that future actions and events might create a situation in Manchuria and China which would limit Soviet gains to those conceded in the treaty and which might persuade Stalin to abide by his promises. This was shown by the hurried steps taken by the Generalissimo to send his troops into Manchuria and North China.

Whatever may be said about the Sino-Soviet Treaty of Friendship and Alliance of 1945 and the related agreements, exchanges of notes, and signed official minutes, Stalin could not be accused of being ungenerous in his promises. It was mainly because of these pledges that the Chinese government was willing to accept the settlement and indeed considered it satisfactory.[199] Two provisions in the documents had direct or indirect bearing on the relationship between the Soviet Union, on the one hand, and the Nationalist government and Chinese Communist party, on the other. In Article V of the Treaty of Friendship and Alliance, the two nations "agree to work together in close and friendly collaboration after the coming of peace and to act according to the principles of mutual respect for their sovereignty and territorial integrity and of non-interference in the internal affairs of the other contracting party." In the exchange of notes relating to the treaty, the Soviet government pledged itself "to render to China moral support and aid in military supplies and other material resources, such support and aid to be entirely given to the National Government as the central government of China."[200]

With reference to the reoccupation of Manchuria by the Chinese government, the Soviet Union made the following commitments. In the exchange of notes mentioned above, the Soviet government "reaffirmed its respect for China's full sovereignty over the Three Eastern Provinces and recognized their territorial and administrative integrity." A separate agreement provided for the appointment of "a Chinese National Government representative and staff" for the territory recovered from Japan. His duties would be "to establish and direct, in accordance with the laws of China, an administration for the territory cleared of the enemy," and "to establish the cooperation between the Chinese armed forces, both regular and irregular, and the Soviet forces in recovered territory." The agreement further provided that "as soon as any part of the liberated territory ceases to be a zone of immediate military operations, the Chinese National Government will

[198] Feis, *The China Tangle*, p. 344.
[199] Pu, "Chung Su tiao-yüeh," *loc. cit.*, p. 123.
[200] *United States Relations with China*, pp. 586, 587–88.

assume full authority in the direction of public affairs. . . ."[201] As noted above, there was also Stalin's promise to begin withdrawing Soviet forces from Manchuria within three weeks after the capitulation of Japan and that three months would be the maximum period necessary for the completion of the withdrawal of troops.[202] These pledges were of such importance to the Nationalists in dealing with the Chinese Communists and reoccupying Manchuria that they were well worth the prices paid, provided the Soviet Union adhered to both the spirit and the letter of these promises.

It was in this light that one must understand the comments made by Chinese officials. On August 16, 1945, Generalissimo Chiang Kai-shek told Ambassador Hurley that he was "generally satisfied with the treaty." On August 29, Madame Chiang Kai-shek, when calling on the President, complimented him on the results of the Sino-Soviet conversations and thanked him for the diplomatic support given by the American government to China.[203] Earlier, Ambassador Harriman reported that Soong said that he was encouraged and that he thought Stalin had accepted the basic principles on which he had taken his stand.[204] Dr. Sun Fo, the president of the Legislative Yüan, hailed the treaty as "a guarantee for a durable peace in the Far East."[205] He emphasized that the Soviet pledges of support for the National government and non-interference in the internal affairs of China were the greatest contribution to Chinese unity.

In the United States the public greeted the treaty with enthusiasm. There were favorable comments even from those who later vehemently condemned the China policy of the United States. An editorial of the September 10, 1945, issue of *Life* magazine reads:

> Two days after Japan gave up, there was announced in Moscow and Chungking an agreement which was as great a victory for common sense as the defeat of Japan was for armed might. The Soong-Stalin treaties contained less ammunition for pessimists than any diplomatic event of the last twenty years. . . . the present prospects of China are a vindication of American policy in Asia for almost fifty years.[206]

[201] Agreement regarding Relations between the Chinese Administration and the Commander-in-Chief of the Soviet Forces after the Entry of Soviet Troops into the "Three Eastern Provinces" of China during the Present Joint Military Operations Against Japan, *ibid.*, pp. 592–93.

[202] *China Handbook, 1950* (New York: Rockport Press, 1950), p. 331.

[203] *United States Relations with China,* pp. 120–21; "Statement of W. Averell Harriman regarding our Wartime Relations with the Soviet Union," *Military Situation in the Far East,* p. 3340.

[204] Feis, *The China Tangle,* p. 344.

[205] *National Herald* (Chungking), August 27, 1945, as quoted by Wu, *op. cit.,* pp. 291–92. See also Cheng, *op. cit.,* p. 274.

[206] *Life,* September 10, 1945, p. 42.

Alfred Kohlberg, later the moving spirit of the "China lobby," wrote, not entirely accurately, that the treaty and the agreements were the tangible results of the efforts of President Truman and his advisers at Potsdam to induce the Russians to reduce greatly their original demands on China. "The success of our Administration officials is deserving every possible praise."[207]

Indeed, the optimism expressed by these American and Chinese comments would have been vindicated had the Soviet Union lived up to the spirit and letter of the treaty and the related documents. As Harriman later commented, the Sino-Soviet agreements "might have saved the Chinese National Government . . . had they been carried out by Stalin"; the inability of the Nationalists to maintain their power was partly "due to the fact that the Sino-Soviet agreements were not honored by Stalin."[208] But these agreements were not destined to be kept because they had been called into being to serve two purposes which, as events proved, could not be accomplished at the same time. First, they were concluded to implement the Yalta Agreement, in order to bring about the Soviet entry into the Pacific war, which inevitably accelerated the emergent shift in the Far Eastern balance of power. Second, they were designed to promote a rapprochement between the Soviet Union and the Nationalist government which would, in turn, pave the way to political and military unity in China. It was hoped that the achievement of political unity would limit Soviet influence in the Far East. In the event, however, the temporary effect of the Sino-Soviet Treaty in weakening the bargaining position of the Chinese Communist party was soon outweighed by the consequences flowing from the presence of the Red Army in Manchuria.[209] The rapid expansion of Chinese Communist forces in Manchuria, which was made possible by Soviet connivance, led to armed clashes in the spring of 1946 in that region. The struggle between the two Chinese parties for control of Manchuria after the withdrawal of Soviet forces was the most important immediate cause of the collapse of the political settlement brought about by General Marshall.[210]

Meanwhile, the initial imbalance of power in the Far East was aggravated by America's rapid demobilization and her unwillingness to use her military power on the Chinese mainland. Within China, the shift in the internal balance of forces was accentuated by the rampant corruption and gross inefficiency exhibited by the Nationalist government in taking over

[207] Quoted by Werner Levi, *Modern China's Foreign Policy* (Minneapolis: University of Minnesota Press, 1953), p. 243, n.
[208] Statement by W. Averell Harriman, *Military Situation in the Far East*, p. 3340.
[209] See chap. viii, below.
[210] See chap. x, below.

the areas liberated from Japanese control. The result was that the strength of the Soviet Union enabled her to clinch the advantages and legal privileges which the Sino-Soviet agreements had given her while the degeneration of the Nationalist government, plus the postwar military weakness of the United States, made it inevitable that the Soviet pledges would not be kept.

CHAPTER VIII

THE

PROGRESSIVE

BREAKDOWN

OF

HURLEY'S

PROGRAM

The arch of the whole structure of American policy from the recall of Stilwell to the dispatch of the Marshall mission was Hurley's program to implement the policy of peaceful unification of China on terms favorable to the Nationalist government. In Hurley's eyes the keystone of this arch was a rapprochement between the Soviet Union and the Nationalist government, which would destroy the Chinese Communists' hope of obtaining Soviet support and bring them to terms. Based upon an overreliance on Stalin's assurances, a misjudgment of the nature of the Chinese Communist party, and a questionable estimate of the relative strength of the Kuomintang and the Chinese Communists, Hurley's program was bound to be frustrated. The progressive breakdown of American policy as interpreted and implemented by Hurley found manifestations in three different areas. First, Hurley failed to work out a political-military settlement between the two sides, and the civil war spread in China after the capitulation of Japan. Second, not long after President Roosevelt sustained Hurley's program over the opposition of the career officials in China, Washington began to move toward a policy of attaching conditions to American assistance to Chiang Kai-shek. Third, the Soviet Union gave subtle but effective support to the Chinese Communists in Manchuria.

The gradual erosion of the Hurley program falls into two phases. The first phase opened in November, 1944, with an apparently hopeful beginning, the acceptance of Hurley's five-point program by the Chinese Communists. It ended in August, 1945, with the race between the two sides to reoccupy as much territory as possible at the time of the surrender of Japan.

The second phase also began encouragingly, with Mao Tse-tung's trip to Chungking to negotiate with the Nationalists. It closed with the spread of the civil war and the resignation of Hurley. What distinguished the second period from the first was the gradual invalidation of the assumptions that a Soviet promise of support for the Nationalist government would force the Chinese Communists to accept its terms and that diplomatic concessions to the Soviet Union would insure Russian support for the Generalissimo and dissuade the Soviet Union from assisting the Chinese Communists.

A. From the Recall of Stilwell to the Surrender of Japan

1. The Miscarriage of Hurley's Program of Establishing a Coalition Government

Hurley's active program to bring the Kuomintang and the Chinese Communist party together unfolded in his first visit to Yenan in November, 1944, not long after Stilwell's recall. There he submitted to the Chinese Communists a five-point draft agreement between the two sides which he had drawn up in Chungking. After two days and nights of "most strenuous and most friendly"[1] discussion, Hurley and Mao produced a revised draft.[2] This document, entitled "Agreement between the National Government of China, the Kuomintang of China and the Communist Party of China," was signed on November 10, 1944, by Mao Tse-tung as chairman of the Central Committee of the Chinese Communist party and Hurley as "personal representative of the President of the United States."[3]

With the purpose of supporting the Nationalist government uppermost in his mind, Hurley sought in his five-point draft agreement to gain for Chiang control of the armed forces of the Communists. Its first point reads: "The government of China, the Kuomintang of China and the Communist Party of China will work together for the unification of all military forces in China for the immediate defeat of Japan and the reconstruction of

---

[1] The adjectives were used by Hurley to describe the atmosphere of the negotiations in a telegram to the secretary of state (Senate Committee on Armed Services and Committee on Foreign Relations, *Hearings on Military Situation in the Far East*, 82d Cong., 1st sess. [1951], p. 3671 [hereafter cited as *Military Situation in the Far East*]).

[2] It cannot be ascertained from materials accessible to the writer to what extent the final draft agreement departed from the draft brought by Hurley from Chungking. Hurley's reports conveyed the impression that the changes were minor. In a sworn statement submitted to the McCarran Committee, Michael Lindsay implied that the Communists produced their own draft and Hurley made some new additions which favored the Communists (statement of Lord Lindsay of Birker [Michael Lindsay], dated June 3, 1952, in Senate Committee on the Judiciary, *Hearings on the Institute of Pacific Relations*, 82d Cong., 1st and 2d sess. [1951–52], p. 5371 [hereafter cited as *Institute of Pacific Relations*]).

[3] For the text of the draft agreement, see Hurley's telegram to the secretary of state, January 31, 1945, *Military Situation in the Far East*, p. 3669.

China."[4] Its fourth point states that "all anti-Japanese forces will observe and carry out the orders of the Coalition National Government and its united National military Council. . . ."[5] As Hurley subsequently explained to the Generalissimo in trying to persuade the latter to accept his program, his five-point draft agreement was "the only document in which there is a signed agreement by the Communists to submit control of their armed forces to the National Government."[6] In exchange, he readily offered the Communists the establishment of a coalition government, representation on a United National Military Council, recognition of the legal status of the Chinese Communist party, and all the civil and political freedoms which were taken for granted in the West and which were considered by Hurley as "innocuous."[7] This was the political meaning of the draft agreement, and General Hurley was obviously rather enthusiastic about it. In an affidavit submitted in June, 1952, to the McCarran Committee, Lord Lindsay of Birker (Michael Lindsay, who worked in Yenan with the Communists from the spring of 1944 to November, 1945) stated that "according to both Chinese and American eyewitnesses, General Hurley signed the Five Point Draft Agreement of 10th November 1944 saying that, though he could not commit his government, he was signing to show that he personally fully approved the draft terms and pledged himself to support them."[8] However, the State Department White Paper states that Hurley signed as a witness.[9]

The Chinese Communists were equally elated by the draft agreement, for it embodied the most important items of the political programs which they had been advocating in the past several months [10] and continued to advocate afterwards.[11] They were perfectly willing to accept the bargain offered by Hurley. Given the political strength of the Chinese Communists and the mass support they enjoyed, Hurley's program could be expected to work to their over-all advantage, if it was accepted by the Nationalist gov-

[4] *Ibid.*
[5] *Ibid.*
[6] Telegram, Hurley to secretary of state, February 18, 1945, *ibid.*, p. 3698; see also p. 3673.
[7] Hurley's telegram to the secretary of state, January 31, 1945 (*ibid.*, p. 3670).
[8] Sworn Statement of Lord Lindsay of Birker, dated June 3, 1952, *Institute of Pacific Relations*, p. 5371.
[9] Department of State, *United States Relations with China* (Washington: Government Printing Office, 1949), p. 74 (hereafter cited as *United States Relations with China*).
[10] See chap. v, above.
[11] In his "On Coalition Government," a political report made on April 24, 1945, at the Seventh National Congress of the Chinese Communist party, Mao stated: "As soon as a new democratic coalition government appears in China, the armed forces of the Chinese liberated areas [*i.e.*, the Communist armed forces] will be immediately handed over to it. And all the Kuomintang troops should be handed over to it at the same time" (Mao Tse-tung, *Selected Works*, [London: Lawrence & Wishart, 1956], IV, 290).

ernment. If it was rejected by the Nationalists, the onus for disunity and civil war would fall on Nationalist shoulders.

Hurley was apparently unaware of these possibilities. Hopefully, he brought the draft agreement back to Chungking and submitted it to the Nationalist government. To Hurley's discomfiture, the government firmly rejected the proposals. Soong told Hurley: "The Communists have sold you a bill of goods. Never will the National Government grant the Communists' request."[12] The Generalissimo argued with Hurley that to accept the proposal of a coalition government would be an acknowledgment of total defeat of his party by the Communists,[13] and that the proposed agreement would eventually lead to Communist control of the government.[14] Underlying these appraisals of the Hurley-Mao draft agreement was a basic distrust of the intentions of the Chinese Communists. As high Nationalist officials told Hurley on several occasions, the support of democratic principles given by the Communists was "merely a ruse which they are using in an effort to obtain control of the government under the Communist one-party rule."[15] Furthermore, the decision of the Nationalist government could not have been unaffected by the growing political strength of the Chinese Communists. This factor was correctly estimated in a memo sent by Secretary Stettinius to the President on January 4, 1945. Stettinius informed Roosevelt that "Chiang is in a dilemma. Coalition would mean an end of conservative Kuomintang domination and open the way for the more virile and popular Communists to extend their influence to the point perhaps of controlling the Government. Failure to settle with the Communists, who are daily growing stronger, would invite the danger of an eventual overthrow of the Kuomintang."[16]

While a correct appraisal of the nature of the Chinese Communist party justified Chiang's rejection of the Hurley program, this was by no means the only reason for his refusal to take necessary steps to liberalize his regime. If it had been, there would have been no explanation for his repressive policies toward the minor political parties which were thoroughly democratic, possessed no independent armed forces, and could not possibly threaten his control, at least for some time to come. Basically, Chiang's whole political program was vitiated by a shortsighted determination to hold on tenaciously to his own power and a corresponding refusal to share power and control with political leaders who did not blindly obey and

[12] Hurley's telegram to the secretary of state, January 31, 1945, *Military Situation in the Far East*, p. 3671.

[13] Telegram, Hurley to the secretary of state, January 31, 1945, *ibid.*

[14] Telegram, Hurley to the President, November 16, 1944, as quoted by Herbert Feis, *The China Tangle* (Princeton, N.J.: Princeton University Press, 1953), p. 216.

[15] Telegram, Hurley to the secretary of state, February 18, 1945, *Military Situation in the Far East*, p. 3678.

[16] Quoted by Feis, *op. cit.*, pp. 219–20.

follow him. This aspect of Chiang's policy fostered a community of interests between the Communists and the minor parties in opposing his monopoly of power and led many anti-Communist and non-Communist leaders to be sympathetic to some of the Communist policies. In the eyes of these political leaders, the Communists were justified in their refusal to relinquish their armed forces before the establishment of a genuine coalition government. Mao adroitly exploited this sentiment. In his *Coalition Government*, he wrote:

> These people [*i.e.*, Chiang and his followers] said to the Communists: "If you give up your army, we shall give you freedom." If these words were sincere, then the parties which had no army should have enjoyed freedom long ago. . . . The Democratic League and the Democratic faction of the Kuomintang had no military force, yet neither of them enjoyed any freedom. . . . Just because they [the workers, peasants, students, intellectuals and bourgeoisie] had no army, they lost their freedom.[17]

Commenting on this passage, Carsun Chang, the leader of the National Social party of China, wrote: "Mao had no confidence in the sincerity of Chiang Kai-shek, when he said the Communist Party would be legalized on condition that it hand over its army to the Government. On this matter it is generally agreed that Mao's point was well taken."[18]

The repressive measures taken by Chiang toward the minor parties and the consequent support given by the latter to the Communists pointed to one basic weakness of American policy in this period. Based upon a misunderstanding of the nature of Chinese communism and motivated by a desire to use Communist forces in the war against Japan, American policy failed to distinguish the problem of liberalizing the nationalist regime to include all non-Communist political elements from the issue of establishing a coalition government with the Communists. As a result, it unwisely demanded the impossible of the Nationalists on the latter issue and did not force them to yield on the former. This failure to separate the two issues enabled Chiang to justify his refusal to liberalize his repressive rule by pointing to the Communist menace and to attribute American criticism of his regime to the inspiration of the Communists. Chiang's policy isolated the Kuomintang from other non-Communist political groups while American policy failed to build up the power and influence of those non-Communist political elements which were oriented toward the United States but were excluded by Chiang from a fair share of power in the government.

[17] The translation of this passage from Mao's *Coalition Government* was taken from Carsun Chang, *The Third Force in China* (New York: Bookman Assoc. 1952), p. 136.

[18] *Ibid.*

Both the Nationalist and American policies worked to the advantage of the Chinese Communist party while each in its own way exacerbated Sino-American relations.

In any case, Hurley could not convince the Generalissimo of the wisdom of his program. Ironically, Chou En-lai joined Hurley in the latter's futile efforts to persuade Chiang to accept the draft agreement.[19] It may be surmised that Chou's endeavors could only have had the effect of strengthening Chiang in his original convictions. Hurley urged Chiang to keep the negotiations alive. At Hurley's suggestion, the Nationalist government submitted a counterproposal, the so-called Three-Point Agreement.[20] The outstanding feature of this counterproposal was the rejection of the idea of a coalition government. The Communists were asked to turn over their armed forces to the Nationalist government. In return, the government was to confer upon the Communist party a legal status, to give a vague and conditional guarantee of political and civic freedoms, and to grant the Communists a place on the National Military Council. It promised to "pursue policies designed to promote the progress and development of democratic processes in government."[21]

In the absence of a democratic political tradition, the value of the first two concessions depended on the good faith of the Kuomintang. In view of the fact that the chairman of the military council, who was Chiang himself, alone made all the major decisions and kept all power in his own hands,[22] membership on the military council meant nothing at all. In the light of the fact that the avowed policy of the Nationalist government in the past sixteen years had always been to end the one-party tutelage and to establish a constitutional regime, the Nationalist promise to promote the development of democracy, reiterated once more, seemed stale. The Kuomintang's proposals would not have been acceptable to the Communists even in 1937 when they had only three divisions of regular forces. In a draft resolution in September of that year, the Central Committee of the Chinese Communist party had decided that

> the Communist Party can participate in the government only when it is changed from one of Kuomintang's one-party dictatorship into an all-nation government of the united front, i.e., when the present Kuomintang government (a) accepts the basic fea-

[19] Telegram, Hurley to the secretary of state, January 31, 1945, *Military Situation in the Far East*, p. 3671.

[20] For the text of the counterproposal, see *United States Relations with China*, p. 75, or Telegram, Hurley to the secretary of state, January 31, 1945, *Military Situation in the Far East*, pp. 3669–70.

[21] *Ibid.*

[22] Tuan-sheng Ch'ien, *The Government and Politics of China* (Cambridge, Mass.: Harvard University Press, 1950), pp. 184–87; F. F. Liu, *A Military History of Modern China* (Princeton, N.J.: Princeton University Press, 1956), pp. 121–22.

tures of the Ten Point Programme for Resistance to Japan and Salvation of the Nation which our party has put forward and, on the basis of them, promulgates an administrative programme; (b) begins to show in actual practice that it sincerely wishes and endeavors to carry out this programme and achieve definite results; and (c) permits the legal existence of the Communist Party's organizations and guarantees the freedom for the Communist Party to mobilise, organise and educate the masses.[23]

Since then, the power and influence of the Communist party had greatly expanded and its regular armed forces had, according to its claims, increased to 900,000 men. The Nationalist government had been gravely weakened by the loss of its best forces in the first six months of the Sino-Japanese War, by Japan's "east China" offensive in 1944, and by the economic and social effects of a long war. The American government had taken the initiative to urge a coalition government on Chiang. The Communist party had formally proposed the establishment of a coalition government as a solution to the political and military crisis. This idea had been spreading among politically-conscious circles. This was the time for the Communists to press on rather than retreat.

So when Hurley tried to persuade the Communists to accept the government's counterproposals, they flatly turned them down.[24] Chou returned to Yenan. In a letter to Hurley in early December, Chou called for the publication of the five-point proposals "in order to inform the public and to bring out the changing attitude of the Government." [25] Obviously, the Communists were negotiating to obtain a settlement on their terms, if possible. If not, they desired to use the negotiations to propagate their views and to influence political opinions in China and abroad. They were confident, and quite correctly, that their political program would gain the support of a large segment of the Chinese people. It is in this light that one must understand the significance of another *démarche* of the Communists. In January, 1945, Mao rejected Hurley's suggestion that he visit Yenan again, together with three top Nationalist officials, to reopen the negotiations. Instead, he proposed convening "a National Affairs Conference" in Chungking, to be attended by delegates of the Kuomintang, the Communist party, and the Democratic League. He added significantly that

[23] Mao Tse-tung, *Selected Works*, II, 241, n. 5. This Draft Resolution had the support of Mao but was probably opposed by some party leaders at the time.

[24] Telegram, Hurley to the President, January 14, 1945, Department of State, *Foreign Relations of the United States: The Conferences at Malta and Yalta, 1945* (Washington, D.C.: Government Printing Office, 1955), p. 346 (hereafter cited as *Yalta Papers*).

[25] Telegram, Hurley to the secretary of state, February 7, 1945, *ibid.*, p. 3673. See also *United States Relations with China*, p. 76.

the proceedings of the conference should be made public and that the delegates should have equal standing and freedom to travel.[26]

Since Hurley's program was to give unconditional support to the Nationalist government, he now endeavored to obtain a settlement on terms which the Nationalists were willing to offer, though he continued to believe that his five-point draft agreement would work out to the advantage of the Nationalist government. Repeatedly, he told the Communists in private negotiations and the Chinese and American public in press conferences that the American government would not supply or otherwise aid the Chinese Communists and that any assistance to them must go through the Nationalist government.[27] In retrospect, this refusal to aid the Communists and the virtual abandonment of his own terms for a political settlement are correct as a matter of principle. But in giving the Generalissimo unconditional support and in failing to urge the Nationalists to undertake long overdue reforms, he identified himself completely with a hopeless cause.

2. The Impasse in Kuomintang-Communist Negotiations

The widespread appeal of the Communist program for a settlement, the rapidly expanding power of the Communist party, and American anxiety to bring about unity put the Nationalist government at a considerable disadvantage in the negotiations. The lack of progress toward unity subjected Hurley's policy to increasing criticism. From the time of the rejection by the Communists of the three-point proposal of the government to the surrender of Japan, three developments in the Kuomintang-Communist negotiations and American policy were visible.

First, the Nationalist government was forced by circumstances to make a series of concessions but always stopped short of accepting the idea of a coalition government. In late January, 1945, the government offered to take certain measures in addition to its previous three-point program. It proposed to set up in the Executive Yüan a new policy-making body of seven to nine men, an organization "resembling a war cabinet."[28] The Chinese Communist party and other parties would be given representation on this organ. The Generalissimo would appoint one Nationalist army officer, one Communist officer, and one American army officer to make recommendations regarding the reorganization, equipment, and supply of the Chinese Communist forces. He would also appoint one American army

---

[26] *Ibid.*, p. 78.

[27] Telegram, Hurley to the secretary of state, January 31, 1945, *Military Situation in the Far East*, p. 3672; press conference in Chungking, February 15, 1945, as quoted in Feis, *op. cit.*, p. 266. For Mao's reaction toward Hurley's statements at a press conference in Washington, April 2, 1945, see Mao, *Selected Works*, IV, 328–29. See also chap. vi, above.

[28] *United States Relations with China*, p. 79.

officer as the immediate commander of Chinese Communist forces for the duration of the war against Japan.[29] On February 3, the Nationalist government offered to convene a "Political Consultative Conference," to be attended by representatives of all parties and by non-partisan leaders. The function of this conference was to consider steps to be taken in terminating the period of political tutelage by the Kuomintang, and in establishing constitutional government, to work out a common political program to be followed in the future, and to decide the form in which members of the parties outside the Kuomintang would take part in the government prior to the inauguration of the constitutional regime.[30] In modified forms and in a different political context, most of these concessions were later incorporated in the agreements between the Kuomintang and the Communists concluded during the Marshall mission.

The second feature of this period was the occurrence of repeated impasses in the negotiations. There was no common basis for an agreement between the two sides. Intensely conscious of the popularity of their political program and the rapidly growing strength of their armed forces, the Communists stood firm on their terms for a settlement. Realizing that the establishment of a coalition government would greatly strengthen the political power of the Communists, Chiang was determined to resist that demand. Apparently, the concessions just mentioned were made by him as part of a belated attempt to avoid the necessity of agreeing to the Communist proposal of setting up a coalition government. Chou En-lai was correct when he characterized the offers made in January as "merely concessions made by the Kuomintang while that party still retained control of the government" and did not meet the Communist demand for a thorough reorganization of the government into a regime run by a coalition of parties.[31] The proposal for convening a Political Consultative Conference was for the Nationalist government a dilatory tactic, substituting talks for action.[32] This offer, in itself, was acceptable to the Communists,[33] for it coincided with Mao's earlier demand for the convocation of a National Affairs Conference. The Communists hoped that such a conference would serve as a forum to publicize their program, pave the way to a coalition government, and become the source of a new legitimacy.

Having made these concessions to strengthen his position, the Generalissimo unfolded his political program in a public address on March 1, 1945. This was the program which, in a modified form, Chiang finally carried out toward the end of 1946, after the failure of the Marshall mission. Its essence

[29] Ibid.
[30] Ibid., p. 81.
[31] Ibid., p. 79.
[32] Cf., Feis, op. cit., p. 221.
[33] United States Relations with China, p. 81.

was the convocation of the National Assembly to adopt a constitution in accordance with which a new government would be instituted to replace the Nationalist government. Meanwhile, the Kuomintang would retain "its power of ultimate decision and final responsibility," though it was willing to give the other parties, including the Chinese Communist party, representation in the government as specified in the proposals made in January.[34]

The significance of this program lay in the fact that the National Assembly would be completely controlled by the Kuomintang. For the delegates to the National Assembly had been elected in 1936 under conditions and regulations which insured the election of Kuomintang members and its faithful supporters.[35] Thus, the constitution adopted would be shaped to perpetuate the rule of the Kuomintang and the new government instituted would not change the reality of Chiang's personal dominance.[36] Under this program Chiang still could claim that he had terminated the Kuomintang tutelage and inaugurated a constitutional regime. But what the Communists wanted, was, first of all, a share of real power in a coalition government rather than the form of a constitutional rule. They promptly denounced the National Assembly as "one-party controlled, deceitful, China-splitting."[37] Quite accurately, they pointed out that it was elected when the people had no freedom and the political parties and groups had no legal status. They did not deign to make counteroffers to the Kuomintang proposals.[38] From then on, the establishment of a coalition government versus the convocation of the National Assembly became the focal point of the political struggle in China.[39] The negotiations reached a complete deadlock. They were not resumed until July when Soong was in Moscow to negotiate with Stalin.[40]

In early July, the Communists submitted a new set of proposals through a group of six minor party and non-partisan leaders who visted Yenan in an effort to break the impasse. In these new proposals, the Communists asked the Nationalist government to call off the National Assembly and to summon, instead, a political conference composed of three members

[34] *Ibid.*, pp. 83–84.
[35] Ch'ien, *op. cit.*, pp. 313–16.
[36] For comments on the "May 5th Draft" of the Constitution, see *ibid.*, pp. 298–306; Paul M. A. Linebarger, *The China of Chiang Kai-shek* (Boston: World Peace Foundation, 1941), pp. 28–40; David W. Rowe, *China among the Powers*, (New York: Harcourt, Brace & Co., 1945), pp. 141–46.
[37] *United States Relations with China*, p. 85.
[38] *Ibid.*, pp. 84–85.
[39] This point must be firmly grasped in order to see clearly that the Communist proposals made later in the Chungking negotiations in the late summer of 1945 represented a retreat on their part and that the political settlement arrived at in January and February of 1946 during the Marshall mission represented a victory for them.
[40] *United States Relations with China*, p. 102.

of the Kuomintang, three members of the Chinese Communist party, three members of the Democratic League, and three members representing other political parties or organizations. General Hurley interpreted this new offer as the Communists' way of playing for time while awaiting the results of the negotiations conducted by Soong in Moscow.

The lack of progress in the Kuomintang-Communist negotiations led to a third development in this period: a gradual drift toward a policy of making American support for Chiang conditional upon a political settlement with the Communists. At first, the attempt of the American foreign service officers in China to challenge Hurley's policy of unconditional support for Generalissimo Chiang was unsuccessful. Shortly before the Generalissimo announced his plan to convoke the National Assembly, the career officers in the embassy at Chungking gained the impression that the Generalissimo's attitude toward the Communists had greatly stiffened and that the situation in China was not developing toward the unity and peace between the two parties which constituted a precondition for the effective prosecution of the war. In a memo dated February 26, they recommended that the United States bypass Chiang Kai-shek and take direct steps "to co-operate with and supply the Communists and other suitable groups who can aid in this war against the Japanese."[41] Undoubtedly, military necessity was, in their mind, "the paramount and immediate consideration." But they also hoped that by this step the United States would exert pressure on the Nationalist government and induce it to reach a settlement with the Communists. Moreover, they expected that the proposed policy would "hold the Communists to our side instead of throwing them into the arms of the Soviet Union." This telegram arrived at the State Department when Hurley was back in Washington. It precipitated a debate between Hurley and the staff of the Far Eastern office of the State Department, who were in general sympathetic toward the views expressed by the career officials in China. In the event, President Roosevelt upheld Hurley's decision to refrain from helping the Communists without Chiang's consent. At Hurley's insistence, several members of the embassy in Chungking were transferred and the political advisers attached to the commanding general in China were recalled.[42]

In spite of Hurley's victory over his critics, his program was bound to be increasingly challenged unless it brought about a political settlement. As the negotiations remained deadlocked, the Far Eastern specialists in the State Department continued to advocate a flexible and realistic policy

[41] For quotations in this paragraph, see *ibid.*, pp. 87–92. For a full analysis of the misconceptions underlying the recommendation, see chap. vi, above.

[42] Feis, *op. cit.*, pp. 271–73; *United States Relations with China*, p. 92; Don Lohbeck, *Patrick J. Hurley* (Chicago: Henry Regnery Co., 1956), pp. 380–83; *Military Situation in the Far East*, pp. 2905–06.

of dealing with all factions in contrast to Hurley's policy of unconditional and exclusive support for Chiang. In time, the State Department advocated a new policy which was quite different from Hurley's program. Its central feature was the use of American assistance as a lever to exert pressure on the Nationalist government while continuing to support it as the still generally recognized central authority. The objectives for which pressure was to be exerted were to promote a broadly representative government with solid popular support and to bring about a settlement between the Kuomintang and the Communists. American support for the Nationalist government, particularly postwar American military assistance to China, was to be conditional upon progress in these areas. This particular feature of conditional support was a return to the Stilwell approach which Hurley had rejected. The immediate consideration lying behind this policy was the effective joint prosecution of the war through the achievement of military unity in China, which would permit the arming of all Chinese forces. The ultimate consideration was to maintain a degree of flexibility to permit co-operation with any other leaders in China in case of the disintegration of the authority of the Nationalist government. This new policy was embodied in an instruction sent to Hurley by the State Department on May 7.[43] On May 28, the State-War-Navy Coordinating Committee, an interdepartmental committee composed of senior representatives of the three departments, adopted a report recommending that the United States make no commitment to assist the Chinese government to create and maintain a modern postwar army and air force until "certain necessary political and economic conditions have been fulfilled by the Chinese Government."[44]

Toward the end of this period, there was also a notable shift in the views of General Wedemeyer, who had heretofore followed unquestioningly Hurley's lead in political matters. On July 10, Wedemeyer told Marshall that polite appeals would not bring about unification in China. To avoid the extension and intensification of armed clashes, he suggested that the United States, in co-operation with the Soviet Union and Great Britain, exercise coercion on both the Kuomintang and the Communists to make concessions to form a coalition.[45]

Hurley's position in China deteriorated sharply. The Communists openly attacked him. They accused him of "going back" on his word which he had given in Yenan in November, 1944, when he signed the five-point draft

[43] Feis, op. cit., pp. 291–93.
[44] Ibid., p. 294.
[45] Ibid., p. 316. The most important passage of this message is quoted in Charles F. Romanus and Riley Sunderland, Time Runs Out in CBI (Washington, D.C.: Government Printing Office, 1959), p. 383. For a discussion of Wedemeyer's view, see Tang Tsou, "The Historians and the Generals," Pacific Historical Review, February, 1962, pp. 41–48.

agreement. They ascribed to Hurley "a decisive role" in stiffening Chiang's attitude toward them. They warned that Hurley's policy was leading China to a civil war, and, in aiding and abetting "the anti-popular forces in China," would plunge the United States into endless woes and troubles.[46] In his concluding speech at the Seventh National Congress of the Chinese Communist party, Mao accused the United States of attempting to undermine the Chinese Communist party.[47] Many non-Communist Chinese leaders found Hurley naïve and vain.[48] His prestige was sinking rapidly in China and with it the influence of the United States. But Hurley remained optimistic. He pinned his hopes on an agreement between the Soviet Union and the Nationalist government, which would, he thought, bring the Communists to terms. This expectation was soon to be frustrated by events.

B. From the Surrender of Japan to the Resignation of Hurley

The events from the surrender of Japan to the resignation of Hurley were significant for three reasons. First, they demonstrated at once the possibilities and the limitations of military assistance and diplomatic support. Second, they revealed the limits imposed on American power by the policy of peaceful unification, by the low priority granted American military operations in China, and by the dismantling of American liaison teams serving with the Nationalist forces. Third, they invalidated the assumptions underlying the Sino-Soviet Treaty of Friendship and Alliance. This last development meant the total bankruptcy of Hurley's program.

1. The Nature, Effects, and Self-imposed Limits of American Military Operations in China

The approaching end of the Pacific war found the main Nationalist forces confined in the southwestern corner of China, hundreds of miles away from the strategically and politically important regions in North and Central China. It is true that the worst military and political crisis had passed with the withdrawal of Japanese forces from their advance

[46] "The Hurley-Chiang Duet is a Washout." *Hsin-hua News Agency*, July 10, 1945; "On the Danger of the Hurley Policy," *Hsin-hua News Agency*, July 12, 1945. It turned out that both of these comments were written by Mao himself (Mao, *Selected Works*, IV, 324–29).

[47] *Ibid.*, pp. 316–18.

[48] Commenting on Hurley's analysis of the relations between the Chinese Communists and the Soviet Union, Carsun Chang wrote: "There was indeed a whiff of freshness in the naive and straight-forward approach of the General towards a problem which the subtlest minds in China had found complicated. It was not without reason that Hurley was nicknamed the 'Big Wind'" (Chang, *op. cit.*, p. 126). See also Theodore H. White and Annalee Jacoby, *Thunder out of China* (New York: William Sloane Assoc., 1946), p. 246. For a defense of Hurley, see George Moorad, *Lost Peace in China* (New York: Dalton, 1949), pp. 45–47.

positions gained in earlier offensives. The opening of the Ledo Road and the conclusion of the North Burma campaign permitted the redeployment of the American-equipped forces back to the main battle fronts in China. The Nationalist forces were even able to launch a limited offensive in Hunan and in the Honan-Hupeh area. But the war ended before the Sino-American operations to open a port in the Canton–Hong Kong area were carried out and before the long projected Chinese "general offensive in the southwest" could be mounted.[49] The Chinese armies were not as well equipped as had been hoped.[50] The sudden end of the war caught both the American and Chinese governments unprepared for the task of re-establishing the authority of the Nationalist government over the whole of China.[51]

Although the Chinese Communists were also caught by surprise, they were in a much better position to exploit the opportunities offered by the surrender of Japan than the Nationalists. Mao asserted in April, 1945, that his army had expanded to 910,000 men and the number of militiamen had grown to more than 2,200,000. The Communists subsequently claimed that at the end of the war they were strongly intrenched in eighteen "liberated areas" in North, South, and Central China, with a total area of 956,000 square kilometers. Their area of activities and operations covered 67 per cent of the areas lost by the Nationalist government. More important, these "liberated areas" comprised some of the most strategic regions of China, along the coast and in the Yellow, Yangtze, and Pearl river valleys. The Communist forces were poised in the vicinity of the principal cities such as Peiping, Tientsin, Nanking, Shanghai, Hankow, Canton, Tsinan, and Loyang.[52]

It is difficult to evaluate the Communists' claims of numerical strength. If they had been as strong as they claimed and if they had actively used their armies against Japan, they could have effectively tied down the Japanese forces, which in 1945 numbered 1,050,000 men in China proper.[53] Only an overwhelmingly large number of regular forces can cope suc-

[49] Liu, op. cit., p. 221; Fung Tzŭ-ch'ao, Chung-kuo k'ang-chan shih ["A History of the War of Resistance of China"] (Shanghai: Chêng-ch'i shu-chü, 1946), pp. 193–95; Romanus and Sunderland, op. cit., chaps. xi and xii.

[50] See chap. iii, above.

[51] Feis, op. cit., pp. 335–36.

[52] K'ang Jih chan-chêng shih-ch'i ti Chung-kuo jên-min chieh-fang-chün ["The Chinese People's Liberation Army during the War of Resistance against Japan"] (Peking: Jên-min ch'u-pan-shê, 1953), pp. 218–20 (hereafter cited as chieh-fang-chün).

[53] Romanus and Sunderland, op. cit., p. 351. A Chinese source shows that at the end of the war, the Japanese had 1,100,000 men in China proper (General Headquarters of the Commander-in-Chief of the Chinese Army, Shou-hsiang pao-kao-shu ["Report on Accepting the Surrender"], [Nanking, 1945], p. 4 (hereafter cited as Shou-hsiang pao-kao-shu). Chalmers A. Johnson puts the size of the regular Communist forces in 1945 at 500,000 (Peasant Nationalism and Communist Power [Stanford, Calif.: Stanford University Press, 1962]), pp. 73–74.

cessfully with guerrillas who have popular support. In their fight against the Communist guerrillas in Malaya, the British employed, at the worst period of their war, fifty armed men, in various capacities as combat troops, supporting troops, police, and home guard, against one guerrilla.[54] In general, it takes between ten and twenty soldiers to control one guerrilla in an organized operation.[55] Conversely, "one guerrilla has effectively tied down or dissipated the usefulness of ten conventional soldiers."[56] But the Chinese Communists obviously were not actively engaged in aggressive actions against Japan's occupation forces. As Chalmers A. Johnson puts it, after their "Hundred Regiments' Offensive" in 1940, the Communists put much greater stress upon "economic guerrilla warfare" than on guerrilla activities of a purely military nature. In 1944 and 1945, the Japanese largely left them alone. Like Chiang, the Chinese Communists were expanding and preserving their forces in preparation for the postwar struggle for power in China. They undoubtedly exaggerated their military strength for political and propaganda purposes to a degree difficult to determine. But the fact remained, and was recognized at the time by American officials, that in case of Japan's defeat or surrender, they were in a good position to take over quickly the vital regions and points still occupied by the Japanese, and thus to contest successfully with the Nationalists for control over China.

The entry of the Soviet Union into the Pacific war brought the moment the Chinese Communists had been waiting for. As early as 1938, Mao had envisaged the development of the Sino-Japanese war in three stages. Starting from the first stage of Japan's strategic offensive and China's strategic defensive, the war would pass through a protracted period of Japan's strategic defensive and China's preparation for the offensive to the final stage of China's strategic counteroffensive to recover the lost territories.[57] He had further prophesied that the strategic counteroffensive would be waged more successfully and vigorously in one locality than in another "on account of the unevenness in China's political and economic development."[58] In this final stage, China's task would be to take advantage of the "favorable international situation" "in order to attain her complete liberation and establish an independent democratic state, which

[54] Letter from Riley Sunderland.
[55] W. W. Rostow, "Countering Guerrilla Warfare," *New Leader*, July 31–August 1, 1960, p. 13.
[56] Colonel George M. Jones, as quoted in *New Republic*, May 22, 1961, p. 3.
For an able discussion of popular support as a condition for successful guerrilla warfare, see Chalmers A. Johnson, "Civilian Loyalties and Guerrilla Conflict," *World Politics*, July, 1962, pp. 646–61.
[57] Mao Tse-tung, "On the Protracted War," *Selected Works*, II (London: Lawrence and Wishart, 1954), 183–91.
[58] *Ibid.*, p. 191.

means at the same time rendering help to the anti-fascist movement of the world."[59]

On August 9, the day after the Soviet Union declared war against Japan, Mao proclaimed that with the Soviet entry into the war, the final stage of the war had arrived. He called on the Communist forces to launch a general offensive throughout the country against the Japanese and puppet forces, to destroy them, to seize their weapons and resources, and to extend vigorously the "liberated areas."[60] On August 10, the day of Japan's conditional acceptance of the Potsdam Declaration, General Chu Teh, the commander in chief of all Communist forces, issued an order to his troops, claiming on the basis of the Potsdam Declaration the right to demand and accept the surrender of Japanese and puppet forces opposing him. He told his troops to exercise this right, to destroy those forces which resisted their demands, and to take over and administer all the cities, towns, and communication centers occupied by the enemy.[61] The next day, General Chu directed four armed groups to march into Manchuria "in coordination with the advance of the Red Army of the Soviet Union into China and in preparation for the acceptance of the surrender of Japanese and puppet forces."[62] He ordered two of his most famous generals to march north from their positions in southern Suiyüan, Chahar, and Jehol provinces to meet Soviet troops driving southward. He told Communist troops in the vicinity of the principal railroads to obtain control of these lines of communication.[63] Unannounced, Communist forces under General Lin Piao marched along the Peiping-Mukden railroad into Manchuria.[64]

The political and military meaning of Chu's order and the troop movements can be seen in a speech made by Mao at meeting of Communist cadres on August 13. Surveying the scene from Yenan, Mao asserted that with the entry of the Soviet Union into the war, the surrender of Japan was a foregone conclusion and that the new task was domestic struggle.[65] In this most serious struggle, the issue was: "to whom should the fruits of

[59] *Ibid.*

[60] "Chairman Mao's Statement concerning the Final Stage of the War of Resistance," in Tai I, *et al.* (ed.), *Chung-kuo hsin-min-chu-chu-i kê-ming shih ts'an-k'ao tzŭ-liao* ["Reference Materials for the History of the New Democratic Revolution in China"] (Shanghai: Commercial Press, 1951), pp. 400–1.

[61] "Orders to Advance Proclaimed by Commander in Chief Chu Teh, Yenan Headquarters," *ibid.*, p. 401.

[62] *Ibid.*, pp. 401–2.

[63] *Ibid.*, p. 402.

[64] *Chieh-fang-chün*, p. 222.

[65] Mao Tse-tung, "The Situation and Our Policy after the Victory in the War of Resistance against Japan," *Selected Works*, IV (Peking: Foreign Languages Press, 1961), 11, 18 (hereafter cited as Mao, *Selected Works*, IV [Peking], in order to distinguish it from the fourth volume of Mao's selected works published by Lawrence and Wishart which covers the period from 1941 to August 9, 1945).

the victory in the War of Resistance [against Japan] belong?"[66] He observed that Chiang, ganging up with "U.S. imperialism," would have the upper hand in the large cities such as Shanghai, Nanking, and Hankow, and would win these prizes. The medium and small cities along the railways in North and Central China would be contested by both sides. The vast rural area in North China and the numerous medium and small towns there would fall into Communist hands.[67] It was possible that for a time the civil war might be restricted in scale and localized as it had been for a long time. But Chiang wanted to launch a country-wide civil war and his policy was set. The Communists must be well prepared for it, no matter when it broke out.[68] The policy of the Communists was to give tit for tat and to fight for every inch of land.

Apparently, Mao was uncertain about the extent of assistance which he could expect from Moscow. On the one hand, he hailed the advance of the Red Army into Manchuria "to help the Chinese people drive out the aggressor"[69] as an unprecedented event in Chinese history. Its immeasurable influence could not be swept away by two atomic bombs. Atomic bombs cannot decide wars and they could not make Japan surrender. It was a mistake to believe that the atom bomb was all-powerful. The theory that "weapons decide everything" was the product of bourgeois mentality. The entry of the Soviet Union into the war was the decisive factor in Japan's surrender. On the other hand, Mao urged his comrades to rely on their own strength and to regenerate themselves through their own efforts rather than through outside help. He declared: "Relying on the forces we ourselves organize, we can defeat all Chinese and foreign reactionaries. Chiang Kai-shek, on the contrary, relies on the aid of U.S. imperialism which he looks upon as his mainstay. . . . But U.S. imperialism while outwardly strong is inwardly weak."[70] He prophesied that the day would come when the United States would find it impossible to back Chiang any longer.[71] By being prepared for a nationwide civil war, the Communists would be able to deal properly with all kinds of complicated situations.[72] "If we do not win," Mao swore, "we would blame neither heaven nor earth but only ourselves."[73]

The Nationalist government lost no time in denouncing Chu's announcement of August 10 as "an abrupt and illegal action." On August 12, Generalissimo Chiang issued an order to the Communist general, telling him

[66] *Ibid.*, p. 16.
[67] *Ibid.*, p. 17.
[68] *Ibid.*, p. 22.
[69] *Ibid.*, p. 21.
[70] *Ibid.*, p. 20.
[71] *Ibid.*, p. 21.
[72] *Ibid.*, p. 22.
[73] *Ibid.*, p. 15.

to direct his forces "to remain in their posts and wait for further instruction" and enjoining him "never again to take independent action."[74] The first answer from the Communists to Chiang's order took the form of a broadcast from Yenan. It denounced Chiang as a "Fascist chieftain" and accused the Nationalist leaders of "treating enemies as friends and friends as enemies" and regarding "Japanese and puppets dearer than their own countrymen and their own countrymen more hateful than the Japanese and the puppets." Appealing to the United States, Great Britain, the Soviet Union, and public opinion in China and abroad, it asserted that the "anti-Japanese troops in liberated China under Commander in Chief Chu Teh have a right to send their representatives directly to participate in accepting a Japanese surrender by the Allies, in military control of Japan, and in the coming peace conference."[75] On August 13, Chu cabled Chiang a reply. Characterizing Chiang's order as "unfair," "contrary to the national interest," and "only beneficial to the Japanese invaders and traitors," Chu told Chiang that "you have issued the wrong order, very wrong indeed and we have to reject it resolutely."[76] On the same day, Chu sent General Yasuji Okamura, the commander in chief of the Japanese forces in China, a cable demanding that the latter order the Japanese troops to surrender to the Communists.[77] The struggle for the control of China was on, with the Communists poised in the most vital regions of China.

What swung the balance in favor of the Nationalist government and averted an imminent Communist victory was American assistance in expeditiously transporting the Nationalist forces by air and sea to strategic points throughout China while Japanese and puppet forces held these areas against the Communists pending the arrival of Kuomintang troops. American landings were also made to occupy important ports to facilitate the movement of Nationalist forces. The first outlines of these military operations were laid down only toward the end of July in anticipation of a Japanese surrender. They envisaged the immediate occupation by American forces of several ports on the mainland of China — Shanghai in the Yangtze Valley, Chefoo on the Shantung Peninsula, and Chinwangtao in North China, just outside of Manchuria.[78] The American government also took the initiative in finding out from Chiang what help was needed. In response to this query, Chiang asked Wedemeyer to plan at once to move

[74] *New York Times*, August 13, 1945, p. 1.

[75] "Text of Broadcast from Yenan," *ibid.*, August 14, 1945, p. 10. This statement was written by Mao for the Hsin-hua News Agency; see Mao, *Selected Works*, IV (Peking), 27–29.

[76] *New York Times*, August 15, 1945, p. 16. This cable was written by Mao for Chu (Mao, *Selected Works*, IV [Peking], 33–34).

[77] Li Shou-k'ung *Chung-kuo tsui-chin ssŭ-shih-nien shih* ["A History of China in the Last 40 Years"] (Taipei, Taiwan: Chung-hua shu-chü, 1954), p. 246.

[78] Feis, *op. cit.*, pp. 334–35; Romanus and Sunderland, *op. cit.*, pp. 389–90.

Chinese government troops into places to be taken by American forces and other key areas. He requested that the American units avoid as far as possible any co-operation with Communist forces. These ideas of Chiang were incorporated in a War Department directive of August 10. This directive to General Wedemeyer provided for the occupation by American forces of key ports and communication centers in China, the rapid transportation of Nationalist forces to key areas, and the turning over of localities occupied by American forces only to agencies and forces accredited by the Nationalist government. But it also ordered Wedemeyer not to support the Nationalist government in a civil war.[79]

In this way, the United States set out to assist the Nationalist government to re-establish its authority in areas occupied by Japan and in so doing strengthened it against the Communists. But this exercise of American power in China was hedged in by three self-imposed restrictions. One was the priority given to the occupation of Japan. Operating in the context of the precipitous end of the war and the projected rapid demobilization of the armed forces, this decision prevented Wedemeyer from doing what he thought was necessary to bolster the position of the government. Seized by a sense of urgency as the Communists were ignoring the order of the government, Wedemeyer asked the Joint Chiefs of Staff to land American forces as soon as possible on a first priority basis. This request was rejected by the Joint Chiefs who also told him that he could expect only a maximum of two American divisions for some time to come.[80] According to Wedemeyer's testimony at the MacArthur hearings, he asked for seven divisions which he intended to employ in Manchuria in order to deter unilateral Soviet action in China. This request was referred to General MacArthur. Uncertain of the reaction of the Japanese toward American occupation, MacArthur refused to make these divisions available.[81]

The second self-imposed limit was the suspension of all training of the Nationalist forces under American supervision, less than ten days after Japan's surrender. This meant the dismantling of the elaborate apparatus of liaison and operational teams which Wedemeyer had built.[82] This action was taken partly in conjunction with the program of general demobilization and partly with a view to transferring the available American personnel to help transport the Nationalist armies to North and East China. Little thought was given to the possible effects of this move in

[79] Feis, *op. cit.*, pp. 335–38; Romanus and Sunderland, *op. cit.*, pp. 391–92, 393–95.
[80] Feis, *op. cit.*, pp. 338–39; Romanus and Sunderland, *op. cit.*, p. 395.
[81] *Military Situation in the Far East*, p. 2415. See also Joseph Alsop, "The Strange Case of Louis Budenz," *Atlantic Monthly*, April, 1952, p. 33; General Albert C. Wedemeyer, *Wedemeyer Reports!* (New York: Henry Holt & Co., 1958), p. 348.
[82] Romanus and Sunderland, *op. cit.*, p. 395.

permanently weakening the military capability of the Nationalist government.[83]

The third self-imposed limit on the exercise of American power was the decision to avoid furnishing direct support to the Nationalist government in the Chinese civil war. With the spread of armed clashes between Nationalist and Communist forces as both raced for the control of China, the contradition between the policy of peaceful unification and the policy of supporting the Nationalist government heightened. Wedemeyer found it difficult to carry out his mission to give full support to the Nationalist forces without also affording direct American assistance to the government troops in fighting the Communists.[84] Short of openly violating the letter of his orders, he endeavored to do everything possible to help the Nationalists. For this purpose, he employed a technique which can best be described in his own words. Wedemeyer testified in the MacArthur hearings:

> I was not permitted, for example, to pick up a Chinese army at point A and move it to B to facilitate the recovery of an area from the Commies by the Chinese Nationalist forces; I was not authorized to use my aircraft for that purpose. But in the process of moving them, I did do exactly that. It was inherent in my instructions that I should recover the areas formerly occupied by the Japanese, so I had to move them into areas that were vacant, and that did cause some friction with the Chinese Communists. . . . Incidentally, sir, it improved the position of the Chinese Nationalists vis-à-vis the Chinese Communists, too.[85]

In spite of Wedemeyer's subtle tactics, the decision not to give direct support to the Nationalists in the civil war and to avoid direct American participation did rule out actions which might have greatly helped the Nationalists. For instance, Wedemeyer found it necessary to refuse Chiang's request to move government forces to Tangku, a strategic point on the mouth of the river leading to Tientsin and on the Peking-Mukden railroad.[86] The most notable case was the cancellation in October of a plan to land a detachment of American marines at Chefoo. This seaport on the northern coast of Shantung was only ninety nautical miles from Dairen and two hundred and fifteen nautical miles from Yingkow and Hulutao — three of the largest ports in Manchuria. Chefoo was serving as a point from which the Communist forces in Shantung were being ferried into Manchuria. On learning of the American plan, General Chu sent two strongly worded protests to Wedemeyer, the second stating that

---

[83] Letter from Riley Sunderland.
[84] Feis, *op. cit.*, pp. 338–39.
[85] *Military Situation in the Far East*, p. 2462.
[86] Feis, *op. cit.*, p. 365, n. 11.

if American forces landed and trouble ensued the full responsibility would fall upon the United States. The plan to land the Marines was canceled after the American transports had hovered off the port for several days.[87] The Chefoo episode set the precedent for subsequent American decisions not to land Nationalist forces at the Manchurian ports of Hulutao and Yingkow which the Soviet forces had allowed the Communists troops to occupy before the American transports carrying Nationalist forces arrived.[88]

Despite these self-imposed limits, American actions achieved spectacular results. Immediately after V-J Day, American air forces lifted three Nationalist armies by air to key points of East and North China, including the three most important cities, Shanghai, Nanking, and Peiping. In the ensuing months, between 400,000 and 500,000 Nationalist troops were moved to new positions. American marines occupied Peiping, Tientsin, the coal mines to the north, and the essential railroads in the area.[89]

This gigantic air and sea lift of Nationalist forces and the landing of the marines would not have been effective in re-establishing the authority of the Nationalist government if, pending their arrival, the Japanese and puppet forces had not garrisoned the contested localities. In assuring the co-operation of the Japanese forces in China, American diplomatic support played a decisive role. In preparing for the surrender of Japan, Washington drafted what was known as General Order No. 1, which was to be issued by the Emperor of Japan according to the terms of surrender. Taking into account Chiang's fear that the Communists would attempt to secure the surrender of the Japanese forces, Washington provided in General Order No. 1 that the Japanese commanders and all air, ground, and sea forces within China (excluding Manchuria), Formosa, and French Indochina north of 16° north latitude were to surrender to Generalissimo Chiang Kai-shek and that all surrenders were to be made only to him or his representatives.[90] In addition General MacArthur warned Japanese Imperial Headquarters of the importance that the United States attached to the surrender of the Japanese forces in China only to the Nationalist government.[91] On August 17, General Marshall informed MacArthur of the view of the State Department that MacArthur ought to make it clear to the Japanese that the Potsdam provision regarding the repatriation of Japanese armed forces applied only to those who surrendered themselves and their arms to Chiang Kai-shek and his subordinates.[92] As Truman noted

[87] Ibid., pp. 365–66. For a detailed description of the episode and a discussion of its significance, see Moorad, op. cit., chap. vi, and p. 93.
[88] Feis, op. cit., pp. 384–86.
[89] United States Relations with China, pp. 311–12.
[90] Feis, op. cit., pp. 341–42; Harry Truman, Year of Decisions (New York: Doubleday & Co., 1955), pp. 439–40.
[91] Feis, op. cit., p. 341.
[92] Ibid., p. 359.

in his memoirs, "This operation of using the Japanese to hold off the Communists was a joint decision of the State and Defense Departments which I approved."[93]

On his part, the Generalissimo acted swiftly to exercise exclusive authority to accept Japanese surrender in the China theater. As early as August 10, four days before the surrender of Japan, he informed his commanders that the Japanese had surrendered unconditionally and ordered them to warn the Japanese troops in the war zones under their jurisdiction not to surrender to Chinese commanders who were not authorized by him to accept surrender.[94] On August 15, he formally ordered General Okamura to stop the military movements of all Japanese forces but to keep temporarily their arms and supplies, to preserve their present positions, to maintain order and communications in their areas, and to await instructions from the Nationalist government.[95] On August 22, General Ho Ying-ch'in, commander in chief of the Chinese army, ordered General Okamura to instruct Japanese forces to allow the passage of Chinese forces dispatched by the designated Nationalist commanders to the occupied areas, but to refuse passage to those Chinese forces without the necessary order from the designated commanders, and to prevent these troops from occupying any city by force.[96] General Ho also told his commanders to make sure that the withdrawal of Japanese forces from the occupied areas was co-ordinated with the movement of Nationalist troops into these regions so as to prevent "bandits" from taking advantage of the situation.[97] The Japanese high command in China co-operated wholeheartedly with the Nationalist government. Actually even before he received the instructions of the Generalissimo, General Okamura had ordered his forces not to surrender its arms to Chinese forces not authorized by the central government to accept their surrender.[98]

In the context of these orders, one passage in Generalissimo Chiang's message to the Chinese soldiers and civilians on the surrender of Japan took on some political significance. Chiang advised the Chinese people:

> I am deeply moved when I think of the teachings of Jesus Christ that we should do unto others as we would have them do unto us and love our enemies. My fellow countrymen know that

[93] Harry Truman, *Years of Trial and Hope: 1946–1952* (New York: Doubleday & Co., 1956), p. 62.

[94] General Headquarters of the Chinese Army, China Theatre, *Ch'u-li Jih-pên t'ou-hsiang wên-chien hui-pien* ["A Compilation of Documents on Handling the Surrender of Japan"], (Nanking, 1945), I, 18.

[95] *Ibid.*, p. 19.

[96] *Ibid.*, p. 42.

[97] *Ibid.*, p. 11.

[98] "Record of Conversations between Commander in Chief Ho and General Okamura," September 10, 1945, *ibid.*, p. 105.

"Remember not evil against others" and "Do good to all men" have been the highest virtues taught by our own sages. We have always said that the violent militarism of Japan is our enemy, not the people of Japan. Although the armed forces of the enemy have been defeated and must be made to observe strictly all the terms of surrender, yet we should not for a moment think of revenge or heap abuses on the innocent people of Japan.[99]

The Generalissimo also moved quickly to obtain the support of the Chinese puppet forces. On August 10, the Generalissimo instructed his commanders in all war zones to incite the puppet forces to shift their allegiance to the Nationalist government, to establish liaison with them, and to use them to control the important points and lines evacuated by the Japanese.[100] The next day he issued a proclamation offering the puppet forces an opportunity to redeem themselves by obeying his orders to remain in their posts, to preserve local order, and to refuse unauthorized incorporation into other forces.[101] The commanders of the puppet forces who availed themselves of this offer were given new appointments by the Military Affairs Commission of the National government and were put under the temporary command of the Nationalist commanders in the various war zones.[102] Most of the commanders of the puppet forces were ideologically and politically closer to the Nationalists than to the Communists. Some of them had fought pitched battles with the Communist forces. A few had originally been high military commanders or officers in the Nationalist army and had shifted their allegiance during the difficult days of the war to the puppet government at Nanking. For those in this last category, shifting allegiance once more was simply returning to their original fold and renewing old comradeship.[103]

With these drastic measures, the Nationalist government succeeded in denying the important cities, towns, and lines of communication to the Communists while its forces were airlifted by the American air force to take them over from the Japanese and puppet forces. Confronted by these maneuvers, the Communists withdrew their major military forces from the Yangtze Valley, concentrated them in the countryside of North China, and dispatched part of them to Manchuria through the port of Chefoo by

[99] Chiang Kai-shek, *Collected Wartime Messages, 1937–1945* (New York: John Day Co., 1946), II, 851.

[100] *Ch'u-li Jih-pên t'ou-hsiang wên-chien hui-pien,* p. 18.

[101] *Ibid.,* pp. 17–18.

[102] *Ibid.,* p. 32.

[103] The most famous cases were Generals Sun Tien-ying, Sun Liang-chêng, and Men Chih-chung. Of the 350,000 puppet troops, the Nationalist government succeeded in incorporating 240,000 men into its army (*Shou-hsiang pao-kao-shu,* pp. 11–12). For a list of commanding officers of the puppet forces who received new appointments from the Nationalist government, see chart 9 in the Appendix.

sea.[104] In this manner, the Nationalist government re-established its authority in Central and South China and occupied some of the most important cities and lines of communication in North China.

2. The Limitations of a Policy of Military Assistance and Diplomatic Support

If the events in this period demonstrated the possibilities of American military assistance and diplomatic support, they also showed their limitations. One obviously limiting factor was the political vitality and military capabilities of the Chinese Communists. While the Communists were making no contests for South and Central China, they made a determined effort to extend their influence in North China and to penetrate into Manchuria. In North China, the Nationalists held the large cities such as Peiping, Tientsin, Paoting, Shihchiachuang, Taiyüan, Tatung, Tangshan, and Chingwangtao and a corridor between them. In addition they held the Lunghai railroad from Hsüchou westward, reoccupied a few large cities such as Tsinan, Weihsien, and Tsingtao, and retained a weak control over some districts in the province of Shantung. But with these exceptions, North China above the Lunghai railroad was in the hands of the Communists. Below the Lunghai railroad, their forces were entrenched in northern Kiangsu, thus controlling its eastern end. They also held on to their guerrilla areas in the provinces of Honan, Anhwei, Hupei, Chekiang, Kwangtung, and Kwangsi and on Hainan Island. They claimed that from August 11 to October 10, they captured and accepted the surrender of 220,000 puppet and Japanese troops,[105] killed and wounded another 10,000, and extended their rule over 197 towns, 315,200 square miles of territory, and 18,717,000 people.[106]

Thus, the Communists had succeeded in linking up their separate "liberated areas" in eastern Shansi, southern Hopei, practically all of Shantung, part of Anhwei, and northern Kiangsu into several regions under their control. They were astride the North China plain. They were in a

[104] At the time of the surrender of Japan, the New Fourth Army under General Ch'ên Yi was operating in the Yangtze Valley (Chieh-fang-chün, p. 222). Toward the end of October contingents from this unit were in control of Hulutao, Manchuria, and they refused to permit the American navy to land Nationalist troops there (Feis, op. cit., p. 385).

[105] The overwhelming majority of the troops which were captured by or surrendered to the Communists were puppet troops. Obviously the figure 220,000 includes the miscellaneous forces serving the local puppet governments, puppet police, etc. According to the official report of the commander-in-chief of the Nationalist army, three divisions of the regular puppet forces went over to the Communists, another three divisions were disarmed by them and still another three divisions were disarmed by the Red Army (Shou-hsiang pao-kao-shu, p. 12). Undoubtedly, the Communists also succeeded in disarming or winning over a small number of Japanese forces (Ch'u-li Jih-pên t'ou-hsiang wên-chien hui-pien, II, 88, 96, 128, 136, 149–50, 152, 157 and 158).

[106] Chieh-fang-chün, p. 222.

position to disrupt the northern sections of China's only two railroads linking the Yangtze River Valley and North China. They cut off Manchuria from the center of Nationalist power. They were also strengthened by the capture of a certain amount of arms, ammunition, and supplies from the puppet and Japanese forces. Admittedly, the Nationalist government, with American military and diplomatic support and with co-operation from Japanese and puppet forces, succeeded in preventing the Communists from achieving hegemony in China. The shift in the balance of forces in a direction favorable to the Communists was also temporarily arrested and the relative strength of the Nationalists vis-à-vis the Communists increased. As Ch'ên Po-ta, a leading Communist theoretician angrily cried, Chiang Kai-shek "robbed the people [i.e., the Communist party] of their fruits of victory and the Japanese bandits became his benefactors."[107] But the Communists were far from being defeated.

The limitations of American policy were also revealed in another direction: the political ineffectiveness of the Nationalist government, which neither military assistance nor diplomatic support could change. The victory over Japan, the reoccupation of Central and South China, and the establishment of a foothold in North China presented Generalissimo Chiang with both a golden opportunity and a serious challenge. Now that Japan had capitulated, Chiang as the national leader of the war of resistance against Japan regained some of his prestige lost during the last few years of the war. His agents and armies were welcomed as liberators by the people of the reoccupied areas. If his government had performed the task of taking over the administration of these territories with even a minimum of efficiency and honesty, its authority would have been greatly strengthened. If he had been less partial toward his own followers and had given other relatively more capable Nationalist leaders a fair chance to demonstrate their ability, the over-all influence of his government would have been enhanced. Yet Chiang and his government characteristically failed to seize the opportunity and to meet the challenge.

In taking over the occupied areas, many of the Nationalist officials were more concerned with appropriating indiscriminately what were classified as "the properties of the Japanese and puppets" for their own use than with the task of setting up the proper administrative machinery, rehabilitating the economy, and planning for reconstruction. The exchange rate between the Nationalist dollar and the puppet dollar was not fixed for some time. Then it was set at the exorbitant rate of 200 puppet dollars to one Nationalist dollar.The people in the liberated areas suddenly found

[107] Ch'ên Po-ta, *Jên-min kung-ti Chiang Kai-shek* ["Chiang Kai-shek, the Public Enemy of the People"] (2d ed.; Tientsin: Hsin-hua shu-tien, 1949), pp. 138–39. See also Liao Kai-lung, *Hsin Chung-kuo shih tsen-yang tan-shêng ti* ["How the New China Was Born"] (Shanghai: Hai-yen shu-chü, 1950).

themselves pauperized. As an editorial of *Ta-kung pao*, a newspaper owned and controlled by persons closely associated with the Political Science group of the Kuomintang, put it,

> [T]he people in the recovered areas kept vigil till dawn. When they saw the flag of the motherland, they were frantically over-joyed. But after several nights of sleep, they discovered that most of them had lost their home and property. . . . Wealth which had taken generations to accumulate was transferred in a twin-kling to those who held gold dollars and Nationalist dollars in their hands.[108]

Two months after the surrender of Japan this leading Chinese newspaper appealed to the government not to lose the confidence of the people when recovering lost territory. A few days later its plea took a desperate form: "Don't lose the confidence of the people *completely*."[109] Still later it la-mented that an "infinite number of people once rejoiced deliriously at the victory over Japan. But now all of us cannot even keep ourselves alive, as if we were plunged into ever deeper water and tormented by ever intense heat of fires."[110] Even in late January, 1946, the situation in the recovered areas was still chaotic. There was uncontrolled inflation, widespread un-employment, shortage of food, and sometimes starvation in many places.[111] American military assistance and diplomatic support had indeed helped re-establish the authority of the Nationalist government in the larger part of China. But the sudden extension of its control over a vast region merely revealed the extent to which the Nationalist government had degenerated in the years of the war. The revitalization of the Nationalist government

[108] *Ta-kung pao*, Chungking, October 27, 1945, editorial, as reprinted in K'ang Tan, *Chung-kuo chih hsin-shêng* ["The New Birth of China"] (Hong Kong: Hsin-shêng Chung-kuo shê, 1948), pp. 46–47. The quote taken from p. 46. Mr. K'ang was an anti-Communist, pro-Nationalist writer.
A strongly anti-Communist American journalist reported the situation in Shanghai as follows: "To describe the liberation of Shanghai is to strain the English language. There is an old Chinese legend entitled *Wu Tze Tung Kuh* [sic] (*Five Sons Became Scholars*) [sic]. Some mordant wit adapted this to Five officials came to Shanghai: one stole gold bars, another seized houses, the third patronized fine restaurants, the fourth sought political power, and the fifth devoted himself earnestly to women. This is a fairly accurate version of what happened when Chungking and Kunming carpetbaggers swarmed into Shanghai, itching for the bright lights and fleshpots of the greatest car-nival city in the East and, of course, the great stocks of Japanese and enemy-alien property, conservatively valued at five billion dollars" (Moorad, *op. cit.*, p. 53).
[109] *Ta-kung pao*, Chungking, October 27, 1945, editorial, *loc. cit.*, p. 47. Emphasis added.
[110] Quoted in Yin Shi, *Chiang Li kuan-shih yü Chung-kuo* ["The Chiang-Li Rela-tionship and China"] (Hong Kong: Freedom Press, 1954), p. 87.
[111] See the dispatches by the correspondents of the *Ta-kung pao* on the situation in the provinces of Shantung and Kwangtung and the cities of Nanking and Peiping. Re-printed as part of the Appendix to Fung, *op. cit.*, pp. 233–70.

was a problem which could not be solved by military assistance and diplomatic support alone.

The task of providing the reoccupied areas with an effective government amidst a civil war would have taxed to the limits the capabilities of the Nationalist government, even if Chiang had effectively mobilized all the talents within the Kuomintang and enlisted the help of all non-Communist leaders. But instead of so doing, Chiang met this serious challenge by a policy of extending the control of his followers as far as possible and preventing other Nationalist leaders from gaining a fair share of power and influence. Soon after the Communist general Chu Teh ordered his troops to receive the surrender of Japan, Generals Li Tsung-jên and Pai Ch'ung-hsi, two of the most capable Nationalist generals who had once been Chiang's political and military rivals, suggested to the Generalissimo that the Nationalist armies closest to the North China front be dispatched immediately to reoccupy that region. Instead, Chiang arranged to have only Central Army units (i.e., troops commanded by generals belonging to Chiang's own Whampoa group) airlifted or shipped by sea from Southwest China to the faraway area of North China. The implementation of this decision caused considerable delay and gave the Communists additional time to expand their control without opposition. Immediately after the end of the war, Chiang also took steps to undercut the power of the provincial leaders. The most conspicuous case was the removal of General Lung Yün as the chairman of Yunnan province. The resentment against Chiang's discriminatory policies sometimes crystallized in defections of provincial forces. In what was the first Nationalist military disaster after the surrender of Japan, a commander in chief of a group army deserted in October with his units to the Communist side and treacherously destroyed almost four army corps of another Nationalist general.[112] Chiang's pursuit of his own narrow power interests prevented him from becoming the national leader of a powerful coalition of non-Communist elements and played into the hands of the Communists. For Mao's tactics had been to win over "middle-of-the-road" forces and to isolate the "die-hards." Included in this category of the "middle-of-the-road" forces were the powerful figures in the provinces who controlled certain localities or had com-

---

[112] Liu, op. cit., pp. 231–32; also 228, 244. Liu's account is based upon Liang Shêng-chün, Chiang Li tou-chêng nei-mou ["The Inside Story of the Struggle between Chiang and Li"] (Hong Kong: Union Asia Press, 1954), pp. 19–20. Liang was a confidant of General Li and wrote the book with the latter's obvious approval.

In an interview with a reporter of the Communist New China Agency, General Kao Shu-hsün, the turncoat Nationalist commander, attributed his defection to discrimination against his troops in the distribution of supplies and to Chiang's policy of eliminating Nationalist forces not under the command of his personal followers (Wei chih-chih nei-chan êrh t'ou-chêng ["To Struggle for the Cessation of the Civil War"] [Chin-Ch'a-Chi jih-pao-shê, 1946, pp. 94–95).

mand of troops. Mao realized that they were basically opposed to the Communists. But he also recognized that "they are also in contradiction with the Kuomintang central government, which is pursuing the policy of seeking its own benefit at the expense of others."[113] His limited hope was that they would "observe a temporary neutrality when we wage struggles against die-hards."[114] Apparently Chiang's discriminatory policies enabled Mao to accomplish more than he expected to achieve.

Still another factor which set limits to the effectiveness of American policy was the presence of the Soviet forces in Manchuria. After the Soviet declaration of war on Japan on August 8, the Red Army marched into China on several fronts. The main Soviet force under Marshal Rodion Malinovsky penetrated into Manchuria from the northwest along the Chinese Eastern Railway. A second Soviet force invaded Manchuria from the north. Both converged toward Harbin and then pushed southward to occupy all of Manchuria. Meanwhile, the Mongolian People's Republic declared war on Japan on August 10. From Outer Mongolia one Soviet force penetrated into and occupied the province of Jehol, and still another Soviet force, supported by Outer Mongolian troops, marched into the province of Chahar and drove toward the strategic city of Kalgan.[115] The advance of the Soviet forces did not stop at the time of the capitulation of Japan on August 14. Nor did it stop at the boundaries of Manchuria where the Soviet forces had been accorded the authority to accept the surrender of Japanese forces.[116] Instead, Soviet forces continued to march into the provinces of Chahar and Hopei and attacked Japanese forces stationed there, in spite of the fact that the Nationalist government had been given the right to accept the surrender of Japanese forces in these provinces and had ordered the Japanese forces to remain in their positions pending the arrival of Nationalist troops. On August 21, Japanese forces were withdrawn from Kalgan under the pressure of Soviet and Mongolian troops.[117]

[113] Mao Tse-tung, "Questions of Tactics in the Present Anti-Japanese United Front," *Selected Works*, (London: Lawrence & Wishart, 1954), III, 196. This paper was an inner-party directive written by Mao for the Central Committee of the Communist party.

[114] *Ibid.*, p. 197.

[115] Liu, *op. cit.*, p. 247; Max Beloff, *Soviet Policy in the Far East, 1944–1951* (London: Oxford University Press, 1953), pp. 37–38; F. C. Jones, *Manchuria Since 1931* (New York: Institute of Pacific Relations, 1949), pp. 223–24.

[116] The American government acquiesced in the Soviet occupation of Jehol and in the Red Army's acceptance of the surrender of Japanese forces there, in spite of Chiang's protest that Jehol should not be included under the geographical designation of Manchuria as used in General Order No. 1 (Truman, *Year of Decisions*, pp. 445–46).

[117] Memorandum from General Okamura to General Ho, September 5, 1945, and accompanying documents, *Ch'u-li Jih-pên t'ou-hsiang wên-chien hui-pien*, pp. 71–76. According to Feis, "Stalin told Ambassador Harriman on August 27, that Chiang Kai-shek had feared that the Red Army would advance to Kalgan and Peiping and unite with the Chinese Communists in those areas. But he explained that he had reassured

As late as August 31, Soviet forces were still advancing and occupied a strategic point inside the border of the province of Hopei.[118] By these military operations in the provinces of Chahar and Hopei, the Soviet forces occupied the vast stretch of territory which linked the "liberated areas" of the Chinese Communists in North China and Inner Mongolia with Manchuria, now controlled by the Red Army. Thus, the Soviet Union put herself in a position to assist the Chinese Communists if she chose to do so. Working against this possibility was the Sino-Soviet treaty and related agreements which pledged the Soviet Union to support the Nationalist government and to help it re-establish its authority in Manchuria.

3. Hurley's Failure To Use the New Opportunity To Obtain a Truce

The military and diplomatic events recounted above — transportation by air and sea of Nationalist troops by the American air force and navy to occupied areas, the landing of American marines, the co-operation given by the Japanese and puppet forces to the Nationalist government, the extensive military penetration of Soviet troops into China, and the conclusion of the Sino-Soviet treaty — provided the background for renewed negotiations between the Nationalists and the Communists. These conversations and Soviet behavior in Manchuria furnished the conclusive test for Hurley's inextricably intertwined assumptions: that a Soviet promise to support the Nationalist government would bring the Communists to terms; that the Soviet Union desired a settlement in China and subscribed to the policy of peaceful unification; and that the Soviet Union would support the Nationalist government, would refrain from aiding the Communists, and had agreed "unqualifiedly" to America's China policy. At first sight, to a limited extent, and for a brief period of time, events seemed to be vindicating Hurley. After having received three invitations from Generalissimo Chiang, Mao Tse-tung climbed down from his cave apartment in Yenan and, accompanied by Hurley, flew to Chungking for the first time on August 28, to take personal charge of the negotiations with the Nationalists.

Two days before his departure, Mao drafted an inner-party circular for the Central Committee, analyzing the current situation and laying down the party's policy. Mao informed the Communists that Chiang had monopolized the right to accept the surrender and that he had strengthened his position by recovering Shanghai, Nanking, and other places, reopening sea communications, taking over the arms of the Japanese forces, and in-

Chiang Kai-shek that he did not want to occupy these areas and he would not" (Feis, *op. cit.*, p. 380). By this time the Red Army had already been in Kalgan for several days. On this point, Stalin was either ill-informed or tried to create a false impression.
[118] *Ch'u-li Jih-pên t'ou-hsiang wên-chien hui-pien*, pp. 76–77.

corporating the puppet troops into his own forces. For the time being, the big cities and important lines of communication would not be in the hands of the Communists. However, in the coming period, the Communists should fight hard and continue their offensive. After another period of offensive operations, it would be possible for the Communists to control most of the areas north of the lower Yangtze River and the Huai River, most of Shantung, Hopei, Shansi, and Suiyüan provinces, all of Jehol and Chahar provinces, and a part of Liaoning Province.

Mao pointed out that during the negotiations, the Kuomintang would certainly demand that the Communists drastically reduce the size of the "liberated areas" and cut down the strength of the "Liberation Army." The Communists were prepared to make concessions. He explained:

> Without such concessions, we cannot explode the Kuomintang's civil war plot, cannot gain the political initiative, cannot win the sympathy of world public opinion and the middle-of-the-roaders within the country and cannot obtain in exchange legal status for our party and a state of peace. But there are limits to such concessions: the principle is that they must not damage the fundamental interests of the people.[119]

It was possible, Mao suggested, that under domestic and foreign pressure the Kuomintang might conditionally recognize the status of the Communist party. A settlement would bring about a new stage of co-operation between the two parties and of peaceful development. In that event, the Communists should strive to master all methods of legal struggle and intensify its work in the Kuomintang areas in the three main spheres: the cities, the villages, and the army. If the Kuomintang still wanted to launch a civil war after the Communists had made concessions, it would put itself in the wrong in the eyes of the whole nation and the whole world and the Communist party would be justified in waging a war of self-defense to crush its attacks.[120]

In the negotiations at Chungking, the Communists gave many signs of wanting to obtain a settlement. They agreed to conduct the negotiations in secret. Neither side disclosed the substance of the conversations and only a brief communiqué was issued after each day of conversation.[121]

[119] Mao, "On Peace Negotiations with the Kuomintang," *Selected Works*, IV (Peking), 49.

[120] *Ibid.*, pp. 47–49.

[121] "Chou En-lai's Report at the Political Consultative Conference on the Talks between the Kuomintang and the Chinese Communist Party," as reprinted in *Chung-kuo wên-ti wên-hsien*, Hsiang Chün (ed.), ["Documents on the Problem of China"] (Tachung ch'u-pan-shê, 1946), p. 118. Chou's account was corroborated by the report of the Nationalist negotiator ("The Complete Text of Shao Li-tzŭ's Report on the Talks between the Kuomintang and the Chinese Community Party," *ibid.*, p. 124).

The Communists took the initiative in offering concrete suggestions and in making concessions while the Nationalist negotiators played the passive role of rejecting or agreeing to the Communist proposals[122]— a role which reflected the strengthened military and diplomatic position of the government. For the first time since 1937, the Communists moderated their demands instead of raising their price for a settlement. As soon as concrete problems were discussed in the negotiations, the Chinese Communists made it clear that they were prepared to make concessions and would not insist on their terms proposed in December, 1944, and January, 1945, such as the establishment of a coalition government and a coalition high command.[123] Instead, they agreed to the holding of a Political Consultative Conference "to exchange views on national affairs and discuss questions relating to peaceful national reconstruction and the convocation of the National Assembly." [124] Here one must note that the question to be discussed was the convocation of the National Assembly rather than the formation of a coalition government. Later, during the Marshall mission when the Communists again pressed for a coalition government, Chou found it necessary to explain away this concession as a mere postponement rather than an abandonment of their demand for the establishment of a coalition government.[125]

As was to be expected, the most intractable long-range issues were the questions of the incorporation of Communist forces into the National army and the problem of political control in the "liberated areas" dominated by the Chinese Communists. Mao as well as Chiang realized that the political power of the Chinese Communists depended on the armed forces and territory under their control.[126] So the Communist negotiators took their stand on these two questions, insisting on their minimum terms after having made some concessions. On the question of incorporating the Communist forces into a National army, the Communists insisted on retaining the control of a minimum of twenty divisions. The two sides reached certain general agreements on this issue but, to use the words of a Nationalist negotiator, many difficulties "still awaited real solution." [127] On the question of the political control of territory dominated by the Communists,

[122] "The Complete Text of Shao Li-tzŭ's Report on the Talks between Kuomintang and the Chinese Communist Party," *ibid.*, p. 125.

[123] *Ibid.*, p. 126.

[124] "Summary of Conversations between Representatives of the National Government and of the Chinese Communist Party," *United States Relations with China*, p. 578.

[125] *Chung kuo wên-ti wên-hsien*, p. 119.

[126] Mao Tse-tung, "Problems of War and Strategy," *Selected Works*, II, 272. This paper is part of the concluding speech delivered at the Central Committee's plenary session on November 6, 1938.

[127] "The Complete Text of Shao Li-tzŭ's Report on the Talks between the Kuomintang and the Chinese Communist Party," as reprinted in *Chung-kuo wên-ti wên-hsien*, p. 123.

not even verbal agreements could be reached. The Communists at first demanded what was in effect recognition by the Nationalist government of the status quo of their eighteen "liberated areas." After this demand was rejected by the government, the Communists asked what amounted to exclusive control of five provinces in North China and Inner Mongolia and a share in the control of six other provinces and four major cities in various parts of China. Then, the Communists slightly reduced their demands to exclusive control of the border region of Shensi-Kansu-Ninghsia and four provinces in North China and Inner Mongolia and a share in the control of two other provinces and three major cities. Finally, the Communists proposed that all the "liberated areas" temporarily retain their status quo until the constitutional provision for the popular election of provincial government officials had been adopted and put into effect.[128] This formula was also rejected by the government.

The abandonment of their demand for coalition government and the insistence on gaining control over provincial and local government indicate that in their weakened position, the Communists were content with preserving their regional influence and temporarily abandoned their hope of gaining political power over the whole country in the immediate future. Regional domination assured them real power and secured control over important territory in which they could maintain intact their political and military organizations and from which they could again try to capture the central government. Control of provincial and local government and retention of a number of Communist divisions were apparently considered to be "the fundamental interests of the people" which set limits to concession.

Intimately linked with the issues of control over local governments and armed forces was the question of the conflicting claims to disarm the Japanese forces and to take over the occupied areas. It was this issue that had been the immediate cause of the increasing armed clashes between the Nationalist and Communist forces. The Nationalist government claimed exclusive authority to send its troops to occupied areas and to disarm the Japanese forces. The Communists claimed the right to disarm the Japanese forces in areas where their forces had been active or had already surrounded the enemy troops. Again, no solution could be found. Thus, on all questions which directly and immediately affected their power position, the Communists insisted on a set of minimum terms which would have at least preserved part of their gains achieved in the eight years of the Sino-Japanese War and would have enabled them to make another advance when a new opportunity came.

It cannot be known to what extent Mao's concessions and his willingness

[128] *United States Relations with China*, pp. 579-80.

to come personally to Chungking stemmed from a feeling of diplomatic isolation produced by the rapprochement between the Soviet Union and the Nationalist government. It also cannot be ascertained to what extent the Communist refusal to compromise beyond a certain point reflected Soviet reassurances through party channels or Soviet connivance or co-operation with Communist forces in their infiltration into Manchuria. But it is interesting to note that the Nationalist-Communist negotiations ran into difficulties as early as September 4,[129] some days before the Chinese Communists were reported to have received help from the Red Army.[130] The Sino-Soviet Treaty probably disappointed the Chinese Communists momentarily in their hope for large-scale Soviet assistance. But apparently it did not diminish their confidence in their own ability to defend the political and military position which they had created for themselves without any significant amount of aid from outside.[131] As a matter of fact, while Mao was negotiating in Chungking, his forces were extending and consolidating their control in the Japanese-occupied areas by attacking puppet forces and isolated Japanese garrisons.[132]

Throughout the negotiations, Hurley was kept informed of developments. As the representative of the most powerful nation on earth, whose action or inaction might turn the balance in favor of one side or the other, Hurley still had great influence, despite his personal fumblings. His views still carried weight and his continued presence in Chungking was formally requested by both parties.[133] Yet Hurley characteristically missed the new

[129] See the report of the Nationalist negotiator as reprinted in *Chung-kuo wên-ti wên-hsien*, p. 123.

[130] On September 8, some Chinese Communist troops were present in Mukden, Manchuria (Feis, *op. cit.*, p. 382, n. 13). On October 3, 1945, the *Times* (London) reported that Chinese Communist armies were penetrating Manchuria and co-operating with Soviet troops in Mukden. On October 30, 1945, the *New York Times* reported that the Russians had allowed the Chinese Communist troops to enter Manchuria as "civilians."

With one rather unimportant exception, all the cases of Soviet co-operation with Chinese Communists on which the Chinese government possessed some firm information took place after September 6 (Chinese Delegation to the United Nations, *China Presents Her Case to the United Nations* [New York, 1949], pp. 16–17, 19, 20–23). It is quite true that as early as August 11, the Chinese Communist high command ordered four armed groups to proceed to Manchuria. But it is uncertain how much the Communist negotiators in Chungking knew at the time of the extent of Soviet co-operation accorded these Communist forces, and how soon. See also Chiang Kai-shek, *Soviet Russia in China* (New York: Farrar, Straus & Cudahy, 1957), p. 144; Moorad, *op. cit.*, pp. 114–15.

[131] Shortly after the conclusion of the Sino-Soviet treaty, the American army observers in Yenan advised Washington that despite their disappointment in the Sino-Soviet treaty, the Communists would continue to fight for the control of China rather than accept the terms offered by the Nationalist government (Feis, *op. cit.*, p. 358). Subsequent events demonstrated the correctness of this forecast.

[132] See this chapter, pp. 311, 317, above.

[133] *United States Relations with China*, p. 107.

opportunity which the recent display of tremendous military power of his country gave him. His approach to the Kuomintang-Communist negotiations was politically deficient even in terms of the policy of avoiding a civil war and bringing about unification by peaceful means. At this crucial juncture, when the two sides were seriously negotiating on the concrete issues dividing them and were coming closer than ever before to a transient accommodation, Hurley did not use his influence to facilitate the search for solutions to the urgent specific problems. Instead, his only contribution to the talks consisted of his efforts in bringing the two sides together and in urging them to keep on talking despite repeated impasses. His advice for the negotiators was to seek an agreement "on basic over-all principles" and to leave the "details" to be worked out in accordance with such principles.

This was precisely the wrong approach. Given the basic conflict in party principles and policies, civil war could have been avoided or postponed, if at all, only by a temporary accommodation which registered the existing balance of forces between the two sides and which was easily enforceable and posed no threat to the political position of either side. Such a temporary accommodation could have been worked out only by solving a series of concrete issues; or to use Hurley's word, "details," over which the two sides were fighting numerous armed clashes. At this time, the most pressing of these issues were the conflicting claims over the authority to disarm Japanese forces and the controversy over political control of the "liberated areas" dominated by the Communists. The only solution to these two questions would have been an arrangement under which China was divided, under some legal and administrative formula, into two zones, one ruled by the Nationalists and the other governed by the Communists, with the Nationalist government exercising some very loose over-all control to give China a semblance of unity, and maintaining a minimum of co-operation in such fields of communication, transportation, currency, internal trade, etc. This was essentially the idea which Colonel Ivan Yeaton, head of the American Army Observer Mission to Yenan, expressed to Hurley at this time.[134] Of less urgency but of fundamental importance was the question of the size of the Communist forces. This could also have been solved, if at all, only on the basis of maintaining the existing ratio between the Nationalist and Communist troops.

Interestingly enough, the Communist proposals offered just such a chance, however slim, of working out a transient arrangement. They were made at a time when the relative strength of the Communists vis-à-vis the Nationalists suffered a momentary decline, and the Communist prospect for an early victory had been darkened by American military assistance to

[134] Feis, op. cit., p. 361.

the Nationalists and the Sino-Soviet treaty. Consequently, these terms were relatively moderate and furnished a basis for a temporary settlement. To be sure, a temporary accommodation along the lines of the Communist proposals would have confirmed the Communists in their position in North China and enabled them to expand when a new opportunity presented itself. But under such an arrangement the political foundations of the Nationalist government would not have been threatened because not even the Communists insisted at this time on the establishment of a coalition government. A settlement on the basis of the maximum concessions made by the Communists would have given the Nationalists a greater advantage than that worked out later by Marshall. It would have been more acceptable to the Nationalists than the latter. It is just possible that American pressure on the Nationalists could have brought about a temporary accommodation, if Hurley had intervened as actively as Marshall subsequently did. A transient settlement would also have given the Nationalists a sorely needed breathing spell to take over the rest of China, including Manchuria, to restore communications, and to stabilize the economy. Since the United States thought it unwise or impractical to intervene militarily on a large scale at this time, it would have been in her interest to promote such a settlement. In all probability, any accommodation could not have lasted very long. But the United States and the Nationalist government would have gained invaluable time.

As it was, Hurley's negative approach meant, in effect, unconditional support for the Nationalist position in the talks; for throughout the period of negotiations, American armed forces were transporting Nationalist forces by air and sea to the occupied area to disarm the Japanese forces. With American aid, Generalissimo Chiang was apparently confident that his forces would win in the race for the control of China. He was highly conscious of his military strength and entirely oblivious of his political and economic weaknesses. Temporarily, he scored some victories over the Communists. In the long run, his policy of fighting a civil war regardless of political and economic circumstances led to his defeat and, with it, the failure of American policy. In this way, Hurley's policy of unconditional support for Chiang militated against his policy of peaceful unification.

Under these circumstances, no agreement could have been reached on the most pressing issue — the conflicting claims over the authority to disarm the Japanese forces, and the related problem of political control over the "liberated areas." To satisfy the public clamor for peace, the two sides agreed to issue a summary of the conversations which emphasized the points of agreement and did not even mention the inability to reach an agreement on the issue of disarming Japanese forces.[135] The negotiations adjourned on October 10, and Mao left for Yenan the next day.

Back in Yenan, Mao made a report to a meeting of Communist cadres on the negotiations in Chungking. Mao observed that Chiang's desire was to maintain his dictatorship and destroy the Communist party, but many objective difficulties stood in his way. Chiang's three main obstacles were said to be the might of the "liberated areas," the opposition to civil war by the people in Nationalist China, and the international situation. Therefore, he had to be a little realistic and invited the Communists to Chungking to negotiate. The Communists were also realistic in going to negotiate with him. As a result of the negotiations, the Kuomintang had accepted the general policy of peace and unity. But words on paper are not equivalent to reality. The Communists must make a greater effort to turn them into reality.

Mao gave two explanations for his offer, made during the negotiations, to give up eight "liberated areas" in southern Kiangsu, Chekiang, southern Anhwei, central Anhwei, southern Honan, Hupeh, Hunan, and Kwangtung. First, the Nationalists would fight for them at all costs, because some of these bases were "right by their beds or in their corridor." [136] It was clear that Mao recognized the difficulty of defending these bases and the advantage of giving them up and concentrating his forces to hold North China. Second, by conceding these bases, the Communists had, according to Mao, completely refuted the Kuomintang's charge that the Communist party just wanted territory and would make no concessions. Thus, the Communists would win the sympathy of the numerous middle elements at home and abroad. For the same reason the Communists made concessions on the problem of armed forces. They demanded the maintenance of only twenty divisions out of their 1,200,000 men or a one to six ratio between the Communist and Nationalist forces. Mao explained, however,

[135] For the text of the summary of the conversations, see Annex 49, *United States Relations with China*, pp. 577–81.

In his conversation with the staff of the American embassy, Chou En-lai said that the only principal point of disagreement was the question of the political control of liberated areas (*ibid.*, p. 108; Feis, *op. cit.*, p. 364). Actually, the lack of an agreement on disarming Japanese forces was an even more pressing problem on which no agreement had been reached and played an even more important part in the ensuing spread of armed conflict. The importance of this unsolved problem was stressed at the time by the usually well-informed *Ta-kung pao*. See *Ta-kung pao*, October, 12, 1945, editorial, as reprinted in *Chung-kuo wên-ti wên-hsien*, pp. 39–44. Chou En-lai himself subsequently admitted that the lack of an agreement on the authority to disarm the Japanese forces was the source of the armed clashes after the adjournment of the negotiations. See Chou's report on January 12, 1946, as reprinted in *ibid.*, pp. 113–20. Chou de-emphasized this problem in his talk to Americans presumably because the United States had previously upheld the authority of the Nationalist government to accept the surrender of Japanese forces in China.

[136] Mao, "On the Chungking Negotiations," *Selected Works*, IV (Peking) p. 56.

that his offer did not mean that the Communists would hand over their guns to the Kuomintang. These must be kept by the Communists.

Mao pointed out that the question of liberated areas had not been solved, and the problem of armed forces had not really been solved either. But if the Kuomintang was to launch civil war again after the Communist concessions, it would put itself in the wrong in the eyes of the whole nation and the whole world, and the Communists would have all the more reason to smash its attack by a war of self-defense. Mao declared: "China's problems are complicated, and our brains must be a little complicated. If they [the Nationalists] start fighting, we fight back, fight to win peace. Peace will not come unless we strike hard blows at the reactionaries who dare to attack the Liberated Areas."[137] To those Communist cadres who would soon leave Yenan for the battlefront, he gave an instruction to "go all out to mobilize the masses, expand the people's forces and, under the leadership of our party, defeat the aggressor and build a new China." [138] Obviously, Mao was preparing for all contingencies. His inclination was "to assume that there would be more difficulties than less," [139] to recognize, analyze, and combat difficulties, and not to try to get things cheaply.

Continued negotiations produced no results. The Nationalist and Communist forces quickened their race for the control of China. The number of armed clashes sharply increased. Clearly, the Sino-Soviet treaty had not brought the Communists to terms, and the negotiations which had begun so hopefully had failed to produce a settlement. One of the major assumptions of Hurley's policy of unconditional support for the Nationalist government was invalidated by events.

4. Soviet Intentions toward China and Soviet Actions in Manchuria

Hurley's belief that a treaty concluded between the Soviet Union and the Nationalist government would bring the Chinese Communists to terms was inseparably interwoven with his other two assumptions: that the Soviet Union subscribed to the policy of peaceful unification and that the Soviet Union would support the Nationalist government and had agreed "unqualifiedly" to America's policy.[140] He seized upon the conclusion of the Sino-Soviet treaty and the related agreements as a vindication of his views. On September 6, 1945, Hurley informed the State Department that the publication of the Sino-Soviet treaty and agreements "has demonstrated conclusively that the Soviet Government supports the National Government of China and also that the two governments are in

[137] Ibid.
[138] Ibid., p. 59.
[139] Ibid., p. 60.
[140] United States Relations with China, p. 96.

agreement regarding Manchuria." [141] He also told Washington in another report that Generalissimo Chiang who had "always doubted the Soviet's position in regard to relations with the Chinese Communists" now shared his confidence in Soviet intentions.[142]

Subsequent events and later research enable us to make a retrospective analysis of Hurley's judgments on Soviet policy and intentions. They vindicate Hurley's belief that the Soviet Union did not desire civil war and wanted a settlement in China, insofar as his belief concerns Soviet policy toward China from the autumn of 1944 to the end of the Pacific war. As Charles B. McLane points out, Soviet policy during this period, particularly after Yalta, was "to urge greater collaboration between the Communists and the Kuomintang for the remainder of the War and to recommend that immediate preparations be made for establishing a coalition government as soon as the war was over." [143] This policy seems to have been based either on uncertainty about the relative strength of the Kuomintang and the Chinese Communists or on a low estimate of Mao's chances of success in an all-out civil war with the Kuomintang.[144] It appears to have been related to Soviet fear of possible American counteraction, as is suggested by the role which the Soviet Union played in the summer of 1945 in terminating the Kazakh uprising in Sinkiang against the Nationalist government.[145] The Soviet Union in her own way supported the American policy of peaceful unification in order that her immediate objectives in the Far East as embodied in the Yalta Agreement could be confirmed by a treaty with the Nationalist government and would not be put into jeopardy by the outbreak of a civil war.

There is evidence that even in the days immediately after the war, Stalin discouraged the Chinese Communists from making a military effort to capture power and urged them to join a coalition government. In 1948, Stalin told Eduard Kardelj, a chief aide of Marshall Tito:

> After the war we invited the Chinese comrades to come to Moscow and we discussed the situation in China. We told them bluntly that we considered the development of the uprising in China had no prospect, and that the Chinese comrades should join the Chiang Kai-shek government and dissolve their army. The Chinese comrades agreed here with the views of the Soviet

[141] *Ibid.*, p. 120.
[142] *Ibid.*, pp. 120–21.
[143] Charles B. McLane, *Soviet Policy and the Chinese Communists, 1931–1946* (New York: Columbia University Press, 1958), p. 209.
[144] *Ibid.*, pp. 181, 264.
[145] Allen S. Whiting and General Sheng Shih-ts'ai, *Sinkiang: Pawn or Pivot?* (East Lansing, Mich.: Michigan State University Press, 1958), pp. 104–10. It should also be pointed out that Stalin assured Soong he would withhold support from the insurgents (see p. 275, above).

comrades, but went back to China and acted otherwise. They mustered their forces, organized their armies, and now, as we see, they are beating the Chiang Kai-shek army. Now, in the case of China, we admit we were wrong. It proved that the Chinese comrades and not the Soviet comrades were right.[146]

As McLane concludes, "the *sense* of these remarks" attributed to Stalin may well be "authentic," insofar as his estimate of the situation in China shortly after V-J Day is concerned.[147] It is also significant that after the war in Europe was over, the French and the Italian Communists buried their arms and joined coalition governments, presumably at Stalin's order. Stalin may very well have pursued the same policy in China.

In 1960, General Lin Piao, a member of the Standing Committee of the Politburo and a vice chairman of the Central Committee, wrote an article on the occasion of the publication of the fourth volume of the *Selected Works of Mao Tse-tung*. In it, he attributed to Mao the sole credit for making the correct appraisal that the Chinese Communists could repulse the attack of the Nationalists and defeat them. Lin stated that "some well-intentioned friends at home and abroad were . . . worried about us."[148] But, according to Lin, "At this critical juncture, on the basis of a Marxist-Leninist analysis of the enemy's strength and ours, Comrade Mao Tse-tung put forward the thesis that all reactionaries are paper tigers."[149] This thesis "swept away the fear that some people had of United States imperialism and the Kuomintang reactionaries and their pessimism regarding the future of the revolution."[150] Lin's phrase, "some well-intentioned friends abroad," can be interpreted as an allusion to Stalin.[151]

If the above analysis is not too wide of the mark, one can conclude that immediately after the war Stalin supported, for a period of time difficult to determine, the American effort to seek amity and establish a coalition government in China. But Stalin's support for the policy of unification did not mean that he would wholeheartedly support the Nationalists, deny assistance to the Chinese Communists, help the Nationalists to establish their authority in China, and "unqualifiedly" support American policy. Soviet behavior in Manchuria at the time soon proved that Hurley interpreted too literally the assurances given by the Russian leaders. It suggests that Kennan's contemporary analysis was much closer to the truth. From early October, 1945, up to May 5, 1946, when the Soviet troops completed

[146] Vladimir Dedijer, *Tito Speaks* (London: Weidenfeld & Nicolson, 1953), p. 331.
[147] McLane, *öp. cit.*, pp. 264–65.
[148] Lin Piao, "The Victory of the Chinese People's Revolutionary War Is the Victory of the Thought of Mao Tse-tung," *Peking Review*, October 11, 1960, p. 9.
[149] *Ibid.*, p. 10.
[150] *Ibid.*
[151] I am indebted to Dr. Allen S. Whiting for this point.

their withdrawal from Manchuria, the Soviet government followed a course of action that called into question Hurley's judgment that the Chinese and Soviet governments were in agreement regarding Manchuria.

First, the Soviet Union interposed obstacles to Nationalist efforts to re-establish authority over Manchuria, facilitated the penetration by the Chinese Communists into Manchuria, and allowed the captured Japanese arms and ammunitions to fall into their hands. Second, she removed large quantities of industrial equipment from Manchuria and endeavored to secure further economic concessions from the Nationalist government. Third, having hindered the Nationalists in their attempts to take over Manchuria, the Soviet Union contrived to postpone three times the withdrawal of her forces from Manchuria, the first two times by agreement with the Nationalist government and the last time by unilateral action. The continued presence of Soviet forces gave the Chinese Communists time to extend their influence and consolidate their newly won position in Manchuria. It was used to back up Soviet demands for the withdrawal of American armed forces from China. It was employed as a means to exact economic concessions from the Nationalist government. Before Hurley resigned on November 27, the Soviet Union had already fully revealed her obstructionist tactics against the Nationalists and her partiality toward the Chinese Communists, although the total impact of Soviet policy was felt only after his resignation. The Soviet Union had, by the mid-autumn of 1945, clinched her gains in Manchuria, had ample opportunity to assess the strength of the Chinese Communists there, and appears "to have been satisfied with alternative policies in China both for themselves and for the Chinese Communists, which were not founded on the presumption of unity and coalition." [152] Since Soviet actions and policies in Manchuria and toward China from early October, 1945, to May, 1946, when the withdrawal of Soviet forces was finally completed, constituted a unified whole a brief account and analysis of them will be given here, even though some of the events belong chronologically to chapter x of this study.

Soviet obstruction of Nationalist attempts to take over Manchuria. — As noted above, the Soviet Union, in the Sino-Soviet treaty and the related agreements and exchange of notes, pledged herself to respect the sovereignty and territorial integrity of China, to refrain from interfering in China's affairs, to render moral support and aid in military supplies and other material resources only to the National government as the central government of China, to respect China's full sovereignty over the Three Eastern Provinces (Manchuria), and to allow the National government "to assume full authority in the direction of public affairs . . . as soon as any part of the liberated territory ceases to be a zone of immediate military

[152] McLane, *op. cit.*, p. 223.

operations." [153] According to the signed minutes, Stalin promised that the Soviet forces would begin withdrawing within three weeks after the capitulation of Japan and that three months would be the maximum period for completion of the withdrawal of troops.[154] By any ordinary reading of these provisions, the Soviet government undertook to assist the Nationalist government to re-establish its authority in Manchuria.

In view of the announced intention of the Chinese Communists to send their forces into Manchuria, the Nationalist government could have effectively taken over this vital region only if its forces could have been rapidly dispatched there. There were three principal routes for the Nationalist armies to reach Manchuria. With the larger part of North China in Communist hands, the shortest way was the sea lane from South and Central China to Dairen and other ports in southern Manchuria. The second and longer route was the sea lane to various ports in North China under Nationalist control. The long overland route linking these ports with the principal Manchurian cities passed through many easily defensible points. It could be easily cut or harassed by hostile forces. The third means of access was by airlift to a limited number of large cities inside Manchuria with large airfields. One of the shortcomings of airlift was the difficulty of transporting in a short period of time a sufficiently large number of troops to any city to keep the confused situation under control.[155] Naturally, the Nationalist government chose the most obvious and the most convenient route of entry.

As early as September 10, the Chinese government asked the United States to provide vessels to transport its troops from Canton to Dairen, hoping that they would get into Manchuria as soon as the Red Army began its withdrawal. On October 1, the Chinese government notified the Soviet ambassador to China of its intention to dispatch its army to the port of Dairen. A disturbing reply came quickly. On October 6, the Soviet ambassador informed the Chinese acting foreign minister that "according to the Sino-Soviet Treaty, Dairen is a commercial port, and that it is a port for the transportation of goods, and not of troops." [156] He further stated that "the landing of troops at Dairen, of whatever nationality, is a violation of the Sino-Soviet Treaty and will be opposed by the Soviet government." The Soviet government was obviously distorting the agreement to serve a political purpose. Not only was the Soviet position not supported by any

[153] *United States Relations with China*, pp. 586, 587, 593.
[154] *China Handbook, 1950* (New York: Rockport Press, 1950), p. 331.
[155] Cf., David J. Dallin, *Soviet Russian and the Far East* (New Haven, Conn.: Yale University Press, 1948), p. 251.
[156] For this and the following quotation, see *China Presents Her Case to the United Nations*, p. 12. See also Tsai I-tien, "Tung-pei ti p'an-chü yü chieh-lüeh" ["The Illegal Occupation and Plundering of the Northeast"] in *Wo-mên ti ti-kuo* ["Our Enemy Nation"] (Taipei: Chung-yang jih-pao-shê, 1952), pp. 136–37.

provision in the agreements, but the exchange of notes in which the Soviet Union affirmed her respect for China's full sovereignty over Manchuria and recognized "the territorial and administrative integrity" of the Three Eastern Provinces [157] clearly showed that the Chinese government was not subject to any other restrictions in its exercise of sovereign rights except those obligations specifically stipulated in the agreement, as the Chinese foreign minister pointed out to the Soviet ambassador.[158] While the American government acted swiftly and effectively in providing shipping for the Chinese troops, it did not give diplomatic support to the Chinese request to enter Dairen or protest against the Soviet refusal.[159] Insofar as the issues arising out of the taking over of Manchuria were concerned, the United States took a detached attitude toward Sino-Soviet relations and also adhered to the policy of not giving direct support to the Nationalists in fighting the civil war.

When in the middle of October the Nationalist forces, carried in American vessels, arrived outside the port of Dairen, there was still no agreement between the Soviet and Chinese governments on a landing at Dairen.[160] But Marshal Malinovsky told General Hsiung Shih-hui, the director of the Generalissimo's headquarters in Manchuria, that the Soviet government would not oppose a landing at three other Manchurian ports — Hulutao, Yingkow, and Antung.[161] Lacking any better alternative, the Nationalist government decided to land its forces at one of the designated ports. On October 25, the Chinese foreign minister told the Soviet ambassador that Chinese troops would land at Hulutao and Yingkow on October 29 in accordance with the arrangement made between Marshal Malinovsky and General Hsiung. On reaching the harbor at Hulutao, the Nationalists found that elements of the Chinese Communist New Fourth Army were in control. After having received an assurance from the Soviet authorities that they would guarantee a landing at Yingkow, the Nationalist forces sailed on American ships to Yingkow. But on arriving, they again found that Yingkow, like Hulutao, was already occupied by the Chinese Communists.[162] Soviet authorities then told the Chinese officials that the port was already garrisoned by armed units of unknown origin and allegiance, and that Soviet government could not be responsible for the security

[157] *United States Relations with China*, p. 587.
[158] Tsai, "Tung-pei ti p'an-chü yü chieh-lüeh," *loc. cit.*, p. 137; *China Presents Her Case to the United Nations*, p. 13. Cf. Wei, *op. cit.*, pp. 195–205.
[159] Feis, *op. cit.*, p. 384.
[160] One of the less important reasons for the Soviet refusal to allow the Nationalists to land at Dairen may have been that the Soviet authorities planned to use the port for loading "war booty" for shipment to Russia. George Moorad reported that the loading in Dairen began on November 12 and was completed on December 5 (*op. cit.*, p. 165).
[161] Feis, *op. cit.*, p. 384.
[162] *Ibid.*, p. 385.

of the landing of Chinese troops.[163] Following the precedent set in the Chefoo episode and motivated by similar considerations, American naval commanders decided against any attempt to land at Yingkow.[164] By these maneuverings, the Soviet Union prevented the Nationalists from using the shortest route to send its forces into Manchuria and compelled the Nationalist forces to make two roundabout detours at sea in futile attempts to land at a Manchurian port. The resultant delay of some five weeks was of great benefit to the Chinese Communists in the race for Manchuria in which every day counted.

Barred from the shortest route to Manchuria, the Nationalists were forced to land at Chinwangtao, a port in North China nearest to Manchuria, and to start a march overland into Manchuria. In their drive into Manchuria along the corridor by the sea, they were attacked by Communist armed groups which were fighting a delaying action against Nationalist advance. The Soviet authorities also refused to give assistance to these Nationalist forces in their overland march in southern Manchuria on the pretext that the Soviet troops in those areas had already been withdrawn.[165] It was not until November 26 that Nationalist forces occupied Chinchow, the first strategic point inside Manchuria.[166] This was some five weeks after the Nationalist forces reached Dairen and were denied entry.

During this same period the Chinese government also hoped to fly its troops into the principal Manchurian cities. But it was informed by the Soviet ambassador on November 13, 1945, that only security forces and gendarmes could be so transported, and that they could proceed to these cities only three or five days before the evacuation of Soviet troops — too short a period of time to airlift enough troops to defend themselves against possible attacks by the Chinese Communists. A Chinese request for a minimum period of one week was rejected by the Soviet government. The Soviet authorities also would not permit the Nationalist government to organize peace preservation units in Manchurian cities by local recruitment. One regiment of peace preservation units which the Nationalist authorities organized in Changchun was suddenly surrounded and disarmed by the Red Army.[167]

While the Soviet authorities were obstructing the Nationalists' attempts to take over Manchuria, they were following a course of action which

[163] *China Presents Her Case to the United Nations,* p. 13.

[164] Feis, *op. cit.,* p. 386.

[165] *China Presents Her Case to the United Nations,* p. 14.

[166] Tung Yen-ping, "Pao-lu O-chün p'an-chü Tung-pei ti ching-kuo," ["An Exposure of the Occurrences during the Illegal Retention of the Northeast by the Russian Army"] in *Wo-mên ti ti-kuo,* p. 169. General Tung, the author, was deputy chief of staff of the Generalissimo's headquarters in Manchuria at that time.

[167] *China Presents Her Case to the United Nations,* p. 14.

helped the Chinese Communist party extend its control over Manchuria, strengthen its armed forces by local recruitment, and obtain captured Japanese arms and ammunition. An estimated 100,000 Chinese Communist soldiers penetrated into Manchuria by land from Inner Mongolia and North China and by sea from Chefoo through the same Manchurian ports the access to which was denied to the Nationalists. Having come unarmed as "civilians," they were soon fully equipped with Japanese arms and ammunition captured by or surrendered to the Red Army.[168]

On December 28, 1945, Mao sent a directive to the Northeast Bureau of the Communist party, urging it to build stable military and political base areas in eastern, northern, and western Manchuria. The base areas were, Mao's directive continued, not to be built in the big cities or along the main communication lines which were or would be occupied by the Kuomintang. They should be built in the cities and vast rural areas comparatively remote from the centers of Kuomintang occupation. Mao pointed out that 100,000 Communist troops had entered Manchuria, that the Communist forces there had been expanded by more than 200,000 and were still growing. He estimated that within a year they would reach 400,000 men.

This phenomenal expansion was made possible by the freedom of action granted, and assistance given, by the Soviet occupation forces. The Soviet authorities allowed the Chinese Communists to recruit new troops. They released many thousands of former Manchoukuo regular soldiers from captivity, some of whom joined the Communist forces. They permitted

---

[168] According to Soviet sources reprinted in a Chinese Communist publication, the Red Army captured:

Airplanes	925	Mortar	1,340
Tanks	369	Machine guns	4,836
Horses and mules	17,497	Rifles	300,000
Depots with munitions		Radio sets	133
and supplies	742	Armored Cars	35
Field artillery	1,226	Motor Vehicles	2,300
		Tractors	125

A total of 594,000 Japanese soldiers and officers and 148 generals surrendered to the Red Army (*Chung-kuo hsin-min-chu-chu-i kê-ming shih ts'an-kao tzŭ-liao*, p. 493). According to Nationalist sources, the Japanese Kwantung army had, at the time of its surrender, on its hands: 1,436 pieces of field artillery, 8,989 machine guns, 11,052 grenade throwers, 3,078 trucks, 104,777 horses, 21,084 supply cars, 815 special vehicles, and 287 command cars (*China Presents Her Case to the United Nations*, p. 16). Presumably, most, if not all, of these arms and munitions fell into the hands of the Chinese Communists.

On their part, the Nationalists took over the following matériel from the Japanese army in China: 685,897 rifles, 30,961 machine guns, 12,446 pieces of artillery (including mortars), 305 tanks, 14,964 armored cars, 18,384 other vehicles, 1,068 airplanes (*Shou-hsiang pao-kao-shu*, pp. 6–7 and Appendix III). These figures indicate that the Japanese arms and ammunition which fell into Communist hands did not in themselves make the Chinese Communists militarily stronger than the Nationalists and could not in themselves account for the Communist victory in China.

the Chinese Communists to organize local government or to take over local governing units which had been organized soon after the Red Army had entered a district. The Chinese Communist forces were also strengthened by the incorporation of some thirty thousand Chinese soldiers who had sought shelter on the Russian border after Japan occupied Manchuria and had been trained by the Russians and who accompanied the Red Army in its march into Manchuria.[169] Under these circumstances, the well-known organizational ability of the Chinese Communists found its full scope. Their shrewd personnel policy also aided them in rapidly establishing their influence in Manchuria. It is noteworthy that three of the four armed groups which Chu Teh ordered to proceed to Manchuria and Jehol immediately after Soviet entry into the war were composed partly of Manchurian forces led by Manchurian officers, who had joined the Communist army at various times.[170] Furthermore, Mao instructed the non-Manchurian cadres "to resolve to become one with the people of the Northeast" and to train large numbers of activists and cadres from among the Manchurians.[171]

Confronted with the obstructionist tactics of the Soviet authorities, and facing a sizable Chinese Communist force, Generalissimo Chiang ordered his troops to halt their advance after the capture of Chinchow on November 26, 1945, rather than press forward to Mukden, the capital of the province of Liaoning. His decision was, to use his own words, "not to proceed with the take-over program but to leave the Russians in illegal occupation of the area in violation of the treaty and to see what they would do to solve the Manchurian question on which world peace and security depended."[172] Shortly before, he had withdrawn from Changchun, the political center of Manchuria, the staff of his headquarters in Manchuria, which, in accordance with the agreement signed on August 14, 1945, with the Soviet Union, he had sent in early October to make preparations for the establishment of civil government for that region. For the Soviet authorities had allowed Chinese Communist troops to enter the city and organize a local government hostile to the mission. Its position had become untenable.[173]

[169] Wu Hsiang-hsiang, *Ti-O ch'in-lüeh Chung-kuo shih* ["A History of Russian Aggression against China"] (Taipei: Chêng-chung shu-chü, 1957), pp. 512–517; Chang, *op. cit.*, pp. 168–69; Robert B. Rigg, *Red China's Fighting Hordes* (Harrisburg, Pa.: Military Service Publishing Company, 1951), p. 252; *China Presents Her Case to the United Nations*, pp. 16–17; Feis, *op. cit.*, p. 381; Liu, *op. cit.*, pp. 227–29.

[170] Tai I, *et al.* (ed.), *op. cit.*, pp. 400–401. One of the commanders was Chang Hsueh-shih, son of Marshal Chang Tso-lin, who controlled Manchuria for more than a decade prior to his assassination by the Japanese in 1928.

[171] Mao, *Selected Works*, IV (Peking), 83.

[172] Chiang Kai-shek, *Soviet Russia in China*, p. 147. Chiang's retrospective account of his decision is corroborated by a telegram sent on November 3 by him to Washington that he intended to postpone entrance into Manchuria until after he had established his authority in North China (Feis, *op. cit.*, p. 403).

[173] *Ibid.*, p. 387; Tsai, "Tung-pei ti p'an-chü yü chieh-lüeh," *loc. cit.*, p. 140; Tung, "Pao-lu O-chün p'an-chü Tung-pei ti ching-kuo," *loc. cit.*, pp. 162–63.

The three postponements of Soviet withdrawal from Manchuria. — Then, the Soviet Union suddenly changed her tactics. On November 17, when the Nationalist mission began its withdrawal from Changchun, the Soviet ambassador delivered a note to the Chinese foreign minister, denying that the Soviet occupation forces had ever given any assistance to the Chinese Communists. This message contended that the presence of the Chinese Communists in certain areas from which the Soviet forces had already withdrawn was the result of the inability of the Chinese government to impose its control. It suggested that if the Chinese government now wished the Soviet forces to delay their withdrawal from Manchuria, the Soviet government could arrange for a postponement of one month or, if necessary, two months. This Soviet note was given point by the fact that as soon as the Soviet forces had withdrawn from the ports and strategic points in southern Manchuria, the Chinese Communist forces had always been present to occupy them. So, two days later, the Chinese government notified the Soviet government that it would extend the deadline for the completion of Soviet withdrawal from December 3 to January 3, after the Soviet and Chinese governments had agreed on an effective plan for the taking over of Manchuria.[174]

To work out such a plan in exchange for the Chinese request for the postponement of Soviet withdrawal, Generalissimo Chiang sent his Soviet-educated son, Chiang Ching-kuo, to Changchun to negotiate with Marshal Malinovsky. Meanwhile, the Chinese and Soviet governments had on November 30 reached an agreement to postpone the withdrawal of Soviet forces for one month to January 3.[175] In his talks with young Chiang on December 5, 1945, Malinovsky gave ready agreement to Chiang's proposal to permit the airlift of one division of Nationalist troops to Changchun and the transportation of two divisions by land to Mukden and promised to guarantee their security. He also stated that the Soviet forces had been pressing forward with the disarming of armed forces not recognized by the government. On his part, Chiang notified Malinovsky on December 9 that the Chinese government agreed to postpone the deadline for the completion of Soviet withdrawal to February 1, 1946, a date proposed by the Soviet authorities in the first talk on December 5.[176] This agreement apparently brightened the prospects of the Nationalist government. Abandon-

---

[174] *Ibid.*, p. 164; Tsai, "Tung-pei ti p'an-chü yü chieh-lüeh," *loc. cit.*, p. 141. Cf. *United States Relations with China*, pp. 123–26.

[175] Tsai, "Tung-pei ti p'an-chü yü chieh-lüeh," *loc. cit.*, p. 143.

[176] *Ibid.*, pp. 164-65. The widely accepted account merely states that the Soviet Union postponed the withdrawal of the Red Army at the request of the Nationalists. While this version of events is technically correct, it says nothing about the origin of the Nationalist request. Nor does it make clear that the Soviet officials were almost as anxious as the Nationalists to retain the Red Army in Manchuria and that the Soviet officials were willing to give specific promise to help the Nationalists in exchange for Nationalist requests for a postponement.

ing his earlier decision, Generalissimo Chiang now ordered his troops to resume their march into Manchuria. On January 5, 1946, the Nationalist government began to airlift its troops to Changchun.[177] On January 26, Nationalist troops entered Mukden in force.[178] Nationalist officials, accompanied by Soviet liaison officers, were flown to ten other major cities and set up municipal governments there.[179] The Nationalists encountered little opposition from the Chinese Communists. For a time, the agreement between Chiang Ching-kuo and Malinovsky worked out relatively well for the Nationalists. But the temporary success emboldened Generalissimo Chiang to advance in Manchuria. It led subsequently to an overextension of the Nationalist forces and ultimately to the loss of the best Nationalist armies. The Generalissimo has since come to regret his change of mind.[180]

It is clear from the above account that in exchange for the Nationalists' requests for a postponement of the withdrawal of the Red Army, the Soviet Union did grant limited help to the Nationalists in their endeavor to take over Manchuria. The Soviet government's desire to postpone the withdrawal of its forces from Manchuria was undoubtedly linked to the continued presence of American marines in North China.[181] When Chiang Ching-kuo visited Moscow in December at the invitation of Stalin, Stalin told him that if the Nationalists allowed a single American soldier to remain in China, the Manchurian question would be very difficult to solve.[182] The Sino-Soviet understanding on the postponement of the Soviet withdrawal enabled Mr. Molotov to claim at the Moscow Conference of the Foreign Ministers of the United States, Great Britain, and the U.S.S.R. that withdrawal of the Red Army from Manchuria had been postponed until February 1 "at the request of the Chinese government."[183] Its diplomatic

---

[177] Tung, "Pao-lu O-chün p'an-chü Tung-pei ti ching-kuo," loc. cit., p. 169.

[178] Chiang, Soviet Russia in China, p. 147.

[179] Tung, "Pao-lu O-chün p'an-chü Tung-pei ti ching-kuo," loc. cit., pp. 174–75.

[180] He wrote in his memoirs: "We should have called off the take-over operations altogether. Then we could have concentrated our armed forces in the Peiping-Tientsin area, held Shanhaikwan and used Chinchow as a forward base. In the meanwhile, we could have submitted the Manchurian problem to the United Nations for a decision and held Soviet Russia responsible for all consequences by appealing to world opinion. In this way our government would have had the necessary military strength below the Great Wall to put down the Communist revolt, control all of North China and use the international deliberations to expose Soviet Russia's design in Manchuria and her eastward advance to the Pacific.

"Owing to domestic and foreign interferences, we failed to adhere to our earlier policy. Instead, we held direct negotiations with Soviet Russia. At the same time we made the mistake of committing the best Government troops to Manchuria only to bog down there-. . . ." (Chiang Kai-shek, Soviet Russia in China, pp. 232–33).

[181] McLane, op. cit., p. 209.

[182] Chiang Ching-kuo "Wo-ti fu-ch'in fan Kung san-shih nien" ["The Thirty Years of My Father's Opposition to Communism"] in Chung-kuo chien-shê ["Reconstruction in China], November, 1957, p. 6.

[183] United States Relations with China, p. 125.

position having been thus strengthened, the Soviet government vigorously pressed for the withdrawal of American forces from China. At the very first meeting, on December 16, Mr. Molotov asked that the question of American troops in North China be discussed. A few days later, he resumed the offensive by suggesting that a date be fixed for the simultaneous withdrawal of American and Russian troops from China. He was insistent in his demand and made repeated efforts to discover what aims, hidden or otherwise, the United States might have toward China.[184] In the end, the Moscow communiqué, issued on December 27, 1945, included a statement which read: "The two Foreign Secretaries were in complete accord as to the desirability of withdrawal of Soviet and American forces from China at the earliest practical moment consistent with the discharge of their obligations and responsibilities." [185]

This was a minor diplomatic defeat for Secretary of State Byrnes. Although no date was fixed for simultaneous withdrawal of American and Soviet troops as Molotov had demanded, this statement put the status of American forces in China, whose presence was eagerly desired by the Chinese government, on the same footing as that of Soviet troops in Manchuria, whose withdrawal was governed by Stalin's pledge given to the Chinese government in August and the latest understanding reached between Chinese representatives and Soviet authorities. Later, the Soviet government was to invoke the Moscow communiqué to denounce the continued presence of American forces in China, after the diplomatic justification for their continued stay, i.e., to assist in disarming and evacuating the Japanese troops, disappeared.

The Soviet government not only played a shrewd political game with incalculable long-term consequences, but also endeavored to extract as much immediate economic advantage as possible. From early September, the Soviet authorities began to carry out a policy of removing the newest, most valuable, and best industrial equipment in Manchuria. The direct damage done to the Manchurian economy was estimated by Edwin W. Pauley, the United States Reparations Commissioner, at $858 million, and the total cost of replacements to offset removals, destruction, and general deterioration was put at $2,000 million.[186] Not content with the removal of industrial assets, the Soviet government took steps to gain a share of control over what remained of heavy industry in Manchuria. On November 24, 1945, Slatekovsky, the economic adviser to Marshal Malinovsky, formally presented to Mr. Chang Chia-ngau, chairman of the Economic Commission of the Generalissimo's headquarters in Manchuria, a proposal for

---

[184] James Byrnes, *Speaking Frankly* (New York: Harper & Bros., 1947), pp. 226–27.
[185] *United States Relations with China*, p. 125.
[186] Edwin W. Pauley, *Report on Japanese Assets in Manchuria to the President of the United States, July, 1946*, p. 37.

joint Sino-Soviet operation of 80 per cent of the heavy industry in Manchuria. It is interesting to note that this proposal was made shortly after the Soviet authorities had given signs of being willing to render the Nationalist government some help in its attempts to take over Manchuria. Apparently, the Soviet government wanted, in addition to postponement of the withdrawal of Soviet forces a price in the economic field.[187]

This additional price the Chinese government was unwilling to pay. On December 4, Mr. Chang told Malinovsky that discussion on Sino-Soviet economic co-operation in Manchuria could begin only after the complete withdrawal of Soviet troops. Then the Soviet authorities advanced another argument for their proposal. On December 7, Slatekovsky informed Mr. Chang that all industrial enterprises in Manchuria should be regarded as "war booty" of the Soviet Union. The Chinese representative took sharp issue with this view. When February 3, the deadline for the complete withdrawal of Soviet forces, drew near, the Soviet Union sought to use the threat of delaying the withdrawal as a lever to exert pressure on the Chinese government. On January 16, Marshal Malinovsky warned Mr. Chang that he would not be able to predict the date of the withdrawal of Soviet troops until the question of economic co-operation had been settled. On January 21, the Soviet ambassador took up the question with the Chinese government through diplomatic channels.[188]

At this point, the American government took a stand on the matter. On February 7, it sent an identical note to the Chinese and Soviet governments. It informed both parties of the concern of the United States about the current discussions relating to the establishment of exclusive Sino-Soviet control over industrial enterprises in Manchuria. It expressed the view that any agreement to that effect would be contrary to the principle of the Open Door.[189] For Generalissimo Chiang, however, the Soviet demand posed a grave dilemma. On the one hand, he naturally was reluctant to relinquish control of important industrial enterprises to the Soviet Union. Furthermore, the Soviet demands and the Soviet plundering of Manchuria aroused widespread resentment in Nationalist China. This spontaneous feeling was exploited by the right wing C.C. clique to stir up violent anti-Soviet and anti-Chinese Communist emotions and to instigate student demonstrations in many major cities.[190] The strong public reaction which temporarily strengthened the political position of the Nationalists and embarrassed the Chinese Communists would have been dissipated if the Generalissimo had yielded to Soviet demands.

[187] Tung, "Pao-lu O-chün p'an-chü Tung-pei ti ching-kuo," loc. cit., p. 175.
[188] China Presents Her Case to the United Nations, pp. 21–28; Jones, Manchuria since 1931, pp. 227–31; Beloff, op. cit., pp. 38–41; Chang, op. cit., pp. 160–68.
[189] United States Relations with China, pp. 123–25, 596–97.
[190] Chang, op. cit., p. 168.

On the other hand, he was now anxious to see the Soviet troops withdrawn from Manchuria as soon as possible. Insofar as Manchuria was concerned his hand had been strengthened by the truce agreement signed on January 10, 1946, under General Marshall's auspices, between the Nationalist government and the Chinese Communists, which gave the government the right to move its forces into Manchuria. In establishing his authority in that region, the assistance or obstruction of the Soviet Union as her forces were being withdrawn would make the difference between success and failure. The Chinese representatives who dealt with the Soviet authorities in Manchuria had gained the impression that, if the Chinese government agreed to the Soviet demands, the Soviet government would not allow the Chinese Communists to play an open part in Manchuria, while permitting them to operate as a purely local force.[191] On the basis of this reasoning, Mr. Chang urged the Generalissimo to approve a list of ten to twenty jointly managed enterprises so that, to use the words of Mr. Chang's brother, "economic cooperation between Soviet Russia and China could be established to serve as a foundation for friendly relations between the two countries."[192] For many days, Generalissimo Chiang wavered between accepting and rejecting Soviet demands. Finally, after several rapid changes of mind, he countermanded at the last moment his earlier order for Mr. Chang to sign an agreement with the Soviet authorities.

While the Chinese government was parrying the Soviet economic demands, the Soviet government disregarded the deadline of February 3 and delayed the withdrawal of its troops under various pretexts such as weather, lack of fuel, etc.[193] As the deadline approached, the Chinese government made many inquiries about the withdrawal. But the Soviet government did not deign to send a formal reply until March 20. On this date, it notified the Chinese government that the withdrawal would be completed by the end of April.[194] Thus, the withdrawal was postponed once more, this time by unilateral action. Meanwhile, the Nationalist government found it increasingly difficult to obtain Soviet co-operation in its attempts to establish local governments in Manchuria. In March, the attitude of Soviet authorities became openly hostile. On March 6, a Chinese Communist newspaper in Changchun which had previously ceased publication on the order of Soviet authorities was again in circulation. Chinese Communist forces attacked and occupied many cities and districts in which Nationalist local governments had been set up with Soviet co-operation. When the Soviet forces began their withdrawal, Soviet authorities refused to disclose to Nationalist representatives the schedule of their withdrawal sufficiently

[191] *Ibid.*, p. 170.
[192] *Ibid.*, p. 168.
[193] Tung, "Pao-lu O-chün p'an-chü Tung-pei ti ching-kuo," *loc. cit.*, p. 166.
[194] Tsai, "Tung-pei ti p'an-chü yü chieh-lüeh," *loc. cit.*, pp. 144–45.

in advance to enable the Nationalist forces to make the necessary preparations. Having made it impossible for Nationalist forces to reach northern Manchuria in time, a high Soviet commander notified a Chinese representative on March 26, that "our [Soviet] troops stationed north of Changchun cannot await the arrival of Chinese Government troops before withdrawal, and that we [Soviet authorities] can only transfer our responsibilities to whatever existing military forces there are."[195] In this manner, the Chinese Communists were permitted to occupy all of Manchuria north of Changchun. After the Soviet forces withdrew from Changchun on April 14, Chinese Communist forces launched a large-scale attack on that city and after four days of fierce fighting, overwhelmed the Nationalist garrison.[196] The battle of Changchun re-ignited the civil war, ended the truce, and led eventually to the breakdown of the whole elaborate program worked out by General Marshall. By the time the Soviet forces completed their withdrawal on May 3, most, if not all, of the gains which had accrued to the Nationalists as the result of the agreement of December 5 were nullified.

The complexity of Soviet policy toward China as revealed in Soviet behavior. — From the above account, it is clear that the Soviet Union rendered invaluable aid to the Chinese Communists and obstructed Nationalist efforts to take over Manchuria. By early November, Soviet behavior had already repudiated Hurley's optimistic assumptions about Soviet intentions toward the Nationalist government and about the relations between the Soviet Union and the Chinese Communists. The basic source of Hurley's error was his failure to grasp the complexity of Soviet policy toward China and to distinguish its temporary manifestation from its essence. Reflecting the basic conflict of interests, both national and ideological, Soviet policy toward China was fundamentally one of hostility toward the Nationalists and support for the Communists. But three factors gave rise to the deceptive impression that Soviet policy was one of support for the Nationalists and indifference toward the Chinese Communists. The first appears to have been the Soviet overestimation of the political viability of the Nationalist government and a corresponding underestimation of the strength of the Chinese Communists. This Soviet calculation ruled out a policy of offensive intervention and of using the Chinese Communists as the chosen instrument to overthrow the Nationalist regime. It led Stalin to base his policy on the assumption that the Kuomintang would continue to be the dominant party and that the Nationalist government would have effective control over Manchuria and China in the near future. As a concession to reality as he saw it, he affirmed the leadership of Chiang Kai-shek in the united front in China and approved the idea of a coalition government as

---

[195] *China Presents Her Case to the United Nations*, p. 15; Tung, "Pao-lu O-chün p'anchü Tung-pei ti ching-kuo," *loc. cit.*, p. 174.
[196] *Ibid.*

a tactical move which, under the circumstances as he saw them, would most effectively serve the interests of the Soviet Union and provide the best opportunity for the Chinese Communists to expand their influence.

But the fundamental policy of hostility toward the Nationalists and support for the Communists found expression in Soviet obstructionism toward the Nationalists in Manchuria and the unobtrusive, but nevertheless effective, assistance given to the Chinese Communists. It was also revealed in Stalin's advice to Chiang to make more concessions toward meeting the Chinese Communists' demands.[197] The apparently contradictory and at the time perplexing behavior of the Soviet Union toward China represented an adjustment of her basic policy to the prevailing circumstances as viewed in Moscow.[198] As Moscow gradually realized the revolutionary potentiality of the Chinese Communists and the political weakness of the Kuomintang, it steadily moved, in the period between Japan's surrender and mid-autumn of 1946, from an outwardly ambiguous policy to a policy of open and firm support for the Chinese Communists.[199]

The second factor which affected Soviet policy was a readiness to arrive at an understanding or to make a deal with the government in power, which would serve the immediate national interest of the Soviet Union. Such a diplomatic deal inevitably entailed a measure of support for the Nationalist government which would strengthen it against the Chinese Communists. But the basic conflict of interests between the Soviet Union and Nationalist China rendered Soviet support for the Nationalists a strictly temporary affair. For in the long run, it was in the interest of the Soviet Union both as an expansionist power and as the center of international communism to have a weak Nationalist China as her neighbor. On the one hand, the weaker the Nationalist government and the more dependent it was upon Soviet support or at least, to use the apt phrase of a Chinese diplomat, "the absence of [Soviet] ill will" the easier it was for the Soviet Union to exact diplomatic concessions from it. The circumstances leading to the conclusion of the Sino-Soviet treaty, the Chinese acquiescence in the postponement of the withdrawal of Soviet troops, and the negotiations in 1949 for Chinese concessions in Sinkiang revealed this aspect of Sino-Soviet relations. On the other hand, when the Nationalist government felt strong enough, it would not hesitate to take measures impinging upon political and ideological interests of the Soviet Union in China. The reassertion of control over Sinkiang by the central government in 1942 and the Nationalist attempts to score a decisive victory over the Chinese Communists

[197] Chiang, *Soviet Russia in China*, p. 151.

[198] Cf. Beloff, *op. cit.*, p. 36; Charles P. Fitzgerald, *Revolution in China* (New York: Praeger, 1952), pp. 93–104; Robert C. North, *Moscow and Chinese Communists* (Stanford, Calif.: Stanford University Press, 1953), p. 222.

[199] McLane, *op. cit.*, chap. v.

immediately after the conclusion of the Sino-Soviet treaty of 1945 were cases in point.

The Soviet Union invariably moved away from a policy of "friendship" for the Nationalists as soon as a policy of supporting them or a diplomatic deal with them had served its purposes. In 1943 when the Soviet Union was gaining the upper hand in the European war and her fear of a Japanese attack lessened, there appeared unmistakable signs of a slight shift in Soviet policy. In that year, Soviet diplomats in China expressed to American officials unequivocal concern over reports of an impending Kuomintang attack on the Communists. By contrast, *Pravda* and *Izvestia* refrained from editorial comment on the New Fourth Army incident of January, 1941,[200] in which the Nationalist forces annihilated the headquarters contingent of the Communist New Fourth Army, killing its deputy commander and capturing its commander. Only shortly after she had wrung important diplomatic concessions from the Nationalist government in the Sino-Soviet treaty of 1945, she hindered the Nationalists in their efforts to re-establish their authority in Manchuria, aided the Chinese Communists there, and strengthened her contact with Yenan.

The third factor limiting the Soviet policy of support for the Communists and hostility toward the Nationalists seems to have been fear of American counteraction. Stalin's wartime profession of his readiness to follow the American lead in China, his expression of support for the Nationalist government, his disavowal of any interest in the Chinese Communists, and the unobtrusive way in which he helped the Chinese Communists in Manchuria — all seem to suggest the presence of this factor. He would push his policy as far as he could but always short of provoking active American intervention on the side of the Nationalists. Indeed, Molotov's attempts, at the Moscow conference of December, 1945, to link the withdrawal of American forces in China with the withdrawal of Soviet troops in Manchuria seems to indicate that Soviet policy at the moment was to prevent American military intervention on a large scale by holding out the possibility of Soviet counterintervention.

One could have understood the complexity of Soviet policy toward China only if one had perceived that this complexity arose out of the necessity for constantly balancing national against ideological interests, immediate against long-range considerations, temporary expediency against fundamental hostility, tactical objectives against strategic aims, the apparent strength of the Nationalists against the potentiality of the Communists, and, finally, Soviet capabilities against the uncertainty about America's intention to intervene. Hurley's naïveté and optimism prevented him from even beginning to tackle this complex problem.

[200] *Ibid.*, p. 149.

5. The Emergence of a New Policy and Hurley's Resignation

By November, 1945, events in China completely refuted two of the three major assumptions of Hurley's program: that a Soviet promise to support the Nationalist government would bring the Communists to terms and that the Soviet Union would support the Nationalists and refrain from aiding the Communists. They also called into question his third assumption, that the Soviet Union subscribed without qualification to the American policy of peaceful unification. Meanwhile, Washington was re-examining the policy in the light of the adverse developments in China for which it was totally unprepared. The precipitous end of the war caught the United States without a postwar program for military assistance in China. The airlift and transportation of Nationalist forces and the landing of American marines had been conceived and justified primarily as measures to effect the surrender of Japan and to wind up the war. It was only in September that the American government decided to complete the re-equipment of thirty-nine Chinese divisions and to enable the Nationalist government to recruit an American military advisory group to help it train its forces.[201] But this initial step toward assumption of greater commitments in postwar China was accompanied by the demobilization of American forces. As of V-J Day, American forces in China numbered approximately 60,000 men.[202] With the landing of 50,000 marines, the total reached 110,000. However, during September 16,000 American troops were returned to the United States. In October, tentative plans were made to begin the withdrawal of marines on November 15 and to deactivate the China theater.[203]

Political and military developments soon convinced American officials in Washington of the impracticality of abruptly terminating American military activities in China. The search for a new policy was given further impetus by the appraisals made by General Wedemeyer of the Chinese situation. On November 14, Wedemeyer told Washington that if Generalissimo Chiang should attempt to expand the area under his control, particularly to push into Manchuria, the marines would be needed indefinitely to hold the key areas in North China now occupied by them. The Chinese Communists, he explained, were fighting hard for North China; the Nationalist government was completely unprepared for occupation of Manchuria in the face of Communist opposition; and the Soviet occupation forces were facilitating the expansion of Communist control and were preventing the Nationalist government from establishing its authority in Manchuria. General Wedemeyer reported that he advised the Generalissimo to consolidate the areas south of the Great Wall and north of the

[201] Feis, *op. cit.*, pp. 368–73; *United States Relations with China*, pp. 338–39, 939.
[202] *Ibid.*, p. 338.
[203] Feis, *op. cit.*, pp. 373–76.

Yangtze and to secure the overland line of communication in North China before making an attempt to take over Manchuria.[204]

In another report, on November 20, General Wedemeyer touched upon the political aspects of the Chinese situation. He was by this time intensely conscious of Nationalist abuses and malpractices in taking over the areas under Japanese control and the consequent serious discontent among the people. He drew the following conclusions with respect to the prospects for Nationalist success in establishing authority in different regions in China. He thought that Generalissimo Chiang would be able to stabilize the situation in the Yangtze Valley and the area south of the Yangtze River, provided he accepted the assistance of foreign administrators and technicians and undertook political, economic, and social reforms through honest, competent civilian officials. As for North China, he expressed the belief that Chiang would be unable to re-establish his authority for months or perhaps even years unless there was a settlement with the Chinese Communists which appeared remote to him. He found it impossible to carry out his directive to avoid involvement in political strife or fraticidal warfare and recommended that either all American forces be removed from China or his directive be changed to justify their presence. As to Manchuria, he felt that occupation of that vital region would be beyond the capabilities of the Generalissimo unless satisfactory agreements were reached with the Soviet Union and the Chinese Communists. Thus, he recommended that a trusteeship over Manchuria by the United States, Great Britain, and Russia be established until such time as the Nationalist government could assume full control over the area — a recommendation which, with a change in terminology, he was to revive in 1947. In two succeeding reports, on November 23 and 26, he told Washington that it was impossible to unify China and Manchuria and to aid the Nationalists to repatriate Japanese forces without involving the American forces in civil war and without providing China with American forces and resources "far beyond those now available or contemplated."[205]

A new program was finally agreed upon in a cabinet meeting on November 27. It had two elements. First, it was decided to postpone the withdrawal of American marines in China and to make preparations for moving additional Chinese armies to the north by sea and for supporting them. A joint memo drawn up by the secretaries of war and navy and sent to the secretary of state on November 26, in preparation for the cabinet meeting, squarely faced the fact that American military assistance to the Nationalists to get the Japanese out of China would involve at least incidental aid to them in the civil war. Second, the American government was

---

[204] United States Relations with China, p. 131; Feis, op. cit., pp. 396–97.
[205] Ibid., pp. 399–402. United States Relations with China, p. 132.

to continue its efforts to bring about a political settlement in China and was to put pressure on Chiang Kai-shek to achieve this aim.[206]

The second element of this new program marked the culmination of a gradual shift toward a policy of conditional support for Chiang which paralleled the gradual erosion of Hurley's policy of obtaining a settlement on Nationalist terms. On September 14, President Truman had told T. V. Soong that the American postwar program for equipping a modern army was contingent upon the understanding that "military assistance furnished by the United States would not be diverted for use in fratricidal warfare or to support undemocratic administration."[207] On October 22, the Coordinating Committee of the State, War, and Navy Departments had adopted a report, stipulating that the United States discontinue her assistance to the development of Chinese armed forces if they "are being used in support of an administration not in conformity with the general policies of the United States, to engage in fraticidal war. . . ."[208] On returning to China from conferences with President Truman, Secretary Byrnes, and the Joint Chiefs of Staff, General Wedemeyer reported to Generalissimo Chiang the President's instructions to Wedemeyer that "the United States positively should not participate in China's military clashes nor could any facilities be furnished for the Central Government's actions against rebellious military elements within Chinese territory."[209] He also informed Chiang:

> They [the Joint Chiefs] declared plainly American military aid to China will cease immediately if evidence compels the United States government to believe that any Chinese troops receiving such aid are using it to support any government which the United States cannot accept, to conduct civil war, or for aggressive or coercive purposes. The degree to which China has obtained political stability and security under a unified government completely representative of the people will be regarded as a fundamental condition governing the United States economic, military, and other forms of assistance.[210]

Thus, the policy of conditional support crystallized into a decision to put pressure on Chiang to obtain a political settlement. This decision represented, in effect, a repudiation of the Hurley approach and a victory for the career officials in the State Department who foresaw the impossibility of getting a settlement on Chiang's terms. On November 27, Hurley resigned and issued a statement blaming the failure of his policy on the oppo-

---

[206] Feis, *op. cit.*, pp. 403–4.
[207] *United States Relations with China*, p. 939.
[208] Quoted by Feis, in *op. cit.*, p. 375.
[209] *Military Situation in the Far East*, p. 555.
[210] *Ibid.*

sition or sabotage of the career officials who, according to him, "sided with the Chinese Communist armed party."[211] In relinquishing his post, Hurley made the first official statement of the conspiracy theory of the China debacle, which was to blossom fully into a witch hunt in the era of McCarthyism. In contrast to this mistrust of his subordinates, Hurley retained complete faith in the intentions of Soviet leaders, despite the events in Manchuria. In his testimony on December 6, 1945, before the Senate Foreign Relations Committee, he made the following ringing declaration of faith:

> [P]lease distinguish between them [the Chinese Communists] and the Union of Soviet Socialist Republics, because they are different, and all of this Marshal Stalin and Commissar Molotov had been telling me, and throughout the entire period of vicissitudes through which we passed so far as I know they have kept their word to me, that, as I stated yesterday, Russia — and this is my own analysis; it is not a quotation — does not recognize the Chinese armed Communist Party as Communists at all. Russia is not supporting the Chinese Communist Party. Russia does not desire civil war in China. Russia does not desire the division of China and the setting up of two governments. Russia desires closer and more harmonious relations with China.
>
> Since these conversations with Mr. Molotov and Generalissimo Stalin, Russia has concluded with China the Sino-Soviet Pact and exchanged letters solemnizing every one of these agreements. I have read that the Soviet has transgressed certain matters that involve the territorial integrity and the independent sovereignty of China, but frankly I have no evidence that would convince me that that is true. I believe that the United States and Russia are still together on policy in China.[212]

Hurley's ambassadorship covered the most crucial period of Far Eastern affairs between Pearl Harbor and the Korean War. During this period, the Soviet Union re-emerged as a Far Eastern power, the Chinese Communists rapidly expanded their power and influence, Japan surrendered, and the struggle for power in China developed into a spreading civil war. When Hurley became the American ambassador, the Kuomintang made certain

[211] The text of Hurley's letter of resignation is printed in *United States Relations with China*, pp. 581–84.

[212] Quoted in *Military Situation in the Far East*, pp. 2894–95. Hurley remained of this opinion at least as late as January, 1946. At that time he told Charles Ross, press secretary for President Truman, that "there is no reason for Byrnes's agitation over Chinese-Russian relations because they are all spelled out in the agreement by the Chinese and Russians signed last July or August" and that "Stalin keeps his words" (Truman, *Years of Trial and Hope*, p. 66).

gestures toward reforms by appointing some of its better elements to high positions in the government, probably with a view to counteracting possible adverse American reaction to the Stilwell crisis. But when Hurley recommended Stilwell's recall, he also repudiated the tactics of pressure and thus failed to seize an unusual opportunity to press the Nationalists to undertake basic reforms. By the end of the period, the Nationalist government clearly showed that it was not capable of effectively taking over the occupied territory or of meeting the Communist challenge. Hurley began his efforts to bring the two Chinese parties together by formulating a set of principles which would have worked to the advantage of the Communists. But at a crucial juncture when the bargaining power of the Communists suffered a decline, he failed to use the influence of his country to bring about a transient political-military accommodation by defining America's position on the all-important matters of "details." His faith in the power of verbal agreement on general principles to control political actions served him poorly in China where the breakdown of the traditional order widened the gap between professed principles and the stark reality of politics. He did not accurately gauge either the discrepancy between the benevolent proclamations of the Nationalist government and its suicidal practices or the divergence between Communist propaganda and actual policies. He was correct in granting military supplies exclusively to the Nationalists and refusing them to the Communists. But the utility of aiding the Nationalists was vitiated by his failure to make American support conditional on fundamental reforms. After Japan's surrender, his optimistic views on Chinese political development and Soviet intentions did not facilitate the retention of America's military power in China. Throughout this crucial period, he was simply swept along by the turbulent political currents in China, without making the political influence of his country a powerful factor in guiding the events. By the time of his resignation, the bargaining power of the Chinese Communists was once again strengthened by internal developments in China and visible changes in Soviet policy. The task of resolving the China tangle which Hurley bequeathed to Marshall was consequently much more formidable than that which had confronted him.

PART THREE

THE LIMITS

OF A

POLICY OF

LIMITED

ASSISTANCE

CHAPTER IX

MARSHALL'S

CHINA POLICY:

INTELLECTUAL

PROCESS

AND

POLICY

DECISIONS

A. Civil Strife and Armed Intervention

In China, General George C. Marshall confronted a range of alternatives: armed intervention; provision of massive military assistance and operational advice to China; support for the Nationalist government short of armed intervention and without providing military assistance on such a scale as would, in his opinion, escalate into armed intervention; standing aloof from the military-political conflict between the Kuomintang and the Communists but granting economic aid to the recognized government; and finally, total withdrawal from China. Marshall did not choose to undertake armed intervention in China. His negative decision rested on the widely shared assumption that American interests in China were not worth a war. This estimate of American interests in China naturally reinforced other assumptions and considerations which predisposed the United States against armed intervention in the Chinese civil war. In turn, the decision against armed intervention shaped or controlled such crucial elements in Marshall's China policy as his efforts to effect a truce between the Kuomintang and the Chinese Communists, his program to bring about a coalition government, his decision to limit the activities of the United States Army Advisory Group, his rejection of General Wedemeyer's recommendations for an expanded program of military assistance, and his negative response to Ambassador John Leighton Stuart's suggestion that the American government advise Generalissimo Chiang to retire.

When Marshall's policy is thus seen as an integrated whole, the relative importance of the various assumptions and considerations in influencing policy decisions can be determined, and the various elements of his policy fall into their proper place. Such a reconstruction enables us to see clearly that all the characteristic ambiguities of America's traditional policy toward China persisted in Marshall's policy. The withdrawal of the United States from China between 1947 and 1949, following President Franklin D. Roosevelt's wartime policy of making China a great power, can then be understood as another phase of the cycles of advance and retreat of the United States in China. In short, Marshall's China policy was a continuation of the traditional policy of the United States and met the same fate that befell its precursor.[1]

1. The Structure of Ends and Means in Marshall's Policy

Soon after Ambassador Hurley abruptly resigned on November 27, 1945, and made public his letter of resignation,[2] President Truman appointed General Marshall as his special representative in China with the personal rank of ambassador.[3] The policy which Marshall was to implement was thoroughly discussed by him and top officials in the State Department. It was again reviewed by him and Secretary of State Byrnes in a meeting with President Truman and Admiral Leahy on December 11 [4] and was outlined in a group of papers, supplemented by an oral understanding. The papers consisted of a letter of instructions from President Truman to General Marshall and three attached documents: a document entitled "United States Policy toward China," a public statement by the President, and a memorandum from Secretary Byrnes to the War Department.[5]

[1] For an account of the cycles of advance and retreat from 1899 to 1937, see A. Whitney Griswold's classic work, *The Far Eastern Policy of the United States* (New York: Harcourt, Brace & Co., 1938).

[2] Chap. viii, above.

[3] Department of State, *United States Relations with China* (Washington, D.C.: Government Printing Office, 1949), p. 132 (hereafter cited as *United States Relations with China*). See also Harry Truman, *Years of Trial and Hope* (New York: Doubleday & Co., 1956), pp. 66–77. The name of General Marshall was suggested by Clinton Anderson, the secretary of agriculture, in a cabinet meeting on November 27 (Walter Millis, *The Forrestal Diaries* [New York: Viking Press, 1951], p. 113).

[4] Truman, *op. cit.*, p. 67; Herbert Feis, *The China Tangle* (Princeton, N.J.: Princeton University Press, 1953), pp. 413–15, 418–20.

[5] General Marshall's role in the writing of his directive and in the formulation of the China policy at this stage was, for a time, a subject of controversy. In the hearings on his nomination as secretary of defense, General Marshall told the Senate Committee on Armed Services on September 19, 1950: "While I was in this room for a week undergoing the Pearl Harbor investigation, the policy of the United States was being drawn up in the State Department, and that was issued when I was on the ocean, going over there" (Senate Committee on Armed Services, *Hearings on the Nomination of General George C. Marshall to be Secretary of Defense*, 81st Cong., 2d sess. [1950], p. 21). In the MacArthur hearings, Marshall, on May 10, 1951, gave a slightly more

The superficially simple program laid down in these papers and in the oral understanding actually comprised an elaborate structure of interrelated ends and means. The "long-range goal" of the United States was defined as "the development of a strong, united and democratic China."[6] This was a continuation of the policy adopted during the war; the words themselves had been popularized by General Hurley. The overriding short-term objective was to support the Nationalist government and to establish its authority, especially in Manchuria, as far as its military capabilities and limited American assistance would permit.[7] This intention found expression in the press release which declared that the United States recognized "the present National Government of the Republic of China as the only legal government in China" and as "the proper instrument to achieve the objective of a unified China."[8] The aim of establishing its authority as widely as possible was revealed in the following statement:

> The United States and the United Kingdom by the Cairo Declaration in 1943 and the Union of Soviet Socialist Republics by adhering to the Potsdam Declaration of last July and by the Sino-Soviet Treaty and Agreements of August 1945, are all committed

detailed account of the writing of the directive. It also minimized his own role and concluded with the statement that "my preparation for going to China was largely a matter in this room of the investigation regarding Pearl Harbor" (Senate Committee on Armed Service and Committee on Foreign Relations, *Hearings on the Military Situation in the Far East*, 82d Cong., 1st sess. [1951], p. 468. [hereafter cited as *Military Situation in the Far East*]). In the same hearings, Secretary of State Acheson gave a different version of the events relating to the preparation of the instructions. It shows that Marshall participated in the task from the beginning (*ibid.*, pp. 1848–49). Acheson's account was fully substantiated by Feis' meticulous narrative of that episode (Feis, op. cit., pp. 413–20).

In his attack on General Marshall, Senator Joseph McCarthy took full advantage of Marshall's erroneous testimony. See the speech made by McCarthy on the Senate floor on June 14, 1951 (*Congressional Record*, XCVII, 82d Cong., 1st sess. [1951], 6580). See also, Joseph McCarthy, *Story of General George C. Marshall* (1952). For a contemporary analysis see Norman Palmer, "Marshall's China Mission," *Current History*, September, 1951, pp. 145–46.

The letter of instructions, the memorandum from Secretary Byrnes to the War Department, and the press release can be found in *United States Relations with China*, pp. 605–9. The statement of policy was printed in Truman's memoirs (Truman, op. cit., pp. 68–71). The press release omitted several significant passages from the statement of policy.

[6] Memorandum from Secretary Byrnes to the War Department, December 9, 1945, *United States Relations with China*, p. 609.

[7] See pp. 352, 355, below. Testifying in the MacArthur hearings, Secretary of State Acheson stated that the American policy was "to give important assistance of all sorts to the Chinese Government and to assist in every way in the preservation of peace in China and the working out of the agreements which were so necessary to enable the Chinese Government to establish itself in those parts of China where it had been before and to get, for the first time, into areas of China where it never had been" (*Military Situation in the Far East*, p. 1842).

[8] Statement by President Truman on United States Policy toward China, December 15, 1945, *United States Relations with China*, p. 608.

to the liberation of China, including the return of Manchuria to
Chinese control.[9]

To achieve this objective, which was justified by the formulas regarding
the unification of China and the evacuation of Japanese troops still remaining in that country,[10] the American government adopted positive
measures, but these, as we shall see, were counterbalanced by the negative
decision that "United States support [for the Chinese government] will
not extend to United States military intervention to influence the course of
any Chinese internal strife"[11] and that "incidental effects of American assistance upon any dissident Chinese element should be avoided as far as
possible." [12] On the positive side, various types of military assistance were
provided to the Nationalist government. United States military and naval
forces were to be maintained in China for the time being [13] — a decision
which had been made in a cabinet meeting on November 27. General
Wedemeyer was instructed to "put into effect the arrangements to assist
the Chinese National Government in transporting Chinese troops to Manchurian ports, including the logistical support of such troops," and to perfect immediately "arrangements for transportation of Chinese troops into
north China."[14] It was also decided to establish a United States military
advisory group in China at the appropriate moment.[15]

At this time, the generally accepted view, shared by General Wedemeyer,
held that the extension of the authority of the Nationalist government into
Manchuria and North China would be impossible without either a political
settlement with the Chinese Communists or American military intervention.[16] Thus, the American government adopted measures designed to
achieve such a settlement. General Marshall was instructed "to persuade
the Chinese Government to call a national conference of representatives
of the major political elements to bring about the unification of China and,
concurrently, to effect a cessation of hostilities."[17] In the public statement

[9] *Ibid.*
[10] At the time of Marshall's arrival only some 200,000 out of approximately 3,000,000
Japanese troops and civilians had been returned to Japan (*ibid.*, p. 690).
[11] Statement by President Truman on United States Policy toward China, December 15, 1945. This was the press release, reprinted in *ibid.*, p. 608.
[12] "United States Policy toward China," reprinted in Harry Truman, *op. cit.*, p. 70.
The press release cited in n. 11 is a public version of this statement, with several important omissions.
[13] *Ibid.*, p. 71, and *United States Relations with China*, p. 608.
[14] Memorandum from Secretary Byrnes to the War Department, December 8, 1945,
ibid., p. 607.
[15] President Truman to General Marshall, December 15, 1945, *ibid.*, p. 606.
[16] For Wedemeyer's view, see *ibid.*, pp. 129–30; Feis, *op. cit.*, p. 402; see also chap.
viii, above.
[17] President Truman to General Marshall, December 15, 1945, *United States Relations with China*, p. 605.

of American policy, President Truman told the warring parties in China:
The Government of the United States believes it essential:

1. That a cessation of hostilities be arranged between the
armies of the National Government and the Chinese Communists
and other dissident Chinese armed forces for the purpose of
completing the return of all China to effective Chinese control,
including the immediate evacuation of the Japanese forces.

2. That a national conference of representatives of major political elements be arranged to develop an early solution to the
present internal strife — a solution which will bring about the
unification of China.[18]

It was in this choice of means to re-establish the authority of the Nationalist government that a basic conflict of policies developed between
the United States and Generalissimo Chiang Kai-shek. The strategy
adopted by the American government was to use the proposal of a broadly
representative government, including the Communists, as a bargaining
counter for gaining control over the Communist armies, and thus to check
Communist influence. President Truman in his public statement declared:

The United States is cognizant that the present National Government of China is a "one-party government" and believes that
peace, unity and democratic reform in China will be furthered
if the basis of this Government is broadened to include other
political elements in the country. . . .

The existence of autonomous armies such as that of the Communist army is inconsistent with, and actually makes impossible,
political unity in China. With the institution of a broadly representative government, autonomous armies should be eliminated
as such and all armed forces in China integrated effectively into
the Chinese National Army.[19]

Since the development of a united and democratic China was not only a
long-term goal but also a means to extend and strengthen the authority
of the Nationalist government, it became an immediate objective of American policy. As President Truman told General Marshall in his letter of
instructions, "Secretary Byrnes and I are both anxious that unification of
China by peaceful, democratic methods be achieved as soon as possible."[20]

In contrast, the strategy of the Generalissimo was, as subsequent events
suggested, to crush the Communists by force, or, at least, to drive them

[18] *Ibid.*, pp. 607–8.
[19] *Ibid.*, p. 608.
[20] *Ibid.*, p. 605.

out of the strategic regions and to reduce them by military means to a negligible factor. For the Nationalist leaders, the elimination of the Communists was a matter of utmost urgency. As Mr. Ch'ên Li-fu, the leader of the C.C. clique was reported to have said later, the Chinese Communists were like a "bad appendix that has to be removed to preserve life."[21]

The American government was aware of this conflict of views over methods of solving the problem of China. Speaking of the necessity of broadening the government to include all major political groups, Secretary of State Byrnes told the War Department:

> This problem is not an easy one. It requires tact and discretion, patience and restraint. It will not be solved by the Chinese themselves. To the extent that our influence is a factor, success will depend upon our capacity to exercise that influence in the light of shifting conditions in such a way as to encourage concessions by the Central Government, by the so-called Communists, and by the other factions.[22]

Thus, the United States government adopted a policy of conditioning large-scale support for the Nationalist government upon the cessation of hostilities and the achievement of unity. President Truman instructed General Marshall:

> In your conversations with Chiang Kai-shek and other Chinese leaders you are authorized to speak with the utmost frankness. Particularly, you may state, in connection with the Chinese desire for credits, technical assistance in the economic field, and military assistance (I have in mind the proposed United States military advisory group which I have approved in principle), that a China disunited and torn by civil strife could not be considered realistically as a proper place for American assistance along the lines enumerated.[23]

The American government further realized that the prospective American military assistance and the Nationalist hope for American intervention would embolden the Nationalist government to seek a military solution to the Communist problem. President Truman's press release specifically ruled out American military intervention.[24] The sentences in the statement of policy concerning the decisions to continue to furnish military supplies, to assist the Nationalists to re-establish control over the liberated areas, including Manchuria, and to set up an American military advisory group

[21] New York Times, July 22, 1946, p. 2.
[22] United States Relations with China, p. 606.
[23] Ibid., p. 606.
[24] Ibid., p. 608.

in China were omitted from the press release.[25] General Wedemeyer was told that pending the outcome of Marshall's discussions with Chinese leaders he was to hold in abeyance further transportation of Chinese troops to North China, except to such North China ports as might be needed for the movement of troops and supplies into Manchuria. He was also instructed that arrangements for transportation of Chinese troops into North China might be immediately perfected but not communicated to the Chinese government.[26] These precautions were also necessary in order to preserve the impartial position of the United States as mediator in the internal Chinese conflict.

The program adopted at this time exerted pressure on the Chinese Communists too, for they had to face the possibility that rejection of the American plan might bring the United States to intervene actively on the side of the Nationalists. As it turned out, however, American pressure on the Nationalist government was far stronger than that on the Communists, because the American program for peace and unity coincided with Communist demands of the moment. Furthermore, American unwillingness to undertake armed intervention in China set a narrow limit on the amount of pressure which the United States could exert on the Chinese Communists.

It cannot be too strongly emphasized that, these facts notwithstanding, the *overriding* objective of the United States was to support the Nationalist government and to establish its authority as far as possible. In the deliberations leading to the final adoption of the program, it was decided that, if the Generalissimo failed to make reasonable concessions to obtain a cease-fire and a political settlement, the United States would continue to support him "to the extent of assisting him to move his troops into North China in order that the evacuation of the Japanese might be completed." [27] This element of Marshall's program was agreed upon but not written into any of the official papers. The rationale behind this decision was stated by General Marshall in the following terms, according to the notes of a meeting on December 11:

> If the Generalissimo . . . failed to make reasonable concessions, and this resulted in the breakdown in the efforts to secure a political unification, and the United States abandoned continued support of the Generalissimo, there would follow the tragic consequences of a divided China and of a probable Russian reassumption of power in Manchuria, the combined effect of

[25] Compare the two statements respectively in Truman, *op. cit.*, pp. 68–71, and in *United States Relations with China*, pp. 607–9.

[26] *Ibid.*, p. 607.

[27] Notes by General Marshall on a meeting with the President, Byrnes, and Leahy, December 11, as quoted in Feis, *op. cit.*, p. 419, n. 15.

this resulting in the defeat or loss of the major purpose of our war in the Pacific.[28]

Marshall recognized that to continue to support Chiang under these circumstances the American government "would have to swallow its pride and much of its policy."[29] But in fact, it was this basic policy of supporting the Nationalist Chinese government, within what were judged to be the capabilities of the United States, which General Marshall endeavored to implement at the beginning of his mission to China and which, according to the State Department White Paper, governed American actions from 1946 to 1949. The establishment of a coalition government including the Communists was only a means to support the Chinese government, one element of a broad political program. To see this element as the over-all purpose of American policy, as the critics of Marshall frequently did, is a gross oversimplification.

Rather, the basic and controlling element in Marshall's policy was the decision against armed intervention and the related decision to refrain from action in China which might escalate into armed intervention. Despite the total collapse of the negotiations between the Kuomintang and the Chinese Communists in November, 1946; despite the rapid deterioration of the political and military position of the Nationalist government in the summer of 1947; and despite Marshall's recognition in February, 1948, of the possibility of an early defeat of the Nationalist government,[30] this decision was strictly adhered to. Nor was its modification effected by the formal repudiation in March, 1948, of the concept of a coalition government including the Communists; the Communist conquest of Manchuria and North China between November, 1948, and January, 1949; the retirement" of Generalissimo Chiang from the presidency in January, 1949; the imminent crossing of the Yangtze River by the Communist forces in April, 1949.

2. The Decision Not To Undertake Armed Intervention

In the complex events from 1945 to 1949, the decision not to undertake armed intervention in China was inextricably intertwined with other factors: first, a misjudgment of the nature and intentions of the Chinese Communist party; second, the incompetence of the Nationalist government and its obstinate resistance to American advice; and third, America's anxiety over the growing influence of communism in Europe and the intensification of disputes with the Soviet Union. There are indications that

[28] *Ibid.*
[29] *Ibid.*
[30] Marshall's testimony before the Committees on Foreign Relations and Foreign Affairs in executive session, *United States Relations with China*, p. 382.

in late 1945 the Chinese Communists were still judged by some high officials in the State Department to be something other than dedicated Communists. In Byrnes' memorandum of December 9, 1945, one of the three documents attached to President Truman's letter of instructions to General Marshall, the term "so-called Communists" was used.[31] But according to his own testimony, General Marshall had no illusions about the Chinese Communists, at least after his arrival in China.[32] Similarly, John Carter Vincent, the director of the Office of Far Eastern Affairs from 1945 to 1947, was, according to his own account, led by the difficulties confronting Marshall in his negotiations with the Chinese Communists to the "definite conclusion" that they were Communists and part of the international Communist movement guided by Russia.[33] Although in the early months of 1949 some American officials probably entertained the idea that Mao would become a Tito,[34] Secretary of State Dean Acheson, in his characterization of the Chinese Communists as a party serving the "interests of a foreign imperialism"[35] in the letter of transmittal in the White Paper, showed that he did not subscribe to this view. The idea of a Chinese Tito was a negligible factor in the decision against armed intervention.

In contrast to the rapidly diminishing influence of the initial misjudgment of Communist intentions, the incompetence of the Nationalist government and its resistance to American advice assumed increasing importance in strengthening America's decision not to intervene by armed force. No one knows to what extent the United States could have been effective in reforming the Nationalist regime, had she actively intervened in Chinese politics. But the fact remains that after the termination of the embargo on arms in May, 1947, the American government did not again resort to strong pressure or intervene actively in Chinese politics, apart from Ambassador John Leighton Stuart's gentle advice and personal activities. One reason for this omission was obviously General Marshall's opinion that no Chinese leader could replace Chiang[36] and that there was no alternative to supporting him within the reasonable limits of American

[31] Truman, *op. cit.*, p. 72, and *United States Relations with China*, p. 606.

[32] Testifying before the MacArthur hearings, Marshall declared: ". . . when . . . I got out to China and looked the ground over, from the very start, . . . there was no doubt that the leadership of this group [the Chinese Communist party] were Marxist Communists, and they so stated in my presence, and insisted, in my presence, that they were" (*Military Situation in the Far East*, p. 378; see also p. 379).

[33] Senate Committee on the Judiciary, *Hearings on the Institute of Pacific Relations*, 82d Cong., 1st and 2d sess. (1951–52), p. 1708 (hereafter cited as *Institute of Pacific Relations*).

[34] *New York Times*, February 14, 1949, p. 10; February 15, 1949, p. 12; February 18, 1949, p. 8; February 21, 1949, p. 5; April 24, 1949, Sec. 4, p. 3.

[35] *United States Relations with China*, pp. xvi–xvii.

[36] Pp. 385–87, below.

capability. But, as we shall see, another reason was American refusal to assume the moral and political commitment to do whatever was necessary to preserve the Nationalist regime in at least a part of China.[37] This commitment would have flowed from active intervention in Nationalist politics. But it would not have been compatible with the prior decision not to use American armed forces in China and the related decision not to give massive military assistance and operational advice in the field. Thus, the decision to refrain from armed intervention inhibited actions to make the Nationalist regime viable. In retrospect, it stands out as the fundamental decision governing China policy from 1945 to 1949.

The decision not to intervene with American armed forces in China stemmed also from considerations other than the misjudgment of Communist intentions and the perception of Nationalist failings. This is evidenced by the fact that such Republican critics of Marshall's policy as Senator William F. Knowland, Senator Owen Brewster, and Representative Walter H. Judd, who were bitter foes of the Chinese Communists and stalwart friends of the Nationalist government, nevertheless concurred in the decision not to use American ground forces in China for combat duties, or at least never publicly advocated such an action.[38] Thus, the decision not to undertake armed intervention must be examined in its own terms.

It should be remembered that events in China moved toward a climax during America's intensified struggle with the Soviet Union over the fate of Europe. Her concerns in Europe formed an increasingly significant element in America's decision against armed intervention in China. America's vital interests in Europe and the Mediterranean decreed that available resources should be devoted to these regions first. In the fifteen weeks of revolution in American foreign policy in 1947, the policy of containment was proclaimed, the program of aid to Greece and Turkey was enacted, and the general concepts of the European recovery plan were formulated. As the Soviet Union continued to push forward with the coup in Czechoslovakia and the Berlin blockade, the United States responded with the North Atlantic alliance and the airlift. These moves were undertaken at a time when the Chinese civil war was entering its decisive phase. Confronted with historic tasks in Europe and a hopeless situation in China, the administration steadfastly adhered to its decision against armed intervention and the related decision against any action which would degenerate into armed intervention. While its critics advocated granting increased military and economic assistance to China, none of them publicly proposed sending American ground forces to China. There was no basic conflict during 1945–49 between "internationalists" and "isolationists" over the

[37] Pp. 389–90, below.
[38] Pp. 363–64, below.

issue of armed intervention on the Chinese mainland. This phenomenal lack of disagreement on a basic issue obliges us to search for the deeper reasons for the decision to refrain from armed intervention which underlay the other elements of Marshall's policy.

3. The Basic Assumption behind American Policy

Armed intervention in civil strife usually involves heavy commitment of a nation's resources, entails a grave risk of counterintervention by a third power, and points only to an uncertain outcome. In the classic balance of power in eighteenth- and nineteenth-century Europe, intervention was admitted to be legitimate only insofar as it was intended to protect the security and vital interests of the intervening power.[39] For the independence and sovereignty of the nation-state were the cornerstones of the international system and non-interference in the internal affairs of another nation was a principle for preserving national independence and for maintaining the flexibility of alignment. The doctrine of non-intervention, however, did not apply to weak nations outside Europe. On the contrary, the powers interfered actively in the internal affairs of these weak nations and, not infrequently, turned them into dependent states or colonies.

By her principle of respecting the territorial and administrative integrity of China and its corollary of non-intervention in Chinese internal affairs, the United States sought to extend the application of the doctrine of non-interference to China. Meanwhile, Wilsonian idealism, the Good Neighbor policy, the Atlantic Charter, the Moscow Four-Power Declaration, and the United Nations Charter — all gave the doctrine of non-intervention the appearance of a self-sufficient and universal principle, seemingly dissociated from the multiple system of balance of power on which it was originally based.

This trend in American thinking was still strong at the end of the Pacific war when the multiple balance of power was being replaced by a bipolar system. Under the new system, each of the two superpowers was the center of a particular philosophy and way of life. The rigid alignment of

[39] Commenting on the principle of intervention in the classical system of balance of power, Lord Brougham, an early nineteenth-century statesman and writer, wrote: "Whenever a sudden and great change takes place in the internal structure of a state, dangerous in a high degree to all neighbors, they have a right to attempt, by hostile interference, the restoration of an order of things safe to themselves, or, at least, to counterbalance, by active aggression, the new force suddenly acquired.

"The right can only be deemed competent in cases of sudden and great aggrandizement, such as that of France in 1790; endangering the safety of the neighboring powers, so plainly as to make the consideration immaterial of the circumstances from whence the danger originated" (Lord Brougham, Works, VIII, 37–38, as quoted in Edward Vose Gulick's Europe's Classical Balance of Power [Ithaca, N.Y.: Cornell University Press, 1955], p. 63).

the two blocs and the ideological dimension of the conflict vitiated the
historic reasons for non-intervention under the multiple system. Thus,
while the long tradition of American thinking continued to restrain the
United States, changes in the international system and the theory and
practice of the Communist movement were placing a premium on intervention as a method in the world-wide struggle for power. More than ever,
non-intervention became a policy designed to hold the ring against possible intervention by a third power while indigenous forces favoring the
non-intervening nation maintained the upper hand in an internal conflict.

In any case and under any international system, the military and political risks involved in armed intervention can be justified and the commitments entailed can be successfully discharged only if the intervening
power has made a prior political decision that her security and vital interests, or at least essential interests, are at stake. Generally speaking, this
decision ought to be based upon long-term considerations reflecting geopolitical reality, which find expression in the historic policy of the nation.
Once a positive decision is arrived at, the feasibility of armed intervention
and its timing, limits, and methods can be determined by weighing
the factor of cost and the chances of success in the light of the estimate of
the interests at stake.

As we have noted, American policy toward China in the twentieth
century contained two contradictory elements: espousal of the principles
of the Open Door and refusal to go to war on behalf of China. America's
pronouncements gave the impression that she had very important stakes
in China. But her concrete actions up to 1941 had consistently been governed by a low estimate of her interests in China.[40] The acceptance of war
with Japan represented only a temporary resolution of the contradiction in
favor of the principle of upholding the integrity of China. The inconsistency
in the traditional policy persisted in the wartime policy of making China
a great power. This grandiose policy was in practice a political means to
keep China in the war. It was meant to be a substitute for America's military presence in the Far East after the war. It implied nothing more than
the circular notion that, to the extent China could become a great power,
America would have important interests in China; otherwise she would
not.[41] After the Stilwell crisis, American officials, including President
Roosevelt, entertained serious doubts that China would soon become a
great power.

Thus, after the Pacific war, the assumption that American interests in
China were not worth a war continued to govern American policy. It

[40] William L. Neumann, "Ambiguity and Ambivalence in Ideas of National Interest
in Asia" in Alexander DeConde (ed.), *Isolation and Security* (Durham, N.C.: Duke
University Press, 1957), pp. 133–58. See chap. i, above.
[41] See chap. ii, above.

found expression in the reluctance of the State Department to define the minimum American interests in China which would be defended by military power. On November 1, 1945, Secretary of War Patterson sent a memorandum to Secretary of State Byrnes requesting political guidance on the question: "What, if any, corollary involvement in *continental* affairs in the Far East do we foresee or accept?"[42] He wanted an answer to this question to determine what military plans must be made against unacceptable aggression in the Orient. Specifically, he suggested that "it would be most valuable to have a clear-cut statement of *minimum interests from which the United States will not retreat in the event of a clash of interests* in the Far East, particularly concerning *Manchuria, Inner Mongolia, North China and Korea.*"[43] The State Department returned a vague reply which plainly revealed its lack of a definite answer to this vital question. It read:

> As to your request for a statement of minimum interests from which the United States will not retreat in the event of a clash in interests in the Far East, the [War] Department might determine in advance the military steps to be taken against possible aggression in the Far East. Department's contribution to political guidance to the Armed Forces can best be made by consistent and close cooperation between the Departments concerned.[44]

[42] "The State Department's Answers to Questions contained in the Memorandum Dated November 1, 1945, from the Secretary of War to the Secretary of State," printed as Appendix XV in John C. Sparrow's *History of Personnel Demobilization* (Washington, D.C. Department of the Army, 1951), p. 493.

[43] *Ibid.* It is interesting to note that Captain H. E. Yarnell asked very similar questions in 1919 (Louis Morton, "War Plan ORANGE," *World Politics*, January, 1959, p. 225).

[44] Sparrow, *op. cit.*, p. 494. As early as 1946 some American officials approached the Chinese scene with the assumption that China could not be a strong ally against the Soviet Union. In a conference of experts on American foreign policy held at the University of Chicago in the late spring of 1946, Mr. Joseph C. Ballantine, who had resigned not long before from his position of special assistant to the secretary of state, assured one of the conferees who had expressed his skepticism of the worth of China as an ally: "I think we would be doing a marked disservice to China, not only to our relations with Russia, if we attempted to build her up as a sort of buffer against Russia. Not only do we have the Russian suspicions, but you have an expectation that cannot be realized. I don't think that anybody in the State Department has any such conception in its plans in connection with military aid to China" (Quincy Wright, *A Foreign Policy of the Unted States* [Chicago: University of Chicago Press, 1947], p. 160). True to the pattern of the traditional policy, the public pronouncements of American officials stressed the vital interests of the United States in China, although the crucial term, "vital interest," was used in contexts that rendered it virtually meaningless. In his statement of December 15, 1945, President Truman said, "It is thus in the most vital interest of the United States and all the United Nations that the people of China overlook no opportunity to adjust their internal differences promptly by means of peaceful negotiation" (*United States Relations with China*, p. 607). In a statement issued in March, 1946, Marshall referred to a "stable" government in China as being "vital" to the United States (*New York Times*, March 17, 1948, p. 26). Like the repeated invocation of the principles of the Open Door, this type of statement empha-

The basic assumption regarding American interests in China played a part in cultivating three considerations which in turn exercised discernible influence on policy decisions. The first was the military postulate that American ground forces should never be used on the mainland of China. The second was the existing military capability at particular times. Both the military postulate and the existing military capability reflected a low but unpublicized estimate of the interests at stake in China. The avowed objective, whether it was the integrity of China or the preservation of the Nationalist government, was beyond the reach of the United States. The third consideration concerned the policies and actions of other powers, who were fully conscious of their interests in China. Toward them, American policy represented merely belated and inadequate responses; and the action or non-action of a third power became too weighty a factor in shaping American decisions. Thus, Japanese aggression in China in the thirties led to war with Japan only after the political and military foundations of the Nationalist government had already been undermined. The lack of direct Soviet support for the Chinese Communists was regarded as an important reason for American abstention from direct military intervention.[45] When the total bankruptcy of American policy seemed imminent, the course of action followed up to that time was justified by pointing to the unimportance of China and by stressing the limits of American capability, which had been set in part by the low estimate of American stakes in China.

4. The Influence of a Military Postulate

In the years between 1946 and 1949, one important consideration governing American policies and actions was that American ground forces should never be used for combat duties on the mainland of China. Testifying in the MacArthur hearings on his thoughts in 1946, General Marshall stated that "I was not only skeptical, but alarmed at the possibilities of the ground involvements in connection with China."[46] The same postulate determined his policies in 1947 and 1948. As he testified in another context, "The real issue was how you would meet this situation without a tremendous commitment of this government on the land area in Asia."[47] The United States Army Advisory Group in China was under specific instruction not to assign its officers and enlisted men to combat units of the

sized the importance of a goal which could not be achieved by a policy based on official thinking. Their only effect was to increase the public's subsequent disappointment in the results of official policy and to magnify the political consequences of America's failure.

[45] Pp. 367–69, below.
[46] *Military Situation in the Far East*, p. 383.
[47] *Ibid.*, p. 465. Emphasis added.

Nationalist forces.[48] In his now famous report, made after a fact-finding mission to China in the summer of 1947, General Wedemeyer recommended a vast expansion of American military and economic aid to China. However, he rejected "active participation in operations by American personnel" as "contrary to current American policy."[49] The American supervision of Nationalist forces which General Wedemeyer envisaged was to be carried on "outside operational areas."[50]

Marshall's reluctance to use ground forces in combat duties on the Asiatic mainland reflected an almost universal feeling in the United States. In the deliberations leading to the enactment of the China Aid Act of 1948, Senator Arthur H. Vandenberg, chairman of the Senate Foreign Relations Committee, stated in his report to the Senate that the broad language of the bill "should not be interpreted to include the use of any of the armed forces of the United States for combat duties in China."[51] Even the most outspoken critics of the Marshall-Truman policy never proposed publicly the use of American ground forces in China for combat duties. In the debate leading to the adoption of the China Aid Act of 1948, Representative Walter H. Judd stated in the House: "Not for one moment has anyone contemplated sending a single combat soldier in. . . . So it is important to make clear when we speak of military aid . . . it is supplies, training and advice, nothing further."[52] In the hearings Mr. William C. Bullitt testified that "you would not send an American soldier except in an advisory status. I do not propose that American troops be sent to China."[53] In reply to the question put by Representative Mike Mansfield whether the sending of military aid might eventually lead to active military participation on the part of the United States, General Claire Chennault said that "there is that possibility, I believe, but I do not feel that it is very probable that that would occur."[54] In a debate on China policy in June, 1949, Senator Tom Connally, a staunch defender of the administration's policy, asked Senator Owen Brewster what he or other Senators would have done to save China and whether they would have sent an army into China. Senator Brewster answered, "I never proposed to send an army into China."[55] On the same occasion, Senator William K. Knowland stated without contradiction that "there has never been a proposal on the

---

[48] *Ibid.*, pp. 558–59.
[49] *United States Relations with China*, p. 811.
[50] *Ibid.*, p. 813.
[51] *Ibid.*, p. 388.
[52] *Congressional Record*, XCIV, 80th Cong., 2d sess. (1948), 3442.
[53] House Committee on Foreign Affairs, *Hearings on United States Foreign Policy for a Post-war Recovery Program*, 80th Cong., 2d sess. (1948), p. 1918 (hereafter cited as *Foreign Policy for a Post-war Recovery Program*).
[54] *Ibid.*, pp. 2222–23.
[55] *Congressional Record*, XCV, 81st Cong., 1st sess. (1949), 8296.

part of those who are critical of the policy we have pursued in the Far East to send an army to China. . . ."[56] General Marshall was right in his estimate that the Nationalists could not win the civil war without direct armed intervention on the part of the United States. He was probably also right in his judgment that providing massive military assistance and operational advice to Nationalist combat units would lead to full-scale intervention. Most of his critics, on the other hand, espoused the ambitious goal of saving China from communism but shrank, for reasons of their own, from publicly advocating the means which would have been indispensable to the achievement of their objective. They did not face squarely the probability that military assistance alone would not enable the Nationalists to defeat their foes.

As the situation in China rapidly deteriorated, this basic military postulate found an additional justification in the tremendous effort necessary to prevent a Communist triumph. It became, to some extent, a self-validating principle. When in December, 1948, the Chinese Communists were annihilating the main Nationalist forces north of the Yangtze and were making preparations to cross the river, Major General David Barr, head of the United States Military Advisory Group, reported to the Department of the Army that he "emphatically" would not recommend a policy of unlimited aid and the immediate employment of United States armed forces, which alone would enable the Nationalist government to maintain a foothold in South China.[57] In rejecting the proposal made by Senator Patrick McCarran to extend a loan of $1.5 billion to China, Secretary of State Dean Acheson wrote Senator Tom Connally, chairman of the Senate Committee on Foreign Relations, on March 15, 1949:

> To furnish the military means for bringing about a reversal of the present deterioration and for providing some prospect of successful military resistance would require the use of an unpredictably large American armed force in actual combat, a course of action which would represent direct United States involvement

[50] *Ibid.*, p. 8297. A possible exception to this generalization was General Wedemeyer, who made the following cryptic statements in the hearings leading to the China Aid Act of 1948: "I do not believe that military participation is necessary *at this time,* sir. I could not develop this subject intelligently for you in open session" (*Foreign Policy for a Post War Recovery Program,* p. 2070). Emphasis added.

In another context he said: "When one is talking about the expenditure of money to accomplish international objectives, one must think in terms of *blood* as well as treasure" (*ibid.*, p. 2068). Emphasis added.

In academic circles, there were advocates of direct military intervention. Professor David Rowe proposed such a policy as early as 1947 (*Institute of Pacific Relations,* pp. 3985–86).

[57] *United States Relations with China,* p. 336.

in China's fratricidal warfare and would be contrary to our traditional policy toward China and the interests of this country.[58]

5. The Factor of Existing Military Capabilities

The belief that it was contrary to the American interest to commit ground forces on the mainland of China should be understood against the background of the rapid demobilization after the Second World War. At the time of the surrender of Germany, the United States Army consisted of approximately 8,290,000 persons.[59] The estimates made by the War Department before Japan's capitulation envisaged the reduction of this mighty force to 2,500,000 men by July 1, 1946, with a figure of 900,000 for the Pacific. The plan for rapid demobilization did not satisfy Congress, nor did the current rate of discharging army personnel. General Marshall had to assure the congressmen in September, 1945, that the War Department was releasing the largest number of men from service as rapidly as possible and that there was "no relationship whatsoever between the rate of demobilization and any future plan of the Army."[60] By the end of 1945, when General Marshall set out on his ill-starred mission to China, the total strength of the army had been reduced to 4,228,936.[61] Although at one time in the second half of 1945 the American armed forces in China were at their peak strength of some 113,000 soldiers, sailors, and marines,[62] the estimate made by the War Department of the authorized strength of the entire Pacific region as of July 1, 1946, envisaged a reduction from 830,000 to less than half that number. Of these, six thousand were to be designated for service in China, and General Wedemeyer feared that reduction by discharges would reduce the available forces to barely three thousand men.[63] By June 30, 1946, when the sporadic fighting in Manchuria began to spread to various points in China proper[64] and when the Soviet press started to give attention and praise to the activities of the Chinese Communists and to express confidence in their potentialities,[65] the total strength of the United States Army had fallen to 1,889,690 men, which represented a decrease of 6,133,614 in a period of nine months since V-J Day.[66] By the

[58] *Ibid.*, p. 1053.
[59] Sparrow, *op. cit.*, p. 359.
[60] *Demobilization of the Army*, Senate Document No. 90, 79th Cong., 1st sess. (September 20, 1945), pp. 1–10.
[61] Sparrow, *op. cit.*, p. 360.
[62] Statement by President Truman on United States Policy toward China, December 18, 1946, *United States Relations with China*, p. 694.
[63] Feis, *op. cit.*, p. 423.
[64] *United States Relations with China*, pp. 170–71.
[65] Charles B. McLane, *Soviet Policy and the Chinese Communists* (New York: Columbia University Press, 1958), pp. 252–56.
[66] Sparrow, *op. cit.*, p. 360.

end of 1946, when General Marshall abandoned his efforts to bring about a political settlement in China, the United States with her world-wide responsibilities had an army of only 1,319,483 men, with 12,000 soldiers and marines in China.[67] On June 30, 1947, shortly before General Wedemeyer embarked on his fact-finding mission to China, the total strength was 989,664 of which the effective strength was only 925,163.[68] In February, 1948, when in Secretary of State Acheson's retrospective view the United States had the last chance to commit her armed forces to the struggle in China,[69] the actual size of the army and air force was 898,000 men, with 140,000 men deployed in the Far East.[70]

No one was more conscious than General Marshall of the limits imposed by military weakness on the policies of the United States. Recalling the fruitless fourth meeting of the Council of Foreign Ministers in Moscow in March and April, 1947, General Marshall told an audience in the Pentagon in November, 1950:

> I remember, when I was Secretary of State, I was being pressed constantly, particularly when in Moscow, by radio message after radio message to give the Russians hell. . . . When I got back I was getting the same appeal in relation to the Far East and China. At that time, my facilities for giving them hell — and I am a soldier and know something about the ability to give hell — was 1⅓ divisions over the entire United States. That is quite a proposition when you deal with somebody with over 260 and you have 1⅓rd. We had nothing in Alaska. We did not have enough to defend the air strip at Fairbanks. . . .[71]

With reference to the situation in China in 1947 and 1948, particularly in regard to General Wedemeyer's recommendations in September, 1947, that the United States extend large-scale military and economic assistance to the Nationalist government, General Marshall testified in the MacArthur hearings:

> There, the issue in my mind, as Secretary of State, was to what extent this Government could commit itself to a possible involve-

[67] Ibid., p. 352; United States Relations with China, p. 634. The number of marines and soldiers in China at the end of 1946 was twice as large as the estimate of 6,000 men to be stationed in China by July, 1946. This change was due to the need for the use of American marines and soldiers to supervise the truce and to keep open the lines of communication.

[68] Sparrow, op. cit., p. 360.

[69] Military Situation in the Far East, p. 1869.

[70] Millis, op. cit., p. 375.

[71] Remarks by the Secretary of Defense at the National Preparedness Orientation Conference, November 30, 1950, p. 15, as quoted in Sparrow, op. cit., p. 380.

ment of a very heavy nature in regard to operations in China it-self. . . .

We would have to make a very considerable initial contribu-tion, and we would be involved in the possibility of very exten-sive continuing responsibilities in a very large area.

At that time, our own military position was extraordinarily weak. I think I mentioned the other day that my recollection is . . . we had one and a third divisions in the entire United States.

As I recall General Wedemeyer's estimates, about 10,000 offi-cers and others would be necessary to oversee and direct those various operations.

In view of our general world situation, our own military weakness, and the global reaction to this situation, and my own knowledge out of that brief contact of mine in China, we could not afford to commit this government to such a procedure.

Therefore, I was not in agreement with undertaking that, nor were . . . the chiefs of staff.[72]

American weakness in conventional forces was not fully compensated by the atomic monopoly which the United States enjoyed. At least up to the time of the Berlin blockade, American officials had not resolved the question of how to turn atomic monopoly into diplomatic bargaining pow-er. This failure was forcefully pointed out by W. Phillips Davison: "The bomb was the only real power the United States had, but no one knew under what circumstances it could be used, or indeed whether it could be used at all."[73] But even if American officials had devoted serious thoughts to the problem of maximizing the political and military utility of the atomic bomb, the ultimate weapon would still have appeared to have no relevance to the civil strife in China. Thus, there was no discussion of its implications, or the lack of them, for the Chinese situation either in the published rec-ords concerning America's postwar policy or in Marshall's retrospective accounts.

6. The Soviet Policy of Non-intervention

In steadfastly adhering to a policy of refraining from direct military intervention in China, the United States was influenced at once by the Soviet policy of non-intervention and by the fear of Soviet counterinterven-tion. Direct military intervention on the part of the United States could be justified, in the American view, only by direct, overt Soviet intervention

[72] *Military Situation in the Far East*, pp. 465–66.
[73] W. Phillips Davison, *The Berlin Blockade* (Princeton, N.J.: Princeton University Press, 1958), p. 155.

or, at least, by large-scale Soviet assistance to the Chinese Communists. But the Chinese Communist armies had already been immensely strengthened by captured Japanese arms and ammunitions in Manchuria which the Soviet Union had allowed to fall into their hands. They had extended their control over the greater part of Manchuria, thanks to the subtle and inconspicuous help rendered by Soviet authorities and to Soviet maneuvers in obstructing Nationalist attempts to take over that region. Against American advice, Generalissimo Chiang moved his best forces deep into Manchuria when the Russian forces withdrew in the spring of 1946. In the fighting which followed, the Chinese Communists proved able to survive the Nationalist offensive in the first phase of the civil war and then to counterattack with increasing ferocity in the later phases. There was no need for the Soviet Union to intervene or to help them with supplies on a large scale. In adhering to the policy of non-intervention, the Soviet Union was following a policy of holding the ring for the Chinese Communists and of discouraging the United States from intervening on the side of the Nationalist government. She was confident of the ability of the Chinese Communists to fend for themselves.

As evidence of Soviet aid or intervention was lacking,[74] the United States found an additional reason for her reluctance to intervene with her armed forces. American officials had an intense fear that, confronted by the Soviet policy of non-intervention, the United States would be condemned by world opinion for her active intervention. Recounting his thoughts on the Chinese situation, General Marshall told a Round Table Conference held in October, 1949, to discuss China policy:

> When it came to Soviet assistance at all, I never could get my hands on it. . . . What did worry me more seriously than anything else was it seemed apparent to me that the Soviets were

[74] Marshall's testimony, *Military Situation in the Far East*, p. 543. See also report of Marshall's statement in the *New York Times*, January 12, 1947, p. 44; and reports of Ambassador John Leighton Stuart to Secretary Marshall, October 29, 1947, and December 16, 1948, in *United States Relations with China*, pp. 832, 895.

General Marshall made this point even more explicitly in an informal remark at a Round Table Conference, called in October, 1949, by the State Department to discuss China policy: "I had officers pretty much all over North China, along the Yangtze and Manchuria, and I always felt that the reports I got were far better than those the Generalissimo received. He was being fooled time and again because the fellow would defend himself, if he withdrew in an ignominious situation, he always made it a great battle with Russian tanks and Russian soldiers. The only thing they did not introduce was the Russian paratroops; they had everything else. I would find out from my people it was a patrol encounter and that went on all the time. Always I was trying to find out anything you could put your finger on that was authentic as to Soviet influence or Soviet help in all this; I never got anything except the influence of what I would call the spiritual or something akin to that" (Transcript of Round Table Discussion on American Policy toward China, as reprinted in *Institute of Pacific Relations*, pp. 1551–1682; the quotation appears on p. 1653).

leaning over backwards . . . in their attitude out there [in China]. . . . Well as far as I could see, what they were preparing themselves for was a case before the United Nations, where they could appear clean as the driven snow and we would have our hands muddied by every bit of propaganda they could put on it. I would probably be the particular lump of mud they would throw on it, and that worried me.[75]

Marshall's sensitive conscience played a part in the vital decision to terminate the China theater of operations and to reduce the strength of the marines in China. General Marshall wrote President Truman from China in February, 1946:

We must clear our hands out here as quickly as possible in order to avoid the Russian recriminations similar to those today regarding the British troops in Greece. I mean by this, we must terminate the "China Theatre of Operations" and in its place quickly develop the military advisory group. . . . Also in this connection, we must move all the Marines out of China but some reconnaissance and transportation and some housekeeping and local guard units.[76]

In explaining the differences between the Greek and Chinese situations, Secretary Marshall told the Committee on Foreign Affairs in February, 1948: "In Greece you have a force which is being supported, according to the report by the United Nations Commission, by bordering states. Now in China we have no concrete evidence that it is supported by Communists from the outside."[77]

7. The Fear of Soviet Counterintervention

The success of the Soviet Union's policy of non-intervention followed a classic pattern of *Realpolitik*. By inspiring a fear of her counterintervention, the Soviet Union managed to hold the ring for the Chinese Communists.[78] Apprehension of possible Soviet actions was intensified by the

[75] Transcript of Round Table Discussion, *ibid.*, p. 1654.

[76] Truman, *op. cit.*, p. 77.

[77] *Foreign Policy for a Post-war Recovery Program*, p. 1555. In explaining the active American policy in Greece, Marshall stated at the MacArthur hearings: "The situation in Greece, however, Senator, I think, was a little different from that in China, because of the proximity of the satellite states which were openly supporting this operation, which we knew were equipping it almost entirely, and which also were protecting these Communist forces, guerrilla forces, by permitting them to retreat across the border and be armed and re-equipped and returned to the fight" (*Military Situation in the Far East*, p. 557).

[78] For a discussion of non-intervention, see Martin Wight, *Power Politics* (London: Royal Institute of International Affairs, 1954), pp. 49–51.

geographic position of the Soviet Union and her posture of strength, despite the American atomic monopoly. When Assistant Secretary of War John J. McCloy returned from China and met with the secretaries of State, War, and Navy on November 6, 1945, he described the American dilemma in the following words: "The Kuomintang must have our support to be able to cope with the situation. If the Russians, however, decide to give active support to the Chinese Communists, then we are in a real mess." [79]

One of the main arguments which General Marshall used in his vain attempts to dissuade Generalissimo Chiang from trying to solve the Communist problem by military means was that the Chinese Communists "would be driven to seek and be dependent upon outside support such as Russian aid" and that the spread of the civil war would afford an ideal opportunity "for the U.S.S.R. to support the Chinese Communists, either openly or secretly." [80] As a soldier, General Marshall was intensely conscious of the strategic position of the Soviet Union. He reminded the Generalissimo that, if Russian aid were given to the Communists, their supply line would be much shorter than his own and much more secure from attack. [81]

There was another political reason for the fear of Soviet intervention in China. Since the United States was refusing to give the Soviet Union a share in the control of Japan, she was apprehensive that the Soviets might disturb the situation in China as a reaction to American policy in Japan. [82] American armed intervention in China or even the mere presence of American troops was thought likely to increase the danger of Soviet intervention.

While the decision not to use ground forces on the Chinese mainland and the rapid demobilization of America's once powerful army were self-imposed limitations, the possibility of Soviet counterintervention in combination with the political and military strength of the Chinese Communists set an external limit to American power and policy. Given a clear recognition of interests at stake, a solution of the problem of American policy toward China would have been to seek a strategic settlement. But the conscious search for a strategic settlement with the Soviet Union was not a predominant mode of thought immediately after the Pacific war. In any case, it presupposed a prior political decision that the United States had certain minimum interests in China important enough to be defended by her armed forces and that a line must be drawn somewhere in China to

[79] Memo of meeting, Byrnes, Patterson, Forrestal, McCloy, Matthews, and Gates, November 6, 1945, in Feis, *op. cit.*, p. 389.
[80] *United States Relations with China*, pp. 176, 189.
[81] Truman, *op. cit.*, p. 88.
[82] Feis, *op. cit.*, chap. xxxiv.

protect these interests. This prerequisite for positive action in China was the very opposite of the basic assumption behind American policy.[83]

Insofar as can be ascertained from published records, there was never a broad strategic plan to hold China or any part of it.[84] In his prepared statement on American policy toward China made at the MacArthur hearings, Secretary of State Dean Acheson outlined three alternatives open to the United States in 1945–46: "to pull out of China"; "to put into China unlimited resources and all necessary military power to try to defeat the Communists, remove the Japanese, and remove the Russians from Manchuria"; and, finally, "to give important assistance of all sorts to the Chinese Government and to assist in every way in the preservation of peace in China and the working out of the agreements [between the Kuomintang and the Chinese Communist party]."[85] Absent from this statement of alternatives was a program to work out, either explicitly and openly or implicitly and under the guise of a loose confederation, a boundary between American-Nationalist and Communist zones of influence which would have fully protected the minimum security interests of the United States and at the same time reflected the relative military and political strengths of the two sides.[86]

8. The Decision Not To Intervene and the Policy of Establishing a Coalition Government in China

General Marshall's program of establishing a coalition government including the Chinese Communists and of unifying the partisan armed forces into a national army was a continuation of the wartime policies of the United States, which Ambassador Clarence E. Gauss and General Patrick J. Hurley had endeavored to implement without success. Holding that the civil war in China could be settled by an elaborate set of formal agreements between the two sides, it assumed that the conflicts could then be confined within a democratic, constitutional framework.[87] But Marshall's postwar program of seeking a political settlement between the Kuomintang and the Chinese Communist party was intimately and explicitly related to the decision not to intervene by the use of American forces. It rested upon the correct military estimate that, without direct American military intervention on a large scale, the Nationalist attempt to suppress the Communists by military means "might end in the collapse of the Government" and "would probably lead to Communist control in China," as

[83] See pp. 359–62, above.
[84] *Military Situation in the Far East*, p. 2759.
[85] Ibid., p. 1842, see also *United States Relations with China*, p. x.
[86] For a perceptive contemporary view, see Paul M. A. Linebarger, "The Complex Problem of China," *Yale Review*, Spring, 1947, p. 513.
[87] For the sources of this erroneous assumption, see chap. vi, above.

General Marshall repeatedly warned Generalissimo Chiang in 1946.[88] Or, to use Secretary of State Acheson's succinct statement, "There was not available force in China to settle these problems by force and therefore you have to resort to negotiations."[89]

It was the hope of some American officials that the political-military settlement sponsored by General Marshall would curb the growing power of the Communist party. As the White Paper on China stressed, the political and military agreements signed by the Kuomintang and the Chinese Communist party during the first three months of the Marshall mission "recognized the preponderant strength of the Kuomintang position in the National Government." [90] In the hearings on the Institute of Pacific Relations, John Carter Vincent, who had played an important role in formulating policy, explained his thoughts in 1945 and 1946: "My concept was that the Communists would come into the Government on a minority basis and that . . . through support of the Chiang Kai-shek government . . . [and] with help from us we could eventually strengthen the Chinese government enough to eliminate the Communists."[91] In other words, the tactic was one of "taking the Communists in in more ways than one by bringing them into a government on a minority basis." [92] At this time, the Communist parties in France and Italy were participating in their governments on a minority basis, and they were later successfully ousted. Responsible American officials may have been influenced at the time by the analogy with the French or Italian situations. Certainly, some tried to justify the Marshall mission by pointing at this parallel. As President Truman wrote in his memoirs, "There was no reason why the Nationalist Government could not be successful in this struggle, as non-Communist governments had been in Europe, if it attended to the fundamental needs of the people." [93]

But this superficially attractive program suffered from a serious flaw. Given the political weakness of the Nationalist government and the popular support enjoyed by the Communists, the political and military settlement between the Nationalist government and the Communists which was indorsed by Marshall might well have worked out to the over-all advantage of the Chinese Communist party, rather than the Kuomintang. The provision for the popular election of the provincial governors and the principle

[88] *United States Relations with China*, p. 176; see also pp. 173–74.
[89] *Military Situation in the Far East*, p. 1897.
[90] *United States Relations with China*, p. 143.
[91] *Institute of Pacific Relations*, p. 1714.
[92] *Ibid.*, pp. 1713–1714. Vincent testified that this idea of "taking the Communists in in more ways ways than one" dated back to a report written by him in 1942, when he was the counselor at the American embassy in Chungking.
[93] Truman, *op. cit.*, p. 90. Mr. Vincent also alluded to this parallel in his testimony before the McCarran Committee (*Institute of Pacific Relations*, p. 1714).

of "a fair distribution of power" between the central government and the provinces as "the highest unit of self-government" [94] would certainly have given the Chinese Communists actual control over several of the most important provinces in North China, Manchuria, and Inner Mongolia. In this respect, the provision for popular election of provincial and local officials would have given the Communists a much greater advantage than their own proposal made in the summer of 1945 for actual control over a specific number of provinces. From the provinces which they would have controlled through elections, the Chinese Communists could have reached out to capture the central government, utilizing the political advantage given them by their participation in a coalition government in the transitional period and the freedom for propaganda and organizational activities granted them under the proposed constitutional principles. The importance which the Communists attached to control over local governments, to their participation in a coalition government, and to the political settlement in general was demonstrated time and again in the controversies leading to the final breakdown of the truce. The political advantages which the political program would have given to the Communists might not have been offset by the military advantages conferred on the Nationalists by the military agreement which was arrived at with Marshall's advice.[95]

General Marshall himself recognized this possibility in his subsequent account of his mission. In explaining what he termed the Communist anxiety to go through with the political agreement, he stated in October, 1949:

> They [the Chinese Communists] undoubtedly felt they could win politically and therefore, if they could avoid the military effort, they were very much better off politically, because they had discipline and indoctrination and they had a solid party; whereas they felt the Kuomintang was just an icing on the top and all its foundations of public support had become almost non-existent . . . so if they could ever get the thing in the political arena they would win, and . . . it would not have been so hard but a rather easy thing for the Communists to dominate the government.[96]

According to Secretary of Navy Forrestal, General Marshall himself also admitted in July, 1946, that the truce of January, 1946, which he had succeeded in obtaining as a preliminary to a general settlement, "had worked out to some extent in favor of the Communists."[97]

[94] Resolution on the Draft Constitution Adopted by the Political Consultation Conference, January, 1946 (*United States Relations with China*, p. 621).
[95] *Ibid.*, pp. 161, 164–66, 168–69, 175–76. For details, see p. 410, below.
[96] *Institute of Pacific Relations*, p. 1656.
[97] Millis, *op. cit.*, p. 174.

B. The United States and Power Relations in Nationalist China

The political and military settlement which some American officials thought would curb the influence of the Communists might have strengthened them unless the unpopular economic and political policies of the Nationalist government had been changed and the Kuomintang rejuvenated, or unless new political forces had been brought into being. In the light of the dynamism of the Chinese Communist party and the weakness of the Kuomintang and other political groups, one is tempted to suggest that the Chinese Communists might even have won in a contest with a reformed Kuomintang and the liberal forces unless the latter had been aided by American economic and military assistance on a large scale, not excluding direct armed intervention. But a new political force could have brought into existence a Chinese government which could have effectively used American aid and which would have given the United States a fair chance of holding a line somewhere in China by direct military intervention.

To bring about these political changes it was necessary to put the greatest possible pressure on the leadership of the Nationalist government. If direct pressure failed to bring about the desired reforms, it was then necessary to effect a change in that leadership, curbing or destroying the influence of some of the groups in control and building up the power of others. Undoubtedly General Marshall saw the urgent need for some fundamental changes in the policies and composition of the Chinese government. Testifying in the MacArthur hearings, General Marshall said:

> And the hope in the matter so far as I saw it was that other parties — the Young China Party, Democratic League and so on . . . and the non-party group could coalesce and the Generalissimo back them, and they would be a group which I would think [sic] have drawn strength from both the other parties, those that were outraged at the character of the operations of the Nationalist Party in its lower echelons, and those that had gone into the Communist Party, who were not real Communists . . . but they were violently antagonistic to the present regime of the Nationalist Government. And it looked as though there would be enough drawn from those groups, together with what existed in the way of an independent group, which was a very small group, to hold the balance of power between the two, along-side of the evident factor to me and to my associates that the Kuomintang Government was utterly incapable of suppressing the Communists by military means.[98]

[98] *Military Situation in the Far East,* p. 638.

The general principle underlying Marshall's remarks, as distinguished from his specific program, was entirely valid. To bring about a change in the balance of force among various political elements in Nationalist China was not only imperative but feasible. Given the rapid disintegration of the Nationalist regime and the Nationalists' dependence on the United States for survival, it would not have been impossible for the United States to bring about drastic changes in the composition and policies of the government if she had adopted a positive program for China and if American officials had been experienced in the art of political maneuver.

1. The United States and the Third Force

Unfortunately, the specific program adopted by General Marshall had several serious flaws both in conception and in execution. His hope that the influence of the small parties and non-party groups would increase depended on his success in achieving a political settlement between the Kuomintang and the Chinese Communist party, under which the liberal groups would become holders of the balance of power. By persisting in his scheme to suppress the Communists at this time, Generalissimo Chiang, intentionally or otherwise, also dealt a fatal blow to Marshall's plan to strengthen the small parties and non-party groups.

Moreover, while General Marshall realized the importance of exerting strong pressure on the Nationalist government to change its policies,[99] American influence and power were, during the larger part of Marshall's mission to China, dissipated in his attempts to seek a settlement on terms which the Kuomintang could not have accepted and which, if implemented, might have benefited the Communists. Little was done at this time to bolster the position of the small parties and other political groups and to curb the arbitrary power of the reactionary groups. Marshall was most careful to avoid partiality toward any group.[100] It was during his mission that two of the most prominent leaders of the Democratic League were assassinated and other liberal leaders were forced to seek asylum in the American consulate in Kunming. It was only after his mission to bring about a political settlement had failed that General Marshall attempted to persuade the small parties and groups to unite and form "a single liberal patriotic organization." [101] He also endeavored to use his influence to bolster the political position of these groups by his informal talks with govern-

---

[99] *United States Relations with China*, pp. 186, 226.

[100] Letter from Professor Knight Biggerstaff, August 31, 1962. For perceptive comments on this failure to support the liberal groups, see John K. Fairbank, "Our Chances in China," *Atlantic*, September, 1946, pp. 37–42; "China's Prospect and United States Policy," *Far Eastern Survey*, July 2, 1947, p. 148; "Can We Compete in China?" *Far Eastern Survey*, May 19, 1948, p. 117; "Toward a Dynamic Far Eastern Policy," *Far Eastern Survey*, September 7, 1949, p. 210.

[101] *United States Relations with China*, pp. 213–14.

ment leaders and his public statement of January 7, 1947, which was issued after his departure from China.[102]

But by this time the small parties and political groups were already badly divided between those who refused to participate in a government dominated by the Kuomintang and those who would enter the government to obtain a nominal share of power and prestige. The former group, oppressed and persecuted by the Nationalist government, had already come increasingly under the influence of the Chinese Communists. The latter group, which, generally speaking, consisted of less capable and influential men, failed to play the role envisaged by Marshall. A program to build up a third force might have had a better chance for success if it had been vigorously implemented at the very beginning of the Marshall mission.

2. The United States and the Various Factions in the Kuomintang

Unlike the Chinese Communist party, the Kuomintang had never been a monolithic organization. Divided into sharply antagonistic factions, it was rent by constantly changing alignments among them. The Generalissimo himself had captured and then retained control over the party by building up the military and political power of a personal following. The Whampoa clique was the personal, military instrument with which he undercut the power of his potential rivals — such men as Generals Li Tsung-jên, Pai Ch'ung-hsi, and Fu Tso-yi — even at the cost of dissipating the over-all strength of the Kuomintang vis-à-vis the Communists. In the political field, the extreme right wing C.C. clique was his principal pillar of strength. Various other groups in the Kuomintang — the Political Science group, the "elder statesmen," and the followers of Sun Fo — served the Generalissimo with varying degrees of loyalty and enthusiasm. But there was a constant struggle for power and maneuvering for position among all these groups, a state of affairs that did not totally displease the Generalissimo, for even among his personal following he maintained control by balancing one faction against another.

Since the Whampoa group and the C.C. clique were factions in control, respectively, of the army and the party, they were the strongest opponents of the changes in government and policies which General Marshall deemed essential to the survival of the Nationalist regime. Yet, with minor exceptions, American equipment and supplies went to the armies commanded by the Whampoa generals and thus, unintentionally, strengthened them vis-à-vis the other military leaders in the Kuomintang. In spite of their better equipment, the armies commanded by Chiang's lieutenants did not, however, distinguish themselves in either the Sino-Japanese War or the

[102] *Ibid.*, pp. 215–18, 686–89.

Chinese civil war, with the exception of the first few months in both cases. In contrast, the provincial armies, poorly equipped but placed in desperate positions where they had to fight for their own survival, frequently gave good accounts of themselves. In the political field, the C.C. clique was just as ineffective in its fight against the Communists. While few Chinese were more fervently anti-Communist than the leaders of the C.C. clique, their narrow intellectual outlook and their determination to monopolize political power led them to pursue restrictive and repressive policies which drove the liberals and intellectuals into the arms of the Communists. While engaging in a life-and-death struggle with the Communists, they were also preoccupied with checking the power of other factions within the Kuomintang. Their tactics played into the hands of the Chinese Communists.[103] The C.C. clique and the Whampoa faction were thus the main obstacles to the pursuit of an effective American policy in China. The success of General Marshall's program to change the composition and policies of the Chinese government hinged upon curbing the power of both groups, remaking them into useful elements in a broad anti-Communist coalition, if possible, and eliminating their most reactionary leaders, if necessary. This was clearly recognized by Marshall. In conversations with several high-ranking government officials shortly before his departure from China, he stressed "the necessity of removing the dominant military clique and the reactionaries from the Government structure" and of creating "an opportunity for the better elements in China to rise to the top." [104]

In late 1946 and the early part of 1947, American actions had the effect of exerting pressure on the Nationalist government to curb the power of the reactionary groups, particularly the C.C. clique, and to strengthen the other groups. In his statement of January 7, 1947, announcing the failure of his mission, General Marshall denounced "a dominant group of reactionaries" in the Kuomintang as severely as he condemned the Communists.[105] In his numerous dispatches, Ambassador Stuart showed that

[103] To cite one specific example, the C.C. clique organized in May, 1947, a series of student demonstrations and strikes to discredit the government which, partly as a result of American pressure, was then under the nominal leadership of the Political Science group. It hoped that the disorders would provide the justification for the establishment of "a strong-arm, right wing government" either through a coup d'état or through winning the elections to be held in the coming autumn (ibid., p. 730). But the leadership in the disturbance organized by the C.C. clique soon passed into the hands of the Democratic League and the Communists. In reporting this incident, Ambassador Stuart commented: "This development [in student agitation] can hardly be displeasing to the CC-CC[sic] clique, which can now claim that lack of public order is attributable to their enemies. Just how much of the agitation is now under Communist leadership is debatable, but it must be assumed that the Communists are present and, if not already active, are prepared to exploit the situation should it become necessary or desirable" (ibid.).

[104] Ibid., p. 218.
[105] Ibid., pp. 687–88.

he was clearly aware of the destructive influence of the C.C. clique. Against the background of the embargo on arms and ammunition, the American "wait-and-see" policy followed by General Marshall in early 1947 militated against the reactionary group and bolstered, to some extent, the influence of the liberal groups. But for several reasons American actions and policies in this direction were too hesitant to be decisive and their effects sometimes neutralized each other. The reactionary groups dominated the Kuomintang long enough to bring about the downfall of the Nationalist regime; and the other factions did not gain sufficient power soon enough to enable them to combine with the liberal groups outside the Kuomintang into a new, effective political force.

3. The American Desire To Introduce Western Institutions to China

American officials in their desire to introduce Western institutions to China did not realize, first, that these Western institutions might have no application at all in China, at least for some time to come; second, that the intended effects of an institutional change might easily be nullified by adroit political maneuvers and other factors; and third, that an institutional change, desirable in itself, might have the consequence of weakening the groups which the United States intended to help. An illustration of the first point is General Marshall's attempt to establish the principle of civil control of the military or at least to check the further development of the domination of civilian authorities by the military. He proposed the setting up of a system of basic military training in China south of the Yangtze River and worked out an arrangement under which he hoped "it would be done in such a manner [that] it would not revitalize the military control of the civil authority." [106] No matter how anxiously the Generalissimo and other Nationalists wanted a system of basic military training to strengthen their own armed forces, the adoption of the system proposed by General Marshall would have gravely weakened, if not destroyed, the basis of their power. In China, the realistic alternatives open to the United States were not civilian control of the military on the one hand or military domination of civil authorities on the other. Rather, the choice was between the continuation in power of a group of generals, including the Generalissimo, who had proved unable to co-operate effectively with the American government, and another group of generals who could probably have acted in concert with the United States and who had showed a greater willingness to work with the liberals, intellectuals, and civilian administrators in China. Naturally, General Marshall's plan came to nothing.[107]

[106] *Military Situation in the Far East*, p. 698.
[107] *Ibid.*

To illustrate the nullification of the intended effects of an institutional change by adroit maneuvers, the following example can be cited. There began in June, 1946, a major military reorganization in China, made partly as a gesture to demonstrate the government's willingness to undertake administrative reforms and partly in pursuance of the resolutions of the Political Consultative Conference of all Chinese political parties and groups — a conference which was held soon after General Marshall arrived in China and which had his blessing. A major objective of those who advocated the change was to establish the principle of civilian supremacy over the military and to enable the other political groups and parties to control the Whampoa clique through the civilian authorities. The military reorganization involved the abolition of the National Military Affairs Commission which had existed outside the Executive Yüan, the highest civilian administrative organ. In its place, a Ministry of Defense was established under the Executive Yüan. The detailed structure of the new ministry closely followed the American concept of unity of control and the organizational pattern of the United States Department of War. Superficially it was based upon American advice.[108] It had the approval of American officials.[109] But in one crucial aspect it departed from American practice: the chief of staff was empowered to ignore or even counteract the directions of the minister of defense.[110] With an eye to American opinion, General Pai Ch'ung-hsi, a leading member of the Kwangsi group and reputedly the best strategist of China, was appointed minister of defense. But General Ch'ên Chêng, a ranking member of the Whampoa clique, was appointed chief of staff. While the chief of staff had direct access to the President — Generalissimo Chiang himself — the new minister of defense had to act through the Executive Yüan. Thus, the hope of establishing civilian control over the military and of promoting the influence of General Pai was largely frustrated.

Sometimes the institutional reforms suggested by American officials had the unintended effect of strengthening the reactionary group whose influence they hoped to curb. After his failure to bring about a political settle-

[108] Ch'ien Tuan-sheng, "The Role of the Military in the Chinese Government," *Pacific Affairs*, September, 1948, p. 249.

[109] During his mission in China, General Wedemeyer told a meeting of the top officials of the Nationalist government: "There must be a streamlined organization and clear-cut enunciation in [sic] the duties of all the ministries and bureaus of the government. April a year ago I discovered that there were over 60 sections in the National Military Council with duplicating functions and conflicting authorities. There was little coordination between the various groups or sections. Actually there were some groups within the National Military Council that were handling matters which had nothing whatsoever to do with national defense matters. Today in the Ministry of Defense we have grouped 60 sections under 6 general heads and reduced the personnel about 50 per cent" (*United States Relations with China*, p. 760).

[110] F. F. Liu, *A Military History of Modern China, 1924–1949* (Princeton, N.J.: Princeton University Press, 1956), p. 231.

ment between the Kuomintang and the Chinese Communist party, General Marshall made a strong effort to persuade the Kuomintang to terminate its one-party rule and to inaugurate a constitutional regime. In the period of political tutelage, the Kuomintang was financed openly and directly from the treasury of the government. The group in control of the party machinery, the extreme right-wing C.C. clique, whose members in general showed no special competence in financial affairs, obtained a relatively small share in the control of the monopolistic and semi-monopolistic economic enterprises of the government. The prospective termination of political tutelage raised the grave problem of financing the hypertrophied party organization and its numerous activities. The only solution was for the C.C. clique to gain control of certain of these economic operations and to venture into commercial and economic activities with an initial capitalization from the treasury or through purchase of government-owned enterprises at a low price.[111]

This expansion of the influence of the C.C. clique into the economic and financial field tended to strengthen its position at the expense of the Political Science group, which the United States sought to help. As Ambassador Stuart reported to Secretary Marshall on April 5, 1947, on the result of the Third Plenary Session of the Kuomintang Central Executive Committee:

> The Chen brothers [leaders of the C.C. clique] are now attempting to insert themselves into the economic field and . . . Chen Li-fu desires to become vice-Chairman of the National Economic Council. . . . [The Political Science group] failed in its objectives to consolidate its hold in financial affairs because the C.C. clique was successful in gaining leadership of the Central Trust. . . . Wong Wen-hao [a leading member of the Political Science group] has said if Chen Li-fu did become vice-Chairman of the National Economic Council, it would be impossible for him, and perhaps others around him, to continue on the Council. . . . On balance, it would appear that the struggle will be continued between the liberals who will control most of the high government positions and have a major interest in the economic world and the C.C. clique largely controlling the Party organization and an influential section of the army, and attempting to inject itself into finance.[112]

The conclusion reached by Ambassador Stuart was that "in the struggle between factions . . . the C.C. clique seems to have emerged in a stronger

[111] Richard E. Lauterbach, *Danger from the East* (New York: Harper & Bros., 1947), p. 357.
[112] *United States Relations with China*, pp. 735–36.

position, to the detriment of other factions."[113] The expansion of the C.C. clique into the financial and economic field had far-reaching consequences, for it weakened confidence in the government among commercial and banking groups,[114] whose active support was a necessary condition for the survival of any non-Communist government in China. This development completed the monopolistic and semi-monopolistic hold of the members of the Kuomintang on the economic life of the country. It gave color to the Communist charge that China was under the merciless and exploitative control of four big families: Chiang, Soong, Kung, and Ch'ên.[115]

Another example of the unintended effect of a new institution was the strengthening of the C.C. group by the pending elections in connection with the inauguration of the constitutional regime. The C.C. group was by far the most disciplined faction in the Kuomintang. By its control over the appointment of magistrates in the hsien, the basic unit of local government in China, and by its domination of the party organization reaching still further down, the C.C. group was the only faction in the Kuomintang which could get out the vote and manipulate the electoral machinery throughout Nationalist China, particularly in the rural areas. Thus, it was not accidental that, as Ambassador Stuart reported on April 5, 1947, "the C.C. clique was putting its main effort into preparation for the elections which would precede the coming into effect of the constitution on December 25, 1947."[116] Commenting on the dependence of Generalissimo Chiang on the C.C. clique, the American ambassador noted:

> The paradox of his position, of which he may be unaware, is that he is being compelled to utilize the qualifications which the C.C. clique can offer. At the same time this clique exploits its preferred position to render more firm its hold on the Party and the country; and with time the Generalissimo therefore may well become less and less able to dispense with them or to circumscribe their activities, which can only serve to aggravate those social conditions basically giving rise [sic] and strength to the Communist movement."[117]

As the date of the elections approached, the American consul general in Shanghai reported on September 22, 1947, according to the White Paper:

[113] *Ibid.*, p. 735.

[114] Ambassador Stuart reported on March 12, 1947: "Evidence of C.C. clique expansion into the financial field will not increase banking and business confidence in government. . ." (*ibid.*, p. 243).

[115] See the book written by a leading Communist theoretician, Ch'ên Po-ta, *Chung-kuo ssǔ ta chia-tsu* ["China's Four Big Families"] (Hsin-hua shu-tien, 1946).

[116] *United States Relations with China*, p. 736.

[117] *Ibid.*, p. 735.

The C.C. clique there was increasing its power and dominating the Kuomintang's preparations to ensure that the successful candidates in the coming elections were "elite" party supporters plus such few political beggars as it may seem expedient to accept as window dressing.[118]

Summing up the outcome of the elections, the China White Paper put it this way: "In the end it was apparent that majority influence in the new National Assembly and the Legislative Yüan would lie with the C.C. clique, the extreme right-wing faction of the Kuomintang."[119] Thus, in their endeavors to introduce into China a set of institutions taken for granted in the West, American officials diverted their energy and influence from the principal task of building up a new political force and of checking the influence of the reactionary group.

When the first National Assembly was meeting to elect a president and vice-president, the American embassy reported to the State Department that "the party bosses of the Kuomintang regarded the establishment of the constitutional government as an exercise in machine politics."[120] On April 26, 1948, Ambassador Stuart cabled Washington:

> Interference of Generalissimo and party machine with elections to Assembly and the new Yuan, with deliberations of Assembly on constitutional amendment question and flagrant intervention in vice-presidential election has [sic] thoroughly convinced those desiring effective constitutional government that Generalissimo intends to use the new constitution as vehicle for continuation of his personal rule in close cooperation with C.C. Clique-dominated party machine and Whampoa clique-dominated High Military Command as has obtained in past.[121]

In the end, however, the military defeats suffered by the Nationalist armies and the general dissatisfaction with the policies of the government created such a widespread resentment against the groups in control that not even Generalissimo Chiang and his following could prevent the election to the vice-presidency of General Li Tsung-jên, the leader of the Kwangsi group and the candidate of the groups demanding reforms. On the surface, it seemed as if the constitution had served as a vehicle for political reform. As a matter of fact, however, the political realities in China did not undergo significant changes, as the impotence and helplessness of the new vice-president clearly demonstrated.

[118] Ibid., p. 263.
[119] Ibid., p. 268.
[120] Ibid., p. 908.
[121] Ibid., pp. 853–54.

4. The Illusion about Generalissimo Chiang

In the postwar years as well as during the Pacific war, Chiang maneuvered the United States into the dilemma of either giving him economic and military assistance on his terms or risking the loss of China. At first, American officials were handicapped by their illusions about the Generalissimo. Chiang did not always flatly reject American advice. Frequently, he accepted American suggestions so long as they could be modified and put into practice in such a way that his power position and that of his personal following would not be affected. After the negotiations with the Communists collapsed, the Generalissimo lent his influence to promote the adoption of a constitution in reasonable accord with the resolutions of the Political Consultative Conference — a step which General Marshall urged strongly on Nationalist leaders.[122] In so doing, Chiang appeared to have exercised a determined personal leadership and worked in concert with all other groups and individuals to oppose the extreme right wing.[123] The adoption of the constitution, which is in many ways an excellent document,[124] was considered by General Marshall to be a great moral victory for the Generalissimo, which "had rehabilitated if not added to his prestige."[125] Thus General Marshall advised the Generalissimo that "he must by his own indirect leadership father a coalition of the minority groups into a large liberal party" and that "the organization of the minority parties into a large liberal group would assist him greatly and he could place himself in the position of the father of his country rather than continue merely as the leader of the Kuomintang one-party government."[126] This advice was given in pursuance of his plan of "building up of the liberals *under the Generalissimo* while at the same time removing the influence of the reactionary."[127]

In April, 1947, the Nationalist government proclaimed the end of the period of political tutelage by the Kuomintang[128] and brought several members of the two minority parties into a reorganized government. In this reorganization, members of the Political Science group were given many of the top positions in the government. These changes brought a certain amount of satisfaction to American officials. As Ambassador Stuart

[122] *Ibid.*, p. 213.
[123] *Ibid.*, p. 214.
[124] The most interesting features of this constitution are the provisions regarding the relations of the president of the Republic, the president of the Executive Yüan, and the Legislative Yüan. This arrangement combines elements from both the presidential system and the cabinet system. In this respect it resembles loosely the constitution of the Fifth Republic of France.
[125] *United States Relations with China*, p. 216.
[126] *Ibid.*
[127] *Ibid.*, p. 213. Emphasis added.
[128] *Ibid.*, p. 245.

reported on April 19, 1947, "The composition of the State Council is as regards the Kuomintang and independents as good as could be expected in the circumstances."[129] On June 18, 1947, the American ambassador informed the State Department:

> He [Generalissimo Chiang] has gone so far in discarding his earlier preconceptions and adopting progressive ideas that I believe he can be influenced to further advance. This will perhaps be slower and much less satisfactory than a more spectacular procedure but it has real possibilities and is perhaps by all odds the most hopeful solution.[130]

Unfortunately, these superficial changes did not modify the actual control of the C.C. clique over the party machinery and the Whampoa clique over the bulk of the armed forces. They did not decrease the dependence of Generalissimo Chiang on these two groups or his trust in them. It is significant that the members of the Kwangsi group and other provincial leaders, such as General Fu Tso-yi, who offered a realistic alternative to the Whampoa clique gained little genuine advantage in the reorganization. It is true that the Political Science group gained the premiership and several important ministries, but this hopeful development was offset by the expansion of the influence of the C.C. clique into the financial and economic field.[131] Under these circumstances, the reorganization meant very little.

American officials were not unaware of these political realities in China as the reports sent by diplomatic and consular representatives in this period clearly showed. But at this time they were still sufficiently impressed with the empty gestures of Generalissimo Chiang to believe that somehow a new political force could be developed under his leadership. This policy of building a new political force under Generalissimo Chiang assumed that he could undergo a moral conversion, abandon his lifelong ideas on government and politics, and sever his relationship with the following which he had relied on to gain and retain control of China — all this without great pressure from the United States. Inevitably, political developments in China disabused them. On February 6, 1948, Ambassador Stuart reported that "increasingly it must be the Generalissimo who must make the decisions and he continues to be the slave of his past and unable to take the drastic measures required."[132] When Generalissimo Chiang relieved General Pai Ch'ung-hsi of the Kwangsi group of his post as minister of defense and rejected his idea of organizing local militia, the American ambassador informed the State Department on June 24, 1948, that "he [Generalissimo

[129] *Ibid.*, p. 746.
[130] *Ibid.*, p. 241.
[131] Pp. 380–81, above.
[132] *United States Relations with China*, p. 267.

Chiang] seems suspicious that the Kwangsi clique have designs against him and is thus alienating, or at least losing the effective cooperation of, men who by every test have been loyal both to him and to the national cause."[133] On August 10, 1948, Ambassador Stuart reported:

> [L]ong experience with him [Chiang] suggests that he is no longer capable of changing and reforming or discarding inefficient associates in favor of competent ones; . . . it [the Nationalist government] ignores competent military advice and fails to take advantage of military opportunities offered, due in large part to the fact that the Government and the military leadership continue to deteriorate as the Generalissimo selects men on the basis of personal reliability rather than military competence.[134]

In a policy review in October, 1948, Secretary Marshall himself told the ambassador that in the light of past experience pressing the Generalissimo for removal of incompetents would not produce promising results.[135]

5. Chiang as the Indispensable Man

After the failure of the Marshall mission, it should have been clear that the Kuomintang and the Chinese Communists could not be brought together under a constitutional regime. If at this time the United States had not been under the illusion of Chiang's indispensability, if she had considered her interests in China vital, and if she had been determined to prevent the Communists from extending their control over the whole of China, the logical course would have been to use her tremendous influence to effect a complete change in the leadership of the government, substituting some other leaders for Chiang. Such a step might have been taken after Generalissimo Chiang's offensives failed to achieve their objectives, when his armies began to suffer reverses, and when the military, economic, and political crisis deepened to such a degree that the Chinese government had to depend upon immediate American assistance for survival.

Certainly, Generalissimo Chiang himself was preoccupied with the thought that it was the policy of the United States in the summer of 1947 to remove him. When the mounting crisis in China led General Marshall to dispatch General Wedemeyer on a fact-finding mission to China, Generalissimo Chiang on August 25, 1947, called Philip Fugh, a Chinese who was Ambassador Stuart's personal secretary, to his residence and asked the American ambassador's confidant whether the dispatch of the Wedemeyer mission meant that the United States wished to force his retirement or re-

[133] *Ibid.*, p. 275.
[134] *Ibid.*, p. 284; see also *Military Situation in the Far East*, p. 698.
[135] *United States Relations with China*, p. 284.

moval.[136] More than a year later, the possibility of advising Chiang to retire did occur to Ambassador Stuart, who by this time was totally disillusioned with Chiang.

As a matter of fact, even without strong pressure or positive advice from the United States, Generalissimo Chiang was forced by political and military events in China to retire from the presidency in January, 1949, though he succeeded in using what remained of his power to prevent his successor from gaining really effective control over Chinese affairs. The real question is not whether American pressure and maneuvers could have been the catalyst in a movement to replace Chiang, but whether the political forces opposing Chiang could have been developed with American help rapidly enough, and whether Chiang could have been replaced soon enough, to make a salvaging operation in China feasible.[137]

But, to the very end, the alternative of building a new political force in China without Generalissimo Chiang was never even seriously considered, let alone implemented. At the time of the Wedemeyer mission, the illusion that Generalissimo Chiang could lead a new political force had not yet dissipated. When disillusionment about Chiang set in, American officials were troubled by the idea that Chiang was the indispensable man whom no one could replace. On April 23, 1948, Ambassador Stuart told Secretary Marshall:

> I do not believe he [Chiang] is conceited or intoxicated with power in the usual sense. Yet he is dangerously self-opinionated and confident that he understands the situation better and has more experience than anyone else. This is all the more tragic be-

[136] *Ibid.*, pp. 258, 826.

[137] Commenting on this problem, Professor George E. Taylor observed: "There was a time when by more purposeful intervention we might have turned the tide in the Kuomintang and have brought about an alliance between the Chinese intellectuals and the modern-minded military on the Nationalist side. This would have meant countenancing what would in effect have been a plot to get rid of Chiang Kai-shek. Today, we have no organized social group to work with at all. The time has long since passed when American assistance could be given to anyone who could use it" (George E. Taylor, "An Effective Approach in Asia," *Virginia Quarterly Review*, Winter, 1950, p. 35). See also Franz Michael, "A Revolutionized Kuomintang," *Far Eastern Survey*, July 28, 1948, pp. 161–64; Woodbridge Bingham, "American Responsibility in China," *Far Eastern Survey*, February 9, 1949, pp. 28–31.

Hanson Baldwin wrote in the *New York Times* that there should be a "thorough clean-up and reformation of the Nanking government" or, alternatively, the present government should be replaced by one or more governments "less wedded to archaic political and military measures." He thought that the United States might have to support individual governors or commanders (*New York Times*, November 9, 1948, p. 4). Later he wrote: "We have it in our power to insist upon reforms in Generalissimo Chiang's Government or to back individual provincial governors or warlords. Aid previously given also could have been on our terms; we have only to review recent events to see that" (*New York Times*, December 4, 1948, p. 4).

cause he is so largely right in these assumptions, and because there really seems to be no one else who could take his place.[138]

The dilemma confronted by the United States as American officials saw it was succinctly stated in the following words of Ambassador Stuart as late as August 10, 1948:

> Universally the Generalissimo is criticized for his ineffective leadership and universally no one can suggest any one to take his place. He is the one who holds this vast country together. Without him disintegration seems inevitable yet . . . unless he can summon the resources to reverse the present trend he will inevitably and in time be discarded.[139]

General Marshall never succeeded in finding a solution to this central dilemma. As he told a conference on China policy sponsored by the State Department in October, 1949, "there was constant pressure to eliminate Chiang Kai-shek, but no one ever suggested anyone [who] could take his place; at least, they never made a suggestion to me that made any impression on my mind, of a man who can handle the situation."[140] Looking at the Chinese scene with this fixed idea, General Marshall found the problem of China insoluble.[141]

This dilemma confronting the United States was no doubt real. But it was also largely created by the political maneuvers of Generalissimo Chiang himself with unintentional help from the United States. While fighting the Communists, he was at the same time trying to undercut the political and military power of the other Nationalist leaders who did not unquestioningly obey him. His policy was the familiar one of rule or ruin. In his domination of the Kuomintang over a period of twenty years, he had built up a powerful following which placed personal loyalty to him above all else. When in early 1948 there was a possibility of General Li Tsung-jên's challenging his absolute control by running for the vice-presidency against Chiang's wishes, the Generalissimo announced his desire to withdraw from the presidential race. Almost immediately, the C.C. clique made known its refusal to co-operate with any government not headed by

[138] *United States Relations with China*, p. 851; see also p. 854.

[139] *Ibid.*, p. 886. Earlier, on June 12, 1948, the American embassy reported to the State Department: "The Generalissimo has dominated the scene for so long, no one stands out as capable of replacing him. . . . We find it difficult to believe that the Generalissimo can be removed from the scene except at the expense of national unity. . . . Should he leave the scene and should regionalism result, the Communist task would be made much more easy" (*Ibid.*, p. 912).

[140] Transcript of Round Table Discussion on American Policy toward China held in the State Department, October 6, 7, and 8, 1949, *Institute of Pacific Relations*, p. 1657.

[141] *Military Situation in the Far East*, pp. 397, 466; see also Millis, *op. cit.*, p. 372.

the Generalissimo and the Whampoa group threatened to go over to the Communists rather than serve under any president other than Chiang.[142] In these circumstances, he naturally appeared to be the only person who could hold China together.

Furthermore, the passive American policy played into his hand. Generalissimo Chiang never allowed the United States to attach any truly effective political conditions to American assistance even when the survival of the Nationalist government depended on large-scale American aid. When in November, 1947, the State Department was considering a program of American assistance to China to the amount of $300,000,000,[143] the Nationalist government handed Ambassador Stuart a memorandum which stated, among other things, that "the American aid to China plan shall contain no political condition other than what may be stipulated in the aid plan for Europe."[144] It informed the American government that while China would, of her own accord, employ American personnel to assist her in planning for financial, monetary, and other administrative reforms, "the employment of these personnel will not, however, be made an international legal obligation of the Chinese government in order to avert infringement on China's sovereignty and administrative integrity."[145] While Congress was debating the China aid bill, Dr. Sun Fo was reported as having said on March 13, 1948, that he feared American aid might infringe on Chinese sovereignty and that China "must insist on the right to reject advice if it is unacceptable."[146] In the end, the China Aid Act of 1948 did not contain any political conditions, though there were provisions regarding the use of economic aid which insured some direct benefits to the Chinese people.

Under these circumstances, the mere prospect of American aid strengthened Generalissimo Chiang's determination to hold on to his power despite the rapidly deteriorating situation. Commenting on the possibility of Chiang's retirement from the government so as to facilitate a political settlement of the civil war, the American embassy reported on March 18, 1948, to the State Department that "we feel sure that he will not do so [i.e., retire] as long as he has any hope that our military assistance to him will be of a scale and scope sufficient to allow him to gain a military decision or to prolong the civil war until such time as other events may force us to intervene decisively in his favor."[147] At this time, the China aid bill had been under consideration in Congress. The subsequent flow of American

[142] United States Relations with China, p. 850.
[143] Ibid., p. 374. This figure was subsequently raised to $570 million in the State Department's proposal. Congress actually appropriated $400 million under the China Aid Act of 1948.
[144] Ibid., p. 377.
[145] Ibid.
[146] New York Times, March 14, 1948, p. 13.
[147] United States Relations with China, p. 907.

economic and military assistance strengthened him vis-à-vis the other dissident Nationalist leaders controlling various provinces. The American embassy reported to the State Department on August 24, 1948:

> The reluctance of the dissidents to make an open break [with Chiang] very likely stems from a new realization that the present Government still performs for them certain indispensable functions. Principal among these at the moment is Nanking's role in channeling American aid to the Provinces. We have made it abundantly clear that we support the Nanking Government. We have also made it plain that we intend to consult the Nanking Government on the allocation of our economic aid, and it is a well-known fact that the disposition of military aid is Nanking's responsibility. In this situation the potential dissident, who cannot dispense with American aid, is bound to Nanking by very strong ties.[148]

6. Intervention and the Problem of Responsibility

The American failure to bring a new political force into existence also arose from American unwillingness to assume the responsibilities that would have come with the exercise of power and the pursuit of an active policy in China. These responsibilities could have been discharged only if the United States had been willing to give large-scale economic and military assistance to China and, if necessary, to intervene with her armed forces to preserve the authority of a pro-American government in at least part of China. Since General Marshall based his policy on the axiom that American ground forces should never be used on the Chinese mainland and since he did not plan, after the failure of his mission, to give large-scale assistance to China, the United States shrank from any action which might have decisively changed the political conditions in China.

On July 17, 1948, Ambassador Stuart called on Generalissimo Chiang to urge him to reconcile his differences with other Nationalist leaders and to unite with them to save China from communism. After having reported his conversations with Generalissimo Chiang, the American ambassador told Secretary Marshall that he could not go further than giving his advice in trying to influence the political development in China. He explained that "any effort to urge him further than I have done would either have to imply much more American aid than is possible or would over-persuade him to relinquish his own judgment."[149] In October, 1948, Changchun, one of the most important cities in Manchuria, was lost to the Communists, and the authority of the government began to disintegrate very rapidly. Ambassa-

[148] Ibid., p. 916.
[149] Ibid., p. 786.

dor Stuart sought instructions on a number of hypothetical questions. One of them was:

> Would we advise the retirement of the Generalissimo in favor of Li Tsung-jen or some other national political leader with better prospects of forming a republican non-Communist government and of more effectively prosecuting the war against the Communist rebels?[150]

To this inquiry, Secretary Marshall replied:

> [T]he United States government cannot place itself in a position of advising the retirement of the Generalissimo or the appointment of any other Chinese as head of the Chinese Government. To offer such advice is to accept responsibility for developments arising from the acceptance thereof and inferentially to commit the United States Government to support the succeeding regime regardless of United States interests.[151]

7. Chiang's Threat To Go It Alone and To Ask for Soviet Help

In his dealings with the United States, Generalissimo Chiang acted on the unshakable conviction that China was indispensable to the United States and that he was indispensable to China. Against the background of the wartime policy of making China a great power and the principles of the Open Door, the passive American policy and American refusal to assume the responsibilities for Chinese affairs failed to make Chiang aware of the possibility of the United States leaving China to her fate. As a result, he felt confident enough to threaten to go it alone in his fight against the Communists and to come to an understanding with the Soviet Union when he hoped to exert pressure on the United States. Thus, the United States was confronted with a paradoxical situation as the military, economic, and political position of the Nationalist government rapidly deteriorated. On the one hand, most of the Nationalist officials and anti-Communist leaders showed an attitude of almost complete dependence on American assistance as the sole means of saving the regime.[152] On the other hand, the Generalissimo frequently proclaimed his determination not to be dependent on American aid. Ambassador Stuart reported on March 3, 1947:

> [T]he Generalissimo is not without hope that the United States will in due course come in some fashion and to some degree to the Government's assistance. There is no doubt he is now increasingly concerned about the rate of financial deterioration and the ability

[150] Ibid., p. 285.
[151] Ibid.
[152] Ibid., pp. 246, 255, 262, 275, 823, 831.

of the Communists to prolong the struggle and create havoc. However, he has made a point of telling Chinese who call upon him that China must stand on its own feet and face the future without American assistance.[153]

Toward the end of General Wedemeyer's mission to China, when it was apparent that unconditional American assistance would not be immediately forthcoming, Generalissimo Chiang proclaimed before the Central Executive Committee of the Kuomintang on September 9, 1947, that China would never again be dependent on the United States for assistance.[154]

To threaten to go it alone was only one aspect of Chiang's tactics. In trying to exert pressure on the United States, Nationalist officials employed the same technique that they had used during the Pacific war. When they were asking for large-scale American assistance, they played upon the American fear of a Soviet-dominated China just as they had exploited the American anxiety over a total collapse of Chinese resistance against Japan. When American assistance was not readily granted, they threatened to seek a rapprochement with the Soviet Union just as they had capitalized on American apprehension of a separate peace between China and Japan. Thus, immediately before the dispatch of the Wedemeyer mission to China, Nationalist officials stressed the material assistance given to the Chinese Communists by the Russians, the Russian aggressiveness in the border regions of China, and the probability of a Russian-dominated China unless large-scale American aid was granted China soon.[155]

Yet when General Wedemeyer's strong criticisms of the Nationalist government aroused their ire and when it was apparent that no large-scale American aid would immediately be given to China, Nationalist officials soon forgot their statements about Soviet ambitions and Soviet support for the Chinese Communists. Instead, they threatened to seek a rapprochement with the Soviet Union. On September 9, 1947, Generalissimo Chiang told the Central Executive Committee of the Kuomintang that China's policy toward Japan was in accord with that of the Soviet Union and that China would have to strengthen her ties with Russia while preserving her traditional friendship for the United States.[156] The Generalissimo's gentle reference to the Soviet Union was expanded upon by the "thinly-veiled suggestions from senior officials of the government obviously intended to convince the [American] Embassy that if aid is not soon forthcoming from

[153] *Ibid.*, p. 235.
[154] *Ibid.*, p. 262.
[155] *New York Times*, June 8, 14, 21, 25, 27, and July 5, 1947, pp. 12, 8, 9, 21, 14, and 4, respectively. See in particular Tillman Durdin's dispatch on the statements made on June 20, 1947, by Dr. Sun Fo, the president of the Legislative Yüan (*ibid.*, June 21, 1947, p. 9).
[156] *United States Relations with China*, p. 262.

the United States, it may be necessary for China to seek assistance from the Soviet Union."[157] Ambassador Stuart further reported that "it has even been suggested to the Ambassador that the Soviet Ambassador to China . . . might be asked to mediate the civil war and that he would be glad to accept."[158] The American ambassador concluded that such talk was "primarily for effect on the United States."[159]

Public statements made by Nationalist officials had an ominous tone. With obvious reference to the Wedemeyer mission, Mr. Ch'ên Li-fu, the leader of the C.C. clique, was reported to have said on September 2, 1947: "Man needs material help but if that help hurts his self-respect, he had better give up material help. If a man keeps his dignity, he can get help, *if not from one source then another.*"[160] Dr. Sun Fo declared that the results of the Wedemeyer mission "will tell China whether it would be better for her to side with the United States or Russia."[161] He explained: "China in the struggle between the powers must adapt herself where it is most advantageous immediately and in the long run. Countries do not ally for the sake of sentiment. Each must consider her national interest."[162] In contrast to their success during the Pacific war, the threats of Chiang and other Nationalist officials failed to achieve their primary objective, which was to draw the United States into the Chinese civil war or, at least, to obtain large-scale economic and military assistance from the United States. Instead, this tactic had the opposite effect and made American officials even more reluctant to pursue an active policy in China.

8. Chiang's Policy of Rule or Ruin

Chiang's policy of rule or ruin was an important factor in his failure to counter successfully Mao's political strategy of isolating the "die-hards," winning over the "middle-of-the-road forces," and developing the "progressive forces." With his narrow outlook and his determination to monopolize all power regardless of consequences, the Generalissimo made it impossible for the Nationalist government under his control to survive on the mainland. With his political and diplomatic skill, he made it equally impossible for other political leaders to replace him. With his recalcitrance and maneuvering he succeeded in implanting a profound sense of despair in the minds of American officials. General Marshall time and again expressed the view that the problem of China was insoluble. According to Secretary of Navy James Forrestal, Secretary Marshall stated at a meeting

[157] Ambassador Stuart to Secretary Marshall, September 20, 1947, *ibid.*, p. 830.
[158] *Ibid.*
[159] *Ibid.*
[160] *New York Times*, September 2, 1947, p. 11. Emphasis added.
[161] *Ibid.*, September 17, 1947, p. 18.
[162] *Ibid.*

of the secretaries of State, War, and Navy on June 26, 1947, that the United States was confronted "by the dilemma created by the incompetence, inefficiency and stubbornness of the Central Government — qualities which made it very difficult to help them." [163] In explaining the difference between American policies in Greece and China, General Marshall stated that in Greece the United States exercised "quite an influence on the Greek Government" through her program of economic and military assistance while in China American effort brought little result.[164] When Marshall, one of the chief advocates of the *quid pro quo* policy during the Pacific war, was giving up that policy in 1947 and 1948, he was also approaching the point of writing China off as a lost cause. To Secretary of State Acheson, the only alternative to the actual policy pursued was "full-scale intervention in behalf of a government which had lost the confidence of its own troops and its own people." [165] This was precisely the alternative which Chiang's political and diplomatic maneuvers presented to the United States. Commenting on this situation, Ambassador Stuart cabled:

> [The] view is not infrequently expressed that he [Chiang] is best asset Communists have. It is ironical therefore that he refuses to turn over active direction of affairs as he has been repeatedly advised to do because this would be in his opinion tantamount to allowing Communists [to] overrun country. [The] issue is thus confused in his mind as apparently in case of many in United States as though American military aid to him were only alternative to complete Communist domination of China. [To maintain in power a man who has lost support of his own people] would arouse greater sympathy for [the Communist] cause and violent anti-American feeling.[166]

Generalissimo Chiang's hold on China also spoiled the case of the American champions of the Nationalist regime. Throughout the period 1946–49, the Chinese government could not make effective use of American assistance, would not wholeheartedly co-operate with the United States, did not accept American advice, and refused to carry out necessary reforms. Even after the military debacles in Manchuria and North China forced Generalissimo Chiang in January, 1949, to step down from the presidency and General Li Tsung-jên took over its formal duties, the Nationalist armies loyal to Chiang refused to take orders from General Li, and Chiang himself in his capacity as leader of the Kuomintang tried to manipulate the political situation from behind the scenes. The result of

---

[163] Millis, *op. cit.*, 285–86; see also *Military Situation in the Far East*, pp. 282, 284, 287, 887, 889.
[164] *Ibid.*, p. 663.
[165] Letter of Transmittal, in *United States Relations with China*, xv.
[166] *Ibid.*, p. 898.

all this was to make it impossible for General Li to defend any part of China.[167] Only purposeful intervention in Nationalist politics over a long period of time by the United States might have forced an early retirement of the Generalissimo and brought about the conditions necessary for successful armed intervention, efficient use of military aid, and effective implementation of American advice. Yet the proponents of Chiang's cause thought, as Marshall did, that there was no alternative to Chiang and drew diametrically opposite conclusions.[168] Thus, the United States debated her policy toward China along lines drawn by the Generalissimo himself.

C. An Examination of the Basic Assumption

When the China debacle was in the making, it became clear that the United States was acting on the assumption that American interests in China were not essential, that China was a liability to her ally, and that she could not possibly be a menace to the United States. In February, 1948, Secretary Marshall told the Committees on Foreign Affairs and Foreign Relations in executive session:

> China does not itself possess the raw material and industrial resources which would enable it to become a first-class military power within the foreseeable future. The country is at present in the midst of a social and political revolution. Until this revolution is completed — and it will take a long time — there is no prospect that sufficient stability and order can be established to permit China's early development into a strong state.[169]

In 1948 and 1949, expert opinions were overwhelmingly on the side of Secretary Marshall. It seemed inconceivable that China after eight years of war with Japan and an immensely destructive civil strife could be a menace to the United States. The task of rehabilitating the devastated country would be tremendous. Even assuming that the Chinese Communists gave the country a relatively efficient and honest government and brought the country some stability, the Chinese would still be confronted

[167] Just prior to his retirement, Generalissimo Chiang had shipped the gold and silver reserve of the government to Formosa, which was under the control of one of his chief lieutenants. Arms and ammunition destined for China under the United States aid program had also been diverted from Shanghai to Formosa (*New York Times*, February 15, 1949, pp. 1 and 12; Yin Shih, *Chiang Li kuan-shih yü Chung-kuo* ["The *Chiang-Li Relationship and China*"] [Hong Kong: Freedom Press, 1954], pp. 114–21; Liang Shêng-chün, *Chiang Li tou-chêng nei-mo* ["The Inside Story of the Struggle between Chiang and Li"] [Hong Kong: Union Asia Press, 1954]).

[168] Some of the American advocates of large-scale American assistance to Generalissimo Chiang openly expressed the view that instead of being a precondition for the effective use of American aid, reform in China was impossible before victory over the Communists was achieved. See *Foreign Policy for a Post-War Recovery Program*, p. 2042.

[169] *United States Relations with China*, p. 383.

with long-range problems of immense proportions. Basic among these would be the reconstruction of the national economy so as to insure a decent livelihood to the Chinese people and the acquisition from the nation's production of a surplus for the support of the government. Evaluating the ability of the new regime to meet these "minimum requirements," the American embassy told the State Department on November 8, 1948, that "here we may fairly question whether the new government has this capacity, and from all indications it would appear that the answer is in the negative."[170] Even if the new government passed this fundamental test of survival, an impoverished and unindustrialized China could not be a menace to the United States and would probably be a liability as an ally. James Reston reported on April 24, 1949: "For China, as the Administration sees it, is not a 'strategic springboard' but a 'strategic morass.' . . . It is a vast unconnected, poorly organized continent of a country, populated by undernourished, highly individualistic people."[171]

Rapid industrialization in China could not be achieved without a revolutionary change in the basic patterns of culture which for thousands of years had been those of an agricultural, family-centered civilization. Admittedly, these basic patterns had been in the process of breaking down in the last hundred years under the impact of the West. But many of the traditional attitudes lingered on, and the development of new social, economic, and political institutions had always lagged behind the demands of the times. In the light of the difficulties that had plagued the Nationalist government and obstructed American efforts to help China, it was easy to conclude that the Chinese Communists would not be able to overcome the cultural obstacles to rapid industrialization.[172] Furthermore, the Chinese Communists would approach the task of industrialization with their imported ideology. As communism clashed violently with the traditional culture of China at many points, it was natural to conclude that the ideological baggage would be an additional impediment to Communist success.[173]

[170] *Ibid.*, p. 918. James Reston reported in April, 1949, that the official information was that the Communists "do not have the administrative personnel to deal effectively with the economic problems of the country. Winning the war, the State Department feels, will be easy for the Communists; running the country will be extremely difficult. . ." (*New York Times*, April 24, 1949, Sec. 4, p. 3).

[171] *Ibid.*, April 24, 1949, Sec. 4, p. 3. Reporting on the views of Washington, C. L. Sulzberger wrote earlier that, "instead of gaining an area replete with the sinews of power, the U.S.S.R. is tending to acquire a major interest in a morass of misery where famine is a calendrical occurrence" (*ibid.*, February 18, 1948, p. 8).

[172] For a most interesting discussion of this question, see Marion J. Levy, Jr., "The Problem of Our Policy in China," *Virginia Quarterly Review*, Summer, 1949, pp. 348–64. Levy's analysis was eminently sensible. No one foresaw the efficiency with which the Chinese Communists swept aside these hindrances.

[173] The American embassy reported on November 8, 1948, that the basic problem of the new regime would "involve the organization of the economy in terms of a new economic and social philosophy which is altogether an import and has no real roots

In contrast to the United States, the Soviet Union, and Western Europe, China was believed to be poor in the natural resources necessary to a high level of industrial development. More important, China was so impoverished that she was considered to lack the ability to accumulate the capital needed for the immensely large initial outlay in any program of rapid industrialization. The Soviet Union was thought to be incapable of supplying China with the necessary amount of economic and technical aid.[174] Thus, the prospect for the rapid industrialization in China was so dim that there was no cause for alarm.[175] From this evaluation of Chinese and Russian economic capabilities flowed an exaggerated notion of the economic dependence of China on the United States. Some thought that the Chinese Communists would have to depend on trade with the United States for the success of their program of rapid industrialization and that their dependence on United States trade and the long tradition of American friendship might serve as a basis for a modus vivendi between the two nations.[176]

There is a kernel of truth in all these analyses. In spite of the amazing initial success of the Communist program of industrialization, the stress and strain stemming from the basic poverty of China and insufficient foreign aid have begun to show. The system of communes, based partly on practical considerations and partly on ideology, contributed to three consecutive years of agricultural crisis. The great leap forward has turned into the great retreat. There is certainly a limit to human endurance even for a people traditionally accustomed to hard work and thrift. Neverthe-

in the country," and that "deep and vital changes will be difficult without doing violence to the Communists' basic, underlying dogma" (*United States Relations with China*, p. 918).

    C. L. Sulzberger reported in February that in Washington analysts were reasoning that the Communist program of revolutionizing China was "an issue of such fundamental and vast scale [that] no compromise is permissible: that the Kuomintang . . . had a revolutionary program. But it foundered upon the reef of Chinese realities" (*New York Times*, February 18, 1949, p. 8).

    [174] George Kennan, then head of the Plans and Policies Division, told a round table conference held in October, 1949, to discuss China policy: "It has been my own thought that the Russians are perhaps the people least able to combine with the Chinese in developing the resources of China and producing anything which in a physical sense would be dangerous to us. . . . China is a competitor with Soviet Siberia for such things as the Soviet government may have to give — and I have heard Stalin express this same thought and I think with complete sincerity" (*Institute of Pacific Relations*, p. 1558).

    [175] C. L. Sulzberger reported in February, 1949: "The State Department view — which is prevailing policy — is that the U.S.S.R., even if it establishes truly cozy relations with Mr. Mao, cannot provide the necessary cadre and assistance for the Chinese to face her fundamental problems and that the Communists will wear themselves out in the slough of misery, just as did General Chiang" (*New York Times*, February 18, 1949, p. 8).

    [176] For example, Derk Bodde, *Peking Diary* (New York: Henry Schuman Co., 1950), p. 265.

less, what these analyses failed to take adequately into account was a new political factor: The ability of a totalitarian party, using all the levers of social control, to manipulate mass attitudes, to organize social life, and to tap surplus labor as a source of capital for the paramount purpose (until 1959, at least) of rapid industrialization. It is a new dimension which American specialists and officials, immersed in the liberal, democratic environment of a free society, naturally failed to gauge. The trend of the social sciences up to that time, which emphasized the determining effects of social forces on political actions, also left them unprepared to appraise correctly a situation in which the political actors deliberately and methodically sought to manipulate the social environment to achieve a preconceived purpose. This deterministic bias, which was a measure of the separation of knowledge from practice, led the West at once to overestimate the difficulties confronted by the Communists and to underestimate the ability of the free world to work out its own destiny. This was one of the basic sources of its complacency as well as its incapability to undertake a bold program to meet the Communist challenge.

These analyses of the difficulties confronting the Chinese Communists were not the only reasons for the absence of a sense of profound crisis. Because of America's traditional friendship for China and her support for Chinese nationalism, many Americans underestimated the hostility of the Chinese Communists toward the United States. Others overestimated the restraining effect of Chinese nationalism and pro-American sentiments in China on the Chinese Communists in their conduct of foreign affairs. Correspondingly, they failed to give adequate weight to ideology as a factor in determining the international behavior of the Chinese Communists. Rightly or wrongly, they expected a conflict between a Communist China and the Soviet Union to take the form of a clash between Chinese nationalism and Soviet domination. As C. L. Sulzberger reported in February, 1949, "Quite plainly the policy makers of the United States are counting upon the historic forces of Chinese nationalism to assert themselves as strongly under a Mao Tse-tung government vis-à-vis the U.S.S.R. as they did under a Chiang Kai-shek government vis-à-vis the United States."[177] Furthermore, the year 1948 witnessed not only the decisive military defeats sustained by the Nationalists but also the sudden rupture in the relationship between Tito and Stalin. This unexpected schism in the seemingly monolithic Communist bloc encouraged some Americans to anticipate the development of a Chinese Titoism, for which all the necessary conditions seemed to be present. As James Reston reported, "Some of our officials believe that Mao Tse-tung and the other Communist leaders will probably show signs of 'Titoism' once they are in control," though "the top officials" discouraged

[177] New York Times, February 15, 1949, p. 12.

this idea.[178] Since then, a dispute between the Soviet Union and Communist China has indeed developed. But the widening breach has assumed the form of a conflict over revolutionary strategy against the West, with Peking urging the adoption of a more militant policy toward the United States.

While Marshall's basic assumption of the unimportance of China has been refuted by events since Peking's intervention in the Korean War, it is a partisan view to attribute to him or other administration officials personal responsibility for the failure of American policy. His program was based on his estimate of the existing limits of American capability and on his judgment of what the American people were willing to do for China. There is every reason to believe that his calculations of these two constraints on American action were correct. The rapid demobilization of the armed forces, the unwillingness of the American people to send their boys to fight in China for a decadent government, and the reluctance to use force without both an unambiguous moral issue and an immediate threat to survival were conditions totally beyond his personal control. The large-scale military assistance proposed by the Republicans was, in Marshall's view, beyond the existing capability of the United States and would entail a serious risk of involving the United States in armed intervention. Armed intervention or any action entailing serious risks of developing into armed intervention could have been a feasible alternative only if the United States as a nation had followed a different approach in foreign affairs and had entertained a different set of assumptions and considerations. Even if there had been such a revolutionary change in thinking, no one can prove conclusively that armed intervention and active interference in Chinese politics could have maintained a non-Communist government in a part of mainland China, or that these actions would have served the national interest rather than courted an even more serious defeat. History may still prove that America's failure in China was a blessing in disguise.

Assuming that the objective constraints on the use of force in China could not have been changed, Marshall's policy of withdrawal from China in order to concentrate American efforts in Europe was the only feasible policy. Immediately after the statement, quoted above, in which Marshall disparaged the importance of China, he added:

[178] *Ibid.*, April 24, 1949, Sec. 4, p. 3. See also reports written by C. L. Sulzberger explaining why some officials expected the development of Titoism in China (*ibid.*, February 14, 1949, p. 10; February 15, 1949, p. 12; February 18, 1949, p. 8; February 21, 1949, p. 5).

In his letter of transmittal in the White Paper on China, Secretary of State Dean Acheson clearly showed that he did not subscribe to this view. He spoke of the Chinese Communists as a party serving the "interest of a foreign imperialism" (*United States Relations with China*, xvi–xvii).

On the side of American interests, we cannot afford, economically or militarily, to take over the continued failures of the present Chinese government to the dissipation of our strength in more vital regions where we now have a reasonable opportunity of successfully meeting or thwarting the Communist threat, that is, the vital industrial area of Western Europe with its traditions of free institutions.[179]

Marshall's program of establishing a coalition government in China was a way to avoid military entanglement. It would have enabled the United States to disengage gracefully from China, although it was not designed to achieve such a purpose. It is not unlikely that the Chinese Communists would, sooner or later, have won control of China under the settlement indorsed by Marshall. But, to use the words of Professor John K. Fairbank, "It seems pretty plain that civil war brought Communist domination in China more rapidly than the alternative of coalition could have done."[180] The avoidable mistake which Marshall committed was that, after events in China had proved the impossibility of a coalition and his mediation effort had collapsed, he failed either to find firm bipartisan support for his policy of limiting American commitments to China or, failing that, to disclose all relevant information and make his policy a subject of public debate at the earliest possible time. In 1947 and 1948, his policy and views, regardless of their intrinsic merits, would in all probability have been indorsed by the American people. Unfortunately, he suppressed the Wedemeyer report of September, 1947, for almost two years and did not take his case to the American public at the appropriate time. His omissions led to a breakdown of bipartisanship and enabled the critics of the administration to charge it with sole responsibility for the China debacle.[181]

No matter what one's evaluation of Marshall's policy and his freedom of action, there cannot be any doubt that Marshall's decision not to undertake armed intervention and the related decision not to provide large-scale military assistance and operational advice to Nationalist China constituted the crucial element of his policy and exercised perceptible influence on its other components. If one cannot demonstrate that armed intervention or massive military assistance could have prevented a total Communist victory, one can at least conclude that the lack of immediate military capability to intervene was a decisive factor in the failure to sustain the Nationalist government, an objective which Marshall sought to achieve. To the extent

[179] *Ibid.*, p. 383.
[180] John K. Fairbank, "America and the Chinese Revolution," *New Republic*, August 22, 1949, p. 13.
[181] For an able analysis of this point, see A. Bradford Westerfield, *Party Politics and Foreign Policy* (New Haven, Conn.: Yale University Press, 1955), chaps. xii–xvi.

that this lack of military power was a product of the rapid demobilization after V-J Day, it was a function of the American people's inability to anticipate the postwar situation in China and to maintain the necessary capability to influence it. To the extent that the political and military developments in China were anticipated by individual officials, the lack of capability was a product of the nation's unwillingness to develop and use military power purposefully to achieve her objectives in China.

One may argue that even if she had been willing to use her armed forces in China, the United States, primarily a naval and air power, could not have done anything effective against the ground forces of the Soviet Union and the Chinese Communists. In other words, it was not merely the existing military capability but also the absolute limits of America's military potential or at least, to use the words of the White Paper, "the reasonable limits" of America's capabilities, which were the ineluctable condition of American policy since the end of the Pacific war. From this point of view, the present balance of power in the Far East, which rests on the confrontation between the ground forces of the Communist bloc on the continent and America's air and sea power based on the island perimeter, was an inevitable development. This line of argument, likewise, cannot be proved or disproved. But one wonders whether this estimate of America's military potential was not itself an expression of the unwillingness of the United States to achieve her political purposes in China by military power. If one directs one's attention beyond the postwar years to American policy toward the Far East since the dispatch of the Hay notes, one finds that its persistent and crucial feature was not the absolute limit set by America's military potential but the unwillingness or, at times, the inability of the United States to develop and use her military power purposefully to achieve her avowed political purpose. After all, in the twenties and thirties, the United States could have developed her immense potential naval power to uphold the Open Door principles against infringement by the island-empire of Japan. During the Pacific war, it was the military objective of securing the unconditional surrender of Japan which shaped political policy rather than the political objectives which guided military strategy. It seems unlikely that this persistent feature of failing to use force purposefully to achieve political objectives should suddenly have disappeared in the postwar years. Seen from this perspective, Marshall's China policy can be interpreted as a new manifestation, under a different set of circumstances, of a persistent feature of American policy and as one more link leading to the present balance of power in the Far East, which was foreshadowed by the abandonment in 1944 of any thought of waging a major campaign on the mainland of China.

In the last chapter, the examination of Marshall's China policy, in order to answer the question of Marshall's failure to achieve his objective of sustaining the Chinese government, was presented in a logical rather than a chronological order. In this and the next two chapters, Marshall's China policy and its continuation under Acheson are viewed in their natural, historical setting. The treatment follows, in the main, the conventional chronological order and will, it is hoped, clarify the question of why the United States did not disentangle herself completely and promptly from China after Marshall's mediation efforts had collapsed. The treatment of substantially the same subject matter first in terms of a logical structure and then in the form of a historical narrative will necessitate a certain amount of repetition. But this will facilitate analysis of the complex problems involved and give a more adequate explanation of why the United States rejected, on the one hand, armed intervention and massive military assistance and, on the other, complete and prompt withdrawal.

A. American Policy and the Foredoomed Settlement in China

1. The Impact of American Policy on Chinese Politics

Marshall arrived in China on December 20, 1945, carrying with him the elaborate program described at the beginning of the last chapter. To understand the impact of Marshall's program, it is necessary to recapitulate briefly the policies of the Kuomintang and the Communists in their political-military struggle. At this time, the Nationalist government enjoyed a five to one superiority in armed forces vis-à-vis the Communists. Thanks to the military assistance given by the United States in airlifting and transporting its troops to Japanese-occupied areas, it was able to re-establish its authority in the big cities and was in a position to reopen important lines of communication in North China. At the same time the position of the Chinese Communists was also strengthened by the extension of their

control in the countryside of North China and, above all, by their acquisition of Japanese arms in Manchuria. But the military superiority still lay
with the Nationalists. Therefore, Generalissimo Chiang pressed forward
his military campaign to drive the Communists from important regions,
while continuing to negotiate with them, partly with a view to satisfying
the public clamor for peace and partly with the hope that under intensified
military pressure the Communists might accept a settlement on his terms.
On their part, the Communists countered the attacks by effectively cutting
Nationalist lines of communication. At the same time, they demanded an
unconditional cease-fire and a cessation of the movement of Nationalist
troops into North China. The Nationalist government would agree to a
cease-fire only on condition that communications between key points be restored first and that the Communists withdraw their troops from places
along the railways.

In the political sphere, the Nationalist government insisted that the
establishment of "unity of military command" i.e., integration of the Communist forces into a national army, was a precondition to the cessation of
its military attacks and that it had to come before the inauguration of constitutional rule and a democratic regime. As the survival of the Chinese
Communists depended on their possession of an autonomous army, their
acceptance of the Nationalist demands would have meant political suicide.
Thus, the Communists argued that the integration of the Communist forces
into a national army could take place only after the establishment of a
democratic coalition government and a constitutional regime. Since the
narrow power base of the Kuomintang contrasted sharply with the popular
support enjoyed by the Communists, the establishment of a genuinely
democratic regime would have doomed the Nationalists to political defeat in the near future. The Kuomintang thus proposed to end its political
tutelage and to inaugurate constitutional rule only in accordance with its
own procedures and on its own terms, making certain that nothing really
important would be changed.

To do this, it took steps to convene a National Assembly which had been
elected in 1936 when the Kuomintang was the sole legal party. This con-
stituent assembly would adopt a constitution, drafted by the Nationalist
government, which provided for an all-powerful president, a weak legislative branch, and a highly centralized unitary government with very little
power left to local governments. These features would guarantee the continued domination of the Kuomintang. In contrast, the Communists called
for a conference of representatives from all parties and groups to discuss
and to pave the way for the adoption of a constitution. This conference
would terminate the one-party rule of the Kuomintang and become the
source of a new legitimacy. As the Communists knew that they could not

hope to capture the executive branch at once, they wanted to have a powerful legislature which would check the powers of a Nationalist cabinet. As they also knew that they could not dominate the central government immediately, they demanded large powers for the provinces and the popular election of provincial governors and other officials on the lower levels of the local governments, feeling that their grass roots support would give them control over important regions.

Maneuvering to gain a semblance of public support for their program to establish a constitutional rule, the Nationalists were not inflexibly opposed to the calling of a conference of all parties and groups, provided that this conference could take place under such political and military circumstances that it would give its stamp of approval to the Nationalist plan of convening the old National Assembly and of adopting a constitution which would enable them to perpetuate their dominance. When its military campaign was gaining momentum in October and November of 1945, the Nationalist government pressed for an early meeting of a Political Consultative Conference of all parties and groups. In contrast, the Communists at this particular time refused to name their delegates to the Conference, so as to avoid negotiating under military pressure; and they used their refusal to back up their demands for an unconditional cease-fire. The deadlock was complete. These impasses reflected the absence of principles shared by the two sides and showed the existence of basic conflicts of interest.[1] While it might have been possible to achieve a temporary modus vivendi on the basis of a division of zones of control or even to set up a coalition government or constitutional regime as a temporary arrangement to gain time, any attempt to achieve a permanent settlement within a constitutional framework was doomed to failure. But this was precisely what General Marshall set out to do.

[1] For the Communist views, see *Hsin-hua jih-pao*, editorial, December 21, 1945, as reprinted in *Hsin Chung-kuo ti shu-kuang* ["The Dawn of New China"] (Hsin-hua jih-pao, 1946), pp. 30–32; "Press Conference of Chou En-lai and General Yeh Chien-ying, Dec. 18, 1945," *ibid.*, pp. 35–41; "The Proposal of the Chinese Communist Delegation for an Unconditional Cease-fire," *ibid.*, pp. 42–43; "Chiang Kai-shek's Speech on New Years' Day and the Political Consultative Conference," editorial in the *Chieh-fang jih-pao*, January 7, 1946, as reprinted in *Chung-kuo wên-ti wên-hsien*, Hsiang Chün (ed.), ["Documents on the Problem of China] (Ta-chung ch'u-pan-shê, 1946), pp. 71–85.

For the Nationalist views, see "Generalissimo Chiang Kai-shek's Speech on New Year's Day," as reprinted in K'ang Tan, *Chung-kuo chih hsin-shêng* ["The New Birth of China"] (Hong Kong: Hsin-shêng Chung-kuo shê, 1948), pp. 163–72; editorial in the Central Daily News, January 17, 1946," as reprinted in Li Hsü (ed.), *Chêng-chih hsieh-shang hui-i chih chien-t'ao* ["An Appraisal of the Political Consultative Conference"] (Nanking: Shih-tai ch'u-pan-shê, 1946), pp. 102–3; editorial in the Central Daily News, January 26, 1946, in *ibid.*, pp. 113–14.

See also chap. viii above; Department of State, *United States Relations with China* (Washington, D.C.: Government Printing Office, 1949), pp. 107–12 (hereafter cited as *United States Relations with China*).

The events in the first three months after Marshall's appointment created the pleasant illusion that the seemingly immense power of the United States, reinforced by his own great prestige, might be able to break the deadlock. Soon after the announcement of the appointment of General Marshall, Wang Ping-nan, the Chinese Communist representative in Chungking, informed the American embassy on December 3 of Yenan's decision to participate in the Political Consultative Conference. The adoption by the Chinese Communists of this more co-operative attitude suggests that they were gravely concerned over the future of American policy. As Wang told the embassy, future developments in China depended even more on American policy than on the meeting of the Political Consultative Conference, and the Communists were eagerly awaiting the arrival of General Marshall and the clarification of the American position. In this conversation, the Communist representative also emphasized the independence of Yenan from Moscow.[2] On December 17, an official spokesman of the Central Committee of the Chinese Communist party in Yenan released a statement which welcomed the Truman declaration of December 15 and pledged its support for the American policy of obtaining a cessation of hostilities, convoking the Political Consultative Conference, terminating the party tutelage of the Kuomintang, and establishing a democratic and united China. He expressed the approval of the Chinese Communist party for the proposal to turn the Communist troops into "a component part of the armed forces of a democratic state."[3] He foresaw "prolonged resistance, misinterpretation and sabotage" on the part of the "anti-democratic" forces.[4] The Nationalist government also expressed its approval of the Truman declaration but, like the Communists, interpreted American policy in its own way.[5] On December 31, 1945, the government announced that the Generalissimo had decided that the Political Consultative Conference would convene at Chungking on January 10, 1946.

But there was also an undercurrent of intensification of the civil strife. In an important political broadcast on New Year's Day, Generalissimo Chiang reiterated his determination to convoke the National Assembly. He did not mention the Political Consultative Conference,[6] which, after President Truman's declaration of December 15 urging an immediate cease-fire and the broadening of the base of the Chinese government, might have had to meet under circumstances quite different from those in October and November, 1945. This significant omission on Chiang's part

[2] Ibid., p. 111.
[3] "The Statement of the Spokesman for the Central Committee of the Chinese Communist Party, welcoming President Truman's Statement," December 17, 1945, as reprinted in Hsin Chung-kuo ti shu-kuang, pp. 18–19.
[4] Ibid., p. 19.
[5] New York Times, December 16, 1945, p. 1.
[6] The text of the speech is printed in K'ang Tan, op. cit., pp. 168–72.

and his program of convening the National Assembly called forth a harsh attack in the official Communist newspaper at Yenan.[7] Meanwhile, the government declared that it was making preparations to take over the province of Jehol, which was partly occupied by Soviet troops and partly by Chinese Communist forces. Nationalist troops were deployed for an attack. The Communists said they would resist and urged an end to the invasion of that province.[8]

2. The Military-Political Settlement of January and February

a. Marshall and the cease-fire agreement of January 10. — In spite of all difficulties, General Marshall succeeded in helping to construct an elaborate structure of agreements to end the internal conflict of China. This edifice consisted of three closely interrelated parts: the cease-fire agreement of January 10, 1946; a set of five resolutions passed by the Political Consultative Conference, meeting from January 10 to 31; and the military reorganization agreement of February 25.

In the formal and informal negotiations leading to the cease-fire, General Marshall exerted his influence to settle two disputes. In the first and more important, he acted decisively in support of the Nationalist position. On January 4, one day after General Wedemeyer had announced that the United States would transport additional Nationalist forces to Manchuria, General Marshall told Chou En-lai, the chief Communist representative, that the United States was committed to the movement of Nationalist troops to Manchuria. Chou then gave his agreement to the inclusion of an exception in the proposed cease-fire order, which permitted the movement of Nationalist troops into that important region. On the second and less important matter, General Marshall supported the Communists. On January 9, the Nationalist government unexpectedly demanded, as a precondition to issuing a cease-fire order, that its forces occupy Chihfeng and Tolun, strategic points in the provinces of Jehol and Chahar respectively. The Communists resolutely refused to accept this demand, arguing that these two places were deep in territory controlled by them since V-J Day. Marshall interceded on behalf of the Communists.[9]

[7] Editorial in Chieh-fang jih-pao, January 7, 1946, as reprinted in Chung-kuo wên-ti wên-hsien, pp. 71–86.

[8] New York Times, January 3, 1946, p. 1; January 5, 1946, p. 5; January 6, 1946, p. 28.

[9] For a contemporary report of General Marshall's role in settling this dispute, see Feng Tzŭ-chao, Chung-kuo k'ang-chan shih ["A History of China's War of Resistance against Japan"] (Shanghai: Chêng-chi shu-chü, 1946), p. 282. For an account of General Marshall's position the question of Chihfeng, see Carsun Chang, Third Force in China (New York: Bookman Associates, 1952), p. 147.

The various dispatches appearing in American newspapers at the time corroborate

On January 10, the Nationalist government and the Chinese Communist party announced an unconditional and immediate cease-fire, with a provision for simultaneous restoration of communications.[10] With regard to Manchuria, it was stipulated in the minutes of the conferences published in the joint statement that the relevant provision in the Order for Cessation of Hostilities "does not prejudice movements of the forces of the National Army into or within Manchuria which are for the purpose of restoring Chinese sovereignty."[11] The agreement also provided for the immediate establishment of an executive headquarters to be composed of three commissioners: one representing the Nationalist government, one representing the Chinese Communist party, and one representing the United States, who was also to be the chairman. Its decisions were to be made by a unanimous vote.[12] Its function was to implement the Order for the Cessation of Hostilities. This was to be discharged by a number of "supervisory and reporting teams."[13] These field teams, consisting of Nationalist, Communist, and American members, were to be sent to areas of conflict or threatened conflict to halt or prevent hostilities.[14] The decision of a field team was to be made by a unanimous vote of its members. During the negotiations for a cease-fire, a committee had been set up consisting of General Marshall, one Nationalist, and one Communist, which was subsequently known as the Committee of Three.

b. *The Political Consultative Conference and the future political balance in China.* — The announcement of the cease-fire furnished a favorable background for the Political Consultative Conference (the PCC). which met from January 10 to January 31. This conference was composed of eight

the statement made by the writer. In his memoirs, President Truman wrote that Marshall persuaded "Chiang Kai-shek to issue an order without reference to Jehol and Chahar" (Harry Truman, *Years of Trial and Hope* [Garden City, N.Y.: Doubleday & Co., 1956], p. 73).

Largely following Freda Utley's account, Senator McCarthy magnified the importance of this episode out of all proportion. He listed it as one of Marshall's four actions in which the American general intervened on the side of the Communists in order to promote their interests (*Congressional Record,* CXVII, 82d Cong., 1st sess. [1951], 6581–82, 6587; Freda Utley. *The China Story* [Chicago: Henry Regnery Co., 1951], pp. 11–12). Senator McCarthy failed to mention Marshall's support for the Nationalist position on Manchuria. The *United States Relations with China* did not mention the Chihfeng episode.

[10] Press release on Order for Cessation of Hostilities, January 10, 1946, in *ibid.,* pp. 609-10. By another agreement, the cease-fire was to be implemented not later than three days after the proclamation of the cease-fire order on January 10. The truce came into effect on January 13.

[11] *Ibid.,* p. 610.

[12] *Ibid.,* and Agreement on Establishment of the Executive Headquarters, January 10, 1946, in *ibid.,* pp. 627–28. Mr. Walter S. Robertson, chargé d'affaires of the American embassy, was named the American commissioner.

[13] *Ibid.,* p. 628.

[14] Memorandum on Operations of the Executive Headquarters, *ibid.,* p. 630. By September, 1946, there were thirty-six teams (*ibid.,* p. 631).

delegates from the Kuomintang, seven from the Communist party, nine from the Democratic League, five from the Youth party, and nine representing the non-party people of the nation, with a total of thirty-eight members.[15] It was held amidst widespread popular desire to end the intermittent civil war which, coming after eight years of war against Japan, was causing immense suffering. Meeting not long after President Truman's statement calling for broadening the base of the government, it was an important link in the American policy of seeking a political settlement in China. Any party taking an intransigent and uncompromising stand would incur the onus of obstructing a peaceful solution of China's problems and risk the displeasure of both the Chinese people and the American government.

Under these circumstances, the conference adopted a political program unfavorable to the Kuomintang. With regard to the procedures leading to the adoption of a new constitution, the PCC resolutions envisaged a thorough reorganization of the government, pending the convocation of the National Assembly. The existing and actually impotent State Council of the Nationalist government was to be reconstituted into a multiparty body and to become "the supreme organ of the Government in charge of national affairs."[16] It was to have both supreme legislative and executive powers. There were to be forty state councilors, half of whom would be Kuomintang members and the other half members of other political parties or prominent social leaders. They were to be nominated by the parties concerned. Any resolution which involved a change in "administrative policy" had to be passed by a two-thirds vote of the state councilors present. This provision was subsequently interpreted to mean that any resolution modifying the PCC resolutions could be passed only by a two-thirds vote. Thus, any party which together with its allies had fourteen seats in the State Council could veto any revision of the PCC resolutions.[17] According to one source, an oral promise was given by Nationalist authorities to the Communist party and the Democratic League that they would have enough seats in the State Council to avail themselves of a veto.[18]

Pending the inauguration of the constitutional regime, the Executive Yüan, the highest executive organ under the State Council, was to be reorganized. This coalition government with a new State Council and a reorganized Executive Yüan was to rule China until the establishment of the constitutional regime. The National Assembly was to meet on May 5 to adopt a constitution, and elections under the new constitution were to

[15] Tuan-sheng Ch'ien, *The Government and Politics of China* (Cambridge, Mass.: Harvard University Press, 1950), p. 376; *United States Relations with China*, p. 111.
[16] Resolution on Government Organization adopted by the Political Consultative Conference, January, 1946, in *ibid.*, p. 610.
[17] *Ibid.*, pp. 139–40, 183–85.
[18] Ch'ien, *op. cit.*, p. 378.

take place six months after its adoption. As for the composition and procedures of the projected National Assembly, the PCC resolutions assured the Communists and their friends, in effect, of a veto on any proposals inconsistent with the PCC resolutions regarding the future constitution and designed by the Kuomintang to perpetuate its power.[19]

The principles laid down by the PCC to govern the revision of the draft constitution drawn up by the government embodied the quintessence of liberal thought in China. But given the nature of the Kuomintang and the Chinese Communist party and the relative strength of the parties in China, a government structure built on the basis of these constitutional principles would very probably have given the Communists a strong position from which they could have proceeded to capture control of the government in the not too distant future. These principles provided for a cabinet form of government with the Executive Yüan responsible to the Legislative Yüan, thus repudiating the Nationalist concept of a government with a strong presidency and an impotent legislature. In the proposed constitutional setup, the province was to be the highest unit of local government, with a provincial constitution. The powers of the province and the central government would be divided according to the principle of "a fair distribution of powers." The provincial governor was to be elected by the people of the province.[20]

These principles were further reinforced by provisions in the Resolution on the Program for Peaceful National Reconstruction which was to serve as a guide for the reorganized government pending the inauguration of constitutional rule. One provision stated that local self-government should be actively pushed forward and that popular elections beginning from the lower administrative units and gradually ascending to the highest unit should be carried out. Provincial, district, and municipal councils were to be established throughout the country at an early date, and district magistrates to be elected by the people.[21] Another provision in this resolution bore directly on the hotly disputed issue which had been the immediate cause of the spread of civil war after the Chiang-Mao negotiations in the late summer of 1945.[22] This stated that, in areas recovered from the Japanese where local government was under dispute, the status quo should be maintained until a settlement was made by a reorganized government, according to the provisions regarding popular election of local governing bodies and the "fair distribution of powers" between the central

[19] *Ibid.*, pp. 319–20. For details, see *United States Relations with China*, p. 619, and Feng Tsŭ-chao, *op. cit.*, pp. 314–21.

[20] Resolution on the Draft Constitution, adopted by the Political Consultative Conference, January, 1946, *United States Relations with China*, pp. 619–21.

[21] Resolution on the Program for Peaceful National Reconstruction, *ibid.*, p. 613.

[22] Chap. viii, above.

and local governments.[23] Given the popular support enjoyed by the Chinese Communists, these provisions would not only have legitimized their *de facto* control over local governments in wide areas of China but would also have enabled them to extend their control into other regions.

In his testimony in the MacArthur hearings, General Marshall emphasized that he had taken no part in formulating the political program laid down by the Political Consultative Conference. He denied that he had personally suggested the formation of a coalition government to the Nationalist government.[24] But coming after Ambassador Gauss's suggestion in 1944 of a "united council of all Chinese parties,"[25] General Hurley's approval of the five-point draft agreement providing for a coalition government,[26] and President Truman's official statement of December 15, Marshall's mission to China gave a new impetus to the movement in China toward the establishment of a coalition government. While the Political Consultative Conference was in session, Generalissimo Chiang asked General Marshall to persuade the Communists to accept the proposals of the government. Marshall countered this request by offering Chiang a draft program which, in President Truman's words, "would convert the Central Government from an agency of the Kuomintang (which it legally was), to a coalition, basing its existence on the national sovereignty of all China."[27] There is scarcely any doubt that Marshall approved of the works of the Political Consultative Conference. In a statement issued on January 7, 1947, after his departure from China, he said that "the agreements reached by the Political Consultative Conference a year ago were a liberal and forward-looking charter which then offered China a basis

[23] *United States Relations with China*, p. 617.

[24] Senate Committee on Armed Services and Committee on Foreign Relations, *Hearing on the Military Situation in the Far East*, 82d Cong., 1st sess. (1951), p. 549 (hereafter cited as *Military Situation in the Far East*).

[25] See chap. v, above.

[26] See chap. viii, above.

[27] Truman, *op.cit.*, p. 74. This draft also contained a bill of rights. In his testimony in the MacArthur hearings, General Marshall referred to this episode in the following words: "Our government had represented [*sic*] its interests in the development of a two-party government, and beyond that I did not touch the matter at all, except to furnish the Generalissimo confidentially our Bill of Rights and *a possible interim set-up* while they were reaching formal constitutional status. I think that was prepared by Dr. Fairchild, I think he is from Yale, who was out there. But that did not enter into their political adjustments in this matter" (*Military Situation in the Far East*, p. 549). Emphasis added. If Truman's account is accurate, then this "possible interim set-up" took the form of a coalition government. The significance of this vague phrase eluded Marshall's questioner, Senator Knowland.

The draft under discussion was prepared by Professor Knight Biggerstaff, now of Cornell University, at the request of Marshall and in accordance with his general views. Marshall himself was an active participant in the final revision of the draft before it was handed over to Chiang (Letter from Professor Knight Biggerstaff, September 10, 1962).

for peace and reconstruction."[28] It is no exaggeration to assert that in reaching these agreements the Chinese delegates to the conference looked after their own interests with one eye and cast a glance at General Marshall with the other. In any case, when the settlement was crumbling after July, Marshall became directly involved in political discussions with the two sides in an effort to resolve the disputes over the implementation of the resolutions adopted by the Political Consultative Conference.[29]

 c. *Marshall's program for integrating Communist forces into a national army.* — The cease-fire agreement of January 10 and the political program adopted by the Political Consultative Conference were the first two major parts of the settlement between the Kuomintang and the Communists. The third part was an agreement of February 25 on the reorganization and the integration of the Communist forces into a national army. General Marshall took an active part in the negotiations leading to this agreement which he also signed in his capacity of "adviser."

 The agreement provided for an army of sixty divisions, with fifty Nationalist divisions and ten Communist divisions. All units other than those provided for in the agreement would be demobilized. This agreement thus preserved the five to one superiority of the Nationalist forces vis-à-vis the Communist forces, while envisaging a deployment of these divisions which would give a fourteen to one superiority to the Nationalist forces in Manchuria, sole Nationalist occupation of Northwest China, and a five to one Nationalist superiority in Central China. The heaviest concentration of Communist forces was in North China, where the ratio was eleven to seven in favor of the Nationalists. This projected deployment would have effectively blocked off any direct link between the Soviet Union and the Communist divisions. The Communist divisions in North China would have been surrounded with overwhelming forces from three sides. This military plan, highly favorable to the Nationalists, would be put into effect simultaneously with the processes of broadening the base of the government and of establishing a constitutional regime. The simultaneous implementation of the political and military agreements represented a compromise between the Nationalist demand that priority be given to the integration of Communist forces into a national army and the initial Communist proposal giving priority to the democratization of the regime. It was a compromise suggested first by Chou En-lai, in his press conference on December 18, 1945, which, according to him, the Communists had been trying for some time to persuade the Nationalist government to accept.[30]

 This political and military settlement was enthusiastically received by

[28] *United States Relations with China*, p. 688.
[29] *Ibid.*, pp. 182–85, and *Military Situation in the Far East*, pp. 549–50.
[30] "The Press Conference of Communist Delegates, Chou En-lai and Yeh Chien-ying," *Hsin Chung-kuo ti shu-kuang*, p. 40.

the Chinese people. The Communists were jubilant.[31] The right-wing Nationalists were openly critical.[32] General Marshall was apparently satisfied with the results of his endeavors. On February 25, President Truman instructed the Secretary of State to conduct the necessary negotiations with the Nationalist government for establishing a United States military advisory group in China with a maximum of one thousand officers and men.[33] On March 11, General Marshall left China for the United States to arrange a loan of $500,000,000 from the Export–Import Bank to China and to secure other aid in the form of shipping and sale of surplus property.[34] With President Truman's backing, he succeeded quickly in gaining the agreement of the various agencies in these matters. In April, he made a report to the Foreign Relations Committee of the Senate on his mission to China. He had the impression that he "was supported" by the committee though there was no formal expression of opinion.[35] Meanwhile, in China, General Wedemeyer set up at the instruction of General Marshall a military mission, which was established under the war powers of the President.[36] Wedemeyer also took steps to withdraw American troops from China. On April 2, he announced that the United States Army in the China theater would be disbanded and the marines would revert to the command of the navy.[37]

After General Marshall returned to China on April 18, the policies set in motion by him moved forward in the United States on their own momentum. In June, bills to provide military advice and assistance to China were introduced in the Senate and the House to give a statutory basis to the military mission.[38] In a hearing before the House Committee on Foreign Affairs on June 19, it was made clear that one of the objectives in granting American assistance to Chinese ground forces was to help China

[31] The Communists held a mass meeting in Yenan to celebrate the successful conclusion of the conference. Addressing the meeting, General Chu Teh urged the Communists to make every effort to implement the resolutions (*Hsin Chung-kuo ti shu-kuang*, pp. 90–94). See also the two editorials of the Communist *Hsin-hua jih-pao* on February 1 and February 2, 1946, as reprinted in *ibid.*, pp. 99–104.

[32] *Central Daily News*, January 17, 1946, editorial; January 25, 1946, editorial (both as reprinted in Li Hsü, *op. cit.*, pp. 102–05, 114–16); Yeh Ch'ing, "A General Appraisal of the Five Principal Resolutions," *ibid.*, pp. 173–209.

[33] *United States Relations with China*, p. 339.

[34] Walter Millis suggested that Marshall hoped that he could bring pressure on the disputing factions in China by his trip to the United States (Walter Millis, with Harvey C. Mansfield and Harold Stein, *Arms and the State* [New York: Twentieth Century Fund, 1958], p. 196).

[35] *Military Situation in the Far East*, pp. 569–70.

[36] *Ibid.*, p. 558; *United States Relations with China*, p. 346. The group was established on March 19, 1946.

[37] *New York Times*, April 2, 1946, p. 19.

[38] *Congressional Record*, XCII, 79th Cong., 2d sess. (1946), 6773, 6979; *United States Relations With China*, p. 340; Norman Palmer, "Marshall's Mission to China," *Current History*, September, 1951, p. 146.

implement the program of integrating the Nationalist and Communist armies.[39] Undersecretary of State Dean Acheson told the committee that General Marshall granted a Communist request that the integration of Communist forces with the other forces "be preceded by a brief period of United States training and by the supply of minimum quantities of equipment."[40] On June 27, the committee reported favorably on the bill. However, no action was taken by the Seventy-ninth Congress. The American army mission continued to depend for its existence on the President's war powers. But events in China developed so quickly in another direction that they left American policies far behind. Even while Marshall was in the United States, the military-political settlement was fast disintegrating.

B. The Breakdown of the Settlement

1. Negotiation, Truce, and War in the Policies of the Kuomintang and the Chinese Communist Party

The process of the breakdown of the settlement and the negotiations after Marshall's return to China formed one of the most intricate chapters of American policy in China and of Chinese history. In Secretary Acheson's words:

> They [the negotiations] are incredibly complex, as complex as only Chinese negotiations can become. One side makes a proposal; the other side says that they will accept one of those proposals, but have four qualifications on each of the others. Then the one making the proposals comes back and will accept certain of the qualifications but has qualifications on those. And after a while it becomes impossible to follow.[41]

It would be unprofitable to recount the details of these negotiations. But if one grasps firmly the fundamentally irreconcilable nature of the conflict and the diametrically opposed positions and policies of the two sides, one can readily delineate the strategies and tactics of the two antagonists which made the breakdown of the settlement inevitable. One can also state the critical issues for which no new solution could be found in spite of Marshall's tremendous efforts. Such a discussion would not only throw light on the general problem of negotiations between two irreconcilable

---

[39] General Marshall's telegram to the committee, June 18, 1946, as reprinted in House Committee on Foreign Affairs, *Assist China To Modernize Her Armed Forces*, 79th Cong., 2d sess. (1946; House Report 2361, to accompany H.R. 6795), pp. 2–3; *Military Situation in the Far East*, p. 602.

[40] Excerpts from Undersecretary of State Acheson's testimony which were read into the *Congressional Record* on May 15, 1951, by Mrs. Edith Nourse Rogers (*Congressional Record*, XCVII, 82d Cong., 1st sess. [1951], 5386). This brief period of training by American officers was specified as 60 to 90 days (*ibid.*, p. 5387).

[41] *Military Situation in the Far East*, p. 1866.

forces, it would also demonstrate the futility of trying to resolve such conflicts by an elaborate structure of formal agreements publicly committing the two sides to detailed terms of concessions and co-operation.

In retrospect, it seems clear that, to say the least, both sides had serious reservations about the possibility of reaching a lasting settlement. The agreements worked out in January and February with the help of General Marshall represented only a deceptive façade behind which each side maneuvered for a better political and military position and hid its own strategies and tactics. Toward the end of his mission, General Marshall was convinced that, to use the words of the United States White Paper of 1949, "the Generalissimo was certainly following a definite policy of force under cover of the protracted negotiations."[42] "In the past [General Marshall] had often felt that the National Government had desired American mediation as a shield for its military campaign."[43] There is no positive evidence that Generalissimo Chiang did not negotiate in good faith in January and February. But subsequent events also suggest that, to state it mildly, he had never ruled out further use of force as one alternative. From available evidence, one cannot determine with certainty whether Chiang's objective was the total elimination of the Communist forces by all-out civil war or was limited to driving them out of the important regions and putting pressure on them to accept a settlement on his terms. But even if his objective was a limited one, his practice of raising his demands and stepping up military attacks after every temporary victory contributed to the expansion of the scope of the fighting and ultimately led to all-out war.

On their part, the Communists never failed to take actions in the field to occupy new territory, to expand their armies, and to increase their influence. These actions were taken when they were clamoring for peace and were justified by them as measures to prepare themselves for a breakdown of the negotiations or a collapse of the settlement. In an article written in 1951 to commemorate the thirtieth anniversary of the Chinese Communist party, General Chu Teh made this point quite clear. According to him, the Chinese Communist party was confronted in 1945 and 1946, on the one hand, with an intense desire for peace on the part of the Chinese people and, on the other, with the determination to wage a civil war on the part of the Generalissimo, who had the support of the United States. Chu wrote:

> Under these circumstances, the Chinese Communist Party, on the one hand, raised resolutely the banners for peace, democracy and unity, and endeavored with the utmost efforts to lead the Chinese people in seeking a way to avoid war and to realize

[42] *United States Relations with China*, p. 90.
[43] *Ibid.*, p. 217.

peace. On the other hand, it mobilized the Party, and all the people and armies in the liberated areas and the people of the whole nation to make full preparations so that it could be in readiness to defeat Chiang Kai-shek's anti-popular and anti-revolutionary military attacks when he resolutely destroyed the peace.[44]

By promoting 'peace, democracy, and unity," the Communists sought to avoid a civil war which they might have lost and to obtain a settlement which would have facilitated the rapid expansion of their influence. By advocating a moderate political program, they endeavored to isolate Generalissimo Chiang and to deprive him further of popular support when he persisted in his attempt to suppress or defeat them by military means.[45] All the while, they took actions to increase their military power and to prepare for a renewal of the civil war. Their dual tactics made peace impossible.

During the whole period of the Marshall mission, the Communists consistently followed this two-pronged policy. After the establishment of the truce in January, the Central Committee repeatedly instructed the Communist cadres in various areas to regard troop training, production, and land reform as their three central tasks. On May 4, it issued a directive changing its policy of reducing rent and interest to that of confiscating the

[44] Chu Teh, "Chung-kuo jên-min tsen-ang chi-pai liao Mei-ti-kuo-chu-i wu-chuang ti Chiang Kai-shek fan-tung-pai" ["How the Chinese People Defeated the American Imperialist-armed, Reactionary Clique of Chiang Kai-shek,"] as reprinted in *Chung-kuo Kung-chan-tang chêng-li san-shih chou-nien chuan-chi* ["Special Compilation Commemorating the Thirtieth Anniversary of the Founding of the Chinese Communist Party"], I (Canton: Jên-min ch'u-pan-shê, 1951), 9–10.

[45] General Chu wrote gleefully: "Thus, when American imperialism and Chiang's reactionary faction of the Kuomintang felt that they had completed their preparations for their anti-popular, anti-revolutionary, large-scale civil war, they had been isolated politically and lost the sympathy of the people of the whole nation." Chu also said that by fighting vigorously for peace, democracy, and unity, the Chinese Communists exposed Chiang's plots to fight a civil war and helped the Chinese people to dissipate their illusions about Chiang through their own experience (*ibid.*, p. 10).

See also Hu Chiao-mu, *Chung-kuo Kung-ch'an-tang ti san-shih nien* ["Thirty Years of the Chinese Communist Party"] (Peking: Jên-min ch'u-pan-shê, 1951), pp. 52–56, and Yeh Hu-shêng, *Hsien-tai Chung-kuo kê-ming shih-hua* ["A History of the Revolution in Contemporary China"] (Peking: Kai-ming shu-tien, 1951), pp. 112–14. For an able contemporary report of the policies of the Communists, see Tillman Durdin's dispatch in the *New York Times*, March 17, 1946, Sec. 4, p. 5. Cf. Lord Lindsay of Birker, "1921 and After," as reprinted in Senate Committee on the Judiciary, *Hearings on the Institute of Pacific Relations*, 82d Cong., 1st and 2d sess. (1951–52), p. 5385 (hereafter cited as *Institute of Pacific Relations*).

It is interesting to note that the *Selected Works* of Mao contain nothing on China's internal situation between December 15, 1945, and July 20, 1946. There are no directives, speeches, or commentaries written by Mao on the negotiations, the truce, the Political Consultative Conference, the agreement on military reorganization, the fighting in Manchuria, and the breakdown of the truce. Available evidence does not permit us even to speculate on the reasons for this omission.

lands of the landlords and distributing them among the peasants.[46] The significance of this directive was that the Communists now abandoned the land policy which they had adopted in 1937 in order to bring about a united front with the Kuomintang and that they reverted to a slightly different version of the policy which they had followed during the first civil war with the Kuomintang. This change in land policy was obviously a measure to mobilize the peasants for the local fighting that was going on in various places despite the truce and for a possible outbreak of all-out war. As Mao pointed out some months later, "The peasants stood with our Party and our army against the attacks of the Kuomintang troops" after the truce had broken down in July wherever the new land policy was carried out firmly and speedily.[47]

Given the profound reservations of both sides about the possibility of a lasting settlement, the collapse of the delicately balanced structure of agreements was inevitable. Soon after the agreements were reached, both sides maneuvered to gain a better position than the settlement granted them. As a result of these maneuvers, the political and military situation was constantly changing; the changed conditions were made the basis of new demands and new negotiations.[48] As the political agreements militated against the interests of the Kuomintang, the Nationalists took actions which cast grave doubts whether they would sincerely honor these agreements. As the provisions in the February agreement regarding the integration of Communist forces into a national army militated against the interests of the Chinese Communist party, the Communists did not take the necessary steps to implement them. In spite of the cease-fire order, both sides took military actions in the field while they were negotiating on unresolved or new issues. Each hoped that certain important cities or areas might be brought under its control so that it would be in a stronger position when the coalition government or the constitutional regime was set up or, alternatively, in a better military posture when the settlement collapsed.[49] Actions on the part of the Kuomintang in the political realm were given as justification for actions on the part of the Communists in the military sphere. Then the actions on the part of the Chinese Communists were in turn cited as reasons why the Nationalist government was forced to take certain military actions against the Communists and to compel the Communists to accept its terms by military pressure. In taking military action against the Communists, the Nationalists relied on their immediate military superiority and sought a quick victory. In refusing to accept a new

[46] Mao Tse-tung, Selected Works, IV (Peking: Foreign Languages Press, 1961) 116, 118, n. 4, 124 (hereafter cited as Mao, Selected Works, IV [Peking]).
[47] Ibid., p. 116.
[48] United States Relations with China, pp. 134–64.
[49] Military Situation in the Far East, p. 1866.

set of terms under military pressure, the Communists counted on their ability to avoid decisive engagements, to prolong the war, and eventually to counterattack. Thus, the fighting was gradually expanded in scope until it became an all-out civil war.

2. The Miscarriage of the Political Program

The process of the collapse of the settlement and the futile negotiations to arrive at a new accord went through three phases, each with its central issues and each leaving unsolved problems to the next. In each of these phases, Generalissimo Chiang moved a step away from the settlement of January and February and toward his own conception of how to deal with the Communists. Likewise, the Communists became increasingly uncompromising in their attitude. During the first phase, the political program laid down by the Political Consultative Conference miscarried. As soon as the PCC adjourned and the military agreement was reached, successful implementation of the agreements became doubtful. There were indications of strong resentments against the resolutions of the conference on the part of powerful groups within the Kuomintang and of opposition by a powerful group of Nationalist generals to any reorganization of the armies which would threaten their interests. Incidents occurred in Chungking and elsewhere which aroused fears that irreconcilable elements in the Kuomintang might sabotage the program worked out by the conference.[50]

At this crucial moment in Chinese politics, a discussion in the United States of the future disposition of former Japanese islands in the Pacific elicited a broadcast from Moscow stating its claim on the Kurile Islands and southern Sakhalin on the basis of a secret agreement made at Yalta.[51] The Yalta Agreement was simultaneously released, on February 12, in the

[50] The most notable instance was "an attack by alleged Kuomintang plainclothes men in a mass meeting held at Chungking to celebrate the success of the PCC." Other instances were also given in the *United States Relations with China*, pp. 143–144, 151. Commenting on these actions, General Marshall wrote in his personal statement issued on January 7, 1947: "They [the dyed-in-the-wool Communists] completely distrust the leaders of the Kuomintang and appeared convinced that every Government proposal is designed to crush the Chinese Communist Party. I must say that the quite evidently inspired mob actions of last February and March, some within a few blocks of where I was then engaged in completing negotiations, gave the Communists good excuse for such suspicions" (*ibid.*, p. 687).

[51] Following a public debate on the question of trusteeship for Pacific bases acquired by the United States, a reporter asked Undersecretary of State Acheson in a news conference about "a secret agreement" at Yalta which gave the Soviet Union possession of the Kuriles. Mr. Acheson replied that the Yalta decision on the subject had been concerned with Soviet occupation of the Kuriles and was not a final territorial decision (*New York Times*, January 23, 1946, p. 10). Acheson's interpretation was disputed by this broadcast from Moscow (*ibid.*, January 27, 1946, p. 19). In his news conference on January 29, Secretary of State Byrnes revealed that the Yalta Agreement had referred to Dairen and Port Arthur as well as the Kuriles and the southern half of Sakhalin. On January 31, President Truman told reporters that the Yalta Agreement would

United States, the Soviet Union, and Great Britain.[52] The publication of the agreement at this time had an unfortunate effect in China. It strengthened the hands of the Nationalist opponents of the Kuomintang-Communist accord, for they were now in a better position to charge that the United States had been sacrificing China's interests to appease the Soviet Union and her Chinese agents by signing the Yalta Agreement and by sponsoring the recent settlement with the Chinese Communists.[53] Their argument was further strengthened by the strained relations with the Soviet Union as a result of Soviet demands for a share of control over Manchurian industries and delay in withdrawing the Red Army from Manchuria after the agreed deadline of February 3. In late February, anti-Soviet student demonstrations, instigated by Ch'ên Li-fu, the leader of the right-wing C.C. clique, broke out in major cities in China.[54]

Against this background, the Central Executive Committee of the Kuomintang met from March 1 to March 17 to pass upon the PCC resolutions. In the meeting, members of the C.C. clique vigorously attacked those responsible for the conduct of Sino-Soviet negotiations in Manchuria.[55] The PCC resolution on the draft constitution was heatedly debated, with many speakers strongly advocating the presidential system and opposing the grant of a high degree of autonomy to the provinces.[56] The aim of these and other moves was to unseat or discredit the moderates of the Kuomintang who were attempting to work out an economic agreement with the Soviet Union in Manchuria and who, with Marshall's help, had negotiated the settlement with the Communists.[57] Although in the end the Central Executive Committee "ratified unanimously" all PCC agreements, it was clear that influential leaders in the Kuomintang wished to revise the PCC resolution on the draft constitution in order to make it conform with the concept of the "Quintuple-Power Constitution" and the Three Principles of the People of which the Kuomintang itself was the authorative interpreter.[58]

be made public if the Soviet Union and Great Britain had no objection (*Department of State Bulletin*, February 10, 1946, pp. 189–90).

[53] *New York Times*, February 12, 1946 p. 10; *Department of State Bulletin*, February 24, 1946, pp. 282–83.

[53] *New York Times*, February 15, 1946, p. 8.

[54] Chap. viii, above.

[55] Chang, *op. cit.*, p. 168; *New York Times*, February 23, 1946, p. 4.

[56] *United States Relations with China*, p. 634. The opposition to the grant of a high degree of autonomy to the provinces took the form of a demand that "provinces should not have their own constitutions," as provided by the PCC resolutions, and the "federalism should be discarded" (*ibid.*, and *China Handbook, 1937–1945* [New York: Macmillan Co., 1947], pp. 760–64).

[57] *New York Times*, March 16, 1946, p. 6.

[58] *United States Relations with China*, p. 144. See also the news release of the official Chinese News Service and the Manifesto of the Central Executive Committee of the Kuomintang, *ibid.*, pp. 634–39, and excerpts from Chiang's speech before the People's Political Council, *China Handbook, 1937–1945*, Supplement for 1946, pp. 760–64.

The Chinese Communist party and the Democratic League countered with the demand that any proposed revisions have the agreement of all parties and that the Kuomintang commit itself to the implementation of the revised PCC program. Meanwhile, they refused to nominate members to participate in a reorganized government. The Chinese Communist party postponed a March 31 meeting of its Central Committee which had been scheduled for the purpose of ratifying the PCC resolutions. The Communists also refused to submit a complete list of their military units as required by the military agreement of February 25. Toward the end of April, the discussions on political matters reached a complete deadlock.[59] It was also at this time that the fighting in Manchuria was moving toward a climax. So long as the issues in Manchuria remained unresolved, there was no prospect that any agreement on political matters could be reached.[60] Thus, the PCC plans to set up a transitional coalition government, to prepare a revised draft constitution, and to convoke the National Assembly on May 5 for the purpose of adopting a new constitution miscarried.[61]

3. The Crisis in Manchuria

The second phase of the breakdown of the settlement overlapped the first and its main issue was the crisis in Manchuria. The cease-fire agreement of January 10, 1946, granted the Nationalist government the right to move its troops into Manchuria for the purpose of restoring Chinese sovereignty as the Soviet troops left. There was a separate provision for the cessation of hostilities which, according to American interpretation, was applicable to Manchuria as well as to other regions of China.[62] On this basis, General Marshall urged the Nationalist government and the Communists to agree to the dispatch into Manchuria of tripartite field teams in order to supervise the truce and to prevent further conflicts. Marshall's proposal met with the approval of the Communists but was adamantly opposed by the government. In the words of the White Paper, "At this stage the National Government seemed determined to incur no restraints on its freedom of action in Manchuria and appeared bent on a policy of complete military occupation of the area and elimination of the Chinese Communist forces if they were encountered."[63] On March 11, the day of his departure for Washing-

---

[59] United States Relations with China, p. 148.
[60] Chang, op. cit., p. 156; Ch'ien, op. cit., pp. 379–80.
[61] According to the minor parties, it was agreed on April 24 by all sides concerned that the convocation of the National Assembly would be postponed and that a new date would be decided by discussion among all parties (United States Relations with China, p. 197).
[62] Ibid., p. 145.
[63] Ibid., p. 146. Testifying in the MacArthur hearings, Marshall stated that the Manchurian crisis was "precipitated largely by the manner in which the Nationalist troop commander proceeded in the case." He said in another context that "he [the com-

ton, General Marshall finally succeeded in persuading Generalissimo Chiang to agree to entry of the field teams into Manchuria. But the authority granted them was not sufficiently broad to bring about a cessation of hostilities. Their activities were also hampered by Nationalist obstructions.[64] Thus, fighting in Manchuria was never effectively stopped.

This already confused situation was further complicated by the withdrawal of Soviet troops which began on April 6. Soviet evacuation of Manchuria left a vacuum which both sides tried to fill. The Nationalist forces pushed forward, not only to take over cities and lines of communication from Soviet troops, but also to establish military control in rural areas occupied by the Communists. On their part, the Chinese Communist forces also rapidly expanded their control in Manchuria, for the Soviet troops were withdrawn in such a way as to facilitate their taking over the evacuated areas. On April 18, the Communist forces captured Changchun which had been garrisoned by the Nationalist forces for several months. The new confidence acquired by the Communists as a result of this development was evidenced by their demand for a revision of the ratio of military strength in Manchuria from the stipulated one Communist division to fourteen Nationalist divisions, to five Communist divisions for fourteen divisions of Nationalist forces.[65] Earlier, they had demanded joint control of Manchuria. They claimed to have 300,000 troops there.[66]

The Communist capture of Changchun was a flagrant violation of the cease-fire agreement.[67] It gave Generalissimo Chiang the needed justification to launch an all-out attack in Manchuria to defeat the Communists. After a month of hard fighting, the Nationalist forces with the American-trained New First and New Sixth Armies as their spearhead defeated the Communist troops and captured the strategic city of Ssŭpingchieh on May 19. Outflanked, outfought, and outnumbered, the Communists suddenly withdrew from Changchun.[68] Flushed with victory, the Nationalist forces disregarded all restraints and pushed toward Kirin and Harbin.

General Marshall made a valiant attempt to stop the fighting in Man-

mander of the Nationalist forces in Manchuria] had needlessly endangered his command and had conducted operations in the hinterland which were extermination, an effort to exterminate all Communists in that region, and they retaliated, of course, and very effectively" (*Military Situation in the Far East*, pp. 543, 544).

[64] *United States Relations with China*, p. 197.

[65] *Ibid.*, pp. 151–54.

[66] *New York Times*, February 16, 1946, p. 1.

[67] *United States Relations with China*, p. 159; Everett D. Hawkins, "War and Peace in Manchuria," *Far Eastern Survey*, January 29, 1947, pp. 18–20. General Marshall thought that this attack on Nationalist forces in Changchun was partly in retaliation for Nationalist assaults in Manchuria (*Military Situation in the Far East*, p. 543).

[68] It cannot be determined from available records whether Chou En-lai's acceptance of Marshall's proposal to evacuate Changchun played a part in the planned withdrawal by the Communists from that city. See pp. 420–21, below.

churia as soon as he came back to China from the United States on April 18, the day the Communists captured Changchun. He endeavored to persuade the Communists to evacuate Changchun voluntarily and to persuade Generalissimo Chiang to halt the advance of the Nationalist forces. His plan envisaged the establishment of an advance echelon of the Executive Headquarters at that city to stop the fighting and to enable the two sides to begin new negotiations. The city was to be turned over to the government within a maximum time of six months. After the Nationalist forces had captured Ssŭpingchieh, Generalissimo Chiang expressed agreement with Marshall's view that the government forces should not at this time occupy Changchun by force. He informed Marshall of his fear that his military commanders in Manchuria were advancing toward that city and said that he was leaving for Mukden to keep control of the situation. On the day he left Chungking, his forces entered Changchun. In spite of both his statements to Marshall and Marshall's new appeals by radio, Generalissimo Chiang took no action to stop the further advance of his troops, which were now pushing on to Harbin.[69] On the contrary, his presence in Mukden at the time of the capture of Changchun and his pronouncements issued in Mukden made it appear that his journey was timed to coincide with a previously planned military triumph. His use of Marshall's official plane for his flight to Manchuria conveyed the impression of Marshall's close connection with the trip.

Worst of all, Marshall, back in Chungking and taking Chiang's words at their face value, succeeded at precisely the same time in persuading Chou En-lai to agree to a halt in the fighting in Manchuria and to a voluntary evacuation of Changchun in return for a cessation of further advance of Nationalist forces.[70] Commenting on this series of events, the White Paper concluded:

> The fact that just as an agreement seemed to be on the verge of being reached the Generalissimo remained absent in Mukden and Peiping for a considerable period while his armies exploited their successful action south of Changchun aroused great suspicion against his good faith and particularly against the impartiality of General Marshall's attitude, since General Marshall had advanced proposals to the Chinese Communists for Communist evacuation

[69] In his memoirs, Chiang wrote: "General Tu [commander of the Nationalist forces] moved up from Ssupingkai to Changchun on May 23. Government troops *were ordered* to push on along the Chinese Changchun Railway with Harbin as their target. . ." (Chiang Kai-shek, *Soviet Russia in China* [New York: Farrar, Straus & Cudahy, 1957], p. 166. Emphasis added). Generalissimo Chiang apparently changed his mind after his arrival in Mukden and decided to push on to Harbin in an attempt to exploit his victory. All reports from the front which he received agreed that the Communists would not be able to fight after the recent defeat (*ibid.*, pp. 166–67).

[70] *United States Relations with China*, pp. 155, 159.

of Changchun and the cessation of further advances by National Government troops which the Communists had accepted.[71]

There began at this time violent Communist propaganda attacks against the alleged support given by General Marshall to the Nationalists in the fighting. The Manchurian crisis temporarily subsided when General Marshall finally succeeded in persuading Chiang and the Communists to issue, on June 6, an order halting advances, attacks, or pursuits by their troops in Manchuria for a period of fifteen days. This truce was later extended to June 30.[72]

4. The Process of Total Collapse

a. The impasse in the negotiations in June. — In the third phase of the breakdown of the settlement, fighting spread throughout China and the country drifted toward all-out civil war while negotiations undertaken with General Marshall as mediator ran into one impasse after another. This third phase began with the period of truce in Manchuria from June 7 to June 30. During this uneasy truce, Generalissimo Chiang presented the Chinese Communists with a series of stringent terms for a settlement with time limits varying from ten to seventy-five days attached to many of these demands.[73] These terms were presented to the Communists against the background of the smashing victory of the Nationalist armies in Manchuria in May. The truce in Manchuria was one of limited duration, and the original cease-fire agreement of January 10 was of doubtful effectiveness and validity. Sporadic but violent fighting took place in various localities, particularly in North China.[74] The freely expressed preference of some Nationalist leaders for a policy of force and their con-

[71] *Ibid.*, p. 159.

[72] Marshall's success in obtaining a truce was considered by Senator McCarthy as the second of Marshall's four interventions on the side of the Communists (*Congressional Record*, XLVII, 82d Cong., 1st sess. [1951], 6587).

Generalissimo Chiang also attributed immense significance to this cease-fire. He wrote in his memoirs: "The second cease-fire order turned out to be the beginning of the Government forces' debacle in Manchuria. If at the time Government pursuit units near Shuangcheng, which is less than 100 kilometers from Harbin, had pressed on toward that city of strategic importance on the Chinese Changchun Railway, Communist remnants in northern Manchuria would have been liquidated and the situation throughout Manchuria stabilized. If the Chinese Communists were driven out of their foothold in northern Manchuria, Soviet Russia would have found no way to send them any more supplies and a fundamental solution to the problem of Manchuria would have been at hand. The subsequent defeat of Government troops in Manchuria in the winter of 1948 was largely due to the second cease-fire" (Chiang, *op. cit.*, p. 168).

Lt. Colonel Robert R. Rigg called the truce "the turning point not only of the Manchurian campaign but of the entire civil war" (*Red China's Fighting Hordes* [Harrisburg Pa.: Military Service Publishing Company, 1951], p. 254).

[73] *United States Relations with China*, pp. 160–61, 165.

[74] *Ibid.*, p. 159.

fidence in a quick victory [75] forcefully reminded the Communists of the possibility of Generalissimo Chiang's launching an all-out attack to enforce his demands.

Generally speaking, in the negotiations during this period the Communists gave the highest priority to the objective of obtaining a cessation of hostilities and an extension of the Manchurian truce, because the short-term military superiority rested with the Nationalists. Their desire to stop the sporadic fighting and to ward off Nationalist military pressure became stronger than their suspicion of American motives. They reversed their position and agreed to the Nationalist demand that the deciding vote be given to Americans on the field teams and in Executive Headquarters regarding matters pertaining to the procedures governing cessation of hostilities.[76] They demanded the issuance of a new order for the termination of hostilities in Manchuria and China proper prior to negotiation on other issues. They made proposals for strengthening the authority of the field teams. They agreed to a formal discussion of the central issue of redistribution of troops in North and Central China after the Generalissimo extended the truce in Manchuria to the end of June.[77]

On the substantive questions, they proposed at first the restoration of the status quo in China proper as of January 13, in accordance with the order for the cessation of hostilities of January 10, and the restoration of original positions in Manchuria as of June 7.[78] This proposal would have worked out to their advantage as they had been much less successful in their military operations than the Nationalists since the first truce had been declared. Later, with new attacks by the Nationalist forces looming on the horizon, they agreed to withdraw their troops under certain conditions from some of the areas claimed by the government and to reduce their forces in others. But they insisted that the Nationalist forces refrain from occupying the area which they would evacuate in accordance with agreements to be reached and during the period of army reorganization. They also demanded that the existing Communist local governments in evacuated areas be maintained.[79] Throughout the negotiations, they expressed concern over the fact that, while they made concessions on military matters, they did not know what the attitude of the government would be later in regard to political questions.[80]

[75] Ibid., p. 161.
[76] Ibid. The proposal to give the American member of a field team the deciding vote was first made by the American branch of the Executive Headquarters. In May, the government adopted this proposal as one of its terms presented to the Communists (ibid., pp. 154–55, 630).
[77] Ibid., p. 164.
[78] Ibid., p. 160.
[79] Ibid., pp. 165–66.
[80] Ibid., pp. 163–64.

To break this impasse, General Marshall prepared a draft proposal. Since he was anxious to prevent the renewal of large-scale fighting which would, he correctly predicted, lead to the collapse of the Nationalist government, Marshall's proposal accepted the basic position of the Communists while favoring the Nationalists in matters of detail. This document provided for the restoration of the status quo in China proper as of January 13 and in Manchuria as of June 7, except where specific exceptions were made.[81] It demanded that the Communists concentrate their forces in specified localities, but asked the Nationalist troops not to move into areas in China proper to be evacuated by the Communists. On their part, the Communists were asked not to station their troops in some of the areas which Generalissimo Chiang wanted the Communists to evacuate.[82] The existing local governments in the evacuated areas were to be maintained.[83]

The Generalissimo found fault with many points of Marshall's draft proposal. In particular he insisted on a change in the civil administration in northern Kiangsu.[84] The Communists were more amenable to Marshall's persuasion. After some discussions with Marshall, Chou En-lai said that he was prepared to consider any formula except that involving a change in the civil administration in northern Kiangsu.[85]

b. Marshall's failure to dissuade Chiang from his policy of force. — Thus the status of local governments, particularly those in northern Kiangsu, remained the only specific issue of any importance to cause a deadlock. But in sharp contrast to his remarkable success in working out a structure of sweeping agreements in January and February, General Marshall failed in June and July to produce a compromise acceptable to both sides. The reasons for this change in Marshall's effectiveness as a mediator are not hard to discover. At this time, Marshall's words carried little weight with Generalissimo Chiang and his advice was frequently rejected. For the Nationalists were now much less dependent on his help in fighting a civil war on a large scale. After the agreements in January and February had been completed, the United States had transported sizable Nationalist forces to Manchuria and North China.[86] This assistance had been rendered

[81] *Ibid.*, p. 167.

[82] *Ibid.*, pp. 166–67. An annex to Marshall's draft proposal provided that the Communist troops would not be garrisoned or concentrated within any of the following areas: all of Anhwei province; Kiangsu, south of the latitude of Hwaian (after an unspecified date) and south of the Lunghai railroad (after an unspecified date); specific points in Shantung province; Chahar, south of the latitude of Kalgan; Jehol south of the latitude of Chengte and Chengte itself; Hupeh-Hunan and all provinces in Manchuria except five northern ones (*ibid.*, p. 646).

[83] *Ibid.*, p. 167.

[84] *Ibid.*

[85] *Ibid.*

[86] In May, General Marshall explained to Chou En-lai that "when the United States had completed the movement of seven National Government armies into Manchuria

to the Nationalists in pursuance of the policy of supporting them to re-
establish their authority as far as possible, particularly in Manchuria. Yet
once the Nationalist military leaders felt strong enough in Manchuria and
North China to defeat the Communists, they paid less heed to Marshall's
advice. They were fully confident of an early victory over the Communists.
If they had any apprehensions about fighting a long and losing war, these
misgivings were offset by the evident belief, to use Marshall's words, that
"they can drag along the United States while carrying out their campaign
of force."[87] At this critical juncture, American policy seemed to be self-
contradictory and vacillating. While General Marshall expressed to Generalissimo Chiang his opposition to the latter's plans, the American government extended lend-lease to China under the terms of the new military aid
agreement of June 28, 1946.[88] A lend-lease "pipeline" credit from the United
States of $51.7 million was provided for China while lend-lease to other
countries was terminated on June 30.[89]

It is clear that sometime in the late spring or early summer Generalissimo
Chiang decided to pursue a policy of force in dealing with the Communists, despite the opposition of General Marshall. The Generalissimo's
mood at this time was vividly revealed in a passage in his memoirs. After
having explained that he rejected "Stalin's second invitation" tendered to
him on May 6 to visit Moscow because he was determined "not to follow
the Russian Communists' consistent strategy toward China, i.e., cooperation
between Kuomintang and the Chinese Communist Party, the joint establishment of a coalition government and complete dependence on Russia,"[90]
he wrote:

> A hidden international current was already lashing at Sino-
> American relations, and China was already being isolated. It was
> no longer possible for China and the United States to work out
> a joint policy toward Soviet Russia on the basis of our common
> interests. Consequently the only thing we could do was to disre-
> gard what attitude and policy the Western nations might or might
> not adopt toward us, and to be prepared, in consonance with our
> own independent policy, to go it alone, if necessary, in combatting
> Soviet aggression to the bitter end.[91]

which it was committed to transport to that area, a total of 228,000 Government troops
would have been moved by American facilities" (*ibid.*, pp. 151–52).
    [87] *Ibid.*, p. 192.
    [88] *Ibid.*, p. 969.
    [89] *Ibid.*, pp. 363, 969.
    [90] Chiang, *op. cit.*, p. 148. There is nothing in the records published by the American
government to support Chiang's report of Stalin's invitations to him to visit Moscow.
    [91] *Ibid.*, p. 149. When Chiang wrote of "combatting Soviet *aggression*," he was ob-
viously referring to what many people would now call "indirect aggression" by the
Soviet Union with the Chinese Communists as the instrument. When he spoke of a

Various items of information scattered here and there in the White Paper show beyond any doubt that by the end of June, Generalissimo Chiang had made up his mind to use force to drive the Chinese Communists from the strategic areas in China proper and to compel them by military pressure to accept his terms for a new settlement. A remark made by General Marshall to the Generalissimo on October 4 showed that Marshall had opposed at the end of June "the whole procedure in prospect for July and August" and that Chiang had assured Marshall that "there would be only local fighting in China proper and no fighting in Manchuria."[92] The Nationalist leader also said confidently to the American general: "Given time, the ripe apple will fall into our laps."[93] At this time, Nationalist military leaders expressed the view that Kiangsu province could be cleared of Communist forces within two months and that the Communists "could be brought to terms from a military standpoint within three months."[94] On June 30, General Marshall pointed out to the Generalissimo that statements issued by Nationalist military leaders indicated that "the Government was washing its hands of any democratic procedure and was pursuing a dictatorial policy of military force."[95] Marshall reminded Chiang of the possibility of violent military ruptures due to "the strong desire of Government military leaders to *settle matters by force for which the National Government plans were complete* and fairly well-known to the Communist Party."[96] In early July, Generalissimo Chiang told Marshall that "it was first necessary to deal harshly with the Communists, and later, after two or three months, to adopt a generous attitude."[97] He also said that "if General Marshall were patient, the Communists would appeal for a settlement and would be willing to make the compromises necessary for a settlement."[98]

"joint policy toward Soviet Russia," he was thinking of a joint policy toward Soviet Russia and the Chinese Communists whom he considered as nothing more than Soviet agents. At this time, Soviet troops had already completed their withdrawal from Manchuria, and there was no question of "Soviet aggression" in the literal sense. The controversy between the United States and China was not so much over the problem of a "joint policy toward Soviet Russia" as over a joint policy toward the Chinese Communists.

[92] *United States Relations with China*, p. 191. The quotations are taken from a paraphrase of a conversation between Marshall and Chiang as reproduced in the White Paper. Testifying in the MacArthur hearings, General Marshall said: "The general effort of the National Government to destroy the power of the Communist regime by military action had its beginnings in June [1946]" (*Military Situation in the Far East*, p. 659).

[93] *United States Relations with China*, p. 214. This statement by Chiang was given as a direct quotation in the White Paper.

[94] *Ibid.*, p. 216. This quotation is taken from the paraphrase of a talk between Marshall and Chiang on December 27, as given in the White Paper.

[95] *Ibid.*, p. 169. This and the following three quotations appeared in the White Paper as paraphrases of records of talks between Chiang and Marshall.

[96] *Ibid.* Emphasis added.

[97] *Ibid.*, p. 197.

[98] *Ibid.*, p. 176.

General Marshall's endeavors to find a new settlement were also frustrated by Communist policies and tactics. The Communists' expressed attitudes toward the United States at this time seemed at first glance to be contradictory but were complementary to each other. On the one hand, they continued to rely on Marshall's mediation to obtain an immediate cessation of hostilities, to ameliorate the Nationalist demands, and to put forth their own terms. These tasks were ably discharged by the suave, persuasive, and urbane Chou En-lai, who always appeared to be conciliatory, moderate, and reasonable. He always professed to trust Marshall. As late as October 10, he assured Marshall that "he did not cast any reflection on General Marshall's action throughout the entire period of mediation."[99] On the other hand, the pronouncements of other leaders and the Communist press castigated American policy with increasing vehemence in the hope of deterring the United States from giving further aid to the Nationalists. On June 26, Mao Tse-tung issued a statement in Yenan attacking the bill introduced in Congress, at the suggestion of the State Department, to provide for the establishment of an American military mission to train the integrated Chinese forces and for the sending of equipment and supplies to China, part of which, according to Undersecretary of State Acheson's testimony, would be given to the Communists.[100] Mao declared that the Chinese Communist party resolutely opposed the dispatch of the mission to China. He demanded that the United States stop all the "so-called military assistance" to China and withdraw all American troops from China.[101]

Interestingly enough, Mao's declaration coincided with a sudden intensification of interest in Chinese affairs on the part of the Soviet press. At this time, Soviet charges of American intervention in China became sharper than in previous months. The Soviet writers expressed greater confidence in the potentiality of the Chinese Communist movement than at any time since the 1920's.[102] On July 7, the Central Committee of the Chinese Communist party issued a statement demanding that the American government stop its "armed intervention in Chinese domestic affairs" and its "instigation of the Chinese civil war."[103] In mid-July, seven American

[99] Ibid., p. 195.
[100] Pp. 411–12, above.
[101] Wei tu-li ho-p'ing min-chu êrh tou-chêng ["Struggle for Independence, Peace and Democracy!"], (Chin-ch'a-chi jih-pao-shê, 1946), p. 17. Naturally, General Marshall was aware of this Communist tactic. He complained to a Communist representative about the "Communist propaganda attacks directed against his personal integrity and honesty of purpose, which were paralleled by repeated private requests from the Communists that he continue his mediation efforts" (United States Relations with China, p. 187).
[102] Charles B. McLane, Soviet Policy and the Chinese Communists, 1931–1946, (New York: Columbia University Press, 1958), pp. 252–54, 256.
[103] Wei tu-li ho-p'ing min-chu êrh tou-chêng, p. 6.

marines were kidnapped and detained by the Communists for several days. On July 29, a marine convoy bound from Tientsin to Peiping was deliberately ambushed by the Communists.[104] The hostile Communist propaganda and the attack on the marines indicated to General Marshall that the Communists now followed a new policy toward the United States.[105]

c. *The embargo and Marshall's renewed efforts.* — In July, Generalissimo Chiang puts his plans into effect. Hostilities spread to various points in China proper. Efforts of the Executive Headquarters and its field teams to stop the fighting were futile. Without consulting the Communists and other parties, and thus violating an understanding with them, the Nationalist government announced on July 4 that the National Assembly would meet on November 12, 1946.[106] This move indicated an intention on the part of the Kuomintang to depart from the procedures provided by the PCC, according to which the Nationalist government would be reorganized into a multiparty government pending the convocation of the National Assembly. Consequently, a Communist spokesman declared that the Communists would participate in the assembly only if certain conditions were met and if the pending political problems were settled satisfactorily.[107] At a time when the truce was rapidly disintegrating, Generalissimo Chiang left Nanking on July 14 for Kuling, a summer resort far away from the capital. The *New York Times* reported that many well informed American and Chinese observers suggested that the Generalissimo left Nanking to give his generals leeway to carry out limited military objectives while he was away from sources of pressure for a peaceful settlement in Nanking.[108] Diplomatic and other qualified sources conceded privately the United States had failed in her prolonged effort to bring peace to China.[109]

On his part, Mao, in an inner-party directive dated July 20, called on the Chinese Communists to smash Chiang's "offensive by a war of self-defense." Mao told his comrades that they could defeat Chiang and should be fully confident of victory. He observed that, although Chiang had American aid, the feelings of the people were against him, the morale of his troops was low, and his economy was in difficulty. To win final victory, the Communists were told to make long-term plans, to abandon temporarily indefensible cities, and to engage in mobile warfare. They were to mobilize the masses by solving the land problem, by improving the livelihood of the people in the "liberated areas," and by meeting the needs of war and at the same time lightening the burden on the people. Mao concluded that

[104] *United States Relations with China*, p. 172.
[105] *Military Situation in the Far East*, p. 543.
[106] *United States Relations with China*, p. 197.
[107] *New York Times*, July 4, 1946, p. 7.
[108] *Ibid.*, July 20, 1946, p. 5.
[109] *Ibid.*, July 21, 1946, p. 1; editorial, Sec. 4, p. 8.

"we rely entirely on our own efforts, and our position is invincible; this is the very opposite of Chiang Kai-shek who depends entirely on foreign countries."[110]

To help him deal with the rapidly deteriorating situation, General Marshall secured the appointment of Dr. John Leighton Stuart, president of Yenching University at Peiping, as American ambassador to China, after the Chinese Communists had expressed their opposition to the appointment of General Wedemeyer who was Marshall's original choice for the position.[111] Then, in the latter part of July, General Marshall took an eventful step, which attracted little attention at the time. On July 22, the *New York Times* published a seven-line report by the Associated Press from Washington to the effect that top American officials had been considering a "shutdown on shipment of arms and ammunition to the Chinese government in the hope that such a move might assist their efforts to bring peace to China."[112] The prohibition on the export of arms and ammunition to China became effective in the United States on July 29 and in the Pacific in mid-August.[113] In explaining this action, the White Paper stated:

> With respect to United States military aid program General Marshall was being placed in the untenable position of mediating on the one hand between the two Chinese groups while on the other the United States Government was continuing to supply arms and ammunition to one of the two groups, namely, the National Government.[114]

Later, the critics of General Marshall were to charge that this embargo of ten months and the delay in shipping supplies to China after the lifting of the embargo led to a shortage of small-arm ammunition which, in their view, was the decisive factor in the military collapse of Nationalist China.[115]

This step had no appreciable effect on the policies of Generalissimo Chiang. He continued to refuse to issue an order for the termination of hostilities. To circumvent the deadlock, General Marshall and Ambassador Stuart proposed the organization of a five-man committee to be composed of Nationalist and Communist representatives under Stuart as chairman,

[110] Mao, *Selected Works*, IV (Peking), 89–92.

[111] General Wedemeyer's testimony, *Military Situation in the Far East*, pp. 2311–12; General Albert C. Wedemeyer, *Wedemeyer Reports!* (New York: Henry Holt & Co., 1958), pp. 364–67; John Leighton Stuart, *Fifty Years in China* (New York, Random House, 1954), pp. 165–66. Stuart's appointment was confirmed by the Senate on July 11.

[112] *New York Times*, July 22, 1946, p. 2.

[113] *United States Relations with China*, p. 356.

[114] *Ibid.*, p. 181.

[115] Utley, *op. cit.*, chaps. i, ii, and iii. Senator McCarthy listed the embargo as the third of the four actions in which General Marshall intervened on the side of the Communists (*Congressional Record*, XCVII, 82d Cong., 1st sess. [1951] 6587).

for the purpose of reaching an agreement for the reorganization of the State Council. They hoped that progress in political discussion would persuade the Generalissimo to agree to a cessation of hostilities.[116] But successes in the field had apparently emboldened the Generalissimo. On August 6, he demanded the fulfilment on the part of the Communists of five conditions within a month or six weeks as a prerequisite to starting discussion on political matters. These terms required the withdrawal of Communist forces from vital positions and lines of communication in Manchuria, North China, and East China. As the White Paper commented, "These terms were more exacting than those at the end of June when the stalemate had been reached."[117] Significantly, as the Communists were quick to point out, Chiang's proposal made no mention of the future disposition of the local governments in areas to be evacuated by the Communists. The Communists continued to adhere to their stand that the existing local governments in disputed areas should be maintained. They also made a demand for simultaneous discussion of political and military questions.

To break this new impasse, the American government took two steps. First, General Marshall and Ambassador Stuart issued on August 10 a joint statement, informing the Chinese public of the deadlock in the negotiations. It pointed out that certain of the unsettled questions related to the disposition of troops and that the most difficult and fundamental issue was the character of local governments to be maintained in the areas evacuated as a result of the military redisposition.[118] This was apparently a move to arouse public opinion in China to bring pressure on the two sides for a compromise. The second step was a personal message dated August 10 from President Truman to Generalissimo Chiang. In it, the President warned the Generalissimo that unless genuine progress was being made toward a peaceful settlement of internal Chinese problems, it would be necessary for the President to redefine and explain the position of the United States to the American people.[119] In conversations with the Generalissimo at this time, General Marshall told the Chinese leader that the policy of the government would probably lead to Communist control in China.[120] Whatever effect these warnings might have had on Generalissimo Chiang, they were weakened by other actions of the American government. On August 30, the American government signed an agreement with the Nationalist government on the sale to China of surplus property in the various Pacific

[116] *United States Relations with China*, pp. 174–75. It was a measure of the deep gulf separating the two sides that, in spite of the tremendous efforts made by Marshall and Stuart, the five-man committee never met. For the two sides made agreement on certain questions preconditions to the meeting of the committee.

[117] *Ibid.*, p. 175.

[118] *Ibid.*, p. 649.

[119] *Ibid.*, pp. 179, 652.

[120] *Ibid.*, p. 176.

islands.[121] At this time, the negotiations between the two governments on a treaty of friendship, commerce, and navigation were also entering their last stage. It was signed on November 4, 1946. It is quite true that, as the State Department emphasized, the treaty was not a move to strengthen the Nationalist government in its civil war with the Chinese Communists and that it had no political significance.[122] But occurring at this critical juncture both the negotiations and the signing of the treaty had unfortunate effects.

The Generalissimo's response to Marshall's and Truman's warnings was twofold. On August 13, he issued a public statement, holding the Communists solely responsible for the breakdown of the negotiations, demanding Communist withdrawal from areas "where they threatened peace and obstruct communications" and asking the Communists to give assurance and evidence that they would carry out the various agreements reached.[123] On August 28, Chiang sent a reply to President Truman's message. Chiang countered the President's demand for a peaceful settlement by arguing that the minimum requirement for the preservation of peace in China was the abandonment by the Communists of "their policy to seize political power through the use of armed force, to overthrow the government and to install a totalitarian regime such as those with which Eastern Europe is now being engulfed."[124] Meanwhile, the Nationalist government continued its offensive in northern Kiangsu, cleared the Communists from the Tsinan–Tsingtao Railway, and captured Chengte, capital of Jehol province, on August 29.[125]

On their part, the Chinese Communists seized upon the Marshall-Stuart statement of August 10 as an occasion to criticize American policy and impugn American motives. On August 11, the official Communist news agency reported that in the opinion of well-informed observers in Yenan the reason for the failure of Marshall's and Stuart's mediatory efforts was the erroneous American policy of supporting "Chiang Kai-shek's dictatorial government."[126] Two days later, the official Communist newspaper published an interesting commentary on the Marshall-Stuart statement. It asserted that the United States had two policies: "One is to assist Chiang in fighting the civil war – this is fundamental; the other is to persuade Chiang to stop the civil war – this is an adjunct or an ornament."[127] It said that Chiang realized the dual nature of American policy and that without hesi-

[121] Ibid., p. 180. The procurement value of the surplus property was estimated at $900 million. The ultimate realization by the United States of this sale was $175 million (ibid., p. 1043).
[122] New York Times, November 4, 1946, p. 1.
[123] United States Relations with China, pp. 177, 649–51.
[124] Ibid., p. 653.
[125] Ibid., p. 178.
[126] Wei tu-li ho-p'ing min-chu êrh tou-chêng, p. 23.
[127] Ibid., p. 31.

tation he "accepted America's artillery and evaded the dove of peace."[128] It suggested that the United States had two choices before her. One was to cease her "one-sided assistance" to Chiang and withdraw her forces from China. The other was to continue her "deceptive" policy of "mediating with one hand and supporting Chiang with the other to oppose the Communists and the people."[129] The next day, a broadcast from Moscow went beyond the Yenan editorial in condemning the Marshall-Stuart statement which was said to mark the beginning of the second phase of American armed intervention in China.[130]

In an interview with Anna Louise Strong in August, Mao charged that "the United States reactionaries" were helping Chiang to fight a civil war. Some people seemed to feel, he said, that "United States imperialism" was terribly strong. The Chinese "reactionaries" were using the strength of the United States to frighten the Chinese people. But it would be proved that "the United States reactionaries," like all reactionaries in history, did not have much strength. Chiang and his supporters, "the United States reactionaries," were, Mao argued, "all paper tigers." Mao asserted: "The atom bomb is a paper tiger which the United States reactionaries use to scare people. It looks terrible, but in fact it isn't. Of course, the atom bomb is a weapon of mass slaughter, but the outcome of a war is decided by the people, not by one or two new types of weapon."[131] Soon after the conclusion on August 30 of an agreement between the American and Chinese governments for the sale of surplus property, the Chinese Communists issued a statement, denouncing the transaction and attributing to it every possible evil purpose. Meanwhile, the Communist forces launched an attack along the Lunghai Railway and began their siege of Tatung in early August. On August 19, shortly after the Nationalist planes bombed Yenan, the Chinese Communists ordered a general mobilization.[132]

In the fighting in July, August, and September, the Nationalist forces succeeded in taking over most of the localities and railways from which the Generalissimo had asked Communists to withdraw. The occupation of these localities by Nationalist forces was followed by the establishment of local governments under Nationalist control. Thus, by his military advances the Generalissimo transformed the five conditions into a *fait accompli*. Thus when Marshall and Chiang met, Marshall gained the impression that all the points covered by his demands would be automatically taken care of by his insistence on continued military occupation of places recent-

[128] *Ibid.*
[129] *Ibid.*, p. 33.
[130] Reprinted in *ibid.*, pp. 25–26. See also *New York Times*, August 11, 1946, Sec. 4, p. 8.
[131] Mao, *Selected Works*, IV (Peking), 97–101.
[132] *New York Times*, August 20, 1946, p. 4.

ly captured by Nationalist forces.[133] The question of local government in these areas was no longer an important issue. The Generalissimo now agreed that this question could be referred to the reorganized State Council.[134]

Having made his five conditions concerning military redisposition a *fait accompli*, in September the Generalissimo turned his attention to political questions. His policy was to compel the Communists by military pressure to accept his terms on political matters or, alternatively, to confront them with accomplished facts. His political program called for an early convocation of the National Assembly, denied the Communists and their allies a veto power in a reorganized State Council, and postponed the reorganization of the Executive Yüan. Despite Marshall's repeated advice, he refused to issue a cease-fire order before agreement on all issues was reached. He told General Marshall frankly that refusing to issue a cease-fire order was "his final trump card in forcing the Communist Party to name its delegates to the National Assembly."[135] Against the background of a series of Nationalist military advances and with the Nationalist government doing all the preparatory work, the National Assembly would meet, a constitution would be adopted, and a constitutional regime would be inaugurated under conditions entirely favorable to the perpetuation of one-party control.

As the Nationalist advance continued, the Communists became even more insistent upon an immediate cessation of hostilities. On the unsettled political issues, the position of the Communists was also diametrically opposed to that of the Generalissimo. They insisted on gaining fourteen seats for themselves and their allies in a State Council of forty members, which would give them the one-third vote necessary to veto any revision of the PCC resolutions. They maintained that the Executive Yüan should be reorganized prior to the convocation of the National Assembly. They resolutely refused to name their delegates to the National Assembly unless there was a cease-fire and the political questions were settled. Thus, no agreement was possible on any of these issues.

While Chou En-lai at Nanking was insisting on a cease-fire, Mao at Yenan issued an inner-party directive on September 16, instructing Communist cadres on the method of concentrating a superior force to destroy the Kuomintang's units one by one. Mao pointed out that this method was most useful when employed against an enemy lacking second-line troops. It was aimed at annihilating the Kuomintang's effective strength. Complete annihilation of the Kuomintang forces, Mao observed, was not only the main source of Communist arms and ammunition but also an important

[133] *United States Relations with China*, p. 183.
[134] *Ibid.*, pp. 183–85.
[135] *Ibid.*, p. 186.

source of Communist manpower through securing the surrender of Nationalist troops. Demonstrating his flexibility in military strategy, Mao told the Communists that during the war against Japan, the dispersal of forces for guerrilla warfare was primary, and the concentration of forces for mobile warfare was supplementary; but in the present civil war, the concentration of forces for mobile warfare should be primary, and the dispersal of forces for guerrilla warfare should be supplementary.[136] In an interview with A. T. Steele on September 29, Mao charged that American policy was "to use the so-called mediation as a smoke-screen for strengthening Chiang Kai-shek in every way."[137]

d. *The Nationalist attack on Kalgan, the convocation of the National Assembly, and the end of American mediation.* – To enforce his demands, the Generalissimo continued his military advance. To check further Nationalist attacks and to gain acceptance of their minimum terms, the Communists played their last card – an open threat to fight a prolonged war. This critical stage in the negotiations was reached when the Nationalists announced on September 30 the start of their military operations against Kalgan, a center of Communist power in Inner Mongolia. On the same day, Chou En-lai informed General Marshall that, if the Nationalist government did not cease its advance toward Kalgan, the Communists would assume that the Government was giving public indication of a "total national split" and of its abandonment of a peaceful settlement.[138] The Nationalist drive against Kalgan led General Marshall to the belief that, to use the words of the White Paper, "the United States Government could not continue to be a third party to the existing procedure under which the Government had been proceeding with its 'local operations' for three months" and that the "campaign against Kalgan could be justified only on a basis of a policy of force."[139] Thus, on October 1, General Marshall sent a memorandum to Generalissimo Chiang warning him that "unless a basis for agreement is found to terminate the fighting without further delays of proposals and counterproposals, I will recommend to the President that I be recalled and the United States Government terminate its efforts of mediation."[140] After further talks with Chiang, Marshall became convinced, as he told the Generalissimo, that "a campaign of force was in progress and that negotiations could be described as a cover for this campaign."[141] He came to the conclusion that "the United States Government was being placed in a position where the integrity of

[136] Mao, *Selected Works*, IV (Peking), 103–6.
[137] *Ibid.*, pp. 109–10.
[138] *United States Relations with China*, p. 188.
[139] *Ibid.*, p. 189.
[140] *Ibid.*
[141] *Ibid.*, p. 191.

its actions could be successfully questioned and that he must, therefore, recommend to President Truman his recall."[142]

On learning through Ambassador Stuart that General Marshall had sent a message to Washington recommending his recall, Generalissimo Chiang agreed to declare a conditional truce of a few days in the Kalgan area.[143] General Marshall withdrew the recommendation for his recall.[144] But this hard-won proposal for a truce was rejected by the Communists on the ground that there should be no time limit to the truce and that they would not negotiate under military pressure.[145] Chou En-lai told Marshall that only a lasting truce would demonstrate that the government did not desire a "total split." As a counterproposal, he demanded that all troops resume the positions held in China proper as of January 13 and in Manchuria as of June 7. He also told Marshall that he would not negotiate under a limited agenda and with a deadline. Instead, he presented as a basis for negotiations a list of detailed points, making clear that the Communists would insist on the implementation of the PCC resolutions. The negotiations now reached a stage where the Communists took a firm and unyielding stand, refusing to make further concessions. The distance between the two sides was greater than ever.

Chou's firm stand reflected an appraisal of the military situation made by Mao in an inner-party directive dated October 1. After three months of fighting in July, August, and September, Mao was more confident of ultimate victory in a protracted war than in early July. He pointed out that a sharp contradiction had arisen between Chiang's overextended battle lines and his shortage of troops and that this contradiction would be the direct cause of Communist victory and Chiang's defeat. Mao explained that of Chiang's more than 190 brigades, nearly half had to perform garrison duties. When his field forces advanced into Communist territory, part or even a majority of them would have to switch over to garrison duty. His effective forces were bound to dwindle as the fighting went on. In the past three months, the Communist forces had destroyed twenty-five Nationalist brigades. He predicted that, after wiping out another twenty-five Nationalist brigades in the next three months or so, the Communist forces would certainly be able to halt Chiang's offensive, to recover part of the territory lost to him, to seize the strategic initiative, and to go over from the defensive to the offensive.[146]

The intransigence of the Communists led Marshall and Stuart to issue

[142] *Ibid.*, p. 192. General Marshall's action in recommending his recall was considered by Senator McCarthy as the last of his four interventions on the side of the Communists (*Congressional Record*, XCVII, 82d Cong., 1st sess. [1951], 6588–89).
[143] *United States Relations with China*, p. 192.
[144] *Ibid.*, pp. 190–93.
[145] *Ibid.*, p. 194.
[146] Mao, *Selected Works*, IV (Peking), 113–14.

a statement on October 8, which gave a factual account of the negotiations and the latest impasse.[147] It was also an implicit criticism of the Communist refusal to accept the Kalgan truce proposal. As no truce agreement was concluded, the Nationalist forces continued their operations against Kalgan. On October 10, Nationalist forces captured not only Kalgan but also Chihfeng, the last Communist stronghold in Jehol province. They were also continuing their advance in northern Kiangsu. The next day, the government announced that the National Assembly would be convened on November 12, as scheduled.[148] A set of eight conditions for cessation of hostilities was also presented to the Communists.[149]

It is a measure of the complexity of Chinese politics that negotiations continued even after these events and despite the Communist threat of a "total national split." In this last month of negotiation, the primary objective of the Communists was to influence the minor parties and groups, with the specific purpose of creating a united front in boycotting the National Assembly.[150]

Meanwhile, the Nationalist forces marched on without much opposition from the Communists. On October 16, Nationalist forces opened an attack on Antung and Chefoo. They occupied the last of the main stations on the Tsinan–Tsingtao Railway and were moving north along the Peiping–Hankow Railway in southern Hopei.[151] By late October, Generalissimo Chiang expressed to General Marshall the view that it was time to halt the fighting. On November 8, he issued an order for all Nationalist troops to cease fire. This unilateral declaration of a cease-fire served, to use his own words, "as a further evidence of the sincere desire of the Government to achieve a lasting peace and political stability."[152] Coming as it did after a series of sweeping military advances, it conveyed a sense of triumph as well as an impression of magnanimity. At the same time, it "still held, in effect, a threat of renewed battle to force a political decision,"[153] as the

[147] *United States Relations with China*, pp. 194, 665–67.

[148] *Ibid.*, pp. 196–97.

[149] *Ibid.*, p. 199. See Chang, *op. cit.*, for a more detailed account of the eight conditions.

[150] It is apparent that at this time the Communists did not expect the negotiations and American mediation to lead to a cease-fire. They reduced their personnel at the Executive Headquarters at Peiping to the point that the Communist branch was practically inoperative. They withdrew their members from all field teams in government-occupied areas in China except at four points. Communist party personnel was gradually withdrawn from Nanking, Shanghai, Chungking, and other cities.

[151] *United States Relations with China*, pp. 190, 200.

[152] *Ibid.*, p. 677.

[153] *Ibid.*, pp. 205–6. Chiang rejected a draft statement prepared by General Marshall, which would announce the cease-fire in such a way as to indicate a desire to reach an immediate agreement with the Communist party for the unconditional termination of hostilities and to agree to an immediate adjournment of the National Assembly after formal convocation so as to hold the door open for further negotiations (*ibid.*, pp. 676–77).

White Paper pointed out. The date set for the convocation of the National Assembly was then only three days away.

Confronted by the Generalissimo with a *fait accompli* in both the political realm and in the disputed territory, the Communists stood fast. Chou En-lai told Marshall that the unilateral action of the government in convening the National Assembly contrary to the PCC resolutions meant a definite "split" in China. The Communist party subsequently informed the government that it would not participate in the National Assembly. The impending meeting of the National Assembly also precipitated a crisis for the minor parties and groups. For the Nationalist government was pressing hard for the submission of a list of their delegates to the National Assembly and postponed its convocation for three days in order to give further time for them to do so.[154] At the same time, the Communists were urging them to take a common stand. The result was a definite split in their ranks. The Democratic League joined the Communist in boycotting the National Assembly, while the Youth party and a badly divided Democratic–Socialist party decided to co-operate with the government. The process of political polarization in a society in revolution had done its work.

The National Assembly was formally convened on November 15. Chou En-lai departed for Yenan on November 19, thus bringing to an end the long period of negotiations begun in January, 1946. Before Chou's departure, General Marshall asked the Communist negotiator to obtain a formal answer from the Communist leaders whether they wished Marshall to continue in his role as mediator.[155] On December 4, Chou sent a message to Marshall from Yenan. It set forth, for transmission to the Generalissimo, terms for reopening negotiations which the government could not be expected to accept. These were (1) dissolution of the National Assembly and (2) restoration of troop positions held as of January 13, in accordance with the first agreement on the cessation of hostilities. Furthermore, Chou's message did not contain a reply to Marshall's request for a definite answer from the Communist party on the question of the continuation of his mediation. The Communist party had, in effect, rejected American mediation.[156]

e. Chiang's miscalculations. — This review of the events from June to November shows that Generalissimo Chiang's actions bore all the marks of a carefully planned program. His policies would have worked out to the interests of his regime if his estimation of its military, economic, and political capabilities had been correct. He told General Marshall on December 1 that the Communist forces could be eliminated in eight to ten months

---

[154] *Ibid.*, p. 207; Chang, *op. cit.*, p. 184.

[155] It was an indication of the embarrassing position occupied by General Marshall that he had, on at least two occasions, told the Communists that if they doubted his impartiality as a mediator, he would withdraw (*United States Relations with China*, p. 195).

[156] *Ibid.*, p. 212.

and that there was no danger for a long time of an economic collapse.[157] It would seem that he also overestimated America's willingness to come to his assistance. At the very moment when the negotiations had completely broken down, two of his chief aides approached General Marshall for financial help.[158] Later, the requests for American economic and military assistance became increasingly insistent as the Nationalist military advances turned into disastrous defeats. Unfortunately for him, his judgments on both of these crucial points was far wide of the mark.

As General Marshall had frankly told the Generalissimo in August:

> The Government had much to lose and little to gain from hostilities at this time, which might end in the collapse of the Government and of the country's economy. The Generalissimo must remember that the long lines of communication and the terrain favored the employment of the Communist guerrilla tactics. . . . He [General Marshall] opposed the policy of the Generalissimo and his immediate advisers because he thought that the procedure of the National Government would probably lead to Communist control in China; the chaotic conditions then developing would not only weaken the Kuomintang but would also afford the Communists an excellent opportunity to undermine the Government.[159]

In a discussion with a high-ranking Nationalist official in July, Marshall had also emphasized that the United States would not underwrite a Chinese civil war.[160] Events in China in the next three years developed in the direction predicted by Marshall and he steadfastly adhered to his policy of refusing to intervene militarily in the Chinese struggle.

But Generalissimo Chiang apparently thought that, as long as he controlled the government of China, the United States would come to his aid sooner or later, notwithstanding his failure to co-operate with General Marshall and to reform his regime. For Chiang had an unbounded faith in his skill in manipulating the international situation to suit his own purposes.[161] His skill in extracting every possible temporary advantage served him well when he had the upper hand, but it tended to make his position untenable when he overestimated his own capabilities and his importance to his allies. In his internal program, he was also bound to fail. For he had never succeeded in providing his regime with a broad social base and in creating a common front of non-Communist forces to confront the Communists with an invincible alliance. He could manipulate individual poli-

---

[157] *Ibid.*
[158] *Ibid.*, p. 210.
[159] *Ibid.*, p. 176.
[160] *Ibid.*, p. 174.
[161] See chap. iv, above.

ticians, but the Chinese Communists were riding on a wave of popular support. He relied solely on his armed forces to crush a popular revolution. In this task, he could only fail, as General Marshall predicted at the time.

After the end of American mediation, General Marshall urged Nationalist leaders to adopt a constitution in consonance with the PCC resolutions. He still hoped that, if such a constitution were adopted and the State Council and the Executive Yüan were reorganized, it might be possible to bring the Communists into the National Assembly. His advice on the adoption of a forward-looking constitution was accepted and implemented by Generalissimo Chiang. On December 18, President Truman issued a statement, reaffirming the policy laid down in his press release of December 15, 1945. He characterized as still sound the plan for political and military settlement worked out in early 1946. He indicated that the United States continued to hope for a peaceful solution of China's internal problems and pledged the United States not to interfere in Chinese affairs and not to become involved in civil strife.[162] On January 6, Marshall's recall was announced by President Truman. Several months before, Marshall had been advised by Truman of the latter's intention to appoint him secretary of state. Shortly after his departure from China, the State Department made public his personal statement about his mission. He attributed his failure to "the complete, almost overwhelming suspicion with which the Chinese Communist Party and the Kuomintang regard each other."[163] For this mutual antagonism, he blamed, on the one hand, "a dominant group of reactionaries who have been opposed to almost every effort I have made to influence the formation of a genuine coalition government," and, on the other, the "dyed-in-the wool" Communists, "who do not hesitate at the most drastic measures to gain their ends."[164] A close reading of Marshall's statement shows that he placed the primary responsibility for the initial breakdown of the settlement on the Kuomintang. In Marshall's opinion, "Irreconcilable groups within the Kuomintang, interested in the preservation of their feudal control of China, evidently had no real intention" of implementing the agreements reached by the Political Consultative Conference in January, 1946.[165] In contrast, the Communists did not "appear last February" to be "irreconcilable."[166] However, in the last stage the Communists assumed, in Marshall's view, a heavy share of the responsibility because of their "unwillingness to make a fair compromise."[167] General Marshall saw the only hope in the "assumption of leadership by the liberals in the Government and in the minority parties, a splendid group of men

[162] *United States Relations with China*, pp. 218–19, 689–94.
[163] *Ibid.*, p. 686.
[164] *Ibid.*, p. 687.
[165] *Ibid.*, p. 688.
[166] *Ibid.*
[167] *Ibid.*

but who as yet lack the political power to exercise a controlling influence."
He expressed the belief that "successful action on their part *under the
leadership of Generalissimo Chiang Kai-shek* would . . . lead to unity
through good government."[168] Thus, an honest effort to bring peace and
unity in China ended in a forlorn hope.

The miscarriage of the political settlement, the progressive disintegration
of the truce, the expansion of local fighting into nationwide civil war,
and Marshall's abandonment of his effort to seek peace were publicly
interpreted by Chou En-lai in a speech on January 10 as a process through
which the true nature of the American policy was exposed. Even Marshall's
statement of January 7 was cited as further proof that the American government had been helping Chiang to extend the civil war.[169] The intense
hostility of the Chinese Communists toward the United States, their confidence in Soviet might, and their depreciations of American economic and
political strength were made emphatically clear in an article which appeared in their official organ at Yenan under the by-line of Lu Ting-yi,
chief of the Department of Information of the Chinese Communist party.
Lu declared that after World War II, the "American imperialists" took the
place of "Fascist Germany, Italy and Japan" and became the fortress of
the world reactionary forces. The only difference which he saw between
the policy of "American imperialism" and that of "Japanese Fascists" toward China was that "the venomous treachery of the means employed by
American imperialism" surpassed that of Japanese imperialism. The "anti-
democratic forces" would of necessity attack the "democratic forces." But
the "democratic forces" would of necessity be victorious. "Capitalist en-
circlement" of the Soviet Union no longer existed. The world reactionary
forces were outwardly strong but hollow inside. They were becoming daily
more isolated. The American economic crisis would arrive "this year or
next." "It may be forecast categorically," he asserted that "the face of
China and the world will be vastly different after three to five years."[170]
On February 1 the Central Committee of the Chinese Communist party
formally declared that it would not recognize any foreign loans, treaties,
agreements, and understandings concluded by the Kuomintang government after January 10, 1946.[171] This statement was aimed at the lend-lease
"Pipeline" agreement of July 14, 1946, the surplus property agreement of
August 30, 1946, and the Treaty of Friendship, Commerce and Navigation
negotiated in 1946 between the United States and the Nationalist government.

These statements by Chou, Lu, and the Central Committee did not mark

[168] *Ibid.* Emphasis added.
[169] *Ibid.*, pp. 706–10.
[170] *Ibid.*, pp. 710–19.
[171] *Ibid.*, pp. 719–20.

a reversal of Communist policy, as the White Paper suggests. They marked the culmination of a process through which the Communist profession in 1944 of friendship for the United States was transmuted into outright hostility by the interaction between the deep-rooted suspicion of the Communists and the ambiguous American policies. The catalyst for this process was the shift of the balance of power in the Far East after 1944. The Chinese Communists must have come to the conclusion in 1947 that the time during which the United States could decisively influence their fortune had passed. The United States had completed her tasks of helping the Nationalist government to expatriate the Japanese and of transporting the Nationalist armies to Central China, North China, and Manchuria. She had terminated the Chinese theater and had reduced her forces in China from the peak strength of 113,000 men to 12,000. On January 29, the State Department had announced the withdrawal of the American personnel in the Executive Headquarters.[172] This action paved the way for the withdrawal of all marines from North China. At the same time, the Soviet Union was holding the ring for the Chinese Communists against possible American military intervention. Professions of friendship no longer served any political purpose. Overt hostility was in harmony with their ideological predisposition. It expressed their resentment against what they believed to be American partiality toward the Kuomintang in the mediation. It put them completely in step with the policy of the Soviet Union and the world-wide Communist movement.

The Chinese Communist leaders were equally optimistic about the military and political developments in China. In an inner-party directive dated February 1, Mao hailed the pending arrival of the new high tide of the Chinese revolution. He observed that the situation in China was about to enter a new stage of development in which "the country-wide struggle against imperialism and feudalism will develop into a great new people's revolution." He noted that, while Chiang's offensive continued, it had become much feebler than before because Chiang could no longer send, due to Nationalist losses and shortage of reserves, large combat-worthy reinforcements from his near areas to attack the Communist bases. As Mao saw it, the political development was equally favorable. The convening of the National Assembly by Chiang had, according to Mao, isolated the Nationalists instead of the Communists. Mao concluded that "our Party and the Chinese people have every assurance of final victory; there is not the slightest doubt about it."[173] Mao's growing confidence paralleled Marshall's pessimistic forecast that all-out civil war might very well lead to the collapse of the Nationalist Government. How did the United States assess the Chinese situation and what policy would she adopt?

[172] *Ibid.*, p. 695.
[173] Mao, *Selected Works*, IV (Peking), 119–25.

CHAPTER XI

PARTIAL WITHDRAWAL,

LIMITED ASSISTANCE,

AND

THE DECISION

TO ABANDON

CHINA

1947–1948

A. The Hypothetical Alternatives and the Middle Course

After the failure of his effort to achieve a political settlement between the Kuomintang and the Communists, Marshall returned to the United States to assume the post of secretary of state. On January 8, 1947, just before he left China, he asked Ambassador Stuart for his opinion on the future policy of the United States toward China. In his usual vague and restrained manner, Stuart outlined three possible courses of action: first, to give active assistance to the Nationalist government, conditioning American aid on Nationalist reform; second, to drift along with no strong program; and third, to withdraw entirely from any participation in Chinese affairs. He added that he was all for the first alternative but would much prefer the third to the second.[1] He realized that, if the United States followed the second course of action, she would antagonize every section of Chinese opinion. "The government leaders would charge us with desertion, the Communists with partisanship, and the intellectuals, speaking for the helpless masses, with imperialistic intrusion."[2] American action would merely prolong the civil war without preventing a Communist victory. The large reservoir of good will for the United States among the Chinese people would be destroyed by the belief that she was supporting a "rotten gov-

[1] John Leighton Stuart, *Fifty Years in China* (New York: Random House, 1954), pp. 178–79.
[2] *Ibid.*, pp. 181–82.

ernment."[3] Anti-American feeling would spread and deepen. Stuart recognized that "if nothing succeeds like success, nothing fails like failure."[4]

The principle underlying Stuart's remarks to Marshall was that either the United States should make an effort sufficient to stem the Communist tide in China or she should do nothing at all. In retrospect, Stuart seems to have been too optimistic about the effectiveness of American military aid and technical advice in changing the balance of forces in China. But the principle itself was sound. Indeed, it was indorsed by persons holding different views on what the China policy of the United States should be. Walter Robertson, chargé d'affaires of the American embassy in China during part of 1945 and 1946 and later one of the chief architects of the tough policy toward Communist China in the Eisenhower administration, told the House Committee on Foreign Affairs on March 4, 1948:

> I think we must face up to whether we, as Americans, are willing to undertake the job of doing what is necessary to be done in China, or if we are not willing to do that. . . . I would rather not do anything because I think you would be likely to lose what you did do.[5]

It was precisely on the basis of the same principle that Professor Nathaniel Peffer opposed the various proposals of giving additional aid to China in the winter of 1947–48. Writing in the *New York Times* on January 25, 1948, Peffer expressed the opinion that the real choice before the United States was between sending a large expeditionary force of 150,000 men to China and letting events run their course. In his view, the measures then proposed by American friends of Generalissimo Chiang to aid the Nationalists would drive the Communists into Russia's arms without enabling the government to defeat them.[6] General Marshall himself apparently subscribed to this conception insofar as it was applied to the European Recovery Program. Asking Congress for $6.8 billion as the cost of the program for the first fifteen months, he was reported to have said in January, 1948: "An inadequate program would involve a wastage of our resources with an ineffective result. . . . Either we undertake to meet the requirements of the program or don't undertake it at all."[7]

Whatever the basic views of General Marshall and the private wishes of other officials, American policy in the two years of 1947 and 1948 shifted erratically in the middle ground marked out by the two realistic alterna-

[3] *Ibid.*, pp. 188, 190.
[4] *Ibid.*, p. 188.
[5] House Committee on Foreign Affairs, *Hearings on United States Foreign Policy for a Post-war Recovery Program*, 80th Cong., 2d sess. (1948), p. 2082 (hereafter cited as *Foreign Policy for a Post-war Recovery Program*).
[6] *New York Times*, January 25, 1948, Sec. 6, pp. 8 ff.
[7] Robert Payne, *The Marshall Story* (New York: Prentice-Hall, Inc., 1951), p. 305.

tives, without following either of them. Starting out in early 1947 with a program of partial withdrawal, the United States adopted in October, 1947, a policy of limited assistance which culminated in the China Aid Act of April, 1948. This program of limited aid was enacted at a time when, according to Dean Acheson's subsequent testimony in the MacArthur hearings, the United States had the last chance to commit unlimited resources and her armed forces to the struggle in China, if she had wanted to do so, and when both the administration and Congress rejected that alternative.[8] The policy of limited assistance thus reached its climax at a juncture when it had even less chance of success than at any time since V-J Day and when its only political effect in China was to identify the United States further with an admittedly hopeless cause.

The program of limited assistance contained in the China Aid Act had scarcely been implemented when the Nationalists suffered disastrous defeats in three crucial battles in September, October, and November. By the end of 1948, Marshall had for all practical purposes written off both mainland China and Formosa. But economic assistance under the China Aid Act was never stopped. Nor was the shipment of arms under the $125 million special fund put at the disposal of the Nationalist government under the same act.[9] The United States thus continued to be entangled in China. Her immobilized position at the center not only deprived her of freedom of action but also incurred for her the liabilities of both a policy of active intervention and a program of prompt withdrawal. The American policy lent color to the Communists' distorted views of the United States, while failing to impress on them American strength and determination. It discarded the Nationalists while intensifying the hostilities of the Communists. The United States sought to avoid war by refraining from military commitments, but continued American entanglement in China intensified Communist hatred and prepared the ground for a military confrontation which was to take place after the neutralization of the Formosa Strait and the crossing of the 38th Parallel by the American forces. How did all this come about?

B. Marshall's Search for a Policy

In July, 1946, when the political-military settlement in China was rapidly disintegrating, General Marshall told Secretary of the Navy James Forrestal that, if the negotiations to preserve the settlement broke down, he would recommend a period of withdrawal so that the United States

---

[8] Senate Committee on Armed Services and Committee on Foreign Relations, *Hearings on the Military Situation in the Far East*, 82d Cong., 1st sess. (1951), p. 1869 (hereafter cited as *Military Situation in the Far East*).

[9] See chap. xii, below.

could take two or three months for reappraisal and re-evaluation of her policy toward China.[10] Shortly after he returned from China and assumed his new office of secretary of state on January 21, the policy of withdrawal was put into effect.[11] On January 29, the American government announced its decision to terminate its connection with the Committee of Three and the Executive Headquarters.[12] This decision made it possible to withdraw the American marines from Peiping, Tientsin, and Tangku where they had been stationed to guard the lines of communication.[13] A guard contingent remained at Tsingtao where the United States Naval Training Group was engaged in training Chinese naval personnel and kept a quiet watch on Russian activities at Port Arthur and Dairen.[14] In the first five months of 1947, the embargo continued in force.

Coming as it did after the failure of the United States and Nationalist China to work out a common policy had completely shattered Marshall's plans for a settlement, this policy of temporary withdrawal was sound. But in retrospect, it seems clear that maximum benefit would have flowed from this period of withdrawal only under two conditions. First, the American withdrawal would have had to be complete rather than partial, thus exerting overwhelming pressure on the Nationalist government to undertake the necessary reforms and to qualify itself for the renewal of American assistance and support. Second, the American government would have had to be able during this period to make a choice between two equally disagreeable alternatives in the light of the Nationalist response. If the pressure arising from America's withdrawal had led the Nationalist government to rejuvenate itself by a change in basic policies or in the top leadership, the indispensable condition for the effective use of large-scale American assistance would then have existed and a policy of holding part of China, by American armed intervention if necessary, might have had a fair chance of success. If the Nationalist government had failed to show the minimum stability and strength to stay in power with American support, the United States could then have promptly dissociated herself with a moribund regime and retained what was left of her freedom of action.

Unfortunately, neither of these two difficult steps was taken. The withdrawal was partial rather than complete. In some measure, this was the

[10] Walter Millis (ed.), *The Forrestal Diaries* (New York: Viking Press, 1951), p. 174.

[11] Department of State, *United States Relations with China* (Washington, D.C.: Government Printing Office, 1949), p. 219 (hereafter cited as *United States Relations with China*).

[12] *Ibid.*, p. 695.

[13] *Ibid.*, p. 219; *Military Situation in the Far East*, pp. 2235–36. In December, 1946, there was a total of less than 12,000 American soldiers, sailors, and marines in China (*United States Relations with China*, p. 694).

[14] In February, 1948, this guard contingent consisted of 2,600 men (Millis, *op. cit.*, p. 376).

result of the momentum of the ambiguous policies and actions of the past. In the first half of 1947, the Nationalist economy was bolstered by the final shipments of UNRRA supplies, totaling $235,108,000,[15] and by the matériel obtained through the surplus property agreement of August, 1946.[16] Both the United States Army Advisory Group and the Naval Advisory Group remained in China. The former was given permission to give advice concerning the organization and equipment of Nationalist units.[17] In April, the President instructed the secretary of the navy to transfer certain ships and floating dry docks to the Chinese government.[18] At a meeting of the Council of Foreign Ministers at Moscow in March, Secretary Marshall gave strong support to Nationalist opposition to the Soviet demand that problems relating to the settlement of the civil war in China be included in the agenda of the meeting.[19]

Furthermore, Marshall's search for a new policy did not lead, either during the period of partial withdrawal or later, to the adoption of one of the two realistic alternatives. Instead, he showed signs of being unable to make the difficult choice. His state of mind in early 1947 can be vividly seen in the following testimony in the MacArthur hearings:

> When I came back I was hard put to find a long-view conclusion in the matter because of the failing structure of the Kuomintang and the determination, organization, and discipline of the Communist group and their undoubted advice and possible support that would occur later from the Soviet government.[20]

[15] John C. Campbell, *The United States in World Affairs, 1947–1948* (New York: Harper & Bros., 1948), p. 190; *United States Relations with China*, p. 363.

[16] Royal Institute of International Affairs, *Survey of International Affairs, 1947–1948* (London: Oxford University Press, 1952), p. 278.

[17] *United States Relations with China*, pp. 346–47. The plan for the establishment of a military advisory group was drawn up under General Wedemeyer's direction shortly after V-J Day. It envisaged a group of 1,000 officers and 2,600 enlisted men from both the army and the navy for the first year or so (General Albert C. Wedemeyer, *Wedemeyer Reports!* [New York: Henry Holt & Co., 1958], pp. 400–401).

On March 31, 1947, Secretary Marshall informed the British and Russian foreign ministers in a note that, after the completion of the withdrawal of the American forces in China, there would remain in China some 6,180 members of the American armed forces connected with the advisory groups (*New York Times*, April 3, 1947, p. 2).

In the spring of 1948, there was a total of 572 officers and 921 enlisted men in China serving in the Army Advisory Group. See Senator Vandenberg's statement to the Senate on March 30, 1948 (*Congressional Record*, XCIV, 80th Cong., 2d sess. [1948], 3668).

[18] Campbell, *op. cit.*, p. 190.

[19] *United States Relations with China*, p. 235. Having recently returned from a trip to China, Representative Mike Mansfield of Montana suggested, in a speech on the floor of the House on February 3, that the United States take the initiative in calling a conference of interested powers to find a settlement of the Chinese civil war (*Congressional Record*, XCIII, 80th Cong., 1st sess. [1947], 767). Mansfield's suggestion elicited no positive response from the State Department. It seems clear that Secretary Marshall had ruled out international mediation as an alternative.

[20] *Military Situation in the Far East*, p. 397.

A year later in a meeting of the National Security Council on February 12, 1948, Marshall read two documents, the gist of which was that the problem of China was "practically insoluble."[21] When the Nationalist government was tottering on the brink of disaster, Marshall's puzzlement turned into despair. He was reported to have said on August 13, 1948: "I wash my hands of the problem which has passed altogether beyond my comprehension and my power to make judgments."[22]

Marshall's growing perplexity mirrored the fact that events in 1947 and 1948 sharpened the dilemma confronting him from the very beginning. The Nationalist setbacks on the battlefield after the summer of 1947 posed in an increasingly more acute form the question of giving large-scale military aid to China and eventual use of American armed forces. The mounting economic and political difficulties confronting the Nationalist government demanded immediate American assistance but at the same time multiplied the condition which in the past had rendered American aid ineffective. Marshall's dilemma was also sharpened by two developments outside of China. The first was the growing criticism of his policy by Republican leaders. The second was the rising tension between the United States and the Soviet Union and the revolutionary change in American policy which found concrete expression in the Truman Doctrine of March 12, 1947, and Marshall's European Recovery Program. Large-scale economic and military aid to Greece and Turkey furnished some Republican leaders with an additional reason to press for the adoption of a positive policy in China. Republican support for the Marshall Plan seemed to require some concession on the part of the administration to the views of Republican leaders on China policy. The lack of a bipartisan policy played into the hands of the Nationalist leaders, who quickly turned the checks and balances in American government to their advantage.[23] They were able to influence American policy through pressure exerted by Republican leaders in Congress.

The lack of a clear-cut policy on the part of the administration, the adoption of a policy of limited assistance under mounting congressional pressure, and the exploitation by the Nationalists of the division of American opinion constituted the main features in the development of American policy in 1947 and 1948. The developing partisan stalemate and the policy of limited assistance are paradoxical in terms of the realistic choices before the United States. But they are understandable as the products of the two inconsistent elements in the traditional pattern of American policy: the hope to preserve American influence and the incapacity to use force.

[21] Millis, *op. cit.*, p. 372.
[22] Payne, *op. cit.*, p. 311.
[23] Daniel S. Cheever and H. Field Haviland, Jr., *American Foreign Policy and the Separation of Powers* (Cambridge, Mass.: Harvard University Press, 1952), pp. 156–57.

C. The Gathering Storm of Republican Criticism

In order to put in historical context the rising Republican criticism of the administration's policy in 1947, it is necessary to recall that during the Marshall mission opposition to Marshall's policy was slight. Appearing in the Town Meeting of the Air on December 27, 1945, Representative Walter Judd gave his blessing to President Truman's statement of December 15, 1945, which formed the basis for Marshall's effort to promote a coalition government in China. Believing "completely in the sincerity of Chiang's desire to achieve a unified, democratic China without further warfare," he expressed the view that the administration's policy would expose the pretenses of the Communists that they supported political unity and democracy.[24] In April when Marshall made a personal report to the Foreign Relations Committee, he left with the impression that he had met with a general acceptance and approval of his policies, though there was no formal expression of opinion.[25] In May, sixty Americans interested in China issued a statement entitled "Manchurian Manifesto," sharply criticizing Soviet actions in Manchuria as a flagrant violation of the Sino-Soviet Treaty and the Yalta Agreement. It called on the American government to support "the demands of the Chinese people for a complete revision of the Yalta agreement."[26] But it made no direct attack on Marshall's policies and activities in China. In July, Senator Owen Brewster, Republican of Maine, was quoted as having said that "the Republican Party will go along with General Marshall in the Chinese situation."[27]

The first sign of dissent from Republican quarters came only on July 26, when Representative Clare Boothe Luce inserted into the *Congressional Record* a letter signed by thirty-eight Americans. This message was prompted by reports of a statement by Undersecretary of State Dean Acheson before the House Foreign Affairs Committee that, as part of Marshall's program to integrate the Communist and Nationalist armed forces, the American government was ready to supply and train Chinese Communist forces prior to their incorporation into a national army. It urged that no further aid or support be given to the Communists. It criticized Truman's statement of December 15 as "an invitation of the Communists to blackmail the Central Government."[28] After armed clashes began to spread in China,

[24] "What Should Be Our Policy in China?" inserted in the *Congressional Record* on January 16, 1946, by Representative Judd (*Congressional Record*, XCII, 79th Cong., 2d Sess. [1946], A107).

[25] Marshall's answer to Senator McMahon's question, in *Military Situation in the Far East*, pp. 569–70. The veracity of Marshall's statement has never been challenged by anyone.

[26] *Congressional Record*, XCII, 79th Cong., 2d sess. (1946), A2763.

[27] *New York Times*, July 8, 1946, p. 10.

[28] This letter was dated July 24, 1946. Among its signers were Alfred Kohlberg, Clarence Streit, Norman Thomas, Freda Utley, William Green, and Sidney Hook (*Congressional Record*, XCII, 79th Cong., 2d sess. [1946], A4494–96).

Life published on September 2 a lengthy editorial asking the United States to give "continuous, whole-hearted and plentiful aid" to the Nationalists, while inviting the Nationalists "to put their own house in order."[29]

Shortly before the Chinese Communists broke off further negotiations with the Kuomintang and rejected American mediation, the mid-term elections of 1946 resulted in a resounding Republican victory and a Republican-controlled Congress. The prestige of the Truman administration was at its lowest ebb, and there was widespread expectation of another Republican triumph in the presidential election of 1948. The division of control over the presidency and the Congress between the two parties intensified the struggle between the two branches of government for the privilege of directing American foreign policy. The likelihood of the Republican party's capturing the presidency in 1948 weakened credence in the Truman administration's capacity to control the long-term policy of the United States. Mr. John Foster Dulles, the principal foreign policy adviser to the Republican party, declared in late January, 1947, in a speech approved in advance by Senator Arthur Vandenberg, the Republican chairman of the Senate Foreign Relations Committee, and Governor Thomas Dewey, the titular head of the Republican party:

> A Democratic President and his Secretary of State can propose, but a Republican Congress can dispose. Foreign diplomats know that, and they suspect what we know — that two years from now, a Republican will be in the White House. So these foreign governments will not take very seriously American proposals which are backed only by the Democratic Party.[30]

There was no dearth of indications that the Republicans were advocating a different policy toward China. On January 11, Senator Vandenberg urged in a speech a shift of emphasis in America's policy toward China so as to encourage the Nationalists to develop a constitutional regime.[31] Advocating a tough policy toward Russia in a statement issued on January 31, Senator Styles Bridges, chairman of the Senate Appropriations Committee, said that the United States could not afford to push China into the Soviet orbit and that she must pledge her support to a nation which had just adopted a democratic constitution.[32] In a speech on February 10, Mr. Dulles called for continued support for the Nationalist government.[33]

[29] *Life*, September 2, 1946, p. 37.
[30] Quoted by Senator Claude Pepper, Democrat from Florida, from the *New York Herald Tribune*, January 26, 1947 (*Congressional Record*, XCIII, 80th Cong., 1st sess. [1947], 789).
[31] *New York Times*, January 12, 1947, p. 46. See also the speech by Senator Pepper, January 15, 1947, and the column by Joseph and Stewart Alsop quoted by Pepper (*Congressional Record*, XCIII, 80th Cong., 1st sess. [1947], 368).
[32] *Ibid.*, pp. 734–35.
[33] *New York Times*, February 11, 1947, p. 6.

The proclamation of the Truman Doctrine on March 12 and the President's request for $400 million in military and economic aid to Greece and Turkey quite naturally led some Republican leaders in Congress to challenge the administration's policy toward China. In a debate on the President's message in the House on the same day, Representative Judd took the occasion to criticize Marshall's effort to bring about a coalition government including the Chinese Communists. He asked Representative John W. McCormack, former majority leader:

> Does not the gentleman feel also that as we stand today at this crossroad we should add to our sense of grave responsibility a sense of regret that in some degree we have been assisting a Communist minority in China in its effort to overthrow the Chinese government, which with all its weaknesses has steadfastly refused to yield to such internal and external pressures as today threaten Greece and Turkey?[34]

The next day, Senator Brewster in a speech in New York called it an anomaly for the United States to help King George fight the Communists while urging Chiang to embrace them.[35]

In the hearings held on March 22 before the House Committee on Foreign Affairs on assistance to Greece and Turkey, Judd also asked Acting Secretary of State Dean Acheson to explain this "contradiction" in American policy. Acheson replied that the current American policy toward China as expressed in Marshall's statement of January 6, 1947, was "not directed toward including Communists in the Government, but making the Government more effective in carrying out the purposes of the Government."[36] He then explained:

> The Chinese Government is not in the position at the present time that the Greek Government is in. It is not approaching collapse. It is not threatened by defeat by the Communists. The war with the Communists is going on much as it has for the last 20 years.[37]

Several months later Acheson was severely criticized for his characterization of the situation of China as nothing serious in comparison to the conditions in Greece.[38] But at the time it seemed to be a reasonable appraisal

[34] *Congressional Record*, XCIII, 80th Cong., 1st sess. (1947), 734–35.
[35] *New York Times*, March 14, 1946, p. 4.
[36] House Committee on Foreign Affairs, *Hearings on Assistance to Greece and Turkey*, 80th Cong., 1st sess. (1947), p. 17 (hereafter cited as *Assistance to Greece and Turkey*).
[37] *Ibid.*
[38] House Committee on Foreign Affairs, *Hearings on Emergency Foreign Aid*, 80th Cong., 1st sess. (November, 1947), p. 24 (hereafter cited as *Emergency Foreign Aid*).

of the two situations. The alarming messages coming in from Greece had reached a climax with a report on February 20 by Ambassador Lincoln MacVeagh informing the State Department that Greece was in danger of complete collapse, economically, psychologically, and militarily, within a matter of weeks.[39] In contrast, the Nationalist forces were still launching large-scale attacks against Communist strong points with outward success, although by the end of February they were compelled to abandon their plans for attacking on all fronts, and the Communists had started a limited offensive in Manchuria.[40] On March 14, the Nationalists began their offensives against Yenan, the Communist capital, and captured it on March 19. The Nationalist chief of staff publicly claimed that the Communists would be defeated in three months.[41] Generalissimo Chiang told Ambassador Stuart that by the end of August or the beginning of September the Communists would either be annihilated or driven into the far hinterland.[42]

These Nationalist claims and the significance of the capture of Yenan were discounted by the American embassy. Its report at this time told of the failure of the Nationalist forces to score a decisive victory and the lowering of morale in Nationalist ranks. But there were no reports of serious Nationalist reverses. While the most serious economic crisis in decades broke out in early February, with prices doubled in a few days and the black market exchange rate tripled in three weeks,[43] the government was able to stabilize the situation by reimposing wartime wage and price controls and by prohibiting all strikes.[44] There were indications that during this period American officials expected a long war of attrition or a stalemate. Well-informed observers such as Nathaniel Peffer, who had recently returned from a trip to China to study "the cultural-relations program" of the State Department, expected a stalemate to ensue in six months or a year. He did not believe that the Communists would be able to conquer the whole of China.[45] In retrospect, it is clear that American officials and observers grossly underestimated the military capabilities of the Communists and, in spite of their severe criticisms of Nationalist failings, overestimated the military strength and political viability of the government. It would appear that this misjudgment with its consequent lack of a sense

[39] Joseph M. Jones, *The Fifteen Weeks* (New York: Viking Press, 1955), p. 131.

[40] *United States Relations with China*, p. 236; Liao Kai-lung, *From Yenan to Peking* (Peking: Foreign Language Press, 1954), pp. 51–53.

[41] *New York Times*, March 21, 1947, p. 17; *United States Relations with China*, p. 808.

[42] *Ibid.*, pp. 237–38.

[43] *New York Times*, February 12, 1947, p. 1.

[44] *Ibid.*

[45] *Ibid.*, May 4, 1947, Sec. 6, pp. 11 ff. Cf. Michael Lindsay, "Military Strength in China," *Far Eastern Survey*, April 9, 1947, pp. 80–82. Lindsay's perceptive analysis of the strength of the Communist forces and the weakness of the Nationalists was subsequently borne out by events.

of urgency was one of the explanations of the failure to adopt a clear-cut policy in the first three months of 1947. But, in extenuation, it should be pointed out that at this time and for more than a year afterward, the Communists themselves expected a long war.

D. The Administration in a Quandary

In April and May, conditions in China took a sharp turn for the worse. A new economic crisis broke out in the latter part of April. Despite controls, prices rose 50 to 100 per cent over a period of a few weeks, and the black market exchange rate made a new jump.[46] In Shantung, Communist forces counterattacked in the latter part of April and smashed another attack by the Nationalists in the middle of May. On May 13, they launched a powerful summer offensive in most of Manchuria and within a few weeks isolated the government units in Kirin, Changchun, and Ssŭpingchieh.[47] On May 30, the American consul general at Mukden warned of the possibility of a sudden debacle which would lay all Manchuria open to the Communists.[48] These Communist successes destroyed completely the Nationalists' hopes of an early victory.

Economic chaos and lack of military success led to political and social unrest. On May 5, a student demonstration in Shanghai started the "antihunger and anti-civil war" movement which soon spread to all other major cities in spite of a Nationalist order on May 18 prohibiting all demonstrations and strikes.[49] Ruthless repressive measures by the government succeeded in averting a nation-wide strike called for June 2. But they led to protests against police violence even among supporters of the government.[50] In May, twenty members of the Legislative Yüan presented a resolution calling for the resumption of peace talks with the Communists. On May 25, the People's Political Council, an advisory body set up in 1938 to give some degree of representation in the government to various non-Kuomintang groups, passed by a large majority a resolution inviting Communist representatives to come to Nanking for discussions on ways and means of bringing about the termination of the civil war.[51] It may very

[46] *New York Times*, April 30, 1947, p. 14; May 1, 1947, p. 16. See also Kia-ngau Chang, *The Inflationary Spiral* (New York: John Wiley & Sons, 1958), pp. 72–74.
[47] *United States Relations with China*, pp. 315–16; Liao, *op. cit.*, pp. 315–16.
[48] *United States Relations with China*, p. 316.
[49] *Ibid.*, p. 238; Dorothy Borg, "Students in Kuomintang China," *Far Eastern Survey*, July 23, 1947, pp. 4–7. For one aspect of the background of the student unrest, see James P. Speer II, "Liquidation of Chinese Liberals," *Far Eastern Survey*, July 23, 1947, pp. 160–62.
[50] A group of liberal legislators in the Legislative Yüan protested police actions. Dr. Hu Shih, president of Peking University, also expressed his disapproval of the highhanded methods of the government (*New York Times*, May 3, 1947, p. 6; June 4, 1947, p. 4).
[51] *United States Relations with China*, p. 240.

A POLICY OF LIMITED ASSISTANCE

well be that these moves were purely political maneuvers designed to pin the sole responsibility for the continuation of the civil war on the Communists. But, even so, the very fact that the Nationalists found it necessary to take these measures indicated the extent to which anti-civil war sentiment had grown in the country.

The proclamation of the Truman Doctrine and the sharp turn of events in April and May in China provided the background for a series of Chinese requests for American aid. The Truman Doctrine had apparently raised the hope of the Nationalist government for obtaining large-scale assistance. The turn of events led it to rely even more heavily than before on renewed American aid for its salvation. From May to June, it made three different requests for large-scale economic aid.[52] To put pressure behind their last request, the Chinese leaders in several statements warned of the dangers of a Communist-dominated China.[53] Secretary of the Navy Forrestal noted in his diary on June 23 that Chinese officials in Washington were "apparently starting another drive around town to enlist further help for the Nationalist government, using particularly the danger of Communism as their chief argument."[54]

These requests confronted officials in the State Department with new complications in working out a policy toward China because they had to be weighed in the light of the administration's global program and Republican demands for a change in China policy. As early as March 5, American officials had begun to give serious thought to the question of granting large-scale economic aid to Western Europe.[55] In a speech in Cleveland, Mississippi, on May 8, Undersecretary of State Dean Acheson, with the advance approval of President Truman, floated a trial balloon for economic assistance to Europe at $5 billion a year for several years. To insure the adoption of such a program, the administration had to enlist the widest possible support. To do so, it had to conciliate Republican critics of its China policy. For the most serious obstacles to its European program were not the advocates of a change in its China policy but the combined force of economy-minded congressmen and unreconstructed isolationists. The Republican-controlled Congress had begun its session on a call made by Speaker Joseph Martin of Massachusetts for an across-the-board cut in income taxes by 20 per cent and sufficient reduction in government spending to make the cut possible.[56] Subsequently, Republican leaders in the House talked of reducing the President's budget of $37.5

[52] Ibid., pp. 364–68.
[53] New York Times, June 8, 1947, p. 12; June 14, 1947, p. 8; June 21, 1947, p. 9; June 25, 1947, p. 2. See chap. ix, above.
[54] Millis, op. cit., p. 285.
[55] Jones, op. cit., pp. 199–206.
[56] Ibid., p. 90.

billion by $6 billion. Although the bill authorizing $400 million to Greece and Turkey had sailed through Congress fairly smoothly, it was only with some difficulty that the administration had avoided a cut of $150 million in its request for $350 million post-UNRRA relief.[57]

Confronted with an economy-minded Congress and deeply preoccupied with the historic task of working out a costly recovery program for Europe, American officials feared that any large-scale assistance to China, which in their opinion would be largely wasted, would entail a decrease in funds available for Europe. The administration thus rejected the Chinese requests. But to conciliate the Republican critics of its China policy so as to win their support for its European program, it had to take some action to help the Nationalists which was subtle enough to avoid the appearance of open intervention in the Chinese civil war and inexpensive enough not to be a drain on American resources. When the American marines withdrew from North China between April and September, 1947, they "abandoned" over 6,500 tons of ammunition and other matériel to the Nationalists.[58] On May 26, 1947, the arms embargo was lifted after having been in effect for ten months.[59] With this action, the period of partial withdrawal came to an end. In June, 130 million rounds of surplus 7.92 rifle ammunition were sold to the Nationalist government at 10 per cent of the procurement cost.[60] On September 15, John Carter Vincent was succeeded by Walton Butterworth as director of the Office of Far Eastern Affairs. Like the lifting of the arms embargo, Vincent's transfer from that important office to serve as minister to Switzerland was a concession to the Republicans.[61] Still a third concession was the dispatch of General Wedemeyer on a "fact-finding" mission to China, announced on July 11.[62]

[57] H. Bradford Westerfield, Foreign Policy and Party Politics (New Haven, Conn.: Yale University Press, 1955), pp. 273–75; Jones, op. cit., pp. 235–37.

[58] United States Relations with China, p. 970; Military Situation in the Far East, pp. 1950, 2235–36. Critics of the administration maintained that the ammunition abandoned would furnish only a six-day supply for the .30 caliber weapons of the Nationalists (ibid., pp. 1952–53).

[59] United States Relations with China, p. 356.

[60] Ibid., p. 975; Military Situation in the Far East, p. 1949. Colonel L. B. Moody, a United States Army Ordnance Corps officer and a critic of the administration's policy, calculated that in December, 1947, the total ammunition in the possession of the Nationalists was, at the normal rate of use, sufficient for only twenty-two days in the case of 7.92 millimeter weapons and for thirty-six days in the case of their .30 caliber United States rifles (ibid., p. 1953; Freda Utley, The China Story [Chicago: Henry Regnery Co., 1951], p. 35). The validity of this calculation depends on the meaning given the phrase "the normal rate of use."

[61] Westerfield, op. cit., pp. 259–60.

[62] In persuading Wedemeyer to go to China, Marshall admitted to Wedemeyer that, in the latter's words, "pressure in Congress (from Congressman Walter Judd, Senator Styles Bridges, and others) and from other sources accusing the Administration of pursuing a negative policy in China were compelling a reappraisal of United States policy" (Wedemeyer, op. cit., p. 382).

This move was suggested by Representative Judd to Secretary Marshall[63] and came as a complete surprise to Ambassador Stuart.[64]

E. The Wedemeyer Mission

According to his retrospective account, Wedemeyer undertook his mission to China to perform a "double task: to convince the Chinese that they must produce proof that American aid would not be wasted; and to convince Washington that such aid must be given."[65] On the one hand, he endeavored to impress upon the Nationalist government that unless it instituted some essential reforms it would not be able to secure American aid. On the other, he sought to show that the security and interests of the United States could be protected only by granting large-scale, long-term assistance to "the presently corrupt, reactionary and inefficient Chinese National Government," to use the words of his subsequent report. He expected the signs of a Nationalist regeneration and his emphasis on the vital necessity of Nationalist reform and American supervision over use of its aid would help him persuade the administration to adopt a program of large-scale aid to China.

General Wedemeyer and the members of his mission arrived in Nanking on July 23, 1947, and spent a month in China visiting the major cities, interviewing Chinese and foreigners, and receiving written communications.[66] In strict conformity with his instructions and probably with a view to generating pressure for reform, Wedemeyer made it clear that he could not make any promise for assistance or indicate what his recommendations would be.[67] After he returned to Nanking at the end of his tour, Generalissimo Chiang asked him to address the high civilian and military officials and told him to give them frankly his observations, impressions, and advice. Urged on by Ambassador Stuart, he accepted the invitation and used the occasion to criticize the government severely and to stress the urgency of various reforms. He attributed the military reverses of the government to its political ineptitude. He took the government to task for its corruption, inefficiency, incompetence, nepotism, oppressive measures against political offenders, and failure to mobilize the foreign and domestic assets of the rich and powerful.[68] He asserted that the Communists could not be defeated by force, for "today China is being invaded by an idea instead of

[63] Wedemeyer's testimony, *Military Situation in the Far East*, pp. 2296, 2312. This is also Judd's view of the origin of the mission (Westerfield, *op. cit.*, p. 260, n. 35).

[64] Stuart, *op. cit.*, p. 185.

[65] Wedemeyer, *op. cit.*, p. 388.

[66] *United States Relations with China*, p. 824.

[67] *Ibid.*, p. 763.

[68] Wedemeyer pointed out to the Nationalist leaders that the Chinese could raise at least one billion United States dollars from their private investments abroad (*ibid.*, p. 761). See also *ibid.*, p. 770.

strong military force from outside."[69] He warned that the government could win the support of the people only by effecting immediate improvements in the political and economic situation and that whether the regime would stand or fall depended on the timeliness and effectiveness of these reforms. His speech was poorly received and the Generalissimo apparently took offense at his devastating criticisms.[70] Pursuing his campaign of urging sweeping reforms on the government, Wedemeyer restated his views in a public statement issued on August 24 at the time of his departure from China. In this, he criticized the apathy, lethargy, and abject defeatism in many quarters, which found expression in the time and effort spent in blaming outside influence and seeking outside help. He concluded with the admonition:

> To regain and maintain the confidence of the people, the Central Government will have to effect immediately drastic, far-reaching political and economic reforms. Promises will no longer suffice. Performance is absolutely necessary.[71]

If General Wedemeyer thought that verbal remonstrances backed by the power to grant or withhold aid could, at this juncture, induce a change of heart on the part of the Nationalist leaders and bring about needed reforms — and indications are that he did so believe — he was totally mistaken. Prior to his departure, General Wedemeyer was given a memorandum by the Chinese government in which it claimed that it had already undertaken most of the internal reforms recommended by the United States.[72] The Nationalist reaction to Wedemeyer's statement of August 24 was made clear in an interview given by Premier Chang Ch'ün to the United Press on September 2. Mr. Chang charged that General Wedemeyer had failed to understand the Chinese situation and had not sought his information impartially.[73] The Chinese official flatly declared that there would be no change in either the domestic or foreign policy of the Chinese government as a result of the Wedemeyer mission.[74]

One reason for this strong Chinese reaction was that General Wedemeyer failed to sweeten his criticism by any hint of the positive recommendations for large-scale aid which he had by that time decided to make. But a more fundamental reason is that sweeping reforms would have militated against

[69] *Ibid.*, p. 759.
[70] *Ibid.*, p. 257. See also Stuart, *op. cit.*, pp. 186–87. However, in his memoirs, Wedemeyer stated that at the end of the speech the Generalissimo and Madame Chiang and a few other officials shook his hand warmly and thanked him (Wedemeyer, *op. cit.*, p. 389).
[71] *United States Relations with China*, pp. 763–64.
[72] *Ibid.*, pp. 259–60.
[73] *Ibid.*, p. 258.
[74] *Ibid.*, p. 815.

the vested interests of the ruling group and probably would have destroyed the whole foundation of its power. The basic fact in China was that there could not have been any genuine reform without a change of leadership at the very top. Such a change could have come about only if the pressure exerted by military reverses and American withdrawal had so shaken the confidence of the top leaders in their ability to remain in control that a new group or combination of groups might have emerged to replace them. But this was precisely the alternative which General Wedemeyer rejected. For he feared that "such a policy would result at some point in the Generalissimo's seeking a compromise with the Chinese Communists" which would give them a dominant position in the government; or that the long period of disintegration might end in the emergence of the Communists as the dominant group.[75] He thus rejected what he called a policy of "no assistance" to China and a policy of "wait and see."[76] Furthermore, General Wedemeyer, like General Marshall, could not envisage a China without Generalissimo Chiang.[77] So he placed all his hope on the ruling group's undertaking the necessary reforms. The hostile reaction on the part of the Nationalist government to his criticism greatly surprised him and caused him serious concern.[78]

Shortly after he left China, General Wedemeyer knew or should have known that he had failed to achieve one of his two interdependent aims, i.e., to convince the Nationalist government that it could not secure American aid without basic reforms. But in spite of the recalcitrance of the Nationalist government, he proposed in his report long-term, large-scale economic and military assistance to China. He apparently believed that strict supervision of the use of American assistance, the presence of American advisers in the military and financial fields, and the continued use of American aid as a lever to exert pressure could still bring about needed reforms and rejuvenate the Nationalist government.[79] His retrospective account of his mission also indicates that his strong criticisms of the Nationalist government and his emphasis on conditioning American aid on reforms were designed in part for domestic consumption. As he wrote in his memoirs:

> My eyes were fixed on America, upon whom the fate of China depended. I hope that by honestly stating all that I found wrong

[75] Wedemeyer's report to the President, *ibid.*, p. 779.
[76] *Ibid.*, p. 778.
[77] *Ibid.*, pp. 768, 778, 779.
[78] *Ibid.*, pp. 258–59.
[79] For example, he wrote in his report: "The purpose of conditional American aid to China should be to facilitate reorganization of her armed forces; to regain public confidence in the armed forces. . . . Such aid could be conditional to foster the emergence of a regime which would develop along lines satisfactory to the United States . . ." (*ibid.*, p. 810).

in China, my *bona fides* in nevertheless advocating aid to her would be established.[80]

In any case, he considered China so important to the United States and the menace of the Russian and Chinese Communists so immediate that he was willing to take a much greater risk than the administration.

In his report of September 19, 1947,[81] General Wedemeyer pointed out that the objectives of the traditional policy of the United States toward the Far East and the principles of the United Nations Charter were jeopardized by "forces as sinister as those operated in the past ten years leading to World War II."[82] For the Soviet Union aimed at progressive expansion of her sphere of control and dominant influence. In achieving this aim in the Far East, she was actively assisted by the Chinese Communists.[83] "A China dominated by Chinese Communists would be inimical to the interests of the United States in view of their openly expressed hostility and active opposition to those principles which the United States regards as vital to the peace of the world."[84] In time of war, an unfriendly China would deny important air and naval bases to the United States and put them in hostile hands to be used to neutralize American air and naval bases in Japan, the Ryukyus, and the Philippines by relatively short-range attacks.[85] A unified China friendly to the United States would not only provide important air and naval bases but, because of its size and manpower, would be an important ally.

Wedemeyer advocated granting the Nationalist government "sufficient and prompt military assistance under the supervision of American advisors in specified military fields."[86] Under this program, the United States would make arrangements for China to purchase military equipment, supplies, and ammunition from the United States. American advice and supervision of Nationalist operations would be extended to include field forces, training centers, and particularly logistical agencies. Wedemeyer rejected "active participation in operations by American personnel" as contrary to current American policy.[87] To avoid involvement in any way in actual combat against Chinese Communists and to prevent charges of

[80] Wedemeyer, *op. cit.*, p. 391.
[81] The report entitled "Report on China-Korea" is printed in *United States Relations with China*, with the portion dealing with Korea omitted, pp. 764–814. For an excellent summary of its content and an able survey of American policy in 1947 and 1948, see Part V, "The Far East," by F. C. Jones in *Survey of International Affairs, 1947–1948, op. cit.*, pp. 274–311.
[82] *United States Relations with China*, pp. 766, 775–76.
[83] *Ibid.*, pp. 813–14.
[84] *Ibid.*, p. 773.
[85] *Ibid.*, p. 809.
[86] *Ibid.*, p. 814.
[87] *Ibid.*, p. 811.

American military intervention, American advice should be carried on outside operational areas, although American personnel were to "provide advice *indirectly* to tactical forces."[88] In his estimation, approximately 10,000
officers and non-commissioned officers would be necessary to provide
advice and supervision down to the regimental level of the Nationalist field
forces.[89] The Army Advisory Group would continue to provide advice on
the general staff level, and American advisers would be placed in the ministry of defense.[90]

Wedemeyer also advocated a program of economic assistance to China
"over a period of at least five years."[91] This program, conditioned upon
Chinese performance and continued progress, would assure an early undertaking of projects essential for China's economic reconstruction and
eventually for stabilization of its currency system. Wedemeyer did not recommend any specific amount of financial aid. He left this to be determined
by Congress acting on the recommendations of the appropriate agencies.
To prepare a program of economic aid by the United States, he recommended the establishment by the Nationalist government of a "high-level
planning and screening agency," with American advisers and a staff of
qualified experts, to work out an over-all priority list of reconstruction
projects. American advisers would also serve in the ministry of finance,
particularly in the fields of budgeting and taxation.[92] Wedemeyer's program envisaged the assumption of vast responsibility by the United States
for the military and economic affairs of China.

General Wedemeyer recognized the vital importance of Manchuria. But
he also knew that it was not within the capabilities of the Nationalist government to defeat the Communists within a short time and eliminate Soviet
influence in that region. He feared that the Chinese Communists might
soon gain military control of Manchuria and announce the formation of
a separatist government and that, following the pattern established for
Outer Mongolia, the Soviet Union might conclude a "mutual support agreement with the Communist regime in Manchuria."[93] He reverted in his
report to a recommendation which he had first made in November, 1945.
This was to establish under the United Nations a five-power "guardianship" in Manchuria, with China, the Soviet Union, the United States, Great
Britain, and France as the guardians. If the Soviet Union should refuse to
participate in such a project, China might then request the General As-

[88] *Ibid.*, p. 813.
[89] Wedemeyer's testimony, *Military Situation in the Far East,* p. 2526. In Greece,
American advice and supervision went down to the battalion level.
[90] *United States Relations with China,* pp. 802, 809.
[91] *Ibid.*, p. 806.
[92] *Ibid.*, pp. 801–2.
[93] *Ibid.*, p. 767.

sembly to establish a "trusteeship" for Manchuria.[94] He thought that the establishment of a "guardianship" or trusteeship for Manchuria would create a buffer zone between the Soviet Union and the areas to the south and thus confine Soviet influence.[95] This recommendation was subsequent-ly characterized by him as "the most important element" of his report.[96]

Wedemeyer's recommendations to the administration fared no better than his efforts to convince the Nationalist government of the necessity of reforms. Secretary Marshall complimented Wedemeyer orally on his re-port but took no action on it. Wedemeyer was told not to disclose the contents of his report to anyone. Officials in the State Department did not discuss the report with him. It was soon apparent that his recommendations were rejected. Marshall rejected Wedemeyer's program for a complex of reasons. In the light of the American weakness in conventional forces and the global situation, both Marshall and the Chiefs of Staff felt that the United States could not commit 10,000 officers and non-commissioned of-ficers to China.[97] In June, 1947, the effective strength of the army was 925,163.[98] Subsequently, Marshall never tired of repeating that there were only one-and-a-third divisions in the entire United States. Marshall also feared that Wedemeyer's program would lead to increasingly deeper com-mitments on the part of the United States. In the MacArthur hearings, Wedemeyer himself admitted under questioning that, as the situation de-veloped, American personnel would have had "to go right into the area of combat and help these Chinese tactically."[99] Marshall was determined not to adopt any measure of military aid which would lead to American military intervention in China. Furthermore, by the time Wedemeyer sub-mitted his report, it was clear that the Nationalist government had rejected his criticisms and would not launch the necessary reforms. The adoption of Wedemeyer's program would merely saddle the United States with serious responsibilities without having gained for the United States recipro-cal commitments from the Nationalist government. These and other rea-sons are reflected in a statement in the White Paper, outlining the basic considerations in the formulation of American policy toward China in October 1947:

> It was recognized that in the main the solution of China's prob-
> lems must largely be a task for the Chinese themselves. A United
> States program of aid to China should not be such as would place

[94] *Ibid.*
[95] *Military Situation in the Far East*, p. 2367.
[96] *Ibid.*
[97] *Ibid.*, pp. 465–66. The army chief of staff was General Dwight D. Eisenhower.
[98] John C. Sparrow, *History of Personnel Demobilization* (Washington, D.C.: De-partment of the Army, 1951), p. 360.
[99] *Military Situation in the Far East*, pp. 2418–19.

the United States in the position of direct responsibility for the conduct of the fighting in China or for the Chinese economy. The United States Government could not virtually take over the Chinese Government and administer its economic and military affairs. Any such undertakings would have involved the United States in a continuing commitment from which it would have been practically impossible to withdraw regardless of circumstances or of Chinese Government actions. Account also had to be taken of the heavy burden of foreign aid which the United States was assuming elsewhere and of the limitation on the extent to which American resources could be drawn upon for foreign aid under the peacetime organization of its economy.[100]

Secretary Marshall also found serious objections to the publication of Wedemeyer's report in its totality. Marshall sent Mr. Butterworth, the new director of the Office of Far Eastern Affairs, to ask Wedemeyer to delete the portions of his report dealing with the establishment of a guardianship or trusteeship for Manchuria. General Wedemeyer refused to comply, and his report was suppressed by Marshall personally.[101] The reason given for the suppression of the report was that Wedemeyer's recommendation of a guardianship or a trusteeship for Manchuria was an impractical one and that "any such recommendation, if made public at that time, would be highly offensive to Chinese susceptibilities as an infringement of Chinese sovereignty, and representing the Chinese Government as incapable of governing Chinese territory."[102]

The suppression of the Wedemeyer report was one of the most unnecessary as well as most unfortunate actions of the administration. Had the report been published, the public debate evoked would have clarified many of the basic issues. If the public had shown its unwillingness to assume the

[100] *United States Relations with China*, pp. 269–70.

[101] Testifying on September 19, 1950, before the Committee on Armed Services on his nomination as secretary of defense, Marshall said: "I did not join in the suppression of the report. I personally suppressed it. I sent General Wedemeyer over there as a last resort to find out what we might do, and when his report came back, a great deal that was happening elsewhere in the world, particularly that part of the world dominated by the Soviets, was not considered" (Senate Committee on Armed Services, *Hearings on the Nomination of General George C. Marshall as Secretary of Defense*, 81st Cong., 2d sess. [1950], p. 22 [hereafter cited as *Nomination of Marshall*]). See also Secretary Marshall's letter to President Truman dated September 25, 1947, as reproduced in Appendix III, in Wedemeyer, *op. cit.*, p. 446.

[102] *United States Relations with China*, p. 260. Marshall said that this was "the major and really the sole reason" for suppressing the report (*Nomination of Marshall*, p. 22).

Senator Vandenberg was told the complete content of the Wedemeyer report by Marshall. He was persuaded that its publication would have been a serious blow to Sino-American relations (Vandenberg's confidential letter to Senator Knowland, December 11, 1948, Arthur H. Vandenberg, Jr. (ed.), *The Private Papers of Senator Vandenberg* (Boston: Houghton Mifflin Co., 1952), pp. 527–28).

costs of a positive policy in China and to risk eventual American participation in the Chinese civil war, the administration would have obtained
some sort of indorsement of its passive policy. If the administration had lost
the debate, it would not have been too late to inaugurate a new policy in
China. In any event, the administration would not have been vulnerable
to charges of concealing vital information from the Congress and the
American people. Furthermore, the report was suppressed on the basis of
an issue not central to the question confronting the United States, which
was whether the United States should give large-scale, long-term assistance
to China. The revelation of Wedemeyer's recommendations concerning
Manchuria would not have strained Sino-American relations any more
than the Yalta Agreement or Marshall's personal statement of January 7,
1947. By becoming suddenly oversolicitous of the susceptibilities of
the Nationalist government, the administration committed an avoidable
mistake.[103]

Many adverse consequences flowed from the Wedemeyer mission. The
announcement of the dispatch of Wedemeyer to China had aroused hopes
in the Nationalist government that large-scale American assistance would
soon be forthcoming.[104] The subsequent disappointment of these hopes
strengthened the right-wing C.C. clique and weakened the moderate Political Science group. In the Fourth Plenary Session of the Central Executive Committee of the Kuomintang meeting in September, 1947, the C.C.
clique consolidated its position.[105] At its insistence and in the face of considerable opposition within the government, the Democratic League was
outlawed.[106] This move played into the hands of the Communists, for it
drove the non-Communist opposition groups into active collaboration with
them.[107] Wedemeyer's public criticism of the Nationalist government in
his farewell statement became grist for the Communists' propaganda
mill.[108] The failure of the Wedemeyer mission to produce large-scale
American aid precipitated many Nationalist hints and threats to seek a
rapprochement with Russia.[109] After the suppression of his report, General

[103] It may very well be that the administration suppressed the report because, as some
of its critics charged, it was not disposed to strengthen the hands of Republican leaders
like Walter Judd (Westerfield, op. cit., p. 260–61). But even taking the administration's
explanation at its face value, the suppression of the report still seems to have been a
mistake.

[104] Stuart, op. cit., p. 185.

[105] United States Relations with China, pp. 826–30.

[106] Ibid., pp. 834–40.

[107] According to the Communists, the outlawing of the Democratic League marked
the end of all attempts to find a "third road" between the Kuomintang and the Communists and gave a great impetus toward the formation of a "revolutionary united front
composed of the various democratic parties" (Liao, op. cit., pp. 72–78).

[108] United States Relations with China, pp. 816–17.

[109] Chap. ix, above.

Wedemeyer began to feel that he "may have been sent to China to allay doubts in Congress and in the country and to provide justification for continuance of the old disastrous China policy."[110] If Wedemeyer was right in his judgment of Marshall's motives, it is obvious that the Secretary's maneuver boomeranged. The Republican critics of his China policy seized upon the suppression of the Wedemeyer report as a new issue in their campaign for larger aid to China.

The advocates of large-scale aid to China found a substitute for the suppressed document in Mr. William Bullitt's famous "Report on China" featured in the October 13, 1947, issue of *Life*. Recently returned from a trip to the Far East, Bullitt offered a three-year plan to save China at a cost of $1,350 million for both military and economic assistance. He urged the immediate delivery of certain stocks of munitions by the United States to China, particularly Manchuria, the placing of American advisers in the training and operation of Nationalist forces, American management of the Chinese services of supply in Manchuria, the building up of thirty new Chinese divisions, and the dispatch of General MacArthur to China as the personal representative of the President. Like Wedemeyer, Bullitt did not feel that Americans should command Chinese units in the field.[111] He was, however, willing to accept even greater responsibility in advising the Nationalists and controlling military affairs. Coincidentally, members of the House Military Affairs Committee called on Generalissimo Chiang on October 11. The Nationalist leader repeated his request for greater American aid, warning that if the Chinese government were finally defeated, it would be the result not of Soviet or Chinese Communist efforts but of American failure to give "promised assistance at a time of desperate need."[112]

F. The Policy of Limited Assistance

In the face of mounting Republican demands, the administration found it necessary to prepare a program for China which would, on the one hand, ward off the rising pressure for large-scale military assistance and, on the other, strictly limit American commitments. What apparently forced the hand of the administration was the necessity of enlisting Republican co-operation to meet the growing economic crisis in Europe. To pass legislation for emergency aid to Europe pending the preparation of the full European Recovery Program, the administration summoned a special session of Congress to meet in November. On September 30, President Truman asked Senator Vandenberg to begin hearings on the ad-

[110] Wedemeyer, *op. cit.*, p. 383.
[111] *Life*, October 13, 1947, pp. 35 ff.
[112] *United States Relations with China*, p. 264.

ministration's proposal to grant interim aid to France, Italy, and Austria. In the latter part of October, the State Department began the formulation of a program of aid to China in what the White Paper called a "redefinition of American policy."[113] It was preparing a proposal for economic aid to China for submission to Congress.[114] On October 27, the American government concluded an agreement with the Nationalist government granting $27.7 million of economic aid to China, earmarked by Congress in the previous spring for post-UNRRA relief.[115] In the same month, the State Department agreed to the participation of the Army Advisory Group in the training activities of a training center in Taiwan.[116] In November, Major General David G. Barr was sent to China to head the Army Advisory Group and was authorized to give operational advice to Generalissimo Chiang on an informal and confidential basis but not to accept responsibility for Chinese strategic plans and operations.[117] The policy of limited assistance was thus launched. It followed a period of five months of indecision after the arms embargo was lifted in May.

This policy of granting limited assistance to China was entirely necessary to guarantee the acceptance by Congress of the administration's programs for Europe. But it did not represent a realistic program for China. In the second half of 1947, Communist forces went on the offensive on a nation-wide scale. In July, August, and September, three Communist columns crossed the Yellow River in their southward advance. In the last four months of 1947, they strongly intrenched themselves in the large region south of the Yellow River and north of the Yangtze, east of the Han River and west of the sea. This bold movement of troops was undertaken when the main Nationalist forces were attacking Communist forces in Shantung and northern Shensi, leaving inadequate garrisons in the central plain. By the close of 1947, Communist units lay in strength along the railroad from North China to Manchuria, constantly interrupting traffic on these lines.[118]

Mao knew that he was winning the war. In a report to the Central Committee of the Communist party on December 25, he declared that China stood at "a turning point in history," "the turning point from growth to extinction for Chiang Kai-shek's twenty-year counter-revolutionary rule." He was so confident of future success that he proclaimed, for the world to ponder, the military principles which had guided the Communist forces to victory and would continue to serve as their guide. He was certain that the Nationalists could neither adopt his strategy nor design effective

[113] Ibid., p. 269.
[114] Senate Committee on Foreign Relations, *Hearings on Interim Aid for Europe*, 80th Cong., 1st sess. (1947), pp. 2–10 (hereafter cited as *Interim Aid for Europe*).
[115] United States Relations with China, p. 367.
[116] Ibid., p. 348.
[117] Ibid., p. 324.
[118] Ibid., p. 317.

countermeasures against it. He was sure that American advice and military aid alone would not save the government forces from defeat. He pointed out that his strategy and tactics were built upon the political foundation of the widespread popular support which he enjoyed and which Generalissimo Chiang had lost. He explained:

> [Our] strategy and tactics are founded on a people's war. No anti-popular army can utilize our strategy and tactics. A vital factor in conquering the enemy is the establishment of strong and powerful political work by the People's Liberation Army based on a people's war and on the solidarity of army and people, the solidarity of commanders and fighters, and the disintegration of the enemy.[119]

Mao was also reported to have said that besides its political and economic weaknesses the Nationalist government suffered from five basic contradictions or defects in the military field which doomed its military efforts to failure. These were, first, the contradiction between the strategic objective of occupying large areas of China and the insufficient number of troops and reserves; second, the contradiction between the same strategic objective and the tactical necessity of concentrating its forces to take the initiative; third, the frictions between the armies commanded by Chiang's personal following and the armies commanded by other Nationalist generals; fourth, the contradiction between the preference for war on the part of a few Nationalist commanders and the anti-war sentiments of the rank and file; fifth, the many defects in the tactical field such as lack of unity of command and failure to utilize American equipment effectively.[120] As will be shown, three months later Marshall also came to the conclusion that the United States must face the possibility of an early collapse of the Nationalist regime.

G. Interim Aid for China and the Intensifying Debate on China

On November 10, the Senate Committee on Foreign Relations and the House met jointly to begin hearings on the administration's proposal to grant interim aid to France, Italy, and Austria. A day before the hearings began, the Republican position on aid to China was once more under-

[119] "The Present Situation and Our Tasks," a report made by Mao Tse-tung to the Central Committee of the Communist party of China, on December 25, 1947. It was published in the United States under the title *Turning Point in China* (New York: New Century Publishers, 1948), p. 9. See Mao Tse-tung, *Selected Works*, IV (Peking: Foreign Language Press, 1961), 157–73 (hereafter cited as *Selected Works*, IV [Peking]).

[120] Sun Han-p'ing, Chung-kuo hsien-tai kê-ming shih chiao-hsüch ts'an-kao ti-k'ang ["A Reference Outline for the Teaching of the History of Revolution in Contemporary China"] (Tientsin: T'ung-shu ch'u-pan-shê, 1955), p. 187.

scored by Speaker Joseph Martin. Martin urged that the proposed program for aid to Europe be expanded to fight communism everywhere in the world, not just in Europe. He said that Congress probably would wish to provide China as well as Western Europe with assistance.[121] In his opening statement, Secretary Marshall asked for $597 million for interim aid to France, Italy, and Austria. He also informed the committees that the Department of the Army would soon present requests for approximately $500 million of supplementary funds for occupied areas during the current year, of which $300 million would be used in Western Germany. As to the full European Recovery Program, Marshall put the tentative estimate at about $1.5 billion for the last three months of the fiscal year 1948 and $6 billion for the fiscal year ending June 30, 1949.[122]

In proposing a series of programs involving huge expenditure in Europe, the State Department found it necessary to make some positive response to Republican demands for aid to China. Thus in his opening statement Marshall also told the committees that a definite proposal for economic aid to China was under preparation in the State Department for early submission.[123] In response to a question by Senator Vandenberg, Marshall said that the administration would ask for $300 million for economic aid to China over a period of 15 months, beginning in April, 1948. This figure, arrived at on the basis of $20 million a month, came very close to the Bullitt estimate of $250 million a year of economic aid needed by China. At this time, the administration did not plan to provide any American funds which could be used by the Nationalist government to purchase military supplies. Furthermore, the administration's program was one of short duration and it was to begin at the same time as the European Recovery Program. This recommendation for economic aid to China was apparently the price which the administration was willing to pay to insure the adoption of the interim aid and the full recovery program for Europe.

The administration's caution was justified by the initial reactions of the Republican leaders to the administration's request for interim aid to Europe as a preliminary to the full Marshall Plan. At one extreme stood Senator Robert Taft whose views at this time reflected the basic attitudes of the isolationist and economy-minded leaders in the Republican party. On November 10, Taft declared that provision for further aid to China had to be considered. The next day, after Secretary Marshall completed his testimony before the congressional committees, Taft said that he was "absolutely opposed" to extending the $2,657 million in additional foreign aid

[121] New York Times, November 10, 1947, p. 1.

[122] Interim Aid for Europe, pp. 2–10.

[123] Ibid., p. 7. It is perhaps not without significance that the State Department began to work on a program of further aid to China in October after Truman asked Senator Vandenberg on September 30 to hold hearings on interim aid to Europe.

which, according to Marshall, was needed for the remainder of fiscal year 1948. In his view, granting aid to Europe would only furnish the Communists with further arguments against the "imperialist" policy of the United States.[124] Later, when the Senate was considering the Marshall Plan, Taft made an unsuccessful attempt to cut more than one billion dollars from the program. He was won over to support full authorization for the European Recovery Program only shortly before the Republican convention.[125]

The hearings on the interim aid program elicited from Representative Judd a systematic statement of his views, many of which were widely shared by the pro-Chiang critics of the administration's China policy – a group of persons whom Westerfield designated the "China bloc."[126] In principle, Judd supported the administration's program for Europe but he conditioned this support on the adoption by the administration of a similar program for China. He informed his colleagues that American assistance and actions had helped turn the tide against communism in Greece, France, and Italy. In his view, however, full European recovery depended on the return to something like the prewar pattern of trade between Europe and Asia. He declared: "[W]e have got to win in Asia, too, or we will ultimately lose in Europe. I cannot myself vote to put some $20,000,000,000 into holding the line on one front and then ignore another front equally vital to our future."[127] To Judd, China was the key to Asia. If China were to be taken by Communists, "how long," he asked, "can India, Malaysia, the East Indies, even the Philippines, resist the pressures?"[128] Judd did not place Asia above Europe in priority, but he believed that a non-Communist Western Europe could not long survive without a non-Communist China.

Judd reported that the Chinese Communists were making rapid progress in destroying the Nationalist government at home while Communist-inspired propaganda since 1944 had succeeded in discrediting it abroad. In the United States, this campaign, Judd charged, "was largely led by about 20 or 30 writers and lecturers and commentators, and by some men who became Far Eastern advisers to our State Department," including some in "what has become widely known as the 'Red cell' in the State Department, the Far Eastern office."[129] These men "have consistently followed the party line with respect to the Chinese Communists."[130] Thus, the Far Eastern experts' accurate appraisal of Chiang's weaknesses, their moral revulsion against aiding a corrupt, oppressive regime, and their underesti-

[124] *New York Times*, November 12, 1947, pp. 1, 7.
[125] Westerfield, *op. cit.*, pp. 289–90.
[126] *Ibid.*, pp. 344, 347.
[127] House Committee on Foreign Affairs, *Hearings on Emergency Foreign Aid*, 80th Cong., 1st sess. (1947), p. 239 (hereafter cited as *Emergency Foreign Aid*).
[128] *Ibid.*
[129] *Ibid.*, pp. 243–44.
[130] *Ibid.*, p. 244.

mation of the Chinese Communist threat were turned into a partisan issue. This partisan attack further complicated the task of policy-making. It rendered the advocacy on realistic grounds of prompt and complete withdrawal a hazardous undertaking merely because the Communists and their fellow-travelers were demanding American withdrawal for reasons of their own.

Judd based his condemnation of the administration's program on the traditional policy of the United States. His task was facilitated by the ambiguities of the traditional policy and by the lack of a commonly accepted understanding of this policy. According to his version of history, a "handful of Communists, fellow-travellers, and misguided liberals"[131] caused "one of the most amazing reversals of history":[132] the abandonment of America's traditional Far Eastern policy at the very moment of its success. As defined by Judd, this policy was to support an independent, sovereign government of China against the encroachment of other powers, even if that government was completely undemocratic, inefficient, and corrupt.[133] It was reversed when President Truman's press release of December 15, 1945, announcing the Marshall mission, declared that American aid would be conditional on the achievement of peace and unity in China. According to Judd, this one sentence, written by an unknown official, informed the Chinese Communists that by blocking peace and unity, they could cut off American assistance to China.

"For us not to help China," Judd declared, "because her government is portrayed as unworthy of support is not only being victims of distorted propaganda; it is ignoring our own history and our own interests."[134] Without naming General MacArthur, Judd reported:

> A great American out in the Far East said to me: "For the first time in our relations with Asia, we have endangered the paramount interests of the United States by confusing them with an internal purification problem in China. It may prove to be the greatest single blunder in the history of the United States."[135]

At this time, the aftermath of the Wedemeyer mission had already shown that no sweeping reforms would be undertaken by the Nationalists. By de-emphasizing the need for reform and by stressing America's historic interests in China, Judd endeavored to justify his program of aid to China. Four months later, MacArthur himself was to state his own ideas in a cable to the chairman of the Committee on Foreign Affairs:

[131] *Ibid.*, p. 246.
[132] *Ibid.*, p. 251.
[133] *Ibid.*, pp. 250–51.
[134] *Ibid.*, p. 250.
[135] *Ibid.*

The international aspect of the Chinese problem unfortunately has become somewhat clouded by demands for internal reform. Desirable as such reform may be, its importance is but secondary to the issue of civil strife now engulfing the land, and the two issues are as impossible of synchronization as it would be to alter the structural design of a house while the same was being consumed by flame.[136]

Judd urged a return to "our basic policy for 100 years" of "standing for the sovereignty, the independence, the territorial and administrative integrity of China." [137] He recommended the adoption of a program of military and economic assistance to enable the Nationalists to eliminate the Communists south of the Great Wall and, at least, to hold their present position in Manchuria. His proposals for military assistance consisted of sending to China "surplus munitions — at little or no cost to us" and an "expanded program of training and advising Chinese forces at all levels." [138] Neither then nor later did he suggest the use of American troops for combat duties in China.

Governor Dewey followed a similar line. In a speech on November 24 which was reported to have been written in consultation with leading Republican members of Congress, Dewey declared that if China fell, all Asia would fall. He compared the free world to a patient with gangrene in two legs, Europe and Asia, and asserted that the patient could not be saved by treating the gangrene in one leg only.[139] The position taken by Representative John M. Vorys, an influential member of the Committee on Foreign Affairs, is of particular interest because he was the outstanding example of a prewar isolationist who became a strong advocate of a program of aid to China and who conditioned his support for the administration's program for Europe on the administration's concessions to his views on China. In 1939, Vorys introduced an amendment to a bill sponsored by the Roosevelt administration to revise neutrality legislation. This amendment provided for an embargo on the shipment of "arms and ammunition" and thus cut the heart out of the bill.[140] Now he stated in the committee that China should be included in the proposal for emergency aid for "all the reasons that apply to Europe." Commenting on the long-term plan for European recovery, he warned that "we must be aware of not only doing too little too late but doing too much too soon in one limited part of the

[136] *Foreign Policy for a Post-war Recovery Program*, p. 2044.
[137] *Emergency Foreign Aid*, p. 250.
[138] *Ibid.*, p. 255.
[139] *New York Times*, November 25, 1947, p. 18.
[140] William L. Langer and S. Everett Gleason, *The Challenge to Isolation* (New York: Harper & Bros., 1952), p. 142.

world, and thus crippling ourselves in the world-wide long pull." [141] He referred with pride to the position he took in 1939 to the effect that it was a great mistake to try to determine America's possible conduct in a future war in Europe before determining her present conduct in the Sino-Japanese struggle in Asia.[142] Thus, Vorys stood somewhere between Taft and Judd in his orientation toward foreign policy.

Some three months later, MacArthur was to make the following ringing declaration of his views on the relation of the United States to Europe and Asia:

> America's past lies deeply rooted in the areas across the Atlantic but the hope of American generations of the future to keep pace with the progress of those of the past lies no less in the happenings and events across the Pacific. While fully availing ourselves of the potential to the east, to our western horizon we must look both for hope of a better life through yet untapped opportunities for trade and commerce in the advance of Asiatic races, and [for] threat against the life with which we are even now endowed.[143]

During the Pacific war, MacArthur had declared:

> Europe is a dying system. It is worn out and run down, and will become an economic and industrial hegemony of Soviet Russia. . . . The lands touching the Pacific with their billions of inhabitants will determine the course of history in the next ten thousand years.[144]

The basic attitude of MacArthur, whose views inspired many of the actions of the China bloc, was thus as "isolationist" toward Europe and "interventionist" toward Asia as Taft's.

Even Senator Vandenberg, upon whose help depended the success of pushing the Marshall Plan through Congress, dissociated himself from the administration's China policy. When he was presenting to the Senate on November 24 the bill for interim aid to France, Italy, and Austria, he expressed regret that the bill did not include interim aid for China and welcomed Marshall's assurance that China would be included in subsequent plans.[145] He again made it clear, just as he had in April, 1947,[146] that he had not been consulted "in any substantial degree regarding Asiatic

[141] *Emergency Foreign Aid*, p. 295.
[142] *Ibid.* Vorys also discussed the link between his own views in 1939 and in the late 1940's in a speech on the floor of the House on April 4, 1949, when the House debated the extension of the China Aid Act of 1948 (*Congressional Record*, XCV, 81st Cong., 1st sess. [1949,] 3826–27).
[143] *Foreign Policy for a Post-war Recovery Program*, p. 2042.
[144] Millis, *op. cit.*, p. 18.
[145] *Congressional Record*, XCIII, 80th Cong., 1st sess. (1947), 10704.
[146] *Ibid.*, p. 3474.

policy." [147] In a debate on December 15 he declared that he had "for some time been out of harmony with our official attitude toward China," and that he had "repeatedly urged a different attitude." [148]

A number of influential Republican leaders were thus united in demanding aid to China. This unity made it necessary for the State Department to propose a program for aid to China which would at least satisfy Vandenberg and conciliate the China bloc. For the greatest danger confronting the global policy of the administration, of which the Marshall Plan was the key, came not so much from the China bloc in Congress, of which Judd and Vorys in the House and Bridges in the Senate were the leading figures, as from the combined forces of the economy bloc and the unreconstructed isolationists, of which Representative John Taber in the House and Taft in the Senate were the spokesmen. Subsequent events show that by making limited concessions to the China bloc, the administration succeeded in averting serious opposition from that quarter to its European program. Indeed, Vorys, Judd, and Bridges all were to lend their support to the Marshall Plan in Congress, while continuing to push their program for China. In the final authorization bill on interim aid, China was named along with France, Italy, and Austria as one of the recipient countries of a total of $597 million in emergency aid. But there was no specific allocation to China or any other country. In appropriating money for interim aid, Congress adopted Vandenberg's suggestion that it appropriate to China $18 million under the post-UNRRA relief act.[149] The amount of money granted China was small but it was a sign that the United States was moving toward a larger program of aid to China.

H. The China Aid Act and the Traditional Dilemma

In the hearings on interim aid and the public debate at that time, much attention was given to Marshall's prospective program of aid to China. The debate clearly showed that the State Department was on the defensive. As noted above, one basic theme of the critics of the administration was that it confused the paramount interests of the United States with an internal purification problem in China.[150] In contrast, the premise of the administration's policy was that without sweeping internal reforms in Nationalist China, American assistance would be wasted and would not save China. As Marshall stated, "Only the Government and the people of China can solve

[147] *Ibid.*, p. 10708.
[148] *Ibid.*, p. 11351.
[149] For some of the high points in the debate and actions taken by Congress, see *ibid.*, 10701–4, 11037, 11296–97, 11344–47, 11679. See also *United States Relations with China*, p. 367; Holbert Carroll, *The House of Representatives and Foreign Affairs* (Pittsburgh, Pa.: University of Pittsburgh Press, 1958), pp. 116–17; Westerfield *op. cit.*, pp. 262–64.
[150] *Emergency Foreign Aid*, p. 250.

their fundamental problems,"[151] and the State Department had been hard put to find a means to help China which would "get about a 70 per cent return in effectiveness of use."[152] Governor Dewey countered this thesis with the assertion that "I do not know whether it [aid to China] would be 50 per cent or 80 per cent effective, and I doubt if anyone knows. Of one thing I am sure, it would be immensely more effective than nothing."[153]

The purely economic nature of the administration's prospective program was another target of Republican criticism. Marshall disclosed that the State Department was working on a program of economic assistance to China which would bring about "a stay of execution in the deterioriation of their [the Chinese] monetary situation. . . ."[154] Judd took Marshall to task by pointing out that economic and financial measures could not arrest further deterioration as long as the military situation continued to go from bad to worse.[155] When Marshall made it clear that his program would not contain any measures to deal with the military situation, Judd asked: "Are we justified in appropriating the tax payers' money as a palliative if we are not prepared to attack the real causes?"[156]

Judd's last question brought out the real dilemma confronting the United States. For the program of military and economic assistance proposed by such persons as Bullitt was precisely nothing more than a palliative. Such a program, particularly American advice and supervision of Nationalist logistical services, might have been the necessary first step. But in itself it would not have been sufficient to stabilize the critical situation. As Marshall was to point out three months later, there was little evidence that the weakness of the government and the deteriorating military structure could be basically changed by foreign aid and "any large-scale effort to oppose the Communists would most probably degenerate into a direct United States undertaking and responsibility, involving the commitment of sizeable forces and resources over an indefinite period."[157] The two realistic alternatives open to the United States were, first, to prepare to intervene with her own armed forces if military assistance and American supervision of Nationalist operations and logistics could not be expected to turn the tide; and, second, to withdraw completely from China as soon as possible. From the beginning, the administration ruled out the first alternative and even the strongest advocates of aid to China refrained from suggesting American military participation.[158] There remained the second alternative. This

[151] Ibid., p. 7.
[152] Ibid., pp. 14, 23.
[153] New York Times, November 25, 1947, p. 18.
[154] Emergency Foreign Aid, p. 23.
[155] Ibid.
[156] Ibid., p. 24.
[157] United States Relations with China, p. 384.
[158] Chapter ix, above.

could have been justified on the ground that it would avoid further identification with an admittedly moribund government, minimize American
defeat, hinder Communist efforts to stir up anti-American sentiments, and,
above all, lessen the chance of an eventual war with the Chinese Communists. But the administration either did not choose it or dared not advocate
it openly. Instead, Marshall repeatedly assured Congress that "we have
been searching . . . with almost complete unanimity for some way to help
[China]."[159] Senator Tom Connally, a staunch defender of the administration's China policy, found it necessary to deny any "disposition on the
part of the State Department . . . to close the door on China."[160] Once this
basic point was conceded, there was no effective argument to resist Republican and Chinese pressure for granting aid to China. The Chinese government shrewdly timed its demands for large-scale assistance to take
advantage of the pressure generated by Congress. On December 22, 1947,
it asked for a four-year program of aid at a cost of one-and-one-half billion
dollars. Of this amount, $500 million of economic aid and another $100
million for military supplies were requested for the first year.[161]

By the time the administration was ready to submit its proposals, it was
compelled to move toward a program of economic assistance to China
which cost almost twice as much as its original plan in November, 1947.
It insisted merely on avoiding any implications of underwriting the Chinese
economy and the Nationalist military efforts. On February 18, President
Truman asked Congress for a grant to China of $570 million over a period
of fifteen months.[162] The total amount requested exceeded slightly Bullitt's
estimate of $450 million a year needed by the Nationalists to purchase
both civilian and military supplies.[163] Although the administration's new
program did not include any provision for military aid, it did not ignore
the military needs of the Nationalist government. The increase of $270
million equaled almost exactly the $274 million of China's reserves of gold
and foreign exchange, as of January 1, 1948. It freed China's own resources
for "purchasing things for their military effort if they wish to do so," as
Marshall testified.[164] Thus, aside from the duration of the program, the
major difference between the administration's program and Bullitt's or
Wedemeyer's proposals was the absence in the former of any provision
committing the United States to supervise Nationalist military operations
and logistics.

Both President Truman in his message of February 17 and Marshall in

[159] *Emergency Foreign Aid*, p. 24.
[160] *Congressional Record*, XCIII, 80th Cong., 1st sess. (1947), 11351.
[161] *United States Relations with China*, p. 377.
[162] *Ibid.*, pp. 379–80.
[163] Bullitt himself recognized this. See his testimony in *Foreign Policy for Post-war Recovery Program*, p. 1910.
[164] *Ibid.*, p. 1596. See also *ibid.*, pp. 1546–47; Westerfield, *op. cit.*, p. 264.

his testimony in the public hearings told Congress that the proposed program would not be adequate to solve the problems of China and that it would at most "retard" the current economic deterioration and provide a "breathing space" for the Chinese government.[165] In a statement read to a joint meeting of the Senate Foreign Relations Committee and the House Foreign Affairs Committee, Marshall frankly admitted "the possibility that the present Chinese Government may not be successful in maintaining itself against the Communist forces." [166] He argued that in order to enable the Nationalist government to reduce the Chinese Communists to a completely negligible factor in China, the United States "would have to be prepared virtually to take over the Chinese Government and administer its economic, military, and governmental affairs."[167] This alternative was rejected for all the reasons given in chapter ix. Marshall thus gave up what Acheson subsequently called the last chance for the United States to intervene with her armed forces in China. According to Acheson, "This matter was laid before the Congress," and "the Congress understood it perfectly" and had the "sound judgment not to choose armed intervention."[168] At this time, the actual strength of the army and air force was only 898,000 men with 140,000 deployed in the Far East.[169]

Marshall realized that his program would not be effective in checking the advance of communism in China. But withholding assistance and complete withdrawal were equally impossible. As Marshall explained, "We are already committed by past actions and by popular sentiments among our people to continue to do what we can to alleviate suffering in China and to give the Chinese Government and people the possibility of working out China's problems in their own way."[170] The traditional attachment to

[165] Truman's message, *Congressional Record*, XCIV, 80th Cong., 2d sess. (1948), 1396. Marshall's testimony, *Foreign Policy for a Post-war Recovery Program*, p. 1545.

[166] *United States Relations with China*, p. 382.

[167] *Ibid.*

[168] *Military Situation in the Far East*, p. 1869.

[169] Millis, *op. cit.*, p. 375. Nowhere in published records can one find an official estimate of the magnitude of American military efforts necessary to stabilize the situation in China. But writing in the *New York Times* in January, 1948, Professor Nathaniel Peffer asserted that only a large American expeditionary force of 150,000 men could do the job (*New York Times*, January 25, 1948, Sec. 6, p. 8 ff). In the hearings on the European Recovery Program and the bill to give aid to China, Wedemeyer expressed the view, contrary to Acheson's retrospective judgment, that military participation by the United States was not necessary "at this time" (*Foreign Policy for a Post-war Program*, p. 2070). But Joseph C. Harsch reported in October, 1958, that the administration rejected a proposal made by Wedemeyer sometime in 1948 to send ten American divisions to hold a line along the Yellow River (*Christian Science Monitor*, October 8, 1958, p. 1). Professor Stefan T. Possony estimates that it would have taken seven American divisions in Manchuria and fifteen divisions in other parts of China to pacify and reorganize China (Stefan T. Possony, *A Century of Conflict* [Chicago: Henry Regnery Co., 1953], p. 323).

[170] *United States Relations with China*, p. 383.

China, now reinforced by a perception of the Communist threat to the United States, found its most vociferous spokesmen in the Republican critics of the administration. To the traditional sentiments and objectives, and thus to the China bloc, some concession had to be made.

It is not accidental that the events accompanying the enactment of a program of renewed assistance to the Nationalist government coincided with official statements proclaiming the burial of the policy of seeking to establish a coalition government in China including the Communists. In the hearings on the foreign aid program before the House Committee on Foreign Affairs, Representative Fulton charged that there had never been a disavowal of the American policy of favoring a coalition government in China and that this was still the official policy. On March 10, Secretary Marshall was asked in a news conference whether this was so. Marshall answered that President Truman's statement of December 15, 1945, urging the Chinese government to broaden its base, was still the American policy. Then, the specific question was raised whether broadening of the base of the Chinese government meant the inclusion of the Chinese Communists. Marshall replied that the Communists were now in open rebellion against the government and that it was for the Chinese government to decide, and not for the American government to dictate, whether or not to include the Chinese Communists.[171] Marshall's answer to the first question was easily misconstrued, for the phrase "broadening the base" in Truman's statement of 1945 clearly meant the inclusion of the Chinese Communists in a coalition government. It was in this light that the press interpreted his reply that the Truman statement of 1945 was still the official policy.[172] Marshall's clarification of his first answer by his somewhat contradictory remark was neglected. The next day, President Truman sought to correct this impression by expressing his hope that the Chinese liberals would be taken into the government and by stating at the same time that "we did not want any Communists in the Government of China or anywhere else if we could help it."[173] These words marked the interment of the policy of a coalition government. But the President did not help to clarify the record when he said that his statement of December 15, 1945, still stood.

The program of limited assistance as embodied in the China Aid Act of April, 1948, and the accompanying appropriations in June were even more inadequate to deal with the turbulent situation in China than the proposal submitted by the administration in February. With the help of Senator Vandenberg and his committee, the administration defeated the attempts of the House to force on the administration a program of military

[171] Ibid., pp. 271–72.
[172] The New York Times, March 11, 1948, p. 6.
[173] United States Relations with China, p. 273.

assistance to China similar to that carried out in Greece under which, as the report of the Committee on Foreign Affairs significantly noted, American military personnel had been engaged, since December, 1947, in providing strategic and tactical advice to the Greek army units down to the divisional level.[174] As a compromise between the House and the China bloc on the one hand and the Senate and the administration on the other, Congress set aside a special fund of $125 million to be "used at China's option for military purposes and in the purchase of urgently needed military supplies."[175] A stipulation put into the appropriation bill by Chairman Taber, under which the special fund must be administered "consistent with the general objectives and the requirements of supervision provided for in the Act for Assistance to Greece and Turkey,"[176] went through the House but lost in the conference committee.[177] As a result of Taber's attempt to cut 30 per cent of the funds asked by the administration, the final appropriation of $400 million (including the $125 million special fund) for a period of twelve months represented a 13 per cent reduction. The lofty purposes of the China Aid Act were, as the preamble put them, to encourage China and her people "to maintain the genuine independence and administrative integrity of China and to sustain and strengthen the principles of individual liberty and free institutions in China." Once again, a verbal affirmation of sweeping principles was juxtaposed with an incapacity to use force in a program of half measures which had no chance of success.

In sum, the China Aid Act represented a compromise between two conflicting views which reflected the inconsistent elements of the traditional policy. Marshall came to be the embodiment of the traditional view that American interests in China were not worth a war, while his Republican critics held to their conception of America's traditional purposes in China. Marshall relied on the principle of non-intervention while his Republican critics appealed to the principle of upholding China's integrity against the encroachment of other powers. Like Theodore Roosevelt and Elihu Root, Marshall was intensely conscious of the limits of American power and China's inability to help herself, while his critics, following William Taft, Charles Evans Hughes, and Henry Stimson, clung tenaciously to the hope that somehow American interests and purposes could be promoted

---

[174] House Committee on Foreign Affairs, *Report on Foreign Assistance Act of 1948,* House Report No. 1585, 80th Cong., 2d sess. (1948), p. 51. Later, American advisers were sent down to the battalion level.

[175] Senator Vandenberg's speech, *Congressional Record,* XCIV, 80th Cong., 2d sess. (1948), 3668.

[176] House Committee on Appropriations, *Report on Appropriations on Foreign Aid,* House Report No. 2173, 80th Cong., 2d sess. (1948), p. 9.

[177] *Conference report, Congressional Record,* XCIV, 80th Cong., 2d sess. (1948), 9292–93.

without the use of American forces. The lack of a bipartisan policy was thus the expression of the inconsistencies and ambiguities of the traditional policy. Meanwhile the pre-1939 active, "interventionist" policy in the Far East, as contrasted with the passive, "isolationist" policy toward Europe, found an echo in the Republican demands that China be included in the administration's policy of containment and economic assistance which was first applied in Europe. The China bloc's demands for concessions to its views as a condition to its support for Marshall's European policies were the growing pains of a nation in the process of making a basic reorientation of her policies and assuming world leadership.

Yet none of Marshall's critics advocated the use of American ground forces in China; nor were there readily available troops for that purpose. Their program was to give large-scale, long-term military and economic assistance to China and to place American advisers with Nationalist units. Some of them such as General MacArthur dismissed the importance of Nationalist reforms in a Sino-American program to defeat the Chinese Communists. Others like Wedemeyer and Bullitt hoped to improve the effectiveness of the Nationalist government by conditioning American aid on Chinese reforms and by American supervision and advice. Marshall, however, was convinced that sufficient personnel to carry out the proposed program was not available. He feared that provision of large-scale military aid and advice would lead to military involvement. He realized that reforms in China were a prerequisite for effective use of American aid. At the same time he came to believe that American pressure and advice would not bring about the desired results and that reforms were not possible under Chiang but that there was no other Chinese leader to replace the Generalissimo. Neither Marshall nor his critics favored active intervention in Nationalist politics to bring about a change in the top leadership.

Thus, a wide gap existed between the critics' objectives and Marshall's estimation of available means. The critics urged making a greater effort in China while Marshall was more ready to abandon the objective of sustaining the Nationalist government. The compromise program of limited aid was necessitated by Marshall's need for the China bloc's support for his European Recovery Program and by the China bloc's inability to impose its views on the administration. In this official program, the discrepancy between end and means was wider than in any policy which the administration or its critics would have followed if either had had a free hand. It was adopted at a less auspicious moment than at any time since the end of the Pacific war. It delayed but did not obviate the necessity of making a clear-cut choice between the China bloc's objective of sustaining the Nationalist government and withdrawal from China. The first choice would have entailed the eventual use of American military power in China and the second choice would have meant the abandonment of the traditional purposes. The long tradition of American policy thus ruled out the timely adoption of a policy of prompt and complete withdrawal as well as a policy of armed intervention.

I. The Effects of the China Aid Act

1. Military Developments and the Anti-American Movement in China

The passage of the China Aid Act marked the culmination of the gradual return to the policy of limited assistance. Such a shift may have been entirely necessary to insure the adoption of the full European Recovery Program and, in this sense, may be said to have served the over-all national interest of the United States. But it did not help to promote the cause of the United States in China. For the military situation in China deteriorated so rapidly in the first half of 1948 that the program could not even delay the outcome of the civil war. It succeeded only in stirring up the most widespread anti-American movement up to that time.

During the debate in the United States over the administration's program of aid to China, the Chinese Communists launched, from mid-December, 1947, to mid-March, 1948, their largest offensive in Manchuria up to that time. This carefully planned attack isolated huge Nationalist forces in three strongholds: Changchun, Mukden, and Chinchow. While Chiang was trying hard to supply his armies in Manchuria, the Communist forces in the northwest scored, in late February and early March, their first great victory. In March, the Communists began placing under the direction of a single government and military command the area between the Lunghai Railway in the south and the Peiping-Suiyüan Railway in the north, between the Tatung-Puchow Railway in the west and the Tientsin-Pukow Railway in the east. They were contemplating the establishment of a Central People's government in 1949.[178]

In Shantung, Communist forces overwhelmed the strategic city of Weihsien on April 29 in a campaign which became a subject of controversy in subsequent congressional hearings. It was cited by the critics of the administration as a prime example of the defeat of the Nationalist forces due to a lack of ammunition which the United States could have supplied to them. To a spokesman of the administration, it symbolized the futility of sending supplies to the central government.[179] In Honan, the Communist forces occupied Loyang in March and Kaifeng in June, two of the key points in the central plains. These Communist victories

---

[178] Mao, *Selected Works*, IV (Peking), pp. 211–15.
[179] *Military Situation in the Far East*, pp. 2998, 2999.

pointed to a most significant military development in China in the first
half of 1948. The Communists for the first time demonstrated their ability
to breach the defenses of well-fortified points held by the Nationalists.
This in turn showed that they mastered the use of artillery and the techniques of demolition and that they could wage positional warfare as well
as guerrilla and mobile warfare. Amidst charges in the United States that
the Nationalists lost the battle primarily because of lack of ammunition,
the Communist forces claimed to have captured in the twelve months between July, 1947, and June, 1948, more than 82 million rounds of ammunition,[180] a figure not far from the 110 million rounds in the hands of the
Japanese army in China proper and Formosa when they surrendered in
1945. In summing up the results of the first two years of the civil war since
July 1, 1946, the Communists declared on July 30, 1948, that the demise
of the Nationalist regime was "not too far away," although they still envisaged "three or four years of hard struggle" before they could unify
China.[181]

The China Aid Act, which reinforced the tie between the United States
and the increasingly unpopular and apparently moribund government of
Chiang Kai-shek, brought about the most widespread and outspoken anti-
American movement up to that time. This anti-American sentiment originated in the commonly held belief that Chiang was leading the country
to ruin and that he could not do so without American support.[182] The
China Aid Act was condemned by a large segment of Chinese opinion as
a factor in prolonging the civil war and strengthening a detested regime.
As the government prohibited anti-government and anti-war propaganda,
the anti-American groups chose an issue on which to attack the United
States which was not related at first glance to internal Chinese politics.
This was the alleged policy of the United States to rearm and rebuild
Japan. As the embassy reported, "The condemnation of our aid is subli-
mated and transformed into an attack on our policies in Japan by student
groups and other elements."[183] In May and June, anti-American demonstrations swept the country. Ambassador Stuart expressed to the State
Department his deep concern that many normally pro-American Chinese
had become receptive to anti-American propaganda.[184]

[180] This figure was taken from a Communist communiqué summarizing the military
developments between July, 1947, and June, 1948, as reprinted in *Ti-san-tz'ŭ kuo-nei
kê-ming chan-chêng kai-k'uang* [A Survey of the Third Revolutionary War in China]
(Peking: Jên-min ch'u-pan-shê, 1954), p. 55.
[181] *Mu-ch'ien hsing-hsi yü wo-mên ti jên-wu* ["The Present Situation and Our Task"]
(Shanghai: Hsin-hua shu-tien, 1949), pp. 151–52.
[182] *United States Relations with China*, p. 906.
[183] *Ibid.*, p. 913.
[184] *Ibid.*, pp. 276–77.

2. American Officials in China Belatedly Adopt a New Approach

American officials began to implement the China Aid Act when the Chinese civil war entered its decisive phase in the second half of 1948. At the outset Washington reaffirmed its policy of avoiding further military commitment. In a meeting on June 4, attended by Secretary Marshall, Secretary of the Army Kenneth C. Royall, General Omar N. Bradley, chief of staff of the army, and General Wedemeyer, director of plans and operations, it was again decided that the United States should not place American advisers with Chinese units in combat areas.[185]

Congress had indicated that the $125 million special grant was to be used as the Nationalist government saw fit. But in China, American officials inaugurated a more positive and aggressive policy in the use of the special fund. In the summer of 1948, Admiral Oscar C. Badger, the commander of naval forces in the western Pacific, Ambassador Stuart, and Mr. Roger D. Lapham, the newly appointed chief of the Economic Cooperation Administration Mission to China, made a tour of North China which was then under the military command of General Fu Tso-yi.[186] Fu was a tested general who had distinguished himself in many battles against the Japanese and the Communists. He was popular with the people and with the troops under his control. But he was not a member of the Whampoa clique, and Generalissimo Chiang's policy of discriminating against military commanders outside of his personal following deprived him of sufficient equipment. He had under his command eleven armies of which four were unequipped and three were poorly equipped. In July, Admiral Badger submitted a list of supplies estimated at a total cost of $16 million which were urgently needed by General Fu and recommended that these be sent to him on a first priority basis. Within a few days the Joint Chiefs approved the sending of these supplies to Fu when they were available. Ambassador Stuart also pushed this project of supplying General Fu. In a conference at Stuart's residence on August 30, attended by Stuart himself, General Barr, and General Ho Ying-ch'in, the minister of national defense, it was agreed that 60 per cent of the total equipment to be sent by the United States under the special grant would be delivered to Shanghai for the defense of East China, 30 per cent would go to Tientsin for the

---

[185] Acheson's testimony, *Military Situation in the Far East,* p. 1854; *United States Relations with China,* p. 284.

[186] This account of this interesting and highly important episode is based on the testimonies of Admiral Badger and General Barr in the MacArthur hearings (*Military Situation in the Far East,* pp. 2745–749, 2964, 2987, 2990–991, 3083). Admiral Badger's testimony was vague about dates and details and was encumbered with obvious errors of fact. General Barr's testimony conflicted at various points with that of Admiral Badger. But a composite picture can be reconstructed by a careful reading of their accounts and the documents, tables, and reports printed in the White Paper. Cf. Possony, *op. cit.,* pp. 347–49.

defense of North China under General Fu's command, and 10 per cent
would be shipped to Tsingtao for the defense of Shantung Peninsula.[187]
For the first time, there was an attempt to bypass the Generalissimo and
to give part of the American supplies directly to Nationalist commanders
who had distinguished themselves in battle.

But the project of shipping arms and ammunition to China under the
$125 million special grant had to find its way slowly through the labyrinth
of American and Chinese bureaucracy and the conflicting purposes of
American and Chinese officials. The first request of the Chinese government for new shipments of arms under the $125 million program was made
only on July 23. This first list gave highest priority to small arms and ammunition. But another request chiefly contained items such as raw materials for the Chinese arsenal program which could not be delivered until
the fall of 1949 and would not have any immediate effects on the battlefield.[188] On receipt of the first Chinese request, the Department of the
Army initiated availability studies and the computation of prices to be
charged the Chinese government. The availability studies and the computation of prices by American officials and the attempts on the part of the
Chinese to get a bargain resulted in a delay of a month.[189] Further confusion was occasioned by the submission on September 20 of a revised list
of requirements by the Chinese ambassador which superseded all previous
Chinese requests. Probably reflecting the rapidly deteriorating military
situation in China, the list included weapons and ammunition primarily.
It nullified most of the work previously done by the Department of the
Army. New availability studies and computations of prices were initiated,
and the Chinese government was asked to show the requirements in the
order of the most urgent priority. It was partly in response to this request
that the Chinese government sent to the Department of the Army on
October 4 a list which specified the destinations and the approximate per-
centage of the supplies to be delivered to different parts of China in accordance with the understanding reached between Ambassador Stuart
and General Ho on August 30. Having received this list, the Department
of the Army took steps on October 5 to implement Admiral Badger's July

[187] *Military Situation in the Far East*, pp. 2990–91.
[188] Statement submitted by Brigadier General T. S. Timberman to the House Committee on Foreign Affairs, June 21, 1949 (*United States Relations with China*, pp.
976–77).
[189] The administration spokesman endeavored to put all the blame for this delay on
the Chinese. See for example General Barr's testimony in the MacArthur hearings
(*Military Situation in the Far East*, p. 3038). The statement submitted by Brigadier
General T. S. Timberman to the House Committee on Foreign Affairs on June 21, 1949,
was slanted to give that impression (*United States Relations with China*, p. 976).
On the other hand, the critics of the administration either blamed the delay on some
mysterious, unknown cause or attributed it to bureaucratic bungling on the part of
the United States. The views of both sides were biased in different degrees.

recommendation to support General Fu in North China and to send supplies to him on a first priority basis. It transmitted the entire list of Chinese requirements to General MacArthur and on October 27 ordered the Far Eastern commander to send to North China all available items on the Chinese list. These supplies, amounting to approximately 1,200 tons of small arms and ammunition with a total value of a little over $2 million, reached Tientsin on November 16.[190] This shipment of supplies, which arrived at its destination four months after Admiral Badger's recommendation, constituted only one-eighth of the supplies which he had urged be sent on a first-priority basis. The only other large shipment of small arms and ammunition, procured through the Department of the Army and sent to mainland China in the remaining days of 1948, was one consignment at a value of $16 million which reached Shanghai on December 1, 1948. Subsequent shipments were diverted at Generalissimo Chiang's request to Taiwan.[191] Of the $125 million special fund, $60.9 million was disbursed during 1948, and $55 million was spent during 1949, leaving a balance of $9 million on January 1, 1950, and $1 million as of February, 1951.[192] None of these expenditures played any significant part in the defense of mainland China.

What evidence we have suggests that a conflict of political purposes between American officials in China and the Nationalist government may have been an important cause for the delay in the shipment of arms to China under the China Aid Act. For some time, Ambassador Stuart had been trying to use the prospect of American aid as a lever to exert pressure on Generalissimo Chiang to select the right men for key posts and to implement a program of reforms. The Generalissimo had outmaneuvered Ambassador Stuart by appealing to his supporters in Congress, who had generated sufficient pressure on the administration to force it to redefine its policy and submit a program of economic assistance to Chiang. As Stuart sadly commented in a dispatch to Secretary Marshall on May 10, 1948, "Any broad or powerful bargaining position vis-à-vis the Chinese Government disappeared on the date Congress passed the China Aid Act of 1948."[193] But Ambassador Stuart was not without hope that in the process of implementing the act he could still exert a certain amount of pressure on Chiang. According to its terms, the use of American economic aid was to be governed by an agreement to be concluded by the two governments. Thus Stuart told Marshall in the same dispatch that the

[190] *Ibid.*, pp. 954, 978; Admiral Badger's testimony, *Military Situation in the Far East*, p. 2747; General Barr's testimony, *ibid.*, p. 2964.
[191] *United States Relations with China*, pp. 953–55; *Military Situation in the Far East*, p. 1930.
[192] *Ibid.*, p. 1929–30.
[193] *United States Relations with China*, p. 993.

United States should use the period of negotiating the bilateral aid agreement to press the Chinese government to undertake measures of self-help and reform. Stuart recommended that the American government display no haste in the negotiations so as to learn at least the identity of the individuals to be appointed to the ministries directly concerned with the aid program, and to extend the period in which American pressure could be applied.[194]

It appears possible that Ambassador Stuart also employed the same tactics of pressure in his endeavor to influence Generalissimo Chiang in the latter's use of the special grant. This seems to be indicated by his initiative in working out a scheme for the distribution of American military supplies between North China and Central China in a conference with Nationalist officials in his residence on August 30, as already recounted.[195] It is probably significant as an indication of Chinese resistance to his suggestion that the scheme of distribution apparently agreed on in August was not sent by the Chinese government to the Department of the Army until October 4.[196] While Ambassador Stuart could use diplomatic influence, the Chinese government had legality on its side. For the legislative history of the China Aid Act had made it clear that the special fund was to be used at the option of the Chinese government. According to the implementing directives, the process of spending the money could be initiated only by specific requests of the Chinese government.[197] Admiral Badger and Ambassador Stuart could advise, suggest, and even use their considerable political influence to push their policy. They had no final authority to use the special fund under the China Aid Act as they saw fit. Admiral Badger's recommendation in July to the Joint Chiefs was merely a suggestion made by an American officer to his superiors and not an official request made by the Chinese government through diplomatic channels in accordance with the procedures laid down by the implementing directives. This conflict of purpose between American and Chinese officials was not conducive to speed.

But even if the shipments of arms had arrived in China several months earlier, they could hardly have averted the four major defeats which the Nationalist forces suffered in the seven months following the inauguration of the China aid program in June. For it was not due to the lack of arms and ammunition that the Nationalist forces lost the first three battles: the battle of Tsinan, the battle of Manchuria, and the battle of Huai-Hai. These three battles brought out, each in its own way, some of the causes of the Nationalist defeat. The Nationalists lost the strongly fortified city

[194] *Ibid.*, pp. 993–94.
[195] Pp. 479–80, above.
[196] *United States Relations with China*, pp. 993–94.
[197] *Ibid.*, pp. 949–50.

of Tsinan on September 23 after the defection of an entire division helped the Communists breach the defenses at a critical point.[198] This outright defection, as well as the immediate surrender of other forces and their failure to stand and fight, had a basic political cause. As the consul general at Tsingtao reported, "Nationalist soldiers and population [in] Shangtung in general no longer consider [that the] Nationalist Government merits continued support in the civil war." [199] The Nationalist forces in Manchuria and the troops sent to reinforce them were totally destroyed in October because they were accustomed to holding fixed points, failed to launch a co-ordinated attack with all their armies, and thus enabled Mao to concentrate his forces to annihilate them one after another. The Nationalist defeat in the battle of Huai-Hai in November and December underlined still another factor contributing to the military debacle. Against the repeated admonitions of Vice-President Li Tsung-jên and General Pai Ch'ung-hsi, the leaders of the Kwangsi group, Chiang decided to meet the all-out attack of half a million Communists at the exposed salient of Hsüchou instead of holding the more easily defensible line of the Huai River. He passed over General Pai and selected two incompetents as commanders for this fateful battle. The Huai-Hai campaign was planned, directed, fought, and lost almost exclusively by generals of the Whampoa clique. Chiang's power interests thus hastened the collapse of the Nationalist regime.

In each of these three battles, the Nationalist forces were vastly better equipped and supplied than the Communist troops, and a large amount of matériel was captured by the latter. General Barr reported on November 16, 1948, that "no battle has been lost since my arrival due to lack of ammunition or equipment. Their [the Nationalists'] military debacles in my opinion can all be attributed to the world's worst leadership and many other morale destroying factors that lead to a complete loss of will to fight."[200] It is possible that, as Admiral Badger charged, the lack of a sufficient reserve of matériel prevented the Nationalists from making plans for offensive actions.[201] Even if this was one of the reasons for the collapse of the Nationalist government, it was a relatively minor factor in one of the most profound social and political revolutions in world history. When asked in the MacArthur hearings for his opinion on the cause of the military defeat of the Chinese Nationalists by the Communists, General Wedemeyer replied: "My military opinion on that, sir, is lack of spirit, primarily lack of spirit; it was not lack of equipment."[202] How could the Nationalist

[198] *Ibid.*, pp. 319, 331.
[199] *Ibid.*, p. 319.
[200] *Ibid.*, p. 358.
[201] *Military Situation in the Far East*, pp. 2762, 2763.
[202] *Ibid.*, p. 2329.

forces have the spirit to fight when the political foundation of the regime had already been eroded?

The early arrival of supplies might have helped General Fu in North China. But after the first three defeats, the Peiping-Tientsin-Kalgan area was surrounded by superior forces on three sides. General Fu could not possibly have held out against overwhelming odds for any length of time. As Dean Acheson testified in the MacArthur hearings:

> By the end of 1948, the struggle in North China had virtually ended with the complete collapse of the Nationalist armies. Eighty percent of all the matériel which we had furnished, both during the war and after, to the Nationalist government, was lost; and seventy-five percent of that is estimated to have been captured by the Communists.[203]

General Fu surrendered Peiping on January 22 under a negotiated agreement with the Communists.

The destruction of the core of the Nationalist forces made it impossible to defend the Yangtze River. General Barr reported on December 28:

> Marked by the stigma of defeat and the loss of face resulting from the forced evacuation of China, north of the Yangtze, it is extremely doubtful if the National Government could muster the necessary popular support to mobilize manpower in this area (South China) with which to rebuild its forces even if time permitted. . . . The complete defeat of the Nationalist Army . . . is inevitable.[204]

3. American Economic Aid and the Chinese Currency Reform

In contrast to the poor handling of the special grant, the economic program of the China Aid Act was effectively implemented. As a result of the lessons learned from the misuse of the UNRRA funds provided to China, the American government insisted on the inclusion in the Economic Aid Agreement, signed on July 3, of provisions for joint supervision of the distribution of United States aid goods within China. Under these provisions, the Chinese government agreed that all United States aid goods should be processed and distributed according to terms, conditions, and prices agreed upon between the two governments. The Chinese government also undertook to achieve a fair and equitable distribution of United States aid food and similar commodities, insofar as possible through rationing and price-control systems in urban centers of China. From the beginning, the E.C.A. mission to China exercised tight control over the

[203] *Ibid.*, p. 1856.
[204] *United States Relations with China*, p. 336.

program of aid. It set out to help the Chinese people and their economy by importing four urgently needed commodities: food, cotton, petroleum, and fertilizer. This program of commodity imports under joint supervision was a major factor in alleviating unrest in China's main urban centers and it succeeded in delivering food and other commodities to the people who were its intended beneficiaries.

But the economic program of the China Aid Act, no matter how effectively implemented, could only have a marginal effect on the Chinese economy, because it was not designed to attack the most pressing economic problem in China, runaway inflation. The inflation in China resulted from two factors directly related to the civil war: the size of the government's budget deficit and the loss of public confidence in the viability of the government. The budget deficit was running at the rate of $50 million a month while economic aid to China amounted only to about $20 million a month. Moreover, the loss of public confidence in the government as a consequence of military defeats sharply affected the value of Nationalist currency. Thus, no purely economic program could stop the inflation.[205] Furthermore, in making an over-all evaluation of the economic program of the China Aid Act, one must ponder the following appraisal by Ambassador Stuart. Stuart, a lifelong missionary, wrote in his memoirs:

> While it [the E.C.A. grant of $275 million] brought some humanitarian relief, yet from the standpoint of American national interests this had to be estimated against the political ill will it helped to aggravate. . . . Perhaps a somewhat cynical moral might be drawn about the futility of mixing philanthropy with politics.[206]

The Chinese government did on its own initiative attempt to check the inflation by a program of currency reform and price and wage control which was proclaimed on August 19. It was enforced by stringent police measures in Shanghai by Chiang Ching-kuo, the Generalissimo's son. But this program could not change the two basic realities in China: increasingly serious military defeats and mounting budgetary deficits. Early in October, a rush away from the new currency started even in Shanghai while price control resulted in a shortage of food and other commodities. The abandonment of price and wage controls on October 31 and the resignation of Chiang Ching-kuo on November 1 meant the total failure of the

[205] Harlan Cleveland, "Economic Aid to China," *Far Eastern Survey*, January 12, 1949, pp. 2–6; Dorothy Borg, "Economic Cooperation Administration and United States Policy in China," *Far Eastern Survey*, August 24, 1949, pp. 197–99; *Economic Aid to China* (Washington, D. C.: Economic Cooperation Administration, 1949).

[206] Stuart, *op. cit.*, p. 245. Stuart also observed that the $400 million had achieved nothing and might better not have been spent (*ibid.*, p. 190).

program.[207] The net effect of this ill-fated attempt was to alienate further the middle classes. For under the currency reform program, all persons holding gold, silver, and foreign exchange were required, under threat of severe punishment, to surrender them to the government in exchange for the new currency, the Gold Yüan, at the rate of one United States dollar to four Gold Yüans. The value of the Gold Yüan collapsed so quickly that by late April and early May, 1949, one United States dollar was worth five million to ten million Gold Yüans. The middle class was, in effect, expropriated. They asked: "Could the Communists be any worse than the Kuomintang?"

J. Mainland China and Formosa Written-off

The disastrous military, economic, and political developments in China during and after the enactment of the China Aid Act brought about two contrasting reactions. On the one hand, the Nationalist government increased its efforts to obtain additional aid from the United States, not only through the normal diplomatic channels, "but also through publicity," as the White Paper put it.[208] On the other hand, the Department of State became even more reluctant than before to throw good money after bad. It adopted a "hands-off" and "wait-and-see" policy. This was shown in Secretary Marshall's rejection of three separate recommendations of Ambassador Stuart in August and October to follow a more positive policy in China.

By August the military defeats suffered by the Nationalist forces and the economic chaos in the big cities had already created powerful public sentiment both within and outside the government in favor of a termination of the civil war through negotiations with the Communists. In view of this development, Ambassador Stuart made three specific recommendations on August 10. First, he suggested that the United States should give continued or increased support to the Nationalist government as the best means to prevent the formation of a "coalition government" including the Communists. Second, if some kind of accommodation between the Nationalists and the Communists could not be prevented, he suggested that:

[American] influence should be used to arrange a cessation of hostilities on a basis of very loose federation with territorial di-

[207] *United States Relations with China*, pp. 278, 400–401, 877–79; *Report by Consultant William C. Bullitt to the Joint Committee on Economic Cooperation Administration Concerning China*, 80th Cong., 2d sess. (December 24, 1948), pp. 1–13. For an interesting sidelight on Chiang Ching-kuo's honest efforts to enforce the program and his conflicts with vested interests, see K. M. Panikkar, *In Two Chinas* (London: Allen and Unwin, 1955), pp. 32–33; *New York Times*, November 1, 1948, p. 1. For the account of an economist, see Chang, *op. cit.*, pp. 82–85.

[208] *United States Relations with China*, p. 279.

vision which would leave as large an area of China as possible with a government or governments free of Communist participation. Third, in the event of a return to regionalism, American economic aid be given to strengthen regional governments.[209]

Stuart's recommendations showed that American officials had learned from bitter experience the fallacy of seeking a genuine coalition government including the Communists. They had also begun belatedly to realize that accommodation with the Communists on a basis of territorial division was the only realistic alternative to fighting a civil war which, without American military intervention, the Nationalist would lose. They also saw at last that the regional leaders furnished an alternative to the moribund central government under Chiang Kai-shek. Stuart's recommendations were in complete accord with his attempts to divert American military supplies to regional commanders.[210] Had it been adopted two or three years earlier, such a policy as Stuart envisaged might conceivably have preserved a part of China under non-Communist control.

But in August, 1948, its chances of success were slim. Thus, it was rejected by Secretary Marshall, who now did not want to take any step which would implicitly place political and moral responsibility on the United States. In an instruction sent to Stuart on August 12, Marshall ruled out any "overt United States opposition to Chinese Government compromise with the Chinese Communists or even secretly expressed opposition, which would become known," while, somewhat inconsistently, he told the ambassador "to overlook no suitable opportunity to emphasize the pattern of engulfment which has resulted from coalition governments in eastern Europe.[211] He dismissed the second suggestion by informing the ambassador that "the United States Government has no intention of again offering its good offices as mediator in China."[212] The next day, the secretary told the ambassador:

> It is not likely that the situation will make it possible for us at this juncture to formulate any rigid plans for our future policy in China. Developments in China are obviously entering into a period of extreme flux and confusion in which it will be impossible with surety to perceive clearly in advance the pattern of things to come and in which this Government plainly must preserve a maximum freedom of action.[213]

[209] *Ibid.*, p. 279.
[210] Pp. 479–82, above.
[211] *United States Relations with China*, p. 280.
[212] *Ibid.*, p. 279.
[213] *Ibid.*, p. 280.

Thus, the policy of "waiting for the dust to settle" for which Dean Acheson was later severely criticized was launched at this time.

The military debacles of Tsinan, Chinchow, and Changchun led to an extensive policy review in late October in the State Department. A series of decisions were reached which mark it as one of the three most significant events in the development of American policy in 1947 and 1948, next only to the rejection of Wedemeyer's recommendations and the decision in early 1948 not to take the last chance to intervene in the Chinese civil war. The policy review seems to have been prompted by a series of cables from Ambassador Stuart asking whether there was any change in American policy. He seems to have suggested the adoption of a more positive program for China under which the American government would press Chiang to remove incompetent leaders, step up aid to China, and expand the function and authority of the Army Advisory Group after prior agreement by Chiang on the acceptance and implementation of American advice.[214] In dismissing these recommendations, Secretary Marshall was able to cite Stuart's numerous dispatches to show how American advice had been ignored in the past and why the policy of granting conditional aid to Chiang would be impossible to implement. Marshall again reminded Stuart forcefully that "direct armed intervention in the internal affairs of China runs counter to traditional American policy toward China."[215] Once more the Secretary of State informed the ambassador:

> To achieve the objective of reducing the Chinese Communists to a completely negligible factor in China in the immediate future, it would be necessary for the United States virtually to take over the Chinese government and administer its economic, military and government affairs. Strong Chinese sensibilities regarding infringement of China's sovereignty, the intense feeling of nationalism among all Chinese, and the unavailability of qualified American personnel in large numbers required argues strongly against attempting such a solution.[216]

Still trying to persuade Marshall to adopt a positive policy, Stuart asked the State Department on October 23, among other things, whether the American government "would advise the retirement of the Generalissimo in favor of Li Tsung-jen or some other national political leader with better prospects of forming a republican non-Communist government and of more effective prosecution of the war against the Communist rebels."[217]

[214] *Ibid.*, p. 284. Stuart's telegram is not printed, but his suggestions can be inferred from Marshall's reply.
[215] *Ibid.*, p. 280.
[216] *Ibid.*, p. 281.
[217] *Ibid.*, p. 285.

Here is another alternative which might have been successfully implemented if the American government had skilfully promoted it over a period of time. But the hour was late and Secretary Marshall did not want to offer any advice which would imply a commitment to support the succeeding regime.[218]

It was also at this time that the State Department ruled out the use of American forces to defend Formosa. This decision was in harmony with Marshall's policy not to intervene militarily in the Chinese internal strife. Once more it revealed the unwillingness of the United States to use her military power to defend her interests in China. It assumed that the United States had a strategic interest in preventing Formosa from falling into the hands of a hostile power, but American occupation or use of Formosa as a base would give her little advantage. It also rested on the belief that the existing condition and strength of American armed forces precluded the possibility of committing any American forces whatever to the defense of Formosa. The American policy was to try by diplomatic and economic means to keep Formosa from falling into hostile hands. According to Acheson's subsequent testimony, this policy was "unanimously recommended to the President by all the departments concerned, and was approved by him."[219] It is apparent that the policy review in the State Department resulted in the conclusion that the United States should not use her armed forces to prevent any part of China from falling into Communist hands.

Ambassador Stuart was certainly disappointed but probably not surprised at the rejections of his recommendations. Nor did the Nationalists place much hope on a drastic change of policy under the Truman administration. While the American government hoped that the China Aid Act would give the Nationalists a breathing space to undertake sweeping reforms and measures of self-help, the Chinese government saw in it nothing but a prelude to increased American assistance under another Republican-controlled Congress and under a new Republican administration.[220] There was much in the developments in American politics to justify this hope. Soon after he was overwhelmingly nominated by the Republican party as its presidential candidate, Governor Dewey stated on June 25 that one of the cardinal principles of his administration, if elected, would be to help China combat Communist influence within its borders and that the United States should provide military advisers, the kind of matériel needed by the Chinese, and far greater financial assistance.[221] His subsequent references to China were less specific. But the repeated pledges

[218] *Ibid.*, chap. ix, above.
[219] *Military Situation in the Far East*, p. 1671.
[220] *United States Relations with China*, p. 877; Stuart, *op. cit.*, p. 219.
[221] *New York Times*, June 26, 1948, p. 1

to bring an end to the "tragic neglect" of China certainly gave the Nationalist government reasons for new hope.[222] At the height of Dewey's campaign and amidst universal expectations of a sweeping Republican victory, Mr. Ch'ên Li-fu, the leader of the extreme right-wing C.C. clique and vice-president of the Legislative Yüan, visited Dewey with a letter of introduction from Generalissimo Chiang. On returning to China he was reported to have said that, if elected, Governor Dewey would take extraordinary measures toward giving military aid to China.[223] Two days before the election Generalissimo Chiang released, on October 31, a lengthy statement in answer to questions submitted by a noted American correspondent. It concluded with the remark: "The center of endeavor in the salvation of Asia must be China. This is the great task unprecedented in human history. I hope that the American people and their statesmen will dedicate their lives to this task."[224]

But the unpredictable American voters confounded the calculations of even the shrewdest politicians. President Truman was re-elected in a great electoral upset on the very same day the Nationalists surrendered Mukden. Truman's electoral victory compelled the Chinese government to appeal once more to the Democratic administration for aid. On November 6, during a meeting of the General Assembly of the United Nations at Paris, Dr. T. F. Tsiang, head of the Chinese delegation, handed Secretary Marshall a message from the Chinese foreign minister. This inquired about the possibility of appointing American army officers to actual command of Chinese army units under the guise of advisers, and the appointment of an officer of high rank to head a special mission to China.[225] Secretary Marshall rejected this oblique request. He emphasized to the Chinese government the inherent difficulties involved in an attempt on the part of a newly appointed foreign official to advise the Chinese government regarding its course of action. Probably having in mind his own experience as well as Stilwell's, he said it would be "a very serious matter for the United States to send an officer to almost certain failure."[226] Dr. Tsiang's initial inquiry was followed by a letter from Generalissimo Chiang to President Truman making the same requests. In addition, the Chinese leader also asked for a firm statement of American policy in support of the Nationalist cause.[227] In response, President Truman called Generalissimo Chiang's attention to Secretary Marshall's recent reply to the Chinese foreign minister. As for

[222] See Dewey's speeches in Salt Lake City, on September 30; in St. Paul, on October 15; and in Cleveland, on October 27, 1948; in *ibid.*, October 1, 1948, p. 17; October, 16, 1948, p. 7; October 28, 1948, p. 24.
[223] Charles Wertenbaker, "The China Lobby," *Reporter*, April 15, 1952, pp. 18–19.
[224] *United States Relations with China*, p. 894.
[225] *Ibid.*, pp. 287, 887.
[226] *Ibid.*, pp. 287, 887–88.
[227] *Ibid.*, pp. 888–89.

Chiang's suggestion for a declaration of American policy, Truman said that his statement of March 11, 1948, expressing the American desire not to have Communists in the Chinese government, and the China Aid Act, extending assistance to China, had made the position of the American government clear.[228]

Coincidental to the Nationalist appeal for additional aid, Senator Styles Bridges, chairman of the Senate Appropriations Committee and of the watchdog committee on foreign aid, denounced the administration's China policy and urged President Truman to call a special session of the Eightieth Congress to consider further aid to China. This demand elicited no positive response from the administration which had just received a new mandate from the people. Not long afterward, two of Senator Bridges' consultants returned from a trip to China and submitted their reports. These clearly indicated the tremendous responsibility and cost which had to be assumed by the United States in any program to save the Nationalist government. Mr. D. Worth Clark, a former Democratic senator who went to China as the consultant to the Senate Appropriations Committee, reported on November 20 that a program to stop the Communists had to include immediate shipment of large supplies of arms and ammunition, combat advice on both the strategic and tactical levels, the assumption by the United States of a major share of the Nationalist government's budget, a minimum loan of $200 million to stabilize the currency, and strict American supervision of expenditure. Clark asserted that nothing less would do the job and anything less would be wasted.[229] The report of Mr. William C. Bullitt, consultant to the Joint Committee on Foreign Economic Cooperation concerning China, emphasized the need for "American direction and control, exercised by a fighting general of the highest qualities, with an adequate staff of able officers." [230] In his judgment, "There is not a single Government general who has the military training and technical skill to handle the over-all problems of logistics involved in meeting the attack of a Communist army of more than 2,000,000 men." [231]

The Nationalist campaign for further aid reached a climax with the arrival of Madame Chiang in Washington on December 1.[232] At his press conference the next day, President Truman declined to comment on the question of sending new aid to China. But he gave a negative answer with

[228] *Ibid.*, p. 889.

[229] *New York Times*, November 21, 1948, p. 1.

[230] *Report by Consultant William C. Bullitt to the Joint Committee on Foreign Economic Cooperation Concerning China*, 80th Cong., 2d sess. (December 24, 1948), p. 12.

[231] *Ibid.*

[232] The advisability of allowing Madame Chiang to come was discussed at a cabinet meeting on November 26. The question was raised by Secretary Marshall and President Truman ruled in favor of it (Millis, *op. cit.*, p. 533).

curt finality when asked about the rumor that the United States was considering sending General MacArthur to China.[233] In her pleas for aid, Madame Chiang asked for three billion dollars over a period of three years. In addition, she renewed the already rejected request for a military mission to China headed by a high-ranking officer and for a forthright declaration of the determination of the United States to halt the expansion of communism in Asia.[234]

In December, the Berlin blockade entered its sixth month and the Western powers were engaged in a costly airlift to supply the city. Europe was more than ever the center of attention. American officials received Madame Chiang with personal courtesy but held firmly to their policy. On December 16, the administration released a statement recapitulating American aid to China to date, putting the total amount at more than $3,884 million. Instead of sending a high-ranking officer to China, the administration not long afterward ordered the Joint United States Military Advisory Group to withdraw from China.[235] In taking these steps, Secretary Marshall did not go as far as some officials in the State Department had recommended. In a cabinet meeting on December 26, Marshall had read a paper, originating in the State Department, which advocated explaining to the American public the inadequacies of the government of Chiang Kai-shek. With the approval of the President, Marshall rejected this recommendation on the ground that such a public statement would administer the final coup de grâce to the Nationalist government.[236]

With the inauguration of the second Truman administration, Marshall was replaced by Dean Acheson as secretary of state. This change marked the end of one tragic phase of the China policy of the United States. From the beginning of his mission to China to the end of his tenure as secretary of state, Marshall adhered consistently to the postulate that the United States should not intervene in the Chinese civil war with her armed forces. His realistic estimate of the relative military and political strength of the Nationalists and the Communists led him to the accurate conclusion that the government could not win the civil war without American participation. Unwilling to abandon his basic postulate, he saw no solution to the problem of China after he failed in his endeavors to seek a political settlement through the establishment of a coalition government. In effect, he aban-

[233] New York Times, December 3, 1948, p. 3. It was reported that General MacArthur did not think that much could be done to arrest the sweep of communism in China (ibid., December 12, 1949, under the by-line of Hanson Baldwin).

[234] Ibid., December 10, 1948, p. 1.

[235] The Joint United States Military Advisory Group was formally established only two months previously, on November 1, 1948, by merging the Army Advisory Group, the Naval Advisory Group, and other American units (United States Relations with China, p. 340).

[236] Millis, op. cit., p. 534.

doned China in order to concentrate American resources and efforts in Europe. Yet he certainly could not and perhaps would not have followed a policy of total and prompt disengagement. To conciliate the Republican opponents of his China policy and to insure the full authorization of his European Recovery Program, he returned to a policy of granting China limited assistance after a period of partial withdrawal. The program of economic and military assistance contained in the China Aid Act was too little and too late to give the Nationalist government much of a breathing space, while it was large enough to elicit the most widespread anti-American movement up to that time. But the course of action followed by the United States was merely a new manifestation of the traditional pattern of American policy. Since the nation was unable either to use the necessary means to achieve her purpose or to define her objectives in the light of available means, her policy necessarily ended in failure. The partisan debate simply dramatized the dilemma between ends and means. The resultant compromises led to an erratic shift in policy without changing its basic course, until events forced the nation to make a choice between the abandonment of China and the use of her armed forces.

CHAPTER XII

DISENGAGEMENT

AND

CONTAINMENT

JANUARY, 1949—

JUNE, 1950

A. The Moral Issues and the Practical Considerations

General Marshall left the thankless and perplexing task of disengagement from China to Dean G. Acheson, who became secretary of state on January 21, 1949. Acheson had served as undersecretary of state from August, 1945, to June, 1947, first under Byrnes and then under Marshall himself. He had been one of the chief contributors to the instructions given Marshall before the latter's departure to China.[1] During Marshall's mission to China, he had been, by prearrangement between Truman and the General, the latter's representative, or to use Marshall's own words, "rear echelon," in Washington.[2] To the hazardous task of disentanglement, Acheson brought his conviction of the correctness of Marshall's policy, his personal courage, and his diplomatic skill. But admitting the defeat of a policy would have been difficult for a nation under any circumstance. It was still more difficult when the policy had been surrounded by a cluster of myths [3] and had remained the object of sentimental attachment, at least for a vociferous group of politicians. The difficulties were multiplied when many of the actions and omissions of the past could easily be distorted to serve a partisan purpose. It was difficult to see that for fifty years a nation had pursued a policy which was doomed to eventual failure by its inherent contradictions. But it was easy to attribute the responsibility for failure to individual officials. While it was embarrassing for critics of the administration to admit that at one time they shared the erroneous judgments of these

[1] Herbert Feis, *The China Tangle* (Princeton, N.J.: Princeton University Press, 1953), pp. 413–20.
[2] Dean Acheson, *Sketches From Life* (New York: Harper & Bros., 1959), pp. 149–54.
[3] See chap. i, above.

494

officials, it was normal human frailty to cast the first stone. Politically risky to advocate openly the use of American forces in China, it was safe to condemn inaction. Acheson was particularly vulnerable to partisan attacks because he lacked an independent base of political power and had to rely almost entirely on the support of the President. His past role in shaping China policy and his loyalty to his subordinates made him a symbol of everything that had gone wrong with American policy toward China. Moreover, his intellectual pre-eminence in official circles eventually made him a target of assaults which can be characterized as nihilistic. Hemmed in by partisan and demagogic attacks, he never had the freedom of action necessary to effect a prompt disengagement and his policy retained some of the ambiguities of the traditional policy.

As noted in the last chapter, the State Department in October, 1948, had, in effect, written off China, including Formosa. From that time to January 21, when Acheson assumed office, the Chinese Communists had completed the conquest of Manchuria, scored another smashing victory in the Huai-Hai campaign, and practically won the battle for North China. The alternatives before the United States were either to defend the Yangtze with American armed forces or to withdraw from China. The Yangtze was a formidable barrier against the advance of the Communists, who had neither a navy nor an air force and lacked experience in amphibious warfare. As General Wedemeyer puts it, the Nationalists "could have defended the Yangtze River with broomsticks if they had the will to do so."[4] Events show that it took the Communists three months to regroup and train their armies for the crossing of the river.

But to adopt the alternative of defending the Yangtze with American forces would have implied a drastic reversal of Marshall's policy at a time when its assumptions were being underscored by developments both outside and inside China. With the cold war more intense and the Berlin crisis unresolved, the use of American forces in China seemed more reckless than ever. President Truman's call for rearmament on March 17, 1948, was followed by little action.[5] The administration's proposal for universal military training was not acceptable to Congress. While selective service was finally re-enacted by Congress, the Joint Chiefs envisaged an increase of the active strength by only 411,000 men to an aggregate of 1,795,000. President Tru-

[4] Senate Committee on Armed Services and Committee on Foreign Relations, *Hearings on the Military Situation in the Far East*, 82d Cong., 1st sess. (1951), p. 2329 (hereafter cited as *Military Situation in the Far East*). American military and naval attachés in China believed that the river could be held for several months if the Nationalist ground, naval, and air forces could be co-ordinated under a unified command and if the soldiers were paid in silver (John Leighton Stuart, *Fifty Years in China* [New York: Random House, 1954], p. 235).

[5] Walter Millis, with Harvey C. Mansfield and Harold Stein, *Arms and the State* (New York: Twentieth Century Fund, 1958), pp. 214–28.

man put the upper limit of the annual expenditure for defense permanently at $15 billion, which was said to be what the American economy could bear. Military strategy was based primarily on America's monopoly of the atomic bomb.

America's subsequent entry into the Korean War shows that a sudden reversal of American policy is possible when a clear-cut moral issue is combined with a perception of the serious consequences of inaction and when a sense of shock overcomes the unwillingness to use force. In the case of China in 1949, however, the moral issue seemed to be ambiguous. As the American consul general at Tientsin reported in March, 1949, Americans in that key port in North China felt that "our global policy of opposition to Communism should not oblige us to support a hopelessly inefficient and corrupt government which has lost the support of its people."[6] The recognition that Chinese communism was genuine communism merely intensified America's dilemma. As Professor John K. Fairbank put it, "China has been going through a social revolution on which the Chinese Communists have capitalized and of which they have taken the leadership."[7] Similarly, awareness of the ties between Moscow and the Chinese Communists did not resolve the moral issue. To quote Fairbank again, "On balance, I am afraid we must put the Communist victory in China down as a case of self-determination, not of outside aggression."[8] Moreover, a Communist-dominated China did not appear to be a serious threat to American interests. As noted in chapter ix, Marshall did not believe that China would soon become a strong power. Some people believed, to use the words of a report indorsed by the International Committee of the National Planning Association, that "the national interests of China in Asia run parallel rather than counter to the interests of the United States."[9] This traditional view underlying the Open Door policy survived the Chinese Communists' vociferous denunciation of "American imperialism." The expectation of a Chinese Titoism on the part of some officials in the early months of 1949 increased American complacency.[10] The Gallup Poll found in several surveys that only a minority favored strong measures to resist Communist expansion in China.[11]

It is possible, though not likely, that if the administration had proposed a strong China policy, public support would have been forthcoming. But

[6] Department of State, *United States Relations with China* (Washington, D.C.: Government Printing Office, 1949), p. 300 (hereafter cited as *United States Relations with China*).

[7] John K. Fairbank *et al.*, *Next Step in Asia* (Cambridge, Mass.: Harvard University Press, 1949), p. 4.

[8] *Ibid.*, p. 18.

[9] Luther Gulick, *A New American Policy in China* (Washington, D.C.: National Planning Association, 1949), p. 22.

[10] See chap. ix, above.

[11] Gabriel A. Almond, *The American People and Foreign Policy* (New York: Harcourt, Brace & Co., 1950), p. 105.

after the breakdown of the Marshall mission, American officials felt that conditions necessary for the efficient use of American aid and effective Sino-American co-operation did not obtain in China. Did the conditions now exist? At first glance, it would seem that the "retirement" of Chiang on January 21, 1949, and the elevation of General Li Tsung-jên as acting president, had removed the major obstacle to the success of an active American policy in China. But a closer look at Chinese political developments shows that this was not the case.

Before Chiang announced his retirement, he had transferred the gold and silver bullion and foreign exchange of the government from Nanking to Formosa.[12] He had requested the American government to ship to Formosa after December, 1948, all the remaining military supplies under the $125 million special grant. He had tightened his political control over that island. After his "retirement," he still controlled the party machinery of the Kuomintang in his capacity as its director general. He interfered with governmental affairs and political policies by behind-the-scene maneuvers and through his personal followers. He retained actual control over the navy and the air force and two major army groups on the mainland, whose active co-operation and effective employment were indispensable for a successful defense of the Yangtze.

Chiang and Li entertained different plans for military operation. Li

[12] *New York Times*, February 15, 1949, p. 1. Chiang's shipment of the gold and silver holdings to Formosa and his refusal to turn them over to Acting President Li were subsequently the subject of a heated debate in September, 1949, between Senator Connally and Senator Knowland on the Senate floor in connection with an amendment to the mutual defense assistance legislation offered by Knowland to give $150 million to the Nationalist government.

Opposing Knowland's amendment, Senator Connally declared on September 7: "I do not think it is fair for the Senator [Knowland] to be making speeches on the floor of the Senate for popular consumption, in an effort to stir up the ragged battalions of those who would throw $2,000,000,000 or $3,000,000,000 more into the rat hole in China in order to resuscitate and bring to life Chiang Kai-shek, who has deserted his people and has gone to Formosa with $138,000,000 in gold in his pocket, money which does not belong to him. It did belong to the government, but he has absconded with it. Why do not they spend that $138,000,000 before they call on us for another hand-out?"

Two days later Senator Knowland let it be known that he was going to address some remarks to Connally on the Senate floor and asked Connally to be on hand. Toward the end of a lengthy speech on China policy, Knowland challenged Connally's statement that Chiang had "absconded" with the $138 million.

Immediately after Knowland had finished his speech, Connally replied: "I want to apologize. I made an error in my statement. . . . I said that Chiang Kai-shek had taken $138,000,000 in gold. I was absolutely in error. He took more than $300,000,000 in gold to Formosa. I did not say he took it to spend for himself. I said it belonged to the Nationalist Government of China. He resigned his position in the Nationalist Government. He is supposed to be a private citizen, and yet he takes the gold that belongs to the treasury of the Nationalist Government" (*Congressional Record*, XCV, 81st Cong., 1st sess. [1949], 12640 and 12758). For a vivid description of this episode, see William S. White, *Citadel* (New York: Harper & Bros., 1956), pp. 5–6.

A POLICY OF LIMITED ASSISTANCE

hoped to defend the Yangtze and, failing that, to defend several provinces in the southwest which were the base of his power. Chiang apparently planned only to fight a delaying action on the mainland so as to gain time to prepare against a Communist assault on Formosa which was under his tight control. While Chiang as president had been vulnerable to the political maneuvers of the Kwangsi leaders, General Li as the acting president was now subject to all the political machinations of Chiang. Li lacked money even to pay his troops, not to mention the necessary financial resources to fight a successful war. He could not obtain American military supplies, which were diverted to Formosa. His orders to the military units commanded by Chiang's followers were not obeyed.[13] All these facts were known to the American government. Defending the Yangtze was a hopeless task. The passive American policy and the program of limited assistance had helped Chiang to stay in power for so long that he had destroyed whatever chances other political leaders might have had for salvaging a part of China.

B. The Perplexing Tasks of Withdrawal

If last-minute armed intervention was not a practical alternative, prompt and complete withdrawal would have been the logical course to follow. But prompt withdrawal was rendered difficult by the same considerations which had made it necessary for Marshall to return to a policy of limited assistance after a brief period of partial withdrawal. It was also hindered by insufficient awareness of the possibility that continued entanglement might increase the chance of an eventual armed clash with the Chinese Communists. The resulting absence of a sense of urgency in withdrawing from China was rooted in the basic assumption behind Marshall's refusal to undertake armed intervention, i.e., that China could not soon be a serious threat to American security.

There was little doubt that State Department officials were advocating and implementing a policy of withdrawal. On January 26, the American government officially terminated its participation in the training of Nationalist forces and recalled General Barr. The next day, the withdrawal of the United States Joint Military Advisory Group was announced.[14] The

[13] *United States Relations with China*, pp. 250, 290–91, 292–304, 403, 901, 921; Yin Shih, *Chiang Li kuan-shih yü Chung-kuo* ["The Chiang-Li Relationship and China"] (Hong Kong: Freedom Press, 1954), pp. 103–28; Liang Shêng-chün, *Chiang Li tou-chêng nei-mo* ["The Inside Story of the Struggle between Chiang and Li"] (Hong Kong: Union Asia Press, 1954), chaps. ii, iii, and iv; F. F. Liu, *A Military History of Modern China* (Princeton, N.J.: Princeton University Press, 1956), pp. 264–67; *Military Situation in the Far East*, p. 1930.

[14] Senate Committee on Foreign Relations, *Hearings on the Nomination of Philip C. Jessup To Be United States Representative to the Sixth General Assembly of the United Nations*, 82d Cong., 1st sess. (1951), pp. 820–21 (hereafter cited as *Nomination of Jessup*).

National Security Council recommended that the American government halt shipment of $60 million in military supplies which remained out of the $125 million special grant.[15] American officials feared that these supplies would simply fall into the hands of the Chinese Communists. In an off-the-record conference on February 5, Senator Vandenberg strongly opposed the recommended action on moral and sentimental grounds. In his opinion, such an action would substantiate the charge that "we are the ones who gave poor China the final push into disaster." He urged that "this blood must not be on *our* hands."[16] President Truman and Vice-President Alben W. Barkley supported Vandenberg. Shipments of arms to Formosa continued. The unexpended balance of the $125 million special fund for arms shipment was never cut off, not even after President Truman's statement on January 5, 1950, announcing the "hands-off-Formosa" policy.[17]

Moralism and sentimentality constituted only one of the factors making it difficult to implement a policy of withdrawal. There were demands for a re-examination of the administration's policy and clamors for a positive program of aid to China. On February 7, fifty-one Republican representatives addressed a letter to Truman, demanding the appointment of a commission to make an immediate re-examination of the situation in China.[18] On February 24, Secretary Acheson explained to thirty signers of the letter in an off-the-record meeting that he could not foresee clearly the outcome in China "until the dust settled."[19] He thus sidestepped their demand.

The following day, Senator Pat McCarran, anti-administration Democrat from Nevada, introduced a bill to provide $1.5 billion in loans for the Nationalist government and to authorize American officers to direct Chi-

[15] The published records do not show whether this recommendation originated in the State Department or the Defense Department. Senator Vandenberg, who recorded this episode in his diary, was silent on this point. Westerfield stated that the proposed action "most probably originated from the State Department" and "was certainly approved by Acheson" (H. Bradford Westerfield, *Foreign Policy and Party Politics* [New Haven, Conn.: Yale University Press, 1955], p. 346).

For Harold Stassen's charge that Dr. Philip Jessup made the recommendation of stopping all supplies to China, see Senate Committee on the Judiciary, *Hearings on the Institute of Pacific Relations*, 82d Cong., 1st and 2d sess. (1951–52), pp. 1068–69 (hereafter cited as *Institute of Pacific Relations*); see also *Nomination of Jessup*, pp. 805–7, 890–98.

[16] Arthur H. Vandenberg, Jr. (ed.), *The Private Papers of Senator Vandenberg* (Boston: Houghton Mifflin Co., 1952), pp. 530–31. See also Harold Stassen's testimony, in *Institute of Pacific Relations*, p. 1068.

[17] See p. 531, below.

[18] *Congressional Record*, XCV, 81st Cong., 1st sess. (1949), 1950–51.

[19] Westerfield, *op. cit.*, p. 347. See also two speeches by Representative Robert Hale, Republican of Maine, in *Congressional Record*, XCV, 81st Cong., 1st sess. (1949), 1950–53; *ibid.*, p. 6137.

The *New York Times* reported the meeting on February 25, 1949, p. 1. Secretary Acheson explained in the MacArthur hearings that this phrase was not meant to denote the administration's policy and that it simply described "my own inability to see very far in this situation" (*Military Situation in the Far East*, pp. 1765–66).

nese troops in the field.[20] On March 10, fifty senators, of whom twenty-four were Democrats, sent and released a letter to Chairman Connally, asking his committee to give the McCarran bill full consideration and hearings.[21] Of the fifty signers, only two were members of the Committee on Foreign Relations. That Senate committee was, broadly speaking, sympathetic toward the State Department's desire to withdraw from China. In the MacArthur hearings, Senator McMahon stated without contradiction that, after a thorough review of the Chinese situation in March, there was complete agreement in the committee that "we had best get out of China as fast as we could" and that "the only point upon which there was some difference of opinion was as to the rate of withdrawal."[22] On March 15, some five weeks before the Communists crossed the Yangtze virtually unopposed, Acheson flatly rejected McCarran's proposal.[23] The 1948 elections and the developments in China had strengthened the hand of the administration. In contrast to its success in 1947 and 1948, the China bloc now failed to force on the administration a program of additional aid to China.

In rejecting the McCarran proposal, however, Acheson found it necessary to make a conciliatory gesture toward the China bloc. Furthermore, Vandenberg's opposition to the halting of arms shipment to Formosa had made it clear that the administration could not suspend economic assistance to China without courting violent reaction from Republican leaders. Acheson thus expressed his willingness to permit the unobligated appropriations under the China Aid Act of 1948 to be spent in a limited period beyond the expiration date of April 2.[24] On the same day, the administration sent Congress a bill to effect this change. In this bill, the administration sought full discretion for the use of the $54 million unexpended fund. It also separated its proposed legislation for China from the bill extending the European Recovery Program. Both of these features were opposed by the China bloc. As finally enacted by Congress on April 14, the bill to extend the European Recovery Program included in substance an amendment proposed by Senator Knowland which qualified the discretion granted the President by limiting the use of the balance appropriated under the China Aid Act to

[20] *Congressional Record*, XCV, 81st Cong., 1st sess. (1949), 1530, 1532–33; *New York Times*, March 11, 1949, p. 13; April 15, 1949, p. 10; *United States Relations with China*, pp. 1053–54.

[21] *New York Times*, March 11, 1949, p. 13. It was the understanding of Senator George D. Aiken, Republican of Vermont, that the letter merely asked the committee to consider the McCarran bill. It was not his intention to ask for aid to China in signing the letter. Senator Connally interpreted the letter to mean that the signers were merely asking his committee "to give attention to the Chinese situation." He asserted that "we have done so, and are continuing to do so" (Statements by Aiken and Connally on March 24, *Congressional Record*, XCV, 81st Cong., 1st sess. [1949], 3085).

[22] *Military Situation in the Far East*, p. 1909.

[23] *United States Relations with China*, pp. 1053–54.

[24] *Ibid.*

non-Communist areas of China.[25] The United States thus continued to be bound to the Nationalists by a program of economic assistance as well as shipment of arms.

The China bloc was hardly satisfied with this meager result. Since it could not force its views on the administration, it intensified its attacks on State Department officials, obviously hoping that these attacks would modify the administration's program of withdrawal, or that a change in personnel would bring about a reversal of policy. These countervailing pressures constituted another obstacle to rapid disengagement. On the same day that Congress adopted the bill to provide the $54 million unexpended fund to China, Acheson's letter of March 15 to Senator Connally commenting on the McCarran bill was made public.[26] The next day, Senator Bridges called for a "full-dress investigation by Congress of the State Department's position toward China." He accused Acheson of "what might be called sabotage of the valiant attempt of the Chinese Nationalists to keep at least part of China free."[27] His attack was strongly supported by McCarran and Knowland.[28] On April 21, the day on which the Communists crossed the Yangtze, Knowland submitted a concurrent resolution providing for an investigation of America's foreign policy in the Far East by a joint bipartisan committee of five senators and five members of the House of Representatives.[29] Such a setup would have given the pro-Chiang congressmen on the House Committee on Foreign Affairs a voice in the investigation.[30] The Senate Foreign Relations Committee pigeonholed Knowland's resolution.

C. The Communist Sweep across the Yangtze River

The conflict over China policy and the immobilized position of the administration created a paradox: only Communist successes could strengthen the hand of the administration over its critics and enable it to carry out its program. As a result, the United States could withdraw only a step ahead of the Communist advance, thus strengthening the impression of her impotence and lack of foresight. The spectacular sweep on April 21 of the Communist forces across the Yangtze confirmed the official view of

[25] For the high points in the legislative history of this bill, see *Congressional Record*, XCV, 81st Cong., 1st sess. (1949), 3237, 3765, 3771, 3823, 3828, 3829; House Committee on Foreign Affairs, *Report on Amending the China Aid Act of 1948*, House Report No. 329, 81st Cong., 1st sess. (1949), p. 5; and *Report on Extension of European Recovery Program*, House Report No. 323, 81st Cong., 1st sess. (1949), Part 2, p. 5; Westerfield, *op. cit.*, pp. 347–50.
[26] *New York Times*, April 15, 1949, p. 10.
[27] *Ibid.*, April 16, 1949, p. 3.
[28] *Ibid.*, April 16, 1949, p. 3; April 17, 1949, p. 25.
[29] *Congressional Record*, XCV, 81st Cong., 1st sess. (1949), 4862.
[30] Westerfield, *op. cit.*, p. 350.

the hopelessness of the Chinese situation. The administration pushed forward its program of disentanglement. Ambassador Stuart, together with the ambassadors of other nations except the Soviet Union, remained in Nanking even after the Communist forces occupied it on April 24. The Soviet Union was the only major power which sent her ambassador to Canton, the new capital of Nationalist China. Throughout May, the Russians continued to negotiate with the Nationalist government with a view to concluding commercial agreements regarding Sinkiang.[31] As a step to justify the administration's policy and to cut the ties to the Nationalist government, Acheson revived a proposal which Marshall and Truman had rejected in November, 1948. He now secured President Truman's approval for the preparation and publication of what was subsequently called the White Paper on China. In the spring, a large number of officials were engaged in this task, with the director of the Office of Far Eastern Affairs, Walton Butterworth, in charge.[32] In June, Philip Jessup, who had successfully negotiated a settlement of the Berlin blockade earlier in the year, was assigned to work on Far Eastern problems. The first task given him was to edit the materials collected and written by subordinate officials.[33]

The smashing military success of the Communists and a private conference with President Truman and Acheson on April 28 had a temporarily sobering effect on Senators Bridges and Wherry.[34] There was a brief lull in the debate over China policy. Only the indomitable Knowland continued his crusade for additional aid to China with undiminished vigor. At his suggestion, General Chennault was brought home to testify before the Armed Services Committee on May 3. Chennault advocated a program at a cost of $700 million a year to support the local and provincial regimes along the peripheral areas in Southwest and Northwest China.[35]

This suggestion was dismissed by Acheson the next day in a flat declaration that American policy remained unchanged. In May, the State Depart-

---

[31] Allen S. Whiting and General Sheng Shih-ts'ai, *Sinkiang: Pawn or Pivot?* (East Lansing, Mich.: Michigan State University Press, 1958), pp. 116–18; Max Beloff, *Soviet Policy in the Far East*, (London: Oxford University Press, 1953), pp. 63–65, 97–101; Henry Wei, *China and Soviet Russia* (Princeton, N. J.: Van Nostrand Co., 1956), pp. 230–32.

[32] Acheson's testimony, *Military Situation in the Far East*, p. 1769; Dean Rusk's testimony before a subcommittee of the Foreign Relations Committee on October 9, 1951, as reprinted in *Nomination of Jessup*, p. 813.

Arthur Krock reported that eighty persons were involved in the preparation of the White Paper. See Krock's column, *New York Times*, August 12, 1949, as reprinted in *Congressional Record*, XCV, 81st Cong., 1st sess. (1949), A5391–92.

[33] Acheson's testimony, *Military Situation in the Far East*, p. 1769; Rusk's testimony, as reprinted in *Nomination of Jessup*, pp. 810–11; Jessup's testimony, *ibid.*, p. 603.

[34] Westerfield, *op. cit.*, p. 350.

[35] *Congressional Record*, XCV, 81st Cong., 1st sess. (1949), 5480–84. In a speech delivered on April 1, Harold Stassen also advocated a similar program (*ibid.*, A2325). See also *Institute of Pacific Relations*, p. 1037.

ment made public its tentative program for granting military assistance to Europe to implement the North Atlantic Pact. On May 17, Knowland served notice on the Senate floor that he would offer an amendment to provide aid to non-Communist forces in China.[36]

D. The Controversy over the Confirmation of Butterworth

Past failures repeatedly came back to haunt the administration. A divisive post-mortem occurred on almost every issue, even if it was only remotely connected with the current policy of the United States. In June, the partisan controversy was rekindled with new intensity by the question of confirming the nomination of Butterworth to the newly created post of assistant secretary for Far Eastern affairs. This debate revealed a widening cleavage along party lines.

It found even Senator Vandenberg openly and severely criticizing the State Department. In the Senate Committee on Foreign Relations, Vandenberg voted "present" on confirmation in spite of the otherwise unanimous approval given by the committee. On June 24, he explained that in his opinion it was a "great mistake," in appointing a new assistant secretary, not "to bring a fresh point of view in the assignment" and "simply to continue the regime which, for one reason or the other, is connected with a very tragic failure of our policy in the Far East."[37] But given the discrepancy between ends and means, and within the limits imposed by the traditional pattern of policy, there could not have been any obvious alternative to the policy that had failed. Vandenberg thus admitted judiciously: "It is a very easy, simple matter to dissociate one's self from a policy. It is not easy to assert what an alternative policy might have been. I concede that it is far easier to be critical than to be correct."[38]

This same dilemma was revealed in the attack by the China bloc and the defense made by the administration's spokesmen. Bridges characterized Butterworth as "the symbol of failure and of a tragic era in our relations with China."[39] Brewster launched into a general attack on the administration's policy.[40] Senator Connally countered with the question "whether there is any member of the Senate who would have voted to send a United States Army to try to settle the controversy between the Chinese factions . . . ."[41] Another bitter debate took place on September 26 and 27 with Senator Knowland playing a prominent part.[42] Senator Fulbright

[36] *Congressional Record*, XCV, 81st Cong., 1st sess. (1949), 6306.
[37] *Ibid.*, p. 8292.
[38] *Ibid.*, p. 8294.
[39] *Ibid.*
[40] *Ibid.*, pp. 8294–97.
[41] *Ibid.*, p. 8296.
[42] *Ibid.*, pp. 13266–70, 13284.

came to Butterworth's defense by pointing out that, if blame was to be ascribed, it certainly had to be attributed to General Marshall or the State Department rather than to a relatively minor official.[43] On September 27, Butterworth was confirmed by a highly partisan vote.[44] The debate over the confirmation of Butterworth did not make easier the task of subordinate officials charged with implementing a policy of withdrawal. It marked the beginning of a process which led to the appointment during the Eisenhower administration of Walter Robertson as assistant secretary of state for Far Eastern affairs — reportedly the choice of the leading members of the China bloc in Congress.

Approximately one month after the debate in the Senate on June 24, the minister of the Chinese embassy in Washington, Dr. Ch'ên Chih-mai, sent a cable to Generalissimo Chiang, making a specific suggestion on the proper method to influence American policy. Ch'ên recommended:

> As far as our activities in the United States are concerned, it seems that [while] we should cover the administration, as well as the legislative branch, we should especially strive for a closer relationship with the latter. There is no danger at all if our procedure strictly follows the laws of the United States, but Dr. Hu Shih [former ambassador to the United States] is opposed to getting in touch with the legislative branch. His opinion is off the beam.[45]

E. Mao's Policy of Leaning to One Side and Acheson's Search for Methods of Containment

When the officials in the State Department were completing their compilation of a defense of the administration's policy in China and when the senators were debating the nomination of Butterworth, Mao Tse-tung made a historic pronouncement on foreign policy on July 1, 1949. In this paper, *On People's Democratic Dictatorship*, Mao declared that China must ally herself "with the Soviet Union, with every New Democratic country, and with the proletariat and broad masses in all other countries." [46] To make his position unmistakably clear and to anticipate possible objections to a policy of joining one camp in opposition to the other, he wrote:

[43] *Ibid.*, pp. 13290–91.

[44] *Ibid.*, pp. 13293–94.

[45] Ch'ên Chih-mai to Generalissimo Chiang Kai-shek, July 21, 1949, inserted in the *Congressional Record* by Senator Wayne Morse of Oregon (*Congressional Record*, XCVIII, 82d Cong., 2d sess. [1952], 3970). On the question of the authenticity of this and other secret messages from the Chinese embassy to the Chinese government, see the statement by Senator Morse, *ibid.*, p. 3970; the letter from Dr. Ch'ên; and another letter commenting on Dr. Ch'ên's explanation, *ibid.*, pp. 4016–17.

[46] Mao Tse-tung, *On People's Democratic Dictatorship* (Peking: Foreign Language Press, 1952), p. 10.

"You are leaning to one side." Exactly. The forty years' experience of Sun Yat-sen and the twenty-eight years' experience of the Chinese Communist Party have convinced us that in order to attain victory and consolidate it, we must lean to one side. According to these experiences, the Chinese people must lean either to the side of imperialism or to that of socialism. There can be no exception. There can be no sitting on the fence; there is no third road. We oppose Chiang Kai-shek's reactionary clique, which leans to the side of imperialism. We also oppose illusions about a third road. Not only in China but throughout the world, one must lean either to imperialism or to socialism. There is no exception. Neutrality is merely a camouflage; a third road does not exist.[47]

Mao was deliberately provocative. For, on the one hand, he did not feel that in the relations between the revolutionaries and the "reactionaries" it made any difference whether one was provocative or not. On the other hand, a clear-cut and provocative statement of position served his purpose of drawing a sharp line between the revolutionaries and the "reactionaries" and of "raising our own morale while deflating the enemy's prestige."[48] Then he proceeded to make explicit the two basic assumptions of his policy of leaning to one side. On the one hand:

In an era when imperialism still exists, it is impossible for a genuine people's revolution in any country to achieve victory without various forms of help from the international revolutionary forces. Even when victory is won, it cannot be made secure without such help.[49]

On the other hand, Mao did not believe that the United States and Great Britain would give aid to a "people's state." If they should trade with and grant a loan to China, they would do so to "ease their own crisis" rather than to "help the Chinese people."[50] These statements further clarified the basic assumptions underlying a declaration issued on April 3 by the Chinese Communists and the leaders of the small parties in China, in which they condemned the North Atlantic Pact and affirmed their intention to march hand-in-hand with "our ally, the Soviet Union" in the event of war. Ideological convictions thus combined with hostility toward the United States to lead Mao to make a sharp break with the age-old Chinese policy of using barbarians to control barbarians.

Mao's statement did not make it easier for the State Department to im-

[47] *Ibid.*
[48] *Ibid.*
[49] *Ibid.*, p. 11.
[50] *Ibid.*, p. 12. See also p. 13.

plement a program of withdrawal. In printing an article by Chennault which advocated a program of aid to save part of China, the editors of *Life* prefaced it with the observation that Mao's article had "shattered the illusion cherished by many an American — the illusion that China's Communists are 'different.'"

Mao's declaration apparently had a sobering effect on official thinking. In contrast to the first four months of 1949, there were now very few reports that officials in the State Department expected an early development of Titoism in China.[51] On July 18, Secretary Acheson sent Mr. Philip Jessup, ambassador-at-large, a top-secret memorandum setting down the policy of containing communism in Asia and instructing Jessup to draw up possible programs of action to achieve this purpose. Acheson told Jessup of his desire "to make absolutely certain that we are neglecting no opportunity that would be within our capabilities to achieve the purpose of halting the spread of totalitarian communism in Asia."[52] In August, Secretary Acheson invited Mr. Everett Case, president of Colgate University, and Mr. Raymond Fosdick, former president of the Rockefeller Foundation, to serve as consultants to the State Department and to work with Jessup in the search for concrete programs of action.[53]

One alternative which had been ruled out was the conclusion of a Pacific pact similar to the North Atlantic Treaty. Acheson was averse to being drawn into the conflicts between the Southeast Asian countries themselves and between them and the European powers. He was conscious of the limits of American resources and power.[54] Furthermore, India, potentially the most powerful non-Communist nation in South Asia, was averse to participation in any bloc and her government thought all discussions of a Pacific pact premature. Japan was under occupation. The other Asian nations could contribute very little real strength to a common cause. The most active Asian advocate of an anti-Communist alliance was none other than Generalissimo Chiang, from whom the American government was seeking to dissociate itself. On July 5, Generalissimo Chiang declared in an interview with an American correspondent that "regardless of whether I hold

[51] On February 14, C. S. Sulzberger reported that the United States clearly recognized "the possibility that while Mr. Mao is a devout Marxist he may also be a 'Titoite' heretic" (*New York Times*, February 14, 1949, p. 10). See also his articles in *ibid.*, February 5, 1949, p. 12; February 18, 1949, p. 8. According to James Reston, some of the American officials believed that Mao Tse-tung and other Communist leaders would rapidly show signs of Titoism once they were in control (*ibid.*, April 24, 1949, Sec. 4, p. 3). See chap. ix, above.

[52] Secretary Acheson's top-secret memorandum for Ambassador Jessup, July 18, 1949, as reprinted in *Nomination of Jessup*, p. 603.

[53] *Ibid.*, pp. 603–4.

[54] See Acheson's statement on May 8, 1949, *Department of State Bulletin*, (May 29, 1949), p. 696; Royal Institute of International Affairs, *Survey of International Affairs, 1949–50* (London: Oxford University Press, 1953), p. 33.

any political office, I cannot give up my revolutionary leadership."[55] At his suggestion, the Kuomintang established in mid-July a new "Extraordinary Committee" with Chiang as the chairman and Acting President Li as one of the two vice-chairmen. This new organization gave Chiang an additional instrument to control political and military affairs in his capacity as the party leader of the Kuomintang. Without even informing Acting President Li beforehand,[56] Generalissimo Chiang flew to the Philippines to pay a visit to President Quirino on July 10.[57] The two Asian leaders announced their intention to issue invitations to a conference for the purpose of discussing an anti-Communist alliance. After his return to Canton, Chiang told the American minister that he had to take the initiative to conclude an anti-Communist alliance because the United States refused to assume the active leadership in Far Eastern affairs.[58] Chiang visited Korea in August, and on August 8 Chiang and President Syngman Rhee urged President Quirino to take steps to summon such a conference. At this time American troops had completed their withdrawal from Korea for more than a month.[59] The previous March, General MacArthur had traced in an interview with a reporter an American line of defense which left out South Korea.[60]

F. The White Paper

While Generalissimo Chiang was flying to Korea to promote his grandiose plan of an anti-Communist alliance, the State Department issued on August 5 the White Paper on China which attributed the failure to counter Communist revolutionary strategy to the basic weakness of Chiang's government. The document was released in the belief that, as Acheson put it subsequently, "the disasters had already overtaken the Nationalist government." [61] The White Paper represented an attempt to justify, before the bar of American opinion, the administration's policy since Pearl Harbor.[62] Acheson's letter of transmittal revealed clearly the dilemma to which the traditional pattern of American policy had led the United States. Acheson conceded that military intervention on a major scale to assist the

[55] *Washington Daily News*, July 5, 1949, as inserted in the *Congressional Record* by Senator Knowland (*Congressional Record*, XCV, 81st Cong., 1st sess. [1949], p. 8820).
[56] Liang, *op. cit.*, pp. 156–63.
[57] Chiang Ching-kuo, *Fu-chung chih-yüan* ["Carrying a Heavy Burden to Reach a Long Distance"] (1960), Part II, pp. 8–10.
[58] *Ibid.*, p. 142.
[59] Harry Truman, *Years of Trial and Hope* (New York: Doubleday & Co., 1956), p. 329. The last of the American troops left Korea on June 29, 1949.
[60] *New York Times*, March 2, 1949, p. 22.
[61] *Military Situation in the Far East*, p. 1770.
[62] Testifying in the MacArthur hearings, Acheson said, "At the time this [*i.e.*, the White Paper] was finally put out, it seemed to me we were in the position where American people had to know what had gone on . . ." (*ibid.*).

Nationalists to destroy the Communists "may look attractive theoretically and in retrospect." But it was "wholly impractical" because "it is obvious that the American people would not have sanctioned such a colossal commitment of our armies in 1945 or later."[63] Acheson's letter also contained an admission that the traditional policy of assisting the Chinese people in resisting domination by any foreign power or powers had failed to achieve its purpose. "In this case," Acheson explained, "the foreign domination has been masked behind the façade of a vast crusading movement which apparently has seemed to many Chinese to be wholly indigenous and national."[64] The only alternative open to the United States was "full-scale intervention in behalf of a Government which had lost the confidence of its own troops and its own people."[65] But intervention "would have been resented by the mass of the Chinese people, would have diametrically reversed our historic policy and would have been condemned by the American people."[66] Acheson concluded:

> The unfortunate but inescapable fact is that the ominous result
> of the civil war in China was beyond the control of the government
> of the United States. Nothing that this country did or could have
> done within the reasonable limits of its capabilities could have
> changed that result; nothing that was left undone by this country
> has contributed to it.[67]

Acheson saw no possibility of the development of a Chinese Titoism. As if to answer Mao's flamboyant proclamation of the policy of "leaning to one side," Acheson declared that "the Communist leaders have foresworn their Chinese heritage and have publicly announced their subservience to a foreign power, Russia, which during the last fifty years, under Czars and Communists alike, has been most assiduous in its efforts to extend its control in the Far East."[68] Echoing the policy of containment stated in his July 18 memorandum to Jessup, Acheson warned that "should the [Chinese] Communist regime lend itself to the aims of Soviet Russian imperialism and attempt to engage in aggression against China's neighbors, we and the other members of the United Nations would be confronted by a situation violative of the principles of the United Nations Charter and threatening international peace and security."[69] As for the distant future, Acheson found hope in the belief that "ultimately the profound civilization and the democratic individualism in China will reassert themselves and she will

[63] *United States Relations with China*, p. x.
[64] *Ibid.*, p. xvi.
[65] *Ibid.*, p. xv.
[66] *Ibid.*, p. xvi.
[67] *Ibid.*
[68] *Ibid.*
[69] *Ibid.*, p. xvii.

throw off the foreign yoke."[70] The United States, Acheson submitted, should "encourage all developments in China which now and in the future work toward this end."[71]

If Acheson hoped that the White Paper would silence his critics and win over public opinion, he was soon disappointed. On the very day it was released, both Senator Knowland and Representative Judd made brief statements on the floor of Congress, asserting that the White Paper and the documents reproduced in it substantiated their criticisms of the administration's policy.[72] Two days later, General Hurley issued a statement calling the White Paper "a smooth alibi for the pro-Communists in the State Department who had engineered the overthrow of our ally, the Nationalist Government of the Republic of China and aided in the Communist conquest of China."[73] On August 19, Judd charged that the State Department omitted sixteen documents and facts which would further support the charges made by the critics.[74] The climax was reached when Senators Bridges, Knowland, McCarran, and Wherry issued a lengthy memorandum, bitterly assailing the White Paper as "a 1,054-page whitewash of a wishful, do-nothing policy which has succeeded only in placing Asia in danger of Soviet conquest."[75] The attack was so intense that Secretary Acheson was obliged to issue a statement in answer to Judd's specific charge of sixteen omissions.[76]

Those who opposed the China bloc's demands for a positive policy were also critical of the White Paper but for diametrically opposite reasons.[77] In a series of three articles, Walter Lippmann refused to accept "Acheson's claim that our China policy was essentially right, and that the result was beyond our control."[78] He desired to know "the causes and the remedies for Chiang's stranglehold on American policy."[79] He wanted an inquiry into the disastrous failure which would be "pursued in the manner of statesmen forming a policy rather than of a lawyer seeking a verdict for his client."[80]

[70] *Ibid.*, p. xvi.

[71] *Ibid.*

[72] *Congressional Record*, XCV, 81st Cong., 1st sess. (1949), 10813, 10875.

[73] *Ibid.*, p. 10941.

[74] *Ibid.*, pp. 11881–82.

[75] *Ibid.*, pp. A5451–54. For the most succinct criticism of the publication of the White Paper by a scholar who was also a critic of the administration's policy, see Paul M. A. Linebarger, "The Failure of Secret Diplomacy in China," *Far Eastern Survey*, September 7, 1949, pp. 214 ff.

[76] *Department of State Bulletin*, September 5, 1949, pp. 350–52, 359.

[77] For a survey of the various comments on the White Paper, see Francis Valeo, *The China White Paper* (Washington, D.C.: Legislative Reference Service, 1949).

[78] Walter Lippmann, "The White Paper: The Chiang Stranglehold," September 12, 1949, as reprinted in *Commentaries on American Foreign Policy* (New York: American Institute of Pacific Relations, 1950), p. 7.

[79] *Ibid.*

[80] *Ibid.*

In his opinion, the White Paper "does not even ask, much less does it answer, the crucial questions."[81]

In China, the White Paper proved to be grist to the Communist propaganda mill. The official Communist organ, *Jên-min jih-pao*, charged on August 19 that the White Paper furnished conclusive evidence of General Hurley's interference in Chinese domestic politics through his policy of supporting Chiang Kai-shek, exposed General Marshall's partiality for the Nationalists in his mediatory efforts, and disclosed the political intrigues of Ambassador Stuart in his attempt to build up the influence of pro-American elements both within and outside the Kuomintang.[82] In five articles written for the *Jên-min jih-pao*, Mao seized upon the White Paper to intensify his attack on the American government, to launch a campaign to destroy the "illusions" of the Chinese liberals about the United States, and to win them over to his cause. Mao characterized the White Paper as a counterrevolutionary document which openly demonstrated "United States imperialist intervention in China."[83] An old hand at trickery and deception, like British imperialism, would not, he averred, have published such a document but

> the newly arrived, upstart and neurotic United States imperialist group — Truman, Marshall, Acheson, Leighton Stuart and others — have considered it necessary and practicable to reveal publicly some (but not all) of their counter-revolutionary doings in order to argue with opponents in their own camp as to which kind of counter-revolutionary tactics is the more clever.[84]

In revealing many of America's "treasured tricks" of the past, the White Paper had become material for the education of the Chinese people. According to Mao, Acheson had made a clean sweep of the illusions about United States humanity, justice, and virtue which the shortsighted, muddle-headed Chinese liberals and democratic individualists had entertained. "It is," Mao declared, "a bucket of cold water particularly for those who believe that everything American is good and hope that China will model herself on the United States."[85]

As for the future American policy, Mao took seriously Acheson's pious

[81] Walter Lippmann, "The White Paper: Mr. Acheson's Conclusion," *ibid.*, p. 1. For an attempt to answer some of the basic questions about the China policy of the United States, see John K. Fairbank, "Toward a Dynamic Far Eastern Policy," *Far Eastern Survey*, September 7, 1949, pp. 209 ff.

[82] *Jên-min jih-pao*, August 19, 1949, p. 2. For an account of other Communist comments on the White Paper, see Knight Biggerstaff, "The Nanking Press: April–September, 1949," *Far Eastern Survey*, March 8, 1950, pp. 53 ff.

[83] Mao Tse-tung, *Selected Works*, IV (Peking: Foreign Languages Press, 1961), (hereafter cited as Mao, *Selected Works*, IV [Peking]).

[84] *Ibid.*

[85] *Ibid.*, p. 430.

declaration that "ultimately the profound civilization and the democratic individualism of China will reassert themselves and she will throw off the foreign yoke." He took it as an indication that the United States would continue to make trouble, placing her hope on the Chinese supporters of "democratic individualism."[86] He declared:

> Make trouble, fail, make trouble again, fail again till their doom; that is the logic of the imperialists and all reactionaries the world over in dealing with the people's cause. . . . This is a Marxist law. When we say "imperialism is ferocious," we mean that its nature will never change.[87]

In contrast, "fight, fail, fight again, fail again, fight again . . . till their victory" was said to be the logic of the people. Mao told the "progressives" that it was their duty to prevent the middle-of-the-roaders and the waverers from being pulled over by the imperialists and to tell the deceived to cast away their illusions about the United States. When these people were won over, "United States imperialism" would be entirely isolated, and Acheson would no longer be able to "play any of his tricks."[88] Let "United States imperialism" and the Kuomintang reactionaries blockade the Chinese Communists for eight or ten years, Mao said, and "by that time all of China's problems will have been solved."[89] Even now, "United States imperialism" and the Kuomintang reactionaries had been defeated. Mao asserted: "It is we who are going to attack them, not they who are coming out to attack us. They will soon be finished."[90]

G. Military Assistance for the "General Area of China"

The China bloc was not deterred by the publication of the White Paper from pressing for military aid to China. Once again it endeavored to use the administration's European program as a peg on which to hang its program for China. In the congressional deliberations on the general military assistance bill implementing the North Atlantic Pact and giving aid to Greece, Turkey, Iran, Korea, and the Philippines, the friends of the Nationalist government both in the Senate and the House proposed amendments to grant military aid to China. In contrast to Marshall's readiness in 1947 and 1948 to make concessions to the China bloc, the congressional supporters of the administration offered strong and effective initial resistance to the China bloc's demands. In the House, two amendments and a

[86] *Ibid.*, p. 428.
[87] *Ibid.*
[88] *Ibid.*
[89] *Ibid.*, p. 438.
[90] *Ibid.*, p. 430.

separate bill to grant military assistance to China failed.[91] In the Senate, Knowland offered an amendment which would grant $125 million for military assistance and provide an American mission to advise the Chinese government.[92] But the combined Committee on Foreign Relations and Committee on Armed Services adopted, by a vote divided strictly along party lines, an amendment offered by Connally granting a $75 million emergency and contingency fund to the President for him to spend or not to spend anywhere in China and the Far East without any detailed accounting to Congress.[93]

Even at this late date, however, the China bloc showed that it was both willing and able to endanger the administration's program for Europe unless it gained some concessions on aid to China. In the House, its defeats on the question of China gave some of its members an additional motive to support an amendment offered by James P. Richards, Democrat of South Carolina, which would cut in half the $1.1 billion requested by the administration for military assistance to the NATO countries with the purpose of prodding them to make integrated arrangements for defense. With strong support from Vorys and Judd, the Richards amendment passed the House by a vote of 209 to 151.[94] In the Senate, some members of the China bloc demonstrated their displeasure by supporting in the combined committees an amendment offered by Senator Walter F. George of Georgia to cut the funds requested for military assistance to Europe by $300 million. George's proposal was defeated by the slim margin of 13 to 10.[95]

Once again a compromise with the China bloc was necessary. The Senate adopted a suggestion offered by Vandenberg, making $75 million available for use in "the general area of China." In the conference committee, the House cut of half the authorization for NATO countries was restored and the Senate provision for $75 million of aid to the "general area of China" was accepted. In the House, both Vorys and Judd reversed their earlier positions and supported the authorization of the amount requested by the administration.[96] The bill passed Congress on September 28, and four weeks later almost the full amount was appropriated. Thus, the United States appeared to the outside world to be tied to the Nationalists by a

[91] Congressional Record, XCV, 81st Cong., 1st sess. (1949), 11013, 11782–91; New York Times, August 16, 1949, p. 1.

[92] Congressional Record, XCV, 81st Cong., 1st sess. (1949), 10737–38.

[93] Westerfield, op. cit., p. 358.

[94] For Vorys' position, see Congressional Record, XCV, 81st Cong., 1st sess. (1949), 11666. For Judd's speech, see ibid., pp. 11787–88. For the House action, see ibid., p. 11807.

[95] New York Times, September 10, 1949, p. 1. For Knowland's statement of September 9, 1949, see Congressional Record, XCV, 81st Cong., 1st sess. (1949), 12757.

[96] For a general account of this episode, see Westerfield, op. cit., pp. 355–59; Holbert Carroll, The House of Representatives and Foreign Affairs (Pittsburgh: University of Pittsburgh, 1958), pp. 127–29.

new program of military assistance. But in reality the China bloc won only an empty victory. At the end of December, as we shall see, the National Security Council supported the State Department's view and rejected a proposal made by the Joint Chiefs to give some military assistance to Formosa in addition to the $125 million appropriated in 1948.[97] The $75 million of military assistance to the general area of China was used entirely in places other than Formosa.[98] The adoption of this program did nothing to enhance American prestige. Nor did it serve to delay the Communist advance in China.

H. The Question of Recognizing the Communist Regime

By ordinary logic, one would expect that the State Department's program of disentanglement from the Nationalist government would be accompanied by a policy of recognizing the Chinese Communists as the governing authority in China. Jessup, for one, thought that as a matter of general principle a policy of non-recognition would not serve any useful purpose.[99] Yet contrary to the widespread impression in the autumn and winter of 1949,[100] the top officials of the administration had not decided on an early recognition of Communist China. It is a measure of the predicament confronting the United States that, at a time when her officials were anxiously cutting her remaining ties with the Nationalist government, they also found it impractical and imprudent to seek to establish as quickly as possible normal diplomatic relations with the Chinese Communists — impractical, it would seem, primarily for reasons of domestic politics and imprudent, as the record shows and as officials subsequently stressed, from the standpoint of American prestige and immediate interests.

The question of recognizing a Communist regime in China was posed a few days after the occupation of Nanking by the Chinese Communists on April 24. Ambassador Stuart, who remained in Nanking to give the Communists "the opportunity to discuss relationships with the United States,"[101] was paid an informal visit by Huang Hua, a Communist official who had been active in the tripartite Executive Headquarters during the Marshall mission. In an informal talk, Huang soon broached the subject of recognition. Stuart replied that the question could only be considered when there emerged a new government which had the acceptance of the Chinese

[97] *Military Situation in the Far East*, pp. 1674, 1808. See also pp. 528–29, below.

[98] *Military Situation in the Far East*, pp. 1345–46; *First Semi-annual Report on the Mutual Defense Program*, House Doc. No. 613, 81st Cong., 2d sess. (1950), pp. 9, 11, 20, 36.

[99] *Nomination of Jessup*, pp. 885–86.

[100] For a documentation of this widespread impression, particularly the recollections of Senator H. Alexander Smith and Harold Stassen, see *ibid.*, pp. 616–20, 713–20, 799–802, 836–38, 856–72.

[101] Stuart, *op. cit.*, p. 236.

people and the ability to maintain relations with other nations according to international standards.[102] In Washington, the State Department expected that a central Communist government would be established around October 10. On May 6, it took steps to convince the governments of the major non-Communist powers with interests in the Far East of "(1) the disadvantages of initiating any moves toward recognition or giving the impression through statements by their officials that any approach by the Chinese Communists seeking recognition would be welcomed and (2) the desirability of concerned western powers adopting a common front in this regard."[103] An informal agreement was reached that the non-Communist powers would consult and inform each other before taking action. But the Australian government made known its view that the Communist central government, when established, should be accorded recognition at the earliest possible moment. The Indian government was considering *de facto* recognition of "the Communist government set up in North China."[104]

The State Department's action in seeking to discourage the other powers from granting early recognition must be understood in the light of the fact that only on April 14 had the Congress included in the bill on the European Recovery Program a provision extending the expiration date of $54 million of unexpended funds for economic aid to the Nationalist government until February, 1950. Any indication on the part of the State Department of a willingness to accord early recognition to Communist China would have clearly flouted the wishes of Congress. Here the matter rested while the Communists called a meeting on June 15 of all anti-Kuomintang parties and groups to make preparations for the convening of a "new Political Consultative Conference" and for the establishment of a Communist-dominated "coalition" government.

On June 24, during the debate between Senator Vandenberg and Senator Connally sparked by the confirmation of the nomination of Butterworth, Senator Vandenberg expressed his hope that there would be no consideration of recognition of a Communist government in China without complete preliminary contact and exploration with the Senate Foreign Relations Committee.[105] On this very day, Senator Knowland released a letter to President Truman signed by sixteen Republican and six Democratic senators, asking the President to make it clear that no recognition

[102] *Ibid.*, p. 247.
[103] Jessup's testimony, *Nomination of Jessup*, p. 615; Acheson's testimony before the Foreign Relations Committee, January 10, 1950, as reproduced in *ibid.*, p. 792; Butterworth's statement to the Round Table Conference held in the State Department, October 6, 1949, as reproduced in *Institute of Pacific Relations*, pp. 1565–66.
[104] *Ibid.*, p. 1566.
[105] *Congressional Record*, XCV, 81st Cong., 1st sess. (1949), 8294.

of the Communist forces was presently contemplated.[106] Taking note of congressional sentiments, Secretary Acheson sent a letter to Senator Connally on July 1, giving assurance that the Foreign Relations Committee would be consulted when the subject came up for decision.[107]

On August 2, three days before the publication of the White Paper, Ambassador Stuart left Nanking for the United States, leaving the embassy at Canton in charge of Counselor-Minister Lewis Clark.[108] On August 14, it was announced that the United States intended to maintain her relations with the Nationalist government. On the diplomatic front, the State Department continued its exchanges of views with other governments. During a meeting of the foreign ministers of the United States, Great Britain, and France in Washington, Secretary Acheson in a talk with Mr. Bevin on September 13 again tried to persuade the latter to act in concert with the United States and once more expressed the view that it would be unwise to recognize Communist China.[109] Bevin indicated to Acheson that the British government could not delay recognition of the Communist regime.[110] On October 1, Mao Tse-tung proclaimed the establishment of the "People's Republic of China" and sent out requests for recognition. The Soviet Union extended recognition the next day. The Soviet satellites soon followed the Soviet lead. On October 3, a spokesman for the State Department declared that the American government would not recognize the Chinese Communist government without consulting Congress. He noted that the Chinese message requesting recognition contained no assurance that the regime was prepared to assume its international obligations.[111]

The question of recognizing the Communist government constituted the most important subject discussed in a rather unusual round table conference held on October 6, 7, and 8, which was called by the State Department and attended by twenty-four leading scholars and businessmen interested in China. There was, to use the words of an impartial participant, a "very general agreement about the desirability of recognizing the Communist government in China and recognizing it fairly soon."[112] The minority view was expressed by Harold Stassen, who pleaded for a delay of at least two years and who was certain of the inability of the Communists to consolidate their control.[113] One of the participants made the

[106] For the text of the letter, see *ibid.*, p. 8406.
[107] Jessup's testimony, *Nomination of Jessup*, p. 615.
[108] Stuart, *op. cit.*, p. 257.
[109] *Nomination of Jessup*, pp. 924, 928.
[110] *Ibid.*, pp. 615, 930. Butterworth's statement at the Round Table Conference, as reproduced in *Institute of Pacific Relations*, p. 1506.
[111] *New York Times*, October 4, 1949, p. 1.
[112] Professor Edwin O. Reischauer's remark in "Transcript of the Round Table Conference" as reproduced in *Institute of Pacific Relations*, p. 1667.
[113] *Ibid.*, p. 1668.

following significant remark which might explain, in part, the hesitations of the State Department.

> Sitting in this room arguing and listening, I think I would say we had come to a state of mind where we would recognize the Communist Government in China but General Marshall has been whispering in my ear for the last few days that a lot of things we were talking about now you cannot get the American public to take right now or the Congress to take. . . . I thing [think?] the procedure would be to watch and wait.[114]

Against this background, Secretary Acheson restated in a news conference on October 12 three main tests to be applied in recognizing a new government: (1) that it control the country it claimed to control; (2) that it recognize its international obligations; and (3) that it rule with the acquiescence of the people who were ruled.[115] If the Communist government could be expected to satisfy the first and third conditions soon, there was little evidence that the second criterion would be met within a very short time. As early as February 1, 1947, the Central Committee of the Chinese Communist party declared that it considered invalid all the treaties, agreements, and loans which the Nationalist government concluded with foreign powers during the civil war. The same point was reiterated on October 10, 1947, in a declaration by the People's Liberation Army. Abrogation of these treaties and agreements was one of Mao's eight conditions for a peace settlement with the Nationalist government. Secretary Acheson was fully aware of this fact.[116]

Furthermore, Mao had adopted a policy "systematically and completely destroying the imperialist domination of China."[117] He had instructed his cadres in March, 1949, that upon entering the big cities their first steps should be to refuse to recognize the legal status of any foreign diplomatic establishments and personnel, to abolish all imperialist propaganda agencies in China, to take immediate control of foreign trade, and to reform the customs system. His hatred and suspicion of the West and ignorance of international affairs had led him to take an extraordinary view of the question of recognition. He thought that the Chinese Communists should not and need not be in a hurry to obtain recognition by "the imperialist countries" even for a fairly long period after total victory over the Kuomintang. He reasoned that "the imperialists, who have always been hostile

[114] Remark by Ernest R. MacNaughton, a banker from Portland, Oregon, ibid., p. 1659. General Marshall, then associated with the Red Cross, attended the conference as a participant and was asked to present his views.
[115] Nomination of Jessup, p. 616.
[116] See Acheson's testimony in an executive session of the Foreign Relations Committee on January 10, 1950, as reproduced in part in ibid., p. 790.
[117] Mao, Selected Works, IV (Peking), p. 370.

to the Chinese people, will definitely not be in a hurry to treat us as equals" and "as long as the imperialist countries do not change their hostile attitude, we shall not grant them legal status in China."[118] Carrying out Mao's policy, the Chinese Communists subjected Americans to all sorts of harassment. In July, Vice-Consul William B. Olive was arrested and beaten by police in Shanghai. On August 17, the American government announced that it was evacuating its embassy and consular staff from Canton which was now threatened by the approaching Communist forces. On October 24, Angus Ward, American consul general in Mukden, and four of his staff, were jailed for a month after he and his entire staff had been put under house arrest for nearly a year. This latest action was considered by the United States to be "in clear violation of established principles of international comity and practice respecting the treatment of consular officials."[119] After their release, Ward and his staff were deported from China. The Chinese Communists were apparently using their treatment of American officials and citizens as one way to demonstrate their ability to defy American power and to deal a blow at American prestige. The Republican senators found in the Communist actions an additional issue on which to attack the administration's China policy.[120] American recognition of the Communist government had to await some change in the international behavior of the Chinese Communists and a calmer political atmosphere at home.

There followed in November and December several exchanges of views between the American and the British governments on the subject. The American position continued to be that the Communists must approach a certain standard of international behavior before recognition could be considered and that the non-Communist powers ought to present a common front. But the more extensive economic interests of Great Britain in China and the vulnerability of Hong Kong predisposed the British government toward an early recognition. More important, the hand of the British government was forced by the anxiety of India to establish a friendly relation with her Communist neighbor. On December 16, Mr. Bevin informed Secretary Acheson of a cabinet decision to extend recognition in early January. In reply, Acheson expressed his regret over the British decision and said that there was nothing he could add to the views previously expressed by him.[121] Following the State Department view, Senator Connally declared on December 29 that he was opposed to recognition of the Chinese Communist government before it was able to

[118] *Ibid.*, p. 371.
[119] *Department of State Bulletin*, November 21, 1949, p. 760.
[120] For example, see Knowland's statement, *Congressional Record*, XCV, 81st Cong., 1st sess. (1949), 5238, 9214.
[121] *Nomination of Jessup*, pp. 624–25, 907.

give absolute assurances of respect for international law, including the protection of foreigners.[122] Thus, there was no substance to the charge that the State Department in effect told the British government to go ahead and recognize Communist China and gave it the impression that the United States would soon follow its action. On December 30, India extended formal recognition to the Chinese Communist government. Pakistan took similar action on January 5. On January 5, 1950, the British government withdrew recognition from the Nationalist government and the next day it accorded *de jure* recognition to the Communist regime. Between January 6 and January 18, Norway, Ceylon, Denmark, Israel, Afghanistan, Finland, Sweden, and Switzerland recognized Peking in rapid succession. On January 10, Secretary Acheson informed the Senate Foreign Relations Committee in executive session of the position taken by the State Department on the question of recognition in its exchange of views and consultations with other governments.[123] He gave no indication that the American government was about to recognize Communist China.

On January 14, the Chinese Communist regime seized the property of the American government in Peking which under the Sino-American Treaty of 1943 had been converted from military barracks used by the marines to consular compounds. In protest, the State Department, carrying out its prior warning, immediately recalled all American official personnel from Communist China and closed all American official establishments. On January 14, Senator Knowland declared that the Communist seizure of American properties in Peking underscored the bankruptcy of America's China policy and suggested that "the men responsible for that policy submit their resignations to the President."[124] Senator Bridges asserted that "if our responsible officials cannot change our policy it is time to change our officials."[125] These and other statements were interpreted by the press as demands for the resignation of Secretary Acheson.[126] The opinion in Congress was that American recognition of the Chinese Communist regime could now be considered out of the question. Secretary Acheson told his news conference on January 18 that the seizure of the consular properties made it an obvious conclusion that the Chinese Communists did not want United States recognition.[127] The American government was actually moving away from rather than toward recognition of the Communist regime.

It seems clear from the above account that recognition of the Communist government was an impractical step for the administration to take

[122] *New York Times*, December 30, 1949, p. 1.
[123] *Nomination of Jessup*, pp. 791–92.
[124] *New York Times*, January 15, 1950, p. 1.
[125] *Ibid.*
[126] *Ibid.*
[127] *Ibid.*, January 19, 1950, p. 1.

so long as the American government, in response to congressional pressure, was still giving economic aid to the Nationalist government. While the State Department was trying to disentangle itself from the Nationalists as quickly as domestic politics permitted, it also endeavored to dissuade the other governments from granting recognition so that the United States would not find itself in an isolated position and a common front of the non-Communist powers could be preserved. Moreover, the State Department appears to have been genuinely concerned about the Chinese Communists' attitude toward their international obligations and about their treatment of foreigners, diplomats, and civilians alike.[128] In view of these considerations, the position taken by the State Department is perfectly understandable and is not as surprising as it appears at first glance.[129]

There was very little left for the State Department to do except to avoid, as far as possible, any further involvement in the Chinese civil war and to allow events in China to unfold themselves. The swift onward march of the Chinese Communist forces seemed to indicate that the demise of the Nationalist government was close at hand. On August 4, General Ch'êng Ch'ien, the chairman of Hunan Province, and General Ch'en Ming-jên, commander of the First Group Army, defected to the Communists and surrendered the northern part of the province. Continued disagreement between Generalissimo Chiang and Acting President Li made it impossible to work out a plan for the defense of the province of Kwangtung.[130] On October 13, the Nationalist government evacuated Canton and moved its capital to Chungking. The Communist forces entered

[128] Stuart, op. cit., pp. 255–56.

[129] In the hearings on the nomination of Jessup as United States representative to the General Assembly of the United Nations in October, 1951, Jessup was harassed by some of the Republican senators for the alleged decision of the State Department to grant early recognition to the Communist government in the fall and winter of 1949 and for the important role which Jessup was supposed to have played in that decision. Jessup was able to refute these charges by citing various evidence and producing the memoranda exchanged between the American and British governments. Jessup summarized the position of the State Department in the following words: "I think the essential fact which is documented in the statement I made, supported by the documents you have seen, is that the Department of State did not at any point reach the conclusion, if I may put it this way, that recognition was just around the corner. They never reached the conclusion that if the British, Indian, and other governments recognized, that we would need to follow" (Nomination of Jessup, p. 659).

The critics of the State Department and Mr. Jessup found fault even with the State Department's position that recognition would be considered only if the new Communist government passed the three tests mentioned above. This attitude led to the following dialogue between two Democratic Senators, ridiculing the Republicans:

"Senator Fulbright: Unless you say 'never' you are just wrong, and yet nobody expects you to say 'never.'

"Senator Sparkman: If you said 'never,' you would be an imbecile.

"Senator Fulbright: And if you do not say 'never,' nobody is satisfied" (Nomination of Jessup, p. 932).

[130] Yin Shih, op. cit., pp. 134–37.

Canton the next day. Three days later, Communist units captured Amoy, the port across the strait from Formosa. On November 20, Acting President Li, a completely defeated man, flew to Hong Kong and shortly afterward arrived in the United States to seek medical care. On December 8, the Nationalist government moved its capital to Taipei, Formosa. Chungking was lost by the Nationalists on December 30. By the end of the year, virtually all of mainland China was in Communist hands. Only a few localities in Southwest China plus Tibet remained to be conquered. On March 1, Generalissimo Chiang resumed the presidency on Formosa.

I. China's Accusation of the Soviet Union in the United Nations

In fighting desperately for its existence, the Nationalist government made a diplomatic move which posed new problems for the State Department. This was the formal complaint which the Nationalist government filed against the Soviet Union in the General Assembly on September 28, 1949, for Soviet violations of the Sino-Soviet Treaty of August, 1945, and the principles of the United Nations Charter.[131] This action was taken by the Nationalist government only three days before the projected inauguration of the "People's Republic of China" on October 1. It was obviously a step to stigmatize the new regime as an illegitimate offspring of Soviet intervention and thus stir up opinions unfavorable to recognition of the Chinese Communist government by the various countries and the United Nations.[132] Concluding a lengthy speech before the Political and Security Committee of the General Assembly on November 25, 1949, Dr. Tsiang expressed his hope (1) that the General Assembly would pronounce judgment on the Soviet Union for obstructing the efforts of the Nationalist government to establish its authority in Manchuria and for giving military and economic aid to the Chinese Communists; (2) that the General Assembly would recognize the cause of China's political independence and territorial integrity as a cause common to all the peoples of the world; (3) that the General Assembly would recommend that all member states desist and refrain from giving further military and economic aid to the Chinese Communists; and (4) that no member state would "accord diplomatic relations" to the Chinese Communist regime.[133]

Subsequently, the Chinese delegation introduced a draft resolution for

[131] New York Times, September 28, 1949, p. 3; Wei, op. cit., pp. 237–38.

[132] This was so in spite of the disclaimer by Dr. T. F. Tsiang, the chairman of the Chinese delegation, that the complaint is "not a question between my government and the Chinese Communists. It is a question between my government and the government of the Soviet Union" (Tsiang's statement before the General Assembly, September 29, 1949, in China Presents Her Case [New York: Chinese Delegation to the United Nations, December, 1949], p. 5).

[133] Ibid., p. 38; United Nations, Official Records of the Fourth Session of the General Assembly: First Committee, 1949, p. 347.

the purpose of translating these hopes, with minor changes, into the findings and recommendations of the General Assembly.[134] Dr. Tsiang explained that, of the four operative clauses of the Chinese draft resolution, the one recommending non-recognition of the Chinese Communists was "the most important." [135]

Meanwhile, the Communist bloc had not been idle. On November 18, Secretary-General Trygve Lie of the United Nations received a cablegram from the Chinese Communist government, demanding that the United Nations immediately deprive the delegation of the Nationalist government of "all rights to further represent the Chinese people in the United Nations so as to conform to the wishes of the Chinese people."[136] This demand by the Chinese Communists furnished the justification for the tactic adopted by the Soviet delegation to counter the Nationalist accusations. On November 15, Mr. Vishinsky declared in the Political and Security Committee that the Nationalist complaint "could not properly be considered since it had been submitted by the Kuomintang ex-Government" and that "his delegation would not participate in the consideration of the question."[137] His position was supported by the Ukrainian, the Polish, the Byelorussian, and the Czech representatives. Ruling on a point of order raised by the Yugoslav delegate, Mr. Lester B. Pearson of Canada, chairman of the committee, upheld the right of the Nationalist delegation to represent China until it was successfully challenged in the proper agency of the General Assembly and in the Assembly itself.[138]

The Chinese draft resolution presented a number of member states in the United Nations with a difficult problem. Most of them had little sympathy with the international behavior of the Soviet Union. But the adoption of the Chinese proposals would limit their freedom of action toward recognition of the Chinese Communist government and thus bar what was thought to be a necessary step to normalize the international situation in the Far East.[139] They were offered a way out of their embarrassment by a joint draft resolution submitted by Philip Jessup and sponsored by the United States, Australia, Mexico, Pakistan, and the Philippines. This joint draft resolution omitted any reference to the issue of recognition of the Communist regime and to the censure of the Soviet Union. It merely

[134] China Presents Her Case, pp. 49–50.

[135] Tsiang's statement before the Political and Security Committee, December 1, 1949, ibid., p. 44.

[136] New York Times, November 19, 1949, p. 6.

[137] United Nations, Official Records of the Fourth Session of the General Assembly: First Committee, 1949, p. 399.

[138] Ibid., p. 340.

[139] In the subsequent debate, the delegates of Australia, Pakistan, and the United Kingdom opposed the Chinese draft resolution on the ground, among others, that member states should not bind themselves for an indefinite period to withholding recognition from the new regime (ibid., pp. 350, 351, 357, 359).

called on all states to be guided by certain general principles in their dealings with China, such as to respect her political independence, to respect the right of the Chinese people to choose their political institutions, to respect existing treaties relating to China, and to refrain from seeking spheres of influence or foreign-controlled regions within the territory of China.[140] There was little doubt that, confronted with the choice between the Chinese draft resolution and the five-power proposal, most member states would opt for the latter. Facing defeat, Dr. Tsiang adroitly asked on December 2 to postpone the vote until December 5.

On December 5, the delegations of Cuba, Ecuador, and Peru came to the rescue of Tsiang by submitting a new joint resolution which would refer the Nationalist complaint to the Interim Committee of the General Assembly.[141] This enabled Tsiang to declare that, if the three-power proposal were adopted, there would be no need to vote on the Chinese draft resolution which would automatically be referred to the Interim Committee.[142] In effect, he withdrew his draft resolution to be reintroduced in the Interim Committee. The three-power proposal, with an amendment submitted by the delegation of Uruguay to strengthen it, was adopted in the Political and Security Committee by a vote of 23 to 19, with the United States in opposition.[143] Since the three-power resolution was procedural in character and was in no way incompatible with the five-power resolution submitted by the United States, the latter was also adopted by 47 votes to 5, with five abstentions.[144] Both of these decisions of the committee were ratified by the General Assembly on December 8. Throughout the debate, Philip Jessup, the principal spokesman of the United States delegation, was unsparing in his attack on Russian imperialism while refraining from condemning the Chinese Communists. No doubt this difference in the American attitude toward the two Communist powers stemmed, in the first instance, from the fact that the Soviet Union rather than the Chinese Communists was the party formally accused by the Nationalist government. But it would seem that the State Department was at this time trying to drive a wedge between the two Communist powers by arousing the nationalistic sentiment of the Chinese against the threat of Soviet imperialism. This intention was also reflected in several official American statements issued in January, 1950. On February 7, 1950, the Interim Committee took up the question of the Chinese appeal but no action was forthcoming.

[140] Ibid., Annex, p. 37.
[141] Ibid., p. 37; United Nations Political and Security Committee, Official Records of the Fourth Session of the General Assembly, 1949, p. 359.
[142] Ibid., December 6, 1949, p. 368.
[143] Ibid., p. 371.
[144] Ibid., p. 372.

J. The Question of Chinese Representation in the United Nations

The question of Chinese representation in the United Nations was closely related to the issue of American recognition of Peking. The actions taken by the State Department toward this question indicated quite clearly a hardening of its attitude toward the Communist regime after the Communist seizure of American properties on January 14 and the announcement of the conclusion of a Sino-Soviet alliance on February 14. The question of Chinese representation in the United Nations came to a head when the Chinese Communist government sent, on January 8, a telegram to the United Nations and the governments of the states represented on the Security Council declaring the presence of the delegate of the "Chinese Kuomintang reactionary remnant clique" in the Security Council to be illegal and demanding his expulsion.[145] Two days later, Mr. Yakov Malik, the Soviet representative on the Security Council, demanded the expulsion of Dr. T. F. Tsiang, the Chinese delegate.

At this time, the United States was not irreconcilably opposed to the admission of the Chinese Communist regime. In the debate, Mr. Ernest Gross, the American delegate, declared that the United States government would vote against the draft resolution submitted by Malik. But he went on to make it clear that the American government considered the question procedural rather than substantive and that his vote against the Soviet motion could not be considered a veto. He declared that his government would "accept the decision of the Security Council on this matter when made by an affirmative vote of seven members." [146] The French delegate also took the same position. On January 13, the Soviet draft resolution was rejected by a vote of six to three with the United Kingdom and Norway abstaining. Thereupon, Malik announced that the U.S.S.R. delegation would not sit on the Council as long as "the representative of the Kuomintang group" had not been excluded from the Council. He reinforced this announcement with the declaration that the Soviet Union "will not recognize as legal any decision of the Security Council adopted with the participation of the representative of the Kuomintang group, and will not be guided by any such decision." [147] His walkout began a Soviet boycott of the United Nations which did not end until one month after the outbreak of the Korean War.

This premature and crude attempt of the Soviet Union to oust the Nationalist delegation from the Security Council was either a grave tactical blunder or a Machiavellian maneuver to isolate Communist China from the West. At this time, five out of the eleven members of the Security Coun-

[145] United Nations Security Council, *Official Records, 459th Meeting*, p. 2.
[146] United Nations Security Council, *Official Records, 460th Meeting*, p. 6.
[147] United Nations Security Council, *Official Records, 461st Meeting*, p. 10.

cil — the U.S.S.R., India, Yugoslavia, Great Britain, and Norway — had already recognized the Chinese Communist government. France and Egypt were expected to extend their recognition soon. If the Soviet delegate had waited a little longer and if the Chinese Communists had subsequently taken no actions to antagonize France and to aggravate the hurt feelings of the United States, the admission of Communist China into the United Nations could not have been delayed.[148] Instead, the Soviet government seemed to many observers to have deliberately courted defeat.[149] The Chinese Communists also took a series of actions which diminished their chance of gaining admission. On January 14, they seized the American consular compound at Peking, as noted. On January 19, Peking radio announced that the Chinese Communist regime had decided to extend diplomatic recognition to the Vietminh government of Ho Chi-minh.[150] In this matter, Peking acted even before Moscow. The effect of this move on French policy was predictable. As Premier Georges Bidault told Trygve Lie later, "France was ready to recognize the new regime, but when Mao and U.S.S.R. recognized Ho Chi-minh recognition on our part was rendered impossible."[151] Likewise, Foreign Minister Robert Schuman confided to Lie that "if it had not been for Peking's support of the Communists in Indochina, France would have voted long since to seat the Chinese Communists."[152]

The Soviet boycott created the gravest crisis confronted by the United Nations up to that time. Secretary-General Lie feared that the Soviet action might be a first step toward the establishment of a rival organization composed of members of the Soviet bloc. He also felt that the Nationalist government, which had already been ousted from the mainland, could no longer represent China in the United Nations.[153] Thus, he took steps to break the deadlock. In a conversation with Secretary of State Acheson on January 21, Lie asked Acheson whether American recognition of Com-

[148] It was thought in the United States that, if the Soviet delegate had not raised the issue prematurely, a proposal to unseat the Nationalist delegate "would certainly be accepted within a few weeks" (*New York Times*, January 11, 1950, p. 1, under the by-line of Thomas Hamilton).

[149] *Ibid.*, January 10, 1950, p. 1. According to Trygve Lie, Secretary-General of the United Nations, Sir Alexander Cadogan, British representative on the Security Council, suspected that "the Soviet attitude was based on a calculated policy of discouraging rather than encouraging recognition of the new Chinese government by either the United States or France. China could thereby be kept more effectively in isolation from the West and under Soviet domination." Sir Alexander expressed these views to Mr. Lie when the latter discussed with him the problem of Chinese representation in the United Nations (Trygve Lie, *In the Cause of Peace* [New York: Macmillan Co., 1954], p. 258).

[150] *New York Times*, January 20, 1950, p. 4.

[151] Lie, *op. cit.*, p. 266.

[152] *Ibid.*

[153] *Ibid.*, pp. 253–54.

munist China would be considered in the foreseeable future. Acheson's answer indicated a hardening of American attitude toward Communist China. He said that the Peking regime scarcely knew what it was doing or what international repercussions its acts had. Recalling the recent seizure of American properties, Acheson declared firmly that the United States would certainly not recognize Peking in such circumstances and was opposed to seating the Communist regime in the United Nations.

After this consultation with Acheson, Lie decided to seek a solution of the issue within the Security Council by trying to persuade two additional members of the council to vote to seat Peking and thus obtain the required majority of seven. But Lie's plan ran into another obstacle. After Malik's walkout on January 13, Peking's seizure of American, French, and Dutch properties on January 14, and Mao's recognition of the Vietminh government on January 19, there was a sudden halt to the rush toward recognition of the Chinese Communist regime which had been gaining momentum since the end of the year when Burma and India had granted diplomatic recognition to Peking. For one reason or another, France, Egypt, Australia, Canada, New Zealand, South Africa, and Mexico – all of whom had been expected to accord recognition soon, withheld their actions. Between January 17, when Switzerland extended recognition, and the outbreak of the Korean War, the Netherlands and Indonesia were the only two nations which recognized Peking. This sudden interruption of the trend toward recognition meant that Peking would not soon be admitted to the United Nations and that the Soviet boycott would not be terminated unless there was a change in the various governments' policies of conditioning a vote in favor of Peking on a prior action of recognition. Thus, the deadlock in the United Nations could be broken only by dissolving the linkage between recognition by the individual governments and representation in the United Nations.

At Secretary-General Lie's request, the Legal Department of the Secretariat prepared in early February a memorandum on the legal aspects of the problem of representation in the United Nations. On the basis of the facts, judicial precedents, and practice, both in the United Nations and in the League of Nations, the memorandum concluded:

> Since recognition of either State or government is an individual act, and either admission to membership or acceptance of representation in the Organization [*i.e.*, the United Nations] are collective acts, it would appear to be legally inadmissible to condition the latter acts by a requirement that they be preceded by individual recognition.[154]

[154] United Nations Security Council, *Official Records, 1950*, Supplement for January 1 through May 31, 1950, Document S/1466, p. 20.

It asserted that the members had made clear by unbroken practice that "a Member could properly vote to accept a representative of a government which it did not recognize, or with which it had no diplomatic relations" and that "such a vote did not imply recognition or a readiness to assume diplomatic relations."[155] As Secretary-General Lie made clear in his memoirs, he hoped that on the basis of this reasoning, France, Egypt, Ecuador, and Cuba — members of the Security Council who did not recognize the Chinese Communist regime — might vote for representation of the Peking government in the council while still withholding recognition.[156] Again, Lie's plan was confounded by another development. On February 14, the conclusion of a Sino-Soviet Treaty of Alliance was announced. The State Department now brought pressure to bear on one of the Latin American countries which, in the light of Lie's memorandum, had planned to support the seating of the Chinese Communists in the Security Council. Neither France nor Egypt gave any sign of preparing to modify their stand.[157]

After the press had learned of Lie's confidential memorandum, Lie made it public on March 8.[158] After its release Mr. Ernest Gross announced that the American government continued to adhere to its earlier position that it would oppose the seating of Peking but would accept a majority decision.[159] In contrast to the situation in January, the State Department now fully realized and had indeed taken steps to make certain that there could not be for the time being a majority in favor of the admission of Peking. Surprisingly enough, the most dispassionate views held by a public figure in the United States were those of John Foster Dulles who subsequently adopted an uncompromising policy toward Communist China when serving as secretary of state in the Eisenhower administration. In a book published on April 18, Dulles wrote that "if the Communist government of China in fact proves its ability to govern China without serious domestic resistance, then it, too, should be admitted to the United Nations."[160] He indorsed the principle of universality and proposed a package deal which would give membership to five nations vetoed by the Soviet Union and three satellite nations opposed by the Western powers.[161] He wrote: "We ought to be willing that all nations should be members without attempting to appraise closely those which are 'good' and those which are

---

[155] *Ibid.*, p. 22.
[156] Lie, *op. cit.*, pp. 257–58.
[157] *Ibid.*, p. 261.
[158] United Nations Security Council, *Official Records, 1950*, Supplement for January 1 through May 31, p. 18; *New York Times*, March 8, 1950, p. 1.
[159] *Ibid.*, March 9, 1950, p. 16.
[160] John Foster Dulles, *War or Peace* (New York: Macmillan Co., 1950), p. 190; *New York Times*, April 18, 1950, p. 1.
[161] Dulles, *op. cit.*, pp. 189–90.

'bad.' "[162] This was substantially the same position as that taken by Trygve Lie.

Lie's memorandum and the State Department's public position greatly disturbed the congressional supporters of Chiang. Failing to appreciate the subtlety of the State Department's action, Senator Knowland warned the department in a speech on the Senate floor on March 10 that the senators were deeply interested in the question of admitting Peking to the United Nations and demanded that the United States repudiate the actions of Trygve Lie.[163] On May 2, a group of thirty-five senators sent a letter to President Truman, urging him to make clear that the United States had no present intention of recognizing the Communist regime and would actively oppose the Soviet move to unseat the Nationalist representatives and to extend membership to Communist Chinese representatives in the United Nations.[164] To this request, President Truman returned a friendly but noncommittal reply.[165] The American position remained unchanged, as Secretary Acheson told an informal session of Congress meeting on May 31 to hear his report on his trip to Europe.[166]

K. The Question of Formosa

Insofar as America's policy toward China is concerned, the decisive question in this period was whether to defend Formosa by military means. If Formosa should fall, the issue of recognizing the Communist regime and granting it membership in the United Nations would automatically lose its political significance. On the other hand, if the United States should commit herself to the defense of this last Nationalist stronghold by her own armed forces or by military assistance, she could not recognize Peking or allow it to be admitted to the United Nations without opposition, unless there was to be an over-all political settlement with the Chinese Communists in the Far East. As noted in the last chapter, the State Department had in October, 1948, ruled out the use of American armed forces to defend Formosa. On August 4, 1949, Secretary Acheson sent a memorandum to the executive secretary of the National Security Council, stating that the fall of Formosa appeared probable and could not be prevented by political and economic measures alone. On August 16, the Joint Chiefs reaffirmed their previous views that "overt" American military action to deny Formosa to the Communists would not be justified. In a memorandum dated August 26, General Wedemeyer, deputy chief of staff for plans and operations,

[162] *Ibid.*, p. 190.
[163] *Congressional Record*, XCVI, 81st Cong., 2d sess. (1950), 3182–84.
[164] *Ibid.*, p. 6492. This request was subsequently indorsed by Herbert Hoover and Senator H. Alexander Smith (*ibid.*, p. 6595).
[165] *Ibid.*, p. 6864.
[166] *New York Times*, June 1, 1950, pp. 1, 5.

suggested to George V. Allen, assistant secretary of state for public affairs, that the latter might consider "information measures" to minimize the "ill effects" of the fall of Formosa on the governments and peoples of western-oriented nations, particularly in the Far East.[167] In September, the Joint Chiefs of Staff advised Secretary of Defense Louis A. Johnson that in their opinion the United States should not even send a military mission to Formosa for the purpose of ascertaining the facts.[168] According to Johnson's retrospective account, he felt that the Joint Chiefs' recommendation was made under political pressure and was influenced by political considerations.[169]

But Republican demands for strong measures to defend Formosa were soon forthcoming. Toward the end of October, Senator H. Alexander Smith of New Jersey returned from the Far East. On November 4, he sent a letter to Secretary Acheson, pleading that the United States should, "under no condition," allow Formosa to fall into the hands of the Chinese Communists. To achieve this purpose, Smith made the following suggestion: if the United States could take the position that Formosa was still technically a part of Japan, the United States, as the occupation power of Japan, could occupy Formosa, with notice to the United Nations that it might be made a trusteeship area. "If this were done," the Republican senator asserted, "the Chinese Communists would be faced with the responsibility of attacking the United States if they attacked Formosa under these conditions."[170] Smith stated these views more positively in his report dated November 29 to the Foreign Relations Committee.[171] He made public his conclusions in a new conference on December 1, implying that General MacArthur supported his position.[172]

On December 8, the Nationalist government moved its capital to Formosa. On the same day, the National Security Council discussed the Formosa situation. The press reported that the American government ruled out any change in its policy not to use American armed forces to defend Formosa.[173] However, Secretary of Defense Johnson asked the Joint Chiefs to make a recommendation from a purely military standpoint without regard to political considerations. The Joint Chiefs reversed their earlier position on the advisability of sending a fact-finding mission to Formosa and suggested that this be done. They also proposed that some military

---

[167] Wedemeyer's memorandum, "Current Position of the United States with respect to Formosa," *Military Situation in the Far East*, p. 2371.

[168] Johnson's testimony, *ibid.*, p. 2577.

[169] *Ibid.*, pp. 2664–65.

[170] Smith's letter to Acheson, *Congressional Record*, XCVI, 81st Cong., 2d sess. (1950), 150.

[171] *Ibid.*, pp. 156–60. See also *Nomination of Jessup*, pp. 875–85.

[172] *New York Times*, December 2, 1949, p. 15.

[173] *Washington Post*, December 9, 1949, p. 1.

assistance in addition to the $125 million appropriated in 1948 should be given to the Nationalists.[174] On December 15, Johnson sent President Truman a memorandum embodying this recommendation.[175] But the State Department adhered to its original stand, arguing that nothing short of the interposition of American armed forces could save the island and that the dispatch of a fact-finding mission would merely court further damage to American prestige and to the American position in the Far East.[176] On December 27, Johnson learned in a conversation with President Truman that, to use Johnson's words, "I had lost my fight on Formosa. . . . I was told . . . that he wasn't going to argue with me about the military considerations but that on political grounds he would decide with the State Department."[177] On December 23, the State Department, acting on General Wedemeyer's suggestion of August 26, sent out a "policy information paper" on Formosa to its missions abroad and to the Voice of America and other agencies. It advised that the loss of Formosa was widely anticipated and that steps be taken to minimize the importance of Formosa and thus the damage to American prestige.[178] On December 29, the National Security Council formally indorsed the view of the State Department.

While the recommendation of the State Department was accepted by the administration, rising demands for a positive policy came from Republican circles. On December 27, Senator Smith again wrote Acheson, urging the administration to begin conversations immediately with Mr. K. C. Wu, the new governor of Formosa, for the purpose of arranging for the occupation of the island by the United States.[179] On December 30, Senator Knowland, who, like Senator Smith, had also returned from the Far East recently, called for the dispatch of a military mission to Formosa.[180] On

[174] *Military Situation in the Far East*, p. 1674.

[175] Johnson's testimony, *ibid.*, p. 2577.

[176] Acheson's testimony, *ibid.*, pp. 1674–75. Writing on December 18, 1949, Hanson Baldwin stated that "to insure the security of Formosa against both possible external assault and internal subversion would probably take more than the ten divisions that the United States now maintains all over the world" (*New York Times*, December 8, 1949, p. 27). At this time, the Nationalists were reported to have on Formosa some 200,000 to 300,000 combat troops, 500 tanks and armed vehicles, 200 combat planes and a small navy of 150,000 tons. The Communists had approximately 100 combat planes which had passed into their hands through defection of the pilots. Foreign observers in Hong Kong thought that it would require about 500,000 to 750,000 troops to make a successful assault on Formosa. The Communists were busily repairing the cruiser "Chungking" which had defected to the Communists and had been severely damaged by the Nationalist air force. This cruiser had heavier guns than any of the vessels in the Nationalist navy. (*Ibid.*, December 21, 1949, p. 9; December 30, 1949, p. 6).

[177] Johnson's testimony, *Military Situation in the Far East*, p. 2578.

[178] The text was declassified by the combined committees conducting the MacArthur hearings (*ibid.*, pp. 1667–69).

[179] *Congressional Record*, XCVI, 81st Cong., 2d sess. (1950), 154.

[180] *New York Times*, December 31, 1949, p. 1.

the same day, Senator Taft suggested in an interview with a newspaper correspondent that Formosa should be kept out of the hands of the Chinese Communists even if it were necessary to send the United States Navy there.[181] On January 2, Senator Knowland released a letter which former president Herbert Hoover wrote him on December 31 in response to his request for an expression of views on the Chinese situation. Hoover suggested that the United States should, if necessary, give the Nationalist government naval protection for its possessions of Formosa and the Pescadores and possibly Hainan Island.[182] Taft immediately indorsed Hoover's recommendation by reiterating at a news conference his demand for the use of the American navy to prevent the Communists from capturing Formosa.[183]

But the Republicans were by no means united on the advisability of taking such a drastic step. Senator Vandenberg declined to comment on the Hoover-Taft proposal. Senator Henry Cabot Lodge, Jr. expressed grave doubts on the wisdom of drawing the line against Communist expansion along the Formosa Strait. Even Judd was not willing to go so far: he wanted only an American military advisory mission for Formosa.[184] However, Senator Knowland's hand was strengthened by a strange coincidence. The day after the release of Hoover's letter, the State Department information guidance paper on Formosa leaked to the press through General MacArthur's command in Tokyo.[185] Knowland promptly seized this opportunity to denounce the State Department for minimizing the strategic importance of Formosa. Senator H. Alexander Smith immediately supported Knowland's demand for the release of the secret document.[186] To the surprise of many, Representative Charles Eaton, the ranking minority member of the Foreign Affairs Committee, came out in support of United States military action to hold Formosa.[187]

On January 4, Acheson took the initiative to seek a conference with the Senate Foreign Relations Committee on January 10 to explain the Chinese situation and the administration's policy.[188] But the Hoover-Taft proposal had stirred up much speculation. The Chinese Communists charged that the United States had arrived at a secret understanding with the Nation-

[181] Ibid.
[182] Ibid., January 3, 1950, p. 1. For the text of the letter, see Congressional Record, XCVI, 81st Cong., 2d sess. (1950), 83.
[183] New York Times, December 31, 1949, p. 1.
[184] Ibid., January 4, 1950, p. 1.
[185] Ibid., p. 14. For the responsibility for the leak, see Acheson's statement, Military Situation in the Far East, p. 1697.
[186] New York Times, January 5, 1950, p. 1. Senator Knowland repeated his demands on the Senate floor on the following day (Congressional Record, XCVI, 81st Cong., 2d sess. [1950], 82, 86–87).
[187] New York Times, January 5, 1950, p. 1.
[188] Ibid.

alists for the occupation of Formosa.[189] Against the background of the profound American aversion to war, Taft's and Hoover's proposals for military action to defend Formosa and Knowland's part in arranging for Hoover's letter rendered the position of the China bloc politically vulnerable. The administration decided to clarify its policy prior to consultation with Congress.[190] Without waiting for Acheson's scheduled meeting with the Foreign Relations Committee, President Truman announced in a statement released by the White House on January 5:

> The United States has no desire to obtain special rights or privileges or to establish military bases on Formosa at this time. Nor does it have any intention of utilizing its armed forces to interfere in the present situation. The United States will not pursue a course which will lead to involvement in the civil conflict in China. Similarly, the United States Government will not provide military aid or advice to Chinese forces on Formosa.[191]

Truman's statement stressed the fact that the Cairo Declaration of December 1, 1943, provided for the restoration of Formosa to China and that the United States and the other Allied powers had accepted since V-J Day the exercise of Chinese authority over the island. The administration thus rejected in categorical terms not only the Hoover-Taft proposal and Senator Smith's suggestion; it also made clear that it had no intention of supplying arms to Formosa by spending the $75 million which Congress had, under a compromise worked out by Senator Vandenberg, authorized in September of 1949 for military assistance for the "general area of China." However, the $9 million unexpended balance of the $125 million special fund was still available to the Nationalists for the purchase of military supplies. This was not cut off. The President's statement meant that no further military aid outside of the $125 million would be given.[192] The words "at this time" in the President's statement did leave a loophole for a change in policy toward Formosa. In his press conference on January 5, Acheson explained that "in the unlikely and unhappy event that our forces might be attacked in the Far East, the United States must be completely free to take whatever action in whatever area is necessary for its own security."[193]

[189] *Ibid.*, p. 18.
[190] Secretary Acheson explained in a press conference on January 5 that "it was the *President's desire* to clarify the situation. . . . It was more important to clarify thinking than it was to go on and have the most desirable of all possible things which is consultation [with members of both parties in Congress]" (extemporaneous remarks by Secretary Acheson at his press conference on January 5, 1950, *Department of State Bulletin*, January 16, 1950, p. 80. Emphasis added).
[191] *Ibid.*, p. 79.
[192] *Military Situation in the Far East*, pp. 1808, 1813, 1820, 1829, 1929–30.
[193] *Department of State Bulletin*, January 16, 1950, p. 87.

Truman's statement immediately became the target of united Republican attack on various grounds. On the Senate floor on January 5, Knowland opened the assault by focusing his criticism on the policy of providing no further military aid to Formosa. He called for a major shake-up in the Far Eastern Division in the State Department, the appointment of General MacArthur as the "co-ordinator" of American policy in the Far East, and the dispatch of a military mission under General Wedemeyer to supervise aid to Formosa. He also called for the utilization of the $75 million appropriated by Congress for shipment of arms to Formosa and the $106 million unexpended funds under the China Aid Act for economic assistance.[194] Taft asserted that "the rejection of any idea of using our armed forces to stop the advance of Communism in the area in question [i.e., Formosa] is wholly inconsistent with what we have agreed to do in stopping Communism in Europe." [195] Senator McCarthy entered the China policy debate by characterizing John S. Service as man "who as a representative of the State Department said that the only hope in Asia was Communism."[196] Senator Vandenberg issued a statement to the press expressing regret that the administration had announced its "conclusions regarding Formosa ahead of a realistic consultation on the subject with the appropriate committees of Congress."[197] Senator H. Alexander Smith charged the administration with bad faith for violating an alleged understanding that no action would be taken on the problem of Formosa without consultation with the Foreign Relations Committee.[198]

But the vehement denunciations by the Republican senators of the President's statement could not cover up the very real possibility that any endeavor to deny Formosa to the Chinese Communists would entail a serious risk of war. The alternatives proposed by Hoover, Taft, and Smith, found little support from the public. Thus, in the Senate debate four days later on January 9, the Republican senators were forced to take a defensive position while the spokesmen for the administration launched their counterattack. In a lengthy speech, Senator Smith stressed the "predominantly

[194] Congressional Record, XCVI, 81st Cong., 2d sess. (1950), 82. The swift advance of the Chinese Communist forces and the rapid contraction of territory under Nationalist control made it impossible to spend the money appropriated under the China Aid Act of 1948 according to plans worked out by the ECA administrators. In the spring of 1949, it was thought $54 million would remain unexpended. In the fall of 1949, the residual funds increased to $94 million. In January, 1950, this figure was $106 million. At this time, the Nationalist government expressed confidence that they could hold Formosa provided they were provided with American economic aid and military supplies (New York Times, January 3, 1950, p. 10).

[195] Congressional Record, XCVI, 81st Cong., 2d sess. (1950), 89.
[196] Ibid., p. 86.
[197] Ibid., p. 103.
[198] Ibid., p. 102.

peaceful and constructive" character of his proposal. He drew a distinction between his suggestion to occupy Formosa and a policy of committing the United States "in an unlimited military way to the Nationalist cause." He explained that by the word "occupation" he did not mean "to imply the sending of American troops to Formosa, but simply the establishment of a joint political authority and responsibility there between ourselves, the Nationalists, and the Formosan people." He asserted flatly that "I do not think it is necessary to send one soldier there." [199]

This last remark was the object of Senator Connally's ridicule in his rebuttal. Connally asked:

> How are we going to occupy it [Formosa] if we do not send an army there? . . . We cannot occupy it with two or three Senators who went there, who, at the firing of the first gun, would go into a hole somewhere (laughter).[200]

Connally confronted the Republican senators with a clear choice between accepting the administration's hands-off policy and risking a war. He demanded:

> Is there any member of the Senate who wishes to send an army to Formosa? Mr. Hoover wants to send the Navy there. The Senaator from Ohio [Mr. Taft] . . . wants to send the Navy there, but they do not have a single spokesman on the floor of this body who will rise and tell the Senate and the country that "I favor sending an army to Formosa."
>
> What do they want to send an army there for? They want to occupy it; they want to take over Formosa. They would say, "According to my formula, in the final analysis we want to intervene in the civil war; we want to run the chance of a war; we want to run the risk of a third world war, on account of Formosa." [201]

As to the idea of "joint occupation," Connally commented: "We would not get very far with joint occupation with Chiang Kai-shek. He would either run the outfit or he would not play, that is all."[202] Furthermore, Connally was now able to link the Republican criticism of the administration's record in China with the Republican proposals for extreme measures. He declared:

> I want to know who the Senators are, and I shall revive the question from time to time, who want to plunge this country, not directly, but possibly, into World War III, in the name of For-

[199] *Ibid.*, pp. 154–55.
[200] *Ibid.*, p. 170.
[201] *Ibid.*
[202] *Ibid.*, p. 172.

mosa, but principally in the name of a bitter attack upon the President of the United States and upon the Department of State.[203]

Connally's attack was so effective that Knowland found it necessary to dissociate himself explicitly from Smith's proposal to occupy Formosa and implicitly from Hoover's suggestion.[204] But Senator Taft held fast to his position. In a Senate speech on January 11, Taft pointed out that the American navy was already deployed in the Formosa Strait and that if the American government should make clear its intention not to permit Communist occupation of Formosa, there would be no Communist attempts at an invasion. Taft explained that such a course of action need not commit the United States to backing the Nationalist government in any prolonged war against the Chinese Communists. He envisaged the possibility of establishing an independent republic of Formosa and was confident of American ability to force the Nationalists to accept such a solution.[205]

While the debate on Formosa was gaining momentum in the United States, Mao Tse-tung arrived in Moscow on December 16 and soon afterward entered into secret negotiations with Stalin himself.[206] These two developments furnished the background for one of the most brilliant as well as the most controversial speeches ever made by Secretary Acheson: his address before the National Press Club on January 12, 1950, entitled "Crisis in Asia — An Examination of United States Policy." Among other things, Acheson defined America's short-term and long-term policy toward China within the general framework of America's basic approach toward Asia. Pointing out that nationalism as the symbol of both freedom from foreign domination and freedom from poverty was the most powerful force in Asia, Acheson asserted that the interests of the United States had been parallel to the interests of the people of Asia. Historically, the United States had always been opposed to the control of China by a foreign power and in favor of the independence of all Asiatic countries. On the other hand, there was a basic conflict between Asiatic nationalism and communism. For "Communism is the most subtle instrument of Soviet foreign policy that has ever been devised and it is really the spearhead of Russian imperialism. . . ."[207] Obviously with an eye on the negotiations in Moscow, Acheson charged:

[203] Ibid.
[204] Knowland protested: "The junior Senator from California has not advocated sending American troops to occupy Formosa. In that respect, I disagree with other points of view." He continued to say that he advocated giving the Nationalist government the same kind of assistance which the United States was rendering Greece (ibid., p. 170).
[205] Ibid., pp. 298–99.
[206] Beloff, op. cit., p. 70; Wei, op. cit., p. 266.
[207] Department of State Bulletin, January 23, 1950, p. 114.

The Soviet Union is detaching the northern provinces of China from China and is attaching them to the Soviet Union. This process is complete in outer Mongolia. It is nearly complete in Manchuria and I am sure that in inner Mongolia and in Sinkiang there are very happy reports coming from Soviet agents.[208]

This contrast between Russian imperialism and America's traditional friendship for China apparently furnished for Acheson the basic justification of the administration's decision not to intervene in the Chinese civil war and not to defend Formosa. It also led him to base America's long-term policy on the possibility of playing Chinese nationalism against the Soviet Union and the Chinese Communists.

Acheson wrote:

We must not undertake to deflect from the Russians to ourselves the righteous anger, and the wrath, and the hatred of the Chinese people which must develop. It would be folly to deflect it to ourselves. We must take the position we have always taken – that anyone who violates the integrity of China is the enemy of China and is acting contrary to our interests.[209]

He asserted that the consequences of Soviet imperialism in China were saddling the Chinese Communists with the most awful responsibility.[210] Recent events have borne out the prophecy of serious conflict between Communist China and the Soviet Union. But it has taken a form quite different from that envisaged by Acheson. Its primary source is a basic disagreement over revolutionary strategy and tactics against the West, with the Chinese Communists advocating a more militant program, placing a heavier reliance on the use of force, and exhibiting a greater willingness to take militant action than the Soviet Union. The dispute has been conducted in terms of ideology rather than national interest. The border regions have not become a significant issue. Chinese nationalism has turned primarily against the United States instead of the Soviet Union.

To deal with the military threat posed by the Communist bloc, which in his opinion was "not the most immediate" menace, Acheson drew a defensive perimeter in the western Pacific which must and would be held by the United States. This defensive perimeter ran along the Aleutians through Japan and the Ryukyus to the Philippine Islands.[211] Formosa was left out-

[208] *Ibid.*, p. 115.
[209] *Ibid.*
[210] *Ibid.*

[211] In his conference with the Senate Foreign Relations Committee on January 10, Acheson had informed the senators of this defense perimeter, and Chairman Connally had told the press about it (*Washington Post*, January 11, 1950, p. 1, under the by-line of Ferdinand Kuhn).

side of this line. The omission of South Korea, which was subsequently thought to have encouraged the North Koreans to launch their attack on June 25, was based on the military assumption that in an all-out war it would be a strategic liability rather than an asset. Apparently, little thought was given to the possibility of local aggression and limited war in that area. The failure to include Southeast Asia indicated that the United States had as yet no firm policy toward its defense. At this time, Ambassador Jessup was on his mission to the Far East and Southeast Asia, searching for a concrete program to contain communism in Asia. He had arrived in Tokyo on January 5 to confer with General MacArthur. He was to meet Generalissimo Chiang on Formosa in the middle of the month and in February to attend a conference at Bangkok, Thailand, of American diplomats stationed in those areas. As to the military security of these areas, Acheson had this to say:

> It must be clear that no person can guarantee these areas against military attack. But it must be clear that such a guarantee is hardly suitable or necessary within the realm of practical relationship. Should such an attack occur — one hesitates to say where such an armed attack could come from — the initial reliance must be on people attacked to resist it and then upon the commitments of the entire civilized world under the Charter of the United Nations which so far has not proved a weak reed to lean on by any people who are determined to protect their independence against outside aggression.[212]

Coming on the heels of Connally's stress of the risk of war in his attack on the proposals of Hoover, Taft, and Smith, Acheson's impressive presentation of the positive aspects of America's Asiatic policy gave the administration considerable advantage. For that policy seemed to avoid any immediate risk of war, drew an easily defensible line to protect America's vital interests, and contained a long-term program for Asia which could be implemented by peaceful means. The Republican critics of the administration had obviously overplayed their hands. As Arthur Krock observed, "Taft, Hoover, Smith and Knowland imperiled their party's campaign against the administration's China policy record by their proposal on Formosa." Moreover, "because of the Republican windfall as to Formosa, Acheson is martially and jubilantly resting a powerful case on administration's policy there."[213] But Acheson's foes quickly found fresh ammunition in a new development. When it was disclosed that the Communists had seized American consular properties in Peking, Knowland and Bridges

[212] *Department of State Bulletin*, January 23, 1950, p. 115.
[213] *New York Times*, January 15, 1950, Sec. 4, p. 3.

demanded indirectly the resignation of Acheson.[214] Again the background of a growing public aversion to adventures in China, the new Republican demands for Acheson's resignation solidified the Democratic ranks. On January 17, the Democratic senators met in a party conference. They were reported to be "practically unanimous in voicing their support for President Truman's hands-off-Formosa policy."[215] The press interpreted the conference to mean "concentrated majority party counterfire to GOP charges of bankruptcy in China policy and Republican demands for Acheson's ouster."[216]

At this point, a group of Republicans in the House under the leadership of Representative Vorys took matters into their own hands. To express their dissatisfaction over the administration's policy in general and its decision on Formosa in particular, they rigorously opposed a bill sponsored by the administration to grant $60 million for economic aid to South Korea for the remaining months of fiscal year 1950. In a debate on the floor, Vorys took the position that in the absence of a comprehensive and sound program for the Far East, economic aid to Korea was money down the "rat hole."[217] Robert Chipperfield, Republican of Illinois, argued that the loss of China rendered South Korea indefensible.[218] Representative Donald L. Jackson, Republican of California, asked: "What kind of policy for the Far East would put économic aid into Korea, which bears no relationship to our national defense, and at the same time refuse a request to put aid into Formosa?"[219] The attack on the aid to Korea bill was so intense that Representative Judd, one of the more responsible and level-headed members of the China bloc, found it necessary to plead with his fellow congressmen that the "mistaken" policies of the administration toward China and Formosa did not justify opposition to aid to Korea even if Formosa was "vital" to the United States and South Korea was not.[220] Joined by economy-minded and non-interventionist Republicans and Southern Democrats, Vorys and his supporters defeated the bill by a margin of one vote. The Republicans opposed it six to one while only three out of four Democrats

---

[214] *Ibid.*, Sec. 1, p. 1. See this chapter, p. 518, above.
[215] Press release, reproduced in *Congressional Record*, XCVI, 81st Cong., 2d sess. (1950), 474.
[216] *Ibid.*, p. 479.
[217] *Ibid.*, p. 636.
[218] *Ibid.*, pp. 639–40.
[219] *Ibid.*, p. 649. Jackson also observed that "South Korea is a Bataan without a Corregidor, a Dunkerque without a flotilla, a dead-end street without an escape" (*ibid.*, p. 644). In contrast, "Formosa is essentially a point in the line of defenses which include Japan, the Philippines, and Okinawa, all essential and vital to the national defense of the United States. Formosa is a tenable position; it is a position which might well be held, it is a position certainly, which should be strengthened if we are going to have any kind of policy at any time in the Pacific area" (*ibid.*, p. 649).
[220] *Ibid.*, p. 651.

supported it.[221] This was the first major setback in Congress for the administration in the field of foreign policy since the end of the war. Once again some members of the China bloc showed their ability to disrupt the administration's program in other areas. Worst of all, the debate publicized the American position that South Korea was indefensible and strategically valueless to the United States. Writing in 1957, Acheson expressed the belief that this action of the House contributed to Soviet miscalculation of the possible American reaction to attack by North Korea.[222] Again, a compromise was worked out. The final bill enacted by Congress combined the Korean aid bill with a provision extending the deadline for the expenditure of the $104 million residual funds under the China Aid Act from February 15 to June 30, 1950.[223] But it was expected that actually only less than $10 million would be spent in Formosa in the extended period and solely for the purpose of continuing the work of the Joint Commission on Rural Reconstruction.[224]

The initial defeat of the Korean aid bill in the House made it clear to the administration that it could do no less than continue economic aid to Formosa in order to insure smooth sailing for its other foreign policy programs. Thus, in the bills passed by both the House and the Senate for general foreign economic assistance for the fiscal year 1951, there was a provision further extending the time limit for the expenditure of the residual funds under the China Aid Act (estimated at $94 million as of June, 1950) from June 30, 1950, to June 30, 1951. The final bill, passed by Congress in May, allocated the residual funds for use "in any place in China and in the general area of China which the President deems to be not under Communist control."[225] It stipulated that "so long as the President deems it practicable, not less than $40,000,000 of such funds shall be available only for such assistance in areas in China (including Formosa)."[226] The ability of the China bloc to influence the administration's policy was weakening. But it was still strong enough to prevent a prompt and complete withdrawal.

L. The Rise of McCarthyism and China Policy

The year which found American policy frozen over the issue of Formosa witnessed the rise of McCarthyism. McCarthyism was fundamentally an underhanded assault on the liberal tradition of America. Given the

---

[221] Westerfield, op. cit., pp. 353–54, 366–67.

[222] Dean Acheson, A Citizen Looks at Congress (New York: Harper & Bros., 1957), pp. 83–84.

[223] Congressional Record, XCVI, 81st Cong., 2d sess. (1950), 1596.

[224] Ibid., pp. 1596, 1600.

[225] Ibid., Part 6, p. 7520.

[226] Ibid. In April, Hainan was lost to the Communists. Therefore in the final bill, Hainan was not mentioned. See also ibid., p. 7526.

moral unity of the American society, it was natural that a fanatical revolt against the prevailing ethos should take a nihilistic character, attacking the established values, institutions, and policies without presenting affirmative answers to the day's pressing problems. Since many of the traditional liberal perspectives found their fullest expression in America's China policy, it was inevitable that this policy should become a major target of McCarthy's onslaught. Since the misjudgment of the nature of Chinese communism, the minimization of the role of ideology in human affairs and thus of the influence of communism as a vital force, the inability to perceive the existence of irreconcilable conflicts in a society, the overreliance on the efficacy of compromise, the corresponding failure to see the need for the use of force, the elevation of non-intervention as a self-sufficient principle, and the tendency to understand alien things in American terms — all exercised perceptible influence on America's China policy,[227] it is not difficult to see that this policy was highly vulnerable to McCarthy's demagoguery. Nor is it surprising that McCarthy's attack on China policy gained him the support for the first time of powerful and respectable Republican leaders. For Hurley in 1945 and Judd in 1947 had already advanced the theory of conspiracy as an explanation of America's failure in China. Frustrated in their efforts to obtain a program of large-scale aid to China, many Republican leaders had, since 1949, intensified their attack on the State Department, demanded an investigation, and asked for a change in personnel. Failing to realize that the defeat of American policy had its roots in assumptions and attitudes which they themselves shared, many Americans expressed their anxieties over Far Eastern affairs by accepting McCarthy's theory of conspiracy as a salve to their wounded pride and by acclaiming or acquiescing in his hunt for non-existent Communists in the State Department as a substitute for a search for a workable policy.[228]

[227] See chaps. vi and ix, above.

[228] Among the eighty-one cases presented by McCarthy to the Senate as bad security risks or worse, only one employee of the State Department, Mr. Val Lorwin, was ever indicted for perjuring himself in denying past membership in the Communist party. In May, 1954, the Justice Department dropped the charge for lack of evidence (James Rorty and Moshe Decter, *McCarthy and the Communists* [Boston: Beacon Press, 1954], p. 14). Richard H. Rovere reported that at one time McCarthy named an ex-Communist in a government agency, who had concealed his past membership. But McCarthy soon dropped the case. According to Rovere, this was about "the closest" McCarthy ever came to turning up a real Communist in the government. This government employee resigned from the government after Rovere brought the case to the attention of an official of that Government agency (Richard H. Rovere, *Senator Joe McCarthy* [New York: Harcourt, Brace & Co., 1959], p. 159).

According to Rorty and Decter, there had been, besides the much mooted case of Alger Hiss, three Communists in the State Department before McCarthy raised the issue of Communist infiltration of the State Department. But they had either been fired or had left the Department: Carl Aldo Marzani in 1946, Julian Wadleigh in 1946, and George Shaw Wheeler in 1947 (Rorty and Decter, *op. cit.*, p. 56). See also Eric Goldman, *The Crucial Decade* (New York: Alfred A. Knopf, Inc., 1956), pp. 133–37; Jack Anderson

Senator McCarthy discovered the issue of Communist infiltration of the State Department quite accidentally in his search for an issue for his re-election campaign in 1952.[229] In his speech made on February 9 at Wheeling, West Virginia, he did not at once focus his attack on officials and experts concerned with China policy, although he did charge John S. Service by name as a man "who had previously urged that Communism was the best hope of China."[230] On February 20, McCarthy delivered a lengthy speech on the Senate floor in response to demands for an explanation of his charges. In this speech, he presented to the Senate his information regarding the Communist leanings of eight-one State Department employees, past and present, whom he identified by numerals.[231] No. 2 of his eighty-one cases turned out to be John Carter Vincent.[232] He was condemned by McCarthy as one of "the Big Three" of the espionage ring in the State Department.[233] He should, McCarthy urged, "not only be discharged but should be immediately prosecuted."[234] The charges leveled against Vincent were concerned with espionage activities rather than Far Eastern policy.[235] According to Rovere, John S. Service was also one of the numbered cases.[236] But McCarthy did move a step closer to the issue of China policy when he asserted that "Research and Intelligence, the Voice of America, and Far Eastern Affairs seem to be the three prime targets [of Communist infiltration]."[237]

It was inevitable that McCarthy's charge of Communist infiltration would soon be linked with the post-mortem over China policy. In the hearings conducted by a Senate Foreign Relations subcommittee under the chairmanship of Millard E. Tydings, McCarthy accused nine persons by name of Communist leanings. Among them four had been connected by by him with America's China policy in one way or another. Almost casually

and Ronald W. May, McCarthy: The Man, the Senator, and the Ism (Boston: Beacon Press, 1952); New York Times, January 26, 1950, p. 14; William F. Buckley, Jr., and L. Brent Bozell, McCarthy and His Enemies (Chicago: Henry Regnery Co., 1954).

[229] Rovere, op. cit., pp. 122–23.

[230] The complete text of McCarthy's speech at Wheeling was nowhere to be found. McCarthy had no copy of it (ibid., p. 127). Nonetheless, McCarthy read in the Senate on February 20 what purported to be his complete Wheeling speech (Congressional Record, XCVI, 81st Cong., 2d sess. [1950], 1954, 1956, 1957).

[231] Ibid., pp. 1954, 1981.

[232] Senate Committee on Foreign Relations, Report on State Department Employee Loyalty Investigation, Report No. 2108, 81st Cong., 2d sess. (1950), p. 95 (hereafter cited as Report on State Department).

[233] Congressional Record, XCVI, 81st Cong., 2d sess. (1950), 1961.

[234] Ibid.

[235] Ibid., pp. 1980–81.

[236] Rovere, op. cit., p. 152. Service seems to have been No. 46. The charges against him centered on the Amerasia case (Congressional Record, XCVI, 81st Cong., 1st sess. [1950], 1967).

[237] Ibid., p. 1960.

he accused Mr. Philip C. Jessup of having "unusual affinity for Communist causes."[238] He characterized Owen Lattimore, director of the Walter Hines Page School of International Relations, Johns Hopkins University, as "an extremely bad security risk" whose "wide knowledge of far eastern affairs and his affinity for the Soviet cause in that area might well have already done this nation incalculable and irreparable harm."[239] He alleged that Lattimore had been "one of the principal architects of our far eastern policy," and had held "numerous positions with the State Department."[240] He elevated John S. Service, then consul general at Calcutta, India, to the position of "one of the dozen top policy makers in the entire State Department on far eastern policy."[241] He declared that "the Communist affiliations of Service are well known."[242] He described Service as "a known associate and collaborator with Communists and pro-Communists . . . consorting with admitted espionage agents."[243] The principal basis of McCarthy's charge was the *Amerasia* case in which Service was arrested in June, 1945, on a complaint that he had transmitted classified material to Philip Jaffe, the editor of *Amerasia*, a periodical specializing in Far Eastern affairs. At that time, a grand jury returned a "no" bill in Service's case by unanimous vote. Up to the time of McCarthy's charge, Service had been cleared thrice by State Department officials looking into his loyalty file.[244]

[238] Senate Committee on Foreign Relations, *Hearings on State Department Employee Loyalty Investigation*, 81st Cong., 2d sess. (1950), p. 28 (hereafter cited as *State Department Employee Loyalty Investigation*).

[239] *Ibid.*, p. 104.

[240] *Ibid.*, p. 92.

[241] *Ibid.*, p. 131.

[242] *Ibid.*

[243] *Ibid.*, p. 140.

[244] It cannot be ascertained whether Jaffe was a Communist. After Service had turned over to Jaffe a number of the reports which he had sent from China to the State Department, he asked Lt. Andrew Roth who had introduced him to Jaffe whether Jaffe was a Communist. Roth answered that Jaffe was not a Communist but "a left-winger and very sympathetic." Harold Isaacs told Service that Jaffe was "bad business" or "bad medicine." The record makes it clear that, soon after Service had given his reports to Jaffe, he began to suspect Jaffe's political affiliation. Service was at least extremely indiscreet in handing over to Jaffe his reports and even more so in continuing his association with Jaffe after he had discovered Jaffe's pro-Communist sympathies. See "Opinion of the Loyalty Review Board in the Case of John Stewart Service," *Institute of Pacific Relations*, pp. 4847–48.

T. A. Bisson testified that Jaffe may have voluntarily and knowingly co-operated or collaborated with Communist party members in furtherance of Communist party objectives. Bisson stated that Jaffe was "connected or associated with Earl Browder" (*ibid.*, p. 4172). For a summary of the *Amerasia* case, see *Report on State Department*, pp. 96–114.

As to the sources of McCarthy's charge, Philip Horton made the following report: "In February, soon after McCarthy's first outburst, Mr. Kohlberg met the Senator for the first time. They needed each other. . . . Over dinner Mr. Kohlberg expounded his thesis that the Institute of Pacific Relations was the instrument of Communist infiltration into the State Department. The Senator was furnished a collection of Mr. Kohl-

Another man named was Haldore Hanson, the chief of the technical co-operation projects staff of the Point Four program. Hanson was charged by McCarthy with entertaining "pro-Communist proclivities" going back to 1938. He was described as "a man with a mission — a mission to com-munize the world. . . ."[245] The charge arose from the fact that in his capacity as a correspondent for the Associated Press, Hanson had spent four months in 1938 with the Chinese Communist armies and had written a book, which contained some praise for the Communists as well as the Nationalists.[246]

In the first four sessions, McCarthy made little headway in convincing the subcommittee or the public of the validity of his charges against the men named by him. Moreover, it developed that he had no new evidence whatsoever to support the accusations against the eighty-one individuals which he had made on February 20 in the Senate. In contrast, Ambassador Jessup, who had flown back from Pakistan to refute McCarthy's charges, won loud applause from the audience at the end of a lengthy statement before the Tydings subcommittee. Jessup stressed the adverse effects of McCarthy's irresponsible charges on the conduct of the nation's foreign policy. To extricate himself from a difficult position, McCarthy made a desperate move. He declared the next day before the subcommittee that he would stand or fall on the single case of Owen Lattimore.[247] Eight days previously, McCarthy had merely called Lattimore "an extremely bad security risk." Now, he characterized Lattimore as "the top espionage agent,"[248] "the top Russian spy,"[249] and "the top of the whole group of which Hiss was a part."[250] This charge shocked the nation and was re-ported on the front page of almost all important newspapers.[251]

Lattimore, however, was not and had never been an employee of the State Department in a strict sense, though in his capacities as editor of *Pacific Affairs*, a prolific writer, American adviser to Generalissimo Chiang, and deputy director of the Office of War Information in charge of Pacific operations, he had undoubtedly had some influence, to a degree difficult to define, on official policy. The charge that he was the top espionage agent was completely groundless. Freda Utley, the first person to expound fully in an official hearing the thesis that Lattimore followed the Communist party line in his writing, was forced to say:

berg's favorite articles and releases, including 'The State Department Espionage Case' by Emmanuel S. Larsen. . ." (Philip Horton, "The China Lobby," *Reporter*, April 29, 1952, p. 2).

[245] *State Department Employee Loyalty Investigation*, pp. 74, 82.
[246] *Report on State Department*, pp. 32–37.
[247] *State Department Employee Loyalty Investigation*, pp. 284–85.
[248] *Ibid.*, p. 285.
[249] *Ibid.*
[250] *Ibid.*, p. 281.
[251] Anderson and May, *op. cit.*, p. 213; Goldman, *op. cit.*, p. 143.

I think that Senator McCarthy was wrong in his original statement that Owen Lattimore is the Soviet Government's top espionage agent in America. I think the Senator underestimated Lattimore. Mr. Lattimore is such a renowned scholar, such an excellent writer, so adept at teaching the American people that they ought to stop opposing the great, good, and progressive Soviet Government, that it is impossible to believe that Moscow would regard him as expendable, as all spies are. To suggest that Mr. Lattimore's great talents have been utilized in espionage seems to me as absurd as to suggest that Mr. Gromyko or Mr. Molotov employ their leisure hours at Lake Success, or at international conferences, in snatching documents.[252]

Senator McCarthy himself was to admit on March 30: "I fear in the case of Lattimore, I may have perhaps placed too much stress on the question of whether or not he has been an espionage agent."[253]

But regardless of the question of its validity, McCarthy's characterization of Lattimore as the top espionage agent raised all the issues of America's China policy. McCarthy now allied himself without reservation with the China bloc in and out of Congress. His charges of Communist infiltration of the State Department found a focus. After an inauspicious beginning in February, it was gaining support by late March.[254] Taft's early reaction to McCarthy's attack had been that "it was a perfectly reckless performance."[255] But on March 22, the very day after McCarthy had charged Lattimore as the top espionage agent before the Tydings subcommittee, the Senate Republican Policy Committee moved toward an indorsement of McCarthy. After a meeting of the Senate Policy Committee of the Republican party, Taft announced that McCarthy's charges were "not a matter of party policy" but that Republican senators were helping him "in his fight" and "reaction seems to be pretty good on the whole."[256] Taft was reported to have said that "if one case doesn't work, try another."[257] On March 25, Senator Bridges told reporters that a group of Republicans would "go after" Acheson in a series of public attacks.[258] Two days later, he delivered a speech in the Senate strongly attacking Acheson. He charged that the Tydings subcommittee was opening "a white-wash factory to make camouflage for the failures of a diplomatic dean of

[252] State Department Employee Loyalty Investigation, p. 768.
[253] Congressional Record, XCVI, 81st Cong., 2d sess. (1950), 4385.
[254] Goldman, op. cit., p. 144.
[255] Rovere, op. cit., p. 135.
[256] New York Times, March 23, 1950, p. 1. Compare Westerfield's interpretation of Taft's statement with that of Rovere (Westerfield, op. cit., pp. 376–77; Rovere, op. cit., p. 135).
[257] Ibid., p. 136.
[258] New York Times, March 26, 1950, p. 1.

fashion." He declared that the wreckage of our diplomatic and military efforts in Europe and Asia was no accident and that "Stalin had help from inside our ranks." He demanded that the Tydings sub-committee find out from Acheson who was responsible for the decision to abandon China.[259]

On March 30, McCarthy made a lengthy speech in Congress, restating his charges of Communist influence in the government. He now centered his attack exclusively on Lattimore, Jessup, Service, Hanson, and the Institute of Pacific Relations, and on the China policy of the United States.[260] He adopted Utley's thesis that Lattimore served Communist interests by propagating the party line. Of Lattimore he said:

> In view of his position of tremendous power in the State Department as the "architect" of our far eastern policy, the more important aspect of his case deals with his aims and what he advocates; whether his aims are American aims or whether they coincide with the aims of Soviet Russia.[261]

He charged that Lattimore's views were followed by the State Department[262] and that "Acheson takes the same position as his counselors on far-eastern affairs — Lattimore, Jessup, and Service."[263] He concluded his speech with the assertion:

> It was not Chinese democracy under Mao that conquered China, as Acheson, Lattimore, Jessup, and Hanson contend. Soviet Russia conquered China and an important ally of the conquerors was this small left-wing element in our Department of State.[264]

The theory of conspiracy which General Hurley had originated was in full blossom.[265] McCarthy not only could draw on the ideas of Alfred Kohlberg (the founder of the American China Policy Association), Mrs. Freda Utley, and a growing body of anti-Communist writers on both the extreme right and left. But in concentrating his attack on the officials and scholars connected with China policy in one way or another, his infamous

[259] *Congressional Record*, XCVI, 81st Cong., 1st sess. (1950), 4118–21.
[260] *Ibid.*, pp. 4372–4408.
[261] *Ibid.*, p. 4385.
[262] *Ibid.*, p. 4386.
[263] *Ibid.*, p. 4407.
[264] *Ibid.*, p. 4407–8.
[265] Hurley had charged that a group of career officials in China and in Washington were "disloyal to the American policy." Hurley's testimony before the Senate Foreign Relations Committee investigating Far Eastern policy in December, 1945, p. 160, as quoted in *Report on State Department*, p. 146.
In his letter of resignation dated November 26, 1945, Hurley said: "The professional foreign service men sided with the Chinese Communist armed party and the imperialist block of nations whose policy it was to keep China divided against itself" (*United States Relations with China*, p. 582). See Part II, chap. viii, above.

crusade also fed upon what the Tydings subcommittee called "the vague uneasiness of many Americans concerning the ascendency of the Communists in China and the decline of the Nationalist government."[266]

Senator Knowland also caught the spirit of the times. As late as March 2, he had attacked Lattimore merely for advocating "a policy of appeasement."[267] Yet on April 5, Senator Knowland delivered a speech in the Senate in which he compared Lattimore's writings with the theses and resolutions of the Sixth World Congress of the Communist International adopted in December, 1928; the Constitution of the Chinese Communist party adopted in July, 1945; a statement on China policy issued in January, 1949, by a front organization of the American Communist party; and an Associated Press report on April 4 of an article in *Pravda*. Knowland asked in what way Lattimore's recommendations differed from the objectives, programs, and policies set forth in the Communist documents.[268] Being an upright man, Knowland refused to be drawn by McCarthy into a discussion of Lattimore's motives, but he did stress "the strange coincidence" between these two sets of views.[269] On June 1, Knowland lent further support to McCarthy by demanding a reopening of the *Amerasia* case.[270] This sustained generalized assault nullified much of the partisan advantage which the administration had gained on the specific issue of Formosa in January. It made disengagement from Chiang more difficult than ever.[271]

At this time, the officials and scholars under McCarthy's attack were still in a strong enough position to launch a forceful counterattack. In his appearance before the Tydings sub-committee, Lattimore openly challenged McCarthy to a debate on China policy.[272] He was able to produce the testimonies of 170 distinguished scholars and experts on his personal integrity and loyalty. He won applause from the audience when he declared that his obligation was to refute McCarthy's charges and establish beyond further challenge the right of American scholars to express their views freely without fear.[273] The Tydings subcommittee issued a report on July 20 totally refuting McCarthy's charges of Communist infiltration and influence in the State Department. It cleared Lattimore, Jessup, Service, Hanson, and Vincent of all of McCarthy's accusations.[274] The Tydings

[266] *Report on State Department*, p. 151.
[267] *Congressional Record*, XCVI, 81st Cong., 2d sess. (1950), 2642.
[268] *Ibid.*, pp. 4804–6.
[269] *Ibid.*, pp. 4828–29.
[270] *Ibid.*, p. 7785.
[271] Westerfield, *op. cit.*, p. 368.
[272] *State Department Employee Loyalty Investigation*, p. 419.
[273] *Ibid.*, p. 826.
[274] It conceded that Service was "extremely indiscreet" in his dealings with Jaffe (*Report on State Department*, pp. 93–94).

report and America's preoccupation with the national crisis ushered in by
the Korean War brought about a brief period of eclipse for McCarthy.[275]

M. The Collapse of American Policy and the Traditional Dilemma

The years 1949 and 1950 witnessed the triumph of the Chinese Communists on the mainland, Mao's proclamation of his policy of leaning to
one side, and the conclusion of the Sino-Soviet Treaty of Alliance. Formosa was expected soon to fall. A half-century's policy was reaching a
point of collapse.

The latest phase in the cycles of advance and retreat of the United
States in China, the Marshall-Acheson program of gradual disengagement
paralleled Theodore Roosevelt's acquiescence in Russia's and Japan's
special positions in Manchuria, Secretary Bryan's note to Japan of March
13, 1915, the Lansing-Ishii Agreement, Hoover's inaction after the Manchurian crisis, and finally the Yalta Agreement. These retreats usually
followed a previous advance and were the products of the inconsistency
between ends and means in American policy. Throughout the fifty-year
period, traditional American methods, which ruled out the purposeful
use of military power, were sooner or later found to be incompatible with
the avowed objectives of maintaining the Open Door and preserving the
territorial integrity of China. Diplomatic support, moral encouragement,
and limited assistance proved unavailing. When the United States was confronted with a choice between the use of force and the acceptance of a
situation created by the actual or potential use of military power by the
other side, retreat followed.

In contrast, all major American advances in China were accomplished
after the United States had taken part in war or had resorted to strong
measures on issues not immediately related to China. The dispatch of
Hay's notes and circular followed the Spanish–American War. The Washington Conference followed the First World War. The refusal to compromise with Japan on the issue of stationing Japanese troops in China
followed the imposition of the total embargo on oil — a measure taken not
so much to defend China as to deter Japan from cutting the British trade
routes and seizing the rich resources in Southeast Asia. The policy of
making China a great power followed Japan's attack on Pearl Harbor.
The landing of American marines and the dispatch of the Marshall mission
followed the end of the Pacific war. These advances were rendered possible when the United States displayed her actual or potential military
power or when her unwillingness to use force on behalf of China was
overcome by a crisis centered elsewhere.

But none of these advances brought about lasting results. In the course

[275] Rovere, *op. cit.*, p. 158.

of time, the United States had to face situations which could not be controlled by peaceful means or by a policy of limited assistance. If the traditional policy was bound to suffer one temporary setback after another before the Second World War, it was doomed to eventual failure by the transformation of the multiple balance of power into the bipolar system. Under the bipolar system, both a policy of containment and a policy of liberation required, in typical cases, a readiness to use military power for their successful implementation. But willingness to use force in China was absent. It was no accident that when the policy of containment was adopted in March, 1947, that policy was not applied to China. It was not until Secretary Acheson had begun to implement the policy of disengagement from China that he instructed Jessup to work out a program to contain the Communists within the boundaries of China. Furthermore, the bipolar system sharpened the inconsistency between the objective of supporting an existing government and the principle of non-intervention. For the bipolar system, together with the theory and practice of the international Communist movement, put a premium on the policy of intervention as a component in either an offensive or defensive strategy. In contrast, the traditional principle of non-intervention inhibited American action. Acheson's letter of transmittal contained an admission of the inadequacy of the traditional policy to deal with a popular movement in China which owed its allegiance to international communism.

While Marshall and Acheson ruled out armed intervention, they did not have the freedom necessary to adopt and implement a policy of prompt withdrawal from China, even if they had desired to do so. The traditional attachment to China, now reinforced by the perception of the threat posed by international communism, found expression in the China bloc's demands for positive action in China. By the first half of 1950, the administration and the friends of Chiang reached a stalemate over China policy. This partisan deadlock was the reflection of the inherent contradiction, now brought to the fore by events, between the two elements of American policy: the objective of supporting China and the unwillingness to use force. In the proposals of Hoover and Taft, there were for the first time suggestions of using American military power to intervene in the Chinese civil war. Subsequent events proved that Taft was right in his belief that the Chinese Communists would not dare challenge the American navy in the Formosa Strait. But these proposals ran into America's aversion to war. Mainland China had been lost. Formosa was not considered important enough to American security to warrant a last-minute armed intervention. The proposals of Hoover and Taft succeeded merely in making the position of the China bloc politically vulnerable, with the result that the Republicans failed to force the administration to undertake military commitments in Formosa.

On the other hand, the administration could not refuse to continue arms shipments and economic aid to the Nationalists without running the risk of jeopardizing its other foreign policy programs. The critics of the administration who held tenaciously to the objective of supporting the Nationalists had demonstrated their capacity for causing trouble. Economic aid and shipment of arms under the unexpended balance of the $125 million special fund would not apparently entail the danger of war. Under these circumstances, the United States continued to be entangled in China and American policy was immobilized at the center. She could not take any initiative because she was unwilling either to use force or to give up her objective. With the United States at odds with herself, the moves of other powers would tip the unstable balance of her policies in one direction or another. If it had come about, Mao's projected assault on Formosa would have enabled the United States to disentangle herself from Chiang. But, in the event, the North Korean aggression on South Korea led to a decision to defend Formosa by force.

Meanwhile, another persistent feature of America's traditional policy reappeared in a new form. Just as it had been in the past, non-recognition as a policy was born of the contradiction between the nation's reluctance to forsake an objective and her incapacity to achieve it by the purposeful use of military power. The friends of the Nationalists advocated non-recognition passionately. The administration adopted it without much conviction as a temporary measure, partly in response to Republican pressure and partly in response to Mao's policy of deliberately provoking the Western powers. Mao's provocative actions and pronouncements stemmed basically from his Marxist-Leninist ideology. But the American policy of sustaining the Nationalist government reinforced his distorted views of the United States while the policy of limited assistance failed to impress on him American strength and determination. It was no accident that Mao responded to the White Paper by fully developing his theme of the unchanging nature of imperialism and by showing his utter contempt for American power. To the extent that the administration was deterred by the provocative acts of the Chinese Communists from recognizing their regime, it was reaping the consequences of its attempt to achieve the objective of sustaining the Nationalist government while ruling out the use of force. It was also harvesting the fruits of its inability to withdraw promptly from China.

Important as was the partisan stalemate in preventing a prompt and complete withdrawal, there was still another related factor, much less obvious but of some significance. When one carefully reflects on the development of American policy from the vantage point of today, one discerns an elusive fact: While American officials were intensely conscious of the immediate dangers of armed intervention, there was no comparable awareness and thus few public discussions of the possibility that a Communist victory could lay the foundation, and continued American entanglement in China could increase the chance, of an eventual armed clash between the Chinese Communists and the United States. Without foreknowledge of the seriousness of a possible Sino-American clash, the very real and ever-present difficulties involved in a policy of prompt disengagement could not have been overcome.

As we have seen, prompt and complete withdrawal would have meant abrupt severance of the ties to a government long supported by the United States, cutting off arms shipments, economic aid, and political bonds. It would have required the abandonment of illusions that parts of China could somehow be denied to the Chinese Communists by a program of limited assistance. It would have involved the relinquishment of any advantage which might have been gained from delaying the total conquest of China by the Communists. It would have entailed the renunciation of a nation to which the United States had been emotionally attached for over a century. It would have had to be undertaken in the face of the Communists' open hostility, defiant challenges, and deliberate affronts.

These emotional attitudes and practical considerations which hindered prompt withdrawal found expression in the views and proposals of the American friends of the Nationalists and their attacks on the administration's policies and its officials. These difficulties could not have been easily and completely outweighed by those disadvantages of continued entanglement which could be seen at the time and which were used as arguments in favor of withdrawal. The capture by Communists of American-supplied arms seemed a trivial matter, involving readily replaceable matériel. The amount of economic aid appropriated but unexpended was small and not a serious drain on American resources. The further loss of American prestige was a serious concern but became less significant in the light of the long American identification with the Nationalists. The rise of anti-Americanism worried American officials, but they continued nonetheless to rely on the supposedly deep-rooted traditional friendship between the United States and China. The argument that continued entanglement would drive the Chinese Communists into the arms of the Soviet Union but withdrawal would promote Chinese Titoism was rapidly weakened and then destroyed by Chinese pronouncements and actions.

All the disadvantages of continued entanglement would have been judged to be as serious as they turned out to be only if the potentiality of China for good or evil had been adequately recognized and the role of ideology in Chinese Communist foreign policy had been correctly judged. Only then could the United States have perceived that the loss of American prestige, the intensified Chinese hostility against the United States, the Chinese Communist leaders' ties with the Soviet Union, and the lack of normal diplomatic relations between the United States and Communist China might lead to an armed clash which might entail a major military effort on the part of the United States. A correct estimate of the dangers involved might in turn have increased the chance of a successful program of prompt withdrawal. But, in the event, American officials and scholars who recommended a program of withdrawal were generally those who did not regard China as a serious menace to the United States or else did not consider ideology a paramount element in future Chinese international behavior. The political figures who did regard a Communist China as a formidable enemy were those who advocated a program of continued assistance to the Nationalists in the vain hope that the Communist advance could be halted or delayed by limited means. While the administration vigorously and successfully opposed any new program of aid to China in 1949 and 1950, it did not advocate and implement a program of prompt and total disengagement with a sense of urgency. This absence of a sense of urgency stemmed from the same basic assumption underlying Marshall's refusal to undertake armed intervention — that China could not soon develop into a strong state and could not readily become a serious threat to the United States. It was also derived from the judgment that the traditional Chinese suspicion of Russian imperialism and the historic Sino-American friendship would soon overcome the ideological bias which bound China to the Soviet Union and engendered hostility to the United States.

The expectation of Chinese Communist impotence or moderation in foreign affairs has turned out to be false. But it was only the last of many unfounded hopes regarding China. It followed the wish that China under the Nationalists could become a great power, the judgment that the Chinese Communists were not dedicated Communists, and the hope that a coalition government could be established. These overly optimistic expectations arose to satisfy a psychological need created by the pattern of America's China policy. For the gap between America's objectives and meager means brought about situations in the Far East over which the United States had no real influence. Yet she could not but hope that somehow things could work out satisfactorily. If Japan had to be eliminated as a significant factor and the United States did not plan to maintain a military presence in China, the only hope for stability in the Far East lay in the possibility of China's emergence as a great and friendly power. If a strife-ridden China could not become a great power and the Kuomintang could not bring about political progress, the only hope lay in a coalition government in which the "so-called Communists" would take part. If the coalition government could not be established and a third force could not be fashioned, the only hope lay in the weakness or moderation of the Chinese Communists. These hopes obviated the necessity of making difficult choices or of accepting what would have looked like impending catastrophe. Many of these illusions also had their roots in America's political tradition.

Up to June, 1950, American policy did achieve one negative result: the avoidance of armed intervention in the Chinese civil war and thus of an immediate military conflict with the Chinese Communists on the mainland of China. But the North Korean aggression against South Korea was to bring about a sudden reversal of the policy of not defending Formosa by force which had been dramatically reaffirmed by Truman and Acheson less than six months before. Despite all its endeavors to avoid that contingency, the administration was to find it necessary to intervene militarily in the Chinese civil war. Once again, the United States was to make a new advance in China as a result of the pressure of events occuring elsewhere. The neutralization of the Formosa Strait was to render an armed conflict with Communist China likely sooner or later, unless it could lead to a political settlement with Peking over the question of Formosa. The crossing of the 38th Parallel and Peking's intervention in the Korean War were to precipitate that conflict sooner than anyone could have expected. The ground for this military confrontation was prepared by the erratic shifts of policy in 1947 and 1948, the partisan debate and deadlock in 1949 and 1950, and the failure to effect a prompt disengagement, which were in turn the expression of the contradictions inherent in American policy. In short, the inconsistencies of the traditional policy did not enable the United States either to achieve her objectives or to avoid the use of her armed forces in dealing with issues relating to China. With the military conflict between Communist China and the United States in Korea, the misfortune of American policy was to become complete.

PART FOUR

THE
IRONIC
FULFILMENT

CHAPTER XIII

THE KOREAN WAR

AND

THE EMERGENCE OF

COMMUNIST CHINA

AS A

GREAT POWER

A. The Soviet Move and the American Reaction

On June 25, 1950, North Korean forces launched a large-scale, carefully planned attack on South Korea. This North Korean aggression was inspired and planned by the Soviet Union,[1] and it appears to have been designed primarily to disrupt the American plan for concluding a separate peace treaty with Japan and to frighten Japan away from America by a demonstration of Communist strength and American weakness. In Soviet calculations, even if it should fail to achieve this principal aim, the conquest of South Korea would improve the defensive and offensive position of the Communist bloc against an eventual American-Japanese alliance.[2] The Soviet plan apparently rested on the assumption that the United

[1] Harry S. Truman, *Years of Trial and Hope* (Garden City, N.Y.: Doubleday & Co., 1956), p. 335. For the testimonies of General Omar Bradley, the chairman of the Joint Chiefs of Staff, and Secretary of State Dean Acheson in the MacArthur hearings, see Senate Committee on Armed Services and Committee on Foreign Relations, *Hearings on the Military Situation in the Far East*, 82d Cong., 1st sess. (1951), pp. 210–11, 1935–36 (hereafter cited as *Military Situation in the Far East*). See also John Foster Dulles, "A Militaristic Experiment," *Department of State Bulletin*, July 10, 1950, p. 49, and his speech before the Commonwealth Club of San Francisco, *ibid.*, p. 207; Alexander L. George, "American Policy-Making and the North Korean Aggression," *World Politics*, January, 1955, pp. 209–32; Allen S. Whiting, *China Crosses the Yalu* (New York: Macmillan Co., 1960), chap. iv; John W. Spanier, *The Truman–MacArthur Controversy and the Korean War* (Cambridge, Mass.: Harvard University Press, 1959), chap. ii.

For a statement of the opposite view, see Wilbur H. Hitchcock, "North Korea Jumps the Gun," *Current History*, March, 1951, pp. 136–44.

[2] Whiting, *op. cit.*, pp. 37–38; George, *loc. cit.*, pp. 214–15; Dulles, *loc. cit.*, pp. 50, 208.

555

States would not defend South Korea with her armed forces. This assumption found support in American actions and statements concerning Korea since 1948.

American commitments in Korea stemmed from actions taken during the Pacific war. In the Cairo Declaration of December 1, 1943, Roosevelt, Churchill, and Chiang Kai-shek announced that "in due course Korea shall become free and independent." The Cairo Declaration was reaffirmed in the Potsdam Declaration of June 26, 1945, to which the Soviet Union adhered upon her entry into the Pacific war. As for the period prior to the establishment of Korean independence, President Roosevelt envisaged, as early as March, 1943, an international trusteeship.[3] This proposal for a transitional arrangement was accepted by Stalin at both the Teheran and the Yalta conferences.[4] In his conversations with Harry Hopkins in May, 1944, Stalin agreed that Korea should be placed under a trusteeship composed of the United States, China, Great Britain, and the Soviet Union.[5] At the time of Japan's surrender, the United States and the Soviet Union agreed on the 38th Parallel as the dividing line for the purpose of accepting the surrender of the Japanese forces in Korea. In the next two years, negotiations between the United States and the Soviet Union to establish a four-power trusteeship for a unified Korea met with no results. After the breakdown of bilateral negotiations, the United States in September, 1947, brought the Korean problem to the General Assembly of the United Nations. The United States now discarded the idea of a four-power trusteeship, and her avowed objective became the establishment of an independent, united Korea.[6] Within the month, however, the Joint Chiefs of Staff were to conclude that, from the standpoint of military security, the United States had little interest in maintaining troops and bases in Korea and that the two American divisions there could well be used elsewhere. Shortly before, General Wedemeyer, in his now famous report, had recommended that American forces be withdrawn concurrently with the withdrawal of Soviet forces from North Korea.[7]

In other words, the United States, by ostensibly emphasizing the ambitious, long-term goal of a united Korea and by bringing the problem to the United Nations, was actually trying to provide a cover for the contem-

[3] Cordell Hull, *Memoirs* (New York, Macmillan Co., 1948), II, 1596.

[4] Department of State, *Foreign Relations of the United States: The Conferences at Cairo and Teheran, 1943* (Washington, D.C.: Government Printing Office, 1961), p. 869; Department of State, *Foreign Relations of the United States: The Conferences at Malta and Yalta, 1945* (Washington, D.C.: Government Printing Office, 1955), p. 770.

[5] Robert E. Sherwood, *Roosevelt and Hopkins* (New York: Harper & Bros., 1948), p. 903.

[6] Leland M. Goodrich, *Korea: A Study of United States Policy in the United Nations* (New York: Council on Foreign Relations, 1956), pp. 7–41.

[7] General Albert C. Wedemeyer, *Wedemeyer Reports!* (New York: Henry Holt & Co., 1958), p. 479; Truman, *op. cit.*, pp. 325–26.

plated reduction of military commitment in South Korea which was judged to be of little importance to her security. As a substitute for military power, the United States sought to invoke the support of the United Nations to uphold her position in South Korea. This structure of avowed objective, actual purpose, prescribed means, and underlying assumption bore a close resemblance to the traditional policy toward China. It was to produce consequences fairly similar to those flowing from the Open Door policy before 1941. It was to invite attack by another power, which the United States would then be obliged to counter with her armed forces. Not long after the United States was to use strong measures, the verbal policy would be transformed into a program to be implemented by force. It was to confront the United States with the dilemma of forsaking an objective to which she had committed her prestige or employing in Korea more manpower and resources than she thought prudent.

After the government in South Korea had been formally inaugurated on August 15, 1948, the American forces began their withdrawal on September 15 as noted in the last chapter. General MacArthur in an interview in early March, 1949, traced an American line of defense which left out South Korea. By the end of June, all American troops had left Korea. In an address on January 12, 1950, Secretary Acheson drew a defense perimeter in the western Pacific which omitted South Korea. All these actions and pronouncements apparently suggested to the Russians that the United States would not defend South Korea against an attack by the North Korean regime. But the well-planned, large-scale attack by North Korean forces across an established boundary suddenly confronted the United States with the clear-cut moral issue of upholding the system of collective security and defending a weak state against armed aggression. It created a crisis which forcefully impressed upon American officials the possibly disastrous consequences of inaction.

The North Korean attack was widely interpreted as a test by the Soviet Union of America's determination to resist open, armed attack by Communist forces. It was assumed that, if the United States failed to resist, other local aggressions would quickly follow and might lead to a general war.[8] President Truman viewed the North Korean attack in terms of Japan's attack on Manchuria, Mussolini's conquest of Ethiopia, and Hitler's aggressions in the thirties.[9] To Secretary Acheson, if the North Korean attack was not repelled, the whole system of collective security would begin to disintegrate; and the system of collective security was one of the bases of American security.[10] To John Foster Dulles, a North Korean success would place Japan "between the upper and lower jaws of the Rus-

[8] George, op. cit., pp. 213, 215–16.
[9] Truman, op. cit., pp. 332–33.
[10] Military Situation in the Far East, pp. 1818–19.

sian bear."[11] Truman also felt that if the United States failed to protect
a country established under American auspices, the peoples in countries
adjacent to the Soviet Union not only in Asia but in Europe, the Middle
East, and elsewhere would be adversely affected.[12]

This new evaluation of America's security interests in Korea, reinforced
by a clear-cut moral issue, led the United States to reverse suddenly her
military strategy in the Far East. On June 27, General MacArthur was
authorized to use American naval and air forces to prevent the Inchon-
Kimpo-Seoul area from falling into unfriendly hands.[13] On June 30, Truman accepted MacArthur's recommendation to employ American ground
forces in Korea.[14] In recommending the use of ground forces in Korea,
MacArthur envisaged "an early offensive action in accordance with his
mission of clearing South Korea of North Korean forces."[15] The commitment of American ground forces on a large scale in Korea constituted not
only a reversal of the strategic plan symbolized by the withdrawal of
American forces from South Korea in 1949. It also represented a departure
from one of the strongly held views of General Marshall to the effect that
American ground forces should not be used on the continent of Asia[16] — a
view which contributed to his refusal to intervene in the Chinese civil
war.[17]

B. The Neutralization of the Formosa Strait

One of the first decisions made after the North Korean attack was
the dispatch of the Seventh Fleet to neutralize the Formosa Strait. Notwithstanding the testimony of Secretary of Defense Johnson to the contrary,[18] this decision was taken in the first day after the North Korean
attack, upon the joint recommendation of the Department of State and the
Joint Chiefs of Staff. According to Secretary Acheson's testimony, the of-

[11] Dulles, "A Militaristic Experiment," loc. cit., p. 50.
[12] Truman, op. cit., p. 339.
[13] Military Situation in the Far East, p. 3192.
[14] Truman, op. cit., pp. 342–43. For the official statement announcing this decision,
see press release by the White House, June 30, 1950, Department of State, United
States Policy in the Korea Crisis (Washington, D.C.: Government Printing Office,
1950), p. 25.
[15] Military Situation in the Far East, p. 1012.
[16] George, op. cit., p. 224.
[17] See chap. ix, above.
[18] Johnson's retrospective account can be summarized as follows: It was he who
injected the issue of Formosa into the deliberations in the evening of June 25 at the
first Blair House meeting. He insisted that "relatively the security of the United States
was more affected by Formosa than Korea." Johnson and Secretary Acheson had a
brief but "really violent" discussion. Then Truman indicated that the question of
Formosa would be discussed later. The decision to dispatch the Seventh Fleet was
made the next day (Military Situation in the Far East, p. 2580). See also Albert L.
Warner, "How the Korean Decision was Made," Harper's, June, 1957, pp. 99–106.

ficials in the State Department and from the Joint Chiefs of Staff worked out together a series of recommendations which included the dispatch of the Seventh Fleet to the Formosa Strait. At the President's request, these recommendations were presented by Secretary Acheson himself at the Blair House meeting on June 25.[19] In his memoirs, President Truman stated that Acheson recommended making a statement that the Fleet would repel any attack on Formosa and that no attacks should be made from Formosa on the mainland.[20] These recommendations were accepted by Truman. The next evening at the second Blair House meeting, the President directed Secretary Johnson to give General MacArthur the instructions regarding the Seventh Fleet.[21] It was also at this meeting that Truman approved the State Department's recommendation to use air and naval force to support the South Korean army—a move which, according to Johnson, "the military neither recommended nor opposed."[22] Truman also approved recommendations for the strengthening of American forces in the Philippines and for increased aid to the French in Indochina. All these decisions were announced by President Truman in a public statement on June 27.

One cannot ascertain from published records whether it was the officials of the State Department or the officers representing the Joint Chiefs who, in their meeting to prepare a joint recommendation, initiated the idea of sending the Seventh Fleet to the Formosa Strait.[23] There is no question that even before the Korean attack, there had been continued pressure on the administration for a change of its policy toward Formosa. When Secretary Johnson and General Bradley came back from a ten-day tour of the Far East just before the North Korean aggression, they brought back with them a memorandum on Formosa prepared by MacArthur which stressed the strategic interest of the United States in denying Formosa to the Communists.[24] How much weight MacArthur's memorandum carried in the deliberations on June 25 cannot be determined.

[19] *Military Situation in the Far East*, p. 2055.

[20] Truman, *op. cit.*, p. 334; *New York Times*, June 28, 1950, p. 1, under the by-line of James Reston.

[21] Truman, *op. cit.*, p. 337.

[22] *Military Situation in the Far East*, p. 2580.

[23] Goodrich observed: "It is quite possible that the neutralization of Formosa was a condition set by the Joint Chiefs for their consent to the State Department's proposal to come to the assistance of the Republic of Korea with armed forces" (Goodrich, *op. cit.*, p. 111).

[24] *New York Times*, June 28, 1950, p. 12, under the by-line of James Reston.

This memorandum was read by General Bradley at the request of Secretary Johnson at the Blair House meeting on the evening of June 25 (Johnson's testimony, *Military Situation in the Far East*, pp. 2579–80; see also Acheson's testimony, *ibid.*, p. 2055). Brigadier General L. Joseph Fortier, director of Theater Intelligence Division of the

There is reason to believe, however, that after the North Korean aggression, Secretary Acheson was quite ready to reverse his policy toward Formosa. The neutralization of the Formosa Strait as well as American actions in South Korea was a step to discourage Communist moves elsewhere, to localize the conflict, and to induce Communist withdrawal in Korea by demonstrating American strength and determination.[25] Thus President Truman, in his statement of June 27, 1950, declared: "The attack upon Korea makes it plain beyond all doubts that Communism has passed beyond the use of subversion to conquer independent nations and will now use armed invasion and war. . . . In these circumstances the occupation of Formosa by Communist forces would be a direct threat to the security of the Pacific area. . . ." [26] Significantly, the President announced at the same time a program of accelerating military assistance to Indochina and the Philippines. Furthermore, domestic politics and the necessity to win wholehearted Republican support for the State Department's policy in Korea made it highly desirable for the administration to reverse its position on Formosa. In sending the Seventh Fleet to prevent an attack on Formosa, the administration adopted, at least as a temporary measure, the policy advocated by Senator Taft and Mr. Hoover. It took a step which was momentarily in line with Senator H. Alexander Smith's suggestion for joint United States–Nationalist occupation of Formosa and went beyond Knowland's and Judd's proposal of sending a military mission and giving military

Far Eastern Command from February, 1949, to September, 1950, flew to Formosa at the invitation of Generalissimo Chiang Kai-shek in late May or early June, 1950. He spent three days in Formosa and stayed in a "very comfortable cottage near where the Generalissimo lived." His mission was to get a first-hand estimate of the situation on Formosa. At the time, the United States government had a consul general and military, air, and naval attachés stationed on the island (General Fortier's testimony, Senate Committee on the Judiciary, *Hearings on the Institute of Pacific Relations*, 82d Cong., 1st and 2d sess. [1951–52], pp. 848–52).

It cannot be ascertained from published records whether or not General Fortier's trip was one of the steps leading to the preparation of General MacArthur's memorandum on Formosa. According to the testimony of Admiral Charles M. Cooke, commander of the Seventh Fleet from December, 1945, to February, 1948, military attachés and diplomatic representatives believed in May, 1950, that Formosa would probably fall before July 15 and a new warning was issued for all Americans to leave Formosa. This appreciation of the military situation was challenged by Admiral Cooke who was in Formosa as a representative of the International News Service. Later, Admiral Cooke served in Formosa as the co-ordinator of the Commerce International–China, an American corporation retaining a group of retired officers, reserve officers, and ex-officers to furnish technical services to the Nationalist government. General Fortier's trip and General MacArthur's memorandum obviously arose from the uncertain situation confronting Formosa (*ibid.*, pp. 1540–41). In the two weeks before the North Korean attack, the Chinese Communist troops opposite Formosa increased from about 40,000 to about 156,000 (*Military Situation in the Far East*, p. 2621).

[25] George, *op. cit.*, pp. 229–30.

[26] *United States Policy in the Korea Crisis*, p. 18.

aid to Formosa.[27] The neutralization of the Formosa Strait temporarily produced bipartisan co-operation on Far Eastern affairs.[28]

Once more, a crisis centered elsewhere overcame America's unwillingness to use force on an issue relating to China. The United States was compelled by the pressure of global events to halt her retreat, to intervene in the Chinese civil war at the last moment, and, temporarily at least, to make a new advance in China. By this time, however, the Chinese Communists were no longer an armed party seeking to seize power; they were the masters of mainland China with a strong alliance with the Soviet Union.

Peking reacted more forcefully than Moscow to President Truman's statement of June 27. For the American government not only abruptly thwarted the Chinese Communists' plan for an early invasion of Formosa but also reopened the whole question of Formosa. President Truman specifically declared that "the determination of the future status of Formosa must await the restoration of security in the Pacific, a peaceful settlement with Japan or consideration by the United Nations." [29] This declaration stood in contrast to his statement of January 5, 1950, announcing the "hands-off" policy and stressing the Cairo Declaration of December 1, 1943, in which President Roosevelt, Prime Minister Churchill, and Generalissimo Chiang Kai-shek stated that Formosa would be returned to the Republic of China.

Mao Tse-tung's immediate reaction was to assert that the American President himself now proved that "his statement [of January 5] was false." [30] Looking through his Marxist-Leninist prism, Mao interpreted this American change in policy to meet a new situation as an "open exposure by the United States of its true imperialist face." [31] In a formal statement on June 28, Foreign Minister Chou En-lai declared: "The fact that Taiwan is part of China will remain unchanged forever. This is not only a historical fact but has been affirmed by the Cairo Declaration, the Potsdam Declaration, and the existing conditions after Japan's surrender." [32] He charged

[27] James Reston reported: "When President Truman on June 27 ordered the United States Seventh Fleet to prevent any attack on Formosa, he had several things in mind. He wanted to localize the Korean War by neutralizing Formosa, and to minimize the political opposition to the Korean War by neutralizing Senators Taft, Knowland, Smith of New Jersey and others who had been condemning his 'hands-off Formosa' policy" (*New York Times*, July 28, 1950, p. 5).

[28] Spanier, *op. cit.*, pp. 62–64.

[29] *United States Policy in the Korea Crisis*, p. 18.

[30] Chairman Mao Tse-tung's comment on President Truman's statement of June 27, a brief talk given on June 28, 1950, at the eighth meeting of the Central People's Government Council in Chang Tao-li, *Why China Helps Korea* (Bombay: People's Publishing House, 1951), pp. 31–32.

[31] *Ibid.*

[32] For the Chinese text see, *Hsin-hua yüeh-pao*, II, No. 3 (July, 1950), 525.

that Truman's statement and the actions of the American navy "constitute armed aggression against the territory of China and total violation of the United Nations Charter." [33] He declared defiantly that "the Chinese people . . . will surely be victorious in driving off American aggressors and in recovering Taiwan." [34] It was apparent from his declaration that Peking would not allow the question of Formosa to be decided at a peace conference over Japan which was then under American occupation or by the United Nations in which the Communist countries were in the minority. An editorial in the *Jên-min jih-pao* on June 29 pointed out that, as late as June 23, Acheson declared that Truman's January 5 statement was still valid.[35] It argued that the Korean situation could not justify the American action in the Taiwan Strait. It appears quite possible that the Chinese Communists had counted on the United States to adhere to the hands-off policy and had derived considerable assurance from every American pronouncement that could be interpreted as a reaffirmation of that policy. The sudden reversal of American policy further increased their distrust of American intentions and their doubt about the reliability of American declarations.

The intensified hostility and distrust toward the United States apparently strengthened Peking's disposition to push its revolutionary interests and to oppose American policies elsewhere in Asia. Both Mao and Chou did not confine their attacks to the reversal of American policy toward Formosa. They viewed American actions in the broad context of Asian affairs. Mao seized upon Truman's statement to denounce American intervention in the "internal affairs" not only of China but also "Korea, the Philippines, Vietnam and other countries." [36] Assuming the role of leadership in Asian affairs, Mao declared that "the affairs of Asia should be administered by the peoples of Asia themselves and not by the United States." He asserted that "United States aggression in Asia will only arouse the extensive and resolute resistance of the people of Asia." He called on the people throughout China and the world to unite and make "adequate preparations to defeat any provocation of American imperialism" which was "outwardly strong but feeble within, because it has no support among the people." [37] Chou charged that "the attack by the puppet Korean government of Syngman Rhee on the Korean People's Democratic Republic at the instigation of the United States government was a premeditated move by the United States, designed to create a pretext for the United

[33] *Ibid.*
[34] *Ibid.*
[35] *Wei-ta ti k'ang Mei yüan Chao yün-tung* ["The Great Movement to Resist the United States and To Help Korea"], (Peking: Ĩên-min ch'u-pan-shê, 1954), pp. 649–51 (hereafter cited as *K'ang Mei*).
[36] Chang Toa-li, *op. cit.*, pp. 32–33.
[37] *Ibid.*

States to invade Taiwan, Korea, Vietnam and the Philippines." [38] Thus from the outset the Chinese Communists did not look at American action in the Formosa Strait in the narrow context of American intervention in the Chinese civil war, but in the broad framework of what they called the "new, premeditated aggressions" of "American imperialism" against the Asian people. They did not define their task as merely taking over Formosa but also as rallying "the people throughout the world who love peace, justice and freedom, particularly the oppressed nationalities and peoples of the East, to rise up and check the new aggressions of American imperialism in the Orient." [39] They took the neutralization of the Formosa Strait as an additional confirmation of their distorted view of the United States. The revolutionary fervor, the ideological perspective, and the mental image of the United States which characterized both Mao's informal talk and Chou's formal statement inevitably affected the Chinese Communist regime's conception of its interests and its duties, its estimate of the external threat, and its appraisal of American intentions. These appraisals were to play an important part in Peking's intervention in Korea after the American forces crossed the 38th Parallel.

The tone and content of Mao's and Chou's statements re-emphasized the Chinese Communists' policy of "joining with revolutionaries" in other countries which was formulated in 1948–49.[40] In turn, this policy was partly the outgrowth of the new aggressive line of international communism which encouraged the resort to armed actions. This new line was inaugurated at the end of 1947 by A. A. Zhdanov's speech at the opening conference of the Cominform.[41] By the summer of 1949, Russian leaders began to stress the importance of the Chinese example for Communist movements in Southeast Asia and allowed the Chinese Communists to take the lead in co-ordinating or guiding them. Flushed with revolutionary fervor and emboldened by their smashing victory over the Nationalists against overwhelming odds, the Chinese Communists accepted without hesitation their new role of leadership in Asian affairs.

In an address to the Trade Union Conference of Asian and Australian countries in Peking on November 16, 1949, Liu Shao-ch'i, a member of the Politbureau, claimed for Communist China the leadership of national revolutionary movements in all other countries of Asia on the basis of the success of the political-military program worked out by Mao Tse-tung. Liu declared: "The path taken by the Chinese people in defeating im-

[38] *Ibid.*, p. 32.
[39] *Ibid.*
[40] H. Arthur Steiner, *The International Position of Communist China* (New York: Institute of Pacific Relations, 1958), pp. 10–11.
[41] Max Beloff, *Soviet Policy in the Far East, 1944–1951* (London: Oxford University Press, 1953), pp. 208–10; Captain Malcolm Kennedy, *A History of Communism in East Asia* (New York: Praeger, 1957), pp. 358–60.

perialism and its lackeys and in founding the People's Republic of China is the path that should be taken by the peoples of various colonial and semi-colonial countries in their fight for national independence and people's democracy." [42] Communist China was the first Communist regime to grant diplomatic recognition to the Democratic Republic of Vietnam on January 18,[43] anticipating a similar action by the Soviet Union on January 30. By 1950 the influence of the Maoist strategy was clearly discernible in the revolutionary program of the Communist parties in Vietnam, the Philippines, and Burma.[44] Up to August of 1950, the Chinese Communists followed a policy hostile, not only to the United States, but also to the established governments in such countries as India, Burma, and Indonesia which had recognized the Peking regime.

At the time the neutralization of the Formosa Strait was thought to be a temporary measure taken in the face of an emergency. It left open the question of the future status of Formosa.[45] But, as we have noted, Chou proclaimed Peking's confidence in driving out "the American aggressors" and in recovering Taiwan.[46] Thus, the neutralization of the Formosa Strait created a new issue between Peking and Washington and produced a basic change in the pattern of conflict among Peking, Washington, and Moscow. The United States had now directly opposed with her armed forces the national interest of China and the revolutionary interests of the Chinese Communist movement. The tension between Peking and Washington was immeasurably heightened. It made insignificant any possible disagreement between Peking and Moscow which may have existed at that time. It even overshadowed any conflict of interests between Moscow and Washington in the Far East. It doomed to failure Acheson's attempt to turn Chinese nationalism against the Soviet Union.

C. The Renewed Conflict over China Policy

Within the United States, the neutralization of the Formosa Strait only temporarily pacified the American friends of Generalissimo Chiang. It enlisted their support for the administration's actions in Korea but did not bring about unity on China policy. It did not make Secretary Acheson

[42] Steiner, op. cit., Appendix A, p. 34.

[43] On January 14, 1950, Ho Chi-minh, the chairman of the Democratic Republic, announced his regime's willingness to establish diplomatic relations with all countries. The next day, the foreign minister of the North Vietnam regime cabled Chou En-lai with a similar request. Chou replied favorably on January 18. For documents, see Hsin-hua yüeh-pao, I, No. 4 (February 15, 1950), 1081.

[44] Shen-yu Dai, Peking, Moscow and the Communist Parties of Colonial Asia (Cambridge, Mass.: Center for International Studies, Massachusetts Institute of Technology, 1954).

[45] Truman, op. cit., p. 339.

[46] P. 562, above.

immune to further attacks. Even at the moment when political unity was momentarily restored, Senator Taft interpreted the neutralization of the Formosa Strait as a reversal by the President of Acheson's policy, attributed to Acheson's hands-off Formosa policy the cause of the Korean War, and demanded the Secretary's resignation.[47] The dispatch of the Seventh Fleet merely marked a turning point after which the United States again became increasingly involved in the Chinese civil war, the heretofore weakening influence of the China bloc was revived and strengthened, and the conflict over China policy was sharpened by the developments in the Korean War.

This conflict over China policy found its most forceful expression in the controversy between the administration and General MacArthur over three issues: the degree of American commitment to Chiang, the neutralized status of the Formosa Strait, and the future of that island. The administration desired to limit its ties to Chiang so as to preserve its freedom of action, while MacArthur wanted an all-out commitment. The administration believed that there was a "basic conflict of interest" between the United States and Chiang; for it was feared that in his burning ambition to use Formosa as a steppingstone for his re-entry to the mainland, Chiang might drag the United States into a war with the Chinese Communists.[48] The administration felt that the adoption of a wrong approach to Chiang and Formosa might destroy the unity of the United Nations. In contrast, MacArthur thought that the United States should back anyone who would fight communism, that Chiang's determination to resist Communist control paralleled the interests and purposes of the American people, and that the administration's policies and the hostile attitudes of the State Department were undermining Chiang.[49]

The administration employed the Seventh Fleet to prevent Nationalist actions against the mainland as well as the projected Communist assault on Formosa. MacArthur felt from the very beginning that the neutralization of the Formosa Strait had given the Chinese Communists "complete immunity" from any countermeasure while they were building up their forces for an attack against Formosa. He suggested that the President withdraw the prohibition against attacking the airfields on the mainland if the Chinese Communists continued to construct airstrips or to build up their position along the Formosa Strait.[50]

Insofar as one can ascertain from published materials, the administration did not have a clear-cut substantive policy for the future of Formosa.

[47] *Congressional Record*, XCVI, 81st Cong., 2d sess. (1950), 9319–23.
[48] Truman, *op. cit.*, p. 351.
[49] *Ibid.*, pp. 352–53; Major General Courtney Whitney, *MacArthur: His Rendezvous with History* (New York: Alfred A. Knopf, Inc., 1956), pp. 373–75.
[50] *Ibid.*, pp. 369–70; Truman, *op. cit.*, p. 353.

It seems to have desired to prevent Formosa from falling into hostile hands by the establishment of "an independent government . . . through the medium of the United Nations." [51] It may have been thinking of an independent Formosa with Formosan self-rule.[52] In contrast, MacArthur could find no evidence for the desire of Formosans for independence. He attributed far greater strategic importance to Formosa than the Joint Chiefs. In his opinion, Formosa in the hands of a hostile power could be used to breach and neutralize America's defense system in the Pacific Ocean. The loss of this defense perimeter "would shift any future battle area 5,000 miles eastward to the coast of American continent, our own home." [53] MacArthur subsequently made this point even more emphatically when he testified in the hearings on his dismissal that "from our standpoint we practically lose the Pacific Ocean if we give up or lose Formosa." [54] His public views at the time implied even to Admiral Forrest Sherman, chief of naval operations, that "we are going to use that [Formosa] as a base from which we would be able to attack objectives in Asia and so on." [55] In contrast, the administration merely wanted to deny Formosa to a hostile power and had no intention to use it for offensive operation. It did not believe that the loss of Formosa to an enemy, to use General Bradley's words, "would jeopardize our position to the extent that we would lose all our other positions in the Pacific." [56]

These conflicts over policy manifested themselves in two significant incidents. On July 31, MacArthur visited Formosa with the prior approval of the Joint Chiefs but not the State Department, which had apparently tried to dissuade him from going at that time. This visit took place six days after Yakob Malik, the Soviet representative on the Security Council, announced that he proposed to return to the council, thus ending the Soviet boycott of seven months. It increased the allies' and neutrals' anxiety over American policy toward China. It played into the hands of Malik's peace offensive. It was considered in Lake Success "a triumph of mistiming." [57] It was also thought to be evidence of lack of co-ordination in American diplomacy. This incident ended when Truman obtained through his emissary, Averell Harriman, a soldier's pledge from MacArthur to support his policy.

The second incident was MacArthur's message to the Veterans of For-

[51] *Ibid.*, p. 352.
[52] For indirect evidence on this point, see MacArthur's comment on Harriman's remarks as reported by the latter, *ibid.*; General Bradley's testimony, *Military Situation in the Far East*, p. 984.
[53] Whitney, *op. cit.*, pp. 377–80.
[54] *Military Situation in the Far East*, p. 53.
[55] *Ibid.*, p. 1591.
[56] *Ibid.*, p. 985.
[57] *New York Times*, August 11, 1950, p. 11, under the by-line of James Reston. See also his dispatch in *ibid.*, August 6, 1950, p. E3.

eign Wars in which MacArthur stated his views on the strategic importance of Formosa.[58] The full text of this message was carried in an American weekly magazine which appeared on August 26. It was sent without the advance knowledge of President Truman, Secretary Acheson, Secretary Johnson, or the Joint Chiefs.[59] It was made known to the world only one day after Ambassador Warren Austin had repeated, in a lengthy letter to Secretary-General Lie, America's strong indorsement of United Nations consideration of the case of Formosa, pledging American support for a full United Nations investigation. Austin's letter was an adroit maneuver to counter Peking's complaint of August 24 of American "aggression" on Taiwan. It represented an effort to gain through the United Nations the allies' and neutrals' support for America's position on Formosa. Successfully executed, it would have extricated the United States from her isolated and vulnerable position on this divisive issue.

MacArthur's message contradicted Austin's letter and gave credence to Peking's charge of American aggression on Taiwan. On August 29, the Peking radio declared that MacArthur's statement constituted a "formal and public admission that Formosa was an indispensable part of America's Pacific line of defense." [60] On September 1, the Soviet radio declared that MacArthur had torn the cover from the real intention of America which was to seize Formosa for the United States.[61] The State Department was distressed not only by the propaganda advantage which MacArthur's message gave the Communists; it was also concerned that to friendly and neutral nations the United States appeared to be speaking with two voices. At the order of President Truman, MacArthur's message was officially withdrawn. But as a result of its publication in the magazine, its full text was known to the world. The Chinese Communists were not impressed by Truman's action in directing MacArthur to withdraw his message. They cited David Lawrence of the *New York Herald Tribune* to the effect that General MacArthur's message was not incompatible with the policy of the State Department and that it was only ill-timed.[62]

Paralleling the growing conflict between the administration and MacArthur, the bipartisan unity temporarily restored at the outbreak of the Korean War was fast breaking down. On August 1, Chairman Guy Gabrielson of the Republican party announced that his party would back American policy in Korea in the November election campaign but would criticize the Truman administration.[63] On August 7, Senator Kenneth S. Wherry of Nebraska, the Republican floor leader, declared that he planned to fix

[58] For the full text, see Whitney, *op. cit.*, pp. 377–80.
[59] Truman, *op. cit.*, p. 356.
[60] *New York Times*, August 29, 1950, p. 17.
[61] *Military Situation in the Far East*, p. 2002.
[62] *Hsin-hua yüeh-pao*, III, No. 1 (November, 1950), 16.
[63] *New York Times*, August 1, 1950, p. 1.

responsibility for the blunder in not recognizing the danger of a Communist invasion of South Korea and demanded the dismissal of Secretary Acheson.[64] A few days later, Senator Taft charged again that the administration's policy in Asia had encouraged the North Korean attack. In a statement made public on August 13, four out of five Republican members of the Foreign Relations Committee accused Truman and Acheson of having invited the Communist assault on Korea.[65] Senator Vandenberg, the ranking Republican member of the committee and the symbol of bipartisanship in foreign policy, was ill. But he saw the text and was "in general agreement with it." [66] The next day, Senator Wherry again demanded the resignation of Acheson and called on President Truman to "get rid of the alien-minded radicals and moral perverts in his administration." [67] Two days later, he followed up his attack on Acheson with the statement that "the blood of our boys in Korea is on his shoulders, and no one else." [68]

Louis Johnson's resignation on September 12 as secretary of defense and the appointment of General Marshall to that post touched off a new round of Republican denunciations. In the debate on September 15 in the Senate over the bill granting President Truman authority to appoint General Marshall, Senator William E. Jenner, Republican from Indiana, shocked that august body by his denunciation of Marshall as "a front man for the traitors," a "living lie," and "either an unsuspecting stooge or an actual co-conspirator with the most treasonable array of political cutthroats ever turned loose in the executive branch of the government." [69] He charged that Marshall had been appointed as secretary of defense for the "frightening purpose of providing the front of respectability to the vicious sell-out not only of Chiang, not only of Formosa . . . but of the American GI's who are fighting and dying even now because of one treachery." [70] The enabling bill was passed on September 15 in both houses, and Marshall's nomination was confirmed by the Senate on September 20 by votes divided almost strictly along party lines.[71] Bipartisanship in foreign policy reached

[64] *Ibid.*, August 7, 1950, p. 2.
[65] *Ibid.*, August 14, 1950, pp. 1 and 10. The four senators were Alexander Wiley of Wisconsin, H. Alexander Smith of New Jersey, Bourke B. Hickenlooper of Iowa, and Henry Cabot Lodge, Jr., of Massachusetts.
[66] *Ibid.*
[67] *Ibid.*, August 15, 1950, p. 1.
[68] *Ibid.*, August 17, 1950, p. 1.
[69] *Ibid.*, September 16, 1950, p. 1. See also, *Congressional Record*, XCVI, (1950), pp. 14913–21. As reprinted in the *Congressional Record* the last part of Jenner's characterization of Marshall reads as follows: "An errand boy, a front man, a stooge, or a co-conspirator for this administration's crazy assortment of collective cutthroat crackpots and Communist fellow-travelling appeasers" (*ibid.*, p. 14917).
[70] *Ibid.*, p. 14916.
[71] *Ibid.*, pp. 14931, 14972–73, 15182; *New York Times*, September 20, 1950, p. 1.

a new low. Secretary Acheson's position was as vulnerable as ever. He had avoided any recommendations which could be considered appeasement of the Communists.[72] But his policies toward Korea and Formosa did not avert Republican attacks on him and on the administration. Only a smashing victory over the Communist bloc could restore the prestige of the administration, brighten its political outlook, and enhance its freedom to seek a diplomatic solution of the question of Formosa.

D. The Crossing of the 38th Parallel

With the neutralization of the Formosa Strait, the American Seventh Fleet and Chinese Communist forces confronted each other. The preponderance of American naval and air power effectively deterred the Communists from attacking Formosa. Soon afterward, Peking moved approximately 30,000 troops from the area opposite Formosa to Shantung. The projected invasion of Formosa was postponed.[73] In retrospect, however, it is clear that given Peking's distrust of American intentions, her determination to occupy Formosa eventually, and her assumption of revolutionary leadership in Asia, a clash between Communist China and the United States was sooner or later likely to occur, if not over Formosa then at other places where terrain, lines of supply, and other geopolitical factors gave Peking a better chance of successfully challenging the United States. What brought this clash about sooner than anyone could have expected was the crossing of the 38th Parallel. What enabled Peking to score a surprising, epochal victory was MacArthur's headlong drive toward the Yalu River. At the roots of the decision to cross the 38th Parallel was a pattern of calculations characteristic of the China policy of the United States. At the root of MacArthur's drive beyond the narrow neck of the Korean peninsula were the same misjudgments underlying the crossing of the parallel, plus MacArthur's pride in his military prowess and the administration's inability to restrain his military movements in spite of the misgivings of the Joint Chiefs and the State Department.

In the early days of the Korean War, the political objective of the United States was merely the restoration of the *status quo ante bellum*.[74] There are indications, however, that as early as the beginning of August the idea of crossing the 38th Parallel came into the mind of important officials. General MacArthur seems to have taken the lead in advocating this idea. In a conference with Harriman on August 6 and 8, MacArthur, who had

[72] *Ibid.*, November 16, 1950, p. 6.
[73] Whiting, *op. cit.*, pp. 62–65.
[74] Truman's remarks at the National Security Council meeting on June 29, Truman, *op. cit.*, p. 341; Secretary Acheson's address before the convention of the American Newspaper Guild June 29, 1950, *Department of State Bulletin*, July 10, 1950, p. 24; *New York Times*, July 15, 1950, p. 1.

conceived of his plan for a landing at Inchon in the first week of the war, told the President's confidant that United Nations-supervised elections could be held within two months after Syngman Rhee's government was re-established in Seoul and that the North Koreans would vote for a non-Communist government when they were sure of no Russian or Communist intervention. He continued that there was no need to change the constitution of the Republic of Korea which provided for 100 seats for the North.[75] The General was obviously thinking of the unification of Korea under the government of Syngman Rhee, for which a military occupation of North Korea would be a prerequisite. Interestingly enough, MacArthur's remarks on Korea drew no adverse comments from Harriman, whose report to Truman showed no sign of hesitancy in criticizing the General's other views.

In a debate in the Security Council on August 17, Ambassador Austin declared that the General Assembly, in adopting its resolutions on Korea in 1947, 1948, and 1949, had sought the establishment by the Korean people of a free, unified, and independent nation, and the holding of free elections throughout all of Korea under the supervision of the United Nations. The United Nations would not want to turn from these objectives now. If all the members of the United Nations would support these objectives, many of the issues would be resolved. Austin ended his speech with these statements: "The opportunity is here. The place is here. The time is at hand. Only the word and the deed are lacking. We are waiting. And while we wait, the strength of the United Nations increases. Its resolution will neither flag nor fail."[76] According to Thomas J. Hamilton of the *New York Times*, this speech by Austin indicated that the United States delegation to the United Nations was entertaining the idea that the resolutions of the General Assembly, together with the Security Council's resolution of June 25, constituted authorization for General MacArthur to continue his advance up to the Soviet border.[77] On September 7, Secretary Acheson declared that crushing the North Korean aggression was by no means the end of the task of the United Nations.[78] Two days later, Dean Rusk, assistant secretary for Far Eastern affairs, stated in a general review of America's Far Eastern policy that "the United Nations must have an opportunity to give effect to its long-standing policy in favor of a free and united Korea along the lines set forth in the resolutions of the General Assembly over the past three years."[79] At the same time, Secretary-General Lie asserted that it would "not be enough" to bring about

[75] Truman, *op. cit.*, p. 357.
[76] United Nations Security Council, *Official Records, 488th Meeting*, August 17, 1950, p. 8.
[77] *New York Times*, August 24, 1950, p. 5.
[78] *Department of State Bulletin*, September 18, 1950, pp. 450–51.
[79] *Ibid.*, p. 467.

the withdrawal of the North Koreans to the 38th Parallel and that "the aim of the United Nations is and must be a united and independent Korea in which all of the people of Korea are able freely to select a government of their own choosing." [80]

MacArthur's remark, Harriman's silence, and the statements by Austin, Acheson, and Rusk were natural developments of American policy. After all, the long-range political objective of the United States since 1947 had been an independent, united Korea through elections supervised by the United Nations. This aim had been frustrated by Soviet obstructions which could not be removed without resorting to force. But the use of American military power to counter the North Korean aggression now opened up the possibility that this long-range objective could be realized. So after a brief interval and with no public debate and apparently insufficient deliberations in official circles, American officials and the public were beginning to think of the Korean War in terms of the unification of Korea even though this objective meant very little in the scheme of American purposes. A verbal policy was in the process of being transformed into a program to be implemented by force, just as the Open Door policy was in 1941. This development came so naturally that American officials and the public gave very little thought to the risks and costs involved.

In a conference in late August with General J. Lawton Collins, army chief of staff, and Admiral Sherman, General MacArthur won their approval for a landing at Inchon. [81] He also secured at this time their agreement that, for the purpose of destroying the North Korean forces, the 38th Parallel would have to be crossed. [82] On the highest level, the formal decision to cross the 38th Parallel was made on September 11 when President Truman approved a recommendation of the National Security Council that "General MacArthur was to extend his operations north of the parallel and to make plans for the occupation of North Korea, if there was no indication or threat of entry of Soviet or Chinese Communist elements in force." [83] On September 15, the day of the Inchon landing, the Joint Chiefs of Staff sent General MacArthur a directive based on the decision of the National Security Council. The Truman administration's program of containment thus did not preclude a policy of liberation which the Republican party later proclaimed with much fanfare but never implemented.

At the time there was overwhelming sentiment for crossing the 38th Parallel in non-Communist circles in the United States, not only on the

[80] *New York Times*, September 9, 1950, p. 1.
[81] Whitney, *op. cit.*, pp. 345–50.
[82] Martin Lichterman, "Korea: Problems in Limited War," *National Security in the Nuclear Age*, ed. Gordon B. Turner and Richard D. Challener (New York: Praeger, 1960), p. 34.
[83] Truman, *op. cit.*, p. 359. Lichterman noted that this was not an order to MacArthur to cross the 38th Parallel, in *loc cit*.

right but also on the left.[84] On September 24, former Attorney General Francis Biddle, national chairman of Americans for Democratic Action, urged continuation "to its conclusion" of the military campaign, to be followed by the setting up of a unified Korea.[85] American officials were almost unanimous in recommending similar action. America's allies and friends also lent their support to this plan. It was only subsequently revealed that George Kennan was opposed to the crossing of the 38th Parallel on the grounds that it would bring Communist counteraction.[86]

General MacArthur's brilliant amphibious attack on Inchon and the total collapse of the North Korean army opened up the immediate possibility of crossing the 38th Parallel. An eight-nation resolution giving tacit approval to the United Nations forces to move into North Korea was submitted to the General Assembly. On September 30, Ambassador Austin declared that "the aggressor's forces should not be permitted to have refuge behind an imaginary line" and that "the artificial barrier which has divided North and South Korea has no basis for existence either in law or in reason." [87]

From Peking, these military and political developments brought increasingly specific warnings against the crossing of the parallel by American forces. On September 22, Peking admitted MacArthur's charge that Communist China had, prior to the North Korean aggression, "furnished substantial if not decisive military assistance to North Korea by releasing a vast pool of combat-seasoned troops of Korean ethnic origin" for service in the North Korean army.[88] She reaffirmed her support for Pyongyang, implying that further assistance would be given. On September 25, General Nieh Jung-chên, the acting chief of staff of the People's Liberation Army, told the Indian ambassador, K. M. Panikkar, that the Chinese did not intend to sit back with folded hands and let the Americans come up to their border.[89] On September 30, Premier Chou En-lai declared in a speech:

> The Chinese people absolutely will not tolerate foreign aggression, nor will they supinely tolerate seeing their neighbors being savagely invaded. Whoever attempt to exclude the nearly 500

[84] *New York Times*, September 24, 1950, pp. E1, E3.

[85] *Ibid.*, September 25, 1950, p. 5. He also urged that the United States should withdraw recognition of Chiang's regime but should grant it recognition as the *de facto* government of Formosa only. The Peking regime would be recognized only if it gave concrete assurance not to intervene in Korea and not to attack Formosa.

[86] *Ibid.*, November 16, 1950, p. 6, under the by-line of James Reston.

[87] Goodrich, *op. cit.*, pp. 130–31.

[88] Statement by spokesman of the foreign ministry, September 22, 1950, as reprinted in *Hsin-hua yüeh-pao*, II, No. 6 (October, 1950), 1961. For MacArthur's charge, see *Military Situation in the Far East*, pp. 1218–22.

[89] K. M. Panikkar, *In Two Chinas* (London: Allen & Unwin, 1955), p. 108.

million people from the United Nations and whoever ignore and violate the interests of this one-fourth of mankind and fancy vainly to solve arbitrarily any Far Eastern problem directly concerned with China, will certainly break their skulls.[90]

On October 1, the South Korean troops had, on the Eighth Army's order, penetrated seven miles into North Korea.[91] On the same day, MacArthur issued his ultimatum, ordering Pyongyang to surrender.[92] The next day, Peking fully defined the *casus belli* in a dramatic manner which was probably intended to convey her sense of urgency. Chou summoned Panikkar to a midnight conference and told the Indian ambassador that if the American forces crossed the 38th Parallel China would be forced to intervene.[93]

Washington dismissed Chou's midnight warning as merely a gambit to influence the pending vote in the General Assembly on the eight-nation resolution.[94] It did not believe that Peking would intervene. On October 7, the General Assembly approved the eight-nation resolution. The next day, American troops crossed the 38th Parallel in force. Less than two months later, they were to run into a gigantic trap carefully laid by the Chinese Communist forces which had begun their movement across the Yalu River in mid-October.

The administration's miscalculation of Peking's intentions does not seem to have stemmed from Acheson's belief that the Chinese Communists were deeply involved in conflict with the Soviet Union and, for that reason, neither would nor could intervene in Korea. There is no doubt that Acheson's long-range policy was to exploit the alleged conflicts between Chinese nationalism and Soviet imperialism. But his actions, such as the neutralization of the Formosa Strait and the attempt to seek a solution of the future status of that island through the United Nations, were dictated by the strategy of containment and were based on the assumption that Peking and Moscow were firm allies, acting in concert at least for the time being. His various statements playing up Sino-Soviet conflict were designed to arouse Chinese nationalism against Moscow, to make more difficult the Russian task of instigating the Chinese Communists to enter the Korean War, and to dissuade Peking from yielding to Soviet pressure or persuasion. Probably they were made also to convince the neutrals at the United Nations that Peking would not intervene and that there was little danger in United Nations' approval of the crossing of the 38th Parallel. The rea-

[90] Chang Tao-li, *op. cit.*, p. 16. For the complete text in Chinese, see *Hsin-hua yüeh-pao*, II, No. 6 (October, 1950), 1218–22.
[91] *New York Times*, October 2, 1950, p. 1.
[92] For text of the ultimatum, see *Military Situation in the Far East*, p. 3482.
[93] Panikkar, *op. cit.*, pp. 109–10.
[94] Acheson's testimony, *Military Situation in the Far East*, p. 1833; Truman, *op. cit.*, p. 362.

sons for the administration's miscalculation must be sought in other, deeper sources.

In his testimony during the MacArthur hearings, Secretary Acheson gave two explanations of the administration's underestimation of the probability of Chinese intervention. The first relates to the administration's estimate of Peking's intentions. The administration realized, Acheson declared, that Communist China had the military capability to intervene in the Korean War.[95] But the administration thought, and quite correctly, that intervention would require the utmost military effort from Peking and that it would entail serious political risks inside China. Above all, the administration was convinced that intervention would weaken rather than strengthen Peking internationally and bring no real advantage to the regime.[96]

The second explanation given by Acheson concerns the administration's estimate of the probable outcome of China's intervention.[97] Prior to the Inchon landing, American observers had credited China with the military capability to tip the balance of victory to the North Koreans and even to push American forces off the peninsula altogether.[98] The brilliant success at Inchon and the smashing victory following it brought about a complete change in the estimate of the military effectiveness of Chinese Communist troops vis-à-vis the United Nations forces. On October 2, one highly placed official in Washington was reported to have said: "I don't think that China wants to be chopped up." [99] Describing Washington's reaction to the warnings transmitted through the Indian government, James Reston wrote: "In spite of the Republican Party's conviction that the Chinese Communists always do the Kremlin's bidding, the chances are that Mao Tse-tung will hesitate to commit suicide." [100] Confidence in the ability of American forces to cope with Peking's intervention was reflected in a directive sent to General MacArthur by the Joint Chiefs of Staff on October 9. This reads in part: "Hereafter in the event of the open or covert employment anywhere in Korea of major Chinese Communist units, without prior announcement, you should continue the action as long as, in your judgment, action by forces now under your control offers a reasonable chance of success." [101] Washington's estimate was later confirmed by

[95] Acheson's testimony, *Military Situation in the Far East*, pp. 1832–35, 2100. For General Bradley's testimony on the same point, see *ibid.*, p. 759.

[96] Acheson's testimony, *ibid.*, p. 2101.

[97] *Ibid.*, p. 1835.

[98] *New York Times*, September 3, 1950, p. E5; September 11, 1950, p. 6, under the by-line of Hanson Baldwin. See also September 3, 1950, p. E3; September 11, 1950, p. 4.

[99] *Ibid.*, October 2, 1950, p. 3.

[100] *Ibid.*, October 1, 1950, p. E3.

[101] Truman, *op. cit.*, p. 362. See also Whiting, *op. cit.*, p. 111; Richard E. Neustadt, *Presidential Leadership* (New York: John Wiley & Sons, 1960), pp. 137–38.

General MacArthur's appraisals. At the conference at Wake Island on October 15, General MacArthur told President Truman and his top advisers, "Had they [the Chinese Communists] interfered in the first or second months, it would have been decisive. We are no longer fearful of their intervention. We no longer stand hat in hand. . . . They have no Air Force. Now that we have bases for our Air Force in Korea, if the Chinese tried to get down to Pyongyang, there would be the greatest slaughter." [102] Since American officials gave Peking the credit of being wise enough not to court disaster, they thought Chinese intervention unlikely. Thus, the impact of Peking's increasingly specific warnings on American calculations and policy was offset by Washington's enhanced confidence in American military might, particularly in the effectiveness of air power to deal with the Chinese forces.

Although the administration miscalculated the intentions of Peking, some of the reasons it gave for its mistake were, to some extent, valid. They also entered into the calculations of the Chinese Communists, as far as we can find out from various published materials. Mr. Chou Ch'ing-wên, the vice secretary-general of the Democratic League, who broke with the Peking regime and fled to Hong Kong in December, 1956, reported that for several days after Chou issued his warning on September 30, high officials in Peking discussed the question whether China should enter the Korean War. Those who opposed Chinese intervention argued that the newly established regime needed peace for reconstruction, particularly when its enemy was a first-rate power. This view was shared even by some generals in the People's Liberation Army.[103] Chou Ch'ing-wên's account was substantiated by contemporary evidence. An editorial in the Jên-min jih-pao on November 6, 1950, found it necessary to state and then to refute the view of those who opposed Chinese intervention.[104]

It emerges from Chou Ch'ing-wên's report that the Chinese Communists carefully weighed the serious risks involved in Chinese participation in the Korean War. The possibility of a Chinese defeat in Korea was taken into account. So was the contingency of an American invasion of the Chinese mainland. According to Chou Ch'ing-wên, Premier Chou En-lai told a group of officials at the time that "if necessary, we are prepared to retreat from the coast to the interior of China and to use the Northwest and the

[102] Senate Committee on Armed Services and Committee on Foreign Relations, *Substance of Statements Made at Wake Island Conference*, 82d Cong., 1st sess. (1951), p. 5.

[103] Chou Ch'ing-wên, *Fêng-pao shih nien* ["Ten Years of Storm"] (2d ed.; Hong Kong: Shih-tai p'i-p'ing shê, 1959), p. 193. An English translation of this book has since appeared. Chou Ching-wen, *Ten Years of Storm* (New York: Holt, Rinehart, and Winston, 1960), pp. 116, 117.

[104] Reprinted in *Hsin-hua yüeh-pao*, III, No. 1 (November, 1950), 3–4.

Southwest as the bases for a prolonged war." [105] Peking also took into consideration the possibility of the United States using the atomic bomb.[106] It will be recalled that on September 25 General Nieh gave Ambassador Panikkar the first indication of Peking's intention to enter the Korean War. On that occasion, the Indian ambassador endeavored to impress upon the Communist deputy chief of staff the ability of the United States to destroy China's industry and cities by aerial bombing and naval bombardment. Nieh replied: "We have calculated all that. They [the Americans] may even drop atom bombs on us. What then? They may kill a few million people. . . . After all, China lives on the farms. What can atom bombs do there?" [107] In early November, the Chinese Communists published no less than three widely distributed articles which contained statements disparaging the effectiveness of the atomic bomb, particularly when dropped in such a country as China. In one of these, Mao Tse-tung was quoted as having said in September, 1946: "The atomic bomb is a paper tiger. It looks fierce but is actually not so." [108] In the early part of November, the Chinese Communists took extraordinary precautions against the possibility of retaliatory air raids. Vital machinery, including rolling mills, was shifted from the South Manchurian industrial region. Peking even issued orders to its regional agencies in Central-South China to prepare for the removal of state-owned industrial components.[109]

What made the Chinese Communists willing to take these grave risks, thus upsetting the administration's calculations, appears to have been their estimate of the threat to their security posed by an American victory in North Korea. In making this estimate, they were influenced not only by the geopolitical importance of Korea to China but also by their image of the United States as the foremost imperialist power. This can be easily seen in several statements published in early November. A joint declaration issued on November 4 by all parties participating in the Peking regime asserted that there were no limits to the aggressive ambitions of imperialists and that, in launching the aggressive war against Korea, the American imperialists certainly did not confine their design to the destruction of the North Korean government but also wanted to invade China, extend their rule over Asia, and conquer the whole world.[110] An editorial in the *Jên-min jih-pao* on November 6 took President Truman's statement of June 27 as proof that the United States had decided to attack China from three

[105] Chou Ch'ing-wên, *op. cit.*, pp. 117, 195.

[106] *Ibid.*, p. 195.

[107] Panikkar, *op. cit.*, p. 108.

[108] *Shih-shih shou-ts'ê* ["Handbook on Current Affairs"], November 5, 1950, p. 45. (hereafter cited as *Shih-shih shou-ts'ê*). Mao made this remark in his interview with Anna Louise Strong in August, 1946.

[109] *New York Times*, November 11, 1950, p. 3; Chou Ch'ing-wên, *op. cit.*, p. 195.

[110] Reprinted in *Hsin-hua yüeh-pao*, III, No. 1 (November, 1950), 6.

directions: Korea, Formosa, and Indochina. Of these three fronts, Korea was, the editorial averred, the most important one. "After the United States will have completed her aggression against Korea, she will then be able to thrust a dagger into China's chest." [111] An outline for propaganda issued by the Chinese Communists pointed out that the United States had already built a network of bases which, according to MacArthur's public admission, had China and the Soviet Union as their targets.[112] President Truman's action in directing MacArthur to withdraw his statement was interpreted as an attempt to cover up America's real intention. The aggressive designs of the United States were said to have arisen out of her endeavor to extricate herself from the crisis created by the rapid decline of the capitalistic world on the one hand and the unprecedented growth of the socialist camp on the other.

With this grim, ideologically colored view of American intentions, the Chinese Communists saw American actions in Korea as a repetition of Japan's course of aggression in the fifty years before the collapse of Japan at the end of the Pacific war. Their ideological perspective did not permit them to distinguish between Japan of yesterday as an expansionist nation and the United States of today as a status quo power. In their eyes, the United States inherited Japan's position in the Far East and was following Tanaka's plan of conquering China and the world. The only difference between the United States of today and the Japan of yesterday was that the United States would not have to stop and consolidate her gains in Korea for as long a period of time as Japan did before attempting to invade Manchuria.[113] The Chinese Communists thus came to the conclusion that China's security was intimately related to the existence of the North Korean regime, that to save one's neighbor was to save onself, and that to defend the fatherland required giving help to the people of Korea.[114] It was this sense of immediate danger which impelled the Chinese Communists to take "voluntary actions to oppose the United States and to help Korea; to protect our homes and to defend our nation." [115] It is probable that this sense of immediate danger was enhanced by MacArthur's pronouncements and actions, and that "the cumulative anxieties of China's leaders may well have focused in their image of an aggressive General MacArthur."[116]

But the Chinese Communists did not enter the Korean War without hope of military victory and political gains. One prominent element of

[111] Reprinted in *ibid.*, pp. 1–4. The quotation was taken from p. 2.
[112] "How To Understand the United States," *Shih-shih shou-ts'ê*, pp. 9–27.
[113] Editorial, *Jên-min jih-pao*, November 6, 1950, as reprinted in *Hsin-hua yüeh-pao*, III, No. 1 (November, 1950), 2–4.
[114] "Joint Declaration of All Democratic Parties," as printed in *ibid.*, p. 6.
[115] Editorial, *Jên-min jih-pao*, November 6, 1950, as reprinted in *ibid.*, pp. 3–4.
[116] Whiting, *op. cit.*, p. 159.

Chinese Communist mentality was the paradoxical combination of a deep sense of insecurity and a tremendous confidence in ultimate victory. This combination was partly a product of ideology and was nurtured by their revolutionary experience. Their sense of insecurity stemmed from their intense hatred and fear of their class enemy. Their confidence in ultimate victory, which found expression in their scorn and contempt for their foe, was derived from their faith in the "scientific" laws of history. This combination of fear and confidence underlay their caution and patience which constituted important factors in their success in the revolutionary war. It was now brought to the fore by their sense of serious danger and the possibility of great gain. Characteristically, the Chinese Communists told the Chinese people in their propaganda to hate, to scorn, and to despise the United States. The Chinese people must hate the United States because she was their implacable enemy. While Secretary Acheson was talking about the traditional friendship of America, the Chinese Communists were teaching their compatriots that from the early nineteenth century onward the United States had consistently followed an aggressive policy toward China which culminated in her support for Chiang Kai-shek in the civil war and her present actions in Korea and Taiwan.[117] The Chinese people were told to treat the United States with scorn because she was a decaying capitalist nation and the headquarters of the declining reactionary camp. They should despise the United States because she was a paper tiger and "certainly" could be defeated.

An earlier article pointed out that the strategic thinking of the United States rested on the use of the atomic bomb and the air force and neglected the ground forces. The army was "the weakest link" in America's military power and the "fatal weakness" was the lack of a sufficient number of troops. The United States could not wage ground warfare on a large scale.[118] The Chinese Communists thus concluded in early November that "the voluntary actions of the Chinese people [i.e., the actions of the Chinese "volunteers"] will give the Korean people boundless encouragement and confidence, and probably can enable them to effect a change in the entire military situation, to annihilate or repulse the American forces which have not yet established a firm foothold, and to force the aggressors to accept a just and peaceful solution of the Korean question."[119] Mao Tse-tung was reported to have given the following retrospective explanation of his decision to intervene in Korea: a victory would

[117] "How To Understand the United States," *Shih-shih shou-ts'ê*, pp. 9–15. This theme, as applied to American policies and activities before 1900, was elaborated in a two-volume work, entitled *Mei-kuo ch'in Hua shih* ["A History of U.S. Aggression against China"], by Ch'ing Ju-chieh (Peking: San lien shu-t'ien, 1952).

[118] "The Strategic Weakness of the American Imperialism," as reprinted in *Hsin-hua yüeh-pao*, III, No. 1 (November, 1950), 11–14.

[119] Editorial, *Jên-min jih-pao*, as reprinted in *ibid.*, p. 4.

at once raise China's international status to a new height; a stalemate between a backward China and a first-rate power would be a victory for China; a defeat would merely entail a repetition of China's war of resistance against Japan.[120] Mao's statement suggests that, in addition to the defense of the Yalu boundary against the imaginary threat of United States "aggression," Peking entered the war to enhance its international prestige, particularly in Asia.

If the pronouncements of the Chinese Communists reflect, in some degree of accuracy, their thinking and if the above analysis is anywhere near the truth, one can conclude that the administration's miscalculations of Chinese intentions rested on an underestimation of the force of ideology in shaping the policies of the Chinese Communists. It did not judge correctly the intensity of their distrust and hostility toward the United States. It failed to gauge their willingness to take well-calculated risks to achieve political gains while warding off serious dangers, a trait which had been planted by their ideology, strengthened by their revolutionary experience, and which had become deeply imbedded in their mentality. Beyond this, there was the inability to take China seriously once the tide of battle in Korea was turned by the brilliant landing at Inchon. American officials apparently refused to believe that China, having been for a hundred years "the sick man of Asia," would dare to oppose or could successfully challenge the triumphant army of the foremost power. The failure to understand fully the nature of the Chinese Communist movement and the underestimation of China's political and military potentiality were the ultimate basis of Truman's and the Joint Chief's assent to MacArthur's proposal to cross the 38th Parallel and of Acheson's hesitant agreement to go along. These misjudgments explained why the decision was not modified in the face of Peking's warnings. American officials still could not free themselves completely from these two basic miscalculations. The first of these had found the most forceful expression in the recommendations of John S. Service and John P. Davies. The second, which had flowered from American disillusionment with Nationalist performance during the Pacific War, had constituted the fundamental reason for General Marshall's decision not to intervene in the Chinese civil war by the use of American troops. If there remained, after the neutralization of the Formosa Strait, any chance for Secretary Acheson to implement successfully his long-range policy of turning Chinese nationalism against Russia, it was destroyed by the administration's decision to cross the 38th Parallel.

It would seem that American officials also were insufficiently aware of the changing pattern of Peking-Moscow-Washington relations which the neutralization of the Formosa Strait had brought about. Acheson and other

[120] Chou ch'ing-wên, *op. cit.*, p. 395.

American officials had time and again sought to play China against the Soviet Union, relying on America's traditional friendship for China and pointing to Russia's past intrusions into China's border regions. Yet in the developing pattern, Peking's anxieties over "America's occupation of Formosa" greatly outweighed any possible concern over Soviet influence in her borderland. The crossing of the 38th Parallel and the subsequent clash between Chinese and American forces were to harden this changing pattern whose significance American officials were slow to recognize.

E. MacArthur's Drive toward the Yalu

General MacArthur's operations in North Korea were initially governed by a directive dated September 27. Under this directive, MacArthur's military objective was "the destruction of the North Korea armed forces." But he was told that "as a matter of policy, no non-Korean ground forces were to be used in the provinces bordering on the Soviet Union or in the area along the Manchurian border." [121] In conformity with this directive, MacArthur envisaged, in his plan of operations submitted the next day, a halt of the non-Korean forces at the Chongju-Yongwon-Hungnam line (see map). This line ran along the narrow neck of the Korean peninsula, ranging roughly from fifty to a hundred miles below the Manchurian border at various points.[122] However, by the time American forces were approaching the restraining line, it was no longer there. For one of the results of the Wake Island Conference, attended by Truman and MacArthur on October 15, was the General's modification and then elimination of the restraining line. On October 17, MacArthur issued a new order moving the restraining line for American forces to a lateral drawn through Chongsanjangsi-Huichon-Pyongwon-Toksili-Pungsan-Songjin, a line which was, at some places, as much as sixty miles north of the original line.[123] This new order was still in accord with the vague directive of September 27. It evoked no adverse reaction from Washington. In retrospect, however, the modification of the restraining line was a move of great military significance. By this order, General MacArthur abandoned the shortest possible line of defense above the 38th Parallel. It was largely in the area between the new and the old lines that the American forces suffered their decisive defeat in late November in the battle for North Korea.

On October 24, MacArthur did away with the restraining line altogether. He advised his field commanders that the initial restrictions were based upon "the possibility of enemy capitulation." He now authorized them "to use any and all ground forces at their commands, as necessary, in

[121] Truman, op. cit., p. 359.
[122] Whitney, op. cit., p. 398; Lynn Montross and Captain Nicholas A. Canzona, The Chosin Reservoir Campaign (Washington, D.C.: U. S. Marine Corps, 1957), pp. 8–9.
[123] Ibid., p. 36.

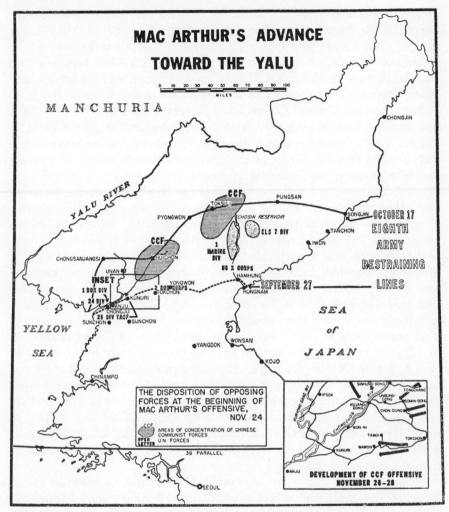

MAC ARTHUR'S ADVANCE TOWARD THE YALU

Sources. — This map is obtained by combining the following three maps: (1) "Eighth Army Advances and Restraining Lines," in Lynn Montrose and Captain Nicholas A. Canzona, *The Chosin Reservoir Campaign* (Washington, D.C.: United States Marine Corps, 1957), p. 4; (2) S. L. A. Marshall, *The River and the Gauntlet* (New York: William Morrow & Co., 1953), p. 15; (3) *ibid.*, p. 181. Used with permission.

order to capture all of North Korea."[124] General MacArthur issued his order of October 24 without having first advised the Joint Chiefs. On October 25, the Joint Chiefs told General MacArthur that his order was not in consonance with their instructions of September 27. They further stated that, while they realized that MacArthur had sound reasons for his new order, they would like to be informed of these reasons. Later in the MacArthur hearings, General Collins cited General MacArthur's order as the one case in which MacArthur violated a directive of the Joint Chiefs, or at least a policy laid down in a directive.[125] General MacArthur immediately replied that the lifting of the restriction was "a matter of military necessity because the Republic of Korea forces were not of sufficient strength and were not sufficiently well led to be able to handle the situation." He explained that he had been given the necessary latitude for modifying the directive of September 27 by a message dated September 30 from Secretary of Defense Marshall. This stated: "We want you to feel unhampered tactically and strategically to proceed north of the 38th Parallel." MacArthur concluded, "I am fully cognizant of the basic purpose and intent of your directive, and every possible precaution is being taken in the premises. The very reverse, however, would be fostered and tactical hazards might even result from other action than that which I have directed. This entire subject was covered in my conference at Wake Island."[126] Once again, President Truman was as much taken by surprise as everybody else. As late as October 26, he reiterated at a press conference that "it was his understanding" that only South Koreans would approach the northern provinces.[127] If Truman's purpose in meeting MacArthur at Wake Island was to establish a more cordial relationship with his field commander, to make certain of MacArthur's faithful implementation of Washington's policies, and to prevent the General from taking provocative action,[128] that aim was not fulfilled.

In late October and early December, the Chinese Communist forces launched two counteroffensives against United Nation troops. Meanwhile the Communist regime started a mass campaign in China, featuring the theme of "hating, despising, and scorning" the United States. All the parties taking part in the regime issued on November 4 a joint declaration vowing support for the movement to oppose America and help Korea "on a voluntary basis." This represented the indorsement by all the parties of the intervention in Korea which was already an accomplished fact. An editorial of the *Jên-min jih-pao* on November 6, scornfully rejected any

---

[124] *Military Situation in the Far East*, p. 1240.
[125] *Ibid.*, pp. 1216, 1230–31, 1239–41, 1314.
[126] Truman, *op. cit.*, p. 372; *Military Situation in the Far East*, p. 1241.
[127] *New York Times*, October 27, 1950, p. 1.
[128] Spanier, *op. cit.*, pp. 107–10.

idea that the United States forces might halt at the Sino-Korean border. It noted that, when American forces were approaching the 38th Parallel, the United States created the impression that American forces would stop at that line. Later, the United States created the impression that American forces would stop some distance from the borders of the Soviet Union and China. But, the editorial charged, events proved these statements to be lies. Now, American troops were approaching the Yalu River. Once again, American spokesmen were laying down a smokescreen by giving verbal assurances that MacArthur's armies would not push beyond the Korean border. The editorial asked: In the light of past experience, were not these statements precisely the sign that American aggressors would push beyond the Korean borders? [129]

On November 7, Chinese and North Korean troops suddenly broke contact with the United Nations forces. This tactical disengagement ushered in a lull on the Korean battlefield. Chinese intervention was now a fact. But there remained the question: What was the purpose and extent of Chinese intervention? Neither Washington nor MacArthur knew. But the administration was much more concerned than MacArthur over a clash with the Chinese Communists. It therefore sought to settle the problem of Chinese Communist intervention by political means while leaving MacArthur's military missions unchanged.[130] It endeavored to reassure Peking of Washington's intention to respect the Manchurian frontier through a six-nation resolution introduced in the United Nations on November 10 and through the public statements made by Acheson on November 15 and by the President himself the next day.[131] It explored the possibility of establishing a buffer zone along the Yalu River. It was prepared to respect China's legitimate interests near the frontier and to grant Peking access to the hydroelectric power generated by installations on Korean soil.[132] Diplomacy was now put ahead of military operations as a means to achieve the unification of Korea.[133] This policy of exploring the possibility of negotiations while leaving MacArthur's directive unchanged rested on two assumptions. First, the Chinese Communists would be willing to negotiate on the basis of a buffer zone and access to power supply in North Korea. Second, General MacArthur's military operations would be successful. Both assumptions turned out to be false.

MacArthur violently opposed any attempt to negotiate with the Chinese

[129] Reprinted in *Hsin-hua yüeh-pao*, III, No. 1 (November, 1950), 3.

[130] Truman, *op. cit.*, pp. 378–80.

[131] *Department of State Bulletin*, November 27, 1950, p. 855; *ibid.*, pp. 852–53. See also U.S. Security Council, *Official Minutes, 530th Meeting*, pp. 22–23.

[132] See the statement by Assistant Secretary of State Dean Rusk, *New York Times*, November 11, 1950, p. 1; *Department of State Bulletin*, December 4, 1950, p. 89; Panikkar, *op. cit.*, p. 115.

[133] Neustadt, *op. cit.*, pp. 140–41.

Communists or to make a conciliatory gesture. He dismissed the importance of the hydroelectric system as a consideration in Peking's calculations. He objected to the idea of a buffer zone on moral and political grounds. He cabled Washington: "To give up a portion of North Korea to the aggression of the Chinese Communists would be the greatest defeat of the free world in recent times; to yield to so immoral a proposition would bankrupt our leadership and influence in Asia and render untenable our position, both politically and militarily." [134] He did not believe that Peking would intervene in full force. He was convinced that a rapid occupation of all Korea would check the Soviet Union's and Communist China's aggressive designs, "before these countries are committed [to a course of action] from which, for political reasons, they cannot withdraw." [135] If the Chinese Communist forces did intervene on a full scale, he was confident that his air power would destroy them.[136] MacArthur was so certain of the overwhelming might of the forces under his command that he launched his final offensive to win the war on November 24, telling his troops that they would be home by Christmas. He split his forces into two groups under two separate commands, with a gap of 20 to 35 air miles between them.[137]

Three days later, the Chinese Communists and North Korean forces met MacArthur's general assault with an all-out counteroffensive. The blow landed "with full speed, full surprise and full shock" against the Republic of Korea II Corps in the central sector.[138] The disintegration of the South Korean forces exposed the right flank of the Eighth Army. With this knowledge and under pressure from numerically superior Chinese Communist forces, the Eighth Army began its withdrawal on November 27. All along the line, the Chinese Communist troops smashed at the United Nations forces. The enemy proved to have amassed a much larger force than previous estimates had indicated. On November 25, Eighth Army intelligence put the enemy strength on its front at 149,000, an increase of

[134] Whitney, op. cit., p. 412.
[135] Ibid., p. 419.
[136] Roy E. Appleman, South to the Naktong, North to the Yalu (Washington, D.C.: Government Printing Office, 1961), pp. 757–65. In reviewing these events, one always wonders to what extent the disagreement between the administration and MacArthur over the method of preventing full-scale Chinese intervention stemmed, as did other controversies, from a fundamental difference in outlook on China policy. As Anthony Leviero of the New York Times pointed out in October, MacArthur disagreed in important respects with the administration's Far Eastern policy, favoring strong acts backed by military force, but the fundamental principle of the administration's Far Eastern policy was that communism, especially in China, could not be overcome by force (New York Times, October 12, 1950, pp. 1 and 6).
[137] Appleman, op. cit., p. 745.
[138] S. L. A. Marshall, The River and the Gauntlet (New York: William Morrow & Co., 1953), pp. 169–70, 172–73, 176; New York Times, November 26, 1950, p. 1; Montross and Canzona, op. cit., p. 146.

95,000 from its estimate of the day before.[139] Three days later the strength of Chinese Communist forces in Korea was put at 200,000. There were actually 300,000 Chinese troops.[140] In a special communiqué on November 28, General MacArthur announced that "we face an entirely new war." This new war began with what S. L. A. Marshall called "one of the major decisive battles of the present century followed by the longest retreat in American history."[141]

Peking accompanied its counterattack in Korea with a diplomatic offensive in Lake Success. On November 24, General Wu Hsiu-ch'üan, the chief delegate of the Peking regime to the Security Council, arrived in New York to attend the Security Council meeting to discuss Peking's complaint of "armed invasion of Taiwan." In a lengthy speech on November 28, Wu ruled out any compromise solution of the question of Formosa. He declared:

> Whatever decision the United Nations General Assembly may take on the so-called question of the status of Taiwan, whether it be to hand over the island to the United States so that it might administer it openly [or] under the disguise of "trusteeship," or "neutralization," or whether it be to procrastinate by the way of "investigation," thereby maintaining the present state of actual United States occupation, it will, in substance, be stealing China's legitimate territory and supporting United States aggression against Taiwan in opposition to the Chinese people. Any such action would in no way shake the resolve of the Chinese people to liberate Taiwan, nor would it prevent action by the Chinese people to liberate Taiwan.[142]

Wu demanded that the Security Council "take concrete steps to apply severe sanctions against the United States for its criminal acts of armed

---

[139] *Ibid.*, p. 140.

[140] Appleman, *op. cit.*, p. 768.

[141] Marshall, *op. cit.*, p. 1. General Whitney asserted that MacArthur had directed his staff to prepare a detailed program for disengagement and withdrawal to be implemented in case of full-scale Chinese intervention (Whitney, *op. cit.*, p. 414). If such a plan existed, no one so far has been able to uncover it. S. L. A. Marshall's meticulous account of the Eighth Army's retreat made no mention of it. On the contrary, he revealed that it was not until November 29 that Major General Lawrence B. Keiser, commander of the Second Division which bore the brunt of the Chinese attack, learned, indirectly and quite accidentally, of the Eighth Army headquarters' plan for withdrawal. Even then, "he did not get a direct order to withdraw and the road by which he should take the division out was not specified" (*op. cit.*, pp. 263–64). On the eastern sector, it was not until November 30 that General Almond directed his divisional commander to draw up a plan and time schedule for extricating the American forces east of the Chosin reservoir area (Montross and Canzona, *op. cit.*, p. 239).

[142] United Nations Security Council, *Official Records, 527th Meeting*, November 28, 1950, p. 10.

aggression against the territory of China, Taiwan, and armed intervention in Korea," and "that the Security Council adopt effective measures to bring about complete withdrawal of American forces from Taiwan and Korea." [143] The violence of Wu's attack on the United States matched the fury of the Chinese Communist assault against the American forces in Korea.

Later, on December 11, Premier Chou En-lai rejected an Indian plea that the Chinese forces halt at the 38th Parallel. He told Ambassador Panikkar that his terms of settlement included the withdrawal of American forces from Taiwan, China's admission to the United Nations, and withdrawal of all foreign troops from Korea.[144] Just as American officials before him, Chou in his hour of victory overestimated his military strength. On December 16, President Truman proclaimed the existence of a national emergency. Only a further test of strength on the battlefield could bring about a restoration of peace.

F. The Korean War and the Demise of the Administration's China Policy

With Peking's intervention and the subsequent stalemate in the Korean War, the neutralization of the Formosa Strait lost its temporary character. These developments spelled the total failure of the administration's policy of disengagement. This failure had its origins in the partisan controversy in the United States. The China bloc's demands for a positive program of aid to the Nationalists and its sentimental attachment to China had necessitated the adoption of a policy of limited assistance in 1947. They had immobilized America's China policy for a year and a half after Marshall had for all practical purposes written off both mainland China and Formosa in October, 1948. This immobility and continued entanglement in China provided the Soviet Union with ample time to prepare for and implement new moves in China and in Korea in order to counter America's policy of building up Japan. Whatever the calculations of the Soviet Union may have been in scheduling the attack on South Korea ahead of Peking's projected assault on Formosa, the aggression in Korea led to the neutralization of the Formosa Strait which further aroused Peking's hostility toward the United States. After American forces crossed the 38th Parallel, Peking intervened. After scoring a surprise victory in North Korea, Communist China, like the United States, refused to halt her forces at the 38th Parallel. We may never know what precise effect the neutralization of the Formosa Strait had on Peking's decision to enter the Korean War or on her subsequent refusal to halt her forces at the 38th Parallel. It may very well be that the crossing of the 38th Parallel by American forces was the sufficient condition for the decisions and actions

[143] *Ibid.*, p. 25.
[144] Panikkar, *op. cit.*, pp. 118–19.

taken by Peking. But one must also remember that the neutralization of the Formosa Strait was one of the most significant events preceding Peking's intervention. It could not but have influenced Peking's decisions. It could not but have lightened Moscow's task in persuading Peking to intervene and to drive American forces out of Korea, if such persuasion was necessary. In any case, the temporary neutralization of the Formosa Strait was followed by the crossing of the 38th Parallel and Chinese intervention which, in turn, basically altered Sino-American relations.

Thus, by the end of 1950, the whole edifice of the administration's policy toward China lay in ruins. The administration had acted to disentangle the United States from the Chinese civil war, but events forced it to intervene at the last moment by neutralizing the Formosa Strait. It had endeavored to dissuade Peking from intervening in Korea, but MacArthur's drive across the 38th Parallel, assented to by the Joint Chiefs and hesitantly by Acheson, brought Peking into the war. It had tried hard to avoid a military conflict between the United States and Communist China, but the decision to march into North Korea paved the way for the defeat of the technologically modern army of the United States by the poorly equipped Chinese soldiers in a terrain even more favorable to the latter than the Chinese mainland. It had attempted to limit America's commitments to the Nationalist government, but the developments of the Korean War after November, 1950, led to a sharp and rapid increase in military aid to Formosa. It had sought a compromise solution of the question of Formosa through the United Nations, but Peking underscored her rejection of any such program by pressing her attack in Korea across the 38th Parallel. It had apparently wished to establish normal diplomatic relations with Peking eventually, but found itself increasingly opposed to recognition of the Communist regime and its admission to the United Nations.[145] It had based its long-term policy on the hope of splitting the Sino-Soviet alliance by turning Chinese nationalism against Russia, but the neutralization of the Formosa Strait and the Chinese intervention in Korea greatly increased Peking's dependence on Moscow and, for the next few years, solidified the unity of the two leading Communist partners.

The decision to cross the 38th Parallel need not have led to the humiliating defeat suffered by American forces if the administration had taken steps to halt MacArthur's drive toward the Yalu. President Truman or the Joint Chiefs could have insisted on maintaining the restraining line

[145] According to James Reston, Acheson was opposed to a British proposal for trying to negotiate a cease-fire at the 38th Parallel in December, 1950. He told the British that, even if the Chinese Communists were brought into the United Nations, recognized by the United States as the government of China, and handed Formosa, they would then probably make demands upon French Indochina and demand a voice in the Japanese peace settlement (*New York Times*, December 6, 1950, p. 8).

for American forces near the narrow neck of Korea.[146] He or they could have countermanded MacArthur's order on October 17 which moved the restraining line sixty miles northward at some points. At the shortest possible line of defense near the narrow neck, the United Nations' forces might have had a better chance of warding off an all-out Chinese assault. Or Truman and the Joint Chiefs of Staff could have countermanded Mac-Arthur's order of October 24 eliminating the restraining line altogether — an order which violated the Joint Chiefs' directive of September 27 or at least a policy laid down in it. Such a step might have prevented some advance elements of the American forces from marching too far into the Chinese trap. In November, the administration might have changed its directive to MacArthur when its diplomatic overtures to Peking met with rebuff. None of these steps was taken because the political objective remained the ambitious one of unification of Korea and the military risks were apparently not thought to be as serious as they turned out to be. After all, China, be it Communist or Nationalist, was not a serious factor in American calculations. The sentimental attachment of the United States to China was not coupled with a respect for Chinese power. Moreover, the administration was in a weak position politically to restrain MacArthur because its China policy had been under severe attack for several years and MacArthur was the symbol of a new approach to Far Eastern affairs. Thus, America's defeat in North Korea had its roots in her policy toward China.

Perhaps a military clash between Communist China and the United States was inevitable because of the ideological component in Peking's foreign policy and the quest for greatness which had always been deeply imbedded in Chinese history and culture and which was reactivated by a revived sense of power and unity after a century of humiliation and defeat. But the failure to withdraw promptly from China between 1947 and 1950, the neutralization of the Formosa Strait, and the decision to cross the 38th Parallel turned potentiality into immediate actuality. It thus deprived the United States of room for maneuver and time for adjustment to the new configuration of power in the Far East. This new configuration of power would in all probability have come into existence over a period of time even if the Korean War had not occurred. For the revolutionary and national interests of an awakened China under Communist leadership clashed sharply with the American policy of containment and with American efforts to bolster non-Communist regimes in Asia. But the Korean War precipitated this emergent international configuration and added to the equation of power new political and emotional factors which otherwise would not have existed.

[146] Neustadt, *op. cit.*, pp. 137–47.

The new configuration of power as it evolved out of the Korean War consists of two main elements. The first is the emergence of China as a powerful nation in the Far East, and the second is a new pattern of conflict among Peking, Moscow, and Washington. The battle in North Korea was the first great victory won by Chinese forces over a major power which had a lasting effect on the outcome of an international war since the Opium War opened the modern era in China.[147] It marked the ironic, partial fulfilment of President Roosevelt's wartime policy of making China a great power. Since the Korean War the balance of power in the Far East has rested on a confrontation between the ground forces of the Communist bloc on the Asiatic mainland and the air and naval power of the United States based on the island perimeter. The Korean peninsula and Southeast Asia have become the objects of the political-military struggle between the two blocs.

Second, the neutralization of the Formosa Strait and Chinese intervention has precipitated a new pattern of relations among Peking, Moscow, and Washington. The unresolved question of Formosa became an obsession with Communist China. As a result, the clash of interests over Formosa between Peking and Washington has tended to overshadow the conflicts between the Soviet Union and the United States. The antagonism between a junior partner in the Communist bloc and the leading nation in the free world has become sharper than the expected tension between the most powerful countries in the two rival camps. The respective positions of Moscow and Peking in the Sino-Soviet alliance have also been basically altered. Moscow's reliance on Peking to promote her foreign policies in Asia has been eclipsed by Peking's dependence on Moscow's support to achieve her most important political objective: the elimination of a rival regime and the attainment of national unity. Peking's diplomatic isolation from the United States has been nearly complete, but Moscow's freedom of maneuver has been greatly enhanced. This change doomed to failure Acheson's policy of playing China against the Soviet Union. It has put the United States in the position of making Peking rather than Moscow the major antagonist with whom no improvement in relations has so far been possible.

Peking's amazing success in a surprise attack and the subsequent prolonged stalemate have been taken by her as confirmation of Mao's concept of the United States as a paper tiger. They have been considered a vindication of his formula of "taking the enemy lightly strategically and

[147] In early 1938, General Li Tsung-jên defeated the Japanese forces at Taiêrhchuang (F. F. Liu, *A Military History of Modern China* [Princeton, N. J.: Princeton University Press, 1956], pp. 199–200). But this Chinese victory in a major battle only temporarily delayed the Japanese advance. It did not constitute the turning point of a war.

taking him seriously tactically," which had always been an important part of Mao's thought but which was to be concisely stated in these terms in November, 1957.[148] The strengthened conviction of the correctness of these ideas was to lead Mao to overestimate the significance of the possession of intercontinental ballistic missiles by the Soviet Union, to attribute strategic superiority to the Communist bloc, and to proclaim that the East wind prevailed over the West wind.[149] This misjudgment in the realm of strategic calculations has not been fully compensated by Peking's caution in tactics. Peking has been advocating a militant policy against the United States wherever and whenever the opportunity has presented itself.

On the part of the United States, the initial defeat and subsequent frustrations aroused deep fear and hostility toward the Chinese Communist regime, all the more because of the previous sentimental attachment to China. This fear and hostility has since replaced traditional friendship as the dominant mood in the American attitude toward China. The United States thus reciprocates Peking's phobia and hatred for Washington. Emotional attitudes and unresolved problems reinforce each other to harden Sino-American antagonism which, in day-to-day struggles, overshadow the long-term Soviet-American rivalry for world leadership.

The courses of action adopted by the Eisenhower administration flowed naturally from the collapse of the Truman administration's policy. To many, the only alternative to a policy that had failed was its logical opposite. The policy of maximum isolation of Peking replaced that of seeking a modus vivendi. The policy of rehabilitating the Nationalist government as a foremost ally in the Far East replaced the policy of limiting America's commitment. Up to at least the end of 1958, the supposition that the Chinese Communist regime was not a lasting phenomenon replaced the assumption that it was here to stay. The policy of going to the brink of war to deter Peking's new moves replaced efforts to reassure China about America's present intentions and to remind her of traditional friendship. The exertion of maximum pressure on the Sino-Soviet bloc as a measure to split the alliance replaced the hope of making Russia the primary target of Chinese nationalism. Meanwhile, Peking has taken upon herself the role of the most uncompromising enemy of the United States in the Communist bloc.

Thus, it has come to pass that after half a century the Open Door policy of John Hay has ended in a confrontation between a bamboo curtain on one side and a total trade embargo on the other. The principle of preserv-

[148] *Comrade Mao Tse-tung on "Imperialism and All Reactionaries Are Paper Tigers"* (Peking: Foreign Language Press, 1958), p. 25.
[149] Donald Zagoria, *The Sino-Soviet Conflict, 1956–1961* (Princeton, N.J.: Princeton University Press, 1962) pp. 164–65, 202, 326; Alice Langley Hsieh, *Communist China's Strategy in the Nuclear Era* (Englewood Cliffs, N.J.: Prentice-Hall, 1962), pp. 76–166.

ing Chinese territorial and administrative integrity has terminated in the reality of two Chinas. Non-intervention in Chinese affairs has passed into an American-enforced *de facto* cease-fire in the civil war. Traditional sympathy for the underdog of the Far East has been superseded by fear of the awakened giant of Asia. Pride in America's moral leadership in China has been replaced by apprehension about Chinese ideological influence in Asia. Missionary and philanthropic activities have given place to political and propaganda warfare. Neighborly dialogue has been supplanted by mutual denunciation. Historic friendship has been consummated in reciprocal hostility. On the horizon looms an ever-present chance of war. One could hardly find a more sobering example of the tragic results produced by a policy of good intentions and high ideals which lacked the foundation of a correlative estimate of self-interest and which was not supported by military power equal to the noble tasks.